IMMIGRATION AND ASYLUM LAW AND POLICY OF THE EUROPEAN UNION

Immigration and Asylum Law and Policy of the European Union

KAY HAILBRONNER

Center for International and European Law on Immigration and Asylum, Universität Konstanz, Germany

KLUWER LAW INTERNATIONAL

THE HAGUE / LONDON / BOSTON

Library of Congress Cataloging-in-Publication Data

Hailbronner, Kay.
Immigration and asylum law and policy of the European Union / by Kay Hailbronner.
p. cm.
Includes index.
ISBN 9041113231 (hc. : alk. paper)
1. Emigration and immigration law--European Union countries. 2. Asylum, Right of--European Union countries. I. Title.

KJE6044 .H35 2000
342.4'842'094--dc21

99-089236

ISBN 90-411-1323-1

Published by Kluwer Law International,
P.O. Box 85889, 2508 CN The Hague, The Netherlands

Sold and distributed in North, Central and South America
by Kluwer Law International,
675 Massachusetts Avenue, Cambridge, MA 02139, USA

In all other countries, sold and distributed
by Kluwer Law International, Distribution Centre
P.O. Box 322, 3300 AH Dordrecht, The Netherlands

Printed on acid-free paper

Printed and bound in Great Britain by Antony Rowe Limited.

Contents

Preface

The author would like to express his thanks to former and present members of the staff of the Research Center for International and European Law on Immigration and Asylum at the University of Konstanz. The present staff of the Research Center, in particular Ulf Häußler, Georg Jochum, Christine Kreuzer, Olaf Müller and Marianne Wiedemann have provided invaluable assistance by preparing drafts of various parts of the book. Volker Gronert, Karoline Kerber, Christian Klos, Claus Weber and Regina Zott have assisted in earlier stages of the work. Sabine Appt has done an excellent job in typing the manuscripts with never-ending patience and great skill. Without the help of all staff members, including many students who have helped in the editorial work, the book would never have been completed.

In consideration of the rapid development of jurisprudence particularly in the field of immigration and asylum law I appreciate any comment or remark as well as suggestions for future improvements.

Kay Hailbronner
Konstanz, February 2000

A

Immigration into the European Union

I. EUROPEAN IMMIGRATION LAW AS AN INTEGRAL PART OF A EUROPEAN INTERNAL MARKET

A European immigration law and policy appears as a logical conclusion of the establishment of the European Internal Market and the abolition of internal border controls which has been achieved for the largest part of the European Union with the entry into force of the Schengen Implementation Convention of 1990 – with the exception, however, of the United Kingdom and Ireland. The establishment of a European Internal Market comprises "an area without internal frontiers in which the free movement of goods, persons, services and capital is ensured in accordance with the provisions of this treaty" (Article 14 ECT). It seems obvious that in achieving the aim of free movement of persons within the European Union one cannot distinguish at the border between third-country nationals and Union citizens, although their legal status is different. Article 62 ECT thus has clarified an ongoing debate on the implications of the Internal Market by obliging the Council to adopt "measures with a view to ensuring, in compliance with Article 14, the absence of any controls on persons, be they citizens of the Union or nationals of third countries, when crossing internal borders".

There is another evident connection between the concept of a European Internal Market and a regulatory framework for entry and residence of third-country nationals. Different national visa regulations as well as different border control regimes will become inefficient when upon entry third-country nationals will be able to move freely from one Member State to the other. The regulatory competence of the Community under ex-Article 100c ECT to establish a list of those countries whose nationals must possess a visa for entering the Community, has therefore, although somewhat reluctantly, been introduced by the Maastricht Treaty as an absolute minimum requirement for any progress in the field of a common European immigration policy.

Finally, the very idea of the European Union as an "area of freedom, security and justice" seems to require a European co-ordination if not harmonization of basic rules on immigration and asylum matters. Hardly surprising, one of the most important driving forces for a European co-operation in immigration and asylum matters was the desire to prevent uncontrolled immigration and illegal entry and sojourn. Therefore, common European guidelines and standards on how to prevent unauthorized entry and illegal behaviour in the context of migration movements were called for. Another driving force was the need to spend spare resources economically. The basic idea of the Dublin Convention has been to use limited resources of Member States economically by giving an asylum seeker only one chance to get a claim for protection examined. It is clear that the very idea of mutual recognition of asylum decisions as well as the principle of exclusive responsibility call for further reaching harmonization of substantive and procedural asylum law.

The same, however, is true with regard to immigrants generally, partly, because one cannot distinguish sharply between asylum seekers on the one hand and immigrants asking for a humanitarian temporary or permanent residence permit on the other hand, partly since it would appear somewhat arbitrary to deny entry and residence on reasons which would be considered sufficient in another Member State. The concept of a European area of "justice" inevitably calls for a certain equalization of basic conditions under which rights can be required and executed. Justice cannot be limited to EU citizens only. The very idea of the progressive establishment of an area of justice (Article 61 ECT) implies that third-country nationals are to be permitted entry and residence under basically the same conditions in the whole European Union and that they are to enjoy basic social rights under the same conditions in any part of the European Union.

The idea of justice and equality, however, must not be used to challenge the existing pattern of distribution of powers between the Community and the Member States. Even within a federal state equality cannot be used as an overriding constitutional concept to rule out existing differences. It will be up to the European Community to draw the balance between the need for an effective European immigration and asylum regime and the legitimate interest of Member States to have their particular cultural, geographical and political preferences with regard to the admission and entry of third-country nationals reflected in European regulations and policies.

To the surprise of many observers, the Amsterdam Treaty in the new title on free movement of persons, asylum and immigration, gave the European Community considerable powers to enact a regulatory framework for European immigration and asylum policy. Title IV ECT remedies some of the most important deficits of the Maastricht Treaty, that is the non-binding nature of intergovernmental co-operation within Title VI TEU. Another major deficit relating to the unanimity requirement in the intergovernmental decision making process has been maintained under Title IV ECT, at least for a period of five years after the entry into force of the Amsterdam Treaty. Under the unanimity requirement substantial progress can hardly be expected. It remains to be seen if the Council after five years will pass a decision that substantial parts of the measures covered in Title IV ECT shall be governed by the co-decision procedure referred to in Article 251 ECT. The European Court as well will probably have to play a substantial role in interpreting the new provisions, particularly if the Council should prove unable to live up to its obligations provided for in Title IV ECT.

The Amsterdam Treaty only partially answers the question how much European immigration and asylum law we need. Compromise between extremes – national or European regulation – is crucial to the further development of European migration policy. A reasonable answer to the question of how much European migration law and policy is necessary should be oriented towards long term interests and should not be blocked by insisting on national sovereignty or mere Euro-activism. There is an obvious need for co-ordination in certain matters in which liberal practice by one member state would undermine restrictive measures by another. Nevertheless, the principle of subsidiarity according to Article 5 ECT requires, that a need for

European action must be proved in detail, as to whether the European or the national level is preferable. National reactions may be favoured, if they are sufficient or – which is not unlikely in some cases – even more efficient.

A common European migration policy is not exempted from external obligations. Agreements binding for the EU Member States under international law and rules of customary law create minimum standards on the treatment third–country nationals receive by Member States. Such obligations will have to be taken into account even if they are not per se obligations of the European Community. The Amsterdam Treaty has made reference to the principles of "liberty, democracy, respect for human rights and fundamental freedoms, and the rule of law, principles which are common to the Member States (Article 6(1) TEU). In addition, the Treaty on European Union provides for a respect of fundamental rights, "as guaranteed by the European Convention for the Protection of Human Rights and Fundamental Freedoms signed in Rome on 4 November 1950 and as a result from the constitutional traditions common to the Member States, as general principles of Community Law" (Article 6(2) TEU). The establishment of a more precise and judicially reviewable set of substantive and procedural rights relating to immigration and asylum measures has yet to be achieved by the European Union, respectively the European Community which is exclusively competent to enact binding legal rules in immigration and asylum matters. This task should not be exclusively left to the European Court of Justice although the European Court will certainly have a very substantial role to play in protecting the human rights of third-country nationals.

By transferring regulatory power from the Member States to the European Community, the scope of application of the European Convention on Human Rights decreases to the extent that the European Community as such is not a contracting party of the European Convention on Human Rights. It remains to be seen to what extent the European Court will apply the obligation contained in Article 6 TEU to respect the fundamental rights as guaranteed by the European Convention for the protection of human rights. There is no obligation of the European Court under the European Convention for the protection of human rights to apply the same principles on the interpretation of the ECHR as the European Court for human rights although one may expect that the European Court will take the judgments of the Strasbourg Court into account when deciding on matters relating to the compatibility of Community action with the ECHR. According to the recent decision of the European Court of Human Rights in the case *Cantoni v France*[1], the Court has argued that it will exercise its jurisdiction over measures of contracting states even if such measures whether of a legislative or administrative measure are completely determined by Community Law. This judgment may be interpreted as the recognition of the thesis that Community Law is only autonomous insofar as it is not subject to the human rights obligations of Member States under the European Convention for the Protection of Human Rights.[2] It

---

1 ECHR, judgment of 15 November 1996, case no. 45/1995/551/637, *Cantoni v France*, RJD 1996-V 1614 = Human Rights Law Journal 1996, 441; cf. *Sebastian Winkler*, EuGRZ 1999, 181 et seq.

2 See *Georg Ress* in Haller (ed.) Staat und Recht, Essays in Honour of Günther Winkler (1997), 897, 922 et seq.

follows that in so far as Member States will have to implement Community Directives on immigration and asylum into national law they will still be subject to judicial review by the European Court of Human Rights. Simultaneously, the European Court of Justice may have to decide on the interpretation and application of Community Law relating to human rights obligations arising from the Treaty. In case of divergent interpretations the European Court of Justice will have to take into account that Member States under the European Convention for the Protection of Human Rights are obliged to comply with binding judgments of the Strasbourg Court. Since under Article 307 ECT rights and obligations arising from the European Convention on Human Rights shall not be affected by the provisions of the Treaty establishing the European Community, human rights obligations of EU Member States under the Convention will have priority in case of a conflict.

Community regulations potentially infringing human rights of third-country nationals, however, are not subject to additional review by the European Court of Human Rights. The question, therefore, may be raised whether the existing provisions are adequate to provide for an efficient procedural mechanism to challenge Community action relating to immigration and asylum law on the reason of non-compliance with international human rights standards. The Treaty provides for immediate access for individuals to the European Court of Justice only in rare instances of decisions of direct and individual concern to the individual.[3] In Title IV matters the power of a national court asked for a preliminary ruling on the validity or interpretation of acts of the institutions of the Community has been severely restricted by Article 68 ECT. Only a court or tribunal whose decision is unappealable under national law shall request the Court of Justice to give a ruling thereon. The question therefore arises whether the procedural scheme established by the Amsterdam Treaty concerning access to judicial review is sufficient to guarantee an effective protection of an individual's rights in immigration and asylum matters. Access to appeal procedures is crucial for any effective protection of human rights. Until the Amsterdam Treaty has entered into force, the existing scheme of judicial national and Community review could perhaps be considered sufficient particularly since the European Court has given the national courts the right to provisionally suspend the validity of Community Acts in combination with a request for a preliminary ruling[4]. Such possibility, however, does not exist in the case of Title IV measures, since lower courts will have no possibility to refer a case to the European Court. It may well be argued that the European Court if asked to decide in a case of immigration or asylum legislation will grant national courts a similar power since otherwise there would be no effective protection available against Community Acts based upon Title IV ECT and challenged on the reason of compatibility with the Treaty or fundamental principles of Community Law. In a

---

3 See Article 230 ECT.

4 See ECJ, judgment of 22 October 1987, case 314/85, *Foto-Frost v Hauptzollamt Lübeck-Ost*, 1987 [ECR] 4199 para 15: National courts may not declare Community legislation invalid. However, national courts may suspend enforcement of a national administrative measure adopted on the basis of a Community regulation: ECJ, judgment of 9 November 1995, case C-465/93, *Atlanta Fruchthandelsgesellschaft mbH and others v Bundesamt für Ernährung und Forstwirtschaft*, 1995 [ECR] I-3761 paras 28-30.

long-term perspective, however, it seems necessary to develop a right of complaint against Community Acts on reasons of violation of an individual right under the Treaty establishing the European Community or international treaties binding for the European Community.

II. Migration to Geographically and Economically Favourable States

1. Migration Movements to the European Union

Migration is determined by geopolitical as well as by economic factors[5]. If one visualises the geographic situation of Europe it must be noted, that migration flows are inevitably directed toward favoured destination countries.[6] Illegal immigration by land is still less risky than by ship or by plane. Effective entry controls can be established at ports or airports relatively easily, when compared to land borders of several hundred kilometres. In addition the price of transport by air and sea may not be insignificant although organized human trafficking which is estimated at 60 – 70 per cent of all illegal entries, indicates that the price of regular transport is of minor importance. Nonetheless a trend towards a globalisation of migration is recognizable.[7]

Great Britain and Ireland can be reached almost exclusively via ship and plane only[8], Spain, Portugal and France are preferred destination countries for migrants from the Maghreb states. Migrants from the African continent will potentially aim for the Mediterranean states.[9] The Mediterranean sea itself is a decisive dividing factor. It must, however be remembered, that the European continent is only less than eight nautical miles away from the African continent at the Street of Gibraltar. An increasing clandestine migration can be observed here. In addition it must be noted, that the migration from the South to the North is long-term in character.[10]

---

5 Gravitation model, see *Fassmann/Münz*, Europäische Migration und die Internationalisierung des Arbeitsmarktes, Innovation und Beharrung in der Arbeitspolitik (1993), 18, 26; *Fassmann/Münz*, Einwanderungsland Österreich, 53; *King* (ed.), Mass Migration in Europe (1995), 21 et seq.; *Faist*, ZSR 1995, 36, 39; *Ronge*, ParlBeilage 7/1993, 16, 23, 27.

6 See e.g. the graphs concerning the relation between third-country nationals and the population in the EEA in the Eurostat Yearbook (1995), 69+75, respectively.

7 *Fassmann/Münz*, Einwanderungsland Österreich, 58; *Eichengreen*, Thinking about Migration, 1, emphasises the decreasing cost of transportation.

8 Apart from the use of the Eurotunnel, which can be easily controlled. Control of external frontiers is naturally easier for island states, see Asyl in Europa, Asyl in der Schweiz, the expert opinion of the ICMPD for the Bundesamt für Flüchtlinge, Switzerland, 37; for Japan see *Fukawa/Vogel* in *Klose (ed.)*, Zuwanderung – Möglichkeiten und Grenzen (1994), 115.

9 Though half the migrants of the world, about 35 million persons, reside in Africa, only a few are able to reach Europe. Most people live in the south of the Sahara and it is very unlikely, that they will have the chance of transport, see *Nuscheler*, International Migration, 55+68; also *Adepoju* in *Appleyard*, Internationale migration today, Vol. I, Trends and prospects (1988), 17 et seq.

10 See parliamentary assembly of the Council of Europe, recommendation 1125 (1990), on the new immigration countries; *Cucó*, Council of Europe, Report on the new immigration countries, Doc. 6211 of 24 April 1990; *Montanari/Cortese* in *King* (ed.), Mass Migration in Europe (1995), 212 et seq., 228; *Cornelius*, Controlling Immigration, 332, 337.

The political changes in middle and eastern European states allowing for free travel have increased the attraction of the European Union, a higher living standard and better employment. Finland, Austria and Germany have their main land borders to these states. The other Scandinavian countries are protected by the Baltic Sea and Finland. An increasing influx of migrants is expected to concentrate mainly on the central part of the EU.[11] The potential of admission of refugees to Scandinavian countries is disregarded to a great extent.[12] The Finish border of over 3,000 km could cause severe security problems in the event of a crisis which leads to forced-migration movements. The new democracies of middle and eastern Europe currently provide – much against their will – a "buffer zone" for the EU. But that buffer is, however only transitional. Once Hungary, Poland and the Czech Republic enter the EU, eastern external borders of the EU may become a main entrance gate to Europe.[13]

2. *Third-country Nationals in the European Union – A Statistical Survey*

At present the legal residence of third-country nationals in the EU does not pose a problem for the political or economic stability of the Union. The net immigration to EU Member States has been registered with 800.000 persons in 1995.[14] An unknown number of third-country nationals immigrate in the EU uncontrolled either as "visa overstayers" or on the basis of false documents or through "green borders".

Third-country nationals account for 12 million, roughly 3,3%, of the 370 million people living in the EU agglomerations. Two-thirds of all third-country nationals reside in the industrial areas of Germany, France and Great Britain. Germany, with 5.9 per cent, has the highest quota of third-country nationals, followed by Austria with 5.6 per cent.[15] The lowest quotas of third-country nationals can be found in

---

11 Asyl in Europa, Asyl in der Schweiz, experts opinion of the ICMPD for the Bundesamt für Flüchtlinge, Switzerland, 16.

12 See *Fassmann/Münz*, Europäische Migration und die Internationalisierung des Arbeitsmarktes, Innovation und Beharrung in der Arbeitspolitik (1993), 25.

13 For the opposite view cf. *Montanari/Cortese* in *King* (ed.), Mass Migration in Europe (1995), 212, 228, who assess the east-west migration as a temporary phenomenon and stress the importance of the south-north migration. For a general survey see *Hönekopp*, Migrationary movements from countries of Central and Eastern Europe – the cases of Germany and Austria, in People on the move, new migration flows in Europe, Council of Europe, Strasbourg (1992), *Hönekopp*, Labour migration for Germany from Central and Eastern Europe – Old and New Trends; Institut für Arbeitsmarkt und Berufsforschung, No. 23, 1997.

14 Figure for 1995; see Eurostat news release 63/96 of 30 September 1996.

15 Eurostat, news release 31/96 of 22 May 1996; see also *Fassmann/Münz*, Europäische Migration und die Internationalisierung des Arbeitsmarktes, Innovation und Beharrung in der Arbeitspolitik (1993), 19 et seq.

Table A

	1987	*1988*	*1989*	*1990*	*1991*	*1992*	*1993*	*1994*	*1995*	*1996*	*1997*	*10 years total*
Austria	7,074	20,795	56,105	71,913	87,651	82,067	40,314	13,107	7,439	4,991	2,575	394,031
Belgium	–1,015	36,668	6,598	19,961	13,321	25,063	17,915	18,388	2,768	16,293	9,984	165,944
Denmark	6,375	664	3,677	8,553	10,880	11,583	11,468	10,556	28,665	17,499	12,043	121,963
Finland	1,080	1,504	5,786	8,604	14,423	9,093	9,092	3,611	4,285	3,938	4,808	66,224
France	44,000	57,000	71,000	8,0000	9,0000	9,0000	7,0000	5,0000	4,0000	35,000	4,0000	667,000
Germany	152,486	497,867	746,078	656,166	602,563	776,397	462,284	315,568	398,263	281,493	94,938	4,984,103
Greece	19,801	27,142	53,852	71,135	87,246	48,878	56,025	27,302	20,859	21,558	2,000	435,798
Ireland	–37,433	–42,822	–27,985	–7,667	5,102	1,716	–3,526	–2,844	5,629	13,236	20,017	–76,577
Italy	–3,880	9,554	16,324	24,212	4,163	181,913	181,070	153,364	94,012	149,745	125,954	936,431
Luxembourg	2,274	2,137	3,719	3,937	4,158	4,272	4,262	4,049	4,576	3,706	3,834	40,924
Netherlands	35,355	27,808	27,260	48,730	49,998	43,185	44,418	20,429	14,929	21,258	27,967	361,337
Portugal	–53,475	–50,195	–57,710	–60,068	–24,644	–9,587	19,954	10,314	5,375	10,246	15,005	–194,785
Spain	–32,805	–20,118	–9,492	1,532	32,279	20,218	24,723	26,648	47,314	47,135	47,433	184,867
Sweden	21,176	29,468	44,235	34,817	24,954	19,756	32,106	50,859	11,648	5,839	6,021	280,879
United Kingdom	21,986	36,072	81,770	68,384	76,416	44,887	90,184	84,249	116,868	100,801	87,500	435,798
European Union	182,999	633,544	1,021,217	1,030,209	1,078,510	1,349,441	1,060,289	785,600	802,630	732,738	500,079	

Spain, Ireland and Finland (0.6 per cent). This supports the thesis that some member states are particularly attractive to migrants due to their level of economic development while geographical proximity seems to be less important.[16]

a) Net Immigration to Europe from 1987 to 1997[17]

Migration patterns differ widely among European Union Member States. This is most clearly shown by the different composition of the foreign population. The main reasons are: the history of colonialism, the recruitment of migration workers, national differences in the recognition of asylum-seekers and refugees, geographical circumstances and specific political and economic links to third states[18]. As yet, the study of migration statistics does not lead to the conclusion that migrants aim for the European Union, but rather for specific EU member states.[19]The most important factor for immigration seems to be the fact that in the host country a substantial number of people of the same language, culture and religion are living. Migration drives migration. People move to an area or town to be close to their own kind of people.

Turkish nationals represent the largest group of third-country nationals (14.7 per cent, 2.6 million at present), 70 per cent of them live in Germany. The high share of Turks can be explained by Germany's intensive migrant recruitment policy in the sixties. The same is true for nationals from former Yugoslavia, who are the second largest group in the EU (7.9 per cent). Again, about 70 per cent of nationals of the Yugoslavia reside in Germany.[20] The war in Yugoslavia led to a significant increase, at least temporarily, of the already high share of former Yugoslav nationals in Germany[21]. Germany received approximately 360,000 civil war refugees, most of them had moved back to Bosnia-Herzegovina by mid 1999.

Geographical and historical factors explain the residence of half of the 1.1 million Moroccans in France. Likewise the presence of the 400,000 US nationals, a quarter of them reside in Britain, a quarter in Germany and 15 per cent in Italy, can similarly be attributed to historical factors.[22]

---

16 "Classical" push–pull model, see *Fassmann/Münz*, Europäische Migration und die Internationalisierung des Arbeitsmarktes, Innovation und Beharrung in der Arbeitspolitik (1993), 26; *Ronge*, ParlBeilage 7/1993, 16; concerning the regional distribution in Germany see *Münz/Ulrich*, Changing Patterns of Migration (1995), 25 .

17 Entire net immigration including nationals, EU/EEA nationals and third-country nationals; Source: Eurostat Bevölkerungsstatistik (Population Statistics), Daten 1995-1998 (1999) 194 et seq.

18 *Muus*, International Migration within and towards the European Economic Area, 14.

19 Cf. SOPEMI – Annual Report (1996), 13.

20 Eurostat, news release 31/96 of 22 May 1996.

21 *Schelter*, ParlBeilage 1-2/1996, 19, 21; a critical view has been presented by *Möschel*, ParlBeilage 3-4/1995, 10, 11, who describes a consensus between the Member States – except Germany – that the unequal share of burden be justified; *Ronge*, ParlBeilage 7/1993, 16, 23, identifies a variable sensitivity in dependence of the distance to the concerned border; see also *Hailbronner*, SZIER 3 (1993), 517 et seq.

22 Eurostat news release 31/96 of 22 May 1996.

Table B

State[23]	*Popu-lation (1000)*	*Nationals*	*Aliens*	*EEA citizens*	*Other States in Europe*	*the Americas*	*Africa*	*Asia*	*Australia and Oceania*	*Others*
Austria	7,795.8	7,278.1	517.7	7,358.2	381.9	9.5	8.5	26.5	0.7	6.2
Belgium	10,143.0	9,233.3	909.8	9,788.9	101.5	20.9	179.5	24.4	0.6	3.6
Denmark	5,251.0	5,028.3	222.8	5,090.7	74.0	9.1	15.7	48.9	1.0	10.5
Finland	5,116.8	5,062.6	32.0	5,062.6	32.0	3.1	7.0	9.7	0.4	1.8
France	56,652.0	53,055.4	3,596.6	54,378.9	315.7	72.8	1,663.1	227.0	2.3	n/a
Germany	81,817.5	74,643.6	7,173.9	76,464.8	4,093.3	183.0	291.2	672.6	9.2	64.6
Greece	10,465.1	10,309.6	155.5	10,354.5	46.1	20.2	13.4	27.1	1.2	n/a
Ireland	3,626.1	3,509.1	3,580.7	n/a	n/a	12.3	n/a	n/a	n/a	n/a
Italy	57,268.6	56,585.0	683.6	56,710.5	131.2	72.4	226.5	113.2	2.9	0.4
Luxembourg	406.6	274.1	132.5	393.9	n/a	n/a	n/a	n/a	n/a	n/a
Netherlands	15,493.9	14,768.5	725.4	14,961.3	238.3	40.1	196.8	71.4	2.5	11.5
Portugal	9,920.8	9,752.4	168.3	9,794.3	1.8	36.7	79.2	6.7	0.5	0.3
Spain	39,741.7	39,242.7	499.0	39,481.4	10.0	108.9	95.7	38.2	0.9	0.3
Sweden	8,837.5	8,305.7	531.8	8,521.9	151.6	33.8	28.7	83.1	1.9	14.3
United Kingdom	57,881.0	5,589.0	1,992.0	56,714.0	135.0	232.0	235.0	437.0	89.0	2.0
EU total	**370,417.4**	**302,637.4**	**20,921.6**	**355,075.9**	**5,712.4**	**842.5**	**3,040.3**	**1,785.8**	**113.1**	**115.5**

23 Own composition on the basis of data material privided in Eurostat Bevölkerungsstatistik (Population Statistics), Daten 1995-1998 (1999), 36 et seq.

b) Share of Non-EEA-Citizens in the EU as of 1 January 1996

EEA nationals enjoy the same right of freedom of movement as EU citizens.[24] It is therefore useful for the evaluating of graphs to disregard nationals of the EEA states. If one takes a look at the non-EEA nationals in the EU, it can be clearly seen, that their relation to the population differs widely. The average share is 2.7 percent. The largest share reside in Germany (6.3 percent) and Austria (5.4 percent). The share of third-country nationals in France (4 percent), Belgium (3.7 percent) and the Netherlands (3.8 percent) is also above average. In contrast to this, there are very few third-country nationals in Finland (0.9 percent), Ireland (0.6 percent), Spain (0.6 percent), Portugal (1.2 percent) and Italy (0.9 percent). The population of non-EEA citizens in the EU is increasing steadily and at the present amounts to about 12 million people.

c) The Employment of Foreign Workers in the EU Member States (1993)

The employment for foreign workers in EU member states as well is by no means homogeneous. The following table shows the share of foreign workers in relation to all employees of the EU member states.

Member State[25]	*EU Citizens*	*Third-country nationals*	*Total*
Belgium	5.9	2.5	8.4
Denmark	0.5	1.4	1.9
France	2.7	3.6	6.3
Germany	2.5	6.2	8.7
Greece	0.2	1.3	1.5
Ireland	2.3	0.6	2.9
Italy	0.2	0.8	1
Luxembourg	34.6	4.0	38.6
Netherlands	1.6	2.3	3.9
Portugal	0.2	0.3	0.5
Spain	0.2	0.3	0.5
United Kingdom	1.4	2.2	3.6
EU total	**1.7**	**3.0**	**4.7**

A remarkably high level of foreign employment is recorded in Belgium, Germany and France. The high quota of Union citizens working in Belgium is notable. Germany has the highest share of third-country nationals among employees (6.2 percent), followed by France (3.6 percent). The particularly high

24 See *infra* Chapter C V 2.

25 Source: *Walwei*, ASP 1996, 15, 24 with reference to Eurostat, Erhebung über Arbeitskräfte, results 1993, published 1995. More recent data have not been available.

level for Germany cannot exclusively be explained by a high rate of admission of third-country nationals. German citizenship law, valid until 1999 has produced many so-called "second- and third generation" descendants of foreign workers. In EU Member States with a different nationality law, partly based on a *ius soli* acquisition of nationality, the second and third generation of foreign workers would usually be counted as nationals.

Nevertheless, roughly corrected high quota of about 5 percent of foreign born third-country nationals remain in Germany[26]. This shows that the foreign employment rate is considerably higher in Germany than in other EU member states. Furthermore, the *ius sanguinis* effect is considerably reduced by the share of "ethnic Germans" from the Soviet Union in the labour market. They are not taken into consideration in the EU statistics, due to their special constitutional status as "Germans" acquiring German citizenship on taking up permanent residence in Germany.

d) Population Development in the European Union in 1998[27]

Member State	*Total Population per 1 January 1998 (1000)*	*Population Increase in 1998 (1000)*	*Net Migration (1000)*	*Total Population per 1 January 1999 (1000)*
Belgium	10,192.3	21.5	11.6	10,213.8
Denmark	5,294.9	18.7	11.0	5,313.6
Germany	82,057.4	–19.4	50.8	82,038.0
Greece	10,511.0	22.1	22.5	10,533.0
Spain	39,347.9	46.3	42.3	39,394.3
France	58,726.9	239.9	40.0	58,966.8
Ireland	3,694.0	50.7	28.5	3,744.7
Italy	57,563.4	49.3	103.2	57,612.6
Luxembourg	423.7	5.5	4.0	429.2
Netherlands	15,654.2	106.0	44.1	15,760.2
Austria	8,075.4	7.4	4.5	8,082.8
Portugal	9,957.3	22.2	15.2	9,979.5
Finland	5,147.3	12.3	4.5	5,159.6
Sweden	8,847.6	6.7	10.9	8,854.3
United Kingdom	59,089.6	157.4	68.0	59,247.0
EU total	**374,582.9**	**746.6**	**461.1**	**375,329.4**

26 *Plender*, Visas and Control of External Border of the Member States, 10, tries to trace the different figures solely to different legal definitions and varying statistical method.

27 Source: *Eurostat* Statistics in Focus, Population and social conditions, no. 12/99, "First results of the demographic data collection for 1998 in Europe".

Figures show that 61.8% of the Member States' increase of population in 1998 is a result of net migration.

3. *The quantity of refugee flows and their geographical distribution*

Larger migration flows or situations of mass migration occur frequently as a result of wars, civil wars, political upheavals and natural disasters. Economic and political turmoil frequently cause problems of control of migratory movements for the EU and its Member States. EU Member States, in particular Germany, have reacted to persistently growing flows of refugees by substantial legislative changes. The German Asylum Reform of 1993, introducing a strict concept of safe third country and abbreviated asylum procedures, – in combination with administrative enforcement measures and a much stricter border control – has brought down the peak of 438,000 asylum seekers in 1992, roughly 75% of all asylum seekers in the European Union, to approx. 99,000 asylum applicants in 1998.[28]

Recently, the civil war in Kosovo and the systematic suppression of the Kosovo Albanian population by Serbian forces has produced an immediate flow of refugees to Western Europe only partly controllable at the European Union's external borders. As usual, political causes of refuge are inseparably connected with economic reasons. From a sociological perspective it seems difficult to draw a dividing line between "political" refugees, "de facto" refugees, trying to escape civil war and political suppression and economic refugees fleeing miserable living conditions. Therefore, refugee issues cannot be separated from the immigration issue on the whole. Refugee movements are part of the migration issue. It is, nevertheless, necessary to maintain a legal distinction between refugees and other migrants.[29]

The following tables and diagrams chart fluctuations in the number of asylum claims in recent years. The number of applications for asylum in EU Member States is compared with figures for classical immigration countries. All data shown are calculated in relation to total population.

[28] UNHCR Statistics – Asylum Seekers in Europe during 1998.

[29] EP, No. 5 of the resolution to the European migration policy of 18 November 1992, A3-0280/92, O.J. 1992 C 337/94.

a) Asylum Claims in Europe 1992-1999[30]

State	1999[31]	1998	1997	1996	1995	1994	1993	1992
Austria	9,830	13,805	6,719	6,991	5,920	5,082	4,744	16,238
Belgium	12,654	21,965	11,575	12,412	11,648	14,456	26,281	17,398
Denmark	3,326	5,699	5,092	5,893	5,104	6,651	14,347	13,884
Finland	1,068	1,272	973	711	854	836	2,023	3,634
France	12,984	22,375	21,416	17,405	20,415	25,884	28,466	28,872
Germany	46,457	98,644	104,353	116,367	127,937	127,210	322,599	438,191
Greece	n/a	n/a	n/a	1640	1282	1107	862	2108
Ireland	1,975	4,626	3,882	1,179	424	362	91	39
Italy	3,268	6,939	1,712	681	1,752	1,844	1,571	2,589
Netherlands	17,431	45,217	34,443	22,857	29,258	52,576	35,399	20,346
Norway	4,450	8,277	2,277	1,778	1,460	3,379	12,876	5,238
Portugal	n/a	n/a	n/a	269	332	614	2090	655
Spain	4,001	6,639	4,975	4,730	5,678	11,901	12,645	11,712
Sweden	5,094	12,844	9,619	5,774	9,047	18,640	37,581	84,018
United Kingdom	30,447	58,000	41,500	37,000	54,988	42,201	28,000	32,300
EU total	**152,985**	**306,302**	**1220,563**	**3533,386**	**3165,207**	**3228,824**	**3569,532**	**3476,42**

b) Distribution of Asylum Claims among EU Member States

The distribution of asylum seekers in the EU is as uneven as the overall distribution of third-country nationals in Europe. Germany in 1998 has continued to receive the largest number of asylum seekers in the EU (99,000), followed by the UK (58,000), the Netherlands (45,000) and Switzerland (41,000). In total, these four countries received 66% of asylum applications lodged in Europe during 1998. A similar trend is shown if the number of asylum claims from 1990 until 1994 are related to the total population. Only Sweden has taken more asylum seekers (2.25%) than Germany with 1.6%. The EU average during that time lies at about 0.68 percent. Only few asylum applications were registered in Finland (0.22%), France (0.32%), Portugal (0.04%), Spain (0.14%) and Greece (0.13%).

The relation between the number of asylum seekers within the past years and the total population must, however, be interpreted with caution. This period of time is

[30] Source: IGC as compiled by Bundesamt für die Anerkennung ausländischer Flüchtlinge (Federal Office for the Recognition of Foreign Refugees), Asylpraxis – Tabellen und Diagramme mit Erläuterungen, 4th ed. (1999) 22. Figures for Greece and Portugal have been taken from Eurostat Bevölkerungsstatistik (Population Statistics), Daten 1995-1998 (1999) 200 et seq. because these states do not participate in IGC. Eurostat data only comprise the years 1985-1996. As regards the other Member States the Eurostat data deviate, though not significantly, from data supplied by IGC. See *Schoenemann* in Heinelt, Zuwanderungspolitik in Europa (1994), 65 et seq. for further data.

[31] The figures include data for January to June except for Italy (January to April).

fixed at random and is chosen to level out short-term variations of asylum claims in one country. In comparison to classical immigration countries it can be seen that many asylum applicants use the asylum procedures to compensate for the lack of other legal immigration opportunities. Recent numbers of 1999 indicate that in Europe an upward trend in asylum claims can be registered while asylum applications in the non-European countries continue to fall, basically due to the development in the United States, where the number of asylum applications fell from 84,800 in the fiscal year 1997 to only 35,000 during the fiscal year 1998.[32] In Europe, the share in the total number of asylum applications lodged in the 29 most important host countries increased from 53% in 1996 to 81% in 1998. In the European Union, the number of applications rose from 252,000 in 1997 to 299,000 in 1998. Although still receiving by far the largest number of asylum applications, Germany recorded a significant decrease in asylum applications in 1998 in contrast to most major EU host countries.[33] Another significant trend seems to be the rapid increase in asylum applications lodged in the Central Eastern European countries, rising from 1997 to 1998 from 9.200 to 16.900. Hungary (plus 573%), Norway (plus 261%), Austria (plus 106%), Belgium (plus 86%) as well as Switzerland (plus 70%) were at the top of European countries with the highest relative increase of asylum seekers. Remarkably, Hungary became the tenth-largest country of destination for asylum seekers in Europe in 1998, while Poland, Rumania and Slovakia recorded a decrease in asylum applications in 1998. The statistics indicate that some European states are more attractive to asylum seekers than others, presumably for geographic, cultural, economical and legal reasons.[34]

4. *The Known and Unknown Factor: Illegal Immigration*

None of the tables and charts previously presented consider the size of clandestine migration. Naturally, exact statistical material does not exist.[35] However, the phenomenon of clandestine migration is an integral part of the migration issue. Illegal migration is frequently attributed to restrictions enacted in 1973, when the labour recruitment programs had been terminated and migrant workers were unsuccessfully encouraged to return home. It has been estimated that after the mid-1980s, undocumented economic migration and asylum inflows accounted for an increasingly large proportion of net immigration into Western Europe. In spite of restrictive admission policies, the number of aliens in Western European countries increased significantly and the arrival of families confirmed the permanent character of the presence of immigrant workers. In addition to legal immigration by family reunion, illegal immigration is generally considered to have become a major factor of the general immigration pattern into Europe including aliens taking

---

32 UNHCR Statistics – Asylum seekers in Europe during 1998.

33 UNHCR Statistics – Asylum Seekers in Europe during 1998.

34 *Münz/Ulrich*, Changing Patterns of Migration (1995), 19; *Hobe*, GYIL 36 (1993), 60, 76, explains the exceptional character of the former asylum law in Germany in a comparative overview.

35 Cf. *Stanley/Rowlands*, Die Rechte von Drittausländern in der neuen europäischen Ordnung (1994), 27.

advantage of the asylum system to file abusive or manifestly unfounded asylum claims. The minimum numbers of illegally present third-country nationals in European countries are estimated for France with 200,000, for Germany with 350,000 plus 300,000 rejected and non deportable asylum seekers, for Italy with 600,000 persons, for Spain with 300,000 and Switzerland with 100,000 persons.[36]

Frequently, European states have reacted to the phenomenon of illegal immigration by programs to regularize the status of illegal immigrants. It seems that legislation and practice in the European countries differs widely as to the national legislation and procedures for regularization of illegal immigrants. In principle, regularization has been held necessary in order to terminate a situation of illegality of those aliens who for legal or factual reasons cannot be deported. Frequently, illegal aliens after a prolonged period of residence become a part of the (irregular) labour force of their host countries and – in spite of their irregular status – a part of the population of the host country. The need to regularize aliens with an irregular status may become stronger with increasing restrictions to achieve a legal status based on valid documents and fulfilment of all necessary requirements in order to get a prolongation of a residence permit.

There are, however, also several arguments which can be raised against legalization programs. First, legalization may send out pull-signals to other potential migrants. Successful illegal immigration may undermine the preventive effect of admission regulations.[37] Entry regulations will become ineffective if illegal immigrants as a rule after a certain time achieve a regular status. Preventive effects cannot be ignored as a tool of immigration control. They also play a significant psychological role. In Germany, for example, the number of asylum seekers from safe countries of origin decreased substantially even before the respective laws were applied. Italian experience indicates that legalization programs may play a major role in the increase of clandestine migration.[38]

Economic arguments may also be advanced against legalization programs. The market value of an illegal employee is based on illegality. Where minimum wages and contribution to social insurance need not be considered an illegal worker may provide services below the costs of a regular employee. Therefore, legalization takes away specific advantages of illegality.[39] Legalization increases the price of formerly illegal workers. A proportionate increase in the price of the products now produced legally or an increase in the demand for new illegal employees may be the result. If illegal employment is not sanctioned adequately, a purely rationally behaving entrepreneur will resort to employing new illegal immigrants in order not to endanger his market position through higher prices.

---

[36] E.g. UNHCR Colloquium on Irregular Migration, Geneva, 25 February 1997, 3; the estimates are reported as having been based on research conducted on basis of clearly elaborated methodology.

[37] Cf. *Stanlay/Rowlands*, Die Rechte von Drittausländern in der neuen europäischen Ordnung (1994), 27.

[38] *Calavita* in *Cornelius et al. (eds.)*, Controlling Immigration (1994), 304, 314.

[39] *Calavita*, id., 317.

III. Migration as a Social and Economic Factor

1. *The Alleged Need for Increased Immigration*

The "ideal migrant" would be an intelligent, healthy young woman of about 20 years of age, with language skills for the destination country, high vocational skills, and financial reserves. She would share democratic convictions, have a clear crime-record and pursue the aim to have children without retiring from working life.

This profile of an "ideal migrant", composing all demand-orientated factors, however, seldom corresponds to real migrants. It is basically a theoretical ideal which would constitute potentially profitable migration for the destination country. The realization of a European migration policy in accordance with the economic needs of the European Union raises a multitude of legal, social and economic issues beyond the scope of this work. It may, however, be necessary to consider more closely a scheme of selection immigration criteria ensuring that persons of high skill fulfilling a certain profile of professional demand will be permitted to migrate into the European Union.

Generally speaking, the decision to leave the country of origin is based upon multiple motives. Monocausal explanations of migration decisions are frequently not sufficient.[40] The common push/pull models may help to understand the reasons for migration, although they are not sufficient to make forecasts about migration movements. Pull migration is explained as "immigration drawn in by a strong economy and sometimes by active government in order to overcome labour shortages" while push migration is "spurred by conditions in the home, or sending country".[41] Only pull migration is seen as economically beneficial. According to such models migration decisions are determined by the following push- and pull-factors:

push-factors:

- international war and annexation
- internal armed conflicts such as civil war, secession, dissolution and revolutionary coups or other internal national or ethnic conflicts
- totalitarian regime with political persecution or genocide
- forced resettlement (e.g. the "ethnic cleansing" in Ex-Yugoslavia)
- discrimination against minorities
- discrimination against majorities (apartheid)
- guerrilla activities and terrorism
- other violations of human rights
- poverty and hunger
- unemployment or permanent low-wage levels

---

[40] See the earliest analysis provided by *Ravenstein*, who founded migration research in the social sciences in 1885, *Blaschke* in *Knapp* (ed.), Migration im neuen Europa (1994), 23, 25.

[41] The definitions are taken from *Breuss/Tesche*, A General Equilibrium Analysis of East-West Migration: The Case of Austria-Hungary (1996), 2. The authors supply detailed references for the distinction they have drawn.

- natural disaster
- ecological devastation

pull-factors:

- state protection of the subsistence level
- unsaturated labour market with higher level of wages
- opportunities for higher education or advanced training
- overall economic prosperity
- family reunion
- striving for luck and cognition
- political stability
- maintenance of the rule of law
- democracy
- pluralism
- effective protection of human rights
- habitable living space

The question why persons actually migrate is, however, dependent on a decision of the individual based upon a highly subjective evaluation of the advantages and disadvantages, as well as of the wishes in case of illegal immigration.[42] Therefore, a policy of migration control is just one of many factors promoting or impeding migration. If push-factors in the European Union producing a flow of migrants do not decrease, the supply of migrants will exceed demand. A reduction of the niveau of prosperity is not desirable and a decrease of the number of conflicts causing migration movements cannot be expected either. Therefore, most likely, many third-country nationals will continue to try to immigrate into the EU. Many of these immigrants will not satisfy the labour market requirements of the EU Member States.

The History of Migration in Europe after the end of World War II can be roughly divided into five phases.[43]

	Period	*Policy charges*	*Gross immigration per year*
Phase 1	1948 – 1964	Freedom of movement granted within the OECD, EEC, Benelux and northern Europe.	500,000
Phase 2	1965 – 1972	Recruitment of migrant workers in Southern Europe, Turkey and Yugoslavia	1,000,000
Phase 3	1973 – 1982	Immigration restriction due to the oil crisis – family reunification.	700,000
Phase 4	1983 – 1988	Increase of asylum seekers.	1,200,000
Phase 5	1989 – present	Intensified harmonization efforts in migration control, common external borders.	2,500,000

---

[42] See e.g. the strong to economic factors adjusted decision process, *Straubhaar* in *Knapp* (ed.), Migration im neuen Europa (1994), 69, 73.

[43] Asyl in Europa, Asyl in der Schweiz, ICMPD expert opinion, 15.

An exact description of the extent and causes of the migration phenomenon can only be made retrospectively. It is impossible to precisely predict the future rate of migration to Europe. Analysis and prognosis are the only way to get an impression of what tomorrow may bring.[44] Such scenarios are susceptible to failure. They may differ significantly from actual migration movements.[45]

The political instability and uncertainty of economic growth in the former Soviet Union may lead to large refugee movements. In case of crises the decisive push-factors will be economic underdevelopment[46] and ethnic conflict.[47] Furthermore, the mid-term demographic development in Africa[48] and Asia may trigger an increase of migration movements to Europe. In the long run the growth of the world population may be stabilized by a change of the fertility behaviour. In the foreseeable future however, world population will increase substantially. An increase from what is now about 5,5 billion up to approximately 9 to 10 billion people is expected by the year 2050. Only if the reproduction rate falls below the replacement fertility level, will the expected population in the year 2200 be the same as today.[49] Even if world population will substantially increase, birth control would be practiced to a much larger degree in the immediate future.

Therefore it is safe to assume that Europe will be confronted with a high and lasting migration pressure in the coming decades.[50] Moreover, one may expect that the world-wide migration potential is much larger than the capacity of western industrial states to admit migrants.[51]

Geographic and economic circumstances lead to an uneven distribution of migrants in the EU. The unproportional burden on some EU Member States caused by migration flows clearly calls for action to share the burden of migration. The abolition of internal border controls enforces the need for further co-operation. Divergent migration policies on the part of any one Member State may undermine stricter national control measures of any other Member States.

---

44 See e.g. The potential of migrants with family links in Germany, in *Hailbronner/Klos/Münz/Ulrich*, Potentiale für die zukünftige Zuwanderung von Ausländern nach Deutschland (1997), 56 et seq., 81; see also, *Eichengreen*, Thinking about Migration, Working Paper (1993), 2; *Sieveking* in Recht und Politik 1992, 135 et seq.

45 *Heinelt*, Zuwanderungspolitik in Europa, 10 with reference to SOPEMI – Annual Report (1992), 123, *Ronge*, ParlBeilage 7/1993, 16, 22; *Thränhardt* in *Heinelt*, Zuwanderungspolitik in Europa (1994), 40; According to initial estimations the migration potential for the former Soviet Union was 40 to 50 million persons. In later estimates a potential of only 2 to 8 million persons was assumed, see *Opitz* in *Knapp* (ed.), Migration im neuen Europa, 60; *Santel*, Migration in und nach Europa (1995), 117; see also *Ghosh* in *Ardittis* (ed.), The Politics of East-West Migration (1994), 217.

46 *Werner*, MittAB 1994, 232, 233, 240.

47 *Öberg/Boubnova* in *King* (ed.), Mass Migration in Europe (1995), 234, 254; *Ronge*, ParlBeilage 7/1993, 16, 22.

48 *Montanari/Cortese* in *King* (ed.), Mass Migration in Europe (1995), 212, 218.

49 See *Birg*, World Population Projections for the 21st Century (1985), 81, 95 et seq., 268 et seq.

50 See COM(94)23 final, 21 (so-called Flynn-Report); further Asyl in Europa, Asyl in der Schweiz, ICMPD experts' opinion for the Bundesamt für Flüchtlinge, Switzerland, 22; *Eichengreen*, Thinking about Migration, 9; *Hellenthal* ZAR (1995), 76; *Öberg* in *King* (ed.), Mass Migration in Europe (1995), 209; *Sadik* in *Klose (ed.)*, Zuwanderung – Möglichkeiten und Grenzen (1994), 14.

51 *Hof*, ParlBeilage 48/1994, 11, 14.

2. *Demographic trends in destination countries*

Demographic trends across the EU are not homogeneous, although a downward trend in birth rates can be seen in most EU Member States[52]. Birth rate decline can be traced back to the level of economic development of a state[53]. It is a structural problem which, even in the long run, is difficult to solve[54]. Changes in the demographic structure will have lasting effects on the gross national product and social security systems of a state. Social security systems may cease to function properly when too many old people for too long time benefit from such systems on the expense of a steadily decreasing work force which has to finance the system. Considerable cuts in basic social welfare payments may be expected. Among the persons most affected by such changes are migrants who are to a much higher degree unemployed or on low paid jobs than the local population[55].

There are several conceivable actions which may be taken to compensate for the aging and declining of the potential workforce. First, productivity could be increased through technological innovation and higher vocational skill.[56] This requires the existence of highly qualified workers and a readiness to keep pace with technological innovation. An increase in the age for retirement may also be necessary. Alternatively or cumulatively pensions will have to be reduced.

Second, an improvement in the employment quota of women is suggested, although an increase in the occupation of women could lead to a further decrease in the number of births[57]. It has been predicted that a higher utilization of the potential workforce represented by women will be at the cost of a lower birth rate.[58] The EU Commission denies a link between female employment and fertility in the EU.[59] The unemployment rate of foreign women differ significantly within the EU from 31.5 per cent (Ireland) to 11.7 per cent (U.K.).[60] Although Italy and Spain have a low female employment quota, the birth rate is also low. This shows that cultural-

---

52 A completely contrary tendency presents itself in the case of the Mediterranean states of northern Africa., see *Montanari/Cortese* in *King* (ed.), Mass Migration in Europe (1995), 212, 218; *Münz* in *Bade*, Das Manifest der 60 (1994), 103.

53 Eurostat found out that the lowest post-WWII fertily rate occured in September 1996. The highest fertility rates exist in Ireland (1,87 child per woman), Finland (1,81), Denmark (1,8) and Sweden (1,74), the lowest in Italy (1,17), Spain (1,18) and Germany (1,24), see Eurostat news release 63/96 of 30 September 1996; cf. COM (96), 60; *Schmid* in *Weidenfeld*, Das europäische Einwanderungskonzept (1994), 89, 92 et seq.; *Schmid/Chruscz* in *Klose (ed.)*, Zuwanderung – Möglichkeiten und Grenzen (1994), 25; *Hof* in Friedrich-Ebert-Stiftung, Europäische Einwanderungspolitik (1995), 12 et seq., 28; *Klauder* in *Bade*, Deutsche im Ausland – Fremde in Deutschland (1992), 458; *Münz* in *Bade*, Das Manifest der 60 (1994), 104.

54 See *Felderer*, ParlBeilage 18/1989, 16.

55 *Richter* ZVersWiss 1995, 647, 652, 658.

56 See the possibilities according to *Schmid/Chruscz* in *Klose (ed.)*, Zuwanderung – Möglichkeiten und Grenzen (1994), 20; cf. also *Miegel* in *Bade*, Das Manifest der 60 (1994), 118 et seq.; *Rürup/Sesselmeier*, ParlBeilage 44/1993, 3, 7 et seq.; *Donges* et al., Einwanderungspolitik (1994), 35 et seq.

57 *Schmid/Chruscz* in *Klose (ed.)*, Zuwanderung – Möglichkeiten und Grenzen (1994), 20, 35;

58 *Hof*, ParlBeilage 48/1994, 11, 19

59 COM (96)60 final.

60 *Kehl/Werner*, The Labour Market Situation of EU and of Third-Country Nationals in the European Union, JAAB (1998), tables 3.2 (numbers from 1983-1995).

historical background and differences in family policy must also be taken into account[61].

Family policy measures could be taken in order to change the demographic trend through a change in the population's attitude towards children. The Swedish example shows that a low birth rate can be influenced. Introduction of a family policy by the state in the years between 1985 and 1990 correlated with an increase of 22 per cent in the fertility rate.[62] Nevertheless, the structurally induced decrease of the birth rate in Germany seems to be irreversible even if the fertility behaviour of the population would change.[63]

Increased migration is frequently suggested as an instrument to influence favourably the demographic structure[64], provided that it were mainly young people who immigrate. It is doubtful whether this could be expected by an open-door migration policy[65]. Furthermore, divergent fertility rates of immigrants should not be overvalued in the long run because the fertility behaviour of immigrants adapts to that of the native population relatively quickly.[66] Migration might be taken into consideration to compensate a demographic deficit as an additional instrument only alongside the indispensable structural changes in the labour market and family policy.

Even if one would try to determine a demand for immigration based on demographic developments in the European Union, it would seem very difficult to identify common European needs and interest. From a demographic perspective, at present only Germany, Italy and Belgium have a potential demand for migration,. There is no need for immigration in Greece and Denmark until the years 2005 and 2010, in Great Britain, France or Spain before 2025.[67] Consequently, a need for European measures to compensate a dwindling potential workforce within the EU vacillates over a period of 30 years. It is therefore difficult to justify a call for action toward a common European reaction to demographic developments. Immigration needs, if there are any, based upon demographic trends can only be identified on national level.[68]

---

61 *Hof*, Europa im Zeichen der Migration (1993), 103, 107.

62 *Coleman*, IMR XXVI (1992), 413, 425; *Calot/Thiede*, DAngVers 1992, 144, 146 for France and Sweden;. see also *Schiffer*, VR 1994, 178, 180.

63 *Hof*, Europa im Zeichen der Migration (1993), 198, 308 et seq.; *Hof*, ParlBeilage 48/1994, 11, 21; *Felderer*, ParlBeilage 18/1989, 16, 22.

64 See EP, D. of the resolution to the European migration policy of 18 November 1992, A3-0280/92, O.J. 1992 C 337/ 94.

65 Cf. *Klauder*, JbchristlSozwiss 35 (1994), 88, 100, 109; *Klauder* MittAB 1993, 477, 486; *Rürup/Sesselmeier*, ParlBeilage 44/1993, 3, 4 .

66 Cf. *Dinkel/Lebok*, ParlBeilage 48/1994, 27, 32; *Schmid*, ParlBeilage 18/1989, 3, 14.

67 *Schmid/Chruscz* in *Klose (ed.)*, Zuwanderung – Möglichkeiten und Grenzen (1994), 38; In contrast to this it is to be noted, that *Rürup/Sesselmeier*, ParlBeilage 44/1993, 3, 9 see an economical need for migration in Germany not until between 2003 and 2008.

68 *Schmid* in *Weidenfeld*, Das europäische Einwanderungskonzept (1994), 89, 116; *Schmid/Chruscz* in *Klose (ed.)*, Zuwanderung – Möglichkeiten und Grenzen (1994), 35 .

3. *Migration and Labour Requirements*

The Parliamentary Assembly of the Council of Europe observes that:

> Immigrants make a significant contribution to the social, economic and political development of industrialized countries. However, if immigration is higher than the capacity of the labour market to absorb new entrants, as observed over recent decades, this may have negative consequences for the social, economic and political stability of industrialized countries.[69]

It accepted in its recommendation of 27 September 1996 that excessive migration can cause negative effects on the destination countries. A harmonized migration policy, as well as national migration policies, must ensure that migrants are socially and politically integrated. Social systems of the welfare state are at stake where uncontrolled migration flows exist. Transnational migration partly contradicts the fundamental principle of national welfare states,[70] although according to the neo-classical approach[71]. Migration movements are in principle always a positive factor in the economy.

Participation in the economic and social life and a fair share in common welfare are indispensable to social harmony. Unrestricted immigration inevitably leads to a struggle for goods[72]. The socially weak will lose this struggle and are in any case those who have to bear the main burden of excessive migration. Unqualified domestic workers and migrants partly crowd each other out in labour market competition.[73]

The economic discussion focuses on the issue whether migrants take those jobs which the local population cannot or does not want to take or also those jobs which otherwise would have been available to reduce unemployment. It seems that a major controversy is whether the emphasis is to be laid on the theories of complement or substitute. It does, however, seem undisputed, that migrants compete with unqualified locals for lower wage jobs.[74] This development is accelerated by structural change which reduce the demand for unskilled labour and

---

69 Parliamentary Assembly of the Council of Europe, Recommendation 1306 (1996) on migration from the developing countries to the European industrialised countries, No. 2, see No. 4; further *Junghanns*, Council of Europe, Report on migration from the developing countries to the European industrialised countries, Doc. 7628.

70 *Donges* et al., Einwanderungspolitik (1994), 7, 28; *Faist*, ZSR 1995, 36, 41.

71 *Hof* in Friedrich-Ebert-Stiftung, Europäische Einwanderungspolitik (1995), 7; *Zimmermann*, SZfVuS 129 (1993), 283, 286; see also the presentation of the different economical theories about migration , *Bauer/Zimmermann* in *van der Erf, Rob and Liesbeth Hee*ring, Causes of International Migration, Proceedings of a workshop, Luxembourg, 14-16. December 1994, Eurostat, (1995), 95, 96.

72 *Hof*, ParlBeilage 48/1994, 11; *Rittstieg*, InfAuslR 1993, 117.

73 *Gieseck/Heilemann/von Löffelholz*, ParlBeilage 7/1993, 29, 34; cf. also *Donges* et al., Einwanderungspolitik (1994), 24; *Hönekopp*, The new labour migration from Eastern Europe (1998), 16; *Rürup/Sesselmeier* in *Klose (ed.)*, Zuwanderung – Möglichkeiten und Grenzen (1994), 65 .

74 Cf. *Hof* in Friedrich-Ebert-Stiftung, Einwanderungskonzeption für die Bundesrepublik Deutschland (1985), 22 et seq.; *Chiodi-Ferro*, Migration (1996), 26; *Zimmermann*, SZfVuS 129 (1993), 283, 291, 293; *Nuscheler*, Internationale Migration (1995), 199, remarks cynically, that, old and sick people will loose their jobs anyway without the competition of migrants.

office work and thus the recruitment of unskilled personnel.[75] Large migratory flows increase the demand for affordable housing. The short-term beneficiaries of excessive migration would therefore appear to be employers and landlords.[76]

The need for immigration is therefore dependent on labour markets.[77] Labour market demand is the classical criterion upon which decisions to admit migrants are based. With an average unemployment rate in the EU at 10.7 per cent and an unemployment rate for non-nationals of 16.7 per cent in 1995, large scale demand for additional work force is not likely.[78] Structural changes, resulting in an increase of qualified work with an over-proportional decrease of unqualified work strongly argue against admission of low skilled immigrants.[79] The mobilization of the EU population of employable age, therefore, is generally given priority, especially in terms of education and further training.[80]

The solution seems to be a coherent European immigration policy based upon a system of selection of young and skilled immigrants according to the economic and social needs of the EU labour market. One must not ignore, however, that on the European level as well as on the national level migration policy decisions are subject to a variety of legal and political considerations such as family reunification, political asylum, humanitarian admission of victims of war and civil war, preferred treatment of nationals of associated countries and the priority of intra-EU labour mobility. An "active" European immigration policy, based upon a selection system and quota of immigrants, can only be envisaged if the labour market demands cannot be satisfied properly by the "ordinary" immigration and internal labour market, including the nationals of Eastern Europe who may legitimately expect to become gradually a part of the EU-labour market. Migrants might cause an increase in the number of unemployed and contribute to the hidden reserve in times of recession.[81]

Moreover, it is essential, if there is to be a positive effect of migration on the social security system, that adequate social insurance contributions are paid. Therefore, migrants need to have jobs with compulsory social insurance

---

75 *Billerbeck*, ZSR (1994), 209, 218; *Junghanns*, Council of Europe, Report on migration from the developing countries to the European industrialised countries, Doc. 7628 of 9 September 1996, *Klauder*, in *Bade*, Deutsche im Ausland – Fremde in Deutschland (1992), 457, 464; this complicates the rise of qualified migrants out of unskilled jobs. cf. *Faist*, ZSR 1995, 108, 118; *Hönekopp*, The new labour migration from Eastern Europe (1998), 14; *Schmid/Chruscz* in *Klose (ed.)*, Zuwanderung – Möglichkeiten und Grenzen (1994), 19.

76 *Afheldt*, ParlBeilage 7/1993, 42, 44-47; *Faist* in ZSR 1995, 36, 40; *v. Loeffelholz* in Friedrich-Ebert-Stiftung, Von der Ausländer- zur Einwanderungspolitik (1994), 53; *Felderer*, ParlBeilage 18/1989, 16, 17; for the situation of competition of migrants from eastern Europe and the German population see *Hönekopp*, The new labour migration from Eastern Europe (1998), 9.

77 Cf. Bundestagsdrucksache (Parliament Document) 13/1070, 792.

78 For the statistical survey see *Kehl/Werner*, The Labour Market Situation of EU and Third-Country Nationals in the European Union (1998) table 3.1.

79 *Coleman*, IMR XXVI (1992), 413, 438, 444; The admission of foreign guest workers (so-called Gastarbeiter) prevented the establishment of new competitive production methods in the German car industry in the seventies, see *Franz*, Zur ökonomischen Bedeutung von Wanderungen und den Möglichkeiten und Grenzen einer Einwanderungspolitik (1993), 19.

80 *Coleman*, IMR XXVI (1992), 413, 443, 455.

81 See *Klauder*, JbchristlSozwiss 35 (1994), 88, 104 .

contributions.[82] In case of persistent high unemployment migration means an economic burden.[83] Only high-skilled migrants may create more jobs than they occupy. There is no perpetuum mobile of migration policy. If there is no lasting stimulation of the labour market, an opening of the EU labour market to third-country nationals may be counterproductive.

4. *Migration Trends*

Fears of large, uncontrolled migration have proved to be unfounded in the case of the Mediterranean states joining the EU.[84] In Germany, immigration primarily resulted from the inflow of third-country nationals. The employment of EU citizens in Germany decreased from 730,000 to approximately 587,000 in 1994. Only recently a minor increase of EU citizens has taken place.

A major influx of migrants to the European Union can be expected from third countries. At present EU net migration is balanced. Although differences between wage levels between some Member States are substantial it is nonetheless possible to achieve a socially acceptable income and living standard in all EU Member States. The economic and social convergence within the European Union is generally said to prevent higher migration flows within the Union. According to polls the main obstacles to intra-EU mobility are inadequate language skills, socio-cultural conditions, insufficient information about job offers and insufficient or expensive accommodation.[85] The need for adjustment caused by structural crises is often fulfilled by regional migration within that Member State. The balance of migration within the EU does not call for controlling or restrictive measures.[86]

IV. Enlargement and Migration

1. *The Effects of Association Agreements and Enlargements of the European Union*

According to Article 310 ECT the European Community has the competence to conclude Association Agreements with other states. The competence to conclude Association Agreements embraces regulations concerning the freedom of movement of citizens of Associated States[87]. Therefore, such treaties may limit policy makers' discretion with respect to defining a European or national migration

---

[82] *Schmähl*, ZVerwWiss 1995, 617, 637.

[83] *Donges* et al., Einwanderungspolitik (1994), 28; *Franz*, ibid., 20; *Klauder*, JbchristlSozwiss 35 (1994), 88, 110; *Klauder* MittAB 1993, 477, 491; *Hof* in Friedrich-Ebert-Stiftung, Einwanderungskonzeption für die Bundesrepublik Deutschland, 22; *Zimmermann*, FAZ 17 of June 1995, 13.

[84] *Werner*, MittAB 1994, 232, 233, 238 et seq.

[85] *Werner*, MittAB 1994, 232, 235.

[86] COM(96)60; *Döring*, SF 1994, 239; *Eichengreen*, Thinking about Migration, Working Paper (1993), 3.

[87] See ECJ, judgment of 30 September 1987, *Demirel v Stadt Schwäbisch Gmünd*, case 12/86, [1987] ECR 3719 para 9.

policy. However, the EEC-Turkey Association Agreement of 1963 remains the only Association Agreement under which free movement has been granted to certain nationals of the associated state. Neither the agreements concluded with Maghreb States nor those recently concluded with the Central Eastern European Countries (henceforth referred to as 'the Europe Agreements' concluded with 'the CEECs') do provide for freedom of movement of nationals of the associated states. Nevertheless, a more liberal treatment of migrants of associated states is an implied part of the structure of the Association Agreements.

Membership of the EU will be the next step for most associated European states. Enlargement of the European Union will take place in the next decade with the accession of certain CEECs, Cyprus and Malta.

Yet the CEECs' present economic situation will still make them more likely to supply push migration, defined by economic analysis as opposite to pull migration. Notably, OECD studies show that migrants from the CEECs tend to be educated, skilled and vital workers[88]. In light of the concern that the expected push migration might accelerate the current employment crisis in the Western European states, there is a risk that the CEECs' accession will pose major challenges to the European Union in the field of migration.[89].

Both migrants from the CEECs and persons who are not nationals of either the CEECs or the EU Member States must be taken into account when speaking of potential migration between CEECs and the EU. Obviously, different legal approaches must be taken to these migration phenomena. CEEC nationals will become EU citizens upon accession of their states of origin while the second group will remain third country-nationals. Prognoses about the prospective post-accession challenges posed by future third country nationals currently resident in the CEECs seem impossible, due to the unavailability of data[90]. The emerging problem must not be underestimated, however, as the Baltic Republics have a high percentage of lawful residents of Russian nationality[91]. Clear estimates about the migration potential between the CEECs and the EU[92] are difficult to obtain. Major challenges are likely to arise from an influx of commuters and the illegally

88 Cf. *Coffey*, Europe – Toward 2001 (1996), 175.

89 *Breuss/Tesche*, A General Equilibrium Analysis of East-West Migration: The Case of Austria-Hungary (1996), 2; see also *Breuss*, Cost and Benefits of EU's Eastern European Enlargement (1995), 15.

90 For instance no estimates were made available by respective authors under the rubrics of prognoses of immigration from Eastern Europe: *Ronge*, ParlBeilage 7/1993, 16, 23 et seq.; or future migration: *Hönekopp*, Old and New Labour Migration to Germany from Eastern Europe, IAB Working Papers No. D-2/10-1996, 16 et seq.

91 See *Behlke*, Das Minderheitenrecht der Republik Lettland (1996) *passim* for a detailed analysis of the situation in Latvia. It should be noted, however, that by the mid-1990s mass movements from the former Soviet bloc had not yet materialised while migration pressure from North Africa in particular has increased; see *Breuss/Tesche*, A General Equilibrium Analysis of East-West Migration: The Case of Austria-Hungary (1996), 6.

92 *Breuss/Tesche*, A General Equilibrium Analysis of East-West Migration: The Case of Austria-Hungary (1996), 4; *Bárta/Richter*, in Europa 1996 – Auswirkungen einer EU-Osterweiterung (1995) 23, 29; *Holnsteiner*, Europa 1996 – Auswirkungen einer EU-Osterweiterung auf die zweite und die dritte Säule (1995), 87 even speaks of 'migration pressure'.

employed, rather than from emigration from the CEECs[93] or due to the fact that baby boomers are soon to enter the CEECs' labour[94] markets. The brain drain problem may be a serious negative side effect for CEECs[95] and will make the implementation of certain restrictions on emigration from these countries to the West[96] unavoidable.

At the same time, doubts have been raised as to whether those CEEC nationals interested in migrating to Western Europe will actually do so when the full freedom of movement is implemented. Analysis of statistical evidence has shown, for instance, that migration patterns were not affected when the restrictions on immigration from Italy were lifted. This fact could support the conclusion that the demand for workers, rather than legal restrictions imposed thereon, is the decisive factor in the development of work migration[97]. After all, migration depends on a complex number of factors[98]. Differences in income and standard of living, employment opportunities, and professional standards of would-be migrants, including language skills[99], all contribute to the decisions made by individuals to take the risks inherent in migration. Travel costs[100] and the existence of "workers' colonies" in Western Europe[101] may also play a role.

2. CEEC Enlargement

Beginning in the early 1990s, the European Union and the Member States started to conclude Europe Agreements with ten CEECs. The agreement with Poland was the blueprint, upon which the other agreements were based[102]. The conclusion of these agreements can be viewed as the first step of a process that will lead to the accession of those CEECs that meet the requirements for becoming EU Member States. The Europe Agreements play the most prominent legal role in the pre-

---

93 *Walterskirchen*, in Europa 1996 – Auswirkungen einer EU-Osterweiterung (1995), 287, 295; *Holnsteiner*, Europa 1996 – Auswirkungen einer EU-Osterweiterung auf die zweite und die dritte Säule (1995) estimates (, 85) that, Austria might face significantly larger numbers of commuters coming from the Slovak Republic, Hungary and the Czech Republic if freedom of movement were introduced.

94 *Walterskirchen*, in Europa 1996 – Auswirkungen einer EU-Osterweiterung (1995), 287, 296.

95 See *van den Bempt & Theelen*, From Europe Agreements to Accession (1996), 48 and the references in the following note.

96 Cf. *Bárta/Richter*, in Europa 1996 – Auswirkungen einer EU-Osterweiterung (1995), 23, 29-30; see also *Merritt*, Abenteuer Osteuropa (1991), 153.

97 See *Gächter*, in Europa 1996 – Auswirkungen einer EU-Osterweiterung (1995), 47, 72-75.

98 Cf. *van den Bempt & Theelen*, From Europe Agreements to Accession (1996), 48 for the factors here discussed.

99 *Breuss/Tesche*, A General Equilibrium Analysis of East-West Migration: The Case of Austria-Hungary (1996), 4 even speak of "language barriers".

100 Cf. *Breuss/Tesche*, A General Equilibrium Analysis of East-West Migration: The Case of Austria-Hungary (1996), 14.

101 *Holnsteiner*, Europa 1996 – Auswirkungen einer EU-Osterweiterung auf die zweite und die dritte Säule (1995), 83.

102 *Guild*, The Europe Agreements, in *Guild* (ed.), The Legal Framework and Social Consequences of Free Movement of Persons in the European Union (1999), 127. For a detailed account of the pre-accession process see *Müller-Graff* in *Maresceau* (ed.), Enlarging the European Union (1997), 27-40 *passim*.

accession process, as they are *pacta de negotiandi* and constitute the duty to enter accession negotiations as soon as CEECs meet the relevant criteria.

The process of enlargement will have a significant impact upon the future European immigration and asylum policy. The accession of more than 100 million people to the European Union will not only put the issue of free movement of labour within the European Union in a completely new dimension; enlargement to Eastern Europe also shifts the burden of external border control and responsibility to deal with illegal immigration and asylum applications to countries that have primarily been transit countries rather than host countries of migrants and refugees seeking protection. The transfer of a regulatory scheme developed under the Schengen Agreement (Schengen Acquis) and within the European Union to countries that did not participate in the elaboration of this system will raise further legal and administrative problems which may require adjustments to the "acquis communautaire".

State	*total area in square kilometers*	*Population in millions per 01 January 1999*[103]
Estonia[104]	45,227	1.446
Latvia[105]	64,589	2.439
Lithuania[106]	65,300	3.701
Poland[107]	312,685	38.667
Hungary[108]	93,030	10.092
Slovenia[109]	20,255	1.978
Slovak Republic[110]	49,035	5.393
Czech Republic[111]	78,866	10.290
Bulgaria[112]	110,994	8.230
Romania[113]	238,391	22.489

[103] See *Eurostat* Statistics in Focus, Population and social conditions, no. 12/99, "First results of the demographic data collection for 1998 in Europe".
[104] O.J. 1998 L 68/3.
[105] O.J. 1998 L 26/3.
[106] O.J. 1998 L 51/3.
[107] O.J. 1993 L 348.
[108] O.J. 1993 L 347.
[109] See O.J. 1999 L 51/3 (26 February 1999). The Europe Agreement concluded with Slovenia entered into force in 1999 because its conclusion was delayed by Italy for almost a year. The agreement had been initialled on 15 June 1995 but signed no earlier than on 10 June 1996 because Italy wanted that certain post-war issues related to Yugoslavian expropriations of Italian citizens in the territory ceded after World War II be settled. See *Vörös/Droutsas*, Die Europa-Abkommen, ZfV (1998), 2, 3.
[110] O.J. 1994 L 359.
[111] O.J. 1994 L 360.
[112] O.J. 1994 L 358.
[113] O.J. 1994 L 357.

Europe and Accession Partnership[114] Agreements have been concluded with ten CEECs. These ten CEECs compromise a total area of about 1,100,000 square kilometers and have a population of about 105,000 million persons.

All accession candidates – except for Romania – share either a common land border or facing coast line with an EU Member State.[115]. The eastern border of Poland alone – which is foreseen as a prospective external EU border – spans a distance of 774 miles.

3. Non-CEECs Interested in EU Membership

In addition to the CEECs, both Malta and Cyprus have expressed interest in becoming EU Member States. As regard Malta there does not exist domestic consensus about the question of whether Malta shall accede to the European Union. While the Maltese government had applied for EU membership in the early 1990s after the 1996 general elections this application had been withdrawn by the new government then in power. The 1998 elections having resulted in a change of government again, Malta has now reactivated her application for EU membership.

Cyprus, as a binational and divided country is in a special situation[116]. Neither the European Communities nor the Member States have recognized the government established after the Turkish intervention in northern Cyprus. The European Union and Cyprus currently negotiate about Cypriot accession regardless of the fact that, according to ECJ jurisprudence, at present political and economic relations are confined to the (southern) Republic of Cyprus[117]. Under the existing EEC-Cyprus Association Agreement only matters of trade form part of the association[118]. Cyprus still has to make major efforts to catch up with the Justice and Home Affairs *acquis*[119]. However, Cyprus will not receive assistance under the PHARE program for that purpose[120]. Apart from that, accession negotiations have to focus on topics such as whether a legal framework must be developed which reconciles Cypriot division and free movement of those Cypriots living under the territorial sovereignty of the non-recognized government established in northern Cyprus. In addition, special arrangements may be necessary for the Turkish population of northern Cyprus is of Turkish ethnicity.

---

[114] Cf. Council Regulation No. 622/98 on assistance to the applicant States in the framework of the pre-accession strategy, and in particular on the establishment of Accession Partnerships, O.J. 1998 L 85/1.

[115] See *Müller-Graff* in *Maresceau* (ed.), Enlarging the European Union (1997), 27, 28.

[116] See *Axt*, in integration 22 (1999), 127 et seq. for a detailed account of the questions related to Cypriot accession.

[117] Cf. ECJ, judgment of 5 July 1994, *The Queen v Minister of Agriculture, Fisheries and Food, ex parte Anastasiou Ltd and others*, case C-432/92, [1994] ECR I-3087 paras 47-55.

[118] See the Agreement establishing an Association between the European Economic Community and the Republic of Cyprus, O.J. 1973 L 133/2 = Greek special edition Chapter 11 Volume 5, 6 = Finnish special edition, Chapter 11 Volume 11 p. 30 = Swedish special edition, Chapter 11 Volume 11 p. 30

[119] Cf. *Axt*, in integration 22 (1999), 127, 134+135.

[120] Cf. *Axt*, in integration 22 (1999), 127, 137.

After all, these questions have quite different a dimension than the questions posed by prospective CEEC accessions. Additionally, CEEC enlargement takes place within a thoroughly drafted legal framework while no similar set of rules exist for Cyprus's potential accession to the European Union.

4. The CEECs' Adaptation to the Justice and Home Affairs Acquis

In its opinions on the CEECs' applications for EU membership in 1997[121], the Commission identified several deficiencies in the implementation of fundamental rights[122], the efficiency of aliens administrations and judicial systems, and in border management facilities and personnel, in the CEECs. PHARE will form part of the framework created by the (prospective) Council Regulation (EC) on co-ordinating aid to the applicant countries in the framework of the pre-accession strategy[123].

The Amsterdam Treaty introduces the aim of establishing an area of freedom, security and justice under Title IV ECT. This change in primary Community law also fuels the need to adjust the pre-accession strategy. Denied entry at the front door several times,[124] the issue of free movement of Eastern Europeans may now sneak in through the back door and finally make its way on to the political agenda. Freedom of movement has in any case been a matter of concern in the course of previous enlargements and will be equally important in the current Accession Agreements negotiations with the prospective new EU Member States. At the same time, EU-CEEC co-operation in the fields of combating clandestine immigration, illegal immigration, the imposition of carrier sanctions shall be increased[125]. Certain elements of such co-operation were already envisaged by the Berlin Declaration of 8 September 1994[126]. The idea of co-operation was later implemented in Article 98 of the Slovenia Agreement, which expressly provides for the establishment of

> a framework for cooperation designed to prevent illegal activities such as ... clandestine immigration and the illegal presence of either party's nationals on the other's territory, with due allowance for the principles and practices of readmission.

---

[121] Bulletin of the European Union, supplements 5-15/97.

[122] Obviously, managing migration involves human rights issues. Cf. *Holnsteiner*, Europa 1996 – Auswirkungen einer EU-Osterweiterung auf die zweite und die dritte Säule (1995), 68-69.

[123] See the amended proposal for a Council Regulation (EC) on co-ordinating aid to the applicant countries in the framework of the pre-accession strategy, O.J. 1998 C 329/13.

[124] See also *Guild*, The Europe Agreements, in *Guild* (ed.), The Legal Framework and Social Consequences of Free Movement of Persons in the European Union (1999), 127: "..the free movement of persons is not an object in itself of the Europe Agreements".

[125] Cf. *Pollet* in *Marescea*u (ed.), Enlarging the European Union (1997), 209, 232-234.

[126] Cf. *Holnsteiner,* Europa 1996 – Auswirkungen einer EU-Osterweiterung auf die zweite und die dritte Säule (1995),73-76.

Member States and the CEECs are discussing the conclusion of a convention modelled upon the Dublin Convention[127]. CEEC visa include the same information as visas issued under European Union auspices[128]. Finally, the CEECs have acceded to the Geneva Convention and the 1967 Protocol. The following States have ratified or lodged a declaration of succession.
Article 8 of the Protocol integrating the Schengen acquis into the framework of the European Union, for example, requires that said acquis "must be accepted in full by all States candidates for admission". In addition, the Member States should also require the CEECs to accede, after joining the European Union, to all agreements concluded under Maastricht's third pillar that have not been re-adopted under Title IV ECT.[129]

State	*Date of entry into force: Geneva Convention*	*Date of entry into force: 1967 Protocol*
Hungary	12 June 1989	14 March 1989
Slovenia	25 June 1991	25 June 1991
Poland	26 December 1991[130]	27 September 1991
Slovak Republic[131]	1 January 1993	1 January 1993
Czech Republic[132]	1 January 1993	1 January 1993
Bulgaria	10 August 1993	12 May 1993
Lithuania	27 July 1997	28 April 1997
Estonia	9 July 1997[133]	10 April 1997
Latvia	29 October 1997[134]	31 July 1997[135]
Romania	5 November 1991	7 August 1991

[127] *Holnsteiner*, Europa 1996 – Auswirkungen einer EU-Osterweiterung auf die zweite und die dritte Säule (1995), 79.

[128] *Holnsteiner*, Europa 1996 – Auswirkungen einer EU-Osterweiterung auf die zweite und die dritte Säule (1995), 80.

[129] Cf. *Holnsteiner*, Europa 1996 – Auswirkungen einer EU-Osterweiterung auf die zweite und die dritte Säule (1995), 72.

[130] Poland has acceded the Convention with the reservation that it does not consider itself bound by Article 24(2) thereof.

[131] Notification of 4 February 1993. The Czechoslovakian Republic had declared its accession to both the Convention and the Protocol earlier. Both instruments took effect for said predecessor state on 24 February 1992.

[132] Notification of 11 May 1993. See also supra previous note.

[133] Estonia has declared that, she considers Articles 23 and 24 of the Convention as recommendatory, and that under Article 25 thereof she will not be bound to deliver certificates in place of the authorities of a foreign country if documentary records necessary for such delivery do not exist in Estonia. Additionally, Estonia will, for a period of five years after the Convention took effect vis-à-vis herself, not issue travel documents under Article 28(1) of the Geneva Convention.

[134] Latvia does not consider itself bound by Articles 8 and 34 of the Convention. Additionally, she reserves the right to designate the place or places of residence of refugees whenever considerations of national security or public order so require. Latvia considers Articles 17(1) and (2), and 24 of the Convention as recommendatory. Finally, Latvia has declared that, in all cases where the convention grants to refugees the most favourable treatment accorded to nationals of a foreign country, she will not interpret this provision as necessarily involving the regime accorded to nationals of countries with which Latvia has concluded regional customs, economic, political or social security agreements.

[135] Latvia has declared that, the reservations made to the Geneva Convention (supra previous note) are applicable in relation to the obligations under the Protocol.

5. *Transitional Arrangements in the course of CEEC Enlargement*

The European Economic Community and the European Union, respectively, had to deal with several cases of enlargement, including the accession of –

- the United Kingdom, Ireland and Denmark in 1973,
- Greece in 1981
- Spain and Portugal in 1986, and
- Austria, Sweden and Finland in 1995.

As was the case in the past, the accession of new Member States will be accompanied by an entire set of comprehensive transitional arrangements. The issue of movement of persons is sure to play a significant role.

Past experience in the enlargement process will be taken into consideration when framing transitional arrangements for new prospective Member States. The Act concerning the Conditions of Accession to the European Communities of the Kingdom of Denmark, Ireland, *the Kingdom of Norway* and the United Kingdom of Great Britain and Northern Ireland and the Adjustments to the Treaties, the Act concerning the Conditions of accession of *the Kingdom of Norway*, the Republic of Austria, the Republic of Finland and the Kingdom of Sweden and the adjustments to the Treaties on which the European Union is founded were the only accession treaties which did not contain comprehensive[136] transitional arrangements with regard to freedom of movement. These Acts dealt solely with certain aspects of social security[137]. The other agreements contained detailed rules on the issue of migration although, at the time of the conclusion of the accession treaties, migration links long existed between the acceding states and the Member States[138]. These provisions dampened any potential massive migration movements[139]. Additionally, the implementation of full freedom of movement caused entirely new migration phenomena only in the case of Portugal[140].

Although the Act concerning the Conditions of Accession of the Hellenic Republic and the Adjustments to the Treaties[141] did not impose any express limitations on the application of Article 39 ECT[142], Article 44 thereof rendered the implementation of the freedom of movement of workers subject to transitional arrangements, as envisaged in regulation 1612/68 and directive 68/360/EEC (see Articles 45-47 of the Act). Additionally, Article 48 of the Act postponed the implementation of certain social rights. A seven year transitional period was implemented for Regulation 1612/68, and was limited to five years with respect to access of family members to the labour market in the Community. States forming

---

[136] Only Protocol No. 3 introduced a specific status of the Channel islands as regards free movement of workers.

[137] By virtue of Annex I to Article 29 of the Act of Accession certain amendments were made to regulation 1408/71 which did, however, not extend to issues of migration; see O.J. 1972 73/1.

[138] Cf. *Gächter*, in Europa 1996 – Auswirkungen einer EU-Osterweiterung (1995), 47.

[139] *Breuss/Tesche*, A General Equilibrium Analysis of East-West Migration: The Case of Austria-Hungary (1996), 4.

[140] *Gächter*, in Europa 1996 – Auswirkungen einer EU-Osterweiterung (1995), 47, 48.

[141] O.J. 1979 L 291/17.

[142] Cf. ECJ, judgment of 30 May 1989, Commission v Hellenic Republic, case 305/87 [1989] ECR 1461, para 15.

the EEC before Greece's accession were allowed to maintain existing restrictions on immigration undertaken with a view to pursuing an activity as an employed person or the taking up and pursuit of paid employment prior to the expiration of the seven year transitional period on 31 December 1987[143]. In addition, Article 130 of the Act allowed the Commission to authorize, of measures aimed at combating serious deterioration in the economic situation of a given area.

The Act concerning the Conditions of Accession of the Kingdom of Spain and the Portuguese Republic and the Adjustments to the Treaties included provision to the extent that Article 39 ECT was applicable only without prejudice to the transitional arrangements[144]. Again, the implementation of the freedom of movement of workers, as envisaged in regulation 1612/68 and directive 68/360/EEC, was postponed until the expiration of transitional period of seven years (see Articles 56-59, 216-219 of the Act). Pre-accession Member States were allowed to maintain, national provisions, or those resulting from bilateral arrangements, which required prior authorization for immigration with a view to pursuing an activity as an employed person and/or taking up paid employment in force until 31 December 1992[145] (see Article 56(1) of the Act). The transitional period was slightly reduced by Council regulation 2194/91[146]. Additional provisions allowed the Commission to authorize measures aimed at combating serious deterioration in the economic situation of a given area, or at the protection of Luxembourg's labour market[147].

Austria, Finland and Sweden acceded to the European Union as EEA Member States. Detailed transitional arrangements with respect to the freedom of movement were unnecessary in this accession, as this freedom had already been introduced by the Treaty establishing the European Economic Area. Accordingly, transitional arrangements did not cover the free movement of persons[148]. However, the existing Member States and Austria did adopt a Joint Declaration on the free movement of workers, which reads as follows:

> Should the accession of Austria give rise to difficulties relating to the free movement of workers, the matter may be brought before the institutions of the Union in order to obtain a solution to this problem. This solution will be in strict accordance with the provisions of the Treaties (including those of the

---

143 ECJ, judgment of 23 March 1983, *Peskeloglou v Bundesanstalt für Arbeit*, case 77/82, [1983] ECR 1085, para 13.

144 Article 55 of the Act (O.J. 1985 L 302/1) reads -

> Article 48 of the EEC Treaty shall only apply, in relation to the freedom of movement of workers between Spain and the other Member States, subject to the transitional provisions laid down in Articles 56 to 59 of this Act.

> Article 215 of the Act contains an identical reservation in relation to the freedom of movement of workers between Portugal and the other Member States.

145 Luxembourg was even allowed to maintain provisions of the mentioned kind until 31 December 1995. See Articles 56(2) and 216(2) of the Act.

146 O.J. 1991 L 206/1 = Finnish special edition Chapter 5 Volume 5, 45 = Swedish special edition Chapter 5 Volume 5, 45.

147 Cf. *Becker*, EU-Erweiterung und differenzierte Integration (1999), 18-19.

148 Cf. *Becker*, EU-Erweiterung und differenzierte Integration (1999), 19, including further references.

Treaty on European Union) and the provisions adopted in application thereof, in particular those relating to the free movement of workers.[149]

This Joint Declaration has no direct binding legal force but qualifies as an instrument of authentic interpretation, as envisaged by Article 31(2)(a) of the Convention of the Law of Treaties[150]. It is, however, of minor importance, as it neither authorizes unilateral action by Austria nor provides for the authorization of such action by the Commission.

Although the Member States and the Commission are unified in support of the requirement that new Member States must accept the entire *acquis communautaire* upon accession to the European Union, they are prepared to accept the adoption of transitional arrangements which enable acceding states to reach Community standards with due consideration to their individual needs. However, preparation for accession plays an equally important role in this process.[151] Accordingly, both the current pre-accession strategy and prospective transitional arrangements must be seen as elements of a differentiated process of integration for the CEECs. That certain transitional provisions governing the free movement of persons will have to be introduced is virtually uncontested[152]. This approach, though somewhat cautious, will enable the CEECs to become EU Member States at an early point in time. The European Union will thus enable the CEECs to participate in European decision-making at a stage when CEEC economies still have to catch up to Western standards, and when the implementation of the free movement of persons will still pose certain economic risks, which are likely to be greater than related benefits for the Western European societies[153]. Which transitional arrangements will eventually be agreed upon, remains a matter of political discretion. It seems to be rather doubtful whether there exist any legal limitations of this discretion[154]. The political dimension of eastern enlargements will be quite different from the changes that originated from the southern enlargements. During the 1980s transitional arrangements only slowed down the implementation of the market freedom accorded to workers, to move within the Community. In the current context, however, freedom of movement is a right enjoyed by all citizens of the Union, though subject to certain limitations and conditions, pursuant to Article 18(1) ECT. Transitional arrangements contained in prospective Acts of Admission

---

149 O.J. 1994 C 241 /388.

150 See *Becker*, EU-Erweiterung und differenzierte Integration (1999), 20. For, detailed analysis see infra B IV 2 c.

151 *Becker*, EU-Erweiterung und differenzierte Integration (1999), 21.

152 See for instance COM(97)2000 final, 41; *Breuss/Tesche*, A General Equilibrium Analysis of East-West Migration: The Case of Austria-Hungary (1996), 14; *Holnsteiner*, Europa 1996 – Auswirkungen einer EU-Osterweiterung auf die zweite und die dritte Säule (1995), 85; Becker, EU-Erweiterung und differenzierte Integration (1999), 13; *Bárta/Richter*, in Europa 1996 – Auswirkungen einer EU-Osterweiterung (1995), 23, 29-30; *Merritt*, Abenteuer Osteuropa (1991), 153.

153 Cf. *Holnsteiner*, Europa 1996 – Auswirkungen einer EU-Osterweiterung auf die zweite und die dritte Säule (1995), 86, for the requirement to balance risks and benefits in regard of the free movement of persons.

154 See *Becker*, EU-Erweiterung und differenzierte Integration (1999), 64-87 for a detailed assessment on the question of whether such outer limits exist.

of individual CEECs would therefore distract from a fundamental freedom which is attached to the core legal relationship between the European Union and its citizens. The need for transitional arrangements notwithstanding, the drafting of such arrangements will require a high measure of political instinct, duly taking into account both the need for effective migration control and the promise of a European Union without internal borders as envisaged inter alia by Article 18 ECT.

B

Immigration, Visa and Asylum Policy in an Area of Freedom, Security and Justice: Title IV of the Treaty establishing the European Community and the Communitarization of the Schengen *Acquis*

The establishment of an immigration control system is obviously closely connected with the abolition of internal border controls and the establishment of the internal market[1]. Title IV ECT, as introduced by the Amsterdam Treaty, will establish a common, though not uniform, legal framework for the regulation of free movement of persons; a European immigration policy will, *inter alia*, deal with entry and sojourn of third-country nationals. The new set of provisions ties ex-Article 100c ECT on visa policy to, by way of communitarization, former third pillar intergovernmental co-operation (as it then was) in the fields of immigration and asylum policy. Additionally, Amsterdam lays the foundations for the communitarization of the Schengen *acquis* (currently placed in the third pillar) while the Council shall concurrently seek and find the appropriate legal bases for each of the provisions and decisions which constitute this *acquis* pursuant to Article 1(1), second paragraph of the Protocol integrating the Schengen acquis into the framework of the European Union (henceforth referred to as the 'Schengen Protocol').

This chapter will focus on various aspects of Title IV ECT, the Schengen Protocol and related instruments. After identifying the general concept underlying its provisions and the reasons for the introduction of Title IV, the scope of EU policy-making related to third-country nationals in terms of substantive European law, the procedures established by Title IV ECT, and related questions of judicial review will be addressed. Additionally, the relationship between the legal framework established by Title IV ECT, and Community powers which regulate European policies affecting nationals of third countries and extend beyond the reach of Title IV ECT, shall be outlined.

I. The Cautious Approach of Title IV ECT to Supranationalization

European Heads of State considered the harmonization of national law regarding alien residents under the auspices of the European Economic Community (as it was then called) as early as 1974 at their Paris summit[2]. In the process of further integration, however, this project was never realized and the regulation of aliens law (including asylum law, which became especially significant due to the growing influx of refugees throughout the 1980s and 1990s) left to the Member States. Member States continue to regard these areas as crucial to maintain their sovereignty.

When drafting Title IV ECT and the Schengen Protocol, the Intergovernmental Conference did not entirely subordinate national control over immigration and asylum policy to EC regulation. Accordingly, the approach towards supranational law-making

1 *Hailbronner*, 35 CML Rev. (1998) 1047, 1048.
2 Paris summit of 9-10 December 1974, communiqué para 10.

within the ambit of Title IV ECT is slightly different from that applied to other branches of Community law. Additionally, Title IV ECT rejects certain jurisprudential methods developed by the European Court of Justice, which have been used to progressively increase the scope of European Treaty law. The Member States have been anxious to retain a certain *domaine réservé* and an active say in its definition; Title IV ECT was framed on this premise. In particular, they have excluded the application of Articles 94 and 308 ECT which exclude a recourse to the *domaine réservé.*

Several features characterize the cautious approach the Member States have taken towards supranationalization.

First, Title IV ECT and the Schengen Protocol can be considered as examples of closer co-operation, as envisaged by Articles 40, 43-45 TEU and Article 11 ECT. The communitarization of Title IV matters and of the Schengen Agreement does not include all EU Member States. The Amsterdam Treaty thus confirms the concept of two categories of Community law, introduced with the UK's refusal to accept the transfer of powers in the field of social policy to the Community. Whether flexibility and closer co-operation may lead to "mixed migration regimes" reflecting the highly divergent interests of different groups of EU Member States, particularly in their refugees policies, remains to be seen.

Second, while ex-Article K.1 TEU viewed asylum policy as a whole, as a matter of common interest within the Maastricht third pillar framework[3], substantive Title IV powers established by Article 63 ECT are confined to specific areas. Neither measures on expulsion and deportation (including the issue of transnational enforcement), nor measures relating to the prevention of migration movements are expressly mentioned in the catalogue. Title IV powers are thus neither comprehensive, nor exclusive, nor exhaustive[4]. Additionally, since Amsterdam's third pillar only provides for police and judicial co-operation in criminal matters, loopholes existent in the catalogue of Title IV powers cannot be filled by the EU framework[5].

Third, the new powers in general allow only for the introduction of minimum standards (Article 63(1)(b-d) and (2)(a) ECT). The term "minimum standard" has been used in first pillar law for the first time in this Title and introduces a new chapter in Community law-making. Articles 94 and 95 (ex-Articles 100 and 100a) ECT provide for harmonization at the European level. Article 95(4) ECT allows for national legislation which exceeds this level of harmonization, but only under exceptional circumstances, and subject to the control of the European Commission[6]. In other words, harmonization can include a minimum standard, but is aimed at the establishment of uniform legal standards. A provision which expressly limits the legislative power to minimum standards, on the other hand, is not aimed at a uniform European legislation, although its application may result in such if all Member States are unwilling to exceed the minimum. Consequently, Title IV ECT leaves the decision to go beyond the common standards of law to the discretion of the Member States.

Fourth, the protocols and declarations related to substantive provisions on immigration, visa and asylum policy include reservations in favour of national foreign

---

3 See *Hailbronner*, in Hummer (ed.), Die Europäische Union nach dem Vertrag von Amsterdam (1998), 179, 180.

4 *Hailbronner* ibid.

5 Cf. *Hailbronner/Thiery* EuR 1998, 583, 587; *Ehlermann* 4 ELJ (1998) 246, 269.

6 See *Klein*, in Hailbronner/Klein/Magiera/Müller-Graff, Handkommentar zum EG/EU-Vertrag (1991), Article 100a para 16.

policy-making. They refute thus the presumption that each internal EC power is tied to a parallel external one (the so-called ERTA effect).

Fifth, the initiative function of the Commission is somewhat restricted by the introduction of a duty to consider proposals presented by Member States, even after it gains the exclusive right of initiative upon the expiry of the five years' transitional period.

Sixth, for a period of five years following the entry into force of the Amsterdam Treaty, adoption of almost all EC legislation will require unanimous approval of the Council. Even after the expiry of this period, as a matter of principle, only a Council decision which has been taken unanimously can bring about change in this respect.

Seventh, and finally, not only has access to the European Court of Justice been limited by restraining referrals for preliminary rulings, but the Court's jurisdiction has also been limited with respect to the maintenance of law and order and the safeguarding of internal security by the Member States in domestic law. Notwithstanding the details of Articles 64(1), 68(2) ECT, and Article 2(1), third paragraph of the Schengen Protocol (which are to be dealt with in detail *sub specie* judicial review), these provisions have established the principle that, in the fields covered by Title IV ECT (including relevant parts of the Schengen *acquis*), the substance of the *ordre public* is to be determined at the national level.

Title IV ECT has been built upon a concept which shifts the meaning of the obligation of co-operation with, and loyalty to, the Community from that laid down in Article 5 of the Treaty towards one which strengthens Member State compentencies and emphasizes the subsidiarity principle to the extent that it establishes a cautious (as opposed to an expansive) method of supranationalization.

At the same time, Title IV ECT extends beyond the mere regulation of the principles of loyalty and subsidiarity. These basic principles have long been an integral part of EU law and there was no need to stress them, albeit implicitly, throughout Title IV ECT. Subsidiarity and loyalty principles form part of the EU *ordre public*. Accordingly, it is for the European Court of Justice to decide upon their application to individual cases. Under Title IV ECT, however, judicial power has been expressly limited for the first time in the history of European integration[7]. In the area of visa policy, Title IV ECT even strips the Court of powers it held under the Maastricht regime. The Member States have, in other words, attempted to retain more than a merely formal position as the masters of the Treaties. Title IV ECT seems to preserve their right to have the last word regarding all procedural and substantive policies on immigration, visa and asylum. Moreover, this concept has not only influenced powers of the European Court of Justice, but also the powers of the Commission and the European Parliament. The Commission, in particular, is no longer the sole motor of integration within the framework of Title IV ECT. It must share the right of initiative with Member States. The Commission is, in addition, completely excluded from influence over national *domaines réservés* for two reasons. First, the Member States will maintain the exclusive right to preserve the *ordre public*, even after they lose the right of initiative. Second, the Commission is, and will be,

---

7 The invocation of ex-Articles 100c(5) ECT and K.2(2) ECT has been regarded as subject to judicial review while doubts have been raised as to "whether the European Court of Justice's attitude to the limitation of public order clauses by means of EC concepts of public order would be applicable." See *Hailbronner* 31 CML Rev. (1994) 969, 992. On the contrary, Article 67(2) ECT expressly excludes the ECJ's jurisdiction entirely.

kept from initiating further integration related to these *domaines réservés*, pursuant to Article 64(1) ECT.

II. The Framework of Community Action under Human Rights and the Geneva Convention

Measures adopted pursuant to Title IV ECT must comply with certain standards contained in international agreements. Article 6(2) TEU binds the Community to respect human rights as embodied *inter alia* in the European Convention on Human Rights. Article 63(1) ECT prescribes that measures on asylum within the ambit of Article 63(1)(a-d) ECT must be taken in accordance with the Geneva Convention of 28 July 1951 relating to the status of refugees[8]. In assessing the meaning of the reference contained in the mentioned provisions it must be borne in mind that Member States are signatories to these agreements while the Community has not acceded to them. Hence, first of all, both references must be interpreted as an affirmation of Member States' clear commitment to their obligations under the European Convention on Human Rights and the Geneva Convention, respectively. These references were, therefore, superfluous were they not to be interpreted as binding for the Community institutions. At the same time, however, such binding legal force does not derive from commitments entered into by the Community under international law since the Community is precluded from participation in these treaties. The extent of binding force attributed to the European Convention on Human Rights and the Geneva Convention must, therefore, be construed in the light of the relevant commitments contained in primary Community law.

1. The European Convention for the Protection of Human Rights and Fundamental Freedoms

The reference to the European Convention on Human Rights forms part of Article 6(2) TEU which provides that –

> [t]he Union shall respect fundamental rights, as guaranteed by the European Convention for the Protection of Human Rights and Fundamental Freedoms ... and as they result from the constitutional traditions common to the Member States, as general principles of Community law.

Reference is, thus, made not only to the Convention itself but equally to the common constitutional traditions of Member States which must be assessed on the basis of comparative evaluation of their constitutional orders. Article 6(2) TEU, therefore, reflects both aspects of human rights protection under the Community legal order. For one, initially the European Court of Justice has held, in *Stauder*, that Community action must comply with –

---

8 Text: 189 U.N.T.S. 150, ratified by all Member States of the European Union.

> the fundamental human rights enshrined in the general principles of Community law and protected by the Court[9].

Moreover, the European Court of Justice has based its human rights jurisprudence on the premise that the Community legal order be an autonomous source of law. Thus, in *Internationale Handelsgesellschaft* the Court has reformulated the principles underlying its human rights jurisprudence to the extent that –

> respect for fundamental rights forms an integral part of the general principles of law protected by the Court of Justice. The protection of such rights, whilst inspired by the constitutional traditions common to the Member States, must be insured *within the framework of the structure and objectives of the Community.*[10]

As to the second aspect, in *Nold* the Court has held that –

> fundamental rights form an integral part of the general principles of law, the observance of which it ensures. In safeguarding these rights, the Court is bound to draw inspiration from constitutional traditions common to the Member States, and it cannot therefore uphold measures which are incompatible with fundamental rights recognised and protected by the Constitutions of those States. Similarly, international treaties for the protection of human rights, on which the Member States have collaborated or of which they are signatories, can supply guidelines which should be followed within the framework of Community law.[11]

The European Convention on Human Rights has attracted further attention following the Joint Declaration by the European Parliament, the Council and the Commission concerning the protection of fundamental rights and the European Convention for the Protection of Human Rights and Fundamental Freedoms stressing –

> the prime importance they attach to the protection of fundamental rights, as derived in particular from the constitutions of the Member States and the European Convention for the Protection of Human Rights and Fundamental Freedoms.[12]

However, even after the adoption of this declaration the European Court of Justice has never directly applied provisions of the European Convention on Human Rights to the cases before it[13].

---

9 ECJ, judgment of 12 November 1969, case 29/69, *Stauder v Stadt Ulm*, [1969] ECR 419 = [1969] Danish Special Edition 107 para 7.

10 ECJ, judgment of 17 December 1970, case 11/70, *internationale Handelsgesellschaft v Einfuhr- und Vorratsstelle für Getreide und Futtermittel*, [1970] ECR 1125 = [1970] Danish Special Edition 235 para 4 (emphasis added).

11 ECJ, judgment of 14 May 1974, case 4/73, *Nold v Commission*, [1979] ECR 491 para 13; cf. judgment of 13 December 1979, case 44/79, *Hauer v Land Rheinland-Pfalz*, [1979] ECR 3247 para 15.

12 O.J. 1977 C 103/1. As to the other political declarations and initiatives see the list in the Opinion of the ECJ 2/94 on the accession of the Community to the European Convention on Human Rights, [1996] ECR I-1759, part III; cf. as to the European Union and human rights *Toth*, 34 CML Rev (1997) 491.

13 The Court only referred to the statement contained in the 1986 Single European Act that –

> Member States are determined to work together to promote democracy on the basis of fundamental rights recognized in the constitutions and laws of the Member States, in the Convention for the Protection of Human Rights and Fundamental Freedoms and the European Social Charter, notably freedom, equality and justice.

in its judgment in ECJ, judgment of 18 May 1989, case 249/86, *Commission v Germany*, [1989] ECR 1263.

Currently, the Court usually applies human rights on the basis that they are embodied in the European Convention on Human Rights and derive from the common constitutional traditions of the Member States[14]. Most likely this way of construction is influenced by the premise that the Community legal order is autonomous from commitments taken by Member States, be it in constitutional or under international law. The Court, in other words, applies the initial premise to the notion of human rights in an unchanged manner. No changes are, therefore, to be expected under the Amsterdam Treaty regardless of the fact that, unlike under ex-Article L TEU, the reference to the European Convention on Human Rights is now covered by the ECJ's jurisdiction pursuant to Article 46(d) TEU because this extension merely confirms a long-standing jurisprudence of the Court[15].

Turning to the Geneva Convention, the relevant reference in primary Community law does not coincidentally refer to the legal orders of Member States. Relevant provisions of the Geneva Convention are, therefore, applicable to cases under Community law regardless of whether they embody principles common to the Member States' legal orders.

The references to both the European Convention on Human Rights and the Geneva Convention imply that any rights held by individuals pursuant to these instruments share the hierarchical rank of primary Community law. Accordingly, they can function as standards of review of Community action only. The jurisprudence of European Court of Justice implies that, though unspoken, the Court employs the same premise. The Court has held that it may not scrutinize Member States' conduct with a view to establishing whether it complies with the European Convention on Human Rights.[16]

In turn, however, this limitation of the scope of the references at issue does not point at either construction or content of the commitment taken by the Community with respect to the European Convention on Human Rights and the Geneva Convention. As regards construction a succession model has been discussed with respect to the European Convention on Human Rights. The reference to both conventions might thus be interpreted such that they bind the Community, by virtue of the fact that all Member States are signatories to the conventions. The reasoning in favour of the succession construction can be summarized as follows. Member States have transferred certain powers to the Community by way of conclusion of the Community Treaties. The Community is to be viewed as Member States' successor in respect of these powers. Taking into account that Member States' powers have been limited by both conventions, the succession covers these limitation as well[17]. Argument has been

---

[14] Cf. ECJ, judgment of 5 October 1994, case C-404/92 P, *X v Commission*, [1994] ECR I-4737 para 17. See also judgment of 14 May 1974, case 4/73, *Nold v Commission*, [1974] ECR 491; judgment of 13 December 1979, case 44/79, *Hauer v Land Rheinland-Pfalz*, [1979] ECR 3727; judgment of 21 September 1989, joined cases 46/87 and 227/88, *Hoechst v Commission*, [1989] ECR 2859; opinion 2/94 of 28 March 1996, *Accession by the Community to the European Convention for the Protection of Human Rights and Fundamental Freedoms*, 1996 [ECR] I-1759 para 32.

[15] Cf. Albors-Llorens 35 CML Rev. (1999) 1273, 1285 et seq.

[16] See ECJ, judgment of 11 July 1985, joined cases 60 and 61/84, *Cinéthèque SA and others v Fédération nationale des cinémas français*, [1985] ECR 2605 para 26; judgment of 30 September 1987, case 12/86, *Demirel v Stadt Schwäbisch Gmünd*, [1987] ECR 3719 para 28.

[17] Cf. *Duvigneau* 25 LIEI (1999) 61, 79 et seq., interpreting *Schermers* 27 CML Rev. (1990) 249, 251 similarly as the present study.

raised that the succession construction derives additional support from the loyalty principle embodied in Article 11 ECT[18].

However, this reasoning is not cogent and it has never been employed by either Strasbourg or Luxembourg jurisprudence. Admittedly, the decision of the (former) European Commission on Human Rights in *M & Co. v Germany* has been regarded as supportive of the succession construction[19]. However, it seems virtually impossible to derive support for that construction from the decision in question. In *M & Co. v Germany* the European Commission on Human Rights has held that –

> it is in fact not competent ratione personae to examine proceedings before or decisions of organs of the European Communities ... This does not mean, however, that by granting executory power to a judgment of the European Court of Justice the competent German authorities acted quasi as Community organs and are to that extent beyond the scope of control exercised by the Convention organs.[20]

The European Commission on Human Rights has further stressed that –

> the Convention does not prohibit a Member State from transferring powers to international organisations

but that nonetheless –

> a transfer of powers does not necessarily exclude a State's responsibility under the Convention with regard to the transferred powers. ... [T]he transfer of powers to an international organisation is not incompatible with the Convention provided that within that organisation fundamental rights will receive an equivalent protection.[21]

The 'equivalent protection' requirement defeats the succession construction because it is irreconcilable with a transfer of limitations resting upon the powers transferred, such transfer of limitations, however, being necessarily implied under the succession construction. Moreover, *M & Co. v Germany* contains a non-ambiguous *dictum* to the extent that –

> [u]nder Article 1 of the Convention the Member States are responsible for all acts and omissions of their domestic organs allegedly violating the Convention regardless of whether the act or omission in question is a consequence of domestic law or regulations or of the necessity to comply with international obligations.[22]

---

[18] See *Hilf*, in Grabitz/Hilf (eds.) EUV/EGV (1995) Article F EUV para 28; *Pescatore*, in Matscher & Petzold (eds.), Protecting Human Rights: The European Dimension, Studies in honour of Gérard Wiarda (1988), 441, 450.

[19] European Commission of Human Rights, decision of 9 February 1990, No. 13258/87, *M & Co. v Germany*, 64 DR 138-146 (1990) = ZaöRV 50 (1990) 865. See *Hilf*, in FS Bernhardt (1995), 1193, 1198.

[20] European Commission of Human Rights, decision of 9 February 1990, No. 13258/87, *M & Co. v Germany*, ZaöRV 50 (1990) 865, 866.

[21] European Commission of Human Rights, decision of 9 February 1990, No. 13258/87, *M & Co. v Germany*, ZaöRV 50 (1990) 865, 867.

[22] European Commission of Human Rights, decision of 9 February 1990, No. 13258/87, *M & Co. v Germany*, ZaöRV 50 (1990) 865, 866.

It seems that in *Cantoni v France*[23] the European Court of Human Rights has implicitly reaffirmed this *dictum*. In holding France liable for her conduct regardless of the fact that this conduct complied with a Community directive the European Court of Human Rights both declined to scrutinise Community law and refused to accept, as a justification of, or an excuse for, alleged infringements of human rights, that Member States lack legislative discretion as to the substantive content of national instruments adopted in order to implement Community directives, as provided for in Article 250 ECT. Indeed, in *Cantoni v France* the relevant Community legislation, modelled upon the French instrument under review[24], was substantially identical with that instrument, and in *M & Co. v Germany* the conduct under review had equally been fully predetermined by Community law[25]. In the light of both *M & Co. v Germany* and *Cantoni v France* there can, therefore, be no doubt that Article 6(2) TEU is the only possible source of the binding force of the European Convention on Human Rights vis-à-vis the Community institutions.

Moreover, the succession construction does not derive support from the European Court of Justice's jurisprudence either. The Court has consistently held Community law is an autonomous legal order, distinct from those of the Member States, and not directly subject to the European Convention for the Protection of Human Rights and Fundamental Freedoms[26]. The European Court of Justice's construction of human rights as general principles of Community law is not, therefore, reconcilable with the succession construction. As early as in *Internationale Handelsgesellschaft* the Court held that –

> the validity of a Community measure ... cannot be affected by allegations that it runs counter to either fundamental rights as formulated by the constitution of that state or the principles of a national constitutional structure[27]

and only accepted to examine whether Community law contains analogous guarantees. Denying, thus, any direct relevance of human rights inherent in the national legal orders of Member States – and one should understand the reference to "the principles of a national constitutional structure" as covering incorporation of commitments taken under international law in accordance with constitutional requirements – the European Court of Justice has declined to accept a succession, by the Community, in limitations resting upon powers transferred by Member States which originate from relevant provisions of their constitutional law. Rather, like international courts do under international law[28], the European Court of Justice has inferred human rights by way of deriving general principles of law on a comparative basis. Moreover, in both international or supranational law general principles have *inter alia* been inferred in

---

[23] ECHR, judgment of 15 November 1996, *Cantoni v France*, RJD 1996–V, 1614 = Human Rights Law Journal (1996), 441.

[24] See *Winkler* EuGRZ 1999, 181 et seq.

[25] See *Giegerich* ZaöRV 50 (1990) 836, 848.

[26] Cf. ECJ, judgment of 5 October 1994, case C-404/92 P, *X v Commission*, [1994] ECR I-4737, para 17. For the opposite view as to the binding force of the EHCR see *Hilf*, in Grabitz/Hilf (eds.) EUV/EGV (1995) Article F EUV para 29.

[27] ECJ, judgment of 17 December 1970, case 11/70, *Internationale Handelsgesellschaft v Einfuhr- und Vorratsstelle für Getreide und Futtermittel*, [1970] ECR 1125 = [1970] Danish Special Edition 235 para 3.

[28] Cf. *Graf Vitzthum* in id. (ed.), Völkerrecht (1997) Part I para 144 for the need to derive general principles of law on a comparative basis.

order to derive implied limitations of powers which have not been expressly limited by state actors when founding such organizations.

Finally, the succession construction does not take sufficient notice of the fact that the obligations resting upon Member States under the European Convention are far from forming a coherent body of law because Member States have not acceded to all additional protocols and have made various reservations to the instruments they have accepted[29].

2. *The Geneva Convention*

Like the commitment taken by the Community with respect to the European Convention on Human Rights the reference to the Geneva Convention contained in Article 63(1) ECT prescribes standards for Community action. Accordingly, Article 63(1) ECT must be interpreted as a self-imposed limitation of the Community's competence with regard to refugee policy. The European Court of Justice may not, therefore, determine whether Member States are acting in accordance with their obligations under the Geneva Convention. Its jurisdiction is confined to determining whether Community institutions have transgressed the limits imposed by the Geneva Convention for the treatment of refugees.

In particular, any interpretation of the Convention which would affect Article 63 ECT's differentiation between Geneva Convention refugee status and temporary protection would corrupt the guiding concept of this Article. The question of whether Member States, in their capacity as Masters of the Treaties, in fact complied with the Geneva Convention when introducing this differentiation into the Treaty establishing the European Community is outside of the jurisdiction of the European Court of Justice.

3. *The Content of the Commitments undertaken by the Community under the European and Geneva Conventions*

After the entry into force of the Maastricht Treaty a dispute arose as to the scope of the reference to the European Convention on Human Rights. The Community, it has been argued, is obliged to respect not only the terms of the Convention as such but also any relevant jurisprudence of the European Court of Human Rights[30]. However, taking into account the premise of the European Court of Justice that the Community legal order is autonomous, considering, further, that Article 6(2) TEU implies equal legal force of human rights regardless of whether they are enshrined in the Convention or "as they result from the constitutional traditions common to the Member States, as general principles of Community law", and, finally, having regard to the possible conflicts between human rights derived from these sources which must be solved "within the framework of the structure and objectives of the Community"[31] it is hardly imaginable that either Member States have intended to bind the European Court of

---

29 Cf. *Duvigneau* 25 LIEI (1999) 61, 80.

30 *Hilf* in Grabitz/Hilf, Kommentar zur Europäischen Union, Art. F para 32; *Ress*, JuS 1992, 985, 990.

31 Cf. ECJ, judgment of 17 December 1970, case 11/70, *Internationale Handelsgesellschaft v Einfuhr- und Vorratsstelle für Getreide und Futtermittel*, [1970] ECR 1125 = [1970] Danish Special Edition 235 para 4.

Justice to the European Court of Human Rights' jurisprudence or that the Luxembourg Court will accept a position inferior to that of the Strasbourg Court. Rather the European Court of Justice will duly consider, as a guideline, relevant jurisprudence of the European Court of Human Rights[32]. Indeed the European Court of Justice has thus far done so[33].

The idea of framing human rights as autonomously as other parts of the Community legal order derives additional support from the character of the judgments handed down by the European Court of Human Rights. Under Article 46 of the Convention such judgments are binding between the parties of a dispute only[34]; complaints under the Convention are not to solve abstract conflicts of law,[35] but those of a particular case. Although Strasbourg judgments imply that defendant States should discontinue a breach of the Convention and change national law and practices[36] it still is a matter of debate whether the Strasbourg jurisprudence has a binding effect for states not involved in particular cases. Such binding effect could certainly be derived from provisions entrusting the European Court of Human Rights with a general power such as to authentically interpret the Convention. Nothing, however, in the European Convention on Human Rights indicates that such general power exists.[37]

Similarly, the European Court of Justice will be autonomous when interpreting the Geneva Convention. At the same time, Member States' practice under the Convention will inform the interpretation of Article 63(1) ECT. When ascertaining the meaning of Geneva Convention provisions the European Court of Justice should apply a technique similar to the elaboration of general principles of Community law. In that course the Court will have to consider that the Geneva Convention has left state actors a large margin of appreciation. In particular, the Court may not prefer restrictive interpretations as developed by the judiciary in some Member States over interpreta-

---

32 See *Klein* in Hailbronner/Klein/Magiera/Müller-Graff, Handkommentar zum EGV/EUV, Article F para 8.

33 See the ECJ cases 46/87 and 227/88 *Hoechst* [1989] ECR 2859, para 18. In this case, the ECJ rendered its own interpretation of Article 8 ECHR and stated that the provision did not apply to business premises. The Court emphasised that no relevant jurisprudence of the European Court of Human Rights existed. (In the meantime, however, the European Court of Human Rights has decided on this issue and applies Article 8 ECHR also to business premises: judgment of 16 December 1992, *Niemitz v Germany*, Series A Vol. 256, 23.

34 *Villiger* Handbuch der EMRK (1993), 150.; *Matscher*, EuGRZ (1982), 517, 526; *Ress* in Bernhardt/Geck/Jaenicke/Steinberger (eds.), Völkerrecht als Rechtsordnung, essays in honour of Hermann Mosler (1983), 719, 727.

35 *Rigaux*, RCJB 38 (1984), 616, 624; *Ress* in *Ress* in Bernhardt/Geck/Jaenicke/Steinberger (eds.), Völkerrecht als Rechtsordnung, essays in honour of Hermann Mosler (1983), 719, 730, para 46.

36 See e.g. *Polakiewicz*, Die Verpflichtungen der Staaten aus den Urteilen des Europäischen Gerichtshofs für Menschenrechte (1993), 63, 156; *Frowein/Peukert*, EMRK-Kommentar, Art. 53 note 6 et seq.; *Velu/Ergec*, La Convention européenne des Droits de l'homme, 1049 et seq., 1052 et seq., para 1217; *Cohen-Jonathan*, La Convention Européenne des Droits de l'Homme, 210; *Villiger*, Handbuch der EMRK (1993), 150, note 242.

37 *Klein* in Mahrenholz/Hilf/Klein, Entwicklung der Menschenrechte innerhalb der Staaten des Europarates (1987), 43, 60; *Velu* in Actes due Sixième Colloque International sur la Convention européenne des Droits de l'homme, Séville 1985 (1988), 533, 595; *Rigaux*, ibid. *Sudre*, RUDH 3 (1991), 259, 269; *Klein*, ibid. *Schermers* in Jacobs/Roberts (eds.), The Effect of Treaties in Domestic Law (1987), 109, 121; *Villiger*, ibid. *Steinberger*, 6 HRJL (1985), 402, 409; *Bartsch* in Les effets des décisions de la Court de justice des Communautés européennes dans les Etats membres (1983), 217, 243-245; *Ress*, ibid. *Matscher*, ibid. *Mosler* in EPIL Instalment 1 (1981), 111, 116; *Rolin*, RDH 6 (1973), 729, 746. For the opposite view see *Polakiewicz*, Die Verpflichtungen der Staaten aus den Urteilen des Europäischen Gerichtshofs für Menschenrechte (1993), 279-354.

tions dominant in other Member States which have retained more political, and administrative discretion under the relevant domestic jurisprudence.

4. *The Competing Jurisdictions of the Strasbourg and Luxembourg Courts*

Community action taken under Title IV ECT is subject to judicial review by the European Court of Justice with a view to the commitments taken under Articles 6(2) TEU and 63(1) ECT. At the same time, however, Member States' related conduct is subject to review by the European Court of Human Rights with a view to the commitments taken by way of accession to the European Convention on Human Rights regardless of the fact that the Strasbourg Court does not directly review Community legislation. As a result, parallel review of Community legislation in Luxembourg and of related legislation or administrative practice of Member States may lead to conflicts where the Courts involved reach different conclusions. Moreover, where only national conduct has been under review the question may arise of whether the EU has to change relevant legislation in order to enable defendant States to discontinue the breach of the Convention by way of changing national law and practices. This question will arise with respect to both directives (*Cantoni v France*) and regulations. In turn, where regulations govern Member States' administrative practice this practice seems to meet the test for reviewability applied by the European Court of Human Rights in *Ireland v. United Kingdom*. In that case the Strasbourg Court held that breaches of the European Convention on Human Rights can result from either the mere existence of a law which introduces, directs or authorizes measures incompatible with the rights and freedoms safeguarded therein, provided that –

> the law challenged ... is couched in terms sufficiently clear and precise to make the breach immediately apparent[38]

or, where such clear and precise law does not exist,

> the decision of the Convention institutions must be arrived at by reference to the manner in which the respondent State interprets and applies *in concreto* the impugned text or texts.[39]

Accordingly, the lack of a clear and precise law at the national level the application of which results in breaches of the Convention does not amount to an excuse or justification of the conduct under review. It seems that, in the light of *M & Co v Germany* and *Cantoni v France*, the lack of a clear and precise law at the national level, and the lack of legislation as such at the national level for reason of the existence of a relevant regulation adopted by the Community must be treated similarly. Otherwise Member States could evade their obligations under the European Convention on Human Rights by mere choice of instrument of Community legislation. Consequently, conduct of national authorities is reviewable and can be in breach of the Strasbourg Convention.

---

[38] See ECHR, judgment of 18 January 1978, *Ireland v United Kingdom*, Series A no. 25, para 240. See also *van Dijk/van Hoof*, Theory and Practice of the European Convention on Human Rights, p. 33.; see also travaux préparatoires (document H (61) 4, 384, 502, 703 and 706).

[39] ECHR, judgment of 18 January 1978, *Ireland v United Kingdom*, Series A no. 25, para 240.

5. *Other Human Rights Treaties*

a) Asylum Policy

The first paragraph of Article 63 ECT does not only refer to the Geneva Convention but equally to "other relevant treaties". Arguably, only such other international treaties are "relevant" to which all Member States are signatories. As far as Member States have declined to take commitments under certain treaties in terms of international law it is most unlikely that they wanted to bind the Community to standards they do not regard acceptable for themselves.

All Member States are bound by some other international agreements relevant to the status of aliens in general and refugees in particular. Most prominent examples are Articles 7, 13 and 17 of the International Covenant on Civil and Political Rights, Article 3 of the Convention against Torture and other Cruel, Inhuman or Degrading Treatment or Punishment and Article 22 of the Convention on the Rights of the Child[40]. The binding force of these provisions must be construed in the same way as the binding force of the European Convention on Human rights and the Geneva Convention.

b) Immigration Policy

No references to international agreements, similar to that related to asylum policy, is contained in the provisions governing immigration policy. However, although the European Union has not committed itself to respect such agreements in that field the second paragraph of Article 63 ECT might bring them into the ambit of Community law. This provision stipulates that –

> Measures adopted by the Council pursuant to points 3 and 4 shall not prevent any Member State from maintaining or introducing in the areas concerned national provisions which are compatible with this Treaty and *with international agreements*. [emphasis added]

This provision contains a requirement that measures adopted by Member States must comply with the obligations each Member State has accepted under international law, respectively. Moreover, one might argue that this compliance requirement implies that prospective Community legislation must equally meet the standards of international agreements – even though no 'succession construction' can be applied to bind the Community to the terms of relevant provisions. However, taking into account the language of Article 63(1) ECT and Article 6(2) TEU whereby the Community is bound to respect the standards contained in international agreements it must be concluded *a contrario* that deliberately Member States have not included a similar clause into the second paragraph of Article 63 ECT. Accordingly, the Community is not bound by the agreements in question.

The European Court of Justice may not, therefore, review Community law as to whether it complies with the provisions in question. It is, however, debatable whether and to which extent the European Court of Justice may scrutinize law and practice of

---

40 See AGIT, Efficient, effective and encompassing approaches to a European Immigration and Asylum Policy, [1999] IJRL [forthcoming].

Member States with a view to ensuring such compliance. In particular, it seems rather unlikely that Member States have intended to establish an ECJ jurisdiction which competes with the competence of the United Nations Human Rights Commission in respect of the International Covenant on Civil and Political Rights. Additionally, it is equally unlikely that Member States have intended to subject to judicial review their conduct with respect to conventions which do not provide for judicial review like the Torture and the Children's Rights Conventions. Consequently, the compliance clause cannot be interpreted as an extension of the European Court of Justice's jurisdiction. The European Court of Justice would face major difficulties if it were to adopt a uniform approach towards the content of Member States' international obligations since Member States have made different reservations to each of the agreements in question. Given these reservations the Court would, moreover, be unable to clearly define the obligations resting upon individual Member States because interpretation of such reservations is within their sovereign power. Nothing indicates that this power has been transferred to the Community level.

Besides the International Covenant on Civil and Political Rights, the Convention against Torture and other Cruel, Inhuman or Degrading Treatment or Punishment and the Convention on the Rights of the Child, only few Member States are bound by other instruments such as the European Convention on the Legal Status of Migrant Workers[41]. Additionally, it has been argued that the International Convention on the Protection of the Rights of all Migrant Workers and their Families and standards set within the framework of the International Labour Organization should also influence European policy-making[42]. This position, however, is hardly convincing from a legal point of view. Nothing indicates that Member States wanted to bind the Community by standards they have not accepted for themselves.

III. THE BACKGROUND OF COMMUNITARIZATION: THE INSUFFICIENCIES OF MAASTRICHT'S LEGAL FRAMEWORK FOR IMMIGRATION AND ASYLUM POLICIES

The Maastricht Treaty introduced a number of provisions dealing with the issues currently governed by Title IV ECT. On the one hand, ex-Article 100c ECT acted as a basis for the common visa policy. This policy has been implemented under the first pillar and does not share the insufficiencies of the framework to be dealt with here. On the other hand, ex-Article K.1 TEU provided for intergovernmental co-operation with respect to asylum policy, rules governing border-crossing at external borders of the Member States and the exercise of controls thereon, immigration policy and policies regarding third-country nationals. Intergovernmental co-operation did not, however, produce the results desired by certain Member States; Member States, consequently, pressed for communitarization during the Intergovernmental Conference at which the Amsterdam Treaty was drafted.

The limits of the intergovernmental approach taken by Title VI TEU are of a primarily structural nature. Additionally, the achievements of intergovernmental co-

---

41 These are France, Italy, the Netherlands, Portugal, Spain, and Sweden.

42 Cf. AGIT, Efficient, effective and encompassing approaches to a European Immigration and Asylum Policy, [1999] IJRL [forthcoming]. However, neither is this Convention in force nor has any Member State, at the time of this writing, signed this Convention.

operation have been rather poor[43]. The Council has adopted priorities for co-operation in the field of justice and home affairs in several resolutions which are, to a certain extent, reiterative[44].

1. The Structural Deficit of Third Pillar Decision-Making

Several authors have drawn attention to the fact that both the Maastricht regime and the Schengen system are inefficient in certain respects.[45] The Maastricht framework, in particular, has been criticized as an obstacle to the abolition of internal border controls, as it did not clearly distinguish between Community legislation and intergovernmental cooperation[46]. There was no consensus among Member States with regard to the division of third-country nationals into 'positive' or 'negative' categories, or under which the visa requirements of states under ex-Article 100c ECT[47] would fall. Moreover, third pillar decision-making within Maastricht's legal framework has not even brought about comprehensive minimum standards regulating all matters of common interest under ex-Article K.1 TEU. Only selected items have been the subject of Joint Positions, Joint Actions or conventions, while draft instruments aimed at creating a comprehensive set of rules have failed in the Council. Additionally, the few third pillar instruments adopted within the Maastricht framework are sources, not of Community, but of international law and, accordingly, have neither direct effect in the domestic sphere nor take precedence over national law. The legal structure of the third pillar has, therefore, been relegated to the status of "legal sandstone" in comparison to the "solid legal granite" formed by the first pillar[48].

---

43 This conclusion is even more evident if regard is had to the ambitious expectations the Council itself had expressed as regards the implementation of the third pillar. See Report of the Justice and Home Affairs Council to the European Council of 11/12 December 1993, 10655/93 JAI 11; the Working Program of 2 December 1993, 10684/93, JAI 12; the Communication from the Commission to the Council and the European Parliament of 23 February 1994, COM(94)23 final; the Communication from the Commission to the Council and the European Parliament on Asylum of 11 October 1991, SEC(91)1857 final; and the Communication on Immigration of 23 October 1991, SEC (91)1855 final. Cf. *Peers* 35 CML Rev. (1999) 1235 et seq. for a detailed account of EU migration policy efforts during the Maastricht era.

44 Cf. Council Resolution of 14 October 1996 laying down the priorities for cooperation in the field of justice and home affairs for the period from 1 July 1996 to 30 June 1998, O.J. 1996 C 319/1 which was replaced by Council Resolution of 18 December 1997 laying down the priorities for cooperation in the field of justice and home affairs for the period from 1 January 1998 to the date of entry into force of the Treaty of Amsterdam, O.J. 1998 C 11/1.

45 Cf. *Hailbronner* 35 CML Rev. (1998) 1047, 1048.

46 *Magiera*, in Burmeister (ed.) Verfassungsstaatlichkeit, Essays in honour of Klaus Stern (1997) 1317, 1324; *Lang*, Gemeinschaftsrecht der Drittstaatsangehörigen (1998), 339.

47 See the detailed discussion of this issue by *Hailbronner* 31 CML Rev. (1994) 969, 979-986. The Commission and the European Parliament argued that ex-Article 100c(1) ECT allowed for drawing up a "positive list" of states, whose nationals are not required to be in possession of a visa when crossing external frontiers. See COM(93)684 final, 40 and the opinion of the European Parliament as published in O.J. 1994 C 128/346. However, the Council has adopted a "negative list" of states whose nationals must be in possession of a visa when crossing the external borders of Member States by virtue of Regulation 2317/95 of 25 September 1995, O.J. 1995 L 234/1. The European Court of Justice has declared void this regulation for procedural reasons (judgment of 10 June 1997, *Parliament v Council*, case C-392/95, 1997 [ECR] I-3213). The Council has subsequently adopted Regulation 574/1999 (O.J. 1999 L 72/2) which does not substantially alter the previous regime.

48 *Müller-Graff* 31 CML Rev. (1994) 493, 495.

Furthermore, the transformation of international agreements concluded by the Member States may take long periods of time[49].

In light of the fact that today's migration phenomena affect the European Union as a whole and that, accordingly, they must be dealt with, on the basis of common principles Maastricht's third pillar decision-making appeared to suffer from a two-fold structural deficit. The decision-making process was insufficient because of the clumsy procedure applied to decision-making, and the decisions lacked binding legal effect.

2. *The Achievements of Third Pillar Co-operation*

Although third pillar decision-making in the fields covered by ex-Article K.1 TEU did not produce the expected results, there are some instruments which – though they dealt mainly with technical, or minor issues – have contributed to the establishment of an area of freedom, security and justice.

Third pillar intergovernmental co-operation previously took one of three forms –

- Joint Positions (see ex-Article K.3(2)(a) TEU), also referred to as "common positions"[50],
- Joint Actions (see ex-Article K.3(2)(b) TEU), and
- Council decisions establishing conventions which the Council recommends to the Member States for adoption in accordance with their respective constitutional requirements (see ex-Article K.3(2)(c) TEU).

In addition, the Council was allowed to promote any cooperation which furthered the pursuit of the objectives of the Union and used the appropriate form and procedures (see ex-Article K.3(2)(a) TEU). The wording of this provision was quite open and required only that cooperation contribute to the pursuit of the objectives of the Union[51]. Accordingly, the forms of action envisaged by ex-Article K.3(2)(a-c) did not bear exclusiveness. The Council regularly enacted instruments of intergovernmental cooperation it deemed appropriate, including non-binding resolutions and recommendations[52].

The Council has adopted two Joint Positions –

- Joint Position of 4 March 1996 on a harmonized application of the definition of the term "refugee" in Article 1 of the Geneva Convention of 28 July 1951 relating to the status of refugees[53], and
- Joint Position of 25 October 1996 on pre-frontier assistance and training assignments[54].

---

[49] For instance, the Dublin Convention determining the State responsible for examining applications for asylum lodged in one of the Member States of the European Communities was signed on 15 June 1990 and entered into force not earlier than on 1 September 1997.

[50] In the English text of Title VI TEU, the phrase "Joint Position" only appears in ex-Article K.3(2) TEU. Ex-Article K.5 TEU stated that Member States shall defend the "common positions" adopted under Title VI TEU within international organisations and, international conferences in which they participate. The Dutch, French, German, Italian, Portuguese and Spanish texts, however, made use of the same phrase in Articles K.3(2) and K.5 TEU. Taking this into consideration there is a strong argument for interpreting ex-Article K.5 TEU as imposing an obligation on Member States to defend Joint Positions adopted under ex-Article K.3(2) TEU. See *O'Keeffe* 32 CML Rev. (1995) 893, 915.

[51] Cf. *Hendry*, GYIL 36 (1993), 295, 311.

[52] Council Recommendations will not be mentioned here. They will be discussed in the appropriate chapters.

[53] O.J. 1996 L 63/2.

The following Joint Actions concerning asylum and immigration policy have been adopted within Maastricht's third pillar –

- Council Decision of 30 November 1994 on a Joint Action adopted by the Council on the basis of ex-Article K.3(2)(b) of the Treaty on European Union concerning travel facilities for school pupils from third countries resident in a Member State[55],
- Joint Action of 4 March 1996 adopted by the Council on the basis of ex-Article K.3 of the Treaty on European Union on airport transit arrangements[56],
- Joint Action of 15 July 1996 adopted by the Council on the basis of ex-Article K.3 of the Treaty on European Union, concerning action to combat racism and xenophobia[57],
- Joint Action of 28 October 1996 adopted by the Council on the basis of ex-Article K.3 of the Treaty on European Union introducing a program of training, exchanges and co-operation in the field of identity documents ('Sherlock')[58],
- Joint Action of 16 December 1996 adopted by the Council on the basis of ex-Article K.3 of the Treaty on European Union concerning a uniform format for residence permits[59],
- Joint Action of 24 February 1997 adopted by the Council on the basis of ex-Article K.3 of the Treaty on European Union concerning action to combat trafficking in human beings and sexual exploitation of children[60],
- Joint Action of 22 July 1997 adopted by the Council on the basis of ex-Article K.3 of the Treaty on European Union, concerning the financing of specific projects in favour of displaced persons who have found temporary protection in the Member States and asylum seekers[61],
- Joint Action of 22 July 1997 adopted by the Council on the basis of ex-Article K.3 of the Treaty on European Union, concerning the financing of specific projects in favour of asylum-seekers and refugees[62],
- Joint Action of 19 March 1998 adopted by the Council on the basis of Article K.3 of the Treaty on European Union, introducing a programme of training, exchanges and cooperation in the field of asylum, immigration and crossing of external borders (Odysseus-programme)[63],
- Joint Action of 26 April 1999 adopted by the Council on the basis of Article K.3 of the Treaty on European Union, establishing projects and measures to provide practical support in relation to the reception and voluntary repatriation of refugees, displaced persons and asylum seekers, including emergency assistance to persons who have fled as a result of recent events in Kosovo[64],
- Joint Action of 27 April 1998 adopted by the Council on the basis of Article K.3 of the Treaty on European Union, concerning the financing of specific projects in

---

54 O.J. 1996 L 281/1.
55 O.J. 1994 L 327/1.
56 O.J. 1996 L 63/8.
57 O.J. 1996 L 185/5.
58 O.J. 1996 L 287/7.
59 O.J. 1997 L 7/1.
60 O.J. 1997 L 63/2.
61 O.J. 1997 L 205/3.
62 O.J. 1997 L 205/5.
63 O.J. 1998, L 99/2.
64 O.J. 1999, L 114/2.

favour of displaced persons who have found temporary protection in the Member States and asylum seekers[65], and

- Joint Action of 27 April 1998 adopted by the Council on the basis of Article K.3 of the Treaty on European Union, concerning the financing of specific projects in favour of asylum-seekers and refugees[66].

Furthermore, the Council has adopted a Decision of 4 March 1996 on an alert and emergency procedure for burden-sharing with regard to the admission and residence of displaced persons on a temporary basis[67]. On the other hand, several draft measures presented by the Commission have not been adopted by the Council. The most important of these are –

- Proposal for a decision, based on ex-Article K.3 of the Treaty on European Union establishing the Convention on the crossing of the external frontiers of the Member States[68],
- Proposal for a Council Directive on the right of third-country nationals to travel in the Community[69], and
- Proposal for a Council Directive on the elimination of controls on persons crossing internal frontiers[70].

3. *Achievements of Intergovernmental Co-operation outside the EU Framework*

The European Union has inherited few instruments of intergovernmental co-operation concluded outside its institutional framework: the Schengen and Dublin Conventions are the most important among these. The Convention Determining the State Responsible for Examining Applications for Asylum Lodged in one of the Member States of the European Communities and measures for its implementation[71] (henceforth referred to as Dublin Convention) is the most noteworthy, since it made Member States responsible for the examination of asylum applications lodged in one of the Member States of the European Communities[72]. It was signed by the EEC Member States on 15 June 1990[73] and introduced a uniform system of regulation in this area. The Bonn

---

[65] O.J. 1998, L 138/6.

[66] O.J. 1998, L 138/8.

[67] O.J. 1996 L 63/10.

[68] COM(93)684 final, O.J. 1994 C 11/6.

[69] COM(95)346 final, O.J. 1995 C 306/5. In the meantime the Commission has submitted a modified proposal: COM(97)106 final, O.J. 1997 C 139/6.

[70] COM(95)347 final, O.J. 1995 C 289/16. In the meantime the Commission has submitted a modified proposal: COM(97)106, O.J. 1997 C 140/21.

[71] O.J. 1997 C 254/1; reprinted in *Meijers, et al.*, Schengen, 148 et seq.; *Hailbronner*, Ausländerrecht, B 11.

[72] For a detailed discussion of the Dublin Convention see *Müller-Graff*, The Dublin Convention: Pioneer and Lesson for Third Pillar-Conventions, in *Bieber/Monar* (ed.), Justice and Home Affairs in the European Union, (1995), 49-63; *Hailbronner* ZAR (1995), 3 et seq.; *Gerlach* ZRP (1993), 164 et seq.; *Ress*, Die Auswirkungen der Abkommen von Schengen und Dublin auf die Asylpolitik der EG, in *Pauly* (ed.), Les accords de Schengen: Abolition des frontières intérieures ou menace pour les libertés publiques?, Maastricht (1993), 79-104; *Stefanini/Doublet*, RMC (1991), 391 et seq.; *Achermann*, Schweizerische Zeitschrift für Asylrecht und -praxis (ASYL) (1990), 12 et seq.

[73] Denmark did not sign the Schengen Convention before 13 June 1991 because she first had to come to an agreement with the other Member States of the Northern Passport Union, cf. Bull. EC (1991) no. 6, clause 2.2.1; Bull. EC (1991) clause 1.4.9; COM(91)237 final para 44.

Protocol of 11 September 1995[74] substitutes the Dublin system for the asylum provisions of the Convention, signed in Schengen on 19 June 1990, implementing the Agreement on the gradual abolition of checks at their common borders, signed in Schengen on 14 June 1985[75] (henceforth referred to as Schengen Implementation Convention – SIC – or Schengen Convention). The Dublin Convention has as yet not been integrated into Community law, although it is almost identical to the Schengen system in its allocation of responsibility for asylum applications. Article 63(1)(a) ECT provides for the adoption of criteria and mechanisms like the ones contained in the Dublin Convention.

A communitarization of Dublin in the form of a regulation[76] would best serve the aim of achieving an Anglo-Irish and Danish opt-in with regard to the allocation of responsibility among Member States for processing asylum applications lodged by third-country nationals[77]. In general, the provisions contained in the Dublin Convention are precise and clearly defined and would meet the regulation requirements for 'direct effect' legislation[78].

The Dublin Convention survived a long waiting period before its entry into force on 1 September 1997[79], as compared to that of the Schengen Convention (19 June 1990 – 26 March 1995)[80]. Schengen's shorter waiting period can be interpreted as evidence of the assumption that outside the EU framework progress may be easier achieved while within the EU intergovernmental co-operation has been usually very time-consuming or too slow to guarantee flexible reactions to urgent problems.

IV. From Maastricht to Amsterdam: Changes and Questions of Transition

The introduction of a comprehensive Title on policies related to immigration, visa, asylum, and third-country nationals (henceforth referred to as European aliens law) into the European Community Treaty, as well as the integration of the Schengen

---

74 The protocol was signed in order to prevent a possible conflict between the Schengen and Dublin agreements pursuant to a resolution of the Schengen Executive Committee (Article 142 SIC) of 26 April 1994. Unlike the Dublin Convention this Protocol has as yet not been published in the Official Journal of the European Communities. According to Article 1 of the Protocol the provisions of Chapter 7 SIC cease to apply after the Dublin Convention enters into force. Indeed, the Dublin Convention entered into force on 1 September 1997 (see O.J. 1997 C 268/1).

75 Unofficial English translations of the Schengen Convention have been published in 30 ILM (1991) 68; IJRL 3 (1991), 773; *Meijers*, et al., Schengen, 155. Quotations of SIC provisions are taken from the reproduction of the unofficial translation provided by the Secretariat-General of the Council of the European Communities (as it then was) as reproduced in ILM.

76 *Marschang*, KJ 1998, 69, 81, Cf. point 36(b)(i) of the Action Plan of the Council and the Commission on how best to implement the provisions of the Treaty of Amsterdam on an area of freedom, security and justice, O.J. 1999 C 19/1.

77 Cf. *Hailbronner/Thiery* EuR 1998, 583, 609.

78 *Hailbronner/Thiery* EuR 1998, 583, 610.

79 See O.J. 1997 C 268/1.

80 The Schengen Convention distinguishes between entering into force (the point, which the contracting parties become bound in international law; internal effectiveness) and bringing into force (the point, which the Member States actually begin to apply the agreement; external effectiveness; see Joint Statement 1(2) of the Final Act to the SIA). It took effect on 1 September 1993 for the original five signatories but was implemented no earlier than 26 March 1995, see *Hailbronner*, Ausländer- und Asylrecht (Textbuch Deutsches Recht) D 8, 67.

acquis into the EU framework[81], puts an end to frequent criticism, which held that ECT provisions do not expressly provide for the adoption of measures in these fields[82]. An outline of the basic structure, and a detailed account of its provisions included in both Title IV ECT and the Schengen Protocol will reinforce this point.

1. The Elements of Amsterdam's Legal Framework

The Amsterdam Treaty regulates immigration, visa and asylum policies through the following mechanisms –

- Title IV ECT,
- the Protocol integrating the Schengen *acquis* into the framework of the European Union (Schengen Protocol),
- the Protocol on the application of certain aspects of Article 14 (ex-Article 7a) of the Treaty establishing the European Community to the United Kingdom and to Ireland, and
- the Protocol on the position of the United Kingdom and Ireland,
- the Protocol on the position of Denmark,
- the Protocol on Asylum for Nationals of Member States of the European Union, and
- the Protocol on external relations of the Member States with regard to the crossing of external borders.

Additionally, the Intergovernmental Conference has adopted the following related Declarations –

- Declaration on the preservation of the level of protection and security provided by the Schengen *acquis*.
- Declaration on Article 62(2)(b) ECT.
- Declaration on Article 63 ECT.
- Declaration on Article 63(3)(a) ECT.
- Declaration on Article 64(1) ECT.
- Declaration on Article 67 ECT.
- Declaration on Article 2 of the Schengen Protocol.
- Declaration on Article 4 of the Schengen Protocol.
- Declaration on Article 5 of the Schengen Protocol.
- Declaration on Article 6 of the Schengen Protocol.
- Declaration relating to the Protocol on asylum for nationals of Member States of the European Union.
- Declaration relating to subparagraph (d) of the Sole Article of the Protocol on asylum for nationals of Member States of the European Union.

---

81 Cf. *Wagner* 25 LIEI (1999) 1 et seq. for a detailed account of the integration of the Schengen *acquis* into the EU's framework.

82 Cf. *Hailbronner*, Möglichkeiten und Grenzen einer europäischen Koordinierung des Einreise- und Asylrechts (1989), 191 et seq.; *Hilf*, in *Hailbronner/Ress/Stein*, Staat und Völkerrechtsordnung, Festschrift für Karl Doehring (1989), 339 et seq.

The Council has already defined[83] and attributed the Schengen *acquis* to legal bases in Community law[84]. Additionally, according to Article 2 of the Council Decision defining the Schengen *acquis* most elements of this *acquis* shall be published in the Official Journal.

2. *Title IV ECT and the Schengen Protocol*

The legal framework of a European aliens law is comprised of a large number of diverse elements and may create major confusion. Indeed, "both the new Title [IV] including its protocols and the Schengen Protocol continued to be disputed right up to the concluding stage of the negotiations of the Amsterdam Treaty"[85]. As a result, the Intergovernmental Conference was not able to draft a coherent set of provisions[86]. Nevertheless, Title IV ECT and the Schengen Protocol have been tied together, indicating the intention to develop a uniform approach towards the implementation of European aliens law. Title IV ECT and the Schengen Protocol work towards identical goals. All primary Community law related to third-country nationals must, therefore, be interpreted such that the various instruments in that field are serving identical aims, thereby developing a uniform set of fundamental principles governing European aliens law.

The development of a European concept of aliens ad asylum law may, however, prove to be problematic in two respects: First, the decision-making processes under Title IV ECT and the Schengen Protocol differ slightly. Second, difficulties in the delineation between follow-up measures to the Schengen *acquis*, as envisaged by Article 5(1) of the Schengen Protocol, and measures unrelated to Schengen but aimed at implementing Title IV ECT[87], may arise.

The decision-making processes under Title IV ECT and the Schengen Protocol differ primarily in their approach to the status of the opt-out Member States – the United Kingdom, Ireland, and Denmark. These differences are to be dealt with in detail *sub specie* opt-out and opt-in provisions. In general, Title IV ECT takes a more restrictive approach towards opt-in by the said Member States than the Schengen Protocol. In particular, except for the possibility to completely renounce her opt-out, Denmark is completely excluded from the implementation of Title IV ECT. As a matter of principle, however, she will participate indirectly in the Schengen follow-up process, under the auspices of international law.

In addition, Article 2(1), third sub-paragraph of the Schengen Protocol suggests that the European Court of Justice is not competent to review the attribution of the elements of the Schengen *acquis* to Title IV ECT legal bases. Jurisdiction of the Court

---

83 Council Decision of 20 May 1999 concerning the definition of the Schengen *acquis* for the purpose of determining, in conformity with the relevant provisions of the Treaty establishing the European Community and the Treaty on European Union, the legal basis for each of the provisions or decisions which constitute the *acquis*, O.J. 1999 L 176/1.

84 Council Decision of 20 May 1999 determining, in conformity with the relevant provisions of the Treaty establishing the European Community and the Treaty on European Union, the legal basis for each of the provisions or decisions which constitute the Schengen *acquis*, O.J. 1999 L 176/17.

85 *Ehlermann* 4 ELJ (1998), 246, 264; *id.* EuR 1998, 367 et seq. and Revue du Marché Unique Européen 1998, 53 et seq. respectively.

86 *Ehlermann* ibid.

87 Cf. *Kortenberg* 35 CML Rev. (1998) 833, 843.

only emerges "in accordance with that determination". This phrase must be interpreted to exclude the determination from judicial review.

In spite of procedure differences, it may be difficult to distinguish Schengen-follow-up decisions from decisions implementing Title IV ECT . Large portions of the provisions of the Schengen Implementation Convention and Title IV ECT in the area of Community competence overlap. Given the requirement that Title IV decision-making –

> which will have the effect of replacing provisions on the abolition of checks at common borders contained in the 1990 Schengen Convention, should provide at least the same level of protection and security as under the aforementioned provisions of the Schengen Convention[88]

the entirety of Title II SIC (abolition of border controls) qualifies for Schengen follow-up.

Neither the Schengen Protocol nor Title IV ECT, however, clearly define the distinction between follow-up measures to the Schengen *acquis* and Schengen-unrelated measures aimed at implementing Title IV ECT under Community law. The Council must obviously make a decision about the route it wishes to take, be that by means of a code of conduct[89] or otherwise, especially in light of the effects this decision will have on the status of the opt-out Member States. The most likely source of conflict arises with respect to Denmark which is bound only indirectly by Schengen follow-up measures. Although some procedural differences apply with regard to the position of the United Kingdom and Ireland, they may participate in the decision-making process, and they may opt-in with respect to individual measures taken under both the Schengen follow-up provisions and Title IV ECT[90].

The attribution of decisions to Schengen follow-up or implementation of Title IV ECT will probably be of a political nature. Article 5(2) of the Schengen Protocol renders the follow-up process "subject to the relevant provisions of the Treaties".

Article 5(2) of the Protocol on the Position of Denmark calls for "appropriate measures" in reaction to a Danish decision not to implement a Schengen follow-up under Title IV ECT. Although this provision is only applicable after the expiration of a six month waiting period it is unlikely that Member States will initiate the difficult process to take appropriate measures under Article 5(2) of the Protocol on the Position of Denmark. Consequently, potential difficulties caused by Danish reluctance to participate in the follow-up to the Schengen *acquis* may be solved more suitably with the decision to adopt a planned measure as Schengen-unrelated implementation of Title IV ECT excluding Denmark from the decision making process altogether.

On the other hand, the choice of any Schengen follow-up procedure would undoubtedly come closer to the aim of developing an area of freedom, security and justice, as it would allow Denmark, albeit only under the auspices of international law, to opt-in.

It follows from the Schengen Protocol that the Council will be able to abolish checks at internal borders by means of a follow-up to the Schengen *acquis*. Only for

---

[88] See the Declaration on the preservation of the level of protection and security provided by the Schengen *acquis*.

[89] A suggestion to this extent has been made by *Kortenberg* 35 CML Rev. (1998) 833, 843.

[90] See Article 5(1), second sub-paragraph of the Schengen Protocol and Article 2 of the Protocol of the Position of the United Kingdom, and Article 4 of the Schengen Protocol and Article 4 of the Protocol of the Position of the United Kingdom, respectively.

policy reasons vis-à-vis the opt-out Member States – particularly Denmark – might the necessity arise to label measures in this field as 'Schengen-unrelated'. With the exception of Denmark's exclusion such decision will not have any negative impacts on the integration process with regard to European aliens law. The procedural and jurisdictional provisions of Title IV ECT, in particular, will apply in either case.

3. The Follow-up of Maastricht's Primary Community Law (Ex-Article 100(c) ECT)

Ex-Article 100c ECT is the only provision which refers to the measures aimed at establishing an area of freedom, security and justice, as introduced by the Maastricht Treaty. While this Article has been repealed by the Amsterdam Treaty, the EU power established therein has been implanted into Title IV ECT. Under the Amsterdam regime, visa regulations (ex-Article 100c(1) ECT) may be adopted pursuant to Articles 62(2)(b) and 63(3)(a) ECT.

Additionally, the technical and procedural provisions which shaped ex-Article 100c ECT have, by and large, become principles applicable to all kinds of Title IV law-making. In particular –

- Article 64(2) ECT provides for the adoption, by the Council, of provisional measures in cases of emergency characterized by a sudden inflow of nationals of third countries, thus resembling of ex-Article 100c(2) ECT.
- Similar to ex-Article 100c(7) ECT the Schengen Protocol provides for continuing legal force of certain instruments adopted outside the single institutional framework of the European Union (here: the Schengen *acquis*) until they have been attributed to Title IV powers.
- Like under ex-Article 100c(4) ECT the Commission's right of initiative is modified by Article 67 ECT. Notably, Article 67(2), first indent ECT in substance repeats ex-Article 100c(4) ECT.
- Article 64(1) ECT safeguards the *domaine réservé* of the Member States applying the same wording as did ex-Article K.2(2) TEU, thereby exceeding the content of ex-Article 100c(5) ECT.
- Especially with regard to its substantive content, ex-Article 100c ECT has been merely substituted for by Articles 62(2)(b) and 63(3)(a) ECT. Existing rules on visas will, therefore, continue to have a legal basis in primary Community law.

Given that Denmark, the United Kingdom and Ireland have participated in adopting the respective *acquis* during the Maastricht era, these rules must now be treated as products of an opt-in of these Member States. Pursuant to Article 4 of the Protocol on the Position of Denmark, she will also participate in the follow-up to the EU visa regime[91].

---

[91] See also *Kortenberg* 35 CML Rev. (1998) 833, 839.

4. *The Effects of the Amsterdam Treaty on Third Pillar Instruments Adopted under the Maastricht Regime*

Title IV ECT does not include any rules governing the future of legal acts adopted under ex-Title VI TEU. Will and can they be transformed into measures under Title IV ECT? Member States had agreed solely to the "soft law" character of third pillar instruments under the Maastricht Treaty. Their legal effects differ substantially from those of Community law, thus rendering Title IV ECT ineligible for automatic transformation. Additionally, the principle of conferred powers presses for attributing these instruments to individual legal bases. This requirement is embodied in Article 2(1), second sub-paragraph of the Schengen Protocol, and also applies to third pillar instruments of the Maastricht era.

As a matter of policy, the *acquis* agreed upon within the framework of Maastricht's Title VI TEU should not be abandoned. The Amsterdam Treaty, however, does not contain express provisions on the fate of this *acquis*. A possible solution may be found in ex-Article 100c(7) ECT and Article 2(1), fourth sub-paragraph of the Schengen Protocol providing that the *acquis* at issue should remain applicable, unchanged in its legal nature and (potentially) binding force, until it is replaced by measures adopted under Title IV ECT.

With regard to judicial review the same principles apply as to the Schengen *acquis* before attribution to Title IV powers.

The re-adoption of elements of the *acquis* under ex-Title VI TEU as instruments of secondary Community law, however, therefore depends on the political will of Member States to cooperate within the framework of Title IV ECT. Member States are, however, prohibited under the Amsterdam rules from following up these instruments on the intergovernmental level, as to do so would conflict with Community powers under Title IV ECT. Member States must, nevertheless, consider the wishes of opt-out Member States to participate in the follow-up process, which is to be dealt with in detail *sub specie* re-adoption of Maastricht third pillar instruments under Title IV ECT.

International treaties concluded by the Member States within the framework of ex-Title VI TEU will undoubtedly remain in force and to be binding under international law. The legal effects of "soft law" adopted under this Title, i.e. Joint Actions and Joint Positions are somewhat unclear. The Amsterdam Treaty itself is silent on the issue; under the Maastricht Treaty the controversy about the legal effects of joint positions has been solved in a pragmatic way. The Joint Positions on a harmonized application of the definition of the term "refugee" excludes a binding effect for national legislatures and courts, but obliges governments to adopt the Joint Position with effect to national administrations. Such limited legal force has not been abolished by the entry into force of the Amsterdam Treaty. Yet, due to their uncertain legal nature, Joint Positions and Joint Actions are "the prime candidates" for replacement by Community legislation under Title IV ECT[92].

The Maastricht Treaty extended the jurisdiction of the European Court of Justice to regulations on the use of information technology for customs purposes[93], as well

---

92 See point 29 of the Action Plan of the Council and the Commission, O.J. 1999 C 19/1.

93 Convention on the use of information technology for customs purposes, O.J. 1995 C 316/33 and protocol to this convention, O.J. 1997 C 151/15.

as to several matters not directly related to aliens law or border controls[94]. Although the extension of the jurisdiction of the European Court of Justice was envisaged by the last sub-paragraph of ex-Article K.3(2) TEU, there should be no doubt that the Court will continue to have jurisdiction as provided for by those instruments. That the Court has been empowered to adjudicate certain issues beyond the scope of the Union Treaties is not without precedent. The 1968 Brussels Convention on jurisdiction and the enforcement of judgments in civil and commercial matters[95], for example, extended the Court's jurisdiction in a similar manner.

V. Structural Aspects of the New Legal Framework

European aliens law under the Amsterdam Treaty raises structural and substantive questions. Some of the structural questions relate to the concept guiding the idea of closer co-operation (also referred to as the 'flexibility'[96], '*à la carte*'[97] or 'pick & choose'[98] concept). European aliens law constitutes a special kind of closer co-operation, subject to rules which differ slightly from those which otherwise guide the Treaties (1). On the other hand, unlike Community law (and, allegedly, other kinds of closer co-operation[99]), policy-making in the field of European aliens law does not imply exclusive treaty making power of the Community, analogous to the ERTA-jurisprudence (2). In general, Title IV ECT strikes a reasonable balance between the need for a common European aliens policy.

1. Closer Co-operation

The most prominent characteristic of European aliens law under the Amsterdam Treaty is that it is to be adopted by way of closer co-operation. The Amsterdam provisions on closer co-operation are based on numerous precedents, dating back to the adoption of the Single European Act[100]. The idea of flexibility finds its roots, *inter alia*, in Articles 15 and 95 ECT (as they are now renumbered), the provisions aimed at establishing the monetary union, and the Social Protocol, which reflect the "rich, if contradictory ideological heritage brought into play by flexibility"[101].

---

94 These instruments are –
- Convention on the protection of the European Communities' financial interests, O.J. 1995 C 316/48 and protocols to this convention, O.J. 1996 C 313/1; O.J. 1997 C 221/11; O.J. 1997 C 151/1
- Protocol on the interpretation, by way of preliminary rulings, by the Court of Justice of the European Communities of the Convention on the establishment of a European Police Office, O.J. 1996 C 299/1
- Convention on the fight against corruption involving officials of the European Communities or officials of Member States, O.J. 1997 C 195/1.

95 O.J. 1972 L 299/32 (unofficial English translation).

96 Cf. *Shaw* 4 ELJ (1998) 63, 69.

97 *Hailbronner*, in *Hummer* (ed.), Die Europäische Union nach dem Vertrag von Amsterdam (1998), 179, 195; *Hailbronner/Thiery* EuR 1998, 583, 584; *Ehlermann* 4 ELJ (1998) 246, 247.

98 *Hailbronner*, in *Hummer* (ed.), id.

99 Cf. *Ehlermann*, 4 ELJ (1998) 246, 258.

100 *Shaw*, 4 ELJ (1998) 63, 68.

101 *Shaw*, 4 ELJ (1998) 63, 69. See *Ehlermann* 4 ELJ (1998) 246, 249 et seq. for the debate following the adoption of the Maastricht Treaty, and for detailed further references.

The Amsterdam Treaty has generally strengthened the concept of closer co-operation although it has been put under strict legal constraints. A future European migration and asylum law may qualify as a prime candidate for closer co-operation, beyond the existing gap between the United Kingdom and Ireland, and Denmark, respectively, on the one side and the rest of EU Member States at the other side, reflected in Title IV Protocols and the Schengen Protocol. Although the very idea of a European migration and asylum law is based on the desirability of a uniform European legal framework, the need may well arise for special legal rules and closer co-operation between a special group of EU Member States based on their common interests which may be different to the interests of other Member States. Immigration and asylum law seems to be particularly prone to such developments since it may affect like few others fields of Community law divergent national interests.

The new framework of closer co-operation does require careful analysis and calls for cautious implementation, as it constitutes a departure from traditional principles of Community law[102]. If it is true that "flexibility suggests a variety of different constitutional and political futures for the European Union, which in turn depend upon future political and socio-economic developments"[103], Member States must limit the extensive use of closer co-operation, and must carefully weigh each departure from traditional Community principles as this might create a fragmented body of European law. The fear "that a schism would progressively emerge in the Community" if further instances of closer co-operation outside the institutional framework of the European Union were to emerge[104] has not been laid to rest by the fact that co-operation has been made subject to substantial requirements of the Amsterdam Treaty. The special regimes of closer co-operation set up by the Schengen Protocol for the Schengen Process and for Title IV ECT matters by the opt-out protocols for the United Kingdom, Ireland and Denmark do exclude the applicability of the general closer co-operation rules as special rules. This does not mean that the general closer co-operation regime of the Articles 40, 43-45 TEU and Article 11 ECT will be *in toto* inapplicable to a future European migration and asylum law. Varying coalitions of Member States may develop. Needs for closer co-operation in particular fields of migration and asylum law will be accommodated, either through formal terms of close co-operation within the legal framework of the ECT or by more informal intergovernmental co-operation outside the Treaty.

The following remarks will focus upon the special closer co-operation regime established by the Schengen Protocol and Title IV Protocols. The general rules governing closer co-operation may influence to some degree the interpretation of these rules.

---

[102] Cf. Deubner, Enhanced Cooperation of EU Member States after Amsterdam (1999) *passim*. See also *Ehlermann* 4 ELJ (1998) 246, 248 as regards ex-Article 100a(4) ECT.

[103] *Shaw* 4 ELJ (1998) 63, 64.

[104] Cf. *Kortenberg* 35 CML Rev. (1998) 833, 835.

a) Title IV ECT and the Schengen Protocol as Examples of Closer Co-operation

Both Title IV law-making and the implementation of the Schengen *acquis* are examples of closer co-operation[105]. This is expressly provided for in the preamble and Article 1 of the Schengen Protocol. Although Title IV ECT has been characterized as "a Title like any other", the "measures adopted under it [being] measures of Community law"[106], there can be no question that Title IV ECT carries all essential features of closer co-operation. Although the opt-outs of the United Kingdom, Ireland and Denmark are based upon a provision in primary Community law, these opt-outs have the same basic structure as opt-outs under Article 11 ECT. The same is true with respect to the Schengen Protocol and the attribution of the Schengen *acquis* to the legal bases of the Treaty establishing the European Community.

Title IV ECT qualifies as an example of closer co-operation and thus continues the policy-making process initiated in conjunction with Schengen. It finds its roots, therefore, in a process previously viewed as the most prominent example of closer cooperation to have emerged outside the EU's single institutional framework. Although this process has been incorporated into Title IV ECT by virtue of the Amsterdam Treaty, the original process contributed greatly to the fears and hopes connected with the idea of closer cooperation. These, in turn, played an important, if not decisive role in the drafting of provisions on closer cooperation and the Schengen Protocol. It is true that, unlike the Schengen Protocol, Title IV ECT is not expressly mentioned in Article 11 ECT. Article 11(4) ECT does, however, include an implicit reference to Title IV ECT in that it renders closer co-operation subject to "all the *relevant*" (emphasis added) ECT provisions. If Title IV ECT constitutes an example of closer co-operation, the provisions contained therein undoubtedly meet the relevance test under Article 11(4) ECT.

By and large, Title IV ECT and the Schengen Protocol follow the procedural lines drawn by the TEU and ECT provisions on closer cooperation and share the most important features of closer cooperation authorized by a Council Decision. Community institution functions are, however, designed somewhat differently. While Article 11 ECT, read together with Article 44(1) TEU and Article 46(c) TEU, does not affect the role of these institutions within the decision-making process[107], Title IV ECT contains genuine institutional provisions which deviate significantly from the norm. On the other hand, as regards the criteria for defining the majority and unanimity requirements, Article 44(1) TEU and, likewise, Articles 1 and 3(2) of the Protocol on the Position of the United Kingdom and Ireland, and Article 1 of the Protocol on the Position of Denmark establish the principle that –

> The qualified majority shall be defined as the same proportion of the weighted votes of the members of the Council concerned as laid down in Article 205(2)

---

[105] This assessment as regards the character of Title IV ECT and the Schengen Protocol has also been reached by *Ehlermann* 4 ELJ (1998) 246, 259 and *Kortenberg* 35 CML Rev. (1998) 833, 836; *Deubner*, Harnessing Differentiation in the EU (1999), 21 et seq. See also *Shaw* 4 ELJ (1998) 63, 75 who notes that the exclusion of the United Kingdom and Ireland from the participation in Title IV measures "provides some evidence as to how Article [11 ECT] might operate".

[106] *Langrish* 23 EL Rev. (1998) 3, 8.

[107] Cf. *Ehlermann* 4 ELJ (1998) 246, 258 as regards the inclusion of judicial Review pursuant to Article 11(4) ECT.

> of the Treaty establishing the European Community. Unanimity shall be constituted by only those Council members concerned.

Consequently, the new role afforded to Community institutions alone create a distinct kind of closer cooperation in Title IV ECT and Schengen Protocol.

Aside from these modifications, the main difference between the Title IV ECT, Schengen and previous regulations lies in the effects the attribution of the products of closer cooperation in the field of European aliens law will have on the *acquis communautaire*. As a matter of principle, Article 11 ECT, read together with Article 43 TEU, excludes the effects of closer cooperation from integration into the *acquis communautaire*, pursuant to Article 43(2) TEU, which limits the duty of loyalty to the Member States participating in the co-operation[108] (see particularly Article 43(1)(e) and (2) TEU). This principle is rebutted in Article 8 of the Schengen Protocol, which provides that –

> [f]or the purposes of the negotiations for the admission of new Member States into the European Union, the Schengen *acquis* and further measures taken by the institutions within its scope shall be regarded as an *acquis* which must be accepted in full by all States candidates for admission.

Schengen-unrelated measures aimed at the implementation of Title IV ECT are arguably designed to form part of the *acquis communautaire*. Notably, the opt-outs with respect to Title IV ECT have been organized such that they do not affect the formal status of this Title as an integral part of primary Community law. Consequently, due to the lack of legislation indicating otherwise, implementation measures for this Title will form a part of secondary Community law. Under Article 11 ECT, on the other hand, only the Council decision authorizing closer co-operation forms part of secondary Community law, as it has its legal basis, and not its source, in Article 11 ECT. Only this decision forms part of the *acquis communautaire*, while other measures adopted under the respective closer co-operation regimes form an *acquis located extra-communautaire* (though it is open to accession by other Member States in accordance with Article 11(3) ECT, and may be commuted to the *acquis communautaire*, should all Member States who opted out initially reverse their decision). The same holds true for Article 11(5) ECT, which stipulates that the said Article does not affect the Schengen Protocol. This provision confirms that the products of closer co-operation reached under the auspices of the Protocol are part of the *acquis communautaire*.

As the Schengen follow-up in the field of European aliens law must comply with the requirements of both the Schengen Protocol and Title IV ECT, this conclusion must apply *a fortiori* to measures adopted pursuant to Title IV ECT alone.

Article 11(5) ECT provides that this Article "shall be without prejudice to the provisions of the Protocol integrating the Schengen *acquis* into the framework of the European Union". The same applies to Title IV ECT by the rule of *lex specialis derogat legi generali*. Beyond the scope of such derogations, there are common issues arising under the general closer co-operation regime as well as in the context of the Schengen Protocol and Title IV ECT.

---

108 *Shaw* 4 ELJ (1998) 63, 71

First, as instruments of primary Community law, the Protocols governing the opt-outs should be regarded as standards of judicial review[109].

Second, as is the case under the general regime governing closer co-operation, there may be some doubt as to whether members of a Community institution elected in an opt-out country should participate in the decision-making process related to such co-operation[110]. The role of the Members of the European Parliament has specifically been questioned[111]. According to Article 190(1) ECT Members of the European Parliament are "representatives [...] of the peoples of the States brought together in the Community"; they cannot yet be regarded as representatives of a single European people. The Treaties are clear on this matter, although they do allow EU citizens regardless of their nationality to vote and stand as a candidates for municipal and European elections in their state of residence (see Article 19 ECT). One could thus regard opt-out Member States as over-represented, if their European Parliament representatives were allowed to vote on closer co-operation proposals. Similar concerns could be voiced about Commission members and judges of the European Court of Justice although neither are to be considered as representatives of Member States. The Treaties have, however, limited the exclusion of the participation of the opt-out Member States to the Council, in order to increase the legitimacy of the decisions taken within the closer co-operation framework, and to ease the way towards a prospective opt-in. This applies to European aliens law in particular, since the incorporation of Title IV into the Treaty establishing the European Community rather than the adoption of Protocols[112], and the provisions governing opt-ins are aimed at encouraging all Member States to participate in the entire creation process of a European aliens policy. Participation of the Members of the European Parliament of opt-out Member States in the decision-making process under Title IV ECT, in addition, might encourage them to act in favour of an opt-in.

Third, Article 11(3) ECT, applies (though *mutatis mutandis*) to British and Irish Title IV opt-ins following the adoption of related Community legislation. This provision states that –

> [a]ny Member State which wishes to become a party to cooperation set up in accordance with this Article shall notify its intention to the Council and to the Commission, which shall give an opinion to the Council within three months of receipt of that notification. Within four months of the date of that notification, the Commission shall decide on it and on such specific arrangements as it may deem necessary.

(A detailed account of related questions will be given *sub specie* opt-in provisions.)

---

[109] Cf. *Kortenberg* 35 CML Rev. (1998) 833, 840 as regards the Protocol on the position of Denmark.

[110] Cf. *Ehlermann* 4 ELJ (1998) 246, 255.

[111] *Ehlermann* ibid.

[112] Cf. the Social Policy Protocol adopted by the Intergovernmental Conference which drew up the Maastricht Treaty.

2. *Implied Treaty Making Powers in Migration and Asylum Law*

a) General Applicability of ERTA-principles

In *ERTA*, the European Court of Justice established the principle that, where certain powers have been conferred on the Community[113], the Council "does not enjoy a discretion to decide whether to proceed through inter-governmental or Community channels"[114] but "that wherever a matter forms the subject of a common policy, the Member States are bound in every case to act jointly in defence of the interests of the Community"[115]. The implied external powers of the Community thus correspond with its internal powers[116]. As expressed by the European Court of Justice: "Only in so far as common rules have been established at internal level does the external competence of the Community become exclusive"[117]. Given that closer co-operation must take place within the single institutional framework of the European Union, and in accordance with the relevant institutional ECT and TEU provisions, action in this area may create ERTA effects similar to those created by Community action[118].

One may argue that areas of closer co-operation, whether based upon the Schengen follow-up process or upon Title IV ECT are necessarily excluded from a treaty making competence of the EC which would incur legal obligations for all EU Member States. It is difficult to imagine international treaties concluded by the "European Countries" with limited internal effect unless the European Countries as subject of public international law are split into two groups – analogous to Community law under Title IV ECT. Such difficulties could, however, be overcome if in fact, based on an opt-in, all EU Member States were bound by an EC comprehensive legislation in migration and asylum matters which according to the ERTA-jurisprudence could result in exclusive treaty making competence. More clarity may be reached by an analysis of the different declarations relating to Title IV measures. In addition, there are several other aspects which may assist in finding an answer whether ERTA-principles have a role to play in Title IV matters. They relate to the ordre-public reservations, the concept of minimum standards and the respect for foreign policy considerations.

---

[113] Cf. ECJ, judgment of 31 March 1971, case 22/70, *Commission v Council* (ERTA), [1971] ECR 263 para 84.

[114] ECJ, judgment of 31 March 1971, case 22/70, *Commission v Council* (ERTA), [1971] ECR 263 para 70.

[115] ECJ, judgment of 31 March 1971, case 22/70, *Commission v Council* (ERTA), [1971] ECR 263 para 77.

[116] See also ECJ-Opinion 1/76 of 26 April 1977, *Laying-up Fund for Inland Waterway Vessels* [1977] ECR 741; judgment of 14 July 1976, cases 3, 4, 6/76, *Kramer*, [1976] ECR 1279; Opinion 1/94 of 15 November 1994, *Competence of the Community to Conclude International Agreements Concerning Services and the Protection of Intellectual Property* (GATS and TRIPS), [1994] ECR I-5267.

[117] ECJ-opinion 1/94 of 15 November 1994, *Competence of the Community to Conclude International Agreements Concerning Services and the Protection of Intellectual Property* (GATS and TRIPS), [1994] ECR I-5267 para 77; cf. ibid. para 89.

[118] An assumption to this extent has been raised for instance by *Ehlermann* 4 ELJ (1998) 246, 258; *Thun-Hohenstein*, Der Vertrag von Amsterdam (1997), 32 et seq.

b) Declarations on Title IV Matters – Legal Nature

First, the Protocol on external relations of the Member States with regard to the crossing of external borders [henceforth referred to as the External Relations Protocol] stipulates that

> [t]he provisions on the measures on the crossing of external borders included in Article 62(2)(a) ECT of Title IV of the Treaty shall be without prejudice to the competence of Member States to negotiate or conclude agreements with third countries as long as they respect Community law and other relevant international agreements.

Second, according to the Declaration on Article 62(2)(b) ECT, foreign policy considerations of both the Union and the Member States shall be taken into account when contemplating measures on the crossing of the external borders of the Member States. Third, the Declaration on Article 63(3)(a) ECT protects the Member States' right to conclude international treaties covering issues of legal immigration, provided that such treaties respect Community law. Finally, Article 64(1) ECT allows Member States to consider foreign policy requirements related to their respective national spheres, and pursuant to the Declaration on this Article, in order to maintain the national *ordre public*. Notably, this Declaration does not mention foreign policy considerations of the EU. Therefore, it seems to verify the understanding that Article 64(1) ECT expresses the recognition of the respective *domaines reservés* of Member States by Community law. While the legal status of the External Relations Protocol is undisputed, as it "shall be annexed to the Treaty establishing the European Community", the Declarations at issue raise a number of questions. First, should they be viewed as matters of legal, rather than political, relevance? Second, if attributed legal relevance, which effects would the Declarations be capable of producing vis-à-vis the Treaty provisions to which they are attached? Finally, to what extent do they exclude ERTA principles, assuming their general applicability in matters of closer co-operation?

Whether Declarations attached to certain Treaty provisions are legal instruments has been put into question with respect to some of the Declarations contained in the Final Act of the Single European Act. The Declaration on Article 8a of the EEC Treaty (Article 14 ECT, as it now is) and the Political Declaration by the Governments of the Member States on the free movement of persons, for example, have created doubts concerning the exact delineation between Community powers and residual powers of the Member States under the Maastricht Treaty[119]. These Declarations did not constitute legal commitments. However, the Declarations discussed here differ significantly from those attached to the Single European Act. The wording of both the Declaration on Article 8a of the EEC Treaty and the Political Declaration on the free movement of persons does not indicate that they were intended for to be legal instruments. Additionally, the former declaration expresses the Conference's "firm political will" to implement the internal market before the end of 1992, while the latter is not only called a political declaration but, moreover, had not been adopted by the Conference drafting the Single European Act. These declarations did not, therefore, impact the delimitation of powers between the EEC (as it then was) and the Member

[119] Cf. the discussion by *Magiera*, in Burmeister (ed.) Verfassungsstaatlichkeit, Essays in honour of Klaus Stern (1997) 1317, 1320-1321.

States[120]. The Declarations on Articles 62(2)(b), 63(3)(a) and 64(1) ECT, however, all commence with the words "The Conference agrees that...", thereby aiming at a, at the very least, quasi-formal character i.e. a "real" agreement under international law[121]. They constitute thus legal, rather than purely political, commitments.

When considering possible legal effects of the Declarations, it is important to remember that they cannot change the content of the Treaty provisions to which they are attached. They are not, however, entirely incapable of influencing this content, provided that they give a distinct meaning to potentially ambiguous expressions. Accordingly, these Declarations must be regarded as instruments of authentic interpretation, as envisaged by Article 31(2)(a) of the Convention of the Law of Treaties, of the provisions to which they relate.

c) The External Relations Protocol

The External Relations Protocol prohibits infringements of Community law by Member States negotiating or concluding agreements with third countries in the field of external border controls. In binding Member States to respect Community law and other relevant international agreements when negotiating or concluding agreements with third countries the protocol clearly indicates the inapplicability of the European Court of Justice's jurisprudence in *ERTA*[122] because under the *ERTA* principles Member States were incompetent to negotiate and conclude agreements with third states in as much as the Community has passed relevant legislation. The External Relations Protocol, therefore, seems to exclude the emergence of ERTA effects in the field of external border controls.

The Protocol, however, can be interpreted in different ways. It either reserves the right of Member States to act on the international level even though, under the ERTA jurisprudence, they would in principle be no longer competent to do so. Or the Protocol implicitly allows for action on the part of Member States only as long as the Community has not adopted comprehensive measures. That raises the question of whether Article 62(2)(a) ECT establishes exclusive Community competence. The wording of the provision is not particularly helpful in finding an answer. Its purpose is to provide for the implementation of measures which gradually abolish internal border controls, as envisaged by Article 61 ECT. Article 61 ECT supports an interpretation whereby the Community may move closer to a comprehensive set of rules. It could be argued, therefore, that Article 62(2)(a) ECT allows for the emergence of exclusive Community competence only if comprehensive (though it might be doubtful whether the Community will ever reach comprehensiveness[123]) measures have been adopted. Such competence notwithstanding, Member States retain the right to conclude international agreements, provided that these comply with substantive

---

[120] Cf. *Magiera*, in Burmeister (ed.) Verfassungsstaatlichkeit, Essays in honour of Klaus Stern (1997), 1317, 1335.

[121] A similar view has been taken by *Thun-Hohenstein*, Der Vertrag von Amsterdam (1997), 35. According to *Thun-Hohenstein* the similarities between the wording of the Declaration on Article 63(3)(a) ECT and the External Relations Protocol indicate similar legal effects of said instruments.

[122] The opposite view has been discussed by *Thun-Hohenstein*, Der Vertrag von Amsterdam (1997), 32.

[123] For instance, *Thun-Hohenstein*, Der Vertrag von Amsterdam (1997), 33 has expressed such doubts.

Community law and other relevant international treaties[124]. As is evident from the French text[125], the Protocol only refers to the substantive content of both respective arrangements and Community law. The Protocol, therefore, cannot be interpreted as a reference to the ERTA-principles. A similar conclusion may be drawn from the requirement that Member States respect other relevant international agreements. This requirement would be unnecessary if the Community were able to prevent Member States from concluding international agreements by implementing them in the form of Community legislation, or by concluding agreements itself[126]. The Protocol thus binds Member States by reference to the duty of loyalty under Article 10 ECT, and obliges Member States to respect other relevant international agreements. Such other relevant agreements may be those concluded by the European Community without, however, attributing any competence to the EC.

d) Foreign Policy Considerations in Visa-regimes

The Declaration on Article 62(2)(b) ECT provides that Member States may take into account foreign policy considerations when adopting rules on visa of no more than three months. Whether this implies exclusiveness or not is, once again, a matter of controversy. The Declaration does not say anything about the competence of Member States relating to visa regulations. It is clear from the wording and spirit of Article 62(2)(b) ECT that at least under the Amsterdam Treaty a uniform comprehensive visa regime is intended, thereby excluding any Member State action in the field of short-term visa requirements. The reference to Member States' responsibilities in the Declaration therefore can only be interpreted as a reference to their general rights and obligations as Contracting States under the Amsterdam Treaty with the particularity, however, that in the exercise of their rights Member States may take foreign policy considerations into account. The background of this clause is the close link of visa requirements with possibly divergent foreign policy considerations. The Declaration makes clear that such foreign policy considerations which may sometimes be bound on national traditions are a legitimate concern in the decision-making process.

e) Declaration on Immigration Policy (Article 63(3)(a) ECT)

According to the second paragraph of Article 63

> [m]easures adopted by the council on immigration policy and the rights of third-country nationals shall not prevent any Member State from maintaining or intro-

---

[124] The same conclusion has been reached by *Winkler*, in *Bergmann/Lenz* (ed.), Der Amsterdamer Vertrag (1998), 45-71 para 17.

[125] The French text of the Protocol reads –

> Les dispositions sur les mesures relatives au franchissement des frontières extérieures prévues à l'article 73 J, point 2), sous a), du titre III A du traité ne préjugent pas la compétence des États membres de négocier ou de conclure des accords avec des pays tiers, *pour autant que lesdits accords respectent* le droit communautaire et les autres accords internationaux pertinents

(emphasis added).

[126] One might think of readmission agreements concluded between the Community and neighbouring states modelled upon the Schengen-Poland readmission agreement.

> ducing [...] national provisions compatible with this Treaty and international agreements.

The Declaration on Article 63(3)(a) ECT contains an expression of agreement, of the Intergovernmental Conference, as regards Member States' right to "negotiate and conclude agreements with third countries ... as long as such agreements respect Community law ". Arguably, the second paragraph of Article 63 ECT thus precludes *ex contractu* exclusive competence of the Community in the fields of Article 63(3) and (4) ECT. At the same time, by way of adopting the Declaration on Article 63(3)(a) ECT Member States have reserved their treaty making power irrespective of the adoption of comprehensive Community legislation.

There are several reasons supporting this conclusion. First, as long as the Community has not yet made use of any exclusive competence pursuant to Article 63, second paragraph ECT Member States retain a sovereign right to conclude treaties. There would have been no need to solemnly confirm this right, particularly since the Declaration refers to only a handful of items contained in Article 63(3) and (4) ECT. Second, the Declaration requires that "arrangements" concluded within its ambit "respect Community law". This wording indicates compliance with the substantive content of both respective arrangements and Community law rather than a mere reference to the ERTA principles. It follows that the implementation of Article 63(3) and (4) ECT is capable of creating ERTA effects, while immigration requirements in the sense of Article 63(3)(a) ECT are excluded from an exclusive treaty-making power of the EC.

f) Ordre-Public Clauses

Obviously, in protecting Member States' rights with respect to the maintenance of law and order and the safeguarding of internal security, the *ordre public* clause contained in Article 64(1) ECT not only allows Member States to take related action, but to that extent also excludes ERTA effects. The Member States would not be able to meet the requirements of this responsibility if they were unable to take action vis-à-vis countries of origin of immigrants posing a threat to their *ordre public*. Thus, Member States may conclude agreements which specifically address such threats. When concluding such agreements, however, Member States must not only consider their *ordre public*, but also the impact of these agreements on foreign relations. Accordingly, the Declaration on Article 64(1) ECT affirms the conclusion that may be drawn upon close reading of the Article itself. Furthermore, the question of the adjudication of ERTA effects does not arise since the jurisdiction of the European Court of Justice is excluded by virtue of Article 68(2) ECT.

VI. The Basic Structure of Title IV Powers

Title IV ECT contains three basic principles for all future action in the field of European immigration an asylum law. First, new "true" Community legislation must be based on Title IV powers. Second, elements of the Schengen *acquis* which regulate aspects of European aliens law must be attributed to Title IV legal bases. Finally, the said *acquis* may only be further developed within the framework established by Title IV ECT.

The Amsterdam Treaty has substantially re-shaped, if not newly established, the legal framework for European aliens law. Aside from the subject matter included in ex-Article 100c ECT, Title IV ECT confers a wholly different set of EU powers. The basic provision of this Title is Article 61 ECT, which (insofar as relevant here) differentiates between –

- "measures aimed at ensuring the free movement of persons in accordance with Article 14" ECT, and
- "other measures".

The Council shall adopt such measures in the fields of -

- external border controls,
- asylum,
- immigration, and
- safeguarding the rights of nationals of third countries

(see Article 61(a) and (b) ECT).

The reference to Article 14 ECT resembles the Preamble of the Schengen Convention, which states that the abolition of internal border controls under the said Convention correspond to the aim of establishing an area without internal frontiers, as envisaged by the Treaty establishing the European Community. Arguably, measures aimed at ensuring the free movement of persons under Title IV ECT are guided by the concept developed in the Schengen Convention.

1. Measures Aimed at Ensuring the Freedom of Movement

As regards the free movement of persons, Article 61(a) ECT provides for the adoption of measures and "flanking measures" directly related to –

- external border controls as envisaged by Article 62(2) and (3) ECT,
- asylum as envisaged by Article 63(1)(a) ECT, and
- immigration as envisaged by Article 63(2)(a) ECT.

Measures concerning the rights of third-country nationals are not covered by this provision.

On the other hand, Article 61 ECT does not refer to measures aimed at abolishing internal border controls as envisaged by Article 62(1) ECT. Nor do these measures qualify as "other measures" in the sense of Article 61(b) ECT, as the latter provisions refer only to Article 63 ECT. One cannot conclude, however, that Article 62(1) ECT falls outside of both categories established by Article 61(a) and (b) ECT, as the purpose of both Article 61(a) and Article 62(1) ECT is to promote the objectives of Article 14 ECT. Article 62(1) ECT thus seems to be excluded from the power to adopt "flanking measures". Although this interpretation might seem surprising at first glance, it becomes more reasonable if Article 61(a) ECT is read in connection with Article 62(2) and (3) ECT. Together, they provide for compensatory measures in the abolition of internal border controls[127], which may be combined with "flanking measures". If Articles 61(a) and 62 ECT are read as such, no specific need for measures "flanking" the abolition of internal border controls exists.

---

[127] See *Thun-Hohenstein*, Der Vertrag von Amsterdam (1997), 32.

2. Other Measures

"Other measures" are not related to border controls, but may cover matters related to asylum and immigration not dealt with by measures aimed at ensuring free movement of persons, as envisaged by Article 14 ECT. Additionally, "other measures" may protect the rights of third-country nationals.

Aside from the difference in the subject-matters covered by Article 61(a) and (b) ECT, the framework for "other measures" differs from that applied to the freedom of movement in the following ways –

- no power to adopt flanking measures exists, and
- the purposes which "other measures" may serve are not limited, except that both categories of measures are intended to the gradual establishment of an area of freedom, security and justice.

Given that the EU has the power to determine the purpose of "other measures", there is arguably no need for a specific power covering "flanking measures". In light of this interpretation, "flanking measures", as envisaged by Article 61(a) ECT, should be regarded as measures which serve a purpose other than that of ensuring the freedom of movement. The power to adopt flanking measures, in other words, functions as a proviso to the limited purpose of measures adopted pursuant to Article 61(a) ECT.

Finally, the power to adopt "other measures", as a matter of principle, is not subject to limitations other than those established by Article 63 ECT while measures aimed at ensuring the freedom of movement may not serve any other purpose.

3. Direct Effects of Title IV Provisions?

The jurisprudence of the European Court of Justice has developed the principle that provisions of Community law have direct effects if they "impose precise and clearly defined obligations [...] which do not require any subsequent intervention by Community or national authorities for their implementation"[128]. An obligation is determined as such if it is not subject to any exception or condition[129]; in other words, if it is "unconditioned and sufficiently precise"[130]. These prerequisites are not met by any of the provisions included in Articles 62 and 63 ECT for several reasons. First, the items referred to in the second paragraph of Article 63 ECT are not bound by a set transition period[131]. Second, the remaining provisions are legal bases for Community action, to be adopted in a decision-making process which includes the exercise of political discretion[132]. In addition, the imposition of the transitional period shows that all provisions included in Articles 62 and 63 ECT require implementation by Community action.

---

128 ECJ, judgment of 1 July 1969, joined cases 2 and 3/69, *Sociaal Fonds voor de Diamantarbeiders v S.A. Ch. Brachfeld & Sons and Chougol Diamond Co.*, [1969] ECR 211 paras 22/23.

129 ECJ, judgment of 4 December 1974, case 41/74, *Duyn v Home Office*, [1974] ECR 1337, para 13.

130 ECJ, judgment of 19 January 1982, case 8/81, *Becker v Finanzamt Münster-Innenstadt*, [1982] ECR 53 para 25. See *Zuleeg* in *v.d. Groeben/Thiesing/Ehlermann*, EUV/EGV Article 1 EGV para 34 for details and further references.

131 These matters were controversial, the time of the conclusion of the Amsterdam Treaty. See *Hailbronner* 35 CML Rev. (1998) 1047, 1050; *Hailbronner/Thiery* EuR 1998, 585, 587.

132 See also *Lang*, Gemeinschaftsrecht der Drittstaatsangehörigen (1998), 359 et seq.

It is a different issue whether the non-fulfilment of the legislative program within the time limit prescribed by Article 61 ECT may give rise to an action for failure to act under Article 232 ECT. The European Court has applied rather strict standards with respect to a successful action. The obligation to act must be in its basic content precise and unconditional. Considering the large scope of political discretion it is unlikely that an action for failure to act under Article 61 ECT will be successful.[133]

VII. Communitarization of the Schengen *Acquis*

1. General Principles and Issues

The Schengen Protocol has functioned as a first step in a twofold process of supranationalization of the parts of the Schengen *acquis*: Article 2(1), second sub-paragraph of the Schengen Protocol provides that "[t]he Council [...] shall determine [...] the legal basis for each of the provisions or decisions which constitute the Schengen *acquis*", and the fourth sub-paragraph of this Article states that "[a]s long as the measures referred to above have not been taken [...] the provisions or decisions which constitute the Schengen *acquis* shall be regarded as acts based on Title VI of the Treaty on European Union". The specific positions of the United Kingdom, Ireland, Denmark, Norway and Iceland[134] notwithstanding, the attribution of parts of the Schengen *acquis* to Title IV powers and other legal bases in the Treaty establishing the European Community has transformed these instruments from those of intra-EU international law[135] to those of (mainly[136]) secondary Community law.

The attribution of elements of the Schengen *acquis* to Title IV legal bases has not affected Denmark (see Article 3(1) of the Schengen Protocol). This provision is obviously modelled on Article 30(4)(b) of the Convention of the Law of Treaties and prevents discontinuation of the *acquis* reached under the Schengen cooperation vis-à-vis Denmark[137] (the effects vis-à-vis Iceland and Norway will be dealt with specifically).

A number of legal questions had to be dealt with by the Council when considering the attribution of the Schengen *acquis* to legal bases contained *inter alia* in Title IV ECT –

- Of which elements is the Schengen *acquis* composed?
- Should the parts of the Schengen *acquis* attributed to Title IV be qualified as directives or regulations – which effect does attribution take?
- What procedural principles apply with regard to the attribution process?
- Is attribution subject to judicial review by the European Court of Justice?
- Which arrangements are necessary vis-à-vis Iceland and Norway?

---

[133] Doubts as to whether an action for failure to act may contribute to exerting pressure upon the Member States have been expressed by *Hailbronner* 35 CML Rev. (1998) 1057, 1050. See also *Thun-Hohenstein*, Der Vertrag von Amsterdam (1997), 31.

[134] The meaning of the unwillingness to join the Schengen club of the United Kingdom and Ireland, and the Danish opt-out will be dealt with sub specie opt-out and opt-in provisions (*infra* XII).

[135] Third pillar decision-making has also been referred to under the label of intergovernmental cooperation with connections to Community law. See *Müller-Graff* 31 CML Rev. (1994) 493, 497; *Hailbronner*, in Hailbronner/Klein/Magiera/Müller-Graff, EUV/EGV (1996), Article K EUV para 12.

[136] Certain parts of the Schengen *acquis* have been attributed to legal bases contained in Title VI TEU.

[137] *Hailbronner/Thiery* EuR 1998, 583, 594.

2. *The Elements of the Schengen* Acquis

An annex to the Schengen Protocol defines the Schengen *acquis* as a compilation of –

- the 1985 Schengen Agreement,
- the 1990 Schengen Convention, including the Final Act and common declarations,
- the Accession Protocols and Agreements to said instruments and related Final Acts and declarations, and
- decisions and declarations adopted by the Executive Committee, as well as acts adopted for the implementation of the Convention by the organs upon which the Executive Committee has conferred decision making powers.

On the one hand, this definition did not resolve problems caused by certain inconsistencies inherent in the decisions and declarations adopted by the Executive Committee[138]. As a result, a final assessment of the Schengen *acquis* has been left to the Council. On the other hand, this definition has excluded the decisions and judgments of the courts of the Member States, and the Association Agreement with Iceland and Norway from the *acquis*[139].

The Council's definition and attribution decisions have excluded certain elements of the Schengen *acquis* from attribution. The Council has observed, in the preamble of its decision, that it must -

> establish for which provisions or decisions constituting the Schengen acquis it is not necessary to determine a legal basis in conformity with the relevant provision of the Treaties.[140]

The Council has given a couple of reasons for excluding certain parts of the Schengen *acquis* from attribution. These reasons are that –

> (a) The provision does not have any binding legal force, and a comparable provision can be adopted by the Council only on the basis of an instrument that has not legal basis in one of the Treaties.
>
> (b) The passage of time and/or events have rendered the provision redundant.
>
> (c) The provision relates to institutional rules which are regarded as being superseded by European Union procedures.
>
> (d) The subject matter of the provision is covered by — and therefore superseded by — existing European Community or Union legislation or by a legal act adopted by all Member States.
>
> (e) The provision has been made redundant by the Agreement to be concluded with the Republic of Iceland and the Kingdom of Norway pursuant to Article 6 of the Schengen Protocol.
>
> (f) The provision concerns an area covered neither by the activity of the Community nor by the aims of the European Union and thus concerns one of those areas in which the Member States have retained freedom to act. This includes

---

[138] *Hailbronner/Thiery* EuR 1998, 583, 608.

[139] *Hailbronner/Thiery* ibid.

[140] Para (3) of the Preamble of the Council Decision concerning the definition of the Schengen *acquis*.

provisions which may be significant only for the purposes of calculating financial claims of or between the Member States concerned.[141]

The Schengen Protocol has not affected the character of the parts of the Schengen *acquis* not attributed to legal bases in Community law. As far as such parts are neither redundant nor superseded they remain, therefore, in the sphere of international law.

3. Legal Nature of the Schengen Acquis

Attribution of the Schengen *acquis* has not included the determination of the character of the instruments attributed. Additionally, the legislative character (directive or regulation) of the Schengen *acquis* following its attribution to a legal base under Title IV ECT is regulated by neither the Schengen Protocol nor the Amsterdam Treaty. As directives and regulations have different legal effects, however, a decision as to their character, as defined by Article 249 ECT, will ultimately have to be made. Arguably, the power to make a decision on the legal basis given to the Council includes the right to determine the legislative character of the elements of the Schengen *acquis*. It is suggested that the Council should attribute the character of regulations to those elements of the Schengen *acquis* which require no further implementation. However, if the Council should opt for a directive rather than a regulation, where appropriate, the question arises as to the effect of such determination. First, should the Council set a time-limit for implementation by Member States[142]? Second, which effects would respective Council decisions take? If a date of implementation could be agreed upon, should the time-limit be regarded as a follow-up decision, subject to Article 5 of the Protocol on the position of Denmark? On the other hand, to what extent would the attribution of the character of a directive affect laws adopted as Schengen Convention implementation measures and already in force in Member States? If it is to be assumed that such laws comply with the duties under the said Convention, does the European Court of Justice have the power to review national implementation measures relating to their compatibility with EC standards? These questions do not find a clear answer in either the Schengen Protocol or the Amsterdam Treaty itself.

4. Judicial Review

While the European Court of Justice has the power to review the attribution of the Schengen *acquis*, it is doubtful whether its jurisdiction extends to reviewing the compatibility of this acquis with the Community Treaties. The elements of the Schengen *acquis* have been given the character of Community law by the Schengen Protocol, which forms part of primary Community law and, as such, is not subject to judicial review[143]. Accordingly, it could be argued that these elements must be deemed

---

[141] Para (4) of the Preamble of the Council Decision concerning the definition of the Schengen *acquis*.

[142] Implementation by way of legislation would become necessary where presently Member States merely apply relevant parts of the Schengen *acquis* in their administrative practice. That follows from the Court's *dictum* in *Technical Circular 'Air'*: ECJ, judgment of 30 May 1991, case C-361/88, *Commission v Germany* (Technical Circular 'Air'), 1991 [ECR] I-2567 para 21 where the Court has held that directives must be implemented "with unquestionable binding force, or with the specificity, precision and clarity required ... in order to satisfy the requirement of legal certainty".

[143] See *Thun-Hohenstein*, Der Vertrag von Amsterdam (1997), 53.

to comply with the provisions of primary Community law to which they are attributed by the Council. A different view can be based on the argument that Schengen *acquis* instruments attributed to Title IV ECT are transformed into secondary Community law and remain as such subject to judicial review like any other legal instrument based upon the Treaty.[144] In support of this argument one may refer to the basic intention of the Schengen Protocol to achieve an incorporation into the legal framework of the Union Treaty rather than excluding it from judicial control. In addition a distinction between the original Schengen *acquis* and follow-up measures with regard to judicial control would raise substantial practical and legal difficulties.

5. *Iceland and Norway*

The reference to "a legal act adopted by all Member States" in para (4)(d) of the Preamble of the Council Decision concerning the definition of the Schengen *acquis* obviously affirms the redundancy of the Schengen asylum provisions. These provisions became by and large inoperative when the Dublin Convention entered into force. Their relevance was, therefore, limited to the legal relationship with the Schengen-*associés*, i.e. Iceland and Norway[145]. However, in the meantime the association of Iceland and Norway has been adapted to the integration of the Schengen acquis into the EU's legal framework, by way of the Agreement concerning their association with the implementation, application and development of the Schengen acquis[146].

By decision of 17 May 1999 the Council has concluded, under Article 6 of the Schengen Protocol, an agreement with the Republic of Iceland and the Kingdom of Norway concerning the latters' association with the implementation, application and development of the Schengen acquis[147]. This agreement replaces the association agreements concluded on 19 December 1996. A convention governing the relationship between the Schengen-*associés* and the United Kingdom and Ireland, is being negotiated.

The Agreement concluded by the European Union and the Republic of Iceland and the Kingdom of Norway on the implementation, application and development of the Schengen *acquis* adjusts the Schengen association to fit the new legal framework of European aliens law. The Agreement creates a specific body, i.e. the Mixed Committee (Article 2), to discuss questions related to the application of the Agreement (Article 11), including the settlement of disputes. The Mixed Committee shall also promote the uniform application and interpretation of the Agreement (Articles 9 and 10). In order to work towards this end, Iceland and Norway shall be given the opportunity to submit position statements or written observations in preliminary ruling proceedings before the European Court of Justice.

---

144 *Kortenberg* 35 CML Rev. (1998) 833, 843.

145 Cf. *Hailbronner/Thiery* EuR 1998, 583, 609.

146 Agreement with the Republic of Iceland and the Kingdom of Norway concerning the latters' association with the implementation, application and development of the Schengen *acquis*, O.J. 1999 L 176/35.

147 O.J. 1999 L 176/36. Additionally, the Council of the one part and Iceland and Norway of the other part have concluded the Agreement in the form of Exchanges of Letters between the Council of the European Union and the Republic of Iceland and the Kingdom of Norway concerning Committees which assist the European Commission in the exercise of its executive powers, O.J. 1999 L 176/53.

As a matter of principle, Iceland and Norway will be bound to accept, implement and apply the measures which amend or build upon the Schengen *acquis* (Articles 2(3) and 8(1) of the Agreement). The European Commission shall, however, informally seek advice from experts of these countries when drafting new legislation (Article 6). Additionally, Iceland and Norway have the right to make suggestions in the Mixed Committee on Agreement-related matters, pursuant to Article 4(4) of the Agreement. In particular, the Agreement strives to establish general agreement on the criteria and mechanisms to be employed in the allocation of responsibility for examining asylum applications lodged in any EU Member State, in Iceland or in Norway (Article 7).

The contracting parties want acts or measures referred to in the Agreement to enter into force simultaneously for the European Union, its Member States, Iceland and Norway. The amount of time associated states need, according to their constitutional requirements, for the implementation of these instruments must thus be taken into account. If special requirements do exist, Iceland and Norway must notify both the Council and the Commission (Article 8(2)(b) and (c)). Iceland must inform Community institutions within four weeks of the date foreseen for the entry into force of respective instruments, at the latest. Norway shall provisionally apply, where possible, the content of such act or measure. If Iceland and Norway fail to fulfil their constitutional requirements, or are unwilling to accept an act or measure which falls within the ambit of the Agreement, the latter shall be considered terminated vis-à-vis the respective state, unless the Mixed Committee decides otherwise within ninety days (Article 8(4)). Disputes irreconcilable under the procedure envisaged by Article 11 of the Agreement will also end in effective termination.

Article 6 of the Schengen Protocol grants a specific treaty-making power to the Council, in that it allows it to sign international agreements related to both the first and third pillars of the Amsterdam Treaty[148]. The Anglo-Irish opt-out notwithstanding, the issue of free movement of persons vis-à-vis third countries will remain a matter of common interest (though this expression no longer bears a distinct legal character) for all EU Member States. Article 6, second paragraph of the Schengen Protocol supports this assumption, in that it stipulates that rules governing the legal effects of the Schengen-association of Norway and Iceland vis-à-vis the United Kingdom and Ireland are to be laid down in an agreement concluded by the Council and approved by unanimous vote.

VIII. Re-Adoption of Maastricht Third Pillar Instruments Under Title IV Powers

Different to the Schengen Protocol Title IV ECT does not provide for an automatic transformation of acts or decisions previously adopted as third pillar instruments now subject to the legislative competence of the European Community. There are no express provisions in the Amsterdam Treaty on the legal effects of such acts nor is there any clause in the Treaty regulating the legal character of intergovernmental third pillar instruments which do not fall under the legislative competence of the Community according to Title IV ECT.

General aspects support the view that third pillar acts remain unaffected in their validity as intergovernmental instruments with limited binding force.

---

[148] *Thun-Hohenstein*, Der Vertrag von Amsterdam (1997), 56.

First, the Amsterdam Treaty does not attribute Maastricht's third pillar *acquis* to legal bases contained in the newly created framework. Second, since the entry into force of the Amsterdam Treaty, Title VI TEU no longer covers the adoption of instruments of European aliens law. Third, this Title includes rules on judicial review (see Article 35 TEU) which deviate substantially from the rules of the Maastricht era and are, thus, incapable of being applied to Maastricht's third pillar *acquis* because neither international nor European law is subject to the jurisdiction of a Court established outside the national sphere, save under express treaty provisions. Treaty interpretation, as a matter of principle, cannot result in the creation of a new jurisdiction. Fourth, and finally, the principle codified in Article 30(3) of the Convention on the Law of Treaties and reflected by ex-Article 100c(7) ECT, namely that instruments adopted under expired legal bases remain in force until their content has been replaced by instruments based on successor norms, supports the view that, the repeal of ex-Articles K.1-K.9 TEU notwithstanding, these provisions continue to legitimize the instruments created in compliance therewith.

It follows that Maastricht's third pillar *acquis* will only change in legal nature if replaced by Community legislation adopted under Title IV ECT. However, such re-adoption will force the United Kingdom and Ireland to decide whether they want to opt in and participate in re-adoption. However, if the United Kingdom and Ireland opt out, the question remains unsolved of whether re-adoption affects the commitments taken by opt-out Member States under the instruments replaced, within the framework of Maastricht's third pillar. This issue is similar to the problem posed by Denmark's Schengen opt-out. A solution may, therefore, found in an analogy to Article 5 of the Protocol on the Position of Denmark.

The re-adoption of instruments enacted under ex-Title VI TEU will not affect international law commitments by Denmark to the other member states. The same applies for the United Kingdom and Ireland, unless these Member States decide to opt-in. This construction proves appropriate as, like Article 3(1) of the Schengen Protocol, it is modelled upon Article 30(4)(b) of the Convention of the Law of Treaties and maintains the legal validity of the *acquis* reached during the Maastricht era[149].

However, Member States participating in decision-making under Title IV ECT must replace intergovernmental instruments, regardless of whether they are substituted for by Community legislation of identical or amended content[150]. As a matter of courtesy, Member States participating in Title IV closer co-operation may invite opt-out Member States to participate in the follow-up on the international level, similar to the relationship between Denmark and Member States envisaged by Article 5 of the Protocol on the Position of Denmark.

IX. Procedural Issues

Title IV ECT includes a number of overlapping procedural provisions. The most important of these is Article 67 ECT, which calls for a transition period of five years. Viewed in the context of the entire process of Community legislation, and compared

---

149 *Hailbronner/Thiery* EuR 1998, 583, 594.

150 Cf. *Hailbronner/Thiery* EuR 1998, 583, 594 including a reference to Article 30(4)(a) of the Convention of the law of Treaties.

to both ex-Article 100c ECT and ex-Title VI TEU, this period might see rather few changes. Areas previously covered by ex-Title VI TEU are now dealt with by way of supranational law-making subject to unanimous vote by the Council. After the expiry of the transition period, certain procedural changes will take effect, while the Council can pass a decision aimed at implementing further procedural and jurisdictional changes, pursuant to Article 67(2), second indent ECT.

During the transition period, two kinds of legislative procedure apply –

- The procedure governed by Article 67(1) and (2) ECT, namely unanimity rule in the Council and consultation of the European Parliament, is applicable to the items envisaged in Articles 62(1), (2)(a), (2)(b)(ii), (2)(b)(iv) and (3), and 63 ECT.
- The procedure framed by Article 67(3) ECT, namely qualified majority rule in the Council and consultation of the European Parliament, is applicable to the matters dealt with in Article 62(2)(b)(i) and (2)(b)(iii) i.e. positive and negative listing, and uniform format for visas.

In addition, the decision-making process related to cases of emergency due to a sudden influx of third-country nationals under Article 64(2) ECT is not subject to the requirements of Article 67 ECT. Unlike Article 62 and Article 63 ECT, Article 64(2) ECT does not refer to Article 67 ECT, nor does it otherwise fall under Article 67 ECT. Article 64(2) ECT, on the other hand, does not allow for the adoption of legislative measures, but only for provisional measures valid for a maximum period of six months.

After the expiry of five years from the date of entry into force of the Amsterdam Treaty, the following principles apply –

- items referred to in Article 62(2)(b)(ii) and (2)(b)(iv) ECT, namely procedures and conditions for issuing visas, and rules on a uniform visa, will be decided upon in co-decision with the Parliament according to Article 251 ECT (see Article 67(3), second indent ECT), and
- the Commission will have the exclusive right to initiative, although it will have to "examine any request made by a Member State that it submit a proposal to the Council" (see Article 67(2)ECT).

Article 67 ECT shows that there are different procedures in visa-related matters during the transitional five years period. A uniform procedure can only be achieved after the transition period if the Council decides according to Article 67(2) ECT to apply the procedure of co-decision to all Title IV matters.

The wording of Article 67 ECT is somewhat vague. It does not leave Council a discretion whether or not to decide upon a transition to the co-decision procedure. On the other hand, there are no criteria in the Treaty for judging whether the Council is obliged to apply the co-decision procedure to any specified Title IV matter. It follows that while Council is obliged to pass a decision according to Article 67(2) ECT it is within its political discretion to determine the scope of application of the co-decision procedure.

Article 67(2) ECT seems to restrict Council's regulative discretion to the introduction of the co-decision procedure. The reference to Article 251 ECT is not only clear in wording, but also serves a specific purpose, i.e. to increase the scope of the procedure of co-decision which has become the only standard procedure besides consultation under Amsterdam's legal framework. Article 67(2) ECT also aims at securing the integration process by extending the scope of application of Article 251

ECT[151]. On the other hand, practical considerations may support a less rigid interpretation granting the Council the power to gradually increase the rights of the European Parliament by a modified co-decision procedure. In the light of the purpose of Article 67(2) ECT and in consideration of its wording, a more flexible interpretation of Article 67(2) ECT seems, however, hardly admissible. Be that as it may; it is at least doubtful whether Council decisions on procedure are subject to judicial review, as they do in fact constitute Treaty amendments. Given their similarity to Treaty amendments and lacking any judicially enforceable standards there is no scope for a judicial review of Council acts under Article 67(2) ECT. If, however, the European Court of Justice were considered as competent to review such decisions it would only be able to either uphold or set aside such decisions.

According to the second indent of Article 67(2) ECT the Council may, furthermore, adapt the provisions relating to the powers of the European Court of Justice in the field of European aliens law. The scope of the Council's discretion with respect to such adaptations is not unlimited. According to Article 67(2) ECT the Council may adapt Court procedure. Adaptation may be interpreted as extending the generally applicable provisions relating to the powers of the European Court of Justice to Title IV matters. Arguably, a broader understanding of the term "adapt" might also include the notion of framing new principles governing the European Court of Justice's powers in the field of European aliens law. Considering the purpose of Article 67(2) ECT, i.e. to assimilate Title IV ECT to the general legal framework of the Treaty, the power of adaptation granted by Article 67(2) ECT to the Council is meant to "normalize" the judicial procedure in Title IV matters rather than to introduce new differentiations and particularities.

The Declaration on Article 67 ECT requires that Community institutions shall aim at "taking and applying this decision on procedures immediately after the end of that [transitional] period". Hence the Commission should already propose the decision on procedures during the transitional period. The Commission has the exclusive right of initiative in this respect because co-initiative under Title IV ECT only refers to Community legislation for reason of the share in competence in this respect.

X. The Scope of Legislative Powers under Title IV

1. Abolition of Internal Border Controls and Compensating Measures

Both the abolition of obstacles to the free movement of persons and the adoption of compensatory measures, as envisaged by Article 61(a) ECT, have been achieved through the Council decision attributing the Schengen *acquis*[152]. Article 62(1) ECT calls for the abolition of internal border controls in the European Union. Article 62(1) communitarizes core elements of the Schengen process and qualifies all measures related to abolition of internal border controls as means to achieve the free movement of persons. Border controls, by definition, are measures aimed at preventing illegal entry of persons constituting a danger to the public order. Accordingly, compensatory measures are considered to be necessary to maintain the level of security considered as necessary to protect the public order. The term "in connection with compensatory

---

[151] Cf. *Ehlermann* 4 ELJ (1998) 246, 250 et seq.
[152] See point 26 of the Action Plan of the Council and the Commission, O.J. 1999 C 19/1.

measures" in Article 61(a) ECT raises some questions relating to the scope of legislative powers under Article 62(1) ECT and the power of Member States to maintain or establish measures to prevent illegal entry of third-country nationals.

Measures employed by national governments to maintain law and order and safeguard internal security have never been confined to border controls. The main purpose of Article 62(2) and (3) ECT is to form a legal basis for compensatory measures with cross-border effects. Accordingly, Member States may maintain existing, or introduce new controls of third-country nationals, as long as these do not undermine the abolition of internal border controls[153]. The concept underlying such controls has been a matter of debate in Community law; the argument has been raised that, under Community law, compensatory measures may only re-establish, but may not extend the level of security which existed before the abolition of internal border controls[154]. However, security levels are not easily quantifiable and statistics maybe manipulated. The effectiveness of measures aimed at establishing a high level of security may change under different political or social conditions. An evaluation of which compensatory measures are sufficient and effective must be left to the political actors. The assessment may be guided by the proportionality principle – both vis-à-vis the Member States which, by the *ordre public* clauses included in Title IV ECT, have the right to maintain internal security, and vis-à-vis the individuals concerned, whose human rights to security (on the one hand) and freedom of movement (on the other) define the parameters to determine compensatory measures. Accordingly, the Community institutions enjoy a margin of political discretion in implementing Articles 62 and 63 ECT. In addition, Article 62(2)(a) ECT calls for the adoption of common standards and procedures for external border controls. This provision covers the entirety of items relevant to external border controls, as regulated by Title II Chapter 2 SIC.

2. *Visa Policy*

Visa policy is the only item of European aliens law which formed part of the Treaty establishing the European Community during the Maastricht era. Accordingly, in providing for visa regulations Article 62(2)(b) ECT allows for both a follow-up of the existing visa regime and for an expansion to include further relevant aspects.

The scope for Community action was rather narrow under ex-Article 100c ECT, and was confined to –

- "drawing up a list of third countries whose nationals must be in possession of a visa when crossing the external borders of the Member States" (ex-Article 100c(3) ECT = Article 62(2)(b)(i) ECT), and
- "measures relating to a uniform format for visas" (ex-Article 100c(3) ECT = Article 62(2)(b)(iii) ECT).

In the area of soft law, the Council has passed a recommendation relating to local consular cooperation regarding visas[155].

---

[153] Cf. *Magiera*, in Burmeister (ed.) Verfassungsstaatlichkeit, Essays in honour of Klaus Stern (1997) 1317, 1337 for the opposite view. The author derives his view from the loyalty principle and the stipulation, under ex-Article B TEU, that the European Union shall build on the acquis communautaire.

[154] *Magiera*, in Burmeister (ed.) Verfassungsstaatlichkeit, Essays in honour of Klaus Stern (1997), 1317, 1330-1331.

[155] O.J. 1996 C 80/1.

In addition to the controversy on the scope of Article 100c(1) ECT, the question of which measures meet the "relating" test under ex-Article 100c(3) ECT has been hotly disputed. The competence for Community action was said to be confined to the establishment of a common visa format, while it did not extend to the question of information contained in a visa[156]. Regulation 1683/95 of 29 May 1995[157] laid down a uniform format for visas and was based on the premise that "measures relating to a uniform format for visas", as envisaged by ex-Article 100c(3) ECT (Article 62(2)(b)(iii) ECT) include the measures necessary to implement a uniform format for visas in general[158], and precautions to be taken against falsification in particular.

On the other hand, ex-Article 100c ECT did not include a competence on substantive requirements for granting visas. The common list of third countries whose nationals must be in possession of a visa and a uniform format for visas both remained formal aspects of visa policy. Confined to legislation on formal aspects of visa policy, the Community could not even adopt conditions for the mutual recognition of visas between Member States. Additionally, ex-Article 100c ECT did not cover Community action aimed at harmonizing the conditions for issuing visas at the Community-wide level[159].

Under the Amsterdam Treaty, Article 62(2)(i) ECT empowers the Community to adopt both positive and negative lists on visa requirements. Article 62(3) ECT allows for measures aimed at the mutual recognition of visas, while Article 62(2)(ii-iv) ECT contemplates measures necessary to justify such mutual recognition, as well as positive and negative lists. In addition, the pre-Amsterdam visa regime under Community law and the visa-related elements of the Schengen *acquis* (Title II Chapter 3 SIC) must be assimilated under the framework created by the Amsterdam Treaty.

3. *Asylum*

a) Reception of Asylum Seekers

Article 63(1)(a) ECT allows for the harmonization of criteria and procedures which divide the responsibility for processing asylum applications among Member States[160]. In relation to other aspects of processing asylum applications, Article 63(1)(b) ECT provides for minimum standards on reception, and Article 63(1)(d) ECT envisages procedures for granting or withholding refugee states under national law. The term "procedures" does not raise major questions with regard to its interpretation; it must be interpreted to cover both administrative and court procedures. Minimum standards adopted under Article 63(1)(b) and (d) ECT will contribute to assimilation of the legal position of asylum seekers in Member States during the asylum determination procedure. However, Member States may grant more favourable legal status and treatment to asylum seekers.

Which matters can be regarded as relating to the "reception" of asylum seekers may, however, be questionable. Clearly, distribution to, and living conditions in, reception facilities are covered by reception minimum standards. Interpreted

---

156 *Nanz*, integration (1992), 126, 133.
157 Regulation 1683/95 of 29 May 1995, O.J. 1995 L 164/1.
158 Cf. *Hailbronner*, 31 CML Rev. (1994) 969, 990.
159 *Hailbronner* 31 CML Rev. (1994) 969, 987.
160 Cf. *Lang*, Gemeinschaftsrecht der Drittstaatsangehörigen (1998), 344.

extensively, the term reception may also to cover family reunification, free movement, identity and travel documents, and social rights, including access to welfare or other forms of public assistance, health care and education, or the labour market. Arguably, the right to protection of an asylum seeker's identity also forms part of the topics to be dealt with under the rubric of "reception". Standards under Article 63(1)(b) ECT may also include the period of sojourn of asylum seekers in reception facilities or collective accommodations. In a narrow reading of Article 63 ECT such aspects are excluded as part of the treatment of refugees *after* reception. A restrictive interpretation would, however, fail to meet the purpose of Article 63 ECT. Minimum standards on reception are to prevent the unfortunate situation that some Member States leave asylum seekers in a rather weak social and legal situation which forces or induces them to move on to other Member States. Minimum standards are to prevent a policy whereby the Member States pursue a deliberate policy of dealing with asylum seekers "in transit" only. It follows that the term reception should include in a wider interpretation these elements that determine the social and legal status of asylum seekers. This interpretation is supported by Article 63(2)(a) which according to its legislative history embraces social benefits. It would hardly make sense to restrict Community competence to refugees and displaced persons within the meaning of Article 63(2)(a) ECT.

b) Minimum Standards of Procedure

Article 63(1)(d) ECT requires the adoption of minimum standards on procedures in Member States for granting or withdrawing refugee status. Obviously, the phrase "granting refugee status" refers to the determination that a person meets the conditions prescribed by Article 1A(2) of the Geneva Convention. Thus, the Council can build upon the Joint Position of 4 March 1996 on the harmonized application of the definition of the term 'refugee' in Article 1 of the Geneva Convention[161]. The term "procedures" covers basic principles governing refugee determination in administrative and judicial proceedings.

In addition, Article 63(1)(d) ECT envisages minimum standards on administrative and court procedures governing withdrawal of refugee status. The provision refers to Article 1C of the Geneva Convention whereby the Convention shall cease to apply to a refugee within the meaning of Article 1 thereof if the circumstances giving rise to the recognition have changed (for details see Article 1C(1-5) of the Geneva Convention).

c) Temporary Protection

The term "minimum standards" is broad enough to make provision for granting temporary protection to "displaced persons", including the procedure of establishing temporary protection, and its relationship to the asylum procedure. It includes provisions on the scope of application of temporary protection regimes, rights accorded to, and duties imposed upon temporarily protected persons, including family reunification, restrictions of free movement, identity and travel documents, and social

[161] O.J. 1996 L 63/2.

rights, including access to welfare or other forms of public assistance, health care and education, or the labour market, humanitarian residence permits, and distribution to, and living conditions in, collective accommodations.

As to the potential beneficiaries of temporary protected status, a major question will be the differentiation between temporary protected status and refugee status, as contemplated by the Geneva Convention because Article 63(2)(a) and (1)(c) ECT differentiates between the two categories, following the pattern established by the national laws of EU Member States. Refugee status at least in the perspective of the Geneva Convention envisages the establishment of a new permanent residence for the persons concerned, while the notion of return once conditions give rise to protection change is inherent in the idea of temporary protection. While only Article 63(1) ECT expressly refers to the Geneva Convention, it cannot be assumed that the Geneva Convention obligations should be restricted to measures under Article 63(1)(c) ECT[162], particularly with respect to the prohibition of refoulement. The reason why only Article 63(1) ECT refers to the Geneva Convention is that the Geneva Convention does not contain any standards as to the temporary protection of refugees and displaced persons in the sense of Article 63(2) ECT. Unless third-country nationals were prevented from applying for asylum after the expiry of temporary protected status, temporary protection schemes do not affect the functioning of the Geneva Convention. The Geneva Convention does not oblige Member States to grant asylum to every asylum seeker fulfilling the requirements of Article 1 of the Geneva Convention. Member States frequently considered themselves free to decide which rights shall be granted to displaced persons in need of protection. Such determination generally is not subject to judicial review.

Additionally, Article 63(2)(a) ECT distinguishes between "displaced persons" and "persons who otherwise need international protection" while Article 63(2) ECT refers to "refugees" and "displaced persons". It is suggested that there is no difference in substance between the two terms. "Displaced persons" refers in a very wide sense to persons who were forced to leave their habitual residence as a result of war, civil war, general violence or breakdown of civil order.

The term "persons who otherwise need international protection" seems to serve primarily as a clause covering all persons who do not fall under any specified general reception programs but would nevertheless be considered as in need of protection due to individual circumstances. This may include persons who had applied for asylum unsuccessfully or persons who are granted a humanitarian residence permit.

d) Sudden Inflows of Third-Country Nationals

Article 64(2) ECT provides for the adoption, by the Council, of provisional measures "[i]n the event of one or more Member States being confronted with an emergency situation characterised by a sudden inflow of nationals of third countries". Ex-Article 100c(2) ECT, conversely, provided for provisional measures related to emergency situations "in a third country posing a threat of a sudden inflow of nationals from that country into the Community". The change of wording seems to indicate a change in

[162] *Winkler*, in Bergmann/Lenz (ed.), Der Amsterdamer Vertrag (1998) 45-71 para 19.

meaning, of the term "emergency situation"[163] because this term now refers to the situation in a Member State rather than in a third state[164].

Measures in reaction to emergency situations as envisaged by Article 64(2) ECT relate to situations which may also qualify for the application of temporary protection regimes because the definition of an emergency situation is very similar to the phrases used in relevant intergovernmental documents and Commission proposals for Joint Actions to be adopted under ex-Article K.3(2) TEU for temporary protection[165]. The question arises how measures according to Article 64(2) may be distinguished from measures establishing a temporary protection scheme. In addition, measures taken under Article 64(2) may also trigger the responsibility of Member States for internal security and public order under Article 64(1) ECT. While Article 64(1) ECT reserves such rights for Member States, Article 64(2) ECT grants the Council an emergency regulatory power. The relationship between national *ordre public* and Community emergency action may cause frictions.

The relevance of emergency situations arising in a Member State and endangering its public order, for the application of Article 64(2) ECT is implicitly required by the fact that both *ordre public* questions and cases of emergency are dealt with in the same Article of the Treaty. Additionally, the fact that Article 64(2) ECT must be applied without prejudice to the right of Member States under Article 64(1) ECT seems to be compelling evidence that Member States have had situations in mind which both trigger the *ordre public* reservation and constitute a case of emergency under Article 64(2).

As to the distinction between temporary protection decisions and provisional emergency measures, it is suggested that temporary protection regimes under Article 63(2)(a) ECT cover the definition of a specific status accorded to displaced persons and persons who otherwise need international protection where these persons have been formally admitted to enter, or stay within the Member States' territories, and the definitions of conditions for admission. Provisional measures, on the other hand, relate to situations where potential beneficiaries of temporary protected status are on their way to one or more Member States[166]. Hence the purpose of provisional measures may well be combating uncontrolled entry of displaced persons. Indeed, under the Commission Proposal for a Joint Action concerning temporary protection of displaced persons the Council would have been required to take "into consideration whether

---

163 The opposite view has been taken by *Winkler*, in Bergmann/Lenz (ed.), Der Amsterdamer Vertrag (1998) 45-71 para 22.

164 See *Hailbronner*, in Hailbronner/Klein/Magiera/Müller-Graff, Handkommentar zum EG/EU-Vertrag (1991), Article 100c paras 26 et seq., for the interpretation that ex-Article 100c ECT referred to emergency situations in third countries.

165 Point 1(a) of Council Resolution of 25 September 1995 on burden-sharing with regard to the admission and residence of displaced persons on a temporary basis, OJ 1995 C 262/1, speaks of persons who "have already left their region of origin to go to one of the Member States". Point 2(a) of the same resolution refers to "a mass influx of displaced persons into the territory of the Member States or a strong probability that the Member States may soon have to cope with such an influx".
See also Article 3(1) of the – now withdrawn – Commission proposal for a Joint Action concerning temporary protection of displaced persons, O.J. 1997 C 106/13 which reads –
In cases of mass influx of persons in need of international protection, the Council ... shall decide to establish a temporary protection regime...

166 Both the German and the French versions of Article 64(2) ECT support this interpretation. The German text speaks of "Zustrom" and the French version uses the term "afflux", both texts thus describing a movement towards the Member State(s) concerned.

adequate protection can be found in the region of origin"[167]. Additionally, Member States were competent to re-introduce visa requirements for displaced persons under the provisional competence provided for in ex-Article 100c(2) ECT[168]. Accordingly, the aim of provisional measures could be to prevent entry of displaced persons into Member States' territories in order to enable the Community to adopt a temporary protection regime appropriate for the respective situation.

Article 64(2) ECT does not define the criteria governing the determination of a given situation as an emergency situation. Arguably, this definition is predetermined politically rather than legally[169]. Article 64(2) ECT applies if a qualified majority of the Member States affected and the Council consider action necessary. Article 64(2) ECT does not exclude Council action in cases in which individual Member States may also take individual action to maintain public order. Article 64(2) ECT, however, provides for a power to react only "for the benefit of the Member States concerned". This excludes action against the wish of the Member States concerned since there is no competence of the Community to define the benefit regardless of the explicit wish of the Member States concerned. The requirement of a "sudden inflow of nationals of third countries" leaves open a large margin of appreciation. There are no standards for the determination of how many third-country nationals qualify as an "inflow" rather than a group "dripping into" the respective Member State, and there does not exist any standard for distinguishing "sudden" inflows from any inflow which might qualify as "pre-expected" or "leisurely", either. Accordingly, it seems to be difficult to provide criteria as to which situations are "emergency situations". Obviously, from an 'integrationist' point of view, it would be better to deal with situations of the kind referred to by Article 64(2) ECT through the adoption of a Council measure rather than by an invocation of the *ordre public* in a given Member State. Consequently, if there were any constraints inherent in Article 64(2) ECT they would not extend further than do those governing the *ordre public* reservation. It is therefore suggested that the constraints that govern Article 64(1) ECT should also be applied to Article 64(2) ECT and that they form a uniform standard for judicial review of all measures taken pursuant to Article 64 ECT.

As to the adoption of measures, proposals from the Commission are to be decided upon by a qualified majority in the Council. Member States thus have no right of initiative in this respect. If, however, a decision on the invocation of the *ordre public* reservation is pending at the national level, the Commission is obliged to examine whether there is a real need for measures under Article 64(2) ECT. Provisional measures will expire automatically after six months by Article 64(2) ECT, or after an earlier date determined by the Council. Article 64(2) ECT does not, however, contain any limitation with regard to a re-adoption of similar provisional measures relating to the same situation after the date of expiration. In this respect one might only doubt whether re-adopting provisional measures instead of adopting Community legislation could infringe the rights of the European Parliament. But in practice, it would be rather difficult to establish that the Council intended to circumvent the participation of the European Parliament by re-adopting provisional measures.

---

[167] Article 3(1) of the – now withdrawn – proposal, O.J. 1997 C 106/13.

[168] *Hailbronner*, in *Hailbronner/Klein/Magiera/Müller-Graff*, Handkommentar zum EG/EU-Vertrag (1991), Article 100c para 28.

[169] *Winkler*, in Bergmann/Lenz (ed.), Der Amsterdamer Vertrag (1998), 45-71 para 22 argues against the existence of such political discretion.

e) The Scope of Minimum Standards in the Light of the Notion of Burden-Sharing

Under Article 63(2)(b) ECT the Council may adopt measures with the aim of promoting a balance of effort between Member States in receiving and bearing the consequences of receiving refugees and displaced persons. The systematic context of Article 63(2)(b) ECT supports a restrictive interpretation of the term "refugee", excluding asylum seekers who are dealt with in Article 63(1) ECT (measures on asylum). The distinction, however, between "asylum seekers" and "refugees " may be difficult to draw. Reported asylum seekers fall into the scope of application of Article 63(2)(b) ECT, where they are granted a humanitarian residence permit or a tolerated status.

Whether the "promotion" of a balance of effort may result in a final and binding imposition of criteria and mechanisms for burden-sharing has deliberately been left open. The term "promotion" seems to indicate a restrictive meaning limiting the role of the Community to a supportive rather than a decisive function. In order to restrict Community competence under Article 63(2)(b) ECT to a mere supportive function which would leave the issue of burden sharing finally within the competence of the Member States, fails to give the provision any useful meaning. Article 63(2)(b) ECT is based on the experience of a gross imbalance of burden arising from the reception of refugees and displaced persons. It is evident that this imbalance cannot be changed by a mere reference to voluntary action of Member States or to their sense of solidarity. Article 63(2)(b) ECT, although worded somewhat vaguely, reflects the common conviction that the aim of achieving a balance of effort can only be reached by measures of the Community obliging Member States to carry a share of the common burden according to certain criteria yet to be defined. The somewhat careful wording "promotion of a balance of effort" indicates that measures under Article 63(2)(b) ECT are not intended to introduce a comprehensive distribution system with equal burdens according to a predetermined scheme. The intention is to make provision for a balance of efforts between Member States rather than replacing Member States' efforts by a Community effort which would make balancing provisions superfluous.

Promoting a balance of effort between Member States also implies some degree of harmonization concerning social rights of refugees and displaced persons. The financial implications of a more balanced reception system require at least a consensus on minimum social standards. This supports an interpretation of Article 63(2)(b) ECT including social rights of refugees and displaced persons.

The proposals and recommendations submitted for burden-sharing confirm the view that Article 63(2)(b) ECT empowers the Community to make provisions for burden-sharing.

In 1995 the European Union has adopted non-binding criteria of reference for burden-sharing that may be supplemented by further criteria in the light of specific situations –

- the contribution which each Member State is making to the prevention or resolution of the crisis, in particular by supply of military resources in operations and missions ordered by the United Nations Security Council or the Organization for Security and Cooperation in Europe and by the measures taken by each Member State to afford local protection to people under threat or to provide humanitarian assistance,

- all economic, social and political factors which may affect the capacity of a Member State to admit an increased number of displaced persons under satisfactory conditions.[170]

f) Establishment of a European Asylum Agency?[171]

Harmonization of reception and asylum determination systems in a long-term perspective may require the establishment of a European Asylum Agency responsible for the determination of asylum claims. Suggestions have been made that such an agency should be entrusted with co-ordination and supervision of all measures governing the status enjoyed by asylum seekers and refugees covered by temporary protection schemes. Moreover, "[i]n the long run exclusive competence should not be excluded".

Whether such an agency will eventually have to be established is a matter of debate. Undoubtedly, the creation of a European Asylum Agency would replace the Dublin Convention system on asylum. Arguably, however, co-operation of competent national authorities as presently conducted under the Dublin Convention is sufficient. Such co-operation already covers assessments of the situations in potential countries of origin – which would be a major task for a European Asylum Agency. Moreover, if the establishment of such an agency would lead to –

> supervision of the application of uniform determination procedures and uniform criteria for protection under the Geneva Convention or for (temporary) protection under European instruments[172]

a comprehensive set of related administrative law would be required, because presently Member States have integrated asylum determination procedures into their general schemes of public administration. If the European Union would adopt such a comprehensive system of administrative law related to asylum determination and refugee treatment procedures, major changes in the general administrative and judicial system would have to be made since the transfer of an essential branch of national administration to the European level would require a European infrastructure of execution of administrative decisions and judicial review and a European judiciary in charge of reviewing asylum decisions taken at the European level. The European Court of Justice is not suited to fulfil such tasks in its present form. Taking into account the importance of separate national administrations and judiciaries for defining Member States' identities, it is hard to imagine that consensus on a European Asylum Agency will be reached in the near future.

---

[170] See Point 4 of the Council Resolution of 25 September 1995 on burden-sharing with regard to the admission and residence of displaced persons on a temporary basis, OJ 1995 C 262/1. However, in both Council resolutions on priorities for JHA co-operation, the examination of temporary protection and burden-sharing does not detail any criteria, nor do these resolutions give reference to the 1995 resolution. See Point 4(f) of the 1996 Resolution, O.J. 1996 C 319/1 and Point 6(f) of the 1997 Resolution, O.J. 1998 C 11/1.

[171] Cf. the suggestion by AGIT, Efficient, effective and encompassing approaches to a European Immigration and Asylum Policy, [1999] IJRL [forthcoming].

[172] AGIT, Efficient, effective and encompassing approaches to a European Immigration and Asylum Policy, [1999] IJRL[forthcoming], Point 11(b).

4. *Immigration*

Article 63(3) ECT provides for measures on immigration policy, namely –

> (a) conditions of entry and residence, and standards on procedures for the issue by Member States of long term visas and residence permits, including those for the purpose of family reunion,
>
> (b) illegal immigration and illegal residence, including repatriation of illegal residents.

Article 64(4) ECT enables the Community to adopt "measures defining the rights and conditions under which nationals of third countries who are legally resident in a Member State may reside in other Member States". Thus, the scope of Title IV ECT is not limited to measures aimed at the prevention of illegal immigration, but also allows for the establishment of an active immigration control policy[173]. Conditions of entry and residence, as envisaged by Article 63(3)(a) ECT, cover items such as the determination of the professional and language skills to be required of third-country nationals for admission to the territory of one of the Member States and granting residence rights if certain conditions, like non-dependency on social welfare, are not met.

Article 63(3)(b) ECT provides for measures related to illegal immigration and residence, including repatriation. This provision covers the treatment of illegal immigrants and illegal residents rather than the determination of reasons which give rise to the termination of lawful residential status. As the criminal justice systems in Member States differ greatly, it is doubtful whether Community legislation may be enacted harmonizing the treatment of criminal aliens. The Schengen Convention contains some basic, primarily procedural rules in this respect[174]. Based on this premise, the communitarization of related elements of the Schengen *acquis* (Articles 23, 25-27, 96-97 SIC in particular) may be considered as sufficient for the implementation of Article 63(3)(b) ECT[175]. In addition, a common regime for rejection at the border, including carrier sanctions, may be adopted as a measure related to illegal immigration under Article 63(3)(b) ECT.

The term "repatriation" only refers to illegal residents. Whether this power may be used to prescribe standards on expulsion and deportation, is highly questionable. One may arrive at an extensive interpretation if the term "repatriation" is understood as a general term which includes both types of measures. However, as a sanction terminating legal resident status, deportation qualifies as a condition of expulsion and is, therefore, not covered by Article 63(3) ECT[176]. The Schengen Convention sets no conditions for deportation. On the contrary, expulsion is equated with involuntary repatriation and in the sense of Article 63(3) ECT. A more restrictive interpretation would cover exclusively procedural matters. The wording does not, however, allow for such a restrictive interpretation. In addition, the purpose of Article 63(3) speaks

---

173 Cf. *Hailbronner* 35 CML Rev. (1998) 1047, 1048.

174 See Articles 96(2) and 97 SIC. These provisions only set the conditions for reporting a third-country national for the purpose of being refused entry but do not limit the Member States' right to implement other reasons for expulsion and deportation in their national law.

175 The same conclusion has been reached by the Council and the Commission. See point 26 of the Action Plan (O.J. 1999 C 19/1).

176 See *Hailbronner* 35 CML Rev. (1998) 1047, 1049.

in favour of an extensive interpretation, covering return means of persons whose residential rights have been terminated. In addition, measures taken to support and encourage the voluntary return of immigrants, including readmission, may be adopted under Article 63(3) ECT[177].

Finally, Article 63 ECT calls for an improved exchange of statistics and information on immigration (and asylum), covering, *inter alia*, the status of third-country nationals under national legislation[178].

5. *The Status of Third-Country Nationals (Article 61(b) ECT)*

Article 61(b) defines the "other measures" relating to third-country nationals under Article 63 ECT as "safeguarding" the rights of third-country nationals. This term may imply restrictive elements as to the powers conferred upon to the Community.

Article 63 ECT includes two different kinds of authorizing clauses. First, Article 63(1-3) ECT focuses on the public policy aspects of measures, and provides for "criteria", "standards", and "conditions". These terms refer to prerequisites drawn up for processing applications for admission to Member States' territories. Given that the function of procedures is to serve basically public interests, it must be concluded that these prerequisites were designed to set a framework for immigration control. On the other hand, Article 63(4) ECT refers to the rights and conditions under which third-country nationals resident in a Member State may reside in other Member States, thus emphasizing individual interests. Read in this context, the term "safeguarding" implies the implementation of rights granted under Community law or public international law binding for all Member States.

Primary Community law guarantees the protection of basic human rights to third-country nationals, but excludes them from the ambit of individual rights accorded to EU citizens by the Community Treaties (namely the market freedoms)[179]. Third-country nationals may only benefit indirectly from the exercise of market freedoms by EU citizens[180]. On the other hand, third-country nationals have been granted certain rights by secondary Community law, the EEC-Turkey Association Agreement and a number of similar instruments. Whether the Community is competent to "safeguard" these rights by way of implementation of Article 63 ECT, however, is questionable. There are specialized procedures under Association Agreements for the implementation of the rights provided for in these Agreements. In addition, such rights were granted before the entry into force of the Amsterdam Treaty and their legal bases are

---

177 Cf. Council document 12028/4/98 REV 4 JAI 31 para 36(c)(ii). No similar observation forms part of the Action plan of the Council and the Commission, O.J. 1999 C 19/1.

178 See point 34 of the Action plan of the Council and the Commission, O.J. 1999 C 19/1.

179 Articles 43(1) and 49(1) ECT expressly refer to nationals of a Member State. See ECJ, judgment of 5 July 1984, case 238/83, *Meade v Caisse d'allocations familiales de la région parisienne*, [1984] ECR 2631 para 7 for the nationality requirement with respect to ex-Articles 48-66 ECT. See also *Salger Droste* in Smit/Herzog, The Law of the European Community, A commentary on the EEC Treaty, § 48.02[2]; *Wölker* in Groeben/Thiesing/Ehlermann, EWGV, Vorbemerkung zu Article 48-50 para 41; *Randelzhofer*, in Grabitz/Hilf, EUV/EGV, Article 48 EGV para 7. On the other hand, arguments have been raised in favour of the application of Article 48 ECT to third-country nationals who are employed in the Community. See *Hilf*, in Hailbronner/Ress/Stein (ed.), Staat und Völkerrechtsordnung, Festschrift für Karl Doehring (1989) 339, 351.

180 Cf. ECJ, judgment of 9 August 1994, case C-43/93, *Vander Elst v Office des Migrations Internationales*, [1994] ECR I-3803 (discused in Chapter C V).

Association Treaty provisions, incapable of covering the adoption of a European aliens law. Moreover, these provisions do not form part of Title IV ECT. As certain provisions other than those contained in Title IV ECT continue to regulate the granting (though in a limited manner) of rights to third-country nationals, these provisions have also conferred the power to safeguard these rights on the organs established by the respective treaties (Association Council). However, Title IV ECT powers must be employed for Community action affecting the status of third-country nationals in as much as Association Agreements do not cover such action. In particular, where Association Councils are confined to adopt non-binding measures, implementation of such measures must be based on relevant Title IV powers, where applicable.[181]

At the same time, the notion of safeguarding human rights establishes certain substantive standards to be met by measures implementing a European immigration control system under Article 63(1-3) ECT. The fact that the Treaty expressly provides for safeguarding the rights of third-country nationals in the field of immigration must be regarded as rejection of the view that immigration issues are entirely governed by public policy interests which exclude the applicability of human rights. This view is the basis of the U.S. Supreme Court's immigration jurisprudence under the plenary power doctrine[182]. As early as in 1889, in the Chinese exclusion case, the U.S. Supreme Court has held that –

> The power of exclusion of foreigners being an incident of sovereignty belonging to the government of the United States, as a part of those sovereign powers delegated by the Constitution, the right to its exercise at any time when, in the judgment of the government, the interests of the country require it, cannot be granted away or restrained on behalf of any one. ... Whatever license ... Chinese laborers may have obtained, previous to the [challenged] act ..., to return to the United States after their departure, is held at the will of the government, revocable at any time, at its pleasure. Whether a proper consideration by our government if its previous laws, or a proper respect for the nation whose subjects are affected by its action, ought to have qualified its inhibition ... are not questions for judicial determination.[183]

This *dictum* must still be regarded as the basic principle of U.S. immigration law, numerous scholarly criticisms notwithstanding. Obviously, Article 61(b) ECT read together with Article 63(1-3) ECT is based on different premises because it renders immigration policy subject to human rights considerations. One must not, however, overestimate the impact of human rights on immigration policy; neither international nor domestic human rights accord a right of entry or admission to the territory of one of the Member States[184]. The sovereign rights of states in migration matters have also been upheld in principle by the jurisprudence of the European Court of Human Rights on Article 8(1) ECHR. The Strasbourg Court has repeatedly denied entry to the territory of the Contracting States for the sole purpose of family reunification. However, Strasbourg case-law has compromised national sovereignty with respect to

---

181 See *infra* XIII 3.

182 See *Legomsky* Immigration and Refugee Law and Policy, 2nd ed. (1997) 12 et seq. for detailed references and a comprehensive discussion of the plenary power doctrine.

183 *Ping v U.S.* 130 U.S. 581 = 9 S.Ct. 623.

184 See *Klos* Rahmenbedingungen und Gestaltungsmöglichkeiten der Europäischen Migrationspolitik (1998), 88-96.

termination of residence, of third-country national long-time residents. Within the scope of application of Article 63(1-3) ECT, human rights may, therefore, primarily impact the procedures applied to claims for entry into the EU, rather than substantial provisions dealing with admission. Third-country nationals in particular may rely upon a right to a fair procedure in immigration and asylum matters.

Article 63(4) ECT allows for "defining the rights and conditions under which nationals of third countries who are legally resident in a Member State may reside in other Member States". This provision raises questions of interpretation because it is framed in somewhat unusual language. When dealing with rights-related regulations, the Community Treaties generally do not use the term "defining"[185]. Unless one concludes that the High Contracting Parties chose this expression accidentally, it must be viewed as distinct from the terms "granting" and "safeguarding". Arguably, "defining rights and conditions" refers to the concept of freedom of movement. As non-EU citizens do not enjoy this freedom under Community law, the notion of "defining" probably means that the Community may only extend certain aspects of freedom of movement to third-country nationals but may not grant them this freedom in its entirety.

It is doubtful whether Article 63 ECT includes measures which govern other aspects of the status of third-country nationals, such as integration and naturalization of immigrants. Both issues are of common interest to all Member States, as formal integration changes the status of former third-country nationals under Community law significantly[186] and naturalization enlarges the scope of application of Union citizenship.

Article 3(d) ECT defines measures adopted under Title IV ECT as "measures concerning the entry and movement of persons". These terms refer to migration issues, but do not speak of the relationship between the migrant and the host society. On the other hand, Article 137 ECT provides for the adoption of rules governing the admission of third-country nationals to the labour market. Employment access may be qualified as an important aspect of integration. This Article thus indicates that substantive integration is subject only to extra-Title IV legal bases for Community action, if any. Indeed, integration into society may be an issue connected with freedom of movement for workers[187]. However, thus far the Community does not enjoy express competence to regulate nationality and citizenship. However, nationality has been

---

185 The expression usually applied to the act of creating new rights or statuses is "granting". See Article 63(1)(d) ECT where it is provided for granting refugee status, and the preamble of the Asylum Protocol which refers to the fact that when concluding the said Protocol the High Contracting Parties acted

BEARING IN MIND that the Treaty establishing the European Community establishes an area without internal frontiers and grants every citizen of the Union the right to move and reside freely within the territory of the Member States.

No less confusing are the German and French texts of Article 63(4) ECT which apply the expressions "*Festlegung*" and "*définissant*". On the other hand, Article 63(1)(d) ECT refers to measures aimed at "*Zuerkennung*", or "*d'octroi... du statut de réfugié*", respectively. And the preamble of the Asylum Protocol does not include the term "defining" either in that it states that the ECT is a Treaty which "*jedem Unionsbürger das Recht* ***gewährt****, sich im Hoheitsgebiet der Mitgliedstaaten frei zu bewegen und aufzuhalten*", that it "***accorde*** *à chaque citoyen de l'Union le droit de circuler et de séjourner librement sur le territoire des États membres*" (emphasis added).

186 Cf. *Klos* Rahmenbedingungen und Gestaltungsmöglichkeiten der Europäischen Migrationspolitik (1998), 118 et seq.

187 See ECJ, judgment of 15 March 1989, joined cases 389 and 390/87, *Echternach and Moritz v Netherlands Minister for Education and Science*, [1989] ECR 723 para 20.

debated by the European Parliament and has given rise to certain observations of the European Court of Justice. Additionally, the argument has been raised that Title IV ECT "concerns an area – namely citizenship – which is specifically excluded from the scope of future closer cooperation arrangements"[188]. It is doubtful, however, whether citizenship falls within the ambit of Title IV ECT. Immigration law usually governs the entrance and sojourn of aliens in their capacity as aliens, while naturalization law contains the conditions for the acquisition of citizenship. As naturalization is virtually ignored in Title IV ECT, however, the very wording of the provisions of this Title seems to rule out a Community power covering naturalization. One might, however, think of a Community power *ex ratione materiae*. Indeed the European Parliament has passed resolutions that call for the adoption of common standards for both acquisition and loss of nationality. Taking into account Declaration No. 2 on nationality of a Member State attached to the Treaty on European Union, however, there seems to be little prospect for realization of the suggestions of the European Parliament. In this Declaration the Maastricht Intergovernmental Conference stated that –

> [t]he Conference declares that, wherever in the Treaty establishing the European Community reference is made to nationals of the Member States, the question whether an individual possesses the nationality of a Member State shall be settled solely by reference to the national law of the Member State concerned. Member States may declare, for information, who are to be considered their nationals for Community purposes by way of a declaration lodged with the Presidency and may amend any such declaration when necessary.

Under the Amsterdam Treaty, this point of view has been reaffirmed by way of the insertion of a third sentence into Article 17(1) ECT which provides that –

> Citizenship of the Union shall complement and not replace national citizenship.

Accordingly, the construction of a power *ex ratione materiae* is not convincing. The Community powers related to immigration and protection of the rights of third-country nationals (Article 63(3) and (4) ECT) do not relate to all issues of substantive, or social, integration. Even if they did, these provisions cannot be used as an inroad for the creation of Community legislation on formal integration, i.e. naturalization. As the German experience has shown, the powers to regulate formal and substantive integration, respectively, are distinct and far from inseparable[189].

Jurisprudence of the European Court of Justice does not indicate otherwise. The Court dealt with issues related to nationality in *Gullung* and *Micheletti*. Both cases did not raise questions of EU citizenship as enshrined in Articles 17 – 22 ECT, because the Court had to give judgment before the entry into force of the Maastricht Treaty. Hence the relationship between nationality of Member States and Community Law had to be determined on the basis of the market freedoms. In *Gullung* the Court held that market freedoms –

> would not be fully realized if a Member State were entitled to refuse to grant the benefit of the provisions of Community law to those of its nationals who are established in another Member State of which they are also a national and who

188 *Shaw* 4 ELJ (1998) 63, 76.
189 Cf. *Häußler* ZAR 1999, 32, 36.

take advantage of the facilities offered by Community law in order to pursue their activities in the first State by way of the provision of services.[190]

In *Micheletti* the Court had to decide whether Member States may treat a person holding dual nationality as a third-country national under legislation providing for the prevalence of the effective nationality if such persons' non-effective nationality links that person to another Member State. The Court strengthened the impact of market freedoms in that it held that –

> it is not permissible to interpret Article 52 of the Treaty to the effect that, where a national of a Member State is also a national of a non-member country, the other Member States may make recognition of the status of Community national subject to a condition such as the habitual residence of the person concerned in the territory of the first Member State.[191]

At the same time, the Court made some observations concerning the relationship between Community Law and nationality legislation as adopted by Member States. According to the Court –

> Under international law, it is for each Member State, having due regard to Community law, to lay down the conditions for the acquisition and loss of nationality. However, it is not permissible for the legislation of a Member State to restrict the effects of the grant of the nationality of another Member State by imposing an additional condition for recognition of that nationality with a view to the exercise of the fundamental freedoms provided for in the Treaty.[192]

This statement, however, remains rather vague. It may be interpreted as a reference to the loyalty principle contained in Article 10 ECT. It is submitted that the Court wanted to reaffirm the principle it has developed in standing case-law that Member States must not adversely affect the exercise of market freedoms irrespective of whether such infringements originate from direct limitations or must be qualified as indirect effects of national legislation which are equivalent to limitations of market freedoms.

Accordingly, neither the resolutions passed by the European Parliament nor the jurisprudence of the European Court of Justice justify the assumption that the Community might regulate nationality. Besides, nationality will finally be based on common principles in Member States anyway. Under the practice of the Council of Europe the European Convention on Nationality[193] is an obligatory requirement for admission to the Council of Europe. This requirement seems to point at a similar (at least political) obligation resting upon the present members of the Council of Europe.

---

[190] ECJ, judgment of 19 January 1988, case 292/86, *Gullung v Conseil de l'ordre des avocats du barreau*, [1988] ECR 111 para 12.

[191] ECJ, judgment of 7 July 1992, case C-369/90, *Micheletti and others v Delegación del Gobierno en Cantabria*, [1992] ECR I-4239 para 11. The Court also referred to the fact that under Directive 73/148 "once the persons concerned have produced one of the documents mentioned in Directive 73/148 in order to establish their status as nationals of a Member State, the other Member States are not entitled to challenge that status .." (id. para 12-14).

[192] ECJ, judgment of 7 July 1992, case C-369/90, *Micheletti and others v Delegación del Gobierno en Cantabria*, [1992] ECR I-4239 para 10.

[193] European Convention on Nationality of 6 November 1997, ETS No. 166

Both present EU Member States and accession candidates are members of the Council of Europe though not all of them have signed, or ratified, this Convention[194].

XI. Institutional Provisions

1. The Right of Initiative

Title IV ECT provides for special procedures. The process of adopting Community legislation is governed by different rules which reflect the close connection between immigration issues and national sovereignty, but do not deviate fundamentally from the general rules. The framework for judicial review similarly deviates from the general rules applicable to national law.

The general scheme of supranational legislation grants the Commission the exclusive right of initiative. The framework created by Title IV ECT, however, is different. During the transitional period, the Commission and the Member States will share a right of co-initiative, except for matters previously dealt with under ex-Article 100c ECT (see Article 67(3) ECT). One might, therefore, ask whether the Commission – the "motor of integration" – has been unduly restricted by Member States through the introduction of co-initiative into Title IV ECT.

During the Maastricht era, ex-Article K.3(2) TEU prescribed for a co-initiative for certain items of third pillar action; this method of allocating the power to initiate the decision-making process on the European level is, therefore, not without precedent. Nevertheless, Member States have reserved their right of initiative in order to ensure that they play an important, if not dominant, role in the course of implementing the core areas of immigration policy covered by Title IV ECT. Only those items on which the disputes were regarded as unlikely to be solved during this period have been exempted from the time-limit. However, the right of co-initiative should not be considered as evidence of a concept aimed at weakening the Commission, rather than at retaining a substantial influence in a sensible area of policy-making. The Commission is to participate in any deliberations on the implementation of Title IV ECT and will thus play its usual role. Second, by binding co-initiative with a time-limit, Member States have emphasized their strong political will to adopt a basic framework of European aliens law in due time. This goal cannot be reached without the support of the Commission. Accordingly, the legislative procedure under Title IV ECT is to expedite this process rather than slow it down.

After the expiration of the transition period, the Commission will have the exclusive right of initiative, but will have to "examine any request made by a Member State that it submit a proposal to the Council" in terms of Article 67(2) ECT. The same provision governed Community legislation under ex-Article 100c(4) ECT. Embodied in the exclusive right of initiative is a unanimous voting requirement with regard to acts which constitute an amendment to Commission proposals under Article 250(1) ECT.

---

[194] The European Convention on Nationality has been ratified by Austria and the Slovak Republic; it has been signed, ratification pending, by Denmark, Finland, Greece, Italy, the Netherlands, Portugal, Sweden, Poland, Hungary, Romania, and the Czech Republic. Belgium, France, Germany, Ireland, Luxembourg, Spain, the United Kingdom, Bulgaria, Cyprus, Estonia, Latvia, Lithuania, and Slovenia have thus far been reluctant to sign the Convention.

The core legal question posed by the Commission's duty to examine Member State requests is that of reviewability, i.e. can Member States force the Commission to act? For items which should have been regulated during the transitional period, the Commission must draw up proposals after the expiration of that period, in order to catch up with existing backlogs. This duty arises from provisions specifying a time-limit. Failure to act is, therefore, subject to Article 232 ECT and may be challenged by the European Parliament. After the expiration of the time-limit, duties no longer exist. The Treaty vests discretionary power in the Commission by defining the obligation resting upon the Commission as a duty to "examine". This reading is supported by provisions contained in both Article 192 and Article 208 ECT, which oblige the Commission to submit proposals as requested.

The Commission's discretionary power is not, however unlimited. Criteria which govern the exercise of this discretion under Article 67(2) ECT may thus be established. One may think of a test of reasonableness[195]. The Commission would have to regard a request as reasonable if the requesting Member State is able to demonstrate that a migration phenomenon which has Community-wide effects exists and thus must be dealt with by Community legislation. Although the Commission must exercise its discretion in favour of drawing up a proposal when the existence of such a phenomenon has been demonstrated, it may be reluctant to do so. A judgment establishing that the Commission failed to act in accordance with such duty should, therefore, be regarded as allowing, by way of a quasi-sanction, for Council deliberations on Community legislation in the areas covered by the initial request for a proposal. A subsequently filed Commission proposal would then become the basis of further legislative efforts, to be undertaken in the course of ongoing deliberations.

In addition, as primary Community law does not prohibit national measures under the minimum standards concept, Member States might be able to use political pressure to encourage the Commission to put forward proposals.

2. *Rights of the European Parliament*

As a matter of principle, Title IV ECT allots the legislative institutions of the Community the role ascribed to them during the early periods of European integration. Council decisions are to be taken by unanimous vote and the European Parliament is to be consulted. This concept is, however, mitigated by the fact that areas communitarized by the Maastricht Treaty are governed by co-decision, and that the other areas under Title IV ECT may be subject to revision after the expiration of the transitional period pursuant to Article 67(2) ECT. The resulting power relationship reflects the scepticism with regard to the question of whether supranationalized immigration and aliens policies will operate more efficiently than related national and intergovernmental efforts. In conferring non-exclusive competence on the Community and in the *de facto* retention of a veto position under the unanimity requirement, Member States have created a procedural situation which promotes national action, and have added to it the national domains reservation embodied in the minimum standards concept governing the substantive areas of European aliens law and policy. Nevertheless, the

---

[195] *Langeheine/van Nuffel*, in Grabitz/Hilf (ed.), EGV/EUV Article 100c ECT para 33 have argued that the Commission has only been obliged to examine whether a request under ex-Article 100c(4) ECT can be qualified as reasonable.

transitional period is designed to be the first step in a gradual process aimed at loosening the ties of immigration to national sovereignty provided, of course, that policy-making on the European level meets the efficiency test in the transitional period.

3. *Powers of the European Court of Justice*

Article 68 ECT has modified the role of the European Court of Justice in the field of European aliens law. Preliminary rulings are limited and a new advisory procedure has been introduced. Additionally, some aspects of the invocation of the *ordre public* clauses contained in Title IV ECT have been excluded[196] from the jurisdiction of the Court.

Article 68(1) ECT requires a national court against whose decisions there is no judicial remedy under national law to request preliminary rulings on cases for which there is no precedent in national law, if it "considers that a decision on the question is necessary to enable it to give judgment". Originally introduced to prevent time-consuming procedures in the field of asylum and immigration, this provision limits individual access to the European Court of Justice[197]. Closer examination of the conditions set by Article 68(1) ECT for referrals of lower courts for preliminary rulings reveals that this provision prescribes the same subject-matters of preliminary rulings as does Article 234 ECT. It also applies a hybrid of the necessity test (applicable to lower instance courts under Article 234 ECT) and the duty to request preliminary rulings (applicable to courts of last instance). It has been said that the sole purpose of this Article is to require courts of last instance to request preliminary rulings[198]. If, however, it was only this duty which was to be introduced, simple repetition of the wording of the third paragraph of Article 234 ECT would have sufficed. While Article 68(1) ECT does not leave the decision on whether there is a need for a preliminary ruling to the discretion of national courts of last instance, it does confer a power of appraisal to national courts on the need to obtain a preliminary ruling to enable it to give judgment. The European Court of Justice held that courts of lower instance have a power of appraisal[199] under Article 234 ECT. As the wording of the respective paragraph of this provision forms part of Article 68(1) ECT, the

---

196 Albors-Llorens 35 CML Rev. (1999) 1273, 1287: Article 68 ECT "has limited the jurisdiction of the Court *ratione materiae*" and (ibid. 1288) "has the effect of destroying the unity of the provisions of the EC Treaty on the Court's jurisdiction".

197 See also Council document 12028/4/98 REV 4 JAI 31 para 30 in which is expressed the assumption that "[t]he entry into force of the Treaty of Amsterdam is likely to have the effect of increasing the case-load of the European Court of Justice". The Action plan of the Council and the Commission (O.J. 1999 C 19/1) does not contain any similar observation.

198 *Thun-Hohenstein*, Der Vertrag von Amsterdam (1997), 39.

199 ECJ, judgment of 16 December 1981, case 244/80, *Foglia v Novello*, [1981] ECR, 3045 paras 15-16. See also ECJ, judgment of 14 February 1980, case 53/79, *Office national des pensions des travailleurs salariés (ONPTS) v Damiani*, [1980] ECR 273 para 5 where the Court has held that –

> [i]t is for the national court, which is alone in having a direct knowledge of the facts of the case and of the argument put forward by the parties, and which will have to give judgment in the case, to appreciate, with full knowledge of the matter before it, the relevance of the question of law raised by the dispute before it and the necessity for a preliminary ruling so as to enable it to give judgment.

This jurisprudence was reaffirmed in the judgment of 30 April 1986, *Criminal proceedings against Lucas Asjes and others, Andrew Gray and others, Andrew Gray and others, Jacques Maillot and others and Léo Ludwig and others*, joined cases 209 to 213/84, [1986] ECR 1425 para 10.

relevant jurisprudence governing the position of courts of lower instance under Article 234 ECT also applies in the cases envisaged in Article 68(1) ECT.

Apart from that, Article 68(1) ECT poses the question which national courts qualify as courts of last instance. This issue is controversial under Article 234 ECT, and has not yet been adjudicated by the European Court of Justice. However, in *Costa v ENEL* the Court, in an *obiter dictum*, referred to the situation in an individual case when ruling on the question whether it could overturn the decision of a national court[200]. The mainstream academic community tends to agree with the spirit of this *obiter dictum*[201]. Article 68(1) ECT thus calls for referrals for preliminary rulings whenever a decision of a national court would be *de facto* non-appealable, i.e. in cases where the only judicial remedy would be 'exceptional' like a constitutional complaint[202].

Furthermore, the argument has been raised that courts of lower instance may be entitled, if not obliged, to refer cases which contest the validity of Community legislation to the European Court of Justice[203]. This assumption is commonly thought to have been modelled on *Foto-Frost*, where the Court held that national courts were incompetent to nullify Community legislation[204]. As Article 68(1) ECT clearly precludes referrals for preliminary rulings, irrespective of the referral's purpose, however, this assumption is not in accord with the relevant Treaty provision.

The advisory procedure introduced by Article 68(3) ECT covers questions on

- the interpretation of Title IV ECT, and
- the interpretation of acts of Community institutions based thereupon

to be brought before the European Court of Justice by the Council, the Commission, or a Member State. The fact that Article 68(3) ECT excludes effects of rulings on *res iudicata* shows that this provision gives rulings the same binding force as preliminary rulings and opinions, pursuant to Article 300(6) ECT. This procedure thus aims to minimize the number of protracted proceedings on preliminary rulings.

A number of procedural and substantive issues must be considered in connection with this advisory procedure. First, there may be some doubt as to whether a Council decision on procedures, as envisaged by Article 67(3) ECT, may include changes, or even a repeal of the advisory procedure[205]. Arguably, the procedure is non-repealable, as it increases the number of types of judicial procedures laid down in the Treaty itself.[206]. Second, the exclusion of effects of ECJ opinions on *res iudicata* has been criticized, not only for weakening the binding force of the Court's jurisprudence, but also for undermining the effects of Community law in general[207]. This view is not convincing. It is a recognized principle that judicial rulings do not affect *res judicata.*[208]. Conversely, retrospective effects of opinions given under Article 68(3) ECT for *res iudicata* could create severe legal uncertainty. Third, the question of

---

200 ECJ, judgment of 15 July 1964, case 6/64, *Costa v ENEL*, [1964] ECR 1411 = Dutch edition, 1203 = Danish edition, 531 = Italian edition, 1129 = German edition, 1253.

201 Cf. *Hailbronner*, in Hailbronner/Klein/Magiera/Müller-Graff, EUV/EGV (1991), Article 177 EGV para 28; *Wohlfahrt*, in Grabitz/Hilf (ed.), EGV/EUV Article 177 para 49.

202 Cf. *Krück*, in *v.d.* Groeben/Thiesing/Ehlermann, EUV/EGV (1997), vol. 4, 5 ed. Article 177 para 69.

203 *Winkler*, in Bergmann/Lenz (ed.), Der Amsterdamer Vertrag (1998), 45-71 para 67.

204 ECJ, judgment of 22 October 1987, case 314/85, *Foto-Frost v Hauptzollamt Lübeck-Ost*, [1987] ECR 4199 para 11-20.

205 Cf. *Thun-Hohenstein*, Der Vertrag von Amsterdam (1997), 40.

206 *Thun-Hohenstein* ibid.

207 *Lang*, Gemeinschaftsrecht der Drittstaatsangehörigen (1998), 351.

208 This principle is laid down in a large number of German statutes governing administrative and court procedures. See for instance § 79(2) of the German Statute on the Federal Constitutional Court.

whether the advisory procedure applies to the elements of the Schengen *acquis* attributed to Title IV legal bases may also arise. The fact that attribution has not transformed Schengen provisions into legislative acts "based" on that Title in the narrow sense of this expression does not exclude that they function as standards of review. Accordingly, the European Court of Justice must also be empowered to interpret them.

Member States have implemented clauses similar to those of the Maastricht era, which protect their discretion in the creation and implementation of unilateral restrictions based on national sovereign powers to maintain public order from interference by Community law[209]. The Maastricht provisions were ex-Articles 100c(5) ECT and K.2(2) TEU; these have been replaced by Article 64(1) ECT.

In addition, the Amsterdam Treaty excludes measures limiting the freedom of movement from ECJ jurisdiction, as they relate to the maintainment of law and order and the protection of internal security (see Article 68(2) ECT read together with Article 62(1) ECT, and Article 2(1), third sub-paragraph of the Schengen Protocol, which in substance have the same wording). Article 64(1) ECT, and Articles 68(2) ECT and 2(1), third sub-paragraph of the Schengen Protocol may all be invoked under the same condition, i.e. in order to maintain law and order, and to safeguard internal security. All subsequent interpretations must take this fact into account. Article 68(2) ECT may be characterized as a special public policy-related clause which refers to ECJ jurisdiction. However, a provision of this kind is a novel phenomenon in Community law. Two questions arise. Must Article 68(2) ECT be interpreted as a limiting factor on the non-justiciability of invocations of the *ordre public* reservation to cases related to the items referred to in Article 62(1) ECT[210]? And, if so, which standards of review should be applied to *ordre public* cases which fall outside of the scope of applicability of Article 68(2) ECT?

The meaning of Articles 64(1) and 68(2) ECT has, thus far, not been examined on the basis of the premise that there is a substantial connection between these provisions. Article 2(1), third sub-paragraph of the Schengen Protocol, moreover, has received little attention to date. However, the partial identity in wording, of the said provisions, points at an interpretative requirement to do so: irrespective of the fact that Articles 62(1) ECT and 2(1) of the Schengen Protocol refer to Community action while Article 64(1) ECT applies to measures taken by Member States. The meaning of Article 64(1) ECT must first be determined, taking its Maastricht legacy into account. The question of whether Article 68(2) ECT has changed this meaning must subsequently be addressed. Only then will it be possible to evaluate the normative concept implemented by the adoption of Articles 64(1) and 68(2) ECT.

During the Maastricht era, the *ordre public* clauses included in ex-Article 100c(5) ECT and ex-Article K.3(2) TEU inspired the debate over whether they were subject to the same interpretation as similar clauses in the Treaty establishing the European Community. Both this assumption[211] and its opposite[212] were considered. Addition-

---

209 See *Hailbronner* 31 CML Rev. (1994) 969, 991 et seq. regarding this aspect of the Maastricht regime.

210 One might read *Thun-Hohenstein*, Der Vertrag von Amsterdam (1997), 39 to this extent. The author argues that the limitation of ECJ juristiction only refers to internal, not external border controls. By giving express reference to the subject-matter dealt with in Article 62(1) ECT as opposed to Article 62(2) ECT *Thun-Hohenstein* implicitly rejects the relevance of Article 68(2) ECT for matters regulated outside Article 62 ECT as well.

211 *Magiera*, in Burmeister (ed.) Verfassungsstaatlichkeit, Essays in honour of Klaus Stern (1997) 1317, 1335.

ally, certain doubts have been expressed about the extent to which they permitted a deviation from Community measures or actions, and whether the ECJ's attitude towards the limitation of public order clauses by means of Community Concepts was applicable in matters falling under ex-Article K.1 TEU[213]. Article 64(1) ECT is an *ordre public* clause[214] and the relevant jurisprudence must thus be examined, in order to determine which position is most compatible with the Title IV framework. The European Court of Justice ruled on *ordre public* issues in a number of cases. The most significant dealt with –

- the meaning of the proviso contained in Article 39(3) ECT, and
- the invocation of the *ordre public* as a limitation of the scope of Community action in the social field.

Article 39(3) ECT's definition of *ordre public* situations diverges somewhat from that of the Article at issue, in that it applies to "grounds of public policy, public security or public health". *Van Duyn v Home Office* dealt primarily with the following questions: first, could the proviso be interpreted as a barrier to the emergence of individual rights within its scope? Second, which actor has the power to define the content of the *ordre public*? As to the first issue, the Court held that –

> a Member State's right to invoke the limitations does not prevent the provisions of Article [39], which enshrine the principle of freedom of movement for workers, from conferring on individuals rights which are enforceable by them...[215]

As to the second question, the Court stated that –

> [i]t should be emphasized that the concept of public policy in the context of the Community and where, in particular, it is used as a justification for derogating from the fundamental principle of freedom of movement for workers, must be interpreted strictly, so that its scope cannot be determined unilaterally by each Member State without being subject to control by the institutions of the Community.[216]

Consequently, the European Court of Justice has held that Article 39 ECT establishes the principle that the freedom of movement may be limited pursuant to the proviso contained in Article 39(3) ECT, which qualifies as an exception under this construction. Moreover, the Court has applied the general methodological rule that exceptional clauses must be interpreted within the limits of their restrictively construed *ratio legis*[217]. – In *Regina v Pieck* the European Court of Justice gave the meaning to Article 39(3) ECT that –

> [t]his restriction must be regarded not as a condition precedent to the acquisition of the right of entry and residence but as providing the possibility, in individual

---

212 *Hailbronner*, in Hailbronner/Klein/Magiera/Müller-Graff, EUV/EGV (1996), Article 100c EGV para 34.

213 *Hailbronner* 31 CML Rev.(1994) 969, 992.

214 Cf. *Thun-Hohenstein*, Der Vertrag von Amsterdam (1997), 31.

215 ECJ, judgment of 4 December 1974, case 41/71, *van Duyn v Home Office*, [1974] ECR 1337 para 7.

216 ECJ, judgment of 4 December 1974, case 41/71, *van Duyn v Home Office*, [1974] ECR 1337 para 18.

217 Ibid. For said principle cf. *Larenz*, Methodenlehre der Rechtswissenschaft, 6. Ed. (1991), 355 et seq. and *Bydlinski*, Juristische Methodenlehre und Rechtsbegriff, 2. Ed. (1991), 440.

cases where there is sufficient justification, of imposing restrictions on the exercise of a right derived directly from the Treaty.[218]

Consequently, the proviso at issue is applicable to individual cases only. Member States may rely upon the proviso only in the implementation of reactive measures; it does not, however, justify preventive national action. Can this interpretation be applied to the *ordre public* clauses contained in Title IV ECT? Before turning to the individual aspect of this proviso, it must be noted that its exercise under Article 39(3) ECT has been rendered subject to the constraints which were affirmed by the European Court of Justice in the quoted judgments, by virtue of Directives 64/221/EEC[219], 68/360/EEC[220] and 73/143/EEC[221]. Arguably, it is these instruments of secondary Community law, rather than the market freedom contained in Article 39 ECT, which impose limitations on the discretionary power which Member States enjoy in the field of immigration control vis-à-vis EU citizens[222]. Even if primary Community law were the source of the limitations on national powers in *ordre public* cases, such limitations would not qualify as emanations of a general principle inherent in Community law with regard to third-country nationals, as the legal frameworks governing the rights of EU citizens and third-country nationals in the field of movement are different in character. As a matter of principle, EU citizens enjoy freedom of movement under primary Community law (cf. Articles 17 ECT and the market freedoms) while third-country nationals do not enjoy this freedom. The invocation of the *ordre public* thus distracts from the fundamental principles of Community law within the scope of the market freedoms, while these principles are not at the basis of Title IV ECT measures[223]. Accordingly, principles derived from provisions governing the free movement of EU citizens may not be applied to third-country nationals by analogy.

At the same time, in addition, the relationship between primary and secondary Community law in the areas covered by Title IV ECT is different to that established by the market freedoms. Article 39 ECT defines the purpose of secondary Community law as the enhancement of the position of the individual created by Community freedoms. On the other hand, secondary Community law designed to implement Title IV ECT only may, though need not, be constitutive for the existence of individual rights. Such legislation will qualify as an exception to the principle embodied in Title IV ECT, which holds that third-country nationals do not enjoy the right to enter the area comprising Member States' territories[224], or to move within this territory. Moreover, the differentiation between reactive and preventive measures, laid down

---

[218] ECJ, judgment of 3 July 1980, case 157/79, *Regina v Pieck*, [1980] ECR 2171 para 9. The Court upheld this dictum in its judgment of 27 April 1989, case 321/87, *Commission v Belgium*, [1989] ECR 977 para 10.

[219] Article 3(1) of Directive 64/221/EEC of 25 February 1964, O.J. 1964 850.

[220] Article 3(1) of Directive 68/360/EEC of 15 October 1968, O.J. (English Special Edition) 1968 (II), 485.

[221] Article 3(1) of Directive 73/143/EEC of 21 May 1974, O.J. 1973 L 172/14.

[222] The judgment of 19 January 1999, case C-348/96, *Calfa*, [1999] ECR 11 paras 26-28 shows that the Member States still have some, though pretty small a margin of, discretion as regards control of intra-EU migration.

[223] This conclusion has also been reached with respect to the *ordre public* clause contained in ex-Article 100c ECT. See *Hailbronner*, in Hailbronner/Klein/Magiera/Müller-Graff, EUV/EGV (1996), Article 100c EGV para 35.

[224] A detailed account of this principle, (humanitarian) limitations thereof, and the relevant provisions in internationals and European law has been given by *Klos* Rahmenbedingungen und Gestaltungsmöglichkeiten der Europäischen Migrationspolitik (1998), 88-96.

in Article 39 ECT, cannot be applied to Title IV ECT. Notably, Title IV ECT does not treat migration as an individual phenomenon, but rather as a mass phenomenon. This conclusion follows from the fact that Title IV ECT does not create any individual rights, but only envisages abstract, general conditions for entry and movement of third-country nationals to govern multiple cases. As preventive measures tend to be based upon a general situation, these measures do not qualify as exceptional under Title IV ECT; only reactive measures qualify as such, as shown by Article 64(2) ECT. Inherent in the notion of immigration control is the prevention of undesired immigration, while freedom of movement is based on the notion of the absence of preventive migration controls[225]. Consequently, the understanding applied to the *ordre public* clause contained in Article 39(3) ECT relates to a legal framework quite different from the one created by Title IV ECT, and cannot be simply copied into the latter.

The European Court of Justice views the *ordre public* as a limitation of the scope open to Community legislation, and thus had to decide whether ex-Article 118 ECT covered Community action in the field of immigration. This provision entrusted the Commission with the task of promoting close co-operation between Member States in the social field. To achieve this end, the Commission had to act in close contact with Member States by making studies, delivering opinions and arranging consultations. In its judgment on the prior communication and consultation procedure on migration policies in relation to non-member countries[226], the European Court of Justice did not accept the assumption that migration policy fell entirely outside the social field, as defined by ex-Article 118 ECT[227]. The Court determined the substantive scope of ex-Article 118 ECT on the basis of an approach which focused on the effects of immigration. The Court then turned to the *ordre public* argument raised by the French Republic. To have ruled in favour of this argument, the Court would have had to treat the *ordre public* as a potential limitation of Community competence. It did not, however, ultimately 'accept' this argument. In the course of defining the scope of ex-Article 118 ECT, the European Court of Justice drew attention to the fact that the employment situation and the improvement of living and working conditions within the Community were bound to be affected by policies pursued by the Member States with regard to workers from third-countries[228] – a position which had also been taken by the Council on several occasions[229]. In particular, the Court defined the scope of the social field under ex-Article 118 ECT as inclusive of –

- the integration of workers who are nationals of third-countries into the workforce, and

[225] Cf. ECJ, judgment of 27 April 1989, case 321/87, *Commission v Belgium*, [1989] ECR 977 para 10-11.

[226] Decision 85/381/EEC of 8 July 1985, O.J. 1985 L 217/25. By virtue of the judgment of 9 July 1987, joined cases 281, 283, 284, 285 and 287/85, *Germany and others v Commission*, [1987] ECR 3203 this decision was declared void insofar as it extended the communication and consultation procedure to cover matters relating to the cultural integration of third-country nationals (see para 3 of the operative part of the judgment).

[227] ECJ, judgment of 9 July 1987, joined cases 281, 283, 284, 285 and 287/85, *Germany and others v Commission*, [1987] ECR 3203 para 18.

[228] ECJ, judgment of 9 July 1987, joined cases 281, 283, 284, 285 and 287/85, *Germany and others v Commission*, [1987] ECR 3203 para 16.

[229] See the resolutions referred to in para 17 of the judgment of 9 July 1987, joined cases 281, 283, 284, 285 and 287/85, *Germany and others v Commission*, [1987] ECR 3203.

- the integration of workers who are nationals of third-countries into society inasmuch as such integration is connected with problems relating to employment and working conditions[230].

On the other hand, the European Court of Justice held that the cultural integration of immigrants does not fall within Community competence under ex-Article 118 ECT because it is aimed at immigrant communities in general, and does not distinguish between migrant workers and other third-country nationals[231]. Moreover, Community competence was seen as subject to inherent limitations, in that it was confined to action dealing with the effects of third-country nationals, on the Community labour market and on working conditions[232].

The French Republic's *ordre public* argument was rejected by the Court. The Court held that –

> [w]hilst it is true that ... Member States may take measures with regard to workers who are nationals of non-member countries ... which are based on considerations of public policy, public security and public health, this does not mean that the whole field of migration policy in relation to non-member countries falls necessarily within the scope of public security.[233]

Now that ex-Article 118 ECT has been replaced entirely by the Amsterdam Treaty (see the successor norm in Article 137 ECT which will be dealt with *infra* and *sub specie* Social Rights of Third-Country Nationals), this case no longer sets a precedent for ECT interpretation. Nevertheless it provides valuable evidence for the construction of the pre-Amsterdam *acquis* by the Court. The European Court of Justice seems to have applied the meaning of the *ordre public* as understood under Article 39(3) ECT, to the argument raised by the French Republic. Supporting evidence was found in the citation of the concerns mentioned in a quoted passage of the latter Article. The Court did not establish a comprehensive distinction between migration of third-country nationals and EU citizens in the judgment on the prior communication and consultation procedure on migration policies in relation to non-member countries. The Court rather seems to have taken the view that the same rules under Community law apply to both kinds of migration phenomena, unless special regimes are established by the Treaty establishing the European Economic Community (as it then was). Title IV ECT, for example, establishes a special regime for the control of migration of third-country nationals. Consequently, the Court's construction of the *ordre public* under ex-Article 118 ECT cannot merely be transferred into the new framework for European aliens law and policy.

The European Court of Justice was not confronted with any cases involving the *ordre public* issue during the Maastricht era. Additionally, unlike the proviso contained in Article 39(3) ECT, which has been implemented at the Community level

---

[230] ECJ, judgment of 9 July 1987, joined cases 281, 283, 284, 285 and 287/85,*Germany and others v Commission*, [1987] ECR 3203 para 21.

[231] ECJ, judgment of 9 July 1987, joined cases 281, 283, 284, 285 and 287/85, *Germany and others v Commission*, [1987] ECR 3203 para 22.

[232] ECJ, judgment of 9 July 1987, joined cases 281, 283, 284, 285 and 287/85, *Germany and others v Commission*, [1987] ECR 3203 para 23.

[233] ECJ, judgment of 9 July 1987, joined cases 281, 283, 284, 285 and 287/85,*Germany and others v Commission*, [1987] ECR 3203 para 25.

by several directives[234], no Community legislation aimed at defining the character of the *ordre public*, as contemplated by ex-Article 100c(5) ECT and ex-Article K.2(2) TEU, has been adopted. The behaviour of the Member States implies that they view these clauses as related to European public policy, rather than to national assessments of the *ordre public*, and subsequent adoption of acts. Article 64(1) ECT, instead, indicates that it is not the task of the Community to adopt rules restricting police powers used to maintain law and order[235]. This conclusion may also be drawn from the *ordre public* provisions in the field of European aliens law, as these differ in framework from Article 39(3) ECT. The latter proviso allows for the limitation of rights, while ex-Article 100c(5) ECT, ex-Article K.2(2) TEU, and Article 64(1) ECT define the preservation of the *ordre public* as the exercise of responsibilities allocated under these provisions. These constructions differ with respect to the relationship between the interests protected. The relationship between a right and the limitation thereof must be seen as based on the premise that the (private) interest protected by the right is of greater importance than the (policy) interest served by the limitation. In the denial of the right to free movement for third-country nationals in primary Community law, the framers of the Treaty, on the other hand, seem to value private interests of third-country nationals less than the freedom of movement for workers under Article 39 ECT.

Notably, the responsibility for the preservation of the *ordre public* resting upon Member States has not been supranationalized. Hence Article 64(1) ECT seems to be based on the unspoken premise that Community action in the field of European aliens law must not interfere with national policies that are aimed at the preservation of the *ordre public*. The interest protected by Article 64(1) ECT is thus a policy interest and responsibility for its realization lies with the Member States. Consequently, the private interest of third-country nationals to migrate within the area comprising Member States' territories does not preclude public interests in the preservation of the *ordre public*. Article 64(1) ECT must, therefore, be interpreted as not only allowing, but also promoting national concepts of public order and internal security[236]. Arguably, this provision has both procedural and substantive effects. On the one hand, it supports the right of Member States to invoke the *ordre public* in a given situation. In particular, Member States carry neither the burden of proof nor of evidence, if this invocation is challenged before the European Court of Justice. Member States may, therefore, use political discretion when determining whether an incident triggers the *ordre public*. While this concept undermines any attempt to establish a uniform understanding of the *ordre public*, the discretion resting in the hands of the Member States is not unlimited. Following the general principle which prohibits fraud of the law, invocations of the *ordre public* will be subject to an arbitrariness test, at the very least. Given the relationship between paragraphs (1) and (2) of Article 64 ECT[237], judicial review will preferably focus on the question of whether respective Member States have established a case of imminent danger for the maintenance of law and order, and of

---

[234] Directives 64/221/EEC (O.J. 1964 850); 72/194/EEC (O.J. 1972 L 121, 32); 75/35/EEC (O.J. 1975 L 14/14). See *Lang*, Gemeinschaftsrecht der Drittstaatsangehörigen (1998), 348 et seq.

[235] *Hailbronner* 35 CML Rev. (1998) 1047, 1053.

[236] See the similar conclusion drawn in an earlier work with respect to the predecessor norms: *Hailbronner* 31 CML Rev. (1994) 969, 992. Cf. *Lang*, Gemeinschaftsrecht der Drittstaatsangehörigen (1998), 352.

[237] See *supra* X 3 d.

internal security[238] – in other words, a case of emergency (though not confined to the sudden influx criterion under Article 64(2) ECT) in a reasonable way.

Article 68(2) ECT[239] excludes measures and decisions in the fields covered by Article 62(1) ECT, and those taken by Member States under invocation of the *ordre public* from the jurisdiction of the European Court of Justice. Article 2(1), third subparagraph of the Schengen Protocol performs the same function for the Schengen *acquis*. It is obviously not possible to downread these provisions to the character of a presumption similar to Article 64(1) ECT. There should be no doubt, however, as to the power of the European Court of Justice to rule on the limits of its jurisdiction. To render a court incompetent to rule on the scope of its own jurisdiction would be unthinkable[240].

Whether the Court's jurisprudence on public order clauses in the Treaty can be assimilated to the provisions at issue is doubtful given the fact that the latter expressly restrict the Court's jurisdiction to a clearly defined area, regardless of the legality of the measures taken. That construction amounts to a substantial departure from the Treaty public order clauses, which, under certain circumstances, justify national restrictions of the market freedoms. Article 68(2) ECT and Article 2(1), third subparagraph of the Schengen Protocol apply to a specific type of Community measure, rather than to national public order exceptions. A national measure to be determined by the criteria laid down in said Articles, is thus generally excluded from the Court's jurisdiction, regardless of any legal objections based upon the Treaty or general principles of Community law. The role of the European Court of Justice will be limited to the application of a plausibility test on the reasons given by Member States to justify an invocation of the *ordre public*. It may not determine whether this reasoning, once its plausibility has been established, can be 'accepted'[241]. In other words, the Court does not have jurisdiction on the question of whether measures which do not obviously lack any relation to the maintenance of law and order and the safeguarding of internal security are permissible under Community law because the provisions at issue define that Community law does not include standards of review for this question.

Under Article 64(1) ECT "maintenance of law and order and the safeguarding of internal security" remain within national sovereignty. The European Court of Justice may review public order decisions only on the basis of an arbitrariness or reasonability test. At the same time, the *ordre public* provisions do not merely restate the principle that the Court "has no ... jurisdiction with regard to national legislation lying outside the scope of Community law"[242]. They contain the implicit assumption, that *ordre public* issues lie outside the scope of Community law.

---

238 *Hailbronner* 35 CML Rev. (1998) 1047, 1052.

239 This passage has been modelled upon previous works. Cf. *Hailbronner* 35 CML Rev. (1998) 1047, 1056 et seq.; *Hailbronner/Thiery* EuR 1998, 583, 596

240 Cf. *Müller-Graff* integration 20 (1997) 271, 280; *Thun-Hohenstein*, Der Vertrag von Amsterdam (1997), 39, 52.

241 It should be recalled that the European Court of Justice made use of this expression in order to repudiate the French Republic's *ordre public* argument in its judgment of 9 July 1987, joined cases 281, 283, 284, 285 and 287/85, *Germany and others v Commission*, [1987] ECR 3203 para 25.

242 This principle has been reaffirmed in a number of judgments. See for instance the judgment of 18 December 1997, case C-309/96, *Annibaldi v Sindaco del Comune di Guidonia and Presidente Regione Lazio*, [1997] ECR I-7493 para 13. See *Winkler*, in *Bergmann/Lenz* (ed.), Der Amsterdamer Vertrag (1998) 45-71 para 70 for the opposite view and for detailed references to the jurisprudence governing the mentioned principle.

XII. Opt-out and Opt-in Provisions

The United Kingdom, Ireland and Denmark were opposed to the communitarization of justice and home affairs matters previously covered by Maastricht's third pillar. They have, however, agreed to the wish of other Member States' to achieve a closer co-operation in these areas. In addition to their opt-out, the United Kingdom and Ireland have also maintained their Common Travel Area, which does not form part of the internal market since the latter "shall comprise an area without internal frontiers in which the free movement of [...] persons [...] is ensured". The Anglo-Irish and Danish opt-outs are governed by the Schengen Protocol and the Protocols on the position of said Member States. Additionally, the Common Travel Area is shielded from the internal market by virtue of the Protocol on the application of certain aspects of Article 14 of the Treaty establishing the European Community to the United Kingdom and to Ireland.

Article 1 of the Protocol on the application of certain aspects of Article 14 of the Treaty establishing the European Community to the United Kingdom and to Ireland entitles the United Kingdom to adopt or exercise comprehensive border controls, contrary to the interpretation of Article 14 ECT, supported until now by the European Commission and some EU Member States[243]. The Protocol thus can be interpreted as an acceptance of the British view that the international market as defined by Article 14 does not necessarily imply abolition of all internal border controls designed to check the immigration of third-country nationals. Article 2 of the said Protocol reserves the same right for Ireland, provided that she maintains the Common Travel Area with the United Kingdom.

According to the Protocol at issue the United Kingdom and Ireland are entitled to exercise such border controls "as [they] may consider necessary" for the purposes of

- verifying the right to enter their territories of citizens of EEA Member States and persons deriving free travel rights from such citizens, or of
- determining whether or not to grant other persons admission to their territories.

Ireland, according to her Declaration to the Final Act, only exercises the rights under the protocol at issue because she wishes to maintain the Common Travel Area with the United Kingdom.

1. Title IV Opt-Out and Opt-In

The Anglo-Irish opt-out from the provision of Title IV ECT is governed by the Protocol on the position of the United Kingdom and Ireland. The United Kingdom and Ireland will not participate in the adoption of measures under Title IV ECT nor will they be bound by any measure or decision based upon this Title. They may, however, participate in the adoption and application of proposed measures under Title IV ECT, if they express their wish to do so within three months after a proposal or initiative has been presented to the Council (see Article 3 of the Protocol; henceforth referred to as initial opt-in). They may also opt-in with regard to Community legislation adopted by the other Member States, subject to admission by the Commission (see Article 4 of

---

[243] *Bardenhewer/Pipkorn*, in: v.d. Groeben/Thiesing/Ehlermann, EUV/EGV vol. 1, 5 ed. (1997), Article 7a para 6; *de Keersmaeker/Pauwels*, in: Smit/Herzog, § 7a.01; *Zacker*, Binnenmarkt und Gemeinsamer Markt – Zwei Begriffe desselben Inhalts?, Recht der internationalen Wirtschaft (RIW) 1998, 489 et seq.

the Protocol read together with Article 11(3) ECT; henceforth referred to as subsequent opt-in). Ireland may also renounce her opt-out, pursuant to Article 8 of the Protocol. Finally, according to her Declaration to the Final Act, Ireland will opt-in to the maximum extent compatible with the maintenance of the Common Travel Area.

The differentiation between initial and subsequent opt-in procedures does not pose specific legal problems. Irrespective of whether the United Kingdom and Ireland participate in the adoption of Community legislation or opt-in after adoption, they may only choose to opt-in fully[244].

In case of an initial opt-in, Article 3 of the Protocol ensures that the United Kingdom and Ireland will not be able to block the decision process. If after a reasonable period of time a measure cannot be adopted with the United Kingdom and Ireland taking part, the Council may adopt such measure without the participation of the United Kingdom or Ireland according to the general provisions applicable in case of non-participation of these States. There may be some doubt as to which period of time is reasonable under Article 3(2) of the Protocol at issue. This question must be resolved by the Council in each individual case, paying special attention to the complexity of the measure proposed, to the aim to make generally applicable Community law, and to the loyalty principle binding both the opt-in Member States and those Member States which participate regularly in the implementation of Title IV ECT[245].

By adopting, pursuant to Article 3(2) of the Protocol, a measure without the participation of the United Kingdom or Ireland the Council implicitly decides that the reasonable period of time has expired. In principle a measure thus adopted can be challenged before the European Court of Justice. The United Kingdom or Ireland, respectively, could argue that the qualification of the relevant period of time as "reasonable" was wrong and that, therefore, the measure taken had been adopted in a defective procedure. The determination of the period of time, however, is not subject to precise legal conditions, but implies a wide margin of political discretion.

The Danish opt-out from both the implementation of Title IV ECT and the Schengen follow-up process is governed by the Protocol on the position of Denmark. In contrast to the situation of the United Kingdom and Ireland, Denmark has only the possibility to inform the other Member States that it no longer wishes to avail itself of all or part of the Protocol. In that case it will be bound to apply in full all measures passed by that time on the basis of Title IV ECT. Denmark may not participate in the adoption of individual measures under Title IV ECT. However, measures building on the Schengen *acquis* are open to a Danish acceptance, notwithstanding the fact that they must be based upon Title IV legal bases[246].

2. *Schengen Opt-Out and Opt-In*

The Protocol integrating the Schengen *acquis* into the framework of the European Union includes provisions related to both the Anglo-Irish and Danish opt-outs. Schengen-related opt-in also appears in Community texts as initial or subsequent opt-in. Article 5 of the Schengen Protocol allows for British and/or Irish participation in

244 Cf. *Hailbronner/Thiery* EuR 1998, 583, 598.
245 Cf. *Hailbronner/Thiery* EuR 1998, 583, 598.
246 Cf. *Thun-Hohenstein*, Der Vertrag von Amsterdam (1997), 55.

the Schengen follow-up process (initial opt-in). Unlike the Protocol on the position of the United Kingdom and Ireland, the Schengen Protocol does not allow for a denial of further participation on the grounds of obstruction. Article 7 of the Protocol on the Position of the United Kingdom and Ireland provides that Article 3 of that Protocol shall be without prejudice to the Schengen Protocol. Therefore the Council does not have the power to adopt a decision without the participation of the United Kingdom or Ireland after a reasonable period of time, once these states have decided to participate in the adoption of measure. To opt in for the purpose of preventing a decision could, however, be considered as a violation of the loyalty principle enshrined in Article 10 ECT. In that case the Member States were entitled to proceed with decision-making without the participation of the United Kingdom and Ireland.

As to subsequent opt-in, two cases must be distinguished. First, the United Kingdom and Ireland may, at any time, request participation in some or all provisions of the Schengen *acquis*. Article 4 of the Schengen Protocol renders such opt-in subject to an unanimous Council decision. Second, subsequent opt-in relating to measures building on the Schengen *acquis* is not provided for in the Schengen Protocol; Article 5 deals solely with initial opt-in[247]. In order to close the gap, Article 4 of the Protocol could be applied by analogy or procedural rules of the Protocol on the position of the United Kingdom and Ireland relating to subsequent opt-ins. It has been argued that Article 7 of the Protocol on the position of the United Kingdom and Ireland render this Protocol inapplicable, as the latter is to operate independently of the Schengen Protocol[248]. As the Schengen Protocol contains no provisions on the specific issue[249], its provisions would not be prejudiced. In addition, the Schengen follow-up procedure in general is governed by the relevant ECT provisions. Therefore, an analogous application of the Protocol on the position of the United Kingdom and Denmark relating to the opt-in procedure would seem to be in line with the system of the Protocol. The same conclusion can be reached by taking into account the purpose of the Protocol. The aim of preventing the fragmentation of the European legal order would be better served through an application of Article 11(3) ECT.

Denmark's situation is determined by its membership of the Schengen Convention and opt-out of Title IV ECT. Full opt-in into Title IV ECT is subject to renunciation of the Protocol on the position of Denmark[250]. According to Article 5, Denmark, within a period of six months after the adoption of a Schengen acquis measure, may decide to implement such a measure within its national law. If it decides to do so it will be obliged by public international law to the other Member States to comply with this decision. Article 5 of the Protocol continues the fiction of a treaty relationship between Denmark and the Schengen Member States even after Schengen has been terminated as an international treaty[251] with relation to Community measures building upon the Schengen *acquis*.

The obligation resulting from an acceptance of a Schengen measure will also be extended to the United Kingdom and Ireland, should they choose to opt-in. Should Denmark decide against an opt-in, the signatories of the Schengen agreements "will

---

[247] Cf. *Kortenberg* 35 CML Rev. (1998). 833, 842.

[248] Cf. *Kortenberg* ibid.

[249] *Kortenberg* id. does not only recognize this fact. Additionally, also build thereon and suggests to extend the reference made to Article 11 ECT by Article 5(1), second sub-paragraph of the Schengen protocol to subsequent options.

[250] Cf. *Hailbronner/Thiery* EuR 1998, 583, 601.

[251] See also *Zimmermann* NVwZ 1998, 450, 453.

consider appropriate measures to be taken". It has been suggested that "it might become necessary to re-establish border controls for people coming from Denmark"[252]. The establishment of new internal border controls obviously would be contrary to the objective laid down in Article 14 ECT and does not comply with Article 62(1) ECT. Member States will have to solve problems and disagreements through political compromise[253].

XIII. Extra-Title IV Legal Bases of Community Action

1. *Extra-Title IV Powers on European Aliens Law?*

During the Maastricht era questions have been raised concerning the scope of the market freedoms and their relationship to ex-Title VI TEU. The debate focused on the question of whether Maastricht's ECT allowed for legislation regulating the status of third-country nationals and whether the Commission and the Council were obliged to make use of existing Community powers rather than allowed to proceed within the new framework of the third pillar[254]. It seems that this debate might be continued and now focus on the relationship between market freedoms and Title IV ECT. In particular, both the exclusiveness of Title IV ECT and the applicability of Articles 94, 95 and 308 ECT have been questioned[255]. Given the limited scope of Title IV ECT, there might indeed be room for a more extensive interpretation of other ECT provisions, which would empower the European Union to take action relating to third-country nationals.

a) The Need to Delineate the Scope of Application of Title IV ECT and of other Legal Bases for Community Action

The issue of harmonization of aliens law with a view to third-country nationals made its way onto the agenda of the European Economic Community (as it then was) at the 1974 Paris summit of the European Heads of States and Governments. Since then the Council, the Commission, the European Parliament and the academic community have been in dispute over the question of whether, and to what extent, the Community may take action in this field. Amendments to the Treaty establishing the European (Economic) Community have intensified the existing disagreement rather than solved the dispute. The internal market concept under the 1986 Single European Act contributed to debates because it envisaged "an area without internal frontiers in which the free movement of goods, persons, services and capital is ensured" (see Article 14 ECT, as it now is). Free movement of persons was said to have been granted to both EU citizens and third-country nationals[256] though Member States

---

[252] *Kortenberg* 35 CML Rev. (1998) 833, 840.

[253] See also *supra* III 2 c.

[254] See *Hailbronner*, in: Hailbronner/Klein/Magiera/Müller-Graff, EUV/EGV, Article K EUV para 17 and *Koenig/Pechstein*, Die Europäische Union, 2nd ed. (1998) at 42 et seq. for detailed references.

[255] *Müller-Graff* integration 20 (1997) 271 at 275.

[256] Cf. *Magiera*, in Burmeister (ed.) Verfassungsstaatlichkeit, Essays in honour of Klaus Stern (1997) 1317, 1334 et seq.

never reached agreement on that point[257] – not even by way of amendment of the Treaty establishing the European Community at the Maastricht intergovernmental conference. Moreover, no attempts have been made to receive guidance from the European Court of Justice[258].

In practice, a pragmatic position was adopted. While the directives and regulations on freedom of movement for workers were clearly restricted to nationals of one of the Member States, provision was made in the Regulation 1408/71 on co-ordination of social insurance benefits for some categories of non-Community nationals, such as recognized refugees, although third-country nationals as such were not included in the Regulation. Based upon the jurisprudence of the European Court of Justice, other market freedoms such as the freedom to provide services were also interpreted as covering at least indirectly the legal status of third-country nationals who can draw benefits from an exercise of a Union citizen's freedom to provide services. In addition, the rights of third-country nationals were affected by Community law protecting general human rights and granting social protection in working conditions and employment generally.

Conversely, the Amsterdam Treaty has resolved the question of whether third-country nationals can derive a right to move freely within the community from the internal market concept. Title IV ECT indicates that they cannot. Nonetheless the pre-Amsterdam dispute must once more be considered. Although no longer relevant for the interpretation of primary Community law as it now stands, this dispute supplies useful guidance for determining the method of delineating the scope of legal bases for Community action vis-à-vis third-country nationals under Title IV ECT on the one hand and extra-Title IV provisions on the other, because its primary focus had been the question of whether the Community could derive implied powers in migration matters from both the Single European Act and the Maastricht Treaty.

b) Delineation of Title IV ECT and extra-Title IV Legal Bases of Community Action

Community law as it stood before the adoption of the Amsterdam Treaty contained a large number of instruments that included provisions governing at least indirectly some aspects of the legal status of third-country nationals. In particular, secondary Community law aimed at implementation of market freedoms and free movement of EU citizens under Article 18 ECT, social rights legislation and association and co-operation agreements contained relevant provisions. Except for ex-Article 118 ECT which has been replaced by a substantially new provision (Article 137 ECT) most legal bases relevant for such Community action have not been changed by virtue of the Amsterdam Treaty. Nevertheless the introduction of Title IV ECT has an influence on the interpretation of these provisions. Title IV ECT and extra-Title IV legal bases for Community action must be interpreted in their systematic context. Assuming that Community law is to form a coherent legal framework, provisions must be interpreted on the basis of the premise that they are constituting a particular part of an interrelated

---

[257] See *Magiera*, in Burmeister (ed.) Verfassungsstaatlichkeit, Essays in honour of Klaus Stern (1997) 1317, 1332 et seq.

[258] See for instance *Hailbronner* 31 CML Rev. (1994) 969, 972 with respect to ex-Articles 238, 117-118 ECT: "Exactly how far the competence of the Community under the provisions mentioned extends has never been tested".

system of rules supplementing each other. It follows that as far as Title IV ECT applies, other provisions of the Treaty establishing the European Community must be deemed to have lost their subsidiary regulatory function.

It has to be noted in this context that the Amsterdam Treaty does not contain a provision similar to ex-Article M TEU. The Amsterdam Treaty is therefore in principle capable of affecting the pre-existing *acquis communautaire*. In turn, Article 47 TEU (as ex-Article M TEU now is) only governs the interrelationship between the Treaties on European Union and establishing the European Community, as respectively amended. Second, the Amsterdam Treaty only gives a clear answer, albeit implicitly, as regards its effects on the pre-existing *acquis*. The instruments adopted under ex-Article 100c ECT are not affected because they continue to have legal bases in primary Community law under Title IV ECT. However, the interpretation of pre-existing powers of the Community derived from other provisions, secondary Community legislation based thereon and related jurisprudence of the European Court of Justice remains an open question. The Amsterdam Treaty did not affect secondary Community law as part of the *acquis communautaire*. Additionally, instruments adopted under ex-Article 118 ECT have continuing legal force under an analogy to Article 30(4)(b) of the Convention of the Law of Treaties. Accordingly, analysis must focus on the interpretation of pre-Amsterdam provisions and on the question of whether, and to what extent, related ECJ jurisprudence as to the scope of application of such provisions can still be regarded as valid.

With the entry into force of the Maastricht Treaty similar questions arose. Like the Amsterdam Treaty, the Maastricht Treaty had not changed the wording of market freedoms which functioned as the core competence norms of Community action capable of affecting the status of *certain* third-country nationals. Like the Amsterdam Treaty, however, the Maastricht Treaty had introduced certain legal bases for action (though, under Maastricht, not necessarily Community action) regulating entry and sojourn of third-country nationals *as such*. It is submitted that the necessary precondition for the introduction of such legal bases has been that Member States in their capacity as Masters of the Treaties have acted on the basis of an, albeit implicit, authentic interpretation of the Treaties. Taking into account that Title IV ECT has by and large communitarized the legal bases introduced by the Maastricht Treaty one can assume that this interpretation has not changed over the years.

c) Delineation of Powers under the Maastricht Traty

Only after the Maastricht Treaty took effect did immigration law and policy make their way onto the European agenda[259]. Even then, however, the Community did not have express powers in the field of aliens law except for those under ex-Article 100c ECT[260], as Member States were only willing to partially compromise their sovereign rights[261]. Nevertheless, since Maastricht the differentiation between Community law governing aspects of the status of third-country nationals related to the functioning of

[259] Cf. Peers 35 CML Rev. (1999) 1235 et seq. for a detailed account of EU migration policy efforts during the Maastricht era.

[260] Cf. *Streinz* EuZW 1998, 137, 141: Title IV ECT is the first Community instrument which confers express competencies related to substantive questions of admission of third-country nationals.

[261] *Hailbronner* 31 CML Rev. (1994) 969, 984.

the common and internal market concepts on the one hand, and European aliens law[262] on the other, is reflected by primary Community law. Examination of the pre-Amsterdam debate shows that this differentiation is based upon a certain, albeit implicit, interpretation by Member States of Community competence vis-à-vis third-country nationals.

However, this implicit interpretation was virtually ignored by some authors who examined whether the Treaty establishing the European (Economic) Community had empowered the Community to act in the areas defined as matters of common interest by ex-Article K.1(1-3) TEU. It was argued that ex-Article K.1(1) TEU was based upon the premise that such alleged Community competence was still valid since this Article provided that Member States shall regard certain areas of aliens law and policy as matters of common interest "without prejudice to the powers of the European Community"[263]. This argument is hardly convincing. Ex-Article K.1 TEU cannot be interpreted as a safeguard clause relating to the interpretation of ECT provisions. Only the powers of the Community, as properly interpreted, by the European Court of Justice in the systematic context of the whole Treaty, should not be affected by Third Pillar provisions.

Under the Maastricht Treaty it has also been argued that market freedoms and complementary social rights were unseparably connected with the status of third-country nationals. ECJ jurisprudence on association agreements to some extent supports this argument. During the Maastricht era delineation was based upon a line of reasoning which usually began with a reference to ex-Article M TEU. This provision stipulates that "nothing in this Treaty [scil.: on European Union] shall affect the Treaties establishing the European Communities or the subsequent Treaties and Acts modifying or supplementing them". This provision was to be regarded as safeguarding the powers conferred on the Community before the entry into force of the Maastricht Treaty. In particular, it was concluded that ex-Title VI TEU was incapable of affecting the ECT powers[264].

The position thus described led to surprising conclusions. The European Court of Justice assumed jurisdiction over third pillar instruments although third pillar instruments were expressly exempted from its jurisdiction. The delineation of the Treaties establishing the European Community and on European Union arrived at a crucial point when the Commission challenged (albeit unsuccessfully) the Joint Action on airport transit arrangements with a motion for annulment[265]. The European Court of Justice refused to accept that its jurisdiction over the issue was excluded by ex-Article L TEU which had exempted third pillar action from the jurisdiction of the Court. Taking into account that this exemption did not extend to ex-Article M TEU the Court concluded that –

[262] Aliens law provisions covered formal aspects of the admission of persons to the territories of Member States (ex-Article 100c ECT), asylum, external border controls, immigration and related policies (ex-Article K.1(1-3) TEU and related procedural and institutional provisions).

[263] See for instance *Schwartz*, in v.d. Groeben/Thiesing/Ehlermann (eds.), EUV/EGV, 5th ed., vol. 5 (1997) Article 235 para 224.

[264] *Müller-Graff* 31 CML Rev. (1994) 493, 500; *Magiera*, in Burmeister (ed.) Verfassungsstaatlichkeit, Essays in honour of Klaus Stern (1997) 1317, 1335 et seq.

[265] ECJ, judgment of 12 May 1998, case C-170/96, *Commission v Council* (Joint action regarding airport transit visas), case C-170/96, [1998] ECR I-2763.

> [i]t is ... the task of the Court to ensure that acts which, according to the Council, fall within the scope of Article K.3(2) of the Treaty on European Union do not encroach upon the powers conferred by the EC Treaty on the Community.[266]

The Court held, moreover, that it has the power to declare third pillar instruments void[267]. Even if, contrary to a correct systematic interpretation of the Treaty, the jurisdiction of the Court were to cover the issue of whether third-pillar action encroaches upon ECT powers the judgments of the European Court of Justice cannot affect instruments adopted under Maastricht's third pillar. Rather the Court's powers would then be confined to holding that such action infringes upon Community law[268], and replacement of these instruments by Community legislation is left in the hands of the legislative Community institutions[269]. This interpretation is supported from a practical point of view because, in the current legal framework, annulment would terminate the legal effects of existing third pillar instruments vis-à-vis the opt-out Member States even where their content is re-adopted under Title IV ECT.

The reasoning by the Commission and the European Court of Justice implies an extensively interpreted concept of the subject-matter safeguarded by ex-Article M TEU, namely the pre-Maastricht *acquis communautaire*. However, the interpretation of ex-Article M TEU, though correct in itself, was irrelevant for the definition of the pre-Maastricht *acquis communautaire*. Ex-Article M TEU only indicated that the *acquis* has not been affected by the 1991 Treaty on European Union but it did not state which elements actually formed part of this *acquis*. Accordingly, the idea of referring to ex-Article M TEU for the purpose of outlining the scope of powers already conferred upon the Community[270] is inherently flawed. Moreover, ex-Article M TEU only stated that nothing *in* the 1991 Treaty on European Union shall affect the Treaty establishing the European Community. This provision did not, therefore, preclude an influence of the Treaty amendments on the interpretation of ECT powers.

d) The Method of Delineation

The dispute carried on during the Maastricht era shows that the delineation of powers cannot be exclusively based on an interpretation of the pre-existing Treaty and previous techniques used *inter alia* to close alleged or existing loopholes in Community competence. The elements of the pre-existing *acquis communautaire* must be distinguished from such techniques then considered necessary to establish a subsidiary competence of the Community. Generally speaking, interpretation has relied upon –

---

[266] ECJ, judgment of 12 May 1998, case C-170/96, *Commission v Council* (Joint action regarding airport transit visas), case C-170/96, [1998] ECR I-2763 para 16.

[267] ECJ, judgment of 12 May 1998, case C-170/96, *Commission v Council* (Joint action regarding airport transit visas), case C-170/96, [1998] ECR I-2763 paras 15-17. The same conclusion has been reached by *Heukels/de Zwaan*, The configuration of the European Union: Community Dimensions of Interinstitutional Action, in *Curtin/Heukels* (eds.) Institutional Dynamics of European Integration – Essays in Honour of Henry G. Schermers II (1994) 195, 224.

[268] Such infringement has the character of failure to act. See *Müller-Graff* 31 CML Rev. (1994) 493, 505.

[269] Cf. *Koenig/Pechstein*, Die Europäische Union, 2nd ed. (1998) paras 125+261.

[270] This idea seems to underlie, for instance, the article published by *Müller-Graff* 31 CML Rev. (1995) 493. See ibid. 504 et seq.

- a larger number of communiqués released by the Heads of States and Governments,
- action plans and draft legislation forwarded by the Commission,
- EP resolutions,
- a newly developing ECJ jurisprudence on EEC-Turkey Council of Association Decision 1/80 and the Maghreb Co-operation Agreements, and
- the European Court of Justice's judgment of 9 July 1987 on the migration policy competence of the Community[271].

Among these, only ECJ judgments may be considered as authentic interpretation of the *acquis communautaire*. This follows from the fact that, in principle, there are only two actors on the European plane empowered to take action with binding force and, therefore, to define elements of this *acquis*[272]. First, the European Court of Justice may rule that a certain power forms part of this *acquis*. Second, all Member States may effect the same through express amendment to the Community Treaties (like they did in Article 8 of the Schengen Protocol). While the relevance of Council practice as a case of authentic ECT interpretation must be carefully examined, the possibility that amendments to the Community Treaties include, at least implicitly, elements of authentic and binding interpretation, cannot be questioned. In particular, implicit authentic interpretation can address the subject-matter of disputes between the non-judicial organs of the European Union over the current scope of Community law, provided that such disputes were not already resolved by the European Court of Justice prior to the entry into force of relevant amendments to the Treaties. Member States may adopt new provisions which govern an issue similar to items already ruled on by the European Court of Justice, but which apply a different wording and legislative concept to the issue. The Member States show thus that the newly introduced clauses shall be without prejudice to the respective jurisprudence and vice-versa – as evidenced by the *ordre public* exceptions contained in Title IV ECT.

Moreover, where dispute arose over the scope of existing powers conferred upon the Community, Member States could express their common view as to which areas lie beyond the scope of relevant powers. The most indicative way to do so was to attach respective declarations to the Final Act of any treaty amending the existing Community Treaties. However, Member States would certainly not have defined, at the Maastricht intergovernmental conference, core aspects of aliens law as a matter of common interest open to intergovernmental co-operation had they been in agreement that the Community were empowered to act in this area under the pre-existing Treaty provisions[273]. The same is true with respect to the adoption of Title IV ECT within the framework of the Amsterdam Treaty.

For these reasons, the relationship between Title IV ECT and powers otherwise conferred upon the Community must be evaluated on the basis of their co-existence. This co-existence is based on the differentiation between admission of third-country-nationals to the territories of Member States and the regulation of their labour market-related and social status. Therefore Community powers which used to govern the

---

[271] ECJ, judgment of 9 July 1987, joined cases 281, 283, 284, 285 and 287/85, *Germany and others v Commission*, [1987] ECR 3203.

[272] The Commission may adopt subordinate legislation provided that it has been entitled to do so by Community legislation. This kind of Community action which is referred to as "Comitology" plays an important practical role. Cf. *Haibach*, Verwaltungsarchiv 90 (1999) 98-111 including detailed references. Given the construction under primary Community law, however, such competencies of the Commission have exceptional character.

[273] That has also been conceded by *Peers* 35 CML Rev. (1999) 1235, 1236.

status of lawful residents will arguably remain applicable to issues unrelated to European aliens law, as construed by Title IV ECT.

2. *The Common and Internal Market Concepts*

The core aims of the pre-Amsterdam European (Economic) Community are embodied in the common and internal market concepts. The internal market defines the Community as "an area without internal frontiers in which the free movement of [...] persons [...] is ensured". Although it is improbable that freedom of movement will be fully extended to third-country nationals, they will undoubtedly, if only indirectly, reap some of the benefits brought about by the implementation of said freedom for EU citizens[274]. Any complete evaluation of the effects of the internal market concept must thus also examine its effects on third-country nationals.

Unlike the expression "internal market", the term "common market" is not expressly defined in the Treaty. The common market is mentioned in Article 2 ECT as an instrument to achieve the economic and social aims of the Community, including inter alia a "harmonious, balanced and sustainable development of economic activities, a high level of employment and of social protection". The common and internal market concepts are not to be regarded as competing or antagonistic, irrespective of the unclear delimitation[275] between the two. Although they are certainly not identical, they overlap to a certain extent[276]; the internal market concept influences the interpretation of the common market idea, and vice-versa.

Disputes during the Maastricht era revolved around the following questions –

- Were the Member States obliged to abolish internal border controls and, if so, should this goal be reached through Community legislation rather than through intergovernmental co-operation?
- Did the Community have the power to regulate freedom of movement of third-country nationals[277]?

Both issues raised certain questions with regard to the interpretation of Articles 3(c) and 14 ECT (as they now are). These Articles are similar in structure, in that neither expressly answers the question of whether the free movement of persons applies solely to EU citizens. The wording of both articles is somewhat ambiguous. On the one hand, the expression "free movement of persons" contained in Articles 3(c) and 14 ECT is not specifically limited to EU citizens (as they now are)[278]. On the other hand, Article 3(c) ECT states that the Community shall pursue its aims "as provided in this Treaty", and Article 14 ECT stipulates that the internal market is to be established "in accordance with the provisions of this Article and of Articles 15, 26, 47(2), 49, 80, 93 and 95" ECT. These references (which were also part of the Maastricht Treaty) do, however, limit the legislative power of the Community. Consequently, the argument that the free movement of persons is determined by

---

274 Cf. *Hailbronner* 31 CML Rev. (1994) 969, 978.

275 *Bardenhewer/Pipkorn*, in: v.d. Groeben/Thiesing/Ehlermann, EUV/EGV (1997), vol. 1, 5 ed. Article 7a para 6; *de Keersmaeker/Pauwels*, in: Smit/Herzog § 7a.01; *Zacker*, Binnenmarkt und Gemeinsamer Markt – Zwei Begriffe desselben Inhalts?, Recht der internationalen Wirtschaft (RIW) 1989, 489 et seq.

276 Cf. *Bardenhewer/Pipkorn* ibid.

277 Cf. *Hailbronner* 31 CML Rev. (1994) 969, 974-977, including further references.

278 Cf. *Magiera*, in Burmeister (ed.) Verfassungsstaatlichkeit, Essays in honour of Klaus Stern (1997) 1317, 1326.

Treaty provisions relating to market freedoms and therefore refers only to EU citizens – as do market freedoms – seems convincing. The same conclusion can be drawn from Article 18 ECT, which expressly grants freedom of movement solely to EU citizens. Additionally, the fact that ex-Article 7a ECT did not include a reference to ex-Article 100c ECT supports the assumption that the internal market concept did not extend to the status of third-country nationals[279]. Third-country nationals thus benefit only indirectly from the implementation of the internal market, but do not derive any individual rights from the concept as such[280]. Finally, rights (so construed) have in principle not been granted to third-country nationals by virtue of secondary Community law.

The Community is to be transformed into an area without internal borders through the common and internal market concepts. This goal includes the notion of the abolition of internal border controls[281]. It simultaneously contemplates freedom of movement for EU citizens, albeit without prejudice to the legal status of third-country nationals, who benefit indirectly from abolition of internal border controls.

3. Article 310 ECT[282] and Association Agreements

The question of whether certain external powers of the EC cover the adoption of Community legislation governing the status of third-country nationals has been discussed primarily in the context of the EEC-Turkey Association Agreement. The Agreement grants Turkish citizens rights, which cover aspects both of admission to the territories of the EU Member States and of the status of resident Turkish citizens. As the Association Agreement was concluded before the Amsterdam Treaty took effect, it is not affected in its content pursuant to international treaty law.

Article 310 ECT confers far reaching competence on the Community to determine the legal status of third-country nationals within the framework of Association Agreements. According to the Court's judgment in *Demirel*, an Association Agreement creates special, privileged links with a non-member state, which in some respect participates in the Community system[283]. Prior to *Demirel* some authors have suggested that Article 310 ECT merely empowers the Community to conclude

---

[279] Notably ex-Article 3(d) ECT included among the activities of the Community for the purposes set out in Article 2 –

> measures concerning the entry and movement of persons in the internal market *as provided for in Article 100c.*

(emphasis added). In thus providing said Article limited the Community powers relating to the movement of third-country nationals to the items included in Article 100c ECT. It follows *e contrario* that freedom of movement as envisaged in Article 3(c) and ex-Article 7a ECT did not extend to third-country nationals. – For the interrelationship of ex-Articles 3(d) and 100c ECT see the judgment in the airport transit visa case: ECJ, judgment of 12 May 1998, case C-170/96, *Commission v Council* (Joint action regarding airport transit visas), [1998] ECR I-2763.

[280] The same conclusion has been reached in an earlier work. See *Hailbronner* 31 CML Rev. (1994) 969, 977.

[281] Cf. *Magiera*, in Burmeister (ed.) Verfassungsstaatlichkeit, Essays in honour of Klaus Stern (1997) 1317, 1326; *Langeheine*, in Grabitz/Hilf, EUV/EGV, Article 100a para 20; *Stüer*, Personenkontrollen an den europäischen Binnengrenzen und ihr Abbau, 256 et seq.

[282] For a detailed account of the questions of competence posed by Article 310 ECT see *Weber*, Der assoziationsrechtliche Status Drittstaatsangehöriger in der Europäischen Union, 25-37.

[283] See ECJ, judgment of 30 September 1987, case 12/86, *Demirel v Stadt Schwäbisch Gmünd*, [1987] ECR 3719 para 9.

international agreements similar in content to internal Community law[284]. However, it is now standing case-law that Article 310 ECT empowers the Community to make commitments to non-Member States in all areas included in the ECT's scope of application, including freedom of movement[285]. The EEC-Turkey Association Agreement and related instruments and jurisprudence support the principle that similar agreements may cover the issue of freedom of movement of third-country nationals. Detailed regulation of the status of Turkish citizens does not bear specific importance with regard to the interpretation of Article 310 ECT itself, but rather refers to individual provisions of the Agreement and related instruments, e.g. the Council of Association Decision No. 1/80.

Association Agreements have frequently been concluded as "mixed agreements" with Member States participating as signatories since they include provisions governing issues which fall within their competence. Prior to the entry into force of the Amsterdam Treaty certain aspects of migration policy were included in Association Agreements although migration policy as such fell outside the scope of Community competence. The Council has stressed in its resolution of 16 July 1985 on guidelines for a Community policy on migration that –

> matters relating to the access, residence and employment of migrant workers from third countries fall under the jurisdiction of the governments of the Member States, without prejudice to Community agreements concluded with third countries.[286]

Moreover, Interim Agreements concluded with CEECs which have implemented "as speedily as possible"[287] those provisions of the Europe Agreements the conclusion of which falls within the exclusive competence of the Communities according to Article 133 ECT, therefore, do not contain provisions governing immigration matters. Commitments undertaken by the opt-out Member States relating to migration under existing Association Agreements are not affected by the transfer of competence to the Community under Title IV ECT.

According to the European Court of Justice, Association Agreements form an integral part of Community law. This construction, however, does not imply that Community law extends to any matter covered by Association Agreements regardless of whether such matter would fall into Community competence. The European Court of Justice found the source of Community competence in respect of freedom of movement for third-country nationals in the extension of market freedoms to nationals

---

284 *Tomuschat* EuR 1977, 157, 159; *Meessen* EuR 1980, 36, 40 et seq.

285 See ECJ, judgment of 30 September 1987, case 12/86, *Demirel v Stadt Schwäbisch Gmünd,* [1987] ECR 3719 para 9; see also *Weber*, Der assoziationsrechtliche Status Drittstaatsangehöriger in der Europäischen Union, 29 et seq. including further references.

286 See the last paragraph of the Preamble of Council Resolution of 16 July 1985 on guidelines for a Community policy on migration (85/C 186/04), O.J. 1985 C 186/3 = Spanish special edition: Chapter 5 Volume 5 p. 10 = Portuguese special edition: Chapter 5 Volume 5 p. 10.

287 These agreements have been concluded as Interim Agreements on trade and trade-related matters between the European Community, the European Coal and Steel Community and the European atomic Energy Community, of the one part, and the CEECs of the other part. By virtue of the Interim Agreement those provisions of the Europe Agreement on trade and trade-related maters have been implemented "as speedily as possible" (see the fifth paragraph of the Preambles of the Interim Agreements) the conclusion of which falls within the exclusive competence of the Communities as conferred by Article 133 ECT. See *Vörös/Droutsas*, Die Europa-Abkommen, ZfV 1998, 2, 4.

of the associated states by virtue of the relevant Association Agreement[288]. Hence Article 310 ECT must be read as implying the power to regulate migration in Association Agreements by way of reference to market freedoms.

Since the Amsterdam Treaty entered into force, the scopes of Title IV ECT and existing Association Agreements overlap, to a certain extent, in regard of migration. The conflict of law which might arise out of this overlap cannot be solved on the basis of the rule *lex superior derogat legi inferiori* because the legal basis of Community legislation under Title IV ECT enjoys the same hierarchical level as Article 310 ECT which covers provisions related to migration policy as contained in Association Agreements. At first sight, therefore, the similarity in hierarchy might point at a need to apply the rule *lex posterior derogat legi priori* in order to remove the overlap. Taking into account, however, the character of Association Agreements as international treaties, this approach seems to be misleading because it does not take notice of the fact that Association Agreements include a commitment vis-à-vis the associated state to the extent that the Community may indeed make use of its power to regulate all issues of migration as envisaged in the Agreement. On that basis Title IV ECT must be read as not affecting Community competence as part of its power to conclude and implement Association Agreements.

This point of view is supported by the fact that existing Association Agreements were signed before the entry into force of the Amsterdam Treaty and hence form part of the pre-Amsterdam *acquis communautaire*. Since the United Kingdom, Ireland and Denmark are not bound by measures adopted under Title IV ECT previous rights and obligations under Association Agreements remain in force as part of the pre-Amsterdam *acquis*.

Notwithstanding the Anglo-Irish and Danish special positions, legal problems remain as to the future implementation of Association Council decisions. Association Agreements do not only envisage binding action of Association Councils but also provide for non-binding resolutions, or recommendations, of such Councils and for a political dialogue being conducted by the High Contracting Parties. Under the current legal framework the legal basis for implementation of such resolutions must be found in the provisions of Title IV ECT. That might, however, cause problems in respect of the position of the opt-out Member States. The United Kingdom, Ireland and Denmark participate in Association Council decision-making and in all relevant fora for political dialogue with associated states. However, as opt-out Member States they may well object to implementation of Association Council Decisions to the extent that such implementation is based upon Title IV ECT. Notwithstanding the question of whether such conduct were to be qualified as an unfriendly act rather than as an evasion from the obligations under the relevant Association Agreement vis-à-vis the associated state, arguably in cases where political commitments in migration matters require implementation by way of the adoption of Community law, insistence on the opt-out status may be considered as irreconcilable with the loyalty principle of Article 10 ECT. The question therefore arises of whether the United Kingdom and Ireland can be regarded obliged to opt in, for the purpose of implementation of political commitments, as envisaged by Article 3 of the opt-out Protocol.

---

[288] See ECJ, judgment of 30 September 1987, case 12/86, *Demirel v Stadt Schwäbisch Gmünd*, [1987] ECR 3719 para 9. The issue will be dealt with in detail sub specie the legal status of Turkish citizens in Chapter C V 3.

It follows that the adoption of Title IV ECT has not changed the agenda for decisions on migration issues with respect to existing associations since Community competence is not affected by Title IV ECT.

4. The Impact of Market Freedoms on the Status of Third-Country-Nationals

Articles 39-42, 43-48, and 49-55 ECT grant market freedoms to Member State nationals only. Hence, the power vested in the Community to implement the market freedoms never included comprehensive competence allowing it to define the legal status of third-country nationals. Moreover, Article 49(2) ECT expressly makes any extension of the scope of application of the freedom to provide services dependent on a Council decision to this end. To date the Council has only extended the freedom to provide services to EEA and CEEC nationals as provided for in the EEA Agreement and the Europe Agreements, respectively.

The exercise of market freedoms by EU citizens and secondary legislation on the implementation of these freedoms may, however, affect the status of third-country nationals. Most notably, secondary legislation on the implementation of market freedoms includes rules governing the legal status of third-country national family members of EU citizens who exercise their market freedoms[289]. The status thus defined is derivative in nature. Consequently, the European Court of Justice has held that family members of EU citizens who neither live nor work in another Member State do not qualify for the rights granted under this status[290].

In addition to family ties, employment relationships also allow third-country nationals to benefit indirectly from the exercise of market freedoms by EU citizens. No Community legislation currently exists in this field, recent Commission proposals still pending[291]. The European Court of Justice, however, has handed down a number of judgments which deal with the indirect effects of the freedom to provide services on the status of third-country national employees. The Court held that Articles 49 and 50 ECT give enterprises established in another Member State the right to provide services by way of posting third-country nationals who are part of the regular work force in the Member State of their establishment. Therefore, Member States may not impose work permit requirements[292]. The Court's reasoning suggests that the requirement to obtain work permits as such – not only the financial burden caused by fees or fines – runs counter to Articles 49 and 50 ECT[293]. The Court did not however rule on the question of whether the host State may require undertakings to obtain documents permitting entry and residence for their third-country national workers. In

---

289 Cf. Articles 10-12 of Regulation 1612/68.

290 See ECJ, judgment of 27 October 1982, joined cases 35 and 36/82, *Morson and Jhanjan v The Netherlands*, [1982] ECR 3723 paras 14-18; judgment of 8 December 1987, case 20/87, *Ministère public v André Gauchard*, [1987] ECR 4879 paras 10-13; cf. judgment of 18 March 1980, case 52/79, *Debauve*, [1980] ECR 833 para 9.

291 Commission Proposals of 12 February 1999 for a Directive on the posting of workers who are third-country nationals for the provision of cross-border services, O.J. 1999 C 67/12; and for a Directive extending the freedom to provide cross-border services to third-country nationals established within the Community, OJ 1999 C 67/17. These proposals are discussed in detail *infra* C I.

292 ECJ, judgment of 9 August 1994, case C-43/93, *Vander Elst v Office des migrations internationales*, [1994] ECR I-3803, para 27.

293 ECJ, judgment of 9 August 1994, case C-43/93, *Vander Elst v Office des migrations internationales*, [1994] ECR I-3803 paras 18-22. See *Khan*, EuZW 1994, 602

principle, therefore, Member States continue to be competent to implement immigration control measures which they deem necessary[294].

Which principles can be derived from this jurisprudence? First and foremost, market freedoms entitle EU citizen as holders of rights. The legal standing of third-country nationals may thus be weak, and render attempts to claim independent rights as family members of EU citizens or employees unsuccessful. The European Court of Justice seems to have reached a similar conclusion when assessing the external Community competence to conclude the GATS agreement. The Court held that "attainment of freedom of establishment and freedom to provide services for nationals of the Member States *is not inextricably linked to the treatment to be afforded in the Community to nationals of non-member countries* ..."[295]. The Community is competent, however, to regulate the position of third-country nationals as a necessary element of the market freedoms. This is shown by the inclusion of family members into the freedom of movement for workers. An observation of the European Court of Justice contained in the GATS opinion also supports this view. According to the Court –

> [a]lthough the only objective expressly mentioned in the chapters on the right of establishment and on freedom to provide services is the attainment of those freedoms for nationals of the Member States of the Community, it does not follow that the Community institutions are prohibited from using the powers conferred on them in that field in order to specify the treatment which is to be accorded to nationals of non-member countries[296].

The European Court of Justice then refers to several pieces of Community legislation none of which, however, includes provisions that expressly allow for the free movement of third-country nationals[297].

Community law as it stands can therefore be interpreted in such a way that implementation of the freedom to provide services and the freedom of establishment may include certain effects, direct or indirect, of such freedoms vis-à-vis third-country nationals. The European Court of Justice has, however, not defined which effects fall within Community competence under Articles 44 and 47(2) ECT. It is submitted that only indirect effects do so, as far as free movement of third-country nationals is concerned. In the GATS opinion the Court merely observed that, under these Articles "[i]t is evident from an examination of those acts that very different objectives may be pursued ..."[298]. It seems, however, that facilitating the movement of third-country nationals within the European Union is no objective that may be pursued in the course

[294] For a detailed analysis of the impact of freedom to provide services on third-country nationals cf. *infra* C V.

[295] ECJ-opinion 1/94 of 15 November 1994, *Competence of the Community to Conclude International Agreements Concerning Services and the Protection of Intellectual Property* (GATS and TRIPS), [1994] ECR I-5276 para 86 (emphasis added).

[296] ECJ-opinion 1/94 of 15 November 1994, *Competence of the Community to Conclude International Agreements Concerning Services and the Protection of Intellectual Property* (GATS and TRIPS), [1994] ECR I-5276 para 90.

[297] Cf. ECJ-opinion 1/94 of 15 November 1994, *Competence of the Community to Conclude International Agreements Concerning Services and the Protection of Intellectual Property* (GATS and TRIPS), [1994] ECR I-5276 paras 92-94.

[298] ECJ-opinion 1/94 of 15 November 1994, *Competence of the Community to Conclude International Agreements Concerning Services and the Protection of Intellectual Property* (GATS and TRIPS), para 91.

of interpreting the freedom of establishment and the freedom to provide services. It is rather doubtful whether Article 3(d) ECT has defined the facilitation of movement of third-country nationals to qualify as an independent objective of the Community. Moreover, said provision expressly renders all relevant policies subject to Title IV ECT.

In addition, a distinction must be drawn between the market freedoms here discussed. The indirect effects of the freedom to provide services vis-à-vis third-country nationals are rather small. Establishment, however, aims at permanent incorporation into the economic system of the Member State in which Union citizens choose to take up self-employed activity. One may imagine that the indirect effect of importing a business implies that third-country national employees essential for running the business were able to move. The European Court has not yet decided whether the freedom of establishment does have such indirect effects vis-à-vis third-country nationals as part of the freedom of establishment of EU-citizens and EU-companies.

5. Article 94 ECT (ex-Article 100 ECT)

Free movement of people falls within the ambit of the concept of the internal market. Usually, Community legislation designed to approximate the legal systems in the Member States in order to facilitate the functioning of the internal market can be adopted under Article 95 ECT. Freedom of movement, however, under Article 95(2) ECT is excluded from the scope of application of Article 95(1) ECT[299].

Article 94 ECT, however, enables the Community to enact directives for the approximation of such laws, regulations or administrative provisions of the Member States as directly affect the establishment or functioning of the common market[300]. Under the Amsterdam Treaty there can be no doubt that the internal market concept makes the abolition of internal border controls an objective of the Community.

The United Kingdom has, however, denied this aim in the past, as well as during the Amsterdam Intergovernmental Conference[301]. The controversy was finally resolved by means of the Protocol on the application of certain aspects of Article 14 (ex-Article 7a) of the Treaty establishing the European Community to the United Kingdom and to Ireland. This Protocol authentically interprets Article 14 ECT[302]. Under the Protocol, the United Kingdom may no longer maintain its view that the abolition of internal border controls is not an objective of the Community while, at the same time, this objective does not have any legal effects vis-à-vis the United Kingdom and Ireland.

Additionally, border controls on non-EU citizens must be renounced if border controls on persons enjoying freedom of movement are to be efficiently abolished[303]. Even though, *prima facie*, the abolition of internal border controls only serves the freedom of movement of EU citizens, third-country nationals will derive *de facto*

---

299 See *Hailbronner* 31 CML Rev. (1994) 969, 984.

300 This view is supported by *Taschner*, in v.d. Groeben/Thiesing/Ehlermann, EUV/EGV, vol. 2/II, 5th ed. (1999), Vorbemerkungen zu Article 100-102 EGV para 3.

301 A Partnership of Nations, The British Approach to the European Union Intergovernmental Conference 1996 at 23.

302 Cf. *Shaw* 4 ELJ (1998) 63, 76.

303 *Hailbronner* 31 CML Rev. (1994) 969, 977.

benefits. In particular, Member States will have to deal with major practical difficulties in enforcing, at their intra-EU borders, restrictions on the entry of third-country nationals lawfully resident in another Member State. In order to maintain a sufficient level of security, compensatory measures will obviously have to be implemented in the absence of border controls. In that respect the Commission has alleged that ex-Article 100 ECT was a suitable legal basis for Community action in the field of European aliens law (as it now is) on two occasions. First, it submitted a proposal for a Council directive concerning the approximation of the legislation of Member States as early as in 1978, in order to combat illegal migration and illegal employment[304]. Second, in July 1995, it submitted proposals for directives concerning free movement of third-country nationals and the abolition of controls on persons at internal borders[305]. Although the view of the Commission is shared by some authors[306] the Council did not agree to the position that free movement for third-country nationals is an objective of the Community and, thus, did not adopt any of the aforementioned proposals.

Article 94 ECT allows for Community action only in the approximation of provisions which directly affect the establishment or functioning of the common market. Interpretation of this provision must have due regard to the fact that free movement for all persons regardless of their nationality is not in itself an objective of the Community. In any event since Title IV ECT has been inserted Article 94 ECT may no longer be applied as a legal basis for the areas covered by this Title according to the principle *lex specialis derogat legi generali.* Conclusively, Article 94 ECT cannot be considered as conferring comprehensive competence in the field of asylum and immigration policy on the Community.

6. *Article 308 ECT (ex-Article 235 ECT)*

Article 308 ECT functions as a subsidiary power for the adoption of measures aimed at achieving Community objectives where the Treaty does not expressly provide for such adoption[307]. Although the exact conditions for the application of Article 308 ECT are controversial – the only true limit may be the prohibition of Treaty amendments[308] – the subsidiary character of Article 308 ECT is undisputed. The European Court of Justice upholds the subsidiarity of this article in that it held that Article 308 ECT –

---

[304] COM(78)86 final, O.J. 1978 C 97/9. The Commission proposal conceded that the EEC Treaty (as it then was) did not expressly provide for Community action aimed at combating illegal migration.

[305] COM(95)346 final and COM(95)347 final.

[306] See, for instance, *Bardenhewer/Pipkorn*, in v.d. Groeben/Thiesing/Ehlermann, EUV/EGV, vol. 2/II, 5th ed. (1999), Vorbemerkungen zu Article 100-102 EGV para 3.

[307] *Schwartz*, in v.d. Groeben/Thiesing/Ehlermann EUV/EGV Art 235 EGV para 2. In its opinion 2/94, Accession by the Community to the European Convention for the Protection of Human Rights and Fundamental Freedoms, [1996] ECR I-1759 para 29 the ECJ speaks of gap-filling. See also ECJ-opinion 2/92 of 24 March 1995, *Competence of the Community or one of its institutions to participate on the third Revised decision of the OECD on national treatment*, [1995] ECR I-521 para 36: ex-Article 235 ECT "enables the Community to cope with any insufficiency in the powers conferred on it"; ECJ-opinion 1/94 of 15 November 1994, *Competence of the Community to Conclude International Agreements Concerning Services and the Protection of Intellectual Property* (GATS and TRIPS), [1994] ECR I-5267 para 89.

[308] See ECJ-opinion 2/94 of 28 March 1995, *Accession by the Community to the European Convention for the Protection of Human Rights and Fundamental Freedoms*, [1996] ECR I-1759. For the opposite view cf. *Grabitz*, in Grabitz/Hilf, EUV/EGV (1986), Article 235 para 4.

> being an integral part of an inter-institutional system based on the principle of conferred powers, cannot serve as a basis for widening the scope of Community powers beyond the general framework created by the provisions of the [ECT] as a whole and, in particular, by those provisions that define the tasks and the activities of the Community[309].

Title IV ECT clearly defines the tasks and activities in the field of European aliens law in a limited manner. This fact, in conjunction with the cautious, non-comprehensive approach taken by Member States, leaves little room for gap-filling[310] after the entry into force of the Amsterdam Treaty.

7. *Social Rights: Article 137 ECT*

Article 137 ECT, unlike its predecessor ex-Article 118 ECT, contains a special provision dealing with Community action in the field of the social rights of third-country nationals. Article 137(3), fourth indent ECT expressly provides for measures governing "the conditions of employment for third-country nationals legally residing in Community territory". Due to its limited wording the scope of application of this Article is confined to measures governing the admission of third-country nationals to the labour market[311]. It does not include admission to Member States' territories, and must not be regarded as a legal basis for European aliens law. There is a clear difference between the admission of legally resident aliens, which is a common feature of national law, to the labour market of respective Member States, and their admission to the territory.

8. *Anti-Discrimination: Article 13 ECT*

Finally, Article 13 ECT may be viewed as a source of Community powers in the field of European aliens law. This Article provides for "appropriate action to combat discrimination based on sex, racial or ethnic origin, religion or belief, disability, age or sexual orientation". Indeed the European (Economic) Community has passed some soft law which deals with aspects of both migration and anti-discrimination. Included among these are –

- Declaration against racism and xenophobia[312],
- Resolution of the Council and the representatives of Member States' Governments meeting within the Council on the response of educational systems to the problems of racism and xenophobia[313], and

---

309 See ECJ-opinion 2/94 of 28 March 1996, *Accession by the Community to the European Convention for the Protection of Human Rights and Fundamental Freedoms*, [1996] ECR I-1759 para 30.

310 Cf. *Hailbronner/Thiery* EuR 1998, 583, 587.

311 Accordingly, the view taken by, *Thun-Hohenstein,* Der Vertrag von Amsterdam (1998), 36 that Article 63(4) ECT were covering measures relating to the admission of third-country nationals to the labour market seems to be rather dubious.

312 O.J. 1986 C 158/1.

313 O.J. 1995 C 312/1.

- Resolution of the Council and the representatives of the governments of the Member States, meeting within the Council concerning the European Year against Racism (1997)[314].

These should not, however, be regarded as model instruments for Community action in the field of European aliens law. Though it allows for action in all potential areas of discrimination currently en vogue, Article 13 ECT has substantially limited the scope of anti-discrimination legislation in several ways. First, the power is limited to provisions created "without prejudice to the other provisions of this Treaty". Article 13 ECT thus does not take precedence over existing Articles, such as Articles 12 or 141 ECT[315]. Second, the Community may only adopt measures based on Article 13 ECT "within the limits of powers conferred by it upon the Community". This phrase has given rise to two possible interpretations[316]. An extensive interpretation reads the phrase "within the limits of the powers" as a reference to the fundamental rules regulating the limits of powers of the institutions in relation to one another, and to the limited compentencies of the Community in areas reserved for the third pillar of the European Union. This interpretation grants the Community a comprehensive power to combat racism in all fields, even those beyond the scope of application of the Treaty[317]. According to a more restrictive interpretation, which is granted by the wording of the provision and its systematic context, the phrase "within the limits of the powers conferred by *it*" (emphasis added) refers to the ECT itself. Article 13 ECT thus empowers the Community to enact anti-discrimination legislation solely in areas in which the Treaty has entrusted the Community with regulatory powers[318]. The Community thus can only pass anti-discrimination regulations in connection with other powers conferred upon it by the Treaty. Read in conjunction with Article 137 ECT, which confers some powers to the Community in its regulation of working conditions, Article 13 ECT might allow the Community to adopt a directive against racism and discrimination in the workplace[319]. Other areas which may be drawn upon are employment, education, culture, and media policies[320].

Finally, Article 13 ECT may play a role in the implementation of Title IV ECT. This does not mean, however, that the Community were obliged to follow a policy of non-differentiation as to the nationality of third-country nationals. Nationality is not mentioned in the catalogue of Article 13 ECT. In addition, Title IV ECT allows the Community a wide amount of discretion with regard to the determination of rights of entry and residence of third-country nationals. Implicit in Title IV ECT is delineation between different kinds of immigrants, e.g. asylum seekers, displaced persons and persons interested in entry into the EU for other reasons (see Article 63(1-3) ECT). Consequently, the adoption of anti-discrimination measures into European aliens law is limited to questions of non-discrimination in the regulation of given status and procedures, but as a rule does not affect the EU's power to grant access to such status

---

[314] O.J. 1996 C 237/1.

[315] Cf. *Langrish*, The Treaty of Amsterdam: Selected highlights, EL Rev. (1998), 3, 15.

[316] Cf. *Bell*, EU Anti-Discrimination Policy, EP working document, Lib 102 en, 02, (1998), 20 et seq.

[317] This interpretation is shared by *Chopin I. and Niessen J.* (eds.), Proposals for Legislative Measures to Combat, Racism and to Promote Equal Rights in the European Union, (1998), 22.

[318] This interpretation is preferred by *Bell*, EU Anti-Discrimination Policy, EP working document, Lib 102 en, 02, 1998, p. 20 and *Langrish*, The Treaty of Amsterdam: Selected Highlights, EL Rev. (1998), 3, 15.

[319] Cf. *Bell*, EU Anti-Discrimination Policy, EP working document, Lib 102 en, 02, (1998), 20.

[320] Cf. the proposals in the Commission's Action-Plan against Racism, COM(98)183 final, 12 et seq.

and procedures, provided, however, that such regulations are not based upon criteria such as race, colour etc. prohibited by human rights instruments.

Outside the scope of market freedoms, the Community maintains the power conferred upon it by the ECJ in conjunction with Association Agreements. In addition, Article 137 ECT allows for Community legislation aimed at integration into the workforce. It is questionable to what extent the provision covers integration of foreign workers into society; its wording is confined to the regulation of "conditions of employment". Responsibility for social and cultural integration has been left to the Member States. Given the wide variety between the societies of the Member States, this conclusion is supported by the subsidiarity principle. An exact borderline, however, may be difficult to draw. Furthermore, the Community does not have the power to use the anti-discrimination policy as a basis for extending rights or privileges under national law to third-country nationals. The powers conferred upon the Community beyond the scope of the market freedoms are thus limited in nature.

XIV. Outlook: Policy Questions Related to Further Supranationalization

Title IV ECT has been called a "labyrinth of new articles and protocols which present the most complex legal challenge of the new Treaty"[321]. As this chapter has shown, however, there are a number of 'red lines' which reduce the complexity of Title IV ECT. In addition, some policy questions, such as the adjustment of procedures after the expiration of the transitional period, and items not covered by Title IV ECT, have been left unsolved by Title IV ECT. These policies must eventually be regulated on the basis of common principles.

From an 'integrationist' point of view, the position of the European Parliament may still be regarded as too weak in the field of European aliens law. However, the consultation procedure under Title IV ECT improves the position of the European Parliament considerably, if compared to its role under the framework of Maastricht's third pillar. One might ask whether this improvement of parliamentary control on the European level is sufficient, given the importance and scope of the instruments provided for by Title IV ECT. In other words, are questions of immigration and asylum, as opposed to visa policy and technical questions of border-crossing, issues to be dealt with in democratic procedures at the supranational, rather than the national level? Title IV ECT cannot be used as the basis of an answer in the affirmative, even in light of its expansive position with regard to further procedural supranationalization. Title IV ECT, it should be noted, has not fully done away with the Member States' prerogative with respect to immigration and asylum policies, but only provides for the establishment of minimum standards. Its objective is not the kind of supranational integration typical of the European process in many other areas. It follows that there is still a need for parliamentary control of the Member States' executive power. National parliaments have made major efforts to improve their position vis-à-vis their governments throughout the course of European integration[322], rendering the argument that control by national parliaments is, by nature, ineffective, unconvincing. On the

[321] *Langrish* 23 EL Rev. (1998) 3, 7.

[322] For instance the German houses of parliament have far-reaching rights under Article 23 of the Basic Law and the federal statutes implementing this Article.

other hand, the introduction of co-decision procedures in Title IV matters will undoubtedly decrease the national parliaments' powers once core issues of immigration and asylum policies will be decided on the European level.

The central question with respect to the role of the European Court of Justice remains the establishment of a framework for future preliminary rulings. Will a regular procedure on referrals for preliminary rulings be introduced after the expiration of the transitional period? As the purpose of preliminary rulings is, *inter alia*, to strengthen the rights granted under Community law, the answer arguably depends on whether rights of third-country nationals are efficiently protected under the present construction. One may argue that the extension of the Court's jurisdictional powers to matters hitherto subject to national sovereignty may well exceed the Court's capacity. The Court so far has shown only little enthusiasm to guarantee an effective protection of individual rights of EU citizens against the EU-regulatory power. It remains to be seen whether the Court will change its perception of the EU legal order with the extension of EU-powers far beyond economic matters into areas closely connected with fundamental rights.

Title IV ECT, as inserted by the Amsterdam Treaty, does not speak of issues such as transnational enforcement of expulsion and deportation. Additionally, it does not envisage explicitly measures aimed at the prevention of migration movements.[323] As these loopholes cannot be closed through the application of Articles 94 and 308 ECT, the only possible way to reach a common approach will be to act outside the single institutional framework of the European Union[324]. Specific aspects of migration movement prevention can be dealt with in the framework of the second pillar. The establishment of a strong connection between Community legislation and related international treaties concluded by Member States in 'gap' areas will promote this process. Various techniques support a legislative process at the national level through which Member States could combine the implementation of given EU directives with the ratification of related treaties, thereby minimizing the amount of time necessary for the ratification process. The entry into force of a piece of Community legislation, for instance, could be made dependent on, or suspended until all Member States have ratified the accompanying international instrument. One might also consider adopting parallel time limits for ratification and implementation. The idea of setting time-limits, it should be noted, is not new to this field. Article 1(1) of the draft Council decision establishing the Convention on the crossing of the external frontiers of the Member States contained a recommendation that the Member States adopt this Convention within a given time-limit. In its explanatory memorandum, the Commission argued that a time-limit would serve the effectiveness of the recommendation given by the Council, pursuant to ex-Article K.3(2) TEU[325].

---

[323] Cf. *Hailbronner* 35 CML Rev. (1998) 1047, 1048.

[324] Cf. *Hailbronner/Thiery* EuR 1998, 583, 587.

[325] COM(93)684 final, 8. See also *Hailbronner*, in Hailbronner/Klein/Magiera/Müller-Graff, EUV/EGV (1996), Article K para 101.

C

Immigration Law – Entry and Sojourn

I. The Need to Develop a Coherent System of European Immigration Law

1. European Immigration Law After Amsterdam: An Overview

Currently, at the European level immigration law comprises –

- a common visa regime,
- common requirements for the crossing of external borders,
- common standards for border controls, and
- common conditions governing the movement of third-country nationals within the European Union.

Relevant instruments are not yet based upon a coherent approach since they originate from different sources and enjoy diverging legal force. Moreover, different actors have applied various underlying policy concepts. In particular, the Schengen States have to a significantly larger extent been ready to enter into binding legal commitments than those Member States whose participation in the adoption of immigration law instruments was confined to the options available under the Maastricht regime. Nevertheless, the Schengen States are far from forming a homogeneous group. The Danish opt-out is the most significant rather than the sole example for the differences in policy approaches. Notwithstanding individual disputes on policy questions, however, communitarization of aliens law under Title IV ECT has made way for adapting the existing provisions and instruments to a uniform concept. In doing so the Community will substantially have to build on the law as it stands. Integration into the framework of the European Union and attribution to EU legal bases of the Schengen *acquis*, which contributes to all aspects of European aliens law mentioned *supra*, has been a major step in this process.

Pending the publication of the communitarized parts of the Schengen *acquis* in the Official Journal of the European Communities it is hardly possible to give detailed account of the law in force. Examination must therefore mainly focus on the Schengen Convention itself.

Moreover, pending the decision on the Anglo-Irish opt-in with respect to certain issues covered by the Schengen acquis some uncertainties remain in regard of the interaction of Community and third pillar instruments adopted during the Maastricht era on the one hand and the Schengen acquis on the other where this acquis would supplement existing regimes.

Finally, the instruments concerned do not govern entry and sojourn of refugees because the Community is bound to respect this Convention under Article 63(1)(a) ECT. Additionally, the second paragraph of Article 5(2) SIC states that entry conditions "shall not preclude the application of special provisions concerning the right of asylum".

2. *The Creation of the Internal Market as the Objective of the Schengen Implementation Convention*

The Schengen Implementation Convention has been an instrument aimed at breaking up the deadlock in EU policy-making with respect to the abolition of internal border controls and compensatory measures which had occurred due to severe disputes between Member States with respect to the scope of the internal market concept. Thus, France and Germany initiated a pressure group of some Member States which agreed to reach the aim of an "area without internal frontiers" on an intergovernmental basis. From the outset, however, the task of this pressure group had been to advance the Community concept of internal market as they understood it. The communitarization of the outcome of the Schengen States' efforts, the Schengen *acquis*, is the 'keystone' of this process. The now communitarized Schengen Agreements originate from the Saarbrücken Agreement signed between France and Germany on 13 July 1984[1]. This Agreement envisaged the gradual removal of the common frontier controls between both States. The Benelux States were later associated with this initiative. On 14 June 1985, the governments of the States of the Benelux Economic Union, the Federal Republic of Germany and the French Republic signed the Agreement on the gradual abolition of checks at their common borders (henceforth referred to as 'the Schengen Agreement'). The Schengen Agreement is a primarily political document, in which the Contracting Parties express the will to decide on future common measures concerning the abolition of the internal border controls[2]. The Agreement took effect immediately after signature. On 19 June 1990 the Schengen States signed the Convention, implementing the Agreement on the gradual abolition of checks at their common borders[3]. All Member States of the European Union except for the United Kingdom and Ireland have acceded to the Schengen

---

[1] Bundesgesetzblatt (BGBl) II 1984, 768.

[2] The Schengen Agreement denominates two categories of objectives. In the short term, the easing of the common frontier controls between the Contracting Parties was to be achieved. Since 15 June 1985, the internal border controls of the Schengen States have no longer been systematic. In order to remove the congestion from the person and goods traffic the customs authorities were carrying out simple visual checks on private vehicles crossing the common borders at a reduced speed without requiring such vehicles to stop. Theoretically this measure should only apply to EU citizens. In the long run, the Agreement envisaged the abolition of the internal border controls on all persons, whatever their origin, and with regard to that aim it contains a large scale programme to compensate the abolition of the border controls. This second objective is the subject-matter of the Schengen Convention.

[3] 30 ILM (1991), 68. See *supra* Chapter B III 3 for further references. A detailed analysis of the Schengen Agreements is undertaken in the following literature: *Joubert & Bevers*, Schengen Investigated: A Comparative Interpretation of the Schengen Provisions on International Police Cooperation in the Light of the European Convention on Human Rights (1996); *O'Keefe*, YEL 1991, 185-221; *Schutte*, 28 CML Rev. (1991), 549-570; *Whitaker*, Georgetown Immigration Law Journal 6 (1992), 191-222; *Würz*, Das Schengener Durchführungsübereinkommen (1997); *Meijers et al.* (eds.), Schengen: Internationalisation of Central Chapters of the Law on Aliens, Refugees, Privacy, Security and the Police (1991); *Nanz* in Bieber/Monar (eds.), Justice and Home Affairs in the European Union, The development of the third pillar, (1995), 29-48.

Agreements[4], prior to the entry into force of the Amsterdam Treaty. Additionally, Iceland and Norway have entered into an association with the Schengen States[5].

Schengen States have concluded the Implementation Convention in order to achieve progress in establishing the area without internal frontiers as envisaged by Article 14 (ex-Article 7a) ECT. This is indicated in the Preamble of the Schengen Convention which expressly states that "the aim pursued by the Contracting Parties coincides with that objective". Since the Schengen Convention became operative on 26 March 1995[6] the common borders of a growing number of Member States may be crossed, at any point, by EU citizens and EEA nationals, as well as citizens of any third country legally present in the Schengen territory, without any form of identity control (Article 2(1) SIC). Originally, the area without internal borders comprised the Benelux states, Germany, France, Spain and Portugal. Subsequently, the Schengen Convention became operative for Italy on 26 October 1997 and for Austria and Greece on 1 December 1997[7]. However, Greece initially only enacted the SIS. Finally, pursuant to Article 2(1) of the Schengen Protocol the Schengen *acquis* now applies to all Member States except for the United Kingdom and Ireland.

The Schengen Implementation Convention had also been an answer to the deadlock of the draft Convention on the crossing of the external frontiers of the Member States in the Council. Immigration ministers had broken off their negotiations on an early draft in June 1991[8]. In December 1993 the Commission

---

4 Cf. the Accession Protocols and Agreements to the 1985 Agreement and the 1990 Implementation Convention with Italy (signed in Paris on 27 November 1990, BGBl. II 1997, 1530), Spain and Portugal (both signed in Bonn on 25 June 1991, BGBl. II 1993, 1902), Greece (signed in Madrid on 6 November 1992, BGBl. II 1996, 2542), Austria (signed in Brussels on 28 April 1995, BGBl II 1997, 966) and Denmark, Finland and Sweden (all signed in Luxembourg on 19 December 1996: Federal Ministry of the Interior (ed.), Schengen-Erfahrungsbericht 1996, 31).

5 The original cooperation agreements signed in Luxembourg on 19 December 1996 are reproduced in *Taschner*, Schengen – Die Übereinkommen zum Abbau der Personenkontrolle an den Binnengrenzen von EU-Staaten (1997), annex 4, 38; see also *Agence Europe* No 6880, 4. The participation of the so-called Northern Union of Scandinavian countries in the SIC created difficulties as under Art 140 SIC only EU countries are entitled to join.

6 The Schengen Convention became operative on 26 March 1995 (see Joint Statement 1(2) of the Final Act of the SIC). The Convention distinguishes between the entering into force (the point at which the contracting parties become bound in international law; internal effectiveness, Art 139, second sentence SIC) and the bringing into force (the point at which the member states actually begin to apply the agreement; external effectiveness). Whilst the Schengen Convention came into force for the Benelux countries, France and Germany on 01 September 1993 (cf. Bundesgesetzblatt, BGBl II 1994, 631), the Executive Committee was not able to establish that seven of the ten Contracting Parties fulfilled the conditions for the application of the agreement until 22 December 1994, and hence pass a resolution to bring the Convention into force, cf. Bulletin der Bundesregierung No. 3, 13 January 1995, 16; Bekanntmachung, 19 December 1995, Bundesgesetzblatt, BGBl II 1996, 242; *Beinhofer*, Bayerische Verwaltungsblätter (BayVBl) 1995, 194. The date set, 26 March 1995, was chosen in consideration of the need of airlines to rearrange flights. Since this date, travellers on internal flights in the Schengen area are no longer subject to identity controls.

7 Decision by the Schengen Executive Committee, 7 October 1997, 2; press information of the BMI (Federal Ministry of the Interior), 7 October 1997.

8 Although the Ministers responsible for immigration had reached agreement on a set of principles in June 1991, which were given formal shape in a Convention, a difference arose in the final stage of negotiations between the United Kingdom and Spain over the territorial application of the Convention with regard to Gibraltar. The point of disagreement was how controls at the port and at the airport

submitted a revised draft of the Convention which took account of the developments after the immigration ministers had broken off their negotiations[9]. The Commission intended, by means of the draft convention, to establish an external borders regime within the framework of Maastricht's third pillar which would have superseded the parallel Schengen regime. However, the Council did not reach consensus on the new draft. The Amsterdam Treaty gave way out of the dilemma in integrating the Schengen acquis into the framework of the European Union, though subject to the territorial limitations resulting from the United Kingdom's and Ireland's unwillingness to participate in the full abolition of internal border controls. In the meantime the Council has attributed the Schengen border regime to legal bases in Community law and has thus communitarized the common external borders regime of the Member States participating in the closer co-operation established under the Schengen Protocol. (These Member States will henceforth be referred to as 'the Schengen States'. In contrast, those States in relation to which the Schengen Convention was operative before the entry into force of the Amsterdam Treaty will be referred to as 'the Schengen group'.) Accordingly, the draft External Borders Convention has become obsolete[10].

A large number of compensatory measures for the removal of the filter function of border controls[11] has been agreed upon in order to prevent the emergence of security deficits due to the realization of free movement of persons within the area comprising Schengen States' territories. The compensatory measures directly related to immigration law are[12] –

---

situated on the Isthmus of Gibraltar should be organised. Both Spain and the United Kingdom feared that the solution might have repercussions on the status of Gibraltar. See Bull.EC (1990) No. 6, para 2.2.1 for the first draft which had been done by the ad hoc immigration group following the program approved by the Madrid European Council ("Palma Document").

9 COM(93)684 final, O.J. 1994 C 11/6. The 1993 draft adapted the earlier draft in line with the requirements of the Treaty on European Union and the European Economic Area (EEA) Agreement. The 1993 draft did not touch the issue of territorial application, thus leaving the dispute over Gibraltar to bilateral solution. Besides technical problems, Member States were also in dispute over the question whether the European Court of Justice should have jurisdiction over the Convention. This jurisdiction was opposed by Spain and Britain, who fear that such a competence would lead to a considerable increase in the workload of the ECJ, and a delay in national proceedings. See Doc. 7574/96 ASIM 80; for the problems of the competence of the ECJ cf. *Hailbronner*, 31 CML Rev. (1994) 969, 989. Finally, for the necessary exchange of information on persons to whom entry into EU territory may not be granted, operation of the Convention on the crossing of the external frontiers of the Member States would have required a European Information System (EIS) parallel to the Schengen Information System (SIS). Cf. *Nanz* in Pauly (ed.), De Schengen à Maastricht (1996), 61, 71 et seq.

10 The Action Plan of the Council and the Commission (O.J. 1999 C 19/1) does not, therefore, envisage the adoption of any measures formerly proposed in the draft External Borders Convention.

11 Whether and how far border controls in fact perform such a filter function is debatable, cf. *Kühne*, Kriminalitätsbekämpfung durch innereuropäische Grenzkontrollen (1991), 41 et seq., wherein the qualitative and quantitative effect is assessed as negligible; also *Weichert*, Informationsbrief Ausländerrecht (InfAuslR) 1990, 258, who nonetheless concedes that border controls are of not insignificant importance as an instrument under aliens law; for the opposing argument see *Lenhard*, Schriftenreihe der Polizei – Führungsakadamie (PFA) 3-4 (1989), 34; *Lintner*, Seminar der PFA, 15-17 June 1992 – Rechtsfragen im Zusammenhang mit dem Schengener Abkommen und seinen praktischen Auswirkungen, 116, supports the filter function of border controls, but does not believe them to be the only effective means of fulfilling this function.

12 The other so-called accompanying measures are directed towards:

- the implementation of uniform principles governing external border controls (Articles 3-8 SIC),
- the adoption of a common visa regime (Articles 9-18 SIC, now superseded by Regulations 1683/95 and 574/99 within their respective scopes of application), and
- the implementation of common conditions gverning the movement of third-country nationals within the area comprising Schengen States' territories.

Since the attribution to EU legal bases relevant SIC provisions constitute the core of the measures aimed at establishing an area of freedom, security and justice.

II. Crossing External and Internal Borders

1. General Requirements for the Crossing of External Borders

a) General Principles and Definitions

Article 3(1) SIC provides that "external borders may in principle be crossed only at border crossing points and during the fixed opening hours"[13]. Definitions of the concepts applied in this provisions are contained in Article 1 SIC under which –

- External borders shall mean the [Schengen States'][14] land and sea borders and their air and sea ports, provided they are not internal borders[15].
- Border Crossing point shall mean any crossing point authorized by the competent authorities for the crossing of external borders.

The principle embodies in Article 3(1) SIC applies regardless of nationality. The (former) Executive Committee[16] has adopted more detailed provisions, exceptions

---

- The intensification of co-operation between national police forces, particularly in the field of hot pursuit and observation (Articles 39-47 SIC)
- Judicial co-operation regarding mutual assistance (Articles 48-58 SIC) and extradition (Articles 59-66 SIC) and the handing over of criminals (Articles 67-69 SIC)
- co-operation in the fight against drugs (Articles 70-76 SIC)
- the creation of a central databank of people and objects (Schengen Information System, SIS, Articles 92-119 SIC).

[13] Article 3(1), first sentence SIC; Article 2(1) EBC; for this duty see § 59(1) of the German Aliens Act (Ausländergesetz) for Aliens; § 3 of the German Passport Act (Paßgesetz) for Germans.

[14] As a matter of principle references to 'the Schengen States' have been substituted for references to 'the Contracting Parties' in all quotations from the Schengen Convention because since the communitarization of this Convention Schengen States are no longer in the position of 'Contracting Parties' of this instrument as this term implies in the usage of international law.

[15] Unter Article 1 SIC, "[i]nternal borders shall mean the common land borders of [Schengen States], their airports for internal flights and their sea ports for regular trans-shipment connections exclusively from or to other ports within the territories of [Schengen States] not calling at any ports outside those territories".

[16] The Executive Committee used to be an intergovernmental authority. According to the first sub-paragraph of Article 2(1) of the Schengen Protocol the Council has been substituted for the Executive Committee. The latter's task was to implement the Schengen Convention in specific fields and to supervise that the provisions of this convention were effectively applied. For details see *Dörr*, Die Öffentliche Verwaltung (DÖV) 1993, 696-705; *Curtin/Meijers*, 32 CML Rev. (1995) 391-442; *Schütz*, AÖR 120 (1995), 509-548.

and arrangements for minor border traffic, and the rules applicable to special categories of maritime traffic. Article 3(2) SIC stipulates that Schengen States "undertake to introduce penalties for the unauthorized crossing of external borders at places other than crossing points or at times other than the fixed opening hours". Thus Article 3(2) SIC does not affect Schengen States' margin of appreciation with respect to determining, at the national level, which penalties are appropriate.

The provisions relating to the crossing of external borders have established a special regime for border crossing at airports. The Schengen Convention distinguishes between external and internal flights. Only internal flights are exempted from border controls. Under Article 1 SIC "[i]nternal flight shall mean any flight exclusively to or from territories of [Schengen States] not landing in the territory of a Third State". According to the same Article "[t]hird State shall mean any State other than the Contracting Parties". That means that safe for an opt-in the United Kingdom and Ireland qualify as Third States because the United Kingdom wanted to maintain border controls for Schengen States' nationals and has therefore insisted on the adoption of the Protocol on the position of the United Kingdom and Ireland. In principle, EEA Member States also qualify as Third States. However, the Kingdom of Norway and Iceland wanted to remove internal border controls and have, for this purpose, entered into the now communitarized association with Schengen States.

Further requirements for border-crossing essentially comprise the duty to submit any necessary documents, as the case may be.

b) Execution of border controls in compliance with uniform principles

Under Article 6(1) SIC external border controls "shall be made in accordance with uniform principles, within the scope of national powers and national legislation, account being taken of the interests of all [Schengen States] throughout the [Schengen States'] territories". A person who has entered a Schengen State is factually able to travel freely within the entire area comprising Schengen States' territories, subject to the conditions laid down in Articles 2(1) and 19-23 SIC. Hence the requirement that competent national border authorities must consider the interests of other Schengen States must be viewed in the light of the fact that Schengen States have in effect delegated the competence to control entry into their territory to those Schengen States situated on borders to third states. The Schengen States thus situated have, therefore, been called "trustees" or "guarantors" in relation to the other Schengen States[17]. Accordingly, the introduction of uniform principles functions as a compensation for the renunciation of sovereignty inherent in the delegation of border control powers[18]. The uniform principles referred to are laid down in Article 6(2) SIC, and in the Schengen Common Handbook. According to Article 6(2) SIC –

---

[17] See *Nanz in* Pauly (ed.), De Schengen à Maastricht (1996), 61, 64; *Epiney* in Heckmann/Tomei (eds.) Freizügigkeit in Europa (1996), 56; *Westphal*, Die Polizei (1995), 114, 115.

[18] See *Rupprecht/Osthus-Schroeder*, Innere Sicherheit im Europäischen Binnenmarkt (1992), 178.

(a) Checks on persons shall include the verification of travel documents and of the other conditions governing entry, residence, work and exit but also checks to detect and prevent threats to the national security and public policy of the [Schengen States]. Such checks shall also cover vehicles and objects in the possession of persons crossing the border. They shall be carried out by each [Schengen State] in accordance with its legislation, in particular as regards searches.

(b) All persons must be subject to at least one check making it possible to establish their identities on the basis of their presentation of travel documents.

(c) On entry aliens must be subject to a thorough check as defined in (a)

(d) On exits checks shall be carried out as required in the interest of all [Schengen States] under the law on aliens in order to detect and prevent threats to the national security and public policy of the [Schengen States]. Such checks shall be made in all cases in respect of aliens.

(e) If such checks cannot be made of particular circumstances priorities must be established. In this connection, entry checks shall in principle take priority over exit checks.

The uniform principles imply, therefore, that EU citizens and EEA nationals must merely establish their identity. Stricter controls in the sense of Article 6(2)(a) SIC may only be carried out if there are grounds for the presumption that the person in question constitutes a threat to national security and public policy. In contrast, aliens are subject to thorough controls as defined in Article 6(2)(a) SIC pursuant to sub-paragraph (c). As a result, the border official conducting controls on aliens considers the cumulated interests of all Schengen States[19].

The Schengen Common Handbook was adopted by decision of the Executive Committee[20]. This handbook contains official instructions for the border police[21]. Its task is to ensure that the surveillance of the external borders is executed in accordance with uniform principles.

Taking into account the references to national contained in Article 6 SIC communitarized SIC provisions do not bestow any competencies on national border authorities with respect to border controls[22].

---

[19] *Epiney* in Heckmann/Tomei (eds.), Freizügigkeit in Europa (1996), 56 note 29.

[20] In Germany, the Schengen Common Handbook is confidential. However, it is published in the Netherlands, see Grensbewakings circulaire (1995), Loseblattsammlung, Staatsverlag; Schengen.

[21] Cf. *Schreiber* in Badura/Scholz (eds.), Wege und Verfahren des Verfassungslebens, essays in honour of Peter Lerche (1993), 532.

[22] Cf. *Westphal*, Die Polizei 1995, 114, 115 who draws particular attention to the issue of searches.

c) Intensified surveillance of the green and blue borders

Article 6(3) SIC provides for usage of mobile units by Schengen States "to exercise surveillance on external borders between crossing points; the same shall apply to border crossing points outside normal opening hours".

Article 6(3) SIC stipulates that the surveillance of the so-called green and blue borders "shall be carried out in such a way as not to encourage people to circumvent the checks at the crossing points". Contrary to concerns expressed by individual authors[23] this principle does not, however, foresee the building of a "Fortress Europe". The policy concept guiding the intensification and coordination of border controls is not to prevent (de facto) refugees and other persons in need of help from entering the territory of Schengen States. The coordinated and tightened surveillance of the external borders is necessary to compensate for the abolition of internal border controls. Moreover, coordinated and tightened surveillance successfully contributes to combating labour and economically motivated illegal immigration, and to combating increased organized crime and trafficking in drugs and human beings.

Figures point at the accuracy of this assumption. In 1997 35,205 persons were registered as illegal entrants to Germany. Most of them entered Germany at the Eastern border. 2,023 persons who, for financial gain, assisted aliens to enter Germany illegally, have been brought to the attention of the authorities. In 64,873 cases, removals have been carried out by German authorities[24]. These figures are not only an indication of the scale of the migration problem, but also evidence of the effectiveness of the filter function achieved by the Schengen external border policy. The price of efficiency in practice, however, is high personnel and technical expenses[25].

As a matter of principle, surveillance of the 'green' and 'blue' borders (land- and sea-borders) is executed by Schengen States' authorities in accordance with national law. However, under Article 6(3) SIC the Council may fix, where appropriate, the surveillance procedures. The Schengen Common Handbook contains certain provisions related to fixed surveillance procedures aimed at ensuring a uniform level of control exercised at all external borders. Accordingly, Schengen States' authorities must act with due regard to relevant SIC provisions and the Handbook. Additionally, Article 7 SIC, as communitarized[26], compels

---

[23] Cf. *Peers* 35 CML Rev. (1998) 1235 et seq., *passim*, who has titled his essay "Building Fortress Europe".

[24] Cf. Federal Ministry of the Interior (ed.), Schengenerfahrungsbericht 1997, 19/20 November 1998, 24 et. seq.

[25] During 1995 approximately 16,900 police officers served at German external borders (9,000 at the borders to Poland and the Republic of Czechoslovakia). In addition, the material resources at German borders reached a maximum of 7 boats, night sensing equipment, 6 helicopters, 306 dogs, and 10 carbon dioxide instruments facilitating the detection of persons being hidden in lorries, cf. Federal Ministry of the Interior (ed.), Themenheft: Ein Jahr Schengen, No. II/1996, 24 May 1996, 2, 11.

[26] Article 7 SIC has been attributed to Article 66 ECT

to the extent that these provisions deal with checks on persons for the purpose of deciding upon nationality/entry and without prejudice to checks for national security purposes and checks for

Schengen States to "assist each other and ... maintain constant close co-operation with a view to the effective exercise of checks and surveillance". To this end, Schengen States shall "exchange all relevant, important information, with the exception of data relating to named individuals, unless otherwise provided in [the] Convention, shall as far as possible harmonize the instructions given to authorities responsible for checks and shall promote the uniform training and retraining of officers manning checkpoints".

In addition, Article 7 SIC provides that "[s]uch co-operation may take the form of the exchange of liaison officers". Exchange of liaison officers serves to mitigate organizational and language difficulties, and contributes to better understanding of respective national administrative structures. Co-operation is not only carried out between the Schengen-States, but also between Schengen-States and neighbouring third countries. These measures have substantially improved the effectiveness of external border controls[27].

2. *Visa Requirements*

Article 2(1) SIC abolishes internal border controls in that it stipulates that "[i]nternal borders may be crossed at any point without any checks on persons being carried out". Under Article 2(1) of the Schengen Protocol this provision is now operative for all Member States except the United Kingdom and Ireland. In the absence of internal border controls, divergent provisions on visas are hardly enforceable. Schengen States have, therefore, decided to harmonize their visa policies[28]. Moreover, irrespective of the dispute on the interpretation of Article 14 (ex-Article 7a) ECT[29], Member States agreed that, upon completion of the internal market and the abolition of border controls, third-country nationals will undoubtedly, if only indirectly, reap some of the benefits brought about by the implementation of freedom of movement for EU citizens[30]. Policy efforts to harmonize visa regimes have started at the intergovernmental level but soon efforts have been made to communitarize the field of visa policy. The Maastricht Treaty provided that visa policy be a matter of common interest of the European Union (ex-Article K.1(2) and (3) TEU) and conferred the power upon the Community to adopt a common visa regime under the conditions of ex-Article 100c ECT. As a second step, the Amsterdam Treaty fully communitarizes visa policy in Article

fiscal purposes, where appropriate, and to the extent that these provisions do not concern forms of police cooperation covered by the provisions of Title III of the 1990 implementing Convention.

27 Cf. Federal Ministry of the Interior (ed.), Jahresbericht Schengen: Erfahrungen und Perspektiven, 26 April 1996, 15.

28 Article 9(1) SIC.

29 The dispute on the correct interpretation of ex-Article 7a (Article 14) ECT is based upon the question whether this provision is applicable to all persons, whether or not they are economically active and irrespective of their nationality, cf. *Weber*, Zeitschrift für Ausländerrecht und Ausländerpolitik, 1996, 25-28; *Peers*, 33 CML Rev. (1996), 7, 9 et seq.; *Magiera* in Burmeister (ed.), Verfassungsstaatlichkeit, (ZAR) essays in honour of Klaus Stern (1997), 1317 – 1338.

30 Cf. *Hailbronner* 31 CML Rev. (1994) 969, 978.

62(2)(b) ECT. Finally, the Schengen Protocol integrated the Schengen visa regime into the framework thus created, and the Council attributed this regime to Article 62(2)(b) ECT as the appropriate legal basis. The common visa regime of the European Union thus comprises –

- Article 62(2)(b) ECT as the relevant legal basis;
- the Community instruments adopted during the Maastricht era under ex-Article 100c ECT, which are –
  - Regulation 1683/95 of 29 May 1995 laying down a uniform format for visas[31] which has communitarized the Schengen uniform format for short-term visas, and
  - Regulation 574/99 of 12 March 1999 determining the third countries whose nationals must be in possession of visas when crossing the external borders of the Member States[32];
- the SIC visa regime as attributed by the Council and as not superseded by the mentioned regulations;
- the intergovernmental instruments adopted pursuant to ex-Article K.3.(2) TEU, in particular the Joint Action on airport transit arrangements of 4 March 1996[33].

a) Negative, positive and grey listing under the SIC

According to Article 9(1) SIC Schengen States must adopt and pursue harmonization of their visa policies "by common agreement". Schengen States have previously defined the term "common agreement" as establishing an unanimousity requirement. Under the current framework a similar requirement results from Article 67(1) ECT, though subject to adoption after the transitional period of five years pursuant to Article 67(2) ECT. The harmonization of the visa policy under the SIC is not, therefore, open for majority voting. Three "confidential" (negative, positive, grey) lists have been adopted by unanimous decisions of the Schengen Executive Committee under Article 9(2) SIC. These listings are attached to the Common Consular Instruction[34]. The Schengen lists have not been communitarized by way of attribution to EU legal bases. Accordingly, they only bind upon the Schengen group.

---

[31] O.J. 1995 L 164/1; COM(94)287.

[32] O.J. 1999 L 72/2. This regulation replaces Regulation 2317/95 of 25 September 1995, O.J. 1995 L 234/1 which has been annulled by the European Court of Justice for reason of non-compliance with procedural clauses. See ECJ, judgment of 10 June 1997, *Parliament v Council*, case C-392/95, 1997 [ECR] I-3213.

See also the Commission communication in pursuance of Council Regulation (EC) No 574/1999 of 12 March 1999 determining the third countries whose nationals must be in possession of visas when crossing the external borders of the Member States, O.J. 1999 C 133/19.

[33] O.J. 1996 L 63/8.

[34] Sch/II-Visa (93) 11, 7 Rev., Brussels, 1994/12/22, annex 1; the Common Consular Instruction is published in *Goudsmit/Steenbergen*, Het Schengenrecht voor vreemdelingen en vluchtelingen (1995); the three listings are also published in the Travel Information Manual (tim) which is monthly issued by a group of carriers.

b) 'Listing' at the Community Level: Regulation 574/99

Regulation 574/1999 applies to visas granted for an intended stay in one or several Member States for a period of no more than three months, or for transit through the territory of one or several Member States. Transit through the international zones of airports and transfers between airports in a Member State is excluded from the scope of the regulation (Article 5). The countries whose nationals need an airport transit visa for transit through the international areas of the airports of Member States are determined by the Joint Action on airport transit arrangements.

It is striking that visa requirements are partly determined by a Community regulation and partly by a Joint Action adopted within the framework of Title VI TEU. This anomaly reflects the controversy about the scope of the competence conferred by ex-Article 100c(1) ECT[35]. The Commission proposal for a Regulation determining the third countries whose nationals must be in possession of visas when crossing the external borders of the Member States included airport transit visas[36]. The European Parliament agreed to the Commission's definition of ex-Article 100c(1) ECT's scope of application[37]. The Council, however, took the view that airport transit visas are not equivalent to visas required when crossing the external borders of the Member States and, therefore, were not covered by ex-Article 100c(1) ECT. As a result, the Council decided to determine the third countries whose nationals are required to be in possession of an airport transit visa through the adoption of the Joint action regarding airport transit arrangements. The Joint Action was subsequently challenged by the Commission. The European Court of Justice, however, upheld the Joint action[38].

Regulation 574/1999 establishes a common list of third countries whose nationals shall be required to be in possession of visas when crossing the external borders of the Member States. The following states are mentioned in the common list:

Afghanistan	Albania	Algeria
Angola	Armenia	Azerbaijan
Bahrain	Bangladesh	Benin
Belarus	Bhutan	Bulgaria
Burkina Faso	Burma/Myanmar	Burundi
Cambodia	Cameroon	Cape Verde
Central African Republic	Chad	China[39]
Comoros	Congo	Côte d'Ivoire
Cuba	Democratic Republic of the Congo	Djibouti
Dominican Republic	Egypt	Equatorial Guinea

[35] See supra Chapter B III 1.

[36] COM(93)684 final, Article 3 of the draft Council Regulation.

[37] Cf. O.J. 1994 C 128/346.

[38] ECJ, judgment of 12 May 1998, case C-170/96, *Commission v Council* (Joint action regarding airport transit visas), [1998] ECR I-2763 paras 22-24. For details see *supra* Chapter B XIII 1 c.

[39] In respect of China, this does not include holders of the Hong Kong Special Administrative Region Passport. Article 2 applies: Member States may decide whether to maintain or review their visa requirements in respect of such persons.

Eritrea	Ethiopia	Federal Republic of Yugoslavia (Serbia and Montenegro)
Fiji	Former Yugoslav Republic of Macedonia	Gabon
The Gambia	Georgia	Ghana
Guinea	Guinea-Bissau	Guyana
Haiti	India	Indonesia
Iran	Iraq	Jordan
Kazakhstan	Kyrgyzstan	Kuwait
Laos	Lebanon	Liberia
Libya	Madagascar	Maldives
Mali	Mauritania	Mauritius
Moldavia	Mongolia	Morocco
Mozambique	Nepal	Niger
Nigeria	North Korea	Oman
Pakistan	Papua-New Guinea	Peru
Philippines	Qatar	Romania
Russia	Rwanda	Sao Tomé and Principe
Saudi Arabia	Senegal	Sierra Leone
Somalia	Sri Lanka	Sudan
Suriname	Syria	Tajikistan
Tanzania	Thailand	Togo
Tunisia	Turkey	Turkmenistan
Uganda	Ukraine	United Arab Emirates
Uzbekistan	Vietnam	Yemen
Zambia		

In addition, the common list mentions Taiwan as an entity and territorial authority not recognized by all the Member States as states. Community law does not establish any criteria for determining which third countries shall be included in the negative list. Hence policy concerns such as prevention of illegal immigration and threats to internal security form the basis of such determination.

Article 2(1-3) of Regulation 574/99 provides that Member States shall determine the visa requirements for nationals of third countries not on the common list, stateless persons, recognised refugees and persons who produce passports or travel documents issued by a territorial entity or authority which is not recognised as a State by all Member States if that territorial entity or authority is not on the common list.

By virtue of Article 1(2) of Regulation 574/99, the visa requirement also applies to nationals of countries formerly part of countries on the common list unless and until the Council decides otherwise. This provision ensures that dismembration or failure of existing states and the emergence of new states do not affect existing visa requirements.

Currently, no positive list of the Community exists. Therefore, Schengen States still apply the Schengen positive list. However, Article 3 of the Regulation provides for further harmonisation to be undertaken during the first half of 2001 if necessary. Moreover, the Action Plan of the Council and the Commission of 3 December 1998 envisages the adoption of a comprehensive visa regime at the Community level which shall comprise –

a regulation on countries:

- whose nationals are exempt from any visa requirement in the Member States of the European Union,
- whose nationals are subject to a visa requirement in the Member States of the European Union (Article 62(2)(b)(i) of the TEC)[40]

According to Article 4 of Regulation 574/99 Members State may –

> exempt nationals of third countries subject to visa requirements under Article 1(1) and (2) from such requirements. This shall apply in particular to civilian air and sea crew, flight crew and attendants on emergency or rescue flights and other helpers in the event of disaster or accident and holders of diplomatic passports, official duty passports and other official passports.

All measures introduced by Member States concerning visa requirements for nationals of third countries not on the common list, for stateless persons, recognized refugees and persons who produce travel documents issued by an entity or authority which is not recognized as a State by all Member States, and which is not on the common list, must be communicated to the other Member States, and to the Commission (see Article 2(4) of Regulation 574/99). The Commission shall publish these measures in the Official Journal for information. The same communication procedure applies to provisions of Member States concerning exemptions from visa requirements.

The Schengen negative list contains some 130 third countries and territorial entities. The Community negative list was modelled on the Schengen list. Originally the Commission proposed to adopt the Schengen list as the Community list[41]. However, the following 28 countries have been removed from the Commission proposal:

Antigua and Barbuda	Bahamas	Barbados
Belize	Botswana	Dominica
Grenada	Kiribati	Lesotho
Marshall Islands	Micronesia	Namibia
Nauru	Northern Mariana Islands	St Christopher and Nevis
St Vincent and Grenadines	Santa Lucia	Samoa (Western)
Seychelles	Solomon Islands	South Africa
Swaziland	Tango	Trinidad and Tobago
Trust territory of the Pacific Islands (Palau)	Tuvalu	Vanuatu
Zimbabwe		

The Schengen list is not, however, irrelevant. Under Article 6 of Regulation 574/99 individual Member States may undertake "further harmonisation ..., going beyond the common list, determining the third countries whose nationals must be in possession of a visa when crossing their external borders." This provision covers

---

[40] See point 36(d)(iii) of the Action Plan of the Council and the Commission on how best to implement the provisions of the Treaty of Amsterdam on an area of freedom, security and justice, O.J. 1999 C 19/1.

[41] Cf. O.J. 1994 C 11/15.

those parts of the Schengen lists not superseded[42] by Regulation 574/99[43] which remain, therefore, applicable in relation to the Schengen group.

Taking into account that Article 6 of Regulation 574/99 does not establish a procedure for the further harmonization envisaged the relevant SIC provision continues to apply, though *mutatis mutandis*. Thus, the negative list may only be amended by unanimous decision of the Schengen group and the amendment must be transformed into respective national laws (cf. Article 9(2) SIC).

In addition, Schengen group has two established merely indicative lists. The positive list contains third countries whose nationals are exempted from visa obligations, and the grey list consists of third countries whose nationals must possess a visa in at least one and, at most, six Schengen group States. As the wording "indicative lists" shows, these listings are not legally binding[44].

c) The SIC Provisions related to Airports and the Joint Action on Airport Transit Arrangements

According to Article 4 SIC entry control must be carried out at the Schengen airport where an external flight first arrives (airport of first entry). Passengers who leave the plane, as well as those who board internal flights, must be checked there. Departure control of passengers on internal flights who transfer onto flights bound for Third States, in contrast, must be carried out at the airport from which the external flight departs. However, the controls on registered baggage are carried out either at the airport of final destination or at the airport of initial departure[45].

The Schengen Common Handbook makes some exceptions to the principles enshrined in Article 4 SIC. In particular, with respect to flights from a Third State with a stop-over in a Schengen State to another Schengen State the handbook provides that passengers may board the internal part of the flight, but are subject to a departure control at the airport of departure and to an entry control at the airport of arrival. Thus, under the above circumstances border controls are carried out on internal flights. This practice, like – allegedly[46] – certain other exceptions contained in the Handbook, is hardly reconcilable with Articles 2(1) and 4(1) SIC.

The Joint Action on Airport Transit Arrangements applies to airport transit visa[47], which are defined in Article 1 as "the authorization to which nationals of

---

42 Cf. *Epiney* in Heckmann/Tonei (eds), Freizügigkeit in Europa (1996), 51, 75.

43 In addition, the visa definition in Article 5 of Regulation 574/99 makes an obvious reference to Schengen including visas valid in several Member States, cf. Peers, 21 E.L. Rev. (1996) 150, 153; *Hailbronner* in Hailbronner/Klein/Magiera/Müller-Graff, Handkommentar zum Vertrag über die Europäische Union (1998), 5th ed., Art. K note 41; *id.*, CML Rev. 31 (1994) 969, 978.

44 Cf. *Hildebrandt* in Heckmann/Tomei *(eds.),* Freizügigkeit in Europa. Migrations- und europapolitische Aspekte des Schengen-Vertrags (1996), 43, 46.

45 The footnote attached to Article 4 with respect to its attribution to Article 62(2)(a) ECT states that – As far as controls on baggage are concerned, Article 4 is superseded by Council Regulation (EEC) No 3925/91 of 19 December 1991 on the elimination of controls and formalities applicable to the cabin and hold baggage of persons taking an intra-Community flight and the baggage of persons making an intra-Community sea crossing.

46 See also *Westphal* in Huber, Handbuch des Ausländer- und Asylrechts, Art. 4 SIC para 5.

47 O.J. 1996 L 63/8.

certain third countries are subject ... for transit through the international areas of the airports of Member States". It creates a negative list of third countries whose nationals shall be required (unless holders of an entry or transit visa for the Member State in question) to possess an airport transit visa, in order to pass through the international areas of airports situated within the territory of Member States (Article 3 of the Joint Action). The aim of this Joint Action is to prevent illegal immigration and applications for asylum in airports.

The following third countries are mentioned in the common list:

Ethiopia	Afghanistan	Eritrea
Ghana	Iraq	Iran
Nigeria	Somalia	Sri Lanka
Zaire		

This negative list is very short, in comparison to that of countries whose nationals shall be required a visa when crossing the external frontiers of Member States under Regulation 574/1999. The requirement of an airport transit visa is an exception to the principle of free transit passage through the international areas of airports established in Annex 9 to the Chicago Convention on International Civil Aviation. States may make exceptions to this general principle by notifying the International Civil Aviation Organization (ICAO) and requiring an airport transit visa. It is, however, important that this possibility be limited as far as possible, so as to avoid unnecessary constraints on the facilitation of international air transport.

According to Article 5 of the Joint Action, Member States remain free to decide whether an airport transit visa should be required of nationals of countries not included on the joint list. Moreover, with implied reference to the Schengen Convention – and in this respect similar to Article 6 of Regulation 574/99 – Article 9 of the Joint Action on airport transit arrangements stipulates that "this Joint Action shall not prevent closer airport-transit harmonization between some Member States, extending in scope beyond the joint list annexed thereto". Hence Schengen States may only introduce airport transit visa requirements for nationals of states not included in the joint list established by the Joint Action but they may not compromise the Joint Action's joint list. Indeed the Schengen group has also drawn up special negative and grey lists for airport transit visas[48]. The legal basis for both lists is Article 11(1)(b) SIC[49]. The Schengen negative list for airport transit comprises eleven third countries whose nationals must be in possession of a transit visa when passing through international areas of airports situated within the territory of one of the Member States.

---

[48] See Annex 3 to the Common Consular Instruction.

[49] For the opposite view see *Westphal* in Huber, Handbuch des Ausländer- und Asylrechts, Art. 11 SIC para 6 et seq.
Aliens who pass through international areas of airports "pass through the territories of the Contracting Parties" in no other sense than aliens passing the territories of the Member States by land. The SIC does not distinguish – like § 59(2) of the German Aliens Act (Ausländergesetz) – between passing the border and passing the office of transit; rather it is geared to the mere being and passing through the territory of the Member States.

Article 6 of the Joint Action provides that Member States are free to determine the airport transit arrangements applicable to statutory stateless persons and refugees.

Similar to Article 4 of Regulation 574/99 the Joint Action allows for exceptions from the visa requirement. Under its Article 4 Member States may provide for exceptions, in particular for -

- crew members of aircraft and ships,
- holders of diplomatic, official or service passports,
- holders of residence permits or equivalent documents issued by a Member State,
- holders of visas issued by a Member State, or by a State which is a party to the Agreement on the European Economic Area.

According to Article 7 of the Joint Action, "Member States shall notify the other Member States and the Secretariat General of the Council of the measures taken" with regard to visa requirements for nationals of third countries not on the common list, for statutory refugees and stateless persons, as well as with regard to exceptions to the visa requirement. Those measures shall be published, for information, in the Official Journal.

Airport transit visas shall be issued by the consular services of the Member States (Article 2(1) of the Joint Action). The conditions of issue of airport transit visas shall be determined by each Member State, subject to Council adoption of criteria governing the requirements for, and issue of visas under Article 2(2) of the Joint Action. According to said provision, moreover, consular services must confirm that the issue of a visa would neither pose a security threat nor increase the risk of illegal immigration. Above all, they must be satisfied that the application for an airport transit visa is justified on the basis of the documents submitted by the applicant, and that, as far as possible, these documents guarantee entry into the country of final destination, in particular by presentation of a visa where so required. Airport transit visas issued by Member States are to conform to the uniform visa format laid down in Regulation 1683/95 of 29 May 1995 (Article 2(3) of the Joint Action).

In order to achieve further harmonization of airport transit arrangements throughout the European Union, the Council Presidency shall draw up and submit a yearly report on progress in this field. The Council shall also examine all proposal for amendments to the joint list (Article 8).

Article 4 of the Joint Action concerns data protection. Without prejudice to relevant more extensive provisions concerning data protection, Article 4 provides that an individual to whom a visa is issued shall have the right to verify the personal particulars entered on the visa and, where appropriate, to ask that any corrections or deletions be made. No information in machine-readable form shall be given on the uniform format for visas unless it also appears in the boxes described in points 6 to 12 of the Annex, or unless mentioned in the relevant travel document.

In 1998 the Council adopted a draft joint action to amend the 1995 joint action of airport transit arrangements.[50] The Parliament approved the draft with some amendments,[51] but after the Treaty of Amsterdam entered in force, the proposal was not further processed. Rather point 36(d)(i) of the Action Plan of the Council and the Commission[52] envisages "the drawing up of a list of countries whose nationals are subject to an airport transit visa requirement (abolition of the current grey list)".

d) Uniform Format for Visas: Regulation 1683/95

The introduction of a uniform visa, under Articles 10 and 11 SIC, valid for the entire area comprised by Schengen States' territories was a major step in the course of harmonization of visa policies under the Schengen Convention. Except for Article 10(2) SIC which has for long become obsolete both these provisions have been attributed to Article 62(2)(b) ECT. Article 10(1) SIC stipulates that the uniform visa "may be issued for visits not exceeding three months". Similarly, Article 5 of Regulation 1683/95 stipulates that –

> For the purposes of [the] Regulation a 'visa' shall mean an authorization given by or a decision taken by a Member State which is required for entry into its territory with a view to:
>
> – an intended stay in that Member State or in several Member States of no more than three months in all,
>
> – transit through the territory or airport transit zone of that Member State or several Member States.

The uniform Community visa has replaced the Schengen visa. The uniform visa is issued on a sticker (the Community sticker has been substituted for the Schengen sticker by virtue of Regulation 1683/95, thus evidencing thus that the Schengen Convention functioned as a 'laboratory'[53] for subsequent EU-wide measures) which fulfils all necessary requirements for the highest level of protection against counterfeiting[54].

---

[50] Draft Joint Action adopted by the Council on the basis of Article K.3 of the Treaty on European Union on airport transit arrangements (10225/98 – C4-0526/98 -98/0915(CNS); not published in the O.J.

[51] O.J. 1998 C 379/387

[52] O.J. 1999 C 19/1.

[53] Further, the SIC has been recognised as an "experimental garden" or as having a "pilot function", to EC initiatives in this area, see *Nanz* in Pauly (ed.), De Schengen à Maastricht (1996), 61, 63; *id.* in Bieber/Monar (eds.), Justice and Home Affairs in the European Union, The development of the third pillar (1995), 29, 44; *Hailbronner* in Rosas and Antola (eds.), A Citizen's Europe: In Search of a New Order, London SAGE (1995), 182, 192; *Hailbronner & Polakiewicz*, Duke Journal Of Comparative & International Law (1992), 49, 60; *Woltjer*, Maastricht Journal of European and comparative law (1995), 256, 257, 259; *O'Keeffe*, 20 E.L.Rev. 1995, 20, 23.

[54] For details see *Hildebrandt* in Heckmann/Tomei *(eds.)*, Freizügigkeit in Europa (1996), 43, 48 et seq.

The preamble of Regulation 1683/95 states that it is essential that the uniform format for visas contain all necessary information and meet very high technical standards, especially those which

The uniform visa entitles its holder, though subject to the modalities of the Anglo-Irish opt-out, to travel freely to all Member States. This right is, however dependent of continuous compliance with entry requirements (Article 19(1) SIC read together with Article 5(1)(a) and (d+e) SIC). To date, only exceptional circumstances justify the imposition of territorial limitations on uniform visas. As a result, third-country nationals significantly benefit from the current regime while prior to 26 March 1995 they had to obtain a visa for each Schengen State they intended to visit individually.

The Schengen group has established three categories of Schengen visas in the Common Consular Instruction: (A) visa on airport transits; (B) transit visa; (C) visa for short visits. Additionally, in order better facilitate border controls and the issuing of visas, as well as to prevent the confusion which could result from different visa designs, the Schengen visa sticker is also used for national visas issued for long visits (cf. Article 18 SIC)[55]. A fourth category (D) has been created for this type of visa. This visa type (D) does not, however, constitute a Schengen visa, but a national visa. No similar visa categories have been adopted under Regulation 1683/93.

Visas issued by the Member States for an intended stay in one or several Member States of no more than three months, or for transit through the territory or airport transit zone of one or several Member States, must conform to the uniform format, as well as the specifications set out in the Annex of the regulation (cf. Articles 1 and 5). This regulation applies to airport transit visas, whereas airport transit visas are excluded from the scope of application of Regulation 574/1999.

Regulation 1683/95 introduced formal specifications for the Schengen visa sticker. Given the limitations inherent in Community competence as conferred by ex-Article 100c ECT, which functioned as the legal basis for the regulation in question, mutual recognition of visas was not provided for. Provision was not either made for the harmonization of visa-issuing and visa-delivery criteria. However, following the integration of the Schengen acquis into the framework of the European Union and the attribution of the visa-related parts of this acquis to Article 62(2)(b) ECT the principle of mutual recognition of visas can be derived from the communitarized SIC provisions. In particular, Article 5(3) SIC stipulates that third-country nationals holding the necessary documents –

> shall be permitted to enter in transit, unless their name is on the national list of persons reported as not [sic!] to be refused entry which is held by the Contracting Party at the external border of which they [sic!] arrive.

Additionally, Article 10 SIC implies that the uniform visa be recognized by all Schengen States in providing not only for its uniformity (paragraph 1) but equally (though this provision has become obsolete) for recognition of national visas prior to its introduction (paragraph 2). It follows *a fortiori* from this provision that the uniform visa must be mutually recognized.

---

safeguard against counterfeit and falsification. It must also be suited for use by all Member States, and bear clearly visible, universally recognizable security features.

[55] Cf. *Nanz* in Bieber/Monar (ed.), Justice and Home Affairs in the European Union (1995), 29, 37 et seq.

Member States may also use the uniform visa format for other purposes. If they choose to do so, they must take appropriate measures to ensure that confusion with the visa referred to in Article 5 of the regulation does not result (Article 7).

The regulation only concerns public, non-secret specifications; these specifications must be supplemented by additional, secret requirements, aimed at the prevention of counterfeit and falsification, and which may not include personal data or references to such data. The regulation establishes a procedure for the establishment of these secret specifications.

The specifications for the uniform visa format are set out in the Annex of Regulation 1683/95. In laying down these specifications, the Council has simultaneously decided on the amount and type of information given by visas. They shall give information, in particular, concerning the issuing Member State, the place and date of issue, the territory for which the visa is valid, the period of validity of the visa, the number of entries and the intended duration of stay.

Further technical specifications, which render the visa difficult to counterfeit or falsify, shall be laid down in accordance with the following procedure prescribed by Articles 2 and 6 of the Regulation. The Commission shall be assisted by a committee composed of representatives of the Member States and chaired by the representative of the Commission. The representative of the Commission shall submit to the committee a draft of the measures to be taken. The committee shall deliver its opinion on the draft within a limited time period laid down by the chairman in accordance with the urgency of the matter. On decisions which the Council is required to adopt on a proposal from the Commission an opinion shall be delivered by the majority laid down in Article 148(2) of the Treaty. The votes of the representatives of the Member States within the committee shall be weighted in the manner set out in that Article. The chairman shall not vote.

The Commission shall adopt the measures envisaged if they are in accordance with the opinion of the committee. If the measures envisaged are not in accordance with the opinion of the committee, or if no opinion is delivered, the Commission shall, without delay, submit to the Council a proposal relating to the measures to be taken. The Council shall act by a qualified majority. If, on the expiry of a period of two months, the Council has not acted, the proposed measures shall be adopted by the Commission, save where the Council has decided against the said measures by a simple majority.

The specifications laid down according to this procedure shall be secret and not be published. They shall be made available only to bodies designated by the Member States as responsible for printing and to persons duly authorized by a Member State or the Commission. Each Member State shall designate one body having responsibility for printing visas. It shall communicate the name of that body to the Commission and the other Member States. The same body may be designated by two or more Member States for this purpose. Each Member State shall be entitled to change its designated body. It shall inform the Commission and the other Member States accordingly (Article 3 of the Regulation).

e) Harmonization of Criteria

Harmonization of criteria for granting the uniform visa forms another important element of the common visa policy. The requirements and modalities for the issuing of the uniform visa are laid down in Articles 12-15 SIC and in the Common Consular Instruction[56]. Articles 12-15 SIC have been attributed to Article 62(2)(b) ECT[57] and hence govern the issuing of Community common visas. According to Article 12(1) SIC the uniform visa "shall be issued by the diplomatic and consular authorities of [Schengen States]" in the country of origin. Article 12(2) SIC provides that the Schengen State of principal destination shall in principle be competent to issue the common visa. Third-country nationals who apply for entry are obliged, under Article 5(1)(c) SIC, to specify their principal destination. If, however, the principal destination cannot be determined, the visa must be issued by the diplomatic or consular post of the Schengen State of first entry.

Under Article 17(3)(c) SIC visas may be issued at the border by the competent border authorities subject to the conditions determined by the Council or, previously, the Executive Committee as laid down in the Schengen Common Handbook. Border authorities may, for instance, issue visas if third-country nationals have not been able to apply for a visa in the country of origin due to lack of time or for other urgent reasons[58]. Hence, border authorities have a certain margin of appreciation under the Schengen visa regime.

According to Article 15 SIC, the uniform visa may, in principle, only be issued if third-country nationals meet the conditions of entry laid down in Article 5(1)(a) and (c-e) SIC. Member States must, therefore, consult SIS in order to establish whether the conditions of entry under this Article are met. That means that if third-country nationals must be refused entry pursuant to Article 96 SIC, any applications for a visa must be dismissed. However, Member States may derogate from the principle of non-issuance embedded in Article 15 SIC. Under Article 5(2) SIC, applicable by way of reference contained in Article 16 SIC, derogations are allowed "on humanitarian grounds or in the national interest or because of international obligations". The territorial validity of visas issued pursuant to this exceptional clause must be restricted to the territory of that Member State, which must in addition inform the other Schengen States[59].

Conversely, Schengen States are not under an obligation to issue a visa for or admit to their territories third-country nationals who meet the conditions of entry contained in Article 5(1) SIC read together with Article 15 SIC. In providing that visas "may be issued" if the relevant conditions are met, Article 15 SIC merely serves the purpose of the Schengen visa regime which is to apply uniform minimum standards for admission of third-country nationals. Nothing indicates that

---

56 The legal basis for these implementory measures of the Common Consular Instruction is Article 17(3)(c) SIC.

57 With respect to Article 14 SIC the relevant Council Decision (O.J. 1999 L 176/17) states that attribution has been done "while recognising that the current rules on the recognition of travel documents are unaffected".

58 Part 2 No. 5 of the Schengen Common Handbook.

59 Cf. Article 16 SIC read together with annex 14 of the Common Consular Instruction.

Member States wanted to compromise their position under international law to determine entry of third-country nationals at their own sovereign will. Communitarization of this part of the Schengen *acquis* has not resulted in any alterations because Title IV ECT is equally based on the idea that third-country nationals cannot claim a right of entry into the territories of Member States regardless of whether relevant entry regimes flow from a supranational or national source.

Article 17(2) SIC entrusts the Council with the task of determining which visas are subject to prior consultation with the central authority of the Schengen State to which the visa application is made, and, where appropriate, with the central authorities of other Schengen States. The (former) Executive Committee has drawn up a list of those third countries for whose nationals central authorities must be consulted before a visa may be issued[60]. The list contains certain Third States, the presence of whose nationals in the area comprising Schengen States' territories is deemed likely to constitute an increased threat to the national security of one or some Schengen States. Since there is no express legal basis for the data exchange being carried out during the consultation procedure, argument has been raised for instance in Germany that until such provision has been established, data should be exchanged only with consent of the applicant[61]. Irrespective of the question of whether there is a statutory basis, tacit agreement of the applicant concerned can be assumed, in that such a visa application implies consent to be checked with regard to the entry requirements.

In order to prevent parallel or successive visa applications (visa-shopping), the consulates and embassies of the Schengen States must cooperate locally[62]. Local cooperation facilitates the achievement of a common evaluation of the conditions favourable to the emergence of migration flows. Moreover, it contributes to ensuring that the common guidelines for the granting of visas are implemented uniformly. The Council adopted a recommendation relating to local consular co-operation regarding visas on 4 March 1996[63]. The aim of this recommendation is to prepare for greater harmonization in visa policy and practice. Pending the possible preparation of joint instructions on the matter, the issuance of visas is governed by Member States' national legislation. The first step towards harmonization is the improvement of information exchange. Each Member State, when issuing its own visas, shall have the necessary information to take the interests of the other Member States into account, especially with regard to the protection of national security and public order, and to the prevention of clandestine immigration.

The Council has recommended that Member States' governments adopt measures necessary to facilitate the exchange of information between Member States' consular services on the criteria for issuing visas and on national security, public order or clandestine immigration risks. Additionally, meetings of the Heads of Member States' consular services and mutual visits of officials responsible for issuing visas have been recommended, in order to improve the exchange of

---

60 Annex 5 of the Common Consular Instruction.

61 Cf. Bericht des Bundesbeauftragten für Datenschutz 1993-1994 of 26 April 1995, 331 et seq.

62 Part VIII Common Consular Instruction.

63 O.J. 1996 C 80/1.

information and increase reciprocal knowledge. At the request of the Council, the consular services shall draw up joint reports on local visa issues which are likely to be relevant to the Council's discussions. The exchange of concrete information concerning visa applications and applicants is also mentioned in the recommendation. Consular services should be able to establish the existence of simultaneous visa applications, and to ascertain earlier visa refusals by another Member State. Exchange of information of this nature is intended to help determine the good faith of visa applicants and their reputation.

Additionally, the Council has adopted a recommendation on the provision for the detection of false or falsified documents in the visa departments of representations abroad and in the offices of domestic authorities dealing with the issue or extension of visas on 29 April 1999[64]. For the purpose of improving the conditions for issuing visas, the Council recommends, in relation to the potential danger of falsified documents, different levels of personal and technical equipment of visa issuing departments.

The rules on common criteria established on the basis of the Schengen system have left certain unsolved matters. In particular, no common policy approaches have been developed with respect to the conclusion of related agreements by individual Member States of the one part and third states of the other. For instance, it has recently been reported that France is negotiating with Algeria on the facilitation of visa applications, providing for up to 150,000 visas to Algerian nationals in 1999[65]. This example shows that Member States still tend to consider visa policy in a traditional manner, i.e. from foreign and national immigration policy points of view. The Schengen conditions on entry and residence are hardly sufficient to ensure that due regard is had of common European interests in formulating national visa policies. It might, moreover, be difficult to enforce the project "to pursue *by common agreement* the harmonization of ... policies on visas" (emphasis added) under Article 9(1) SIC even within the current framework. The language of Article 9(1) SIC must be considered rather weak, thus establishing a political commitment rather than a legal one. Even when respecting that Schengen States should continue to be entitled to advance national concerns, harmonization by way of definition of minimum principles related to common interests and policy guidelines is strongly suggested because a regime based on territorial validity of visas for multiple states requires the definition of common interests. Additionally, binding consultation requirements for areas beyond the scope of such basic common interests should be established. Neither the definition of basic common interests nor the introduction of consultation requirements may, however, compromise the Member States' right, under the second paragraph of Article 63 ECT, to introduce and maintain national provisions on entry and residence of third-country nationals. The Action Plan of the Commission and the Council envisages the adoption of measures related to "procedure and conditions for issuing visas by Member States (resources, guarantees of repatriation or accident and health

---

[64] O.J. 1999 C 140/1.
[65] Migration News Sheet, August 1999, E 3.

cover)"[66]. Arguably, a formal procedure should involve the Commission with respect to the formulation of visa policy guidelines. In addition, harmonization of procedures on applying for visas, examining and deciding on visa applications in consulates and embassies are of particular importance in order to prevent an increasing number of "visa-overstayers" and persons applying for third-term visas in order to immigrate into the European Union. Practical experience shows that in particular countries a very high percentage of visa applications are used to evade existing immigration requirements. In terms of numbers the abuse of visas for tourist and short-term visit purposes is of much larger significance than the use of falsified documents or falsified visa stickers.[67]

Particular attention should be drawn to visas for study purposes. The large majority of nationals of some third countries apply for visas for the purpose of studying in a Member States only as a pretext to take up employment. Successful completion of a study and subsequent return to the country of origin seems thus to be sometimes exceptional in certain circumstances. However, the common interest at the European level should be to prevent such developments and their negative effects such as brain-drains, which the Third States concerned will and do suffer from. Similarly, visa abuse also relates to fictitious business contacts which frequently involve falsified or convenience invitations.

It may be assumed that such practices are a common challenge of visa regimes of all Member States in specific countries of origin. It is indispensable to arrive at a systematic exchange of information on such practices, including information on rejections of visa applications in order to prevent "visa shopping". In addition, there should be common European guidelines, adapted to the special circumstances of the different countries of origin, on how to effectively combat increasing abuse of visa applications to evade existing immigration restrictions.[68]

3. *Entry for Short-Term Visits*

The communitarized SIC provisions distinguish between conditions for third-country nationals entering for short and long terms. Short term stays may not exceed three months. The Schengen entry regime is related to short-term visits only. In turn, admission of aliens for long-term stays is subject to the national laws of Schengen States. Even those Member States which have chosen to cooperate in the Schengen framework did not reach consensus with respect to entry regimes of long-term stays since their social and labour market legislations deviate substantially. This task will, therefore, be one of the core projects to be pursued within the framework of the Amsterdam Treaty.

Schengen States have reached agreement on the conditions of entry for short-term visits. Admission of third-country nationals is dependent on certain uniform minimum conditions laid down in Article 5(1) SIC. These uniform conditions are

---

66 Action Plan of the Council and the Commission, O.J. 1999 C 19/1 point 36(d)(i).

67 This information is based on personal interviews with members of German embassies and consulates, i.e. in Morocco and Egypt.

68 *Schattenberg* in Hailbronner/Weil (eds.), From Schengen to Amsterdam (1999), 23, 26 et seq.

based on the premise that admission of third-country nationals by one Schengen State must respect the interests of both the admitting State and of all other Schengen States[69]. According to Article 5(1) SIC, a third-country national may be permitted entry to the territories of the Member States for a maximum period of three months, provided that he meets the following requirements –

- in possession of a valid document or documents permitting them to cross the border, as determined by the Executive Committee;
- in possession of a valid visa if required;
- if applicable, submits documents substantiating the purpose and conditions of the planned visit and has sufficient means of support, both for the period of the planned visit and to a return to their country of origin or to travel in transit in a Third State, into which their admission is guaranteed, or is in position to acquire such means legally;
- has not been reported as a person not to be permitted entry;
- is not considered to be a threat to public policy, national security or the international relations of any of the [Schengen States].

a) Defining the Notion of "Alien"

Entry requirements apply to "aliens" only. Under Article 1 SIC an alien is "any person other than a national of a Member State of the European Communities". Conditions of entry are not, therefore, applicable to EU citizens. Taking into account the obligations entered into by the Community under international law they are not applicable to EEA-nationals under Chapters 1 to 3 of Title III of the EEA Agreement, which in principle extend market freedoms to EEA nationals, either.

b) Possession of Travel Documents and Visa

Third-country nationals must be in possession of a valid travel document which authorizes border-crossing. Travel documents to be considered valid are enumerated in annex 4 of the Schengen Common Handbook. Additionally, if required, they must be in possession of a visa valid for the length of stay envisaged unless exempted from the visa requirement by national law.

---

[69] Cf. *Nanz* in Bieber/Monar (eds.), Justice and Home Affairs in the European Union, (1995), 29, 35; *Epiney* in Heckmann/Tomei (eds.), Freizügigkeit in Europa (1996), 51, 60.

c) Sufficient Means for and Purpose of Visit

The obligations to prove sufficient means or of being in a position to legally acquire the means for self-support during the intended period of sojourn and transit costs and to produce documents justifying the purpose of the intended stay or transit have been give a more concrete feature in the Schengen Common Handbook[70]. The amount of money required for proof of 'adequate resources' is annually fixed by Schengen States in annex 7 of the Handbook[71]. Proof of sufficient means of subsistence may be submitted in cash, credit cards, traveller's cheques or other appropriate guarantees[72]. In addition, third-country nationals may acquire sufficient means of subsistence lawfully during a short visit. The short visit can, thus, also be granted for the purpose of pursuing an economic activity, provided that the third-country national concerned meets respective national prerequisites.[73]

The obligation to submit documents relating to purpose and conditions of the planned visit has been criticized as an infringement on privacy (Article 8 ECHR), especially where one must substantiate in detail the relationship with the persons one plans to visit[74]. It has been argued that such a violation of privacy does not pass the proportionality test of Article 8 of the European Convention on Human Rights. Whether this provision actually applies to entry requirements is a matter of debate. However, even assumed that the obligation to declare the purpose of the visit be an intrusion into privacy, such intrusion would be justified in accordance with the limitations resting on Article 8 of the European Convention on Human Rights. The requirement to control the purpose of the visit constitutes a suitable and necessary measure to determine whether a third-country national must be considered a threat to public policy, national security or the international relations of a Schengen State. The issue of whether the national interests of security and public order or the individual privacy interests take priority cannot be determined in abstract fashion but must be determined on a case-by-case basis. Moreover, as long as the sovereign right of states to refuse entry of aliens is upheld, it must be concluded *a maiore ad minus* that the obligation to submit necessary documents for the purpose of being granted entry is justified by the sovereign right in question.

---

70 Before the adoption of the Schengen Common Handbook conditions of entry have been criticized. The Handbook can, therefore, be regarded as a response of Schengen States to this critique. See *Steenbergen* in Meijers et al (eds.), Meijers et al (eds.), Schengen: Internationalisation of Central Chapters of the Law on Aliens, Refugees, Privacy, Security and the Police (1991), 56, 66; *Epiney* in Heckmann/Tomei (eds.), Freizügigkeit in Europa (1996), 51, 61.

71 Set amounts have not, however, been introduced in Germany. In German practice the guideline is 50 DM (€ 125,56) per day, plus travel costs.

72 Cf. *Westphal* in Huber (ed.), Handbuch des Ausländer- und Asylrechts, Art. 5 SIC (1996) para 20.

73 Cf. *Westphal* in Huber, Handbuch des Ausländer- und Asylrechts, Art. 5 SIC para 22.

74 See *Steenbergen* in Meijers et al (eds.), Schengen: Internationalisation of Central Chapters of the Law on Aliens, Refugees, Privacy, Security and the Police (1991), 56, 66; *Epiney* in Heckmann/Tomei (eds.), Freizügigkeit in Europa, (1996), 51, 61.

d) Reporting Aliens for the Purpose of Being Refused Entry

Entry to the territories of Schengen States must be refused where a third-country national has been reported as a person not to be permitted entry. The term 'reported' is defined in the Schengen Convention as to include those third-country nationals listed in the Schengen Information System (SIS)[75] for reasons laid down in Article 96 SIC[76]. The decision to report is taken in compliance with the respective domestic legislation of the reporting State. Article 96(2) SIC stipulates that this decision "may be based on a threat to the public order or national security and safety which the presence of an alien in national territory may pose". The paragraph in question also names cases in which this may in particular be so. These cases comprise

- convictions of an offence carrying a custodial sentence of at least one year, and
- serious grounds for believing the commission of serious offence, including those referred to in Article 71 SIC[77], or the existence of genuine evidence of an intention to commit such offences in the territory of a Schengen State.

Qualifying the cases of threat to public order or national security as "particular" examples Article 96(2) SIC does not establish exhaustive grounds for reporting of third-country nationals for the purpose of being refused entry. Schengen States may, therefore, introduce additional grounds provided that they reflect public order or national security concerns. Additionally, Article 96(2) SIC leaves a wide margin of appreciation to Schengen States' legislation with respect to the determination of grounds for registration in the SIS. For one, reference is made to "national security". This phrasing indicates that national concepts of "security" shall be recognised at the European level rather than superseded by a uniform European approach. To the same end, in defining offences carrying a custodial sentence of at least one year as a potential case of threat to public order or national security Article 96(2)(a) SIC implies that policy decisions taken with a view to periods of sentences, at the national level, shall be fully respected.

Article 96(3) SIC provides that decisions with a view to reporting aliens[78]

> may also be based on the fact that an alien has been the subject of a deportation, removal or expulsion which has not been rescinded or suspended, including or accompanied by a prohibition on entry or, where appropriate, based on non-compliance with national regulations on the entry or residence of aliens.

Again, national *ordre public* concepts must be recognised under the reference to national regulations on entry or residence of aliens. Consequently, the

---

75 On the SIS see *Bäumler*, Computer und Recht (CR) 1994, 487; *Wehner* in Heckmann/Tomei (eds.), Freizügigkeit in Europa (1996), 129 – 178; *Scheller* in Juristenzeitung (JZ) 1992, 904; *Riegel* in Die Öffentliche Verwaltung (DÖV) 1991, 311.

76 The provisions on the SIS, including Article 96 SIC, are pending attribution to EU legal basis.

77 Article 71 SIC has been attributed to Articles 34, 30 and 31 TEU.

78 Thus, if an alien is reported in the SIS by German authorities because of a deportation or expulsion order, the alien is refused entry according to § 8(2) read together with § 60(1) German Alien Act (AuslG). For details see *Hailbronner*, Ausländerrecht, § 60 para 42; *Westphal*, Die Polizei (1995), 114, 116 et seq.

determination of the ordre public concept underlying the reporting of aliens for the purpose of being denied entry is based upon the same premise as the ordre public provisions contained in Title IV ECT. As a result, the position of individual third-country nationals has not been significantly changed by the integration of the Schengen reporting regime into the framework of the European Union. Certainly, the fact that concepts of public order or national security may differ between Schengen States will sometimes result in a third-country national being reported by one State and refused entry by another on that basis, even though his behaviour would not have constituted grounds for reporting in the second State.

If, under Article 5(2) SIC, a Schengen State admits any third-country national who has been reported on the grounds specified in this provision, that State must restrict the permission to enter to its territory and inform the other Schengen States accordingly.

e) Public Policy and National Security: Article 5(1)(e) SIC

Finally, third-country nationals must be refused entry if they are "considered to be a threat to public policy, national security or the international relations of any of the [Schengen States]". However, concepts of public policy vary among Schengen States. Nevertheless, third-country nationals must meet the public policy requirements not only of the Schengen State they wish to enter but equally those of all other Schengen States. As a result, if third-country nationals are to be considered as a threat to the ordre public of a single Schengen State they may not be granted a Schengen-wide visa. Consequently, on a narrow reading of Article 5(1)(e) SIC the Schengen State whose ordre public definition is the strictest would be able to set the standards for all Schengen States as regards the granting of visas. Obviously, however, such narrow reading would render nugatory Schengen States' commitments to undertake to adopt a common visa policy rather than to continue insisting on each and every specifically national concern. Utmost insistence would certainly fail the arbitrariness test suggested with respect to invocations of the national *ordre public*[79].

f) Individual Rights, Direct Applicability and Judicial Review

As an international treaty originally the Schengen Convention primarily introduced obligations of its signatories under international law. However, taking into account that international treaties may be self-executing the question has been discussed before the communitarization of the Schengen regime of whether some SIC provisions take direct effect. Currently, attributed SIC provisions and related instruments bind upon Schengen States in their capacity as Community law. However, their legal force vis-à-vis individuals must be considered separately. Arguably, neither SIC provisions nor decisions of the Executive Committee,

[79] See supra Chapter B XI 3.

though attributed to EU legal bases, qualify for imposing self-executing obligations. These provisions and instruments have not acquired the character of a Community regulation by virtue of attribution. Nothing, however, in the jurisprudence of the European Court of Justice can be relied upon to construe self-executing obligations resting upon individuals under Community law unless such obligations derive from regulations of the Community. Article 6(1) SIC supports this interpretation since it provides that border controls shall be made, *inter alia*, "within the scope of national powers and national legislation". Similar references to national law are contained in numerous SIC provisions. Additionally, the initial purpose of the adoption of the Schengen Convention i.e. to establish a coordinated system of entry conditions, indicates that the task of implementation of the Schengen border control regime has been assigned to national legislatures. SIC provisions and decisions of the Executive Committee do not, therefore, either bestow certain powers upon border authorities[80] or impose duties on third-country nationals who wish to enter the area comprising Schengen States' territories.

However, it is a matter of debate whether third-country nationals can derive any rights from SIC provisions or decisions of the Executive Committee on analogy to the European Court of Justice's jurisprudence with respect to Community directives. This question requires assessment of individual provisions rather than an answer in the abstract. The would-be furthest reaching position enjoyed by third-country nationals were according to them a right of entry. However, Article 5(1) SIC stipulates that "entry ... *may* be granted to an alien who fulfils the ...conditions" (emphasis added) laid down in this paragraph. Read in its systematic context with Article 5(2) SIC, under which "[e]ntry to the territories of the Contracting Parties must be refused to any alien who does not fulfil all the above conditions" Article 5(1) SIC merely limits Member States' margin of appreciation with respect to decisions on granting or refusing entry of third-country nationals at external borders of the Schengen States. Providing that "entry ... may be granted" Article 5(1) SIC does not either accord a right to third-country nationals to be granted entry under its conditions or limit Schengen States' sovereign power to refuse entry of third-country nationals in accordance with their respective legal orders. Similarly, Article 5(2) SIC is also addressed to the Schengen States only.

In turn, no personal rights can be derived from the exceptional clause contained in Article 5(2) SIC. Under this clause Schengen States may grant entry to third-country nationals who do not fulfil the entry conditions of the respective Schengen State if that State "considers it necessary to derogate from that principle on humanitarian grounds, in the national interest or because of international obligations". In referring to "considerations" taken by Schengen States the exceptional provisions contained in Article 5(2) SIC are far from meeting the European Court of Justice's test for direct applicability because entry is conditional on the very considerations referred to. The question of whether a third-country national, having been denied access to a Schengen State's territory, does not even involve, therefore, any issues to be judicially resolved at the European level. Hence third-country nationals may only challenge respective decisions for reason of

---

[80] Cf. *Huber*, NVwZ 1996, 1069, 1070.

alleged misuse of discretionary power subject to the conditions laid down in relevant national law[81].

As a result, Schengen States' obligations under Community law derived from Article 5 SIC are confined to implementation of the Schengen criteria for refusal of entry. Obligations envisaged in this Article do not take direct effect on either border authorities or third country nationals[82]. Hence respective national legislation of Schengen States must provide for the execution of entry conditions[83]. Taking account the European Court of Justice's jurisprudence in "Technical Circular 'Air'"[84], Schengen States must lay down these criteria by way of legislation rather than in administrative guidelines governing the use of discretionary application of statutory provisions phrased in general terms.[85]

Moreover, the Schengen Common Handbook[86] and the Common Consular Instruction do not take direct effect[87]. Individuals cannot, therefore, rely on provisions of the Handbook or the Instructions to enforce any rights. In turn, neither the Handbook nor the Instructions as such impose any duties on individuals. The Handbook is binding for border authorities only, and the Common Consular Instruction contains official instructions for the consulates and embassies of Schengen States designed to ensure that SIC visa provisions are applied according to the uniform principles adopted.

In contrast, Article 2(1) SIC[88], providing for the abolition of internal border controls, and Articles 5(3), 18, 19 and 21 SIC are directly applicable. These provisions (comprising transit and short-stay rights for aliens who hold certain national residence permits and visas) meet the relevant test of the European Court of Justice. They do not require any further measures for implementation[89]. The mentioned provisions share the precedence of Community law over national law on passports and entry requirements[90] within their respective scopes of application.

---

81 Cf. *Huber*, Neue Zeitschrift für Verwaltungsrecht (NVwZ) 1996, 1069, 1070; *Steenbergen* in Meijers (ed.), Schengen – Internationalisation of central chapters of the law on aliens, refugees, security and the police (1991), 56, 64 et seq. Misuse of discretionary powers may, however, prove rather difficult to establish.

82 See *Westphal*, Die Polizei (1995), 114, 116; *Hailbronner*, Ausländerrecht, § 60 para 39.

83 The relevant provisions in German law are §§ 59(1), 60(2) and 70(1) of the German Aliens Act (Ausländergesetz). See *Hailbronner*, Ausländerrecht, § 60 para 39 et seq. and, for the opposite view, *Westphal*, Landes- und Kommunalverwaltung (LKV) 1996, 154, 155; *id.* in Huber, Handbuch des Ausländer- und Asylrechts, Art. 5 SIC para 23 et seq.

84 ECJ, judgment of 30 May 1991, case C-361/88, *Commission v Germany* (Technical Circular 'Air'), 1991 [ECR] I-2567.

85 Prior to the communitarization of the Schengen acquis adminsitrative decision-making that duly took into account the Schengen criteria was sufficient; cf. *Westphal*, Landes- und Kommunalverwaltung (LKV) 1996, 154.

86 See *Westphal* in Huber, Handbuch des Ausländer- und Asylrechts, Schengener Durchführungsübereinkommen (1998), B 651, Article 17 note 2.

87 See *Westphal* in Huber, Handbuch des Ausländer- und Asylrechts (1998), Schengener Durchführungsübereinkommen, B 651, Article 17 note 3.

88 Cf. *Westphal*, Landes- und Kommunalverwaltung (LKV) 1996, 154

89 Cf. *Epiney* in Heckmann/Tomei (eds.), Freizügigkeit in Europa (1996) 58; *Westphal*, Landes- und Kommunalverwaltung (LKV) 1996, 154; *id.* in Huber, Handbuch des Ausländer- und Asylrechts, Art. 5 SIC para 39.

90 The same view has been taken by this author previous to the communitarization of the Schengen *acquis*. See *Hailbronner*, Ausländerrecht, § 60 para 37 et seq.

4. Conditions of Intra-EU Movement of Third-Country Nationals

a) Requirements for the Free Movement of Third-Country Nationals

The abolition of internal border controls enables third-country nationals to move freely within the territory of Schengen States. This privilege will not, however, be extended to all third-country nationals. Under the Schengen system, third-country nationals may travel freely for up to three months within the Schengen territory under the following conditions.

According to Articles 5(3) and 25 SIC third-country nationals who hold a residence permit[91] and/or a return visa issued by a Member State are permitted to enter the territory of the other Schengen States and remain, in transit, unless their name appears on the national list of persons not to be permitted entry held by the Member State at the external border at which they arrive. These provisions privilege third-country national lawful residents in a Schengen State in that they enable third-country nationals concerned to return to their State of residence without any further requirements. In particular, within the ambit of Articles 5(3) and 25 SIC, third-country nationals need not necessarily meet the conditions of Article 5(1) SIC. Accordingly third-country national lawful residents are not obliged to present valid travel documents other than a passport evidencing that they hold a residence permit[92].

According to Article 18 SIC, the holder of a national visa issued for visits of more than three months may –

> transit through the territories of the other [Schengen States] in order to proceed to the territory of the [Schengen States] which issued the visa, unless he fails to fulfil the conditions of entry or he is on the national reporting list of the [Schengen State] through the territory of which he seeks transit.

Under Article 19(1) SIC third-country nationals “holding a uniform visa who have legally entered the territory of a [Schengen State] may move freely within the territories of all [Schengen States] throughout the period of validity of their visas, provided they fulfil the conditions of entry”.

Third-country national lawful residents enjoy freedom of movement subject to Article 21 SIC. Thus they –

> “may, under cover of [the residence permit held] and of a travel document, both documents being valid, move freely within the territories of the other [Schengen States] provided [they fulfil] the conditions of entry ... and [are] not on the national reporting list of the [Schengen State] concerned”.

---

91 Residence permit is defined in Article 1 SIC as an authorization of any type issued by a Contracting Party giving the right of residence within its territory. This definition shall not include temporary admission to reside within the territory of a Contracting Party for the purpose of processing of an application for asylum or an application for a residence permit. Residence permits considered valid are *exemplary* enumerated in annex 4 of the Schengen-handbook (more than one hundred documents).

92 Cf. *Westphal* in Huber, Handbuch des Ausländer- und Asylrechts, Art. 5 SIC para 41.

Persons who meet these requirements must no longer apply for visas if they wish to enter another Schengen State for a short term visit. Besides, school pupils holding the nationality of a Third State benefit from Council Decision 94/795 of 30 November 1994 on a joint action adopted by the Council on the basis of Article K.3(2)(b) of the Treaty on European Union concerning travel facilities for school pupils from third countries resident in a Member State[93]. According to Article 1 of this Joint Action Member States shall not, in principle, require a visa of third-country national school pupils legally resident in another Member State and seeking to enter its territory either for a short stay or transit under further specified conditions.

Third-country nationals not subject to a visa requirement enjoy freedom of movement according to Article 20(1) SIC. This provision is not directly applicable because its implementation by measures taken at the national level, determining which third-country nationals do not need a visa are necessary because the positive list is not legally binding[94]. The right thus accorded is, moreover, subject to the reporting requirement laid down in Article 22 SIC.

In contrast, third-country nationals whose stay is subject to restrictions, under Article 5(2) SIC, to the territory of one Member State, do not enjoy free movement. The same applies to aliens who hold a visa in which validity is subject to territorial limitation[95]. In practice enforcement of restrictions of movement will turn out to be difficult. Nonetheless, the Schengen Convention contains provisions supportive of enforcement of such restrictions. Third-country nationals who no longer meet the conditions of entry are obliged to leave the territory of a Schengen State without delay (Article 23(1) SIC). On failure to fulfil this obligation they must in principle be expelled. Under Article 23(4) SIC "[e]xpulsion may be effected to the country of origin or to any other State to which the third-country nationals in question may be permitted entry"[96]. Effectiveness of this provision is highly dependent on internal control.

b) Reporting Requirement

According to Article 22 SIC, third-country nationals who have legally entered the territory of a Schengen State must report to the competent national authorities. This provision aims at ensuring that third-country nationals do not stay longer than the maximum period of three months during the six months following the date of first entry in the territory of the Member States[97]. Schengen States may determine that "[s]uch declaration may be made ... either on entry or, within three working days of entry, within the territory" of the Schengen State concerned. Most Schengen States

---

[93] O.J. 1994 L 327/1

[94] Cf. *Westphal* in Huber, Handbuch des Ausländer- und Asylrechts, Art. 20 SIC para 3.

[95] Cf. Article 19(3) SIC read together with Articles 10(3) and 16 SIC.

[96] Unless they are granted residence (Article 23(3) SIC) or unless it has been otherwise agreed with another Member State (Article 23(4) SIC).

[97] See *Charpentier* in Pauly (ed.), Les accords de Schengen, (1993) 65, 71.

were, however, reluctant to act in accordance with this obligation[98]. Under the current framework continuous failure to implement Article 22(1) SIC will qualify as failure to fulfil an obligation under the Treaty establishing the European Community.

The reporting requirement has been criticized as a classic example of the replacement of external border controls with internal ones[99]. Regardless of its practical relevance, which has been considered low,[100] the reporting requirement qualifies as a compensatory measure. Accordingly it serves the Community aim of establishing an area of freedom, security and justice which comprises, *inter alia*, the adoption of measures compensatory for the abolition of internal border controls.

5. *Practical Experiences and the Need for Further Development*

a) Visa Policy

The core aim of the common policy related to controls of external borders is to strengthen the prevention of illegal immigration with a view to deterring third-country nationals from illegally migrating to the European Union in their countries of origin rather than at the external borders of Member States[101]. This policy has to a large extent been successful.

Between 26 March 1995 and 31 March 1996 approximately 2.5 million, in 1997 approximately 1.6 million Schengen visas were issued by German consulates and embassies alone[102]. This figure points at the effectiveness of the Schengen visa regime. The practical functioning of the visa regime can be further verified by the fact that, initial problems with respect to technical questions of the consultation procedure under Article 17(2) SIC having been solved, the number of territorially limited national visas granted has been kept to a minimum. Additionally, Schengen States mutually represent one another in issuing visas where individual Schengen States do not maintain consulates in a certain Third State. Moreover, visa granting fees have been harmonized as well[103]. Finally, the Schengen visa system has also

---

98 For the reasons for this reluctance, see *Guimezanes* in Pauly (ed.) Schengen en panne (1994), 5, 22. In Germany, for example, a reporting requirement has only been established for children who are under sixteen years of age, and who do not need a residence permit. Cf. § 38 of the German Aliens Act (Ausländergesetz) and §§ 13, 2 of the Ordinance on the Implementation of the Aliens Act (Durchführungsverordnung zum Ausländergesetz); for details see *Hailbronner*, Ausländerrecht, § 38 AuslG para 2 et seq.

99 Cf. *O'Keeffe* in Schermers (ed.), Free movement of Persons in Europe (1993), 515, 518 et seq.; *id.*, YEL 1991, 185, 194; *Steenbergen* in Meijers et al (eds.), Schengen: Internationalisation of Central Chapters of the Law on Aliens, Refugees, Privacy, Security and the Police (1991), 56, 72 affirms that the reporting requirement weakens the abolition of the internal borders.

100 Cf. *Epiney* in Heckmann/Tomei (eds.), Freizügigkeit in Europa (1996), 51, 69.

101 Cf. *Epiney* in Heckmann/Tomei (eds.), Freizügigkeit in Europa (1996), 51, 65.

102 Cf. Federal Ministry of the Interior (ed.), Themenheft: Ein Jahr Schengen, No. II/1996, 24 May 1996, 2, 3. For the 1997 figure cf. Federal Ministry of the Interior (ed.) Schengenerfahrungsbericht 1997 (19/20 November 1998), 30.

103 Cf. annex 12 of the Common Consular Instruction.

functioned as a laboratory for EU measures: The uniform visa format regulation, the regulation determining those third-countries whose nationals must be in possession of a visa when crossing the external borders of Member States, and the Joint Action on airport transit arrangements are largely modelled on the Schengen uniform visa sticker and negative listings.

Although this has clearly been a success story of the Schengen group's efforts, Member States must continue to harmonize visa policy within the framework of the Amsterdam Treaty with respect to negative and positive listing, thus gradually abolishing the grey list of those Third States on which no consensus has been reached[104]. Currently the absence of a Third State from the negative list may simply indicate that only one Member or Schengen State is unwilling to impose visas on the nationals of a particular country. In the absence of a harmonized and binding positive list, there is nothing to prevent all other Member or Schengen States from imposing visa requirements on nationals of any State left off the negative list. A legally binding positive list would, therefore, be a desirable next step in the harmonization of national visa policies[105] Prospective Community legislation must, therefore, serve the aim to continue harmonization of visas along the lines of the negative and the positive listings drawn up by Schengen States[106].

In addition, in order to prevent the Schengen visa regime from being partially undermined, residence permits and passports must be better protected against imitation and falsification. Approximately eighty different residence documents have the same effect as a visa and falsifications of passports which pretend nationality of countries whose nationals are exempted from visa obligations intensify the risk of illegal immigration. The high security requirements and standards currently applied to visas must, therefore, also be extended to these documents[107]. The adoption of Joint Action of 16 December 1996 concerning a uniform format for residence permits[108] must be considered the first step in that direction, the importance of which may not be underestimated.

---

[104] Cf. Schengen annual report of the Central Group, Sch/C(96) 17, 2. Rev., 18 April 1996, 14.

[105] The decision of the Executive Committee to abolish the grey list on 1 January 1999 (cf. Federal Ministry of the Interior (ed.), Schengen-Erfahrungsbericht 1997, 19./20. November 1998, 31 et. seq.) is a major step in this direction. However, currently the Schengen grey list still consists of Columbia (information given by an official of the German Federal Ministry of the Interior). Moreover, Schengen States seem to act rather slowly when implementing obligations under international law in the Schengen framework. For instance the monthly issued Travel Information Manual (tim) for September 1999 still referred to visa requirements imposed upon nationals of States who have recently been placed upon the Schengen positive list.

[106] Cf. *Hailbronner*, 31 CML Rev. (1994), 969, 979; *Hildebrandt* in Heckmann/Tomei *(eds.)*, Freizügigkeit in Europa. Migrations- und europapolitische Aspekte des Schengen-Vertrags (1996), 43, 52 with respect to the need that similar efforts be made by the Schengen group.

[107] Cf. Federal Ministry of the Interior (ed.), Jahresbericht Schengen: Erfahrungen und Perspektiven, 26. April 1996, 18; *Hildebrandt* in Heckmann/Tomei (eds.),Freizügigkeit in Europa (1996), 43, 53.

[108] Joint Action of 16 December 1996 adopted by the Council on the basis of Article K.3 TEU concerning a uniform format for residence permits, O.J. 1997 L 7/1.

b) The Rule of Law

Due consideration must, moreover, be given to the role to be played by the rule of law within the area of granting visas and admission. Criticisms of the current regime have their fundamental basis in the accumulation of entry conditions in the absence of a duty to admit aliens who fulfil all entry conditions[109]. In addition, argument has been raised that Member States' use of national public policy concepts constitute an accumulation of restrictions and that the support of the foreign policy of one of the Contracting Parties by refusing admission of a third-country national be inconsistent with international obligations of respective Member States to admit the persons concerned. Related criticisms focus on the questions of whether third-country nationals whose visa application or entry into the area comprising Member States' territories has been denied are entitled to be issued with a reasoned decision, and whether they can have reviewed decisions with a view to reporting them in the SIS.

Two basic premises must be taken into account when answering the criticisms raised. First, third-country nationals do not enjoy, in ordinary circumstances, a right to enter any Member State. And, second, procedural due process rights such as the right to written reasons for a decision adversely affecting one's interests require, as a prerequisite of their very existence, that such interests have been recognized by law, that is, have been accorded the character of individual rights. One may, therefore, conclude that a person not entitled to enter a State equally lacks entitlement to be informed of reasons for any given denial of entry. Similarly, it is highly questionable if reporting decisions must necessarily be reviewable.

Attributed SIC provisions seem to be based upon the premises referred to in the previous paragraph. These provisions do not compel Schengen States to either justify, or to inform the reported alien of refusal of entry. Accordingly, third-country nationals must seek recourse to the courts subject to the perhaps rather strict conditions established by national law of the respective Schengen State. In turn, the Schengen Convention accords a right to third-country nationals to have reporting decisions reviewed. Under Article 111(1) SIC –

> Any person may, in the territory of each [Schengen State], bring before the courts or the authority competent under national law an action to correct, delete or provide information or obtain compensation in connection with a report concerning him.

Notably, Article 111 SIC does not give a right to access to the courts. Moreover, pending attribution to an EU legal basis, the obligation created by this provision remains one of international law, though arguably self-executing. From a practical point of view this provision will not, however, contribute to a significant increase of cases because third-country nationals must not be notified of their having been reported. Article 111(1) SIC must be thus interpreted since it expressly provides

[109] See *O'Keeffe*, YEL 1991, 185, 190 et seq.; *Steenbergen* in Meijers et al (eds.), Schengen: Internationalisation of Central Chapters of the Law on Aliens, Refugees, Privacy, Security and the Police (1991), 56, 65 et seq.; *Epiney* in Heckmann/Tomei (eds.), Freizügigkeit in Europa, (1996), 51, 62 et seq.

for access to information. Claiming to be informed of whether someone is registered in the SIS is the prototype claim aimed at provision of information. In many circumstances third-country nationals will not therefore acquire knowledge of reporting decisions unless having been denied entry[110].

Moreover, frequently Member States do not give written reasons for refusal of a visa application or denial of entry. In principle, public interests override any private interest to be granted relevant information since it would be virtually impossible to furnish reasons for millions of relevant decisions. It is reported that since the entry into force of the Schengen Convention, in Germany approximately six million visa have been issued according to the Schengen rules[111]. One may assume that there is an even larger number of visa refusals. Taking into account that generally no one has an individual right to be issued a visa or granted entry, substantive human rights under either international treaties or constitutional law are not affected by refusal of a visa application. A different approach must only be taken with respect to such exceptional circumstances as non-refoulement at the border and certain cases of family reunification. Nevertheless, however, aliens have a legitimate, though not legally recognized, interest to be informed about the reasons for any given refusal and to have corrected a decision based on unlawful or incorrect assumptions. National law may, therefore, accord more favourable treatment to third-country nationals concerned.

Taking into account the weak position of third-country nationals under the law as it stands there is no more than a marginal role for the European Court of Justice with respect to visa and entry issues. Taking into account that the Schengen Protocol has established an irrebuttable presumption that the Schengen acquis as attributed by the Council is *in toto* in conformity with primary Community law and that, moreover, the visa-related parts of this acquis do not affect Schengen States' competence to refuse issuance of visas in accordance with relevant national law it is hard to imagine that any questions might arise which require referral for preliminary ruling to the European Court of Justice. In particular, the Court's jurisprudence cannot be relied upon according to which the Court may review Member States' conduct with a view to testing compliance with human rights requirements where Member States either implement Community law on behalf of the Community or act under express derogation from Community law[112]. In the current pretext, however, Member States mainly act on the basis of their sovereign position as masters of their territories, which has not been compromised by the Amsterdam Treaty but rather expressly been recognized in Community law under Article 64(1) ECT.

After all, therefore, applicable relevant due process rights inherent in Community law must be regarded as having been limited by virtue of the SIC provisions communitarized by the Schengen Protocol which enjoys equal hierarchical quality as primary Community law and exempts SIC provisions from

---

110 Cf. *O'Keeffe*, YEL 1991, 185, 191; *Steenbergen* in Meijers et al (eds.), Schengen: Internationalisation of Central Chapters of the Law on Aliens, Refugees, Privacy, Security and the Police (1991), 56, 68.

111 *Schattenberg*, in Hailbronner/Weil (eds.), From Schengen to Amsterdam (1999), 23,26.

112 Cf. Duvigneau 25 LIEI (1999) 61, 68, including further references.

judicial review with a view to compliance with any part of primary Community law whatsoever. The legitimate interest of aliens to be furnished with written reasons for given denials of visas may, however, be recognized at the national level although no general requirement of giving written reasons for a negative decision can be recommended for practical reasons.

With respect to review of reporting decisions the question of *quis iudicabit* has not yet been settled. In a recent case the French Conseil d'État assumed competence to rule on the legality of registering foreign nationals in the Schengen information system. Under French law the authorities, in motivating their refusal to grant a visa, must inform the applicant of the Schengen State which requested the registration of this person in the SIS in order to allow him to exercise a right of appeal before the authorities of the state responsible for having him listed in the SIS. The Conseil d'État decided that it was competent to rule on the registration of foreign nationals in the SIS even though this was not done by the French authorities. Consequently, a decision by the German authorities to list somebody in the SIS was considered as unlawful by the French Court since the reason cited by the German authorities was not among the reasons listed in Article 96(2) and (3) of the Schengen Convention. The Conseil d'État therefore quashed the decision to refuse a visa[113]. This jurisprudence gives rise to a number of issues concerning judicial protection under the Schengen regime[114]. It seems hardly acceptable that national courts decide on the basis of diverse judicial systems and procedural rules on the application of Schengen rules. Since the European Court of Justice is clearly not equipped to deal on a day-to-day basis with issues of interpreting the Schengen rules on visa and entry permits, there is, however, no alternative to national judicial control. To the extent that national administrative decisions are based upon the decisions of other EU Member States, national courts must be considered as competent to review the legality of decisions such as registry within the Schengen system.

It is not the role, however, of courts to review the legality according to foreign law standards. Thus, judicial review would be limited to controlling the compliance with Schengen standards and internally applicable legal standards. In a long-term perspective, however, the establishment of a European Administrative Appeal Court would seem to be necessary.

c) Public Policy

Decisions on entry taken by border officials are primarily based upon the public policy concept of their States since border officials cannot usually be expected to, and do not know all relevant public policy provisions of, and their interpretation by, other Schengen States. That might give rise to concerns with a view to a lack of uniformity of the concepts underlying decisions on entry. However, in practice security risks are unlikely to arise. Public policy concepts of Schengen States are

---

[113] For a preliminary report on the decisions of 9 June 1999 in the case Hamssaoui and Forabosco, No. 190384 et 198344 see Migration News Sheet, August 1999, 2.

[114] See *Hubert*, in Hailbronner/Weil (eds.), From Schengen to Amsterdam (1999), 65, 69.

largely identical, especially in the field of criminal offences. Hence by adhering to national public policy concepts of individual States, border officials indirectly enforce the legitimate security interests of all Schengen States. Similarly, the position of third-country nationals concerned is not adversely affected by the lack of a uniform European public policy concept because Schengen States, in principle, share the same traditions and interests with regard to their security interests as well as to their humanitarian commitments.

III. ILLEGAL IMMIGRATION AND ANTI-TRAFFICKING MEASURES

1. The Problem of illegal immigration and trafficking

During the last decade illegal immigration and trafficking in migrants have substantially increased. Hence this issue has been attached growing importance on the international agenda. Illegal immigration and trafficking in human beings are rather complex phenomena. Complexity is not only factual in nature but equally relates to legal questions. In particular, "illegality" is not an objective concept but subject to definition by relevant legal instruments. Hence "illegality" covers situations which are substantially different in nature and require different analysis and treatment.

The notion of "illegality" is defined at both the European and the national levels. National laws of Member States define the notion of illegality of immigration in slightly different manners. Additionally, to date European law primarily governs certain conditions of entry of third-country nationals for short term and residence of several groups of privileged third-country nationals. In turn, national laws of entry and residence apply to entry of non-privileged third-country nationals for long terms. Subject to the relevant provisions illegal entry results from non-compliance with entry requirements including all necessary formalities, as the case may be, while 'illegal' foreign residents are those who have no residence permit for the host country[115]. This definition, however, may be too wide since it covers aliens whose residence permit has expired but who may nevertheless be entitled to a prolongation of such residence permit. Unless an application for renewal of a residence permit implies a fiction of legal residence according to national law[116], third-country nationals may be temporarily without a residence permit, either due to their own fault or due to the fault of the aliens authorities. However, this category of third-country nationals need not to be focused on when formulating concerns with respect to common measures against illegal immigration. Rather concerns must focus on the increasing number of third-country nationals entering a Member State without fulfilling the legal requirements for entry such as visa and valid travel documents, and those remaining in a Member State regardless of expiry or termination of their residence permit while not being entitled to prolongation or issuance of any new permit. The latter

[115] Cf. *Lederer* in Europäisches Forum für Migrationsstudien (ed.), On the Politics and Economics of Illegal Migration, (1997), 1.

[116] See § 69 of the German Aliens Act.

category, however, also comprises third-country nationals whose presence is tolerated for humanitarian or alike reasons although they do not hold a residence permit, and who may eventually be "legalized". It follows that the term "illegal aliens" covers a very large group of persons in quite different situations. A prospective European regime against illegal immigration, to be developed on the basis of relevant parts of the Schengen *acquis* and to be adopted under Article 63(3) ECT must, therefore, be flexible enough to enable action appropriate for responding to all relevant factual situations.

Dimension and forms of illegal immigration put an additional obstacle to the establishment of a common definition of illegal immigration. Since the end of the Cold War and especially in the aftermath of the armed conflicts in former Yugoslavia, large groups of refugees and immigrants made their way to western countries with an eye to permanent settlement. In the absence of a common legislation and policy on immigration, illegal immigration initially took the form of an abuse of the asylum procedure, particularly in Germany where 438,000 asylum claims[117] were registered in 1992. The reaction of States was to stop illegal immigration by a change of asylum or immigration policies[118]. Member States adopted measures to tackle the abuse of their asylum procedures; they accelerated the recognition and return processes, for instance by introducing fast track procedures and conclusion of readmission agreements with transit countries and countries of origin on the basis of the concepts of "safe third country" and "safe country of origin"[119]. These reforms, however, although successful, have not been as effective as desired. While the number of asylum claims decreased[120], the number of illegal immigrants outside the asylum determination procedure increased. As a result, to a large extent only the forms of illegal immigration have changed. Currently, illegal immigrants try to cross borders clandestinely and undocumented, hidden in cars, lorries, coaches, trains or aircraft and live undetected in the country, without applying for asylum or recognition as a refugee. Others try to cross the border with the help of forged documents. Finally, others simply remain in Western countries after their visa have expired (so-called "visa overstayers")[121]. Many illegal immigrants illegally join the labour force of the State they stay in.

The following facts highlight this development. In 1997, 35,205 persons were detained after attempting to cross the German border illegally. This is an increase of 30.3 per cent if compared with data for 1996[122]. In Germany, the number of detected falsifications of documents by people without resident status increased

---

[117] Cf. further details and facts above A I 3.

[118] Cf. the recent development in the OECD-Countries, SOPEMI, Trends in International Migration, annual report (1998), 53-62 and older reports.

[119] Cf. for example the reform of the German asylum law: Federal Ministry of the Interior, Recent Developments in the German Law on Asylum and Aliens, IJRL 6 (1994), 265; *Hailbronner*, IJRL 5 (1993), 31-65; *Lehnguth/Maassen/Schieffer*, Rücküberführung und Rückübernahme (1998), 80.

[120] Cf. the figures *supra* Chapter A II 3 a.

[121] Cf. for the forms of illegal immigration: *Lederer* in Europäisches Forum für Migrationsstudien (ed.), On the Politics and Econmics of Illegal Migration (1997), 2-3.

[122] Cf. German Minister of Interior, Schengenerfahrungsbericht 1997 (Experiences with Schengen Report 1997), 24.

from about 4000 cases in 1992 to approximately 9000 in 1996[123] – an increase of more than 100 per cent. In addition, the number of sanctioned illegal employment cases in Germany increased from 23,100 in 1992 to 55,300 cases in 1996[124]. The number of illegal resident non-nationals for France is estimated at 200,000, for Germany at 750,000, for Italy at 600,000, and for Spain at 300,000[125]. These estimations include both detected cases and an estimate of non detected cases.

Obviously restrictive immigration and asylum policies of Member States have not diminished the attraction of Western Europe for people who live in countries where economic problems, civil wars, unsustainable population growth, or natural or environmental disasters severely impact on daily life.

At the same time, mass migration movements affect western European States very differently. The flight of a half million people out of Rwanda has hardly affected immigration quotas in western Europe. On the other hand, however, a large number of Kurdish immigrants made their way from Iraq and Turkey to the borders of Member States in 1997 and 1998. The obvious difference between these phenomena can be partially explained by the fact that for refugees it is easier to organize and finance a journey from the Middle East, than a trip from Rwanda to Western Europe. A more compelling reason, however, takes the feature of the "immigration chain". For instance Kurds usually move to countries where they may expect to find a familiar environment with a substantial number of people of the same ethnic origin and in similar economic conditions since networks existing in "migrants' colonies" will provide some kind of work even under conditions of unemployment, in a black labour-market.

Additionally, it should not be underestimated that immigration is an expensive undertaking, the commonly held assumption that it is primarily the poor who migrate to Western Europe is, in most cases, incorrect.[126]

Restricting the opportunities for migrants to legally enter the 'welfare zone' of Member States has brought about an increase in the illegal market for trafficking in human beings. Refugee smuggling have become a very lucrative "business". Estimated fees range from several hundreds to 50,000 US$. For example, a Kurd who wishes to migrate to Western Europe must pay 1,000-2,500 US$ for the passage to Greece and an additional fee of 10,000 US$ for the passage to Germany[127]. The International Organisation for Migration estimates that four million people each year are moved by traffickers[128]. Trafficking is thus a market

---

[123] Source: Polizeiliche Kriminalstatistik (statistics on criminal law investigations made by the police), cf. figure at *Lederer* in Europäisches Forum für Migrationsstudien (ed.), On the Politics and Economics of Illegal Migration (1997), 11.

[124] Source: Ministry of Labour and Welfare, Federal Office of Labour, *Lüpke* Bekämpfung illegaler Beschäftigung in der Bundesrepublik Deutschland (1997), Federal Labour Office (conference paper).

[125] Source: UNHCR, IGC/UNHCR Colloquium on irregular migration, anti-trafficking measures and their impact on the movement and protection of persons in need of international protection, Geneva 1997 (conference paper: Do the control measures adopted by European governments for the purpose of preventing illegal immigration have an impact on refugee protection?).

[126] Cf. *Griesbeck*, ZFIS 1998, 266, 267.

[127] Cf. the example given in Migration News Sheet, June 1998, 6.

[128] Cf. *International Organisation for Migration*, Trafficking in Migrants, Quarterly Bulletin, No. 16 (1997), 1.

with a annual volume of approximately 10 billion US$. It is not surprising that a market of such a volume has received the attention of international organized crime networks. Trafficking in human beings is as lucrative an illegal market as that for the smuggling of drugs, weapons, stolen cars or for the extortion of "protection fees". The same actors often 'deal' on a wide range of illegal markets. Italian, Russian, Turkish or Yugoslav Mafia-gangs, the Chinese and Vietnamese triads, and South American cartels control much of the "business". Services rendered to the clientele of these organizations is highly professional in nature; crime syndicates efficiently utilise their connections to obtain legal visas, legal or forged birth certificates and passports. They are often aided by corrupt government officials in sending, transit and receiving countries, and their work is made easier by the absence of adequate legislation and enforcement. Smuggling of migrants into Western Europe takes place overland, via Eastern European countries, as well as by sea to the coastlines of the Northern Mediterranean countries like Italy, France or Spain. The journey is not without risk for those smuggled. The route through transit countries can be, in itself, life-threatening, as migrants must often stay hidden for days in containers without sufficient air supply[129]. Moreover, traffickers in human beings are increasingly involved in the business of prostitution. Young women and even minors are moved from East to West, where they are forced to serve in brothels. They forcibly work to pay their fees for the journey to Western Europe often for the same organization which has organized the traffic[130]. While these facts represent only a short overview of a highly complex, multi-faceted problem, they support the view that only a comprehensive strategy can succeed in the fight against illegal immigration and trafficking in human beings. Such a strategy must include effective legal instruments and monitor the economic and social conditions in countries of origin and transit. This task can be undertaken much more effectively at the European level.

2. *Legislative Measures against Illegal Immigration and Trafficking at the European Level*

The legal regime of the Maastricht Treaty allowed for the establishment of restricted measures against trafficking and illegal immigration at the European level only. The lack of Community competencies with respect to immigration policy, as well as its lack of competence to impose sanctions of a criminal law character[131] have limited the range of measures at the European level to the government cooperation allowed for under Maastricht's Title VI TEU. In the early 1990s, Member States regarded the issues of combating illegal immigration and

[129] Cf. *Kyle*, Transparent Economies and invisible Workers: Human Smuggling under Global Economic Liberalism, Presentation at Conference, Dilemmas of Immigration Control in a Globalizing World, European University Institute, Florence 11-12 June 1998; *Griesbeck*, ZFIS 1998, 266, 268, *Severin*, Aus Politik und Zeitgeschichte B 46/97, 11 et seq.

[130] Cf. *IOM*, Trafficking in Migrants, Quarterly Bulletin, No. 15, (1997), 1; *IOM*, Trafficking in Migrants, Quarterly Bulletin, No. 18, (1998), 2.

[131] Cf.the opinion of Advocate-General Verloren van Themat in case 117/83, *Karl Könecke GmbH v Bundesanstalt für landwirtschaftliche Marktordnung*, [1984] ECR 3291 para 4.2

criminal trafficking as parts of their sovereign *domaines réservés*. Notwithstanding the limited scope of action under the previous framework, Member States' cooperation during the Maastricht era in the area of illegal immigration has led to the adoption of a number of important instruments. The first instrument adopted to combat clandestine immigration, residence and work was the Council Recommendation of 30 November 1994, which called for the adoption of a standard travel document for the expulsion of third-country nationals.[132]

The Council adopted two further recommendations in the following year: Council Recommendation 96/C5/01 of 22 December 1995 harmonized means of combating illegal immigration and illegal employment, and improved related control measures[133], as well as Recommendation 96/C5/02 (approved on the same day) on concerted action and cooperation in carrying out expulsions[134]. Recommendation 96/C5/01 is aimed at better coordination of the implementation of expulsions with respect to illegally resident third country nationals. The Council has recommended that the residence situation of a foreigner be verified in accordance with national law through an identity check (para 2). Control of the residence situation should also be carried out on other occasions, such as the time of application for social benefits of an alien or employment recruitment of any foreign worker (para 4-5). The Recommendation further called *inter alia* for the establishment of a central file of foreign nationals, which contains information on the administrative situation of foreign nationals with regard to residence, and which records any refusal of authorization to reside and all expulsions (para 8) and measures to improve security of the documents against fraud.

a) Cooperation in Expulsion

Recommendation 96/C5/01 aims at improving control mechanisms. To this end it has been twinned with Recommendation 96/C5/02[135] on concerted action and cooperation in carrying out expulsions. Expulsions concerning third-country nationals whose presence is unauthorized are often difficult to enforce due to a lack of identity or travel documents. As a result, the Council has recommended a number of measures in three different areas. First, the Council recommended improvement of cooperation measures and principles in the procurement of the necessary documentation; for instance stricter adherence by Member States to the provisions on presumption of nationality detailed in the standard readmission agreement adopted by the Council on 30 November 1994[136] and, where necessary travel documents cannot be obtained, to issue the standard travel document adopted by the Council on 30 November 1994[137]. The recommendation further proposes principles of cooperation to facilitate transit for the purpose of expulsion where

[132] O.J. 1996 C 274/18.
[133] O.J. 1996 C 5/1.
[134] O.J. 1996 C 5/3.
[135] Cf. O.J. 1996 C5/3.
[136] O.J. 1996 C 274/20.
[137] O.J. 1996 C 274/18.

respective administrative acts have been issued by another Member State. These provisions address the problems of escort and the transit procedures. Finally, the Council has recommended principles to which Member States should adhere when undertaking a joint, concerted effort to enforce expulsions. In general, this recommendation primarily relies on the principle of responsibility of the state which decided in favour of an expulsion. A third-country national may be returned to the territory of the Member State which originally adopted the expulsion if, for some reason, the expulsion cannot be carried out (para 5(f)). The Member State whose cooperation has been requested for carrying out the expulsion by air is entitled to refuse to allow expulsion to be carried out from its territory. Member States have been allowed a wide range of discretion in this area of cooperation.

b) Illegal Employment

A further recommendation of the Council addresses illegal employment of third-country nationals. Council Recommendation (96/C304/01) of 27 September 1996 on combating illegal employment of third-country-nationals[138] envisages the implementation of sanctions in the national law of Member States and the coordination, cooperation and exchange of information between enforcement agencies. First, the Council has recommended that criminal or administrative penalties be imposed on those who employ illegal workers, as well as those who encourage, facilitate or promote illegal employment. Illegal labour trafficking shall be punished as a criminal offence. The Council also hopes to eliminate the added profits and other advantages won by employers who hire illegal workers. Second, the Council has recommended that Member States adopt the measures necessary to coordinate the activities of the competent services or authorities, including support during inspections or in emergency situations.

c) Marriages of Convenience

The latest measure aimed at combating illegal immigration is the Council Resolution of 4 December 1997 on measures to be adopted on the combating of marriages of convenience[139]. A marriage of convenience is defined as a marriage concluded between a Member State national and a third country national, with the sole aim of circumventing the rules of entry and residence. The Resolution defines the grounds upon which a marriage may be suspect, such as the absence of matrimonial cohabitation, or if information provided by spouses about their respective personal details does not correlate. Additional factors which may indicate a marriage of convenience are –

---

[138] O.J. 1996 C 304/1.

[139] O.J. 1997 C 382/1.

- the lack of an appropriate contribution to the responsibilities arising from the marriage;
- the spouses have never met before their marriage;
- the spouses do not speak a language understood by both; or
- a sum of money, determined by contract, was exchanged at the time of marriage.

Marriage dowries are excluded from this provision, if the rite of dowry is common practice in the country of origin. Previous marriages of either spouse may also function as grounds for investigation. Finally, the Resolution also lists possible sources of information to be utilized in the investigation of a suspected marriage of convenience. If there is evidence supportive of the assumption that a marriage is one of convenience, Member States shall issue a residence permit to the third-country national on the basis of that marriage only after close examination of the case. Such examination may involve separate interviews with each spouse. As general rule, residence permits granted on the basis of the third-country national's marriage must be withdrawn, revoked or not renewed if the marriage turns out to be one of convenience. Third country nationals shall, however, be granted the opportunity to contest or have reviewed a decision to refuse, withdraw or not renew a residence permit before a national court or a competent administrative authority. Originally the Resolution called upon Member States to implement, in national law, the measures proposed by 1 January 1999.

d) Trafficking of aliens and exploitation

The above mentioned measures taken by the Council under Maastricht's legal framework can be viewed as attempts to gradually develop minimum harmonization and cooperation with respect to some major features of illegal immigration. Additionally, European measures have also been taken with a view to combating trafficking in human beings. The Commission had proposed a Regulation on the development and consolidation of democracy and the rule of law and respect for human rights and fundamental freedoms envisages measures to promote operations supporting action taken against various forms of exploitation or trafficking in human beings, in particular with regard to women and children[140]. This regulation should have been based on Article 177(2) (ex-Article 130u) ECT, had the Council decided to adopt it. Currently, since the Amsterdam Treaty has conferred more comprehensive competence on the Community than ex-Article 130u ECT, future legislation in this area is more likely to build upon this proposal rather than its being submitted once more.

Some additional legal measures have been adopted under Maastricht's third pillar. The increase in trafficking in human beings in the last few years has garnered the attention of the Justice and Home Affairs Council. Two Joint Actions are of primary importance in this context. Both instruments extended the mandate

---

[140] COM(97)357 final, O.J. 1997 C 282/14 (cf. Article 2 g).

of the Europol Drugs Unit and improved its equipment[141]. According to these Joint Actions the Europol Drug Unit shall function as a non-operational team for the exchange and analysis of information and intelligence in the areas of trafficking in human beings and crimes involving clandestine immigration networks. A directory of specialized competencies, skills and expertise in the fight against international organized crime, as it relates to drug trafficking and trafficking of human beings, has also been established. Measures which specifically address these two areas were created in light of the fact that international organized crime networks are not only involved in drug trafficking, but also in trafficking in human beings.

Moreover, the Justice and Home Affairs Council also adopted the Joint Action of 24 February 1997 concerning action to combat trafficking in human beings and sexual exploitation of children[142]. This Joint Action was initiated by the Belgian government, as a political reaction to the cases of sexual exploitation of children in Belgium which evoked world-wide public uproar and caused a crisis in the Belgian political system. The Joint Action envisages the adoption of minimum standards of criminal law in Member States. Member States shall review existing law and practice with a view to classifying trafficking and sexual exploitation of persons and children as criminal offences punishable by effective, proportionate and dissuasive criminal penalties (Title II A a, b). Further, according to the Joint Action several measures related to criminal procedure and investigation shall be implemented. [143] Member States shall criminalize trafficking and sexual exploitation (Title I B c, d), at least in cases where this offence is committed, wholly or partly, on its territory. Each Member State shall take the measures necessary to ensure that adequate investigation powers and techniques are in place, in order to support the investigation of all offences and effective prosecution. All prosecutions must comply with the rights of defence and privacy of the persons subject to those measures (Title II E). In addition, each Member State must provide the protection necessary for witnesses who provide information, as well as appropriate assistance for victims and their families (Title II F). In order to improve and streamline the investigation process, authorities responsible for investigation and punishment should cooperate (in accordance with national law) with governmental or non-governmental services with relevant experience in the fight against trafficking in human beings and sexual exploitation of children. The immigration, social security and tax authorities, for example, must give special attention to problems connected with trafficking in human beings and sexual exploitation of children. In cases which merit special attention, these services should advise those authorities on their own initiative, if there is reason to believe that one of these offences has been committed. They should provide authorities

---

[141] Joint Action of 29 November 1996 adopted by the Council on the basis of Article K.3 of the Treaty on European Union, concerning the creation and maintenance of a directory of specialized competences, skills and expertise in the fight against international organized crime, in order to facilitate law enforcement cooperation between the Member States of the European Union O.J. 1996 L 342/2; Joint Action of 16 December 1996 adopted by the Council on the basis of Article K.3 of the Treaty on European Union extending the mandate given to the Europol Drugs Unit, O.J. 1996 L 342/4.

[142] Cf. O.J. 1997 L 63/2.

[143] Cf. further procedural commitments in Title II C, D.

with all useful information, either upon request or of their own initiative and, if appropriate, function as experts in the investigation and indictment procedures (Title II G). Member States are to coordinate the competent authorities, in order to ensure the full effectiveness of the fight against trafficking in human beings and sexual exploitation of children (Title II H). Authorities must also pay due regard to the contributions of non-governmental organizations, which aim to combat such offences by virtue of their Statutes, to the fight against trafficking in human beings and sexual exploitation of children (Title II I).

The Joint Action commits Member States to "the widest possible judicial cooperation in the investigations and judicial processes" relating to trafficking in human beings and sexual exploitation. This concept includes exchange of information and effective mutual assistance in criminal matters.

As the Joint Action discussed aims to fight against the sexual exploitation of children and adults, the offences of trafficking in human beings are covered only in so far as trafficking in human beings is undertaken for financial profit and involves sexual exploitation. The problems of trafficking of illegal immigrants are not, therefore, specifically addressed by the Joint Action. The Joint Action should be viewed as both a reaction to concrete problems like the Dutroux affair in Belgium and part of the general strategy in the fight against illegal immigration and trafficking.[144]

In its Resolution of 26 June 1997 on unaccompanied minors who are nationals of third countries[145] the Council has repeated its concerns with respect to trafficking in minors. The Council has pointed at the need that –

> Member States, mindful of the particular vulnerability of minors, should take all measures to prevent and combat the trafficking and exploitation of minors, and cooperate in this regard.

Finally, the Joint Action of 21 December 1998 on making it a criminal offence to participate in a criminal organization in the Member States of the European Union[146] aims at setting minimum standards for the criminal law of Member States. Member States shall make participation in a criminal organization a criminal offence. In the context of the Joint Action, "a criminal organization shall mean a structured association, established over a period of time, of more than two persons acting in concert, with a view to committing offences which are punishable by deprivation of liberty or a detention order of a maximum of at least four years or a more serious penalty, whether such offences are an end in themselves or a means of obtaining material benefits and, where appropriate, of improperly influencing the operation of public authorities" (Article 1). However, a group which organizes

---

[144] In this context is also to mention the amended proposal for a European Parliament and Council Decision adopting a programme of Community action (the DAPHNE Programme) (2000-2004) on measures aimed to prevent and protect against violence against children, young persons and women (O.J. 1999 C 162/11). One of the objectives of these instrument is "to raise public awareness about violence and the prevention of and protection against violence against children, young persons and women, including trafficking for the purpose of sexual exploitation, commercial sexual exploitation and other sexual abuse" (Annex II).

[145] O.J. 1997 C 221/3.

[146] Cf. O.J. 1998 L 351/1.

the transport of illegal immigrants cannot, by this definition, be regarded as a criminal organization in every case. Definition as such depends on the measure of punishment set out for the offences committed in connection with the trafficking.

On 29 April 1999 the Council adopted Recommendation 1999/C140/01 on the provision for the detection of false or falsified documents in the visa departments of representations abroad and in the offices of domestic authorities dealing with the issue or extension of visas[147]. This recommendation suggests measures for dealing with the phenomena of an increasing number of visa applications based on false facts and documents.

Legal measures taken by the European Union in the areas of illegal immigration and trafficking can be seen as activities which promote the establishment of minimum standards. These measures alone cannot, however, solve the problem. Real progress in the fight against trafficking in humans beings will require a more far-reaching perspective, as well as the integration of Middle and East European States in a unified concept to combat this problem. This challenge has been recognized by both the European Union and its Member States. The problem of illegal immigration and trafficking is integrated in the accession programs of the European Union, as shown by the establishment of the Budapest Process as a forum for discussion of this problem.

3. *Cooperation with Central and Eastern European States*

a) The Budapest Process

The so-called "Budapest Process" is an international panel created to discuss matters relating to immigration on a high level. In the Budapest Process experts and ministers or their representatives meet to discuss migration matters and give recommendations. This international panel is primarily connected with the accession of Central and Eastern European Countries to the European Union. One prerequisite for membership imposed upon the ten associated States in Central and Eastern Europe is the alignment of their immigration policy with that of the European Union. Not only these States, but also the States neighbouring the European Union and associated CEECs, will undoubtedly have to take these harmonization efforts into account and eventually adapt to the new common entry control regime. This harmonization process will also have to be extended to matters relating to illegal immigration. In addition, the Budapest Process has invited international organizations and other western countries such as the United States, Australia and Canada to participate in its discussions.

The Budapest Process produced two remarkable documents addressing the problem of illegal immigration. The recommendations of the Conference of Ministers on the prevention of illegal migration, held in Prague on 14-15 October 1997, must first be mentioned[148].

---

[147] Cf. O.J. 1999 C 140/1.

[148] For the entire text see Migration News Sheet, No. 177/97-12 (December 1997), 3-6.

The recommendations proposed 55 concrete measures to further harmonize legislation to combat trafficking in aliens, pre-entry and entry control, return to countries of origin and readmission agreements, information exchange, technical and financial assistance to Central and Eastern European States and cooperation. The harmonization of legislation to combat trafficking begins with a common definition of the term 'trafficking in aliens'. The conference recommended that "a common understanding of the term "trafficking in aliens" should include activities taken deliberately to facilitate the border crossing or residence of an alien in the territory of the State, contrary to the rules and conditions applicable in such a State." (para 1)[149]. Defined as such, trafficking, as well as attempted trafficking and aiding and abetting, should be regarded as criminal offences (para 2). This offence should be punished with a maximum imprisonment of at least two years , or under aggravating circumstances, 3 years (para 5). The conference also suggested the confiscation of proceeds obtained as a result of trafficking in aliens, as well as of the means of transport owned by traffickers and their accomplices used for trafficking in aliens (para 6). In addition, the conference regards the following kinds of behaviours as criminal offences:

- Illegal border-crossing should be punished with fines, and under aggravating circumstances, short term imprisonment.
- The production and use of fraudulent documents should result in a maximum imprisonment of at least 3 years. Such documents should be confiscated, and proceeds from levied fines should be used to continue the fight against these activities.
- Employment of illegal migrants should be punished with sanctions which include a maximum imprisonment of at least 6 months, fines, and confiscation of proceeds won by illegal employment.

Harmonization of criminal law in these matters must be accomplished through an extension of the scope of national legislation on trafficking in aliens, so that nationals and other persons residing within the territory of a Member State and who facilitate illegal entry into any state are punishable by law. In addition, an *acquis* of relevant international instruments should be fully implemented in all participating States. The following instruments should be included in this *acquis* –

- the 1950 European Convention on Human Rights and its additional protocols;
- the 1951 Geneva Convention on the Status of Refugees and the 1967 New York Protocol;
- the 1979 Convention on the Elimination of all forms of Discrimination against Women;
- the 1984 Convention against Torture and Other Cruel, Inhuman or Degrading Treatment or Punishment;
- the 1989 Convention on the Rights of the Child;
- the 1957 European Convention on Extradition and its additional Protocol of 1978;

---

[149] The number is related to the number of the recommendation.

- the 1959 European Convention on Mutual Assistance in Criminal Matters and its 1978 Protocol;
- the 1981 European Convention for the Protection of Individuals with regard to Automatic Processing of Personal Data; and
- the 1990 Convention on Money Laundering, Search, Seizure and Confiscation of the Proceeds for Crime.

Additionally, a number of recommendations were made with a view to harmonizing minimum standards for entry control and visa regimes. The Conference recommended *inter alia* –

- the use of information programs in countries of origin and transit, in order to prevent illegal migration;
- the adoption of measures to establish the identity of improperly documented aliens and to exchange related data at the international level;
- the introduction of the ICAO technical standards for the issuing of passports and visas, and of systems based on machine readable passports and visas;
- the creation of sanctions against carriers who conduct illegal transport services and/or fail to identify improperly documented passengers, by which fines may be levied and carriers may be held liable for the return costs; and
- the gradual adaptation of visa and transit visa regimes, procedures for issuing visas, and border control practices to the relevant policies and regulations adopted by the European Union.

The third group of recommendations addresses the problems of return and readmission. The recommendations propose the return of persons concerned directly to their countries of origin as the most favourable option. In order to achieve this goal, the Conference recommended measures to further facilitate voluntary return, as well as identification of undocumented immigrants. The measures recommended are joint actions vis-à-vis countries in which the readmission of citizens and cooperation in transit, or readmission by issuing standard travel documents or consular laissez passer documents is generally problematic. The recommendations also establish several common principles for readmission agreements. Participating States should attempt to conclude readmission agreements which contain clauses on nationals, on citizens of third countries, on transit for the purpose of return, and on protection of personal data. Readmission agreements should be flexible and adhere to a standard format and return should be conducted as quickly as possible. The conference called for the creation of a model bilateral readmission agreement of the European Union, acceptable to all participating States. Finally, the conference recommended that readmission clauses be inserted in all general cooperation agreements between Member States and third countries.

The last group of recommendations addresses the cooperation between the participating States, as well as technical and financial assistance. Cooperation between States includes the exchange of information on illegal migration. The purpose of this exchange is to create an information system compatible with systems applied in all participating States for the monitoring and analysis of illegal migration and trafficking. The technical and financial aid should be linked to existing European Union programs, e.g. PHARE, STOP and TACIS, as well as relevant international organizations, e.g. UNHCR, The Council of Europe, IOM, Interpol and ICMPD.

b) The Enlargement of the European Union

The Budapest Process is connected with another process, the enlargement of the European Union by the accession of the Central and Eastern European States. The time period in which the European Community will develop the new policy in areas of asylum and immigration under the regime of the Amsterdam Treaty will roughly coincide with the period in which the enlargement negotiations enter their crucial phase[150]. It should also be mentioned that most accession candidates are countries of transit or origin of illegal immigration or organized trafficking in human beings. The European institutions consider that in many of the applicant countries significant efforts have still to be made in the fight against organized crime, particularly traffic in human beings[151]. It can be argued that there is consensus between all European institutions and the Member States that substantial efforts are a precondition for an accession of the Central and Eastern European States and Cyprus to the EU.

The Council expressed this expectation in two instruments which give some guidelines to the accession states. This instrument is the Pre-accession Pact on organized crime between the Member States of the European Union and the applicant countries of Central and Eastern Europe and Cyprus, approved by the Justice and Home Affairs Council on 28 May 1998[152]. This Pre-Accession Pact is aimed at combating all forms of organized crime, including trafficking in human beings and organized illegal immigration by a better and closer cooperation between the EU and the Central and Eastern European States and Cyprus. In a number of principles the Council laid down a detailed program of measures which consist of a harmonization of law and an intensive exchange of information and know how.

The Pre-Accession Pact follows the guidelines worked out by the conferences of the Budapest Process. More than the Pre-Accession Pact a number of Council decisions concerning the accession of some Central and Eastern European States express the need for significant progress in the field of combating illegal immigration and trafficking as a precondition of an accession to the European Union. The Council adopted on 30 March 1998 decisions on the principles, priorities, intermediate objectives and conditions contained in the accession partnership with Hungary, Poland, Romania, Slovakia, Latvia, Estonia, Lithuania, the Czech Republic, Bulgaria and Slovenia[153] In a midterm priority the Council

[150] Cf. EP Resolution on the implications of enlargement of the European Union for cooperation in the field of justice and home affairs, O.J. 1998 C 138/214, para K.
[151] Cf. EP Resolution on the implications of enlargement of the European Union for cooperation in the field of justice and home affairs, O.J. 1998 C 138/214, para F.
[152] O.J. 1998 C 220/1.
[153] O.J. 1998 L 121/1.

demands of all these countries to contribute to the fight against organized crime (in particular trafficking in human beings) and corruption. These states must also align their visa policy with that of the Union and complete the alignment on international conventions. Finally, the Council demands an implementation of migration policy and asylum procedures, notably in view of the Schengen acquis. These documents lay down the political strategy of the EU to integrate the problems of illegal immigration and trafficking in human beings in the enlargement process. This integration is consequent and necessary. The European Union will eventually become an area of freedom, security and justice, in which the free movement of persons is assured (Article 2 TEU). This aim can only be fulfilled if the enlargement process is also integrated in the process of developing legislative and administrative structures which are in accordance with this aim.

4. Perspectives of a future European policy against illegal immigration and trafficking

The problem of illegal immigration and trafficking cannot be solved by national measures. This is the consequence of the free movement of persons within the European Union. Even an EC policy in this area might be insufficient. Such a policy will only be successful if the transit States and the States of origin can be integrated in a comprehensive concept to combat the illegal migration and trafficking. This is the concept of the Budapest Process and it will be the concept of the European Union in the following years. The Council and the Commission adhered to this concept in the Action Plan on how best to implement the provisions of the Treaty of Amsterdam on an area of freedom, security and justice adopted on 3 December 1998 at the Council meeting in Vienna[154]. In the Action Plan the Council and the Commission announced to take *inter alia* the following measures in a delay of two years after the entry into force of the Treaty of Amsterdam –

- an assessment of countries of origin in order to formulate a Country specific integrated approach (point 36(a))[155];
- the implementation of Eurodac (point 36(b)(ii))[156];
- the establishment of a coherent EU policy on readmission and return (point 36(c)(ii));
- combating illegal immigration through, *inter alia*, information campaigns in transit countries and in the countries of origin (point 36(c)(iii));
- further harmonization of Member States' laws on carriers' liability (point 36(d)(iv)); and
- comprehensive harmonization of visa regulations.

---

[154] O.J. 1999 C 19/1.

[155] O.J. 1999 C 19/1.

[156] Cf. Proposal for a Council Regulation (EC) concerning the establishment of "Eurodac" for the comparison of the fingerprints of applicants for asylum and certain other aliens, COM(99)260 final – CNS 99/0116, see infra E III 8.

Within five years the Council will adopt measures to improve the possibilities for the removal of person who have been refused a right of stay through improved EU-coordination, implementation of readmission clauses and development of European official (Embassy) reports on the situation in countries of origin (point 38(c)(i)).

In the context of illegal immigration and trafficking the Council will also adopt measures in the area of police and judicial cooperation. Within two years the Council will make the fight against illegal immigration networks one of the priorities of operational cooperation, particularly by using national units as a network of national contact points responsible for dealing with them. The Council will also identify the behaviour in the field of organized crime for which it is urgent to adopt measures establishing minimum rules relating to the constituent elements and to penalties. This examination could include offences such as trafficking in human beings, sexual exploitation of children.

The work of the European institutions continues in the direction of a European migration strategy. In May 1999 the Council drafted some guidelines of such a strategy integrating external aspects of migration. A European migration strategy will aim to eliminate or reduce the root causes of asylum-seeking and migration in countries of origin. The EU will achieve this aim by an active human rights policy, conflict prevention, economic and development cooperation and the promotion of democratic structures in countries of origin. This integrated approach will combine a wide variety of foreign, external economic, development, social and home affairs policy measures.[157]

IV. Third-Country Nationals Privileged with respect to the Exercise of Market Freedoms by EU Citizens

1. Family Members of EU Citizens

The Treaties establishing the European Community and the European Union do not contain any provisions dealing specifically with the legal status of third-country nationals. Nevertheless, Community law has granted certain rights to family members of EU citizens as an inherent part of the exercise of market freedoms, particularly the freedom of movement. Community legislation has defined the following categories of persons eligible for family reunification[158] –

- spouses,
- children of less than 21 years of age,
- dependent children over the age of 21,
- dependent relatives in the ascending line of both the EU citizen exercising free movement and his spouse, and

[157] Cf. Council of the EU, Guidelines for a European migration strategy, Council Doc. 8815/99, 28. May 1999, 5.

[158] See Article 10 of Regulation 1612/68, Article 1 of Directive 73/148/EEC, Article 1(2) of Directive 90/364/EEC, Article 1(2) of Directive 90/365/EEC, Article 1 of Directive 93/96/EEC. Article 1 of Regulation 1251/70 applies the definition included in Regulation 1612/68 by way of reference.

- any other family members who are dependent on, or live under the roof of a person entitled to freedom of movement.

However, not all legal instruments on freedom of movement grant a right to family reunification to all relatives in the mentioned categories. Moreover, rights granted to third-country national family members by secondary legislation are derivative in nature. Their existence is conditional on both the exercise of the right to free movement by an EU citizen, and the actual existence of a family relationship[159]. Not included in these categories are divorcés and persons involved in non-marital relationships. The legal position of these groups of persons shall, therefore, be discussed in a separate paragraph of this chapter.

The legal situation of privileged third-country nationals has primarily been shaped by the jurisprudence of the European Court of Justice relating to the market freedoms. The concept of Union citizenship and a resulting right to move freely within the European Union (now Article 18 ECT), introduced by the Maastricht Treaty, has not yet had significant influence on the legal situation of family members of EU citizens. The internal market concept embodied in the Single European Act and the Maastricht Treaty having signalled that freedom of movement within the Communities shall be dismantled from the limitation to the exercise of market freedoms, the European Court of Justice will sooner or later have to deal with Article 18 ECT and related secondary Community law.

This paragraph will, first, describe the *acquis communautaire* developed in relation to market freedoms. Article 18 ECT and related instruments shall be discussed and the question be addressed of whether the principles established by the European Court of Justice can be applied to these instruments. Analysis will then focus on the relevance of other provisions of primary Community law for the law governing entry and sojourn of third-country national family members of EU citizens. Finally, the conditions of entry and sojourn of third-country national family members of EU citizens shall be described.

a) The Market Freedoms and Secondary Community Law aimed at their Implementation

The legal status of third-country national family members of EU citizens is particularly influenced by Articles 39, 43 and 49 ECT and secondary Community law aimed at their implementation. The freedom of movement for workers under Article 39 ECT entails the right to enter, move freely and stay within the territories of Member States. Articles 43 and 49 ECT stipulate that restrictions of the freedoms of self-employed economic activity "shall be prohibited". In *Royer* the European of Justice has held that these provisions –

---

[159] *Cremona* EL Rev. 20 (1995), 87,93

> have the effect of conferring rights directly on all persons falling within the ambit of [these] Articles, as later given closer articulation by regulations or directives implementing the Treaty.[160]

The Court has expressly referred to the fact that "[t]his interpretation has been recognized" by all relevant measures of secondary community law, thus claiming congruence of its jurisprudence and the practice of other Community institutions under the Treaty.[161] However, in the same judgment the Court held that –

> the right of nationals of a Member State to enter the territory of another Member State and reside there for the purposes intended by the Treaty – in particular, to look for or pursue an occupation or any other activity as employed or self-employed persons, or to rejoin their spouse or family – is a right conferred directly by the Treaty, or, as the case may be, by the provisions adopted for its implementation.[162]

Accordingly, the European Court of Justice has drawn a distinction between rights accorded to nationals of the Member States (EU citizens, as they now are called) by the Treaty establishing the European Community and such rights as accorded to EU citizens by virtue of secondary Community law. However, the Court has not yet attributed the right to family reunification to either primary or secondary Community law. Rather, its jurisprudence remains ambiguous on that point. In *Echternach* the Court again observed that –

> the right of nationals of a Member State to enter the territory of another Member State and reside there for the purpose of seeking or pursuing an occupation or rejoining their spouses or families is a right conferred directly by the Treaty or by the provisions adopted for its implementation.[163]

This ambiguity notwithstanding, the reasoning of the European Court of Justice in *Singh* strongly suggests that, in principle, primary Community law implies the right to family reunification of EU citizens exercising freedom of movement because the withholding of this right would result in an obstacle to the freedom of movement for persons and thus run counter to Article 3(1)(c) ECT[164].

At the same time, the Court has not ruled, in *Royer* and *Echternach*, on the legal position enjoyed by third-country national family members of EU citizens because both cases arose from facts which did not involve third-country nationals. Although Article 39 ECT contemplates the right of "free movement of workers", not "free movement of EU national workers", ECJ jurisprudence has not extended

---

[160] ECJ, judgment of 8 April 1976, case 48/75, *Royer*, [1976] ECR 497 para 23.

[161] ECJ, judgment of 8 April 1976, case 48/75, *Royer*, [1976] ECR 497 paras 24-28.

[162] ECJ, judgment of 8 April 1976, case 48/75, *Royer*, [1976] ECR 497 para 31. This passage was quoted in the judgment of 18 May 1989, case 249/86, *Commission v Germany*, [1989] ECR 1263 para 9.

[163] ECJ, judgment of 15 March 1989, joined cases 389 and 390/87, *Echternach and Moritz v Netherlands Minister for Education and Science*, joined cases 389 and 390/87, [1989] ECR 723 para 25. In a similar way of reasoning the Court has referred to rights of family members "which Article 48 of the Treaty and Regulation No 1612/68 afford" them, *ibid.* para 12.

[164] Cf. ECJ, judgment of 7 July 1992, case C-370/90, *The Queen v Singh*, [1992] ECR I-4625 para 15.

this right to non-EU citizens. The Court's *dicta* thus still being good law, Articles 39, 43 and 49 ECT guarantee free movement of persons to EU citizens only[165]. Third-country nationals cannot, therefore, claim any rights under those Articles.

Although third-country national family members of EU citizens have not been accorded personal rights by the Treaty EU citizens themselves may claim family reunification, regardless of whether their family members possess the nationality of a third country[166]. Free movement of workers (Article 39 ECT) and self-employed persons (Articles 43, 49 ECT) would be severely impeded if family members were prevented from accompanying EU citizens because of their nationality. Implied in the freedom of movement for workers is, therefore, a right to family reunification held by EU citizens exercising their respective right to free movement. Although the European Court of Justice was never requested to expressly address this issue there can be no doubt that it would hold as suggested here. The European Court of Justice's *dictum* in *Echternach* clearly supports this assumption. The Court held that –

> [t]he equal treatment, in relation to national workers, to which workers of a Member State who are employed in another Member State are entitled as regards the benefits granted to members of their families, contributes to their integration in the society of the host country, in accordance with the aims of the freedom of movement for workers.[167]

Undoubtedly, one cannot draw a distinction between EU citizen and third-country national family members as regards the beneficial effects for integration of EU citizen workers into host societies. Similarly, the Court in *Singh*[168] paid no attention to the fact that the family member concerned was a third-country national. That reinforces the argument that, as regards family reunification, no distinction may be drawn that is based upon the nationality of family members of EU citizens who exercise their market freedoms.

It follows that the exercise of the freedom of movement of Union citizens, granted by the Treaty, implies as an integral component the right to live together with a citizen's family members. Secondary Community law only implements this right, but may not restrict it, subject to the limitations provided for by the Treaty itself. Third-country nationals, however, on the legal basis of market freedoms and Union-citizenship do not acquire an independent, individual right of immigration and residence since their affiliation with a Union citizen does not result in the extension of Union citizenship to family members. Consequently, they are not entitled to family reunification on their own.

---

165 Cf. *Hailbronner*, CML Rev. (1994), 969, 974; for the opposite view see *Alexander* EJIL 1994, 199, 200.

166 Cf. *Hailbronner*, Essays in honour of Ulrich Everling (1995), 399, 409

167 ECJ, judgment of 15 March 1989, joined cases 389 and 390/87, *Echternach and Moritz v Netherlands Minister for Education and Science*, [1989] ECR 723 para 20. The Court made the point that family reunification supports integration again in its judgment of 18 May 1989, case 249/86, *Commission v Germany*, [1989] ECR 1263 para 11.

168 ECJ, judgment of 7 July 1992, case C-370/90, *The Queen v Singh*, [1992] ECR I-4625.

The legal construction of indirect (derived) benefits does not exclude the granting of individual rights by secondary Community law to third-country national family members. Such rights have been granted to family members of Union citizen workers by Regulation 1612/68 relating to equal treatment in social benefits and equal access to schooling and professional formation. There is nothing in the Treaty preventing the extension of Union citizens' rights to family members. EU citizenship cannot be interpreted as an exclusive concept of rights which must not be extended to third-country nationals

Family reunification cases often gave rise to certain doubts as to whether Community law was applicable at all. Usually such doubts arose when EU citizens wanted their third-country national family members to be admitted to their home countries. Market freedoms generally require a cross-border-link. Hence freedom of movement is inapplicable to cases of "workers who have never exercised the right to freedom of movement within the Community"[169]. The argument put forward to support this requirement is that it is the purpose of market freedoms under Article 3(1)(c) ECT to abolish all obstacles to the establishment of the common market[170]. Nationals of a Member State are therefore not entitled to claim market freedoms in their internal relations with their own Members State containing no cross-border element[171]. Cases lack cross-border relevance where the only factor which takes them out of a purely national context is the fact that nationals of a Member State live in a Member State other than that in which they practise their profession[172]. This principle, developed by the European Court, in *Werner*, has rightly been criticized by Advocate General La Pergola. In *Huijbrechts*, a subsequent case, he argued that an EU citizen exercises his right to freedom of movement under the Treaty establishing the European Community simply by moving his residence from one Member State to another Member

[169] ECJ, judgment of 27 October 1982, joined cases 35 and 36/82, *Morson and Jhanjan v Netherlands*, [1982] ECR 3723 para 17. The Court has upheld this principle in its judgments of 17 December 1987, case 147/87, *Zaoui v Caisse regional d'assurance*, [1987] ECR 5511 para 15; of 18 October 1990, joined cases C-297/88 and 197/89, *Dzodzi v Belgian State*, [1990] ECR I-3763 para 24; of 28 January 1992, case C-332/90, *Steen v Deutsche Bundespost*, [1992] ECR I-341 para 9; of 22 September 1992, case C-153/91, *Petit v Office national des pensions*, [1992] ECR I-4973 para 8; of 16 December 1992, case C-206/91, *Poirrez v Caisse d'allocations familiales*, [1992] ECR I-6685 para 11; and of 5 June 1997, joined cases C-64 and 65/96, *Ücker and Jacquet v Land Nordrhein-Westfalen*, [1997] ECR I-3171 para 16-18.

[170] See ECJ, judgment of 27 October 1982, *Morson and Jhanjan v Netherlands*, joined cases 35 and 36/82, [1982] ECR 3723 para 15.

[171] This point is stressed by the European Court of Justice in its judgment of 18 October 1990, *Dzodzi v. Belgian State*, joined cases C-297/88 and 197/89, [1990] ECR I-3763 which relates to a Belgian statute that has extended Community treatment to Belgians.

[172] ECJ, judgment of 26 January 1993, *Werner v Finanzamt Aachen-Innenstadt*, case C-112/91, [1993] ECR I-429 para 16.

State[173]. However, the European Court resolved *Huijbrechts* without touching the issue of freedom of movement[174]. Hence *Werner* still applies as a precedent.

Conversely, cross-border relevance cannot be denied in cases triggering both national law and Community law. In particular, Community law is applicable to cases where EU citizens return to their home country after exercising the freedom of movement under Community law[175]. In *Singh*, the Court reaffirmed that –

> the provisions of the Treaty relating to the free movement of persons are intended to facilitate the pursuit by Community citizens of occupational activities of all kinds throughout the Community, and preclude measures which might place Community citizens at a disadvantage when they wish to pursue an economic activity in the territory of another Member State.[176]

Moreover, holding that –

> [a] national of a Member State might be deterred from leaving his country of origin ... if, on returning ... the conditions of his entry and residence were not at least equivalent to those which he would enjoy under the Treaty or secondary law in the territory of another Member State[177]

and that –

> [h]e would in particular be deterred from so doing if his spouse and children were not also permitted to enter and reside in the territory of his Member State of origin...[178]

the European Court of Justice established the principle that not only Member States of different nationality than an EU citizen exercising his freedom of movement but also the respective EU citizen's country of origin must not put obstacles to such free movement[179]. It should be noted that this principle is equally embodied in Article 2(4) of Directive 68/360 which prohibits the imposition of exit visa requirements by Member States upon their nationals who exercise free movement.

---

173 See the Opinion of Mr. Advocate General La Pergola, delivered on 3 October 1996, in case C-131/95, *Huijbrechts v Commissie voor de behandeling van administratieve geschillen ingevolge artikel 41 der Algemene Bijstandswet in de provincie Noord-Brabant*, [1997] ECR I-1409.

174 ECJ, judgment of 13 March 1997, *Huijbrechts v Commissie voor de behandeling van administratieve geschillen ingevolge artikel 41 der Algemene Bijstandswet in de provincie Noord-Brabant*, case C-131/95, [1997] ECR I-1409 *passim*.

175 See ECJ, judgment of 7 July 1992, *The Queen v Singh*, case C-370/90, [1992] ECR I-4625. The United Kingdom had raised the argument that a Community national who returns to establish himself in his country of origin ... enters and remains in that country by virtue not of Community law but of national law (para 14).
The European Court of Justice admitted that this were so in principle (ibid. para 22) but nevertheless held that the case of *Mr Singh* was concerned with the freedoms of movement and establishment (ibid. para 23). Indeed, it appears from the grounds of the judgment that *Mr Singh* had been employed in Germany (ibid. para 3) before returning to the United Kingdom.

176 ECJ, judgment of 7 July 1992, *The Queen v Singh*, case C-370/90, [1992] ECR I-4625 para 16. The Court has held in almost identical language in its judgment of 7 July 1988, case 143/87, *Stanton and another v Inasti*, [1988] ECR 3877 para 13.

177 ECJ, judgment of 7 July 1992, *The Queen v Singh*, case C-370/90, [1992] ECR I-4625 para 19.

178 ECJ, judgment of 7 July 1992, *The Queen v Singh*, case C-370/90, [1992] ECR I-4625 para 20.

179 Cf. ECJ, judgment of 7 July 1992, *The Queen v Singh*, case C-370/90, [1992] ECR I-4625 para 23.

Although in *Singh* the Court only had to deal with return migration where the EU citizen concerned had left his country of origin accompanied by his spouse the principle pronounced by the European Court of Justice must equally apply to cases where such EU citizen marries in another Member State.

The requirement of cross-border relevance does not prevent Member States from extending the scope of application of market freedoms to purely internal situations. Community law on freedom of movement could thus be extended to a State's own nationals and their family members regardless of a cross-border-link. The European Court of Justice has assumed jurisdiction over such cases, reasoning that if –

> the content of a provision of Community law is applicable ... to the purely internal situation underlying the dispute ..., the national court is entitled to request the Court for a preliminary ruling on the terms laid down by the provisions of Article 177 ...[180]

The Court's *dictum* gives rise to the question of whether national courts are merely entitled to request preliminary rulings or rather obliged to do so if the relevant conditions as prescribed by Article 234 ECT are met. Arguably, the European Court of Justice would hold national courts liable to request preliminary rulings if the conditions for mandatory requests are met. On that point, the Court's observation that –

> it is manifestly in the interest of the Community legal order that, in order to forestall future differences of interpretation, every Community provision should be given a uniform interpretation irrespective of the circumstances in which it is to be applied[181]

lacks any ambiguity.

De lege ferenda, the Commission has unsuccessfully proposed the elimination of the cross-border relevance requirement[182]. There are very good reasons for a change. The criteria used by the Court to draw the borderline appears frequently as unconvincing. What exactly constitutes a cross-border-link is hardly clear if one takes as a decisive element making use of market freedoms. A Union citizen making use of his rights as a recipient of services (tourist), however, would not be entitled to claim Union citizen treatment when returning to his home country. What constitutes the difference from a Union citizen, having exercised his freedom of movement as a worker in another Member State (*Singh*)? The concept of European Union citizenship and the idea of the European Union as an area of justice should give rise to consideration whether the limitations of application of freedom of

---

[180] ECJ, judgment of 18 October 1990, *Dzodzi v Belgian State*, joined cases C-297/88 and 197/89, [1990] ECR I-3763 para 41.

[181] ECJ, judgment of 18 October 1990, *Dzodzi v Belgian State*, joined cases C-297/88 and 197/89, [1990] ECR I-3763 para 37.

[182] Proposal for a Council Directive amending Directive 68/360/EEC on the abolition of restrictions on movement and residence within the Community for workers of Member States and their families, COM(88)815 final, as amended by COM(90)108 = O.J. 1990 C 119/12. Apparently, negotiations on the proposal have not proceeded since the 1990 amendment.

movement deriving from the traditional cross-border-requirement should be abolished.

b) The Concept of Family Members

To date no Community concept exists as to the meaning of the terms 'spouse', 'relative' and 'family member'[183]. Thus, reference must be made to the practice of the Community institutions which have consistently referred to national legal orders when the necessity arose to define the notion of "family members"[184]. As a matter of principle, therefore, it is for the Member States to define who are the relatives of persons exercising freedom of movement, provided that such definition cannot be regarded as an obstacle to said freedom.

Several questions arise. First, how firm must family ties be to qualify for family reunification? And can the meaning of the term 'spouse' be dissociated from traditional concepts of marriage? Second, what attitude does Community law take towards sham marriages? Third, which children or relatives in the ascending line qualify as dependants under Article 10(1) of Regulation 1612/68 and Article 1(1) of Directive 73/148/EEC? Fourth, what is the meaning of "any member of the family" under Article 10(3) of Regulation 1612/68 and Article 1(2) of Directive 73/148/EEC? These questions bear particular relevance because Regulation 1612/68 and Directive 73/148/EEC have limited family reunification to such family members. Other family members do not enjoy similar rights since Member States only need to "facilitate" (Regulation 1612/68) or "favour" (Directive 73/148/EEC) their admission. However, once restrictions of EU-wide free movement of third-country nationals are removed to a greater or lesser extent admission of relatives beyond the nuclear family might be increasingly important an issue.

The lack of a Community concept of the terms 'spouse', 'relative' and 'family member, endangers a uniform application of Community law, a fundamental principle frequently recognised by the European Court of Justice[185]. Interpreting these terms as a reference to national law would leave it to the Member States to determine the scope of their obligations under Community law – an interpretation which the European Court has repeatedly rejected in its jurisprudence on the

---

183 The only relevant definition was included in paragraph (4) of the Annex to Regulation 1612/68. This annex has, however, been deleted by virtue of Article 1(8) of Regulation 2434/92, O.J. 1992 L 245/1= Finnish special edition Chapter 5 Volume 5 p. 160 = Swedish special edition Chapter 5 Volume 5 p. 160. It stated that –

> The expression "family ties" means ties of marriage or relationship to the second degree between an employer and a worker, and ties of relationship to the first degree between two workers.

This definition related to the previous version of Article 16(3)(a) of Regulation 1612/68 on terms and conditions for EU-wide notification of vacancies. It cannot, therefore, be generalized.

184 See the relevant Joint Declarations of the High Contracting Parties of all Europe Agreements, and of the EU-Tunisia Co-operation Agreement. These Declarations will be discussed further in the relevant parts of this chapter. See also Article 1(f)(i) of Regulation 1408/71.

185 See, for instance, ECJ, judgment of 18 October 1990, joined cases C-297/88 and 197/89, *Dzodzi v Belgian State*, [1990] ECR I-3763 para 37.

market freedoms. The need to uphold legal certainty by clear legal concepts will ever increase because the factual concepts of 'family' are undergoing continuous changes. Moreover, immigration might contribute to such changes where immigrants from non-western cultural backgrounds practice different family concepts. Whether bigamist marriages, admissible under religious rules of an immigrant's home country, qualify as family, may be doubtful. The German Federal Administrative Court has expressed serious doubts as to whether polygamists can be integrated into Western societies and has, therefore, concluded that the second wife of a bigamist could not claim, under German constitutional law, to be admitted to German territory in order to conduct 'marital' life because the constitutional protection of marriage were confined to protecting monogamous marital life[186]. However, attitudes may change, and other Member States might take different attitudes. For instance, some Member States tolerate or even recognize same-sex 'marriages' while other Member State disagree in principle. The European Court of Justice has held that –

> any interpretation of a legal term on the basis of social developments must take into account the situation in the whole Community, not merely in one Member State[187].

To date the European Court of Justice has only had to deal with stability of family ties. The Court has ruled that status as a family member is not dependent on the quality of family ties. The Court held twice that third-country national family members may claim rights accorded under secondary Community law notwithstanding the fact that they had separated from their respective spouse and instituted divorce proceedings[188]. This jurisprudence is based on a principle according to which the formal validity of the marital relationship is to be judged on the basis of the national law of the state of residence. As a result, where national law of conflicts refers to the legal order of a non-Member State this law might be decisive for the case of a person seeking family reunification. Indeed, a German Administrative Court has held that a person married to an EU citizen under Nigerian tribal law is eligible for family reunification[189]. It is doubtful, however, whether mere existence of a formal marital relationship may be considered as sufficient for enjoying a right to family reunification. Family reunification serves the actual protection of marriage and family. Relevant provisions imply, therefore, the existence of a real relationship between the persons concerned, regardless of whether they live under the same roof permanently. Such a relationship does, however, no longer exist where divorce proceedings have been formally instituted

---

186 Bundesverwaltungsgericht (Federal Administrative Court), decision of 4 April 1986, Bayerische Verwaltungsblätter (BayVBl) 1986, 294; see also the Court's judgment of 30 April 1985, BVerwGE 71, 228, 230. Additionally, the Court denied second wife of a bigamous marriage possible rights under Article 8 of the European Convention on Human Rights: Federal Administrative Court, judgment of 18 September 1984, NJW 1984, 2775.

187 ECJ, judgment of 17 April 1986, *Netherlands v Reed*, case 59/85, [1986] ECR 1283 para 13.

188 ECJ, judgment of 13 February 1985, *Diatta v Berlin*, case 267/83, [1985] ECR 567 para 20; and of 7 July 1992, *The Queen v Singh*, case C-370/90, [1992] ECR I-4625 para 12.

189 Verwaltungsgericht (Administrative Court) Koblenz, judgment of 25 November 1993, InfAuslR 1993, 97.

or where separation has lasted so long that the discountenance of a marital relationship has become evident.[190]

To date, the European Court of Justice has not specifically dealt with sham marriages. However, in *Singh* the Court observed that –

> As regards the risk of fraud referred to by the United Kingdom, it is sufficient to note that ... the facilities created by the Treaty cannot have the effect of allowing the persons who benefit from them to evade the application of national legislation and of prohibiting Member States from taking the measures necessary to prevent such abuse.[191]

This statement, though an *obiter dictum* in *Singh*, reflects consistent jurisprudence of the Court[192]. National courts have dealt with the issue of sham marriages. According to German administrative jurisprudence, Member States can examine the seriousness of marriage if third-country nationals ask for a residence permit in order to join an EU citizen[193]. Where it is established that a marriage is a sham no right to sojourn can be claimed[194].

Under Article 10(1)(a) of Regulation 1612/68 and Article 1(1)(c) of Directive 73/148/EEC children are eligible for family reunification if they are under the age of 21 or, regardless of their age, are dependants of the EU citizen worker exercising free movement[195]. There is no firm age limit for family reunification of children. Moreover, Article 10(1)(b) of Regulation 1612/68 and Article 1(1)(d) of Directive 73/148/EEC provide that relatives in the ascending or descending line of both the EU citizen worker and his spouse are eligible for family reunification under the same condition.

Family reunification, thus, depends on the interpretation of the term "dependency". In *Lebon,*[196] the notion of "dependency" was interpreted extensively.[197] The European Court of Justice decided that dependency did not require a legal entitlement to financial support nor a proof that the dependent child is in fact unable to earn a living. [198]The Court held, therefore, that –

---

[190] Cf. *Hailbronner*, Ausländerrecht, D.1 § 7 Aufenthaltsgesetz/EWG paras 12-13 (1998).

[191] ECJ, judgment of 7 July 1992, *The Queen v Singh*, case C-370/90, [1992] ECR I-4625 para 24.

[192] The Court referred to its judgments of 7 February 1979, *Knoors v Secretary of State for Economic Affairs*, case 115/78, [1979] ECR 399 para 25; and of 3 October 1990, *Bouchoucha*, case C-61/89, [1990] ECR I-3551, para 14: ECJ, judgment of 7 July 1992, *The Queen v Singh*, case C-370/90, [1992] ECR I-4625 para 24.

[193] Cf. Article 4(3) of Directive 68/360/EEC.

[194] Verwaltungsgerichtshof (Administrative Appeal Court) Baden-Württemberg, judgment of 2 January 1995, InfAuslR 1995, 97, 98.

[195] The jurisprudence of the European Court of Justice does not apply these conditions to the exercise of the right accorded to children of EU citizens under Article 12 of Regulation 1612/68. See judgment of 4 may 1995, *Landesamt für Ausbildungsförderung v Gaal*, case C-7/94, [1995] ECR 1031 paras 22-25. This issue shall be dealt with in detail sub specie Social Rights of Third-Country Nationals.

[196] ECJ, judgment of 18 June 1987, *Centre public d'aide sociale v Lebon*, case 316/85, [1987] ECR 2811

[197] ECJ, judgment of 18 June 1987, *Centre public d'aide sociale v Lebon*, case 316/85, [1987] ECR 2811 para 20.

[198] European Court of Justice, judgment of 18 June 1987, *Centre public d'aide sociale v Lebon*, case 316/85, [1987] ECR 2811 para 20.

> the status of dependent member of a worker's family ... is the result of a factual situation, namely the provision of support by the worker, without there being any need to determine the reasons for recourse to the worker's support.[199]

Member States have retained more or less unfettered discretion with respect to granting family reunification to relatives other than spouses and relatives in the descending and ascending lines. As a matter of policy, however, in the course of adoption of a uniform European system of immigration control that issue will be the subject of Community legislation.

c) Conditions of Entry

Article 10(3) of Regulation 1612/68 requires that "the worker must have available for his family housing considered as normal for national workers in the region where he is employed". The European Court of Justice has regarded this requirement as a limitation of the principle of free movement and, therefore, interpreted it restrictively. The Court has held that Article 10(3) of Regulation 1612/68 "does not require that the member of the family in question must live permanently with the worker"[200]. This conclusion derives support from Article 11 of the Regulation which permits that family members concerned –

> shall have the right to take up any activity as an employed person throughout the territory of that same state, even if they are not nationals of any Member State.

Moreover, the housing requirement applies at the time when the right to family reunification is exercised. Subsequent changes in housing conditions do not affect the status to be accorded to third-country national family members upon joining the EU citizen worker concerned[201]. Member States may, however, adopt provisions aimed at preventing abuse by workers who supply adequate housing only temporarily in order to obtain the right to be reunified with members of their family[202]. Under current German legislation giving up sufficient housing within six months after the family has been reunified qualifies as such abuse[203]. This provision has been introduced after previous legislation had been declared inconsistent with Regulation 1612/68[204] and has not been either tested by the

---

[199] ECJ, judgment of 18 June 1987, *Centre public d'aide sociale v Lebon*, case 316/85, [1987] ECR 2811 para 24.

[200] ECJ, judgment of 13 February 1985, *Diatta v Berlin*, case 267/83, [1985] ECR 567 para 18.

[201] See ECJ, judgment of 18 May 1989, *Commission v Germany*, case 249/86, [1989] ECR 1263 para 12.

[202] Cf. ECJ, judgment of 18 May 1989, *Commission v Germany*, case 249/86, [1989] ECR 1263 para 14.

[203] § 7(10) of the Statute on Entry and Residence of Nationals of the European Economic Community (Aufenthaltsgesetz/EWG); cf. *Hailbronner*, Ausländerrecht, D.1 § 7 Aufenthaltsgesetz/EWG para 17 (1998).

[204] ECJ, judgment of 18 May 1989, *Commission v Germany*, case 249/86, [1989] ECR 1263.

European Court of Justice or criticized by the Commission as being in breach of Community law.

d) Non-Discrimination

Article 12 ECT stipulates that within the scope of application of the Treaty establishing the European Community any discrimination on grounds of nationality shall be prohibited. Prohibition of discrimination only refers to EU citizens. Thus, non-discrimination under Article 12 ECT and the market freedoms run parallel. The European Court of Justice has consistently held that Article 39 ECT "gives more specific expression" to the principle enshrined in Article 12 ECT[205]. The Court held similarly with respect to freedom of establishment in *Van Ameyde v UCI*:

> In the respective spheres of the right of establishment and the freedom to provide services Articles 52 and 59 guarantee the application of the principle laid down by Article 7. It follows therefore that if rules are compatible with Articles 52 and 59 they are also compatible with Article 7.[206]

Consequently, though in principle applicable to cases concerning family members of EU citizens[207] Article 12 ECT does not affect the status of third-country nationals.

e) Freedom of Movement under Article 18 ECT

The Maastricht Treaty has linked freedom of movement to EU citizenship as enshrined in Article 17 ECT. This provision as such has, therefore, never been capable of according personal rights to third-country nationals. Moreover, Article 18 ECT does not compromise the well-established differentiation between cases with and without cross-border relevance. The European Court of Justice has emphasized that –

> citizenship of the Union, established by Article [17 ECT], is not intended to extend the scope *ratione materiae* of the Treaty also to internal situations which have no link with Community law.[208]

---

[205] ECJ, judgment of 27 October 1982, *Morson and Jhanjan v Netherlands*, joined cases 35 and 36/82, [1982] ECR 3723 para 14. The Court has reaffirmed this view, though in slightly different language, in its judgment of 17 April 1986 *Netherlands v Reed*, case 59/85, [1986] ECR 1283 para 21.

[206] ECJ, judgment of 9 June 1977, *Van Ameyde v UCI*, case 90/76, [1977] ECR 1091 para 27. The Court reaffirmed this position in its judgment of 26 January 1993, *Werner v Finanzamt Aachen-Innenstadt*, case C-112/91, [1993] ECR I-429 para 20.

[207] Cf. ECJ, judgment of 13 July 1983, *Forcheri v Belgium*, case 152/82, [1983] ECR 2323 paras 7+18. This case concerned, however, social rights.

[208] ECJ, judgment of 5 June 1997, *Ücker and Jacquet v Land Nordrhein-Westfalen*, joined cases C-64 and 65/96, [1997] ECR I-3171 para 23.

Prior to the entry into force of the Maastricht Treaty three instruments of Community legislation to implement freedom of movement were adopted which could now be based on Article 18(2) ECT[209]. These instruments shall, therefore, be discussed in the present section.

Article 1(2) of Directive 90/364 and Article 1(2) of Directive 90/365 accord rights to family reunification to spouses and dependent children of EU citizens, and to dependent relatives in the ascending line of both the EU citizen and his spouse. Under Article 1(2) of Directive 93/96 spouses and dependent children may join an EU citizen student in another Member State. However, EU citizens and their family members may only settle in another Member State if they and their family members are sufficiently insured against sickness and are unlikely to become dependent on the social welfare system of the host Member State during their presence[210].

To the extent that the Directives at issue use the language applied in Regulation 1612/68 and Directive 73/148/EEC they obviously intend to extend respective concepts of family ties and dependency to the categories of persons concerned. This view is reaffirmed by the fact that Directives 90/364/EEC, 90/365/EEC and 93/96/EEC all include references to certain social rights provisions of Regulation 1612/68.

As a matter of policy, from a generous approach towards family reunification one might criticize the provisions contained in the Directives presently discussed as too restrictive[211]. However, such criticism cannot allege that the limitations of family reunification lack congruence with primary Community law. The Treaty establishing the European Community does not include any provisions which could be employed as standards of review of the Directives. Moreover, nothing in the judgments mentioned points at standards of eligibility for family reunification under primary Community law. Additionally, all relevant ECT provisions stipulate for the implementation of free movement by way of adoption of secondary Community law. The legislative Community institutions must, therefore, be competent to shape the scope of family reunification i.e. define both the categories of family members eligible for family reunification and any necessary conditions for the exercise of that right. The legislative institutions may, therefore, render certain family members ineligible for family reunification, or impose conditions such as to protect national health care and public assistance systems.

f) The TEU's Reference to the European Convention on Human Rights

Standards of review of Community legislation governing family reunification might, however, be derived from Article 8(1) of the European Convention on

---

[209] Directives 90/364/EEC, 90/365/EEC and 90/366/EEC. However, after the European Court of Justice had declared void the last mentioned Directive the Council has re-adopted the content of this instrument as Directive 93/96/EEC.

[210] See Article 1(1) of Directive 90/364, Article 1(1) of Directive 90/365 and Article 1(1) of Directive 93/96/EEC.

[211] Cf. *Peers*, 33 CML Rev. (1996) 7, 16.

Human Rights. The increasing importance of family reunification is confirmed by a growing number of judgments of the European Court of Human Rights. Community institutions must have due regard to this jurisprudence because Article 6(2) TEU binds the European Union to respect fundamental rights, as guaranteed by the Convention. The Court of Justice has held that –

> Regulation No 1612/68 must also be interpreted in the light of the requirement of respect for family life set out in Article 8 of the Convention for the Protection of Human Rights and Fundamental Freedoms. That requirement is one of the fundamental rights which, according to the Court's settled case-law, restated in the preamble to the Single European Act, are recognized by Community law.[212]

The European Court of Human Rights as yet has not derived a right to entry and residence for family members from Article 8(1) of the European Convention of Human Rights. Although Article 8(1) of the Convention obliges contracting states to take the protection of an actually existing marriage or family into account when deciding on measures terminating a third-country national's residence, the Court has constantly held that Article 8(1) of the Convention cannot be interpreted as granting aliens a right to choose the country in which they could live safely with their spouses and children. The Court has therefore refused to deduce a right to family reunification as long as the family could live together in the home country of the spouse or family member asking for a right of entry or residence. Only in exceptional circumstances under which there is no alternative country of residence available, could a right to family reunification be deduced from Article 8 of the European Convention on Human Rights. The European Court of Human Rights, thus, has been careful to avoid far-reaching conclusions in immigration matters. It can therefore be assumed that Community law as it stands complies with the European Convention of Human Rights although some peripheral questions of non-compliance might eventually arise. Accordingly, Article 8(1) of the Convention is unlikely to effect major change of the Community legal order.

g) Immigration and Residence Control Measures

Family members of an EU worker have the right to take up employment anywhere in the Member State of the worker's residence regardless of their nationality[213]. The purpose of relevant provisions prohibits residence restrictions. Third-country national family members of EU citizens have, therefore, the right to free movement within the Member State.[214]

---

[212] ECJ, judgment of 18 May 1989, *Commission v Germany*, case 249/86, [1989] ECR 1263 para 10.

[213] Article 11 of Regulation 1612/68, Article 2(2) of Directive 90/364/EEC, Article 2(2) of Directive 90/365/EEC, Article 2(2) of Directive 93/96/EEC.

[214] See Article 6(1)(a) of Directive 68/360/EEC, Article 5 of Directive 73/48/EEC. Moreover, Article 2(2) of Directive 90/365/EEc and Article 2(2) of Directive 90/365/EEC have declared Article 6(1)(a) of Directive 68/360/EEC applicable by way of reference. It should be noted, however, that Directive 93/96/EEC has not included a similar reference to Article 6(1)(a) of Directive 68/360/EEC though referring to other provisions of this Directive. Arguably, therefore, Member States need not

Member States may not resort to immigration control measures either. Although they may require visas from third-country national family members of EU citizens they are bound to afford "to such persons every facility for obtaining any necessary visas"[215]. Moreover, third-country national family members shall be issued a residence document equivalent to that issued to the EU citizen upon whom they are dependent[216]. Thus, the rights of entry and of residence are inseparable[217]. In practice, therefore, as far as residence permits are concerned, Member States must and do accord the same treatment to family members of EU citizens regardless of their nationality. Derogations from the status enjoyed by family members are prohibited irrespective of their nationality, save on grounds of public policy, public security or public health[218]. According to jurisprudence at the national level the right of residence is, however, not even affected by illegal entry. The Administrative Appeal Court of Hessen has held that a third-country national spouse of an EU citizen is entitled to an albeit provisional, right of residence in spite of illegal entry[219].

Community legislation requires Member States to issue residence documents which are characterized as "proof of the right of residence" by relevant provisions[220]. Holding that under these provisions a spouse's "right to residence is to be evidenced by the issue of a residence permit"[221] the European Court of Justice has reaffirmed that such documents are only of a declaratory nature and cannot be regarded as constituting a family member's right of residence in the issuing Member State. Recent Community legislation has reiterated this decision of the Court[222].

h) Scope of the Right of Residence and Loss of Status

The right of residence of family members is dependent on the respective right enjoyed by the EU citizen worker. Workers acquire the right to permanent residence after certain periods of time encompassed in Article 2 of Regulation 1251/70. According to Article 3(1) of the said Regulation their family members acquire an independent right of permanent residence if their sponsor has acquired permanent resident status, provided that they are residing with the EU citizen

---

accord the same treatment, under Community law, to EU citizens, students and their family members as to other EU citizens exercising free movement.

215 Article 3(2) of Directive 68/360/EEC, Article 3(2) of Directive 73/148/EEC.

216 Article 4(4) of Directive 68/360/EEC, Article 4(3) of Directive 73/148/EEC, Article 2(1) of Directive 90/364/EEC, Article 2(1) of Directive 90/365/EEC, Article 2(1) of Directive 93/96/EEC.

217 *Cremona*, LIEI 21 (1995) 87, 100

218 Article 10 of Directive 68/360/EEC, Article 8 of Directive 73/148/EEC, Article 2(2) of Directive 90/364/EEC, Article 2(2) of Directive 90/365/EEC, Article 2(2) of Directive 93/96/EEC.

219 Hessischer Verwaltungsgerichtshof (Administrative Appeal Court), judgment of 2 November 1995, 13 TH 1700/94, InfAuslR 1996, 340.

220 Article 4(2) of Directive 68/360/EEC, Article 4(1) of Directive 73/148/EEC.

221 ECJ, judgment of 18 October 1990, *Dzodzi v Belgian State*, joined cases C-297/88 and 197/89, [1990] ECR I-3763 para 46.

222 Article 2(1) of Directive 90/364/EEC, Article 2(1) of Directive 90/365/EEC, Article 2(1) of Directive 93/96/EEC.

worker. In both cases the right of permanent residence includes a right to remain after termination of participation in the labour market.

The right of residence enjoyed by family members being dependent upon the status of the sponsor the question arises under what circumstances third-country national family members lose their privileged status. Termination of family ties is one reason. Another reason is maturity as defined by regulation 1612/68. After reaching the age of 21 children lose their right to residence if they are no longer dependants. The permanent resident status, acquired under Article 3(1) of Regulation 1251/70 is not independent of such circumstances. Article 6(1)(c) of Regulation 1251/70 stipulates that residence permits issued under the Regulation may be issued periodically though for a minimum period of five years. Article 3 of Regulation 1251/70 cannot be understood either as dissociating permanent resident status of family members from the family ties with their sponsors or as a dispensation from other conditions placed upon family reunification in terms of relevant secondary Community law.

Termination of family ties does not however, include the death of the sponsor. Article 3(2) of Regulation 1251/70 stipulates that, after the death of an EU citizen worker, "members of his family shall be entitled to remain there permanently" in the Member State of their residence under certain conditions such as a two year time-limit for the exercise of this right. However, children only acquire the right to permanent residence until their 21st birthday after the death of their parents. The privileged status of non-dependent children expires at the age of 21 regardless of whether their sponsor is alive under Article 10(1)(a) of Regulation 1612/68. Moreover, as a matter of policy no reason can be found why under the circumstances described, non-employed adult family members should enjoy a better status than persons participating in the labour market.[223]

2. *Close Persons without Family Ties*

a) Divorcés

Currently, Community law does not accord any rights to third-country national divorcés. Thus, the legal position of third-country national spouses might be particularly weak. In her case before the European Court of Justice *Mrs Diatta* argued that

> if co-habitation of the spouses were a mandatory condition, the worker could at any moment cause the expulsion of his spouse by depriving her of a roof[224].

Similarly, one might argue that under the present conditions third-country national spouses live in the Community at risk of losing their right to residence at any time due to termination of the marital relationship.

---

[223] *Hailbronner*, Ausländerrecht, D.1 § 7 Aufenthaltsgesetz/EWG para 8 (1998).
[224] ECJ, judgment of 13 February 1985, *Diatta v Land Berlin*, case 267/83, [1985] ECR 567 para 10.

It is obvious that the loss of a residence right in case of a divorce or separation may lead to considerable hardship, particularly if the circumstances giving rise to the divorce or separation are caused by a person disposing of an unrestricted right of residence. The Panel charged with an enquiry into issues relating to the free movement of persons[225] describes the situation as follows:

> In the event of divorce, the interested party may find him- or herself, from one day to the next, deprived of the right to stay in the Member State where he/she was hitherto resident. The precariousness of this situation is hard to accept, in particular as it may be used to the disadvantage of such persons. It is not rare for them (most often women) to be subjected during marriage to the threat of divorce. Even in the event of the marriage being dissolved, Community law should continue to offer some legal protection to the spouse who is a third-country national, in particular with regard to his/her right of residence. The fact that the third-country national may have exercised certain rights in the Community during his/her marriage creates objective ties whose effects exceed the duration of the marriage. Such is the case in particular where there are common children or where the spouse has exercised his/her right to pursue a profession. Accordingly it is suggested not only that national authorities be invited to take into account this situation but also that the various Community provisions applicable to the right to remain, should be amended so as to recognise a right of residence for the divorced spouse who is a third-country national.[226]

The suggestions of the Panel are reflected, although to a varying degree, in the national laws of Member States who increasingly grant a separate right of residence to spouses, provided, however, that marriage has lasted for a certain time. From a immigration law point of view one may argue that there is no reason to maintain a right of residence once the primary purpose for granting a residence permit has disappeared. In addition, an independent right of residence even after a very short period of time may result in subsequent immigration of family members and spouses of the divorced foreign national. Finally, the attractiveness of marriage of convenience may be considerably increased if an independent residence right is acquired automatically even after a very short period in the host state followed by a subsequent divorce. On the other hand, there is clearly a need to avoid the difficulties and precariousness of a situation of divorced spouses as described by the High Level Panel. Member States try to find a balance by requiring a certain period of time after which an independent right of residence may be acquired. Frequently there are in addition hardship clauses providing for the case that a spouse has been the victim of domestic violence or unacceptable treatment by the spouse. The European Commission taking up the proposals of the High Level Panel has suggested a change to Article 10 of Relation 1612/68 by granting third-country national family members a general right of residence in the Member State

[225] See Report of the High Level Panel on the Free Movement of Persons (Veil-Report) of 18 March 1997.

[226] Op.cit. at p. 70.

of residence if the marriage is dissolved, on condition that they have lived in that country under the terms of this Article for a period of three consecutive years.[227] This provision may appear to some as too restrictive. It does, however, reflect in general a fair balance of interests, taking into account the right of third-country nationals who have established some ties with the country of residence. There are, however, cases in which a three-year period may appear as too restrictive, particularly if a divorce is based upon violent behaviour of a spouse. Therefore, a hardship clause seems to be necessary.

b) Non-Marital Relationships

The European Court of Justice has declined to accord any rights under Article 10(1) of Regulation 1612/68 to non-married companions regardless of whether their relationship can be considered stable[228]. In *Reed*, however, the Court decided that Member States granting under national law a right of residence to a non-married partner of a national must grant equal treatment to a non-married partner of a Union citizen. The Court has regarded the right to reunion with a non-married partner as a social advantage as referred to in Article 7(2) of Regulation 1612/68 because

> the possibility for a migrant worker of obtaining permission for his unmarried companion to reside with him, where that companion is not a national of the host Member State, can assist his integration in the host society and thus contribute to the achievement of freedom of movement for workers[229].

Accordingly, Member States that allow for reunion of non-married couples must not discriminate on the basis of nationality.

Given the lack of a coherent social development as to the recognition of same-sex 'marriages' in the Community equal treatment applies to such relationships as well. The same is true with respect to polygamous relations. Where Member States allow for 'family' reunification with more than one partner at a time they may not treat differently their nationals and nationals of other Member States.

A European immigration law, however, cannot disregard the fact that the social environment relating to the recognition of non-marital relationships has changed. Under the domestic law of most EU Member States as well as under Community law the term "spouse" does not include an unmarried partner. The Panel on the Free Movement of Persons[230] has pointed out that the "family group" is undergoing rapid change and that a growing number of people, often with children, form *de facto* couples. The Panel recommended, on the basis of the *dictum* in *Reed*, that if a Member State grants rights to its own unmarried nationals living together, it must grant the same rights to nationals of other Member States, and that a study should be made of practice in the Union. The study should identify the criteria which, in

---

[227] COM (1998) 394, final, 27.
[228] ECJ, judgment of 17 April 1986, *Netherlands v Reed*, case 59/85, [1986] ECR 1283 para 15.
[229] ECJ, judgment of 17 April 1986, *Netherlands v Reed*, case 59/85, [1986] ECR 1283 para 28.
[230] See Veil-Report, op.cit.

the Member States, provide for non-married couples to be treated in the same way as married couples, as well as the extent to which this assimilation applies.[231]

Although it seems fairly obvious that to some extent unmarried relationships should be included in a European immigration regime, particular problems arise from the special nature of such relationships. As long as there are no formal requirements stated by law, it will be extremely difficult to evaluate under immigration law aspects the sincerity of a non-marital relationship. In the absence of a formal registry procedure implying some legal obligations as to inheritance rights, maintenance etc. no test can be invented to verify whether non-marital relationships satisfy conditions analogous to those which have to be fulfilled by spouses. Some Member States have introduced some formal procedures for registering non-marital relationships. Until a European regime can be devised, it would be useful to draft some minimum standards which have to be fulfilled in order to qualify as a non-married companion being entitled to a right of residence for the purpose of reunification with a partner.

As a matter of policy, one might think of Article 13 ECT influencing reunion with non-married partners, same-sex partners and of polygamous 'families'. Arguably, living in polygamous structures or in an unmarried partnership can be qualified as a specific sexual orientation. However, it has already been established that Article 13 ECT is without prejudice to the EU's power to grant access to any status under European aliens law. The Community may not, therefore, adopt measures aimed at easing access of non-married, or same-sex partners and of polygamous 'families' by way of anti-discrimination measures.

3. Posted Workers: The Freedoms to Provide Services and of Establishment

Article 49 ECT provides that –

> restrictions on freedom to provide services within the Community shall be prohibited in respect of nationals of Member States who are established in a State of the Community other than that of the person for whom the services are intended.

According to Article 50 ECT the person providing a service is entitled to

> temporarily pursue his activity in the State where the service is provided, under the same conditions as are imposed by that State on its own nationals.

Under Article 49 ECT the freedom to provide services is accorded to EU citizens only. To date, save for certain provisions contained in the EEA Agreement and the Europe Agreements no Community legislation exists under which third-country nationals can either exercise, or derive indirect benefits from the exercise of EU citizens of, the freedom to provide services. ECJ case law, however, has allowed third country nationals to benefit indirectly from this market freedom if they are employees of an undertaking established in the Community which posts them

---

[231] Op. cit. at p. 51.

abroad temporarily in order to provide services in a Member State other than the State in which they are lawfully and habitually employed. Community and national legislation covers certain aspects of the posting of workers for the provision of cross-border services.

a) Legal Issues of the Posting of Workers

The European Court of Justice dealt with the legal status of posted workers in *Rush Portuguesa*[232] and in *Vander Elst*[233]. Both cases arose with respect to cross-border posted workers who did not, at the time they were posted, enjoy the freedom of movement for workers while their employer was able to claim freedom to provide services. In both cases the European Court of Justice did not expressly address the issue of whether Member States may in any way limit access of posted workers to their territories. *Rush Portuguesa* does not touch the issue of residence permits at all, while it appears from the grounds of *Vander Elst* that national requirements for access to the territory had been complied with[234]. Hence the question of access to the labour market was the core issue of the judgments to be discussed here. In *Vander Elst* the Court had to consider whether Moroccan posted workers could be required to hold a work permit. The Court decided that the freedom to provide services

> preclude[s] a Member State from prohibiting a person providing services established in another Member State from moving freely on its territory with all his staff and preclude[s] that Member State from making the movement of staff in question subject to restrictions such as a condition as to engagement in situ or an obligation to obtain a work permit.[235]

Additionally, the Court in *Rush Portuguesa* held that the freedom of movement for Portuguese workers and the derogation therefrom provided for in the Act of Accession for a transition period were irrelevant to the case. According to the Court the purpose of this derogation was the prevention of possible disruptions of the labour markets of the pre-accession Member States. Temporarily posted workers could not cause such disruption. The Court pointed at the fact that such workers "return to their country of origin after the completion of their work

---

232 ECJ, judgment of 27 March 1990, case C-113/89, *Rush Portuguesa v Office national d'immigration*, [1990] ECR I-1417. Already before, in its judgment (Full Court) of 3 February 1982, *Seco/EVI*, joined cases 62 and 63/81, [1982] ECR 223, the Court had held that social security contributions for posted workers required from their employers without any corresponding social security benefit for the respective workers were contrary to Community law, in particular ex-Articles 59 and 60 ECT. That case, however, did not raise questions with regard to entry or residence of the workers in question.

233 ECJ, judgment of 9 August 1994, case C-43/93, *Vander Elst v Office des Migrations Internationales*, [1994] ECR I-3803.

234 ECJ, judgment of 9 August 1994, case C-43/93, *Vander Elst v Office des Migrations Internationales*, [1994] ECR I-3803 para 19.

235 ECJ, judgment of 27 March 1990, case C-113/89, *Rush Portuguesa v Office national d'immigration*, [1990] ECR I-1417 para 12.

without at any time gaining access to the labour market of the host Member State"[236].

Furthermore, the Court added that any condition as to engagement *in situ* or obligation to obtain a work permit would discriminate against the provider of services in relation to competitors established in the host Member State whose activities are not subject to similar conditions. The Court held that any such conditions would affect the ability to provide services as such[237]. In *Vander Elst* the Court reinforced this position:

> Article 59 of the Treaty therefore requires not only the elimination, against a person providing services who is established in another Member State, of all discrimination on the ground of his nationality but also the abolition of any restriction, even if it applies without distinction to national providers of services and to those of other Member States, when it is liable to prohibit or otherwise impede the activities of a provider of services established in another Member State where he lawfully provides similar services.[238]

As a result, third country-national workers may benefit indirectly from their employers' freedom to provide services although they do not enjoy freedom of movement.

This jurisprudence has provoked concerns as to possible distortions of labour markets by way of wage dumping and social dumping. The dumping issue was expressly addressed in *Vander Elst* in an *obiter dictum*. The European Court of Justice observed that the application of the legal framework established in the 'sending' Member State as regards working conditions or remuneration, and the field of social security, to posted workers excludes any substantial risk of workers being exploited or of competition between undertakings being distorted in the 'receiving' Member State[239]. This *dictum* must be viewed in connection with the Court's jurisprudence related to imposition of specific requirements on persons providing services. The Court held that such requirements

> cannot be considered incompatible with the Treaty where they have as their purpose the application of rules governing such activities. However, the freedom to provide services [...] may be restricted only by provisions which are justified by the general good and which are imposed on all persons or

---

236 ECJ, judgment of 27 March 1990, case C-113/89, *Rush Portuguesa v Office national d'immigration*, [1990] ECR I-1417 para 18. The Court reinforced this point of view in its judgment of 9 August 1994, case C-43/93, *Vander Elst v Office des Migrations Internationales*, [1994] ECR I-3803 para 21.

237 ECJ, judgment of 27 March 1990, case C-113/89, *Rush Portuguesa v Office national d'immigration*, [1990] ECR I-1417 para 12.

238 ECJ, judgment of 9 August 1994, case C-43/93, *Vander Elst v Office des Migrations Internationales*, [1994] ECR I-3803 para 14. The Court also referred to its judgment of 25 July 1991 in case C-76/90, *Saeger v Dennemeyer*, [1991] ECR I-4221 where it held almost identically in paragraph 12. This view was confirmed for instance in the judgments of 10 may 1995, case C-384/93, *Alpine Investments BV*, [1995] ECR I-1167 para 35/39, and of 28 March 1996, case C-272/94, *Guiot & Climatec*, [1996] ECR I-1905 para 10.

239 ECJ, judgment of 9 August 1994, case C-43/93, *Vander Elst v Office des Migrations Internationales*, [1994] ECR I-3803 para 25.

> undertakings operating in the said state in so far as that interest is not safeguarded by the provisions to which the provider of the service is subject in the Member State of his establishment.[240]

Additionally, the Court held that requirements of the aforementioned –

> must be objectively justified by the need to ensure that professional rules of conduct are complied with and that the interests which such rules are designed to safeguard are protected.[241]

Standards of protection of workers qualify as professional rules of conduct if regarded from the point of view of respective employers. Hence working conditions or remuneration and social security as implemented by Member States can be justified under the jurisprudence of the European Court of Justice. Indeed the Court held, in *Rush Portuguesa*, that –

> Community law does not preclude Member States from extending their legislation, or collective labour agreements entered into by both sides of industry, to any person who is employed, even temporarily, within their territory, no matter in which country the employer is established; nor does Community law prohibit Member States from enforcing those rules by appropriate means.[242]

Standards of protection of workers adopted by Member States are, however, different. Moreover, non-discrimination provisions included in existing association or cooperation agreements[243] do not stipulate for equality of treatment for third-country national workers throughout the European Union but within the framework of each individual Member State. Hence discrepancies between standards applicable to domestic workers and posted workers have not been abolished under the jurisprudence in *Rush Portuguesa* and *Vander Elst*.

---

240 ECJ, judgment of 17 December 1981, case 279/80, *Webb*, [1981] ECR 3305 para 17. The Court had already reached a similar conclusion in its judgment of 18 January 1979, joined cases 110 and 111/78, *Ministère public and another v van Wesemael and others*, [1979] ECR 35 para 28. This jurisprudence has been reaffirmed in the judgments of 4 December 1986, case 205/84, *Commission v Germany*, [1986] ECR 3755 para 27, of 26 February 1991, *Commission v Italy*, case C-180/89, [1991] ECR I-709 para 17, and of 26 February 1991, *Commission v Hellenic Republic*, case C-198/89, [1991] ECR I-727 para 18.

241 ECJ, judgment of 4 December 1986, case 205/84, *Commission v Germany*, case 205/84, [1986] ECR 3755 para 27.

242 ECJ, judgment of 27 March 1990, case C-113/89, *Rush Portuguesa v Office national d'immigration*, [1990] ECR I-1417 para 21, quoting from the judgment of 3 February 1982, joined cases 62 and 63/81, *Seco v EVI*, [1982] ECR 223 para 14. The Court reinforced this jurisprudence in its judgments of 9 August 1994, case C-43/93, *Vander Elst v Office des Migrations Internationales*, [1994] ECR I-3803 para 23, and of 28 March 1996, case C-272/94, *Guiot & Climatec*, [1996] ECR I-1905 para 12.

243 The Court noted, in *Vander Elst*, that the Moroccan posted workers' employment contracts fell subject to Articles 40 and 41 of the Co-operation Agreement between the European Economic Community and the Kingdom of Morocco which stipulate that all discrimination based on nationality between Community workers and those of Moroccan nationality, with regard to working conditions or remuneration, and social security, must be eliminated. See ECJ, judgment of 9 August 1994, case C-43/93, *Vander Elst v Office des Migrations Internationales*, [1994] ECR I-3803 para 24.

After an increase of cross-border provision of services Germany decided to act against wage dumping and social dumping by way of enacting the Federal Statute on Labour Conditions applicable to Cases of Cross-Border Services[244]. Similar concerns were raised at the European level and finally led to the adoption of Directive 96/71/EC which establishes a nucleus of mandatory rules for minimum protection to be accorded to posted workers. Article 3(1) of Directive 96/71/EC defines comprehensive minimum standards as regards terms and conditions of employment of posted workers which Member States must ensure. Article 3(1) of Directive 96/71/EC also determines the sources of domestic law which Member States may choose for the purpose of achieving the aims of the Directive, namely

- law, regulation or administrative provision, and/or
- collective agreements or arbitration awards which have been declared universally applicable i.e. which, according to Article 3(8), must be observed by all undertakings in the geographical area and in the profession or industry concerned.

Taking into account that Directive 96/71/EC mainly focuses on social rights of posted workers the question remains which scope of action national governments have retained in respect of controlling entry and sojourn of posted workers.

Rush Portuguesa and *Vander Elst* take precedence over national work permit requirements in so far as posted workers are concerned, provided that such workers are lawfully and habitually employed by a provider of services established in a Member State. Member States may, in other words, not inhibit the exercise of the freedom to provide services by way of rendering posted workers subject to the conditions prescribed for access to national labour markets because, according to the European Court of Justice, posted workers do not seek such access. This jurisprudence resembles principles established with respect to the free movement of goods and must, therefore, be understood as prohibiting work permit requirements even where such documents are issued either as a pure formality or on mere request[245]. In the meantime Member States have adjusted their legislation and administrative practice to the *Rush Portuguesa* and *Vander Elst* principles in that respect[246]. However, the mentioned principles also limit, to a certain extent,

---

[244] Arbeitnehmer-Entsendegesetz of 26 February 1996, Bundesgesetzblatt (BGBl) (1996) I, 227; see *Hold*, AuA, 1996, 113; *Webers*, Der Betrieb 1996, 574; *Lorenz*, Europäisches Arbeits- und Sozialrecht (EuroAS) 1996, 29.

[245] ECJ, judgment of 15 December 1971, joined cases 51 to 54/71, *International Fruit Company NV and others v Produktschap voor groenten en fruit*, [1971] ECR 1107 para 5 et seq., concerning the free movement of goods. Until 1996, Germany did not comply with the principle described. The Bundesanstalt für Arbeit had issued an Administrative Circular (Dienstblatt-Runderlaß No. 72/59; see *Borgmann*, Entsendung drittstaatsangehöriger Arbeitnehmer durch EU-Unternehmen nach Deutschland, Zeitschrift für Ausländerrecht und Ausländerpolitik (ZAR) 1996, 119; *Marschner*, Neue Zeitschrift für Arbeitsrecht (NZA) 1996, 186) which tied the employment of third-country nationals to a work permit irrespective of the *Vander Elst* principles. This requirement was eventually dropped after Commission criticized the Federal Republic of Germany for non-compliance with *Vander Elst*. See the reply of Commissioner *Monti* of 6 October 1995 to a parliamentary question of MEP *Gaigg*, E-2468/95, O.J. 1996 C 9/51.

[246] Germany's Foreign Office promulgated a circular of 29 July 1996 to all Diplomatic and Consular Representations according to which third-country nationals permanently resident in a Member State may provide services in Germany for limited time without needing a work permit. Austria replaced,

Member States' competence to restrict entry of posted third-country national workers pursuing dependent economic activity within the framework of the provision of services. Member States have, however, not taken any steps aimed at amending their relevant immigration legislation. The Commission has proposed a directive to this extent[247].

Cross-border provision of services poses a number of legal questions not yet settled. First, which kinds of services fall within the ambit of the *Rush Portuguesa* and *Vander Elst* principles? Second, which rules govern access of posted workers to the territories of Member States? Third, do these principles also govern establishment? Finally, to what extent does Directive 96/71/EC limit national discretion in respect of adopting mandatory minimum standards for the protection of posted workers?

b) Definition of Posted Work

National work permit requirements are prohibited for posted third-country national workers only. Hence a clear definition must be given for the concept of posted work. This definition can be based on the twofold characterization ascribed to posted work in the relevant jurisprudence. On the one hand, posted work is said to be "temporary" in nature. One may, therefore, ask when it ceases to be so. On the other hand, the meaning of the qualification of posted workers as "lawfully and habitually employed" requires further consideration.

The qualification as "temporary" refers to the period third-country national workers are posted into a Member State. In *Vander Elst* workers had been posted for one month while in *Rush Portuguesa*, reputedly, this period extended to half a year, although this is not ascertainable from the judgment[248]. It is suggested that no fixed time-limit can be prescribed to determine the temporary nature of posted work. Every project involving the provision of services of posted workers must be assessed individually. Certainly, posting of workers would cease to be temporary in nature if workers were subsequently posted to provide services in the framework of two or more projects. Arguably, an outer time-limit can be derived from Member States' legislative distinction between temporary and permanent employment in their regular labour markets.

The questions referred to the Court in *Vander Elst* dealt specifically with employees "lawfully and habitually" employed by an undertaking[249]. The Court did

---

in 1997, the *Entsendebewilligung* (precondition for taking up employment) by a system in which the employer (or the employee) must merely inform competent labour authorities that he is going to provide services in the territory of that Member State. Provided the complicance with certain conditions the labour authorities issue declaratory *EU-Entsendebestätigungen*. See Article 18(12-16) *Ausländerbeschäftigungsgesetz (AuslBG)*, BGBl. No. 218/1975, as amended by law, BGBl. I No. 78/1997.

[247] Proposal for a Directive on the posting of workers who are third-country nationals for the provision of cross-border services, COM (99)3 final, O.J. 1999, C 67/12.

[248] Cf. *Cholewinski*, Migrant Workers in International Human Rights Law (1997), 301 n. 86.

[249] ECJ, judgment of 9 August 1994, case C-43/93, *Vander Elst v Office des Migrations Internationales*, [1994] ECR I-3803 para 10.

not define lawful and habitual employment as a distinct concept under Community law. *Vander Elst* might, therefore, have a limited dimension only. Member States seem to have retained the competence to define the meaning of lawful and habitual employment. However, any minimum duration requirement for employment may well be considered an obstacle to the provision of services. Arguably, such a requirement impedes practices common in the construction business characterized by highly irregular employment, high turnover of staff, and which must be able to react flexibly to fluctuating levels of available work. Comparison with the relevant Community legislation on social rights of EU citizens shows that the treatment of posted workers has not been tied to previous periods of employment. EU-posted workers remain subject to the social legislation of the 'sending' country regardless of whether they belongs to the regular staff or are engaged with a view to being posted (cf. Article 14(1) Regulation 1408/71)[250]. Similarly, the concept of lawful and habitual employment as referred to in *Vander Elst* might simply reiterate the Court's view that posted workers do not seek access to the national labour market of the host Member State after having fulfilled their contractual obligations. Then, it has been argued, it would be likely that the Court, should it be asked to review this matter once again, might drop the "lawful and habitual employment" qualification[251]. On the other hand, however, the requirement of lawful and habitual employment may be indispensable to distinguish posted work from loan employment. The European Court of Justice has ruled as early as in 1981 that Member States may

> subject the provision of manpower within their borders to a system of licensing in order to be able to refuse licences where there is reason to fear that such activities may harm good relations on the labour market or that the interests of the workforce affected are not adequately safeguarded.[252]

because

> the provision of manpower is a particularly sensitive matter from the occupational and the social point of view[253].

Member States do not encroach upon a loan employer's freedom to provide services if they require the latter to meet those requirements for pursuit of his activities not already complied with under the laws applicable where the loan employer is established[254]. Obviously, provision of services in kind can be a means to circumvent conditions and requirements governing the provision of employees. Such circumvention can, however, be combated by thoroughly applying the

---

[250] O.J. 1971 L 149/2 = English Special Edition Series I 71 (II) p. 416. The *Administrative Commission for Migrant Workers* has expressed the view referred to in its Decision No. 162 of 31 May 1996 concerning the interpretation of Articles 14(1) and 14b (1) of Regulation 1408/71, on the legislation applicable to posted workers (OJ 1996 L 241, 28) para 2(b). However, this decision is not binding.

[251] *Peers*, EL Rev. 20 (1995), 303, 307.

[252] ECJ, judgment of 17 December 1981, case 279/80, *Webb*, [1981] ECR 3305 para 19.

[253] ECJ, judgment of 17 December 1981, case 279/80, *Webb*, [1981] ECR 3305 para 18.

[254] ECJ, judgment of 17 December 1981, case 279/80, *Webb*, [1981] ECR 3305 para 19.

requirement that posted workers must be lawfully and habitually employed. The European Court of Justice held, in *Rush Portuguesa*, that –

> it must be acknowledged [...] that an undertaking engaged in the making available of labour, although a supplier of services within the meaning of the Treaty, carries on activities which are specifically intended to enable workers to gain access to the labour market of the host Member State.[255]

In the event of nationals of third countries being excluded from a Member State's labour market the provision of loan employees would obviously circumvent any provision covering such exclusion.[256] Member States must, therefore, be competent to ascertain whether any undertaking proving services "is not availing itself of the freedom to provide services for another purpose, for example that of bringing his workers for the purposes of placing workers or making them available"[257]. However, according to the European Court of Justice this competence is not unlimited. Checks introduced by Member States

> must observe the limits imposed by Community law and in particular those stemming from the freedom to provide services which cannot be rendered illusory and whose exercise may not be made subject to the discretion of the authorities.[258]

Consequently, Member States may introduce any control measures short of enabling their authorities to take decisions regarding admission on a discretionary basis. Moreover, the Council has acknowledged the need to combat abuse in the field of cross-border loan employment in a recent resolution[259]. Nevertheless, the jurisprudence of the Court remains vague, to a certain extent[260]. In *Vander Elst* the Court was therefore invited by Advocate General Tesauro[261] to further develop the implications of its *dicta* in *Rush Portuguesa*. However, the Court declined to do so.

---

[255] ECJ, judgment of 27 March 1990, case C-113/89, *Rush Portuguesa v Office national d'immigration*, [1990] ECR I-1417 para 16.

[256] Cf. ECJ, judgment of 27 March 1990, case C-113/89, *Rush Portuguesa v Office national d'immigration*, [1990] ECR I-1417 paras 16 and 17.

[257] ECJ, judgment of 27 March 1990, case C-113/89, *Rush Portuguesa v Office national d'immigration*, [1990] ECR I-1417 para 17.

[258] ECJ, judgment of 27 March 1990, case C-113/89, *Rush Portuguesa v Office national d'immigration*, [1990] ECR I-1417 paras 16 and 17. Similar qualifications concerning control measures can be found for instance in the judgment of 11 November 1981, case 203/80, *Casati*, [1981] ECR 2595 para 27(concerning the free movement of capital) and in the judgment of 15 December 1976, case 41/76, *Donckerwolcke*, [1976] ECR 1921 para 30 et seq. (free movement of goods).

[259] Council Resolution of 22 April 1999, O.J. 1999 C 125/1.

[260] Cf. *Hailbronner*, in Europäisches Wirtschafts- und Steuerrecht (EWS) 1997, 401, 405.

[261] See Advocate General *Tesauro's* opinion in case C-43/93, *Vander Elst v Office des Migrations Internationales*, [1994] ECR I-3803 para 27.

c) Migration Control (Visa Requirements and Registration Duties)

Rush Portuguesa and *Vander Elst* left unaffected the differentiation between access to the labour market and access to the territories of Member States. Particularly, notice must be taken of the fact that in *Vander Elst* the European Court of Justice analyzed French law applicable to posted workers and established that this law differentiates between legislation concerning the immigration and residence of aliens and the work permit requirement. Observing that "a short-stay visa is not equivalent to a [work] permit" the Court concluded that the work permit requirement "is intended to regulate access to the French labour market for workers from non-member countries" only.[262] Taking into account that the Moroccan posted workers held Belgian work permits[263] *Vander Elst* might *mutatis mutandis* apply, to the question of which conditions govern access to the labour market in Member States, the principle that goods admitted to the market for goods in one Member State cannot be barred from the market of another Member State save for compelling reasons[264], rather than affect Member States' competence to regulate migration. Hence it is suggested that the *Rush Portuguesa* and *Vander Elst* principles do not either override public policy considerations or prohibit Member States from making legislative efforts aimed at preventing abuse of the conditions for admission of posted workers to Member States' territories.

The European Court of Justice has not yet decided whether or not freedom to provide services prohibits Member States from requiring visas for posted third-country national workers. In particular, the Court's remark in *Vander Elst* that the workers concerned held valid short-stay visas[265] may be interpreted either way.

The argument has been forwarded that under *Rush Portuguesa* and *Vander Elst* Member States no longer enjoy any discretion with regard to the admission of third-country national employees of undertakings making use of their freedom to provide services. Rather, it is said, Member States were obliged to issue entry visas to such workers for the length of time necessary to provide the services required of them by their employer[266]. However, prior to the adoption of relevant community legislation under Title IV ECT Community law did not affect Member States' competence to monitor the movement of third-country nationals. In his opinion on *Vander Elst* Advocate General Tesauro dismissed the need for work permits *inter alia* for the reason that Member States have other means of controlling such movements within their territory. Public policy and security requirements, expressly provided for by Articles 39(3) and 46(1) ECT, allow Member States to make the movements of those individuals subject to specific controls and permits;

---

262 ECJ, judgment of 9 August 1994, case C-43/93, *Vander Elst v Office des Migrations Internationales*, [1994] ECR I-3803 para 20.

263 Cf. ECJ, judgment of 9 August 1994, case C-43/93, *Vander Elst v Office des Migrations Internationales*, [1994] ECR I-3803 para 19.

264 Cf. ECJ, judgment of 20 February 1979, case 120/78, *Rewe v Bundesmonopolverwaltung für Branntwein (Cassis de Dijon)*, [1979] ECR 649 para 14.

265 See ECJ, judgment of 9 August 1994, case C-43/93, *Vander Elst v Office des Migrations Internationales*, [1994] ECR I-3803 para 19.

266 *Khan*, EuZW 1994, 602; *Peers*, EL Rev. 20 (1995), 303, 307.

in particular, through enforcement of entry visa and residence permit requirements[267].

The Court does not seem to question the legality of these requirements in any way. In an earlier case – *Watson and Belmann* – the Court ruled that Community law, by creating the principle of freedom of movement for persons and by conferring on any person falling within its ambit the right of access to the territory of the Member States (for the purposes intended by the Treaty), does not restrict the power of Member States to adopt measures enabling national authorities to have an exact knowledge of population movements affecting their territory[268], even with regard to EU citizens. Under this jurisprudence the obligation to report one's presence to the host Member State's authorities does not infringe Community law, provided that such formalities do not restrict the freedom of movement or limit rights accorded by the Treaty. In particular, provisions establishing a time-limit for reporting one's arrival only encroach upon the market freedoms if such a time-limit is fixed unreasonably[269]. Moreover, the Court is likely to apply even more generosity to controls on the movement of nationals of non-member countries. It is expected to allow Member States to choose between entry-visas, residence permits or mere declaration of arrival requirements. Given the wide range of conditions specific to certain sectors (as they have been recognized in particular for the construction industry[270]), Member States must have a wide discretion in the organization of effective controls of the movements of posted workers. Consequently, Member States may introduce the means of control they deem necessary.

Member States must, however, respect that providers of services who employ third-country nationals falling within the ambit of the *Vander Elst* principles, are entitled to have their employees admitted to the territories of other Member States. It is rather doubtful, however, whether employees themselves may claim for admission in order to fulfil labour contracts because no obligations resting upon Member States can be derived from relevant work relationships. The reasons Member States may invoke for denying necessary documents are, therefore, limited[271]. In particular, it is submitted that public policy concerns can justify

---

[267] See Advocate General *Tesauro's* opinion delivered on June 1, 1994, case C-43/93, *Vander Elst v Office des Migrations Internationales*, [1994] ECR I-3803 para 23.

[268] ECJ, judgment of 7 July 1976, case 118/75 *Watson and Belmann*, [1976] ECR 1185 para 17 et seq.

[269] In its judgment of 12 December 1989, case C-265/88, *Messner*, [1989] ECR 420 para 9 et seq., the Court found that a time-limit of three days could not be regarded as reasonable.

[270] See ECJ, judgment of 28 March 1996, case C-272/94, *Guiot & Climatec*, [1996] ECR I-1905 para 16.

[271] In Germany, according to Administrative Circulars of the Foreign Office of 8 August 1995, and of 29 July 1996, the firm or foreign enterprise, in order to get entry-visa for its third-country national employees under the *Vander Elst* regime, must have a seat in one of the EU-member States. The activity of such enterprise in Germany must be of a temporary nature. Beginning and end of the services to be provided in Germany must be laid down explicitly. The third-country national must be permanently and regularly employed by the enterprise making use of the freedom to provide services. As already mentioned above, the test is whether the third-country national belongs at least for one year to the enterprise. His occupation and residence in the sending country must be legal. An additional requirement is a right of access to the labour market and a residence permit in the sending country, enabling the third-country national to return to the sending country after termination of his

denial of access of posted third-country nationals to a Member State's territory only for reasons covered by Article 46(1) ECT.

Additionally, it has been suggested that third-country nationals enjoying derivative rights as employees of an EU company may enjoy indirect protection against termination of residence (expulsion or deportation from a Member State), except in accordance with the principles applied to EU citizens. Arguably, less far reaching protection might hinder the rights of Union companies providing services in another Member State[272]. A judgment of the Baden-Württemberg Administrative Appeal Court can be read to the same effect. The Court had to rule on the expulsion of a third-country national who had been employed by an Italian company in Germany without holding a residence or work permit. Holding that European Community law concerning freedom to provide services was applicable, the Court concluded that the worker's expulsion would have violated Community law if the Aliens Office had not adequately considered the fact that the third-country national had been employed under the Community privilege to provide services in Germany[273]. Violations of formal requirements alone cannot, therefore, justify an expulsion. However, this judgment cannot be interpreted as an extension of principles established under Community law to expulsion and deportation of Union citizens since the judgment's core issue was an alleged restriction of the freedom to provide services rather than a limitation of a potential freedom of movement which, indeed, has never been granted to third-country nationals.

The Schengen Convention provides that short-stay visa requirements are to be abolished between those Member States party to the Convention. Short-stay visas are defined as visas not exceeding three months (see Articles 10 and 11 of the Convention). According to Article 21(1) SIC an alien holding a residence permit issued by one of the Contracting Parties may, by virtue of that permit and of a travel document, both documents still being valid, move freely within the territories of the other Contracting Parties, provided he fulfils certain entry conditions referred to in Article 5(1)(a), (c) and (e) of the Agreement, and he is not on the national reporting list of the Contracting Party concerned[274].

---

employment in Germany. Finally, the third-country national, participating in the social insurance system of the sending country, must prove that there is a guarantee for an adequate medical supply in Germany in case of illness or labour accident. Whether even these requirements would stand an action brought before the ECJ depends on an evaluation based on the principle of proportionality. Austria has also changed her *Fremdengesetz* (Aliens Act), BGBl. I No. 75/1997, in order to comply with the *Vander Elst* principles. See BGBl. I No. 86/1998.

[272] See *Peers*, CML Rev. 33 (1996), 7, 47 et seq.

[273] Verwaltungsgerichtshof (Administrative Appeal Court) Baden-Württemberg, judgment of 7 December 1994, NVwZ 1996, 817.

[274] According to Article 5(1)(a), (c) and (e) SIC, referred to in Article 21(1) SIC, an alien must be in possession of a valid document or documents permitting him to cross the border, as determined by the Schengen Executive Committee (a), he has to submit documents substantiating the purpose and the conditions of the planned visit and must have sufficient means of support, both for the period of the planned visit and to return to his country of origin or to travel in transit in a Third State, into which his admission is guaranteed, or be in a position to acquire such means legally (c), and he must not be considered to be a threat to public policy, national security or the international relations of any of the Contracting Parties (e). For details concerning the entry regime under the Schengen Implementation Agreement see *supra* C I.

The Schengen Convention does not include specific rules concerning short stays for working purposes. National aliens legislation, however, frequently limits access to the territory to cases where the person concerned does not want to take up employment during his short stay.[275] However, any argument to the extent that under the Schengen Convention it would have been unnecessary for an employer like Mr. *Vander Elst* to obtain visas for his workers to perform services lasting one month would not be convincing. The Schengen Convention primarily aims at a common visa policy with respect to short-term visas (see Article 9(1) SIC). The question of whether someone needs a visa or a residence authorization for being granted entry into a Member State for the purpose of work touches different aspects of admission to the territory. Visa requirements have a formal character while the need to obtain a residence authorization must be characterized as a substantive requirement for entry. Accordingly, the communitarization of the Schengen *acquis* under the Amsterdam regime as such does not result in a change with respect to substantive requirements for entry as established at the national level.

Member States may oblige third-country nationals to declare their arrival within their territory. Similarly, according to Article 22 SIC, an alien resident within the territory of one of the Contracting Parties, who enters the territory of another Contracting Party, may be obliged to report his presence, in accordance with the conditions imposed by each Contracting Party, to the competent authorities there.

Furthermore, there may be other duties of registration aimed at controlling the observance of certain working conditions also applicable to posted workers pursuing activities in that country. In Germany, according to § 3 of the Federal Statute on Labour Conditions applicable to Cases of Cross-Border Services, before an employer falling within the scope of that legislation starts any activities, he must forward the following information to the competent State Labour Office (Landesarbeitsamt):

- names of the workers employed,
- duration of the work, and
- place of work.

In addition, the employer must assure compliance with the relevant provisions on labour conditions for all employees. The information required shall enable labour authorities to monitor that mandatory working conditions, and minimum rates of pay in particular, are observed. Similar, but even more detailed information has to be transmitted in advance to public bodies in charge of managing the system of paid annual holidays by virtue of special collective agreements declared universally applicable[276]. However, each of these duties runs the risk of infringing

[275] Cf. § 1(1) of the German Regulation Implementing the Aliens Act (Verordnung zur Durchführungs des Ausländergesetzes – DVAuslG). Under this provision third-country nationals who wish to take up employment need a residence authorization for entry into Germany.

[276] In Germany, the body responsible for the so-called *Urlaubskassenverfahren* in the construction industry is the *Urlaubs- und Lohnausgleichskasse der Bauwirtschaft (ULAK)*. Legal basis are certain provisions in special collective agreements, in particular § 8 *Bundesrahmentarifvertrag für das Baugewerbe (BRTV)* and § 59 *Tarifvertrag über das Sozialkassenverfahren im Baugewerbe (VTV)*.

upon the freedom to provide services enjoyed by undertakings established in other Member States, as they are liable to "prohibit, impede or render less advantageous"[277] the activities of a provider of services. The European Court of Justice will probably apply strict scrutiny to the question of whether such requirements can be justified by overriding concerns of public interest. The Court has held that where no such justification can be found where relevant public interests are already protected by the rules of the State where the provider of services is established or where the same result can be achieved by less restrictive rules. Several Belgian provisions have successfully been challenged before the Court[278].

d) The *Rush Portuguesa* and *Vander Elst* Principles and the Freedom of Establishment

Under the *Vander Elst* principles EU-based employers may temporarily post third-country national workers to another Member State in order to provide services. The argument may be raised that similar principles govern the freedom of establishment. Articles 43-48 ECT might be relied upon if an undertaking established in one Member State wishes to transfer an employee to an agency or branch in another Member State. Provided that the European Court of Justice were to abandon the concept of "lawful and habitual" employment, undertakings might even gain the right to hire third-country nationals legally resident in another Member State, possibly limited solely to employment with the establishing company. Arguably, any restriction on transfer or hiring under these conditions could be viewed as a non-discriminatory rule that hinders companies' freedom of establishment[279].

The emphasis placed on the temporary nature of the provision of services in *Vander Elst* seems to support the assumption that at the present stage of Community law these principles cannot be extended to cases in which an employer operates in another Member State via permanent establishment. Indeed, in *Vander Elst* the Court expressly distinguished between services and establishment, holding that –

> a Member State may not make the provision of services in its territory subject to compliance with all the conditions required for establishment and thereby

---

This system was extended to posted workers from other Member States by virtue of § 1(1) of the Federal Statute on Labour Conditions applicable to cases of Cross-Border Services.

[277] These qualifications have been used as elements of definition of infringements of the freedom to provide services, by the European Court of Justice in its judgment of 28 March 1996, case C-272/94, *Guiot & Climatec*, [1996] ECR I-1905 para 10.

[278] ECJ, judgment of 23 November, 1999, joined cases C-369/96 and C-376/96, *Arblade & Leloup/Sofrage*.

[279] Cf. for instance *Peers*, CML 33 Rev. (1996), 7, 39; *id.*, EL Rev. 20 (1995), 303, 308; *Cholewinski*, Migrant Workers (1997), p. 301, n. 86. According to *Peers*, CML 33 Rev. (1996), 7, 39, 41 et seq., albeit such general rights are likely to be rejected by the ECJ, there should be at least a right to hire third-country nationals in 'managerial or supervisory posts' or those who qualify as 'key personnel' in accordance with Article 44(3)(f) ECT.

deprive of all practical effectiveness the provisions whose object is to guarantee the freedom to provide services.[280]

This reasoning implies that Member States may require at least some of these conditions in the case of establishment, subject to the usual necessity and proportionality tests[281]. In light of the fact that employment under the establishment regime will normally entail an extended period of residence in the other Member State[282], these workers will, in reality, form an integral part of the labour market of that country. Member States may, as a result, demand work permits for third-country national workers from those companies established within, and fully economically integrated into, their territory, even if the Court has prohibited this requirement with regard to undertakings supplying services on a temporary basis.

e) Recent Commission Proposals for EC Directives in the Field of Provision of Services

In February 1999 the Commission proposed two directives to be adopted by the Community which shall be discussed in this section, namely:

- Proposal for a Directive of the European Parliament and of the Council on the posting of workers who are third-country nationals for the provision of cross-border services[283], and
- Proposal for a Council Directive extending the freedom to provide cross-border services to third-country nationals established within the Community[284].

In its proposal for a Directive on the posting of workers who are third-country nationals for the provision of cross-border services the Commission suggests the introduction of a new document, namely an EC service provision card which, under Article 2(1) of the Commission Proposal, shall be issued by the Member State where the provider of services is established if –

(a) the worker resides in that Member State, in accordance with its legislation;

(b) he is affiliated to the social security scheme in the Member State responsible for the risk of sickness or industrial accident, or else is insured against the risk of sickness or industrial accident during his posting to one or more other Member States.

---

280 ECJ, judgment of 9 August 1994, case C-43/93, *Vander Elst v Office des Migrations Internationales*, [1994] ECR I-3803 para 17. See also the judgments of 26 February 1989, case C-154/89, *Commission v France*, [1991] ECR I-659 para 12; and of 25 July 1991, case C-76/90, *Säger v Dennemeyer*, [1991] ECR I-4221 para 13.

281 See *Cremona*, Citizens of Third Countries: Movement and Employment of Migrant Workers within the European Union, LIEI 21 (1995), 87, 101.

282 This is also conceded by *Peers*, CML Rev. 33 (1996), 7, 39.

283 Commission Proposal of 12 February 1999, O.J. 1999 C 67/12, COM(99)3 final.

284 Commission Proposal of 12 February 1999, O.J. 1999 C 67/17, COM(99)3 final.

According to Article 2(2) and (3) of the Commission Proposal the EC service provision card shall be issued for half year or a year, dependent on the period of employment before it is issued, and it shall be renewable if the conditions as to its issue are fulfilled once more. Under Article 2(5) of the Commission Proposal –

> [t]he Member State issuing the EC service provision card may not regard posting for the provision of services in another Member State as being an interruption of the posted worker's period of residence or paid activity.

This provision would allow for subsequently posting workers.

As regards rights accorded by the proposed directive, Article 2(4) of the proposal stipulates that –

> [t]he EC service provision card shall be a separate document belonging to the service provider, which he puts at the disposal of the posted employed worker described therein. ...

This provision seems to reflect that employees cannot derive but indirect benefits from the exercise of their employer's freedom to provide services.[285] However, the Commission proposes that any Member State –

> shall permit the entry and residence of a worker who is a third-country national to its territory for the purpose of one or more provisions of services, if such person is in possession of the EC service provision card, and of an identity card or passport valid for the period during which the services are to be provided (Article 3(1) of the Commission Proposal).

Moreover, according to the second paragraph of that Article Member States may not –

> require from *the posted worker* or the service provider in his capacity as employer
>
> (a) an entry or exit visa;
>
> (b) a residence permit other than that specified in paragraph 3; or
>
> (c) a work permit or permit for access to a job; or
>
> (d) impose any obligation equivalent to those in points (a), (b) and (c)

(emphasis added). This provision indicates that under the proposed directive third-country national posted workers shall be accorded an individual right as to access to the territories of Member States where their employer wants to provide services.

Article 3(2) of the Commission Proposal limits the migration control competence by the prohibition of visa and residence permit requirements. Article 3(3) of the proposal imposes an obligation on Member States to issue residence permits to posted third-country national workers if their employer declares that the

---

[285] Article 3(4) of the Commission Proposal reflects the same basic construction in that it provides for legal remedies being available to the service provider in his capacity as employer in connection with decisions that fail to observe equality of treatment under this paragraph.

total period required for the service provision or provisions in question exceeds six months out of a period of twelve months, provided that respective Member States require providers of services to declare, before any of their workers enters the territory, the intended presence of that posted worker, the period of presence provided for and the service provision or provisions for which he is to be posted. Further limitation of national competence in the field of migration control is included in Article 4(2) of the proposal which stipulates that –

> Member States may not derogate from this Directive except on grounds of public order, public security or public health, in which case Directive 64/221/EEC shall apply *mutatis mutandis.*

The reference to Directive 64/221 though only mutatis mutandis supports an interpretation whereby posted third-country nationals enjoy the same treatment as EU-citizens concerning restrictions and termination of residence. Substantial differences between the legal situation of posted workers and EU citizens enjoying full freedom of movement appear to be neglected by such an interpretation, particularly with relation to the main purpose of Directive 64/221 as a major instrument to achieve full freedom of movement and to eliminate any obstacles that may prevent EU citizens from making use of the freedom of movement. The privileges derived from the freedom to provide services are in no way intended to achieve similar purposes with regard to a posted third-country worker. The reference therefore fails in substance.

Limitations of competence in the field of migration control affect, however, not only host Member States. According to the second sentence of Article 2(5) of the Commission Proposal

> The issuing Member State may not refuse, under national regulations, the readmission to its territory of the posted worker, for any reason whatsoever.

"Any reason" taken literally would preclude readmission in cases where residence titles have expired or have been withdrawn. "Any reason whatsoever" would even preclude readmission in cases where otherwise the issuing Member State could invoke compelling reasons of public policy. The second sentence of Article 2(5) of the Commission Proposal would result in equal treatment of nationals of host Member States and third-country national workers posted from that Member State with respect to readmission. In so providing the Commission proposal would clearly go beyond the standards governing readmission as they now stand. In principle a duty to readmit a posted worker appears as a reasonable consequence of issuing a service card. By issuing a service card to be accepted by the host state the issuing state has to carry a certain responsibility in case of a failure of the posted worker's assignment. Such failure, however, is not always adequately dealt with by an unconditional duty of readmission. Direct expulsion to a home country may be a more efficient way to deal with serious disturbances of public order. In addition, termination of residence permits should be executed directly by the host state rather than by a complicated procedure of readmission to the issuing state.

The Commission has submitted Articles 47(2) and 55 ECT as a legal basis. Under the current legal framework only the indirect effects of market freedoms may be regulated on the basis of Articles 47(2) and 55 ECT. *Rush Portuguesa* and

Vander Elst show that such indirect effects only cover issues related to the status of posted workers in the labour market of the host Member State, including the question of whether such workers may be required to hold work permits. As far as conditions for entry and sojourn of third-country national posted workers are concerned the draft directive must be based on Title IV ECT.

The Commission suggests that providers of services could equally include, in necessary declarations to the host Member States' competent authorities, a service provision or provisions for which they post workers. This provision would allow for provision of services by way of subsequently posting the very same workers. This provision read together with Article 2(3) and (5) of the Commission Proposal, under which renewal of EC service provision cards must be granted regardless of whether workers concerned are subsequently posted in a way amounting to permanent posting, shows that providers of services could post third-country national workers *ad infinitum*. It is difficult to see how a distinction can be drawn between temporary posting of workers to provide services and cross border provision of manpower. The proposal thus tends to eliminate immigration control with regard to third-country posted workers altogether, an aim which had at least in principle been recognised as legitimate by the European Court in *Vander Elst* and *Rush Portuguesa*.

Finally, the Commission proposal aims at equality of treatment with respect to certain social rights not covered by Directive 96/71/EC. Article 3(4) of the draft directive stipulates that –

> In order to facilitate the provision of services, any Member State in which a service is carried out shall ensure equality of treatment between third-country nationals and citizens of the Union posted as workers for the purpose of provision of services as regards the recognition of diplomas, certificates and other qualifications acquired within the Community with a view to performing the activity concerned, and issued by a competent authority of a Member State.

f) Third-Country National Providers of Services

The draft proposal is based upon Article 49(2) authorizing the Council to extend freedom to provide services to individuals of a third country who provide services and are established within the Community by a qualified majority decision. Unlike the draft directive on posting of workers the draft directive on extension of the freedom to provide services does not raise legal concerns as to the Member States' competence to control migration. The Treaty authorization to extend the provision of Chapter 3 of the ECT to third-country nationals implies that all provisions applicable to EU-citizens as providers of services apply also to third-country nationals by way of a Council decision. To that extent, Member States have irrevocably lost their power to restrict or control entry and residence of third-country nationals, provided, however, that third-country nationals act within the scope of application of the freedom to provide services. This implies as well that third-country providers of services established in a Member State may post third-country nationals under the same conditions as any EU-citizens making use of the freedom to provide services.

In its proposal for a Directive extending the freedom to provide cross-border services to third-country nationals established within the Community the Commission suggests the extension of the freedom to provide services to third-country nationals established in a Member State for at least twelve months, provided that the person concerned is not either a recipient of services or a provider of services in the transport sector, or also an employee (see Article 1(2) and (3) of the draft directive). Third-country national providers of services shall be issued with an EC service provision card similar to the EC service provision card issued to third-country national posted workers pursuant to Article 2(1) of the draft directive. Similarly, the EC service provision card shall be issued for a renewable period of one year (Article 2(2) of the draft directive). As regards admission to the territory of host Member States and readmission to the territory of the Member State of establishment the draft reiterates the substantive content of the proposal for a Directive on the posting of workers who are third-country nationals for the provision of cross-border services.

g) National Discretion in Respect of the Protection of Posted Workers

Unable to prevent posted workers, including third-country nationals, from entering their territory, some Member States have extended national legislation or collective labour agreements on minimum working conditions to such workers. Thus, Member States pursued two aims. On the one hand, they wanted to establish minimum protection for posted workers in order to prevent exploitative conditions. On the other hand, Member States wanted to make the engagement of posted workers economically less attractive. This practice distracts from the principle laid down in Article 6(2)(a) of the Rome Convention on the law applicable to contractual obligations of 19 June 1980[286] (henceforth referred to as the Rome Convention) in terms of which a contract of employment shall, in principle and in the absence of choice, be governed by the law of the country in which the employee habitually carries out his work in performance of the contract, even if he is temporarily employed in another country. Member States could, however, invoke Article 7(2) of the Rome Convention under which they may apply their mandatory rules of law to the contract, irrespective of the law otherwise applicable. Although the European Court of Justice did not refer to Article 7(2) of the Rome Convention it reached a similar conclusion in its relevant *obiter dicta* in *Rush Portuguesa* and *Vander Elst*.

Directive 96/71/EC concerning the posting of workers in the framework of the provision of services[287] which aims, according to paragraph (5) of its Preamble, at creating "a climate of fair competition and measures guaranteeing respect for the

[286] O.J. 1980 L 266/1.

[287] Directive 96/71/EC of the European Parliament and of the Council of 16 December 1996, O.J. 1997 L 18/1.

rights of workers" expressly refers to the quoted provisions of the Rome Convention. However, paragraph (11) of the Preamble adds that –

> according to the principle of precedence of Community law laid down in its Article 20, the said Convention does not affect the application of provisions which, in relation to a particular matter, lay down choice-of-law rules relating to contractual obligations and which are or will be contained in acts of the institutions of the European Communities or in national laws harmonized in implementation of such acts.

Under Article 20 of the Rome Convention Member States are, therefore, prohibited from evading the provisions contained in Directive 96/71/EC by way of invocation of Article 7(2) of the Rome Convention.

Directive 96/71/EC *inter alia* extends minimum wages and minimum paid annual holidays to posted workers primarily employed in the construction business. Obviously, such conditions compromise the competitive advantages of those suppliers of services who are established in a Member State with lower standards than the State where services are to be supplied. These conditions might, therefore, have effects equivalent to limitations of the freedom to provide services. The jurisprudence of the European Court of Justice with respect to the free movement of goods reinforces such concerns. According to the Court, national price regimes are prohibited by Article 30 ECT as measures having an effect equivalent to quantitative restrictions even if minimum prices for goods were applicable without distinction to domestic and imported products.[288] However, the Court's approach to the services sector as contained in the *obiter dicta* in *Rush Portuguesa* and *Vander Elst* seems to be more generous. Nevertheless, Member States may not apply protective standards where providers of services are subject to equivalent standards in their country of establishment[289]. Hence Member States' legislative discretion is subject to the terms of the Directive since its validity has not been challenged before the European Court of Justice regardless of possible doubts as to whether Directive 96/71/EC really aims at making it easier for persons to supply services as required by Articles 47(2) and 55 ECT.

Some Member States have already taken legislative steps based upon similar concerns as Directive 96/71/EC. Relevant national instruments must be construed in accordance with the terms of this Directive. Germany's Federal Statute on Labour Conditions applicable to Cases of Cross-Border Services provides that provisions in collective agreements in the construction business relating to payment and vacation apply equally to foreign employees and workers employed in Germany. The law is applicable to the construction business, as well as to certain other businesses present on construction sites. In case of violation fines may be imposed and employers may be excluded from the admission to public contracts. Corresponding collective agreements have been declared universally

---

288 ECJ, judgment of 24 January 1978, case 82/77, *van Tiggele v Netherlands*, [1978] ECR 25 para 13/14, (minimum prices of gin); see also judgment of 29 January 1985, ECJ, judgment of 29 January 1985, case 231/83, *Cullet v Leclerc*, [1985] ECR 305 para 23/25, (national rules on fuel prices).

289 ECJ, judgment of 23 November 1999, joined cases C-369/96 and C-376/96, *Arblade & Leloup/Sofrage*.

applicable. In France the state-fixed minimum wage *salaire minimum de croissance (SMIC)* as well as other working conditions have been declared applicable to all persons providing services.[290] Austria requires that foreign workers must be paid comparable wages to nationals if they are employed in Austria for more than one month.[291]

In addition, national law may require providers of cross-border services to submit any information necessary for surveillance of obligations under national law. Requirements of that kind must not, however, exceed what is necessary for effective implementation of such obligations. In particular, where the submission of documents issued in the 'sending' country is possible these documents must be regarded as sufficient.[292]

V. Privileged Third-Country Nationals: Treatment in Association Agreements

1. Relevant Agreements

Association agreements, concluded on the basis of Article 310 ECT, create special, privileged links between associated non-Member States and the Community[293]. Subject to the relevant provisions of association agreements nationals of certain associated states enjoy a privileged status as workers or as self-employed persons, as the case may be.

To date the Community has concluded the following association agreements[294]:

- the Agreement establishing an Association between the EEC and Turkey[295], including the Additional Protocol[296],
- the Maghreb Cooperation Agreements with Algeria[297] and Morocco[298], and the Euro-Mediterranean Agreement with Tunisia[299] (which has replaced the Cooperation Agreement with Tunisia),
- the Lomé Convention[300],

---

290 See *Décret* 94-573 of 11 July 1994, Journal Officiel 12 July 1994, p. 10041.

291 See Article 7 *Arbeitsvertragsrechts-Anpassungsgesetz – AVRAG*, BGBl. No. 459/1993.

292 *Hailbronner*, in Europäisches Wirtschafts- und Steuerrecht (EWS) 1997, 401, 408 et seq.

293 This is consistent ECJ jurisprudence since *Demirel*: ECJ, judgment of 30 September 1987, case 12/86, *Demirel v Stadt Schwäbisch Gmünd*, [1987] ECR 3719.

294 The association agreement with Greece was replaced by the 1981 Act of Accession. The Cooperation Agreement with former Yugoslavia has been denounced by virtue of Council Decision 91/602/EEC of 25 November 1991, O.J. 1991 L 325/23 = Finnish special edition Chapter 11 Volume 19 p. 16 = Swedish special edition Chapter 11 Volume 19 p. 16.

295 O.J. 1963, 3687 = O.J. 1977 L 361/1 (English Edition) = OJ, English Special Edition 1973 C 113/1.

296 O.J. 1973, L 293/1.

297 O.J. 1978, L 263.

298 O.J. 1978, L 264.

299 O.J. 1998, L 98. This Agreement replaces the Co-operation Agreement concluded in 1978 (O.J. 1987, L 265/2).

300 O.J. 1991, L 229/3 = Finnish Special Edition Chapter II vol. 17, 59 = Swedish Special Edition Chapter II vol. 17, 59.

- the Europe Agreements concluded with the CEECs: Hungary, Poland, the Czech Republic, the Slovak Republic, Romania, Bulgaria, Estonia, Latvia, Lithuania and Slovenia[301],
- the EEA Agreement[302], and
- the Euro-Mediterranean Interim Association Agreement on trade and cooperation between the European Community, of the one part, and the Palestine Liberation Organization (PLO) for the benefit of the Palestinian Authority of the West Bank and the Gaza Strip, of the other part[303].

Moreover, Euro-Mediterranean Agreements are awaiting ratification by Member States, assent by the European Parliament having been given, with

- Morocco[304]
- Israel[305], and
- Jordan[306].

A further Euro-Mediterranean Agreement with Egypt has recently been concluded. Notably, the EC-Israel, EC-Jordan and EC-Egypt Agreements provide *inter alia* for cooperation in combating illegal immigration. For instance, Article 57 of the EC-Israel Agreement provides that –

> The Parties shall cooperate with a view in particular to:
>
> – defining areas of mutual interest concerning policies on immigration;
>
> – increasing the effectiveness of measures aimed at preventing or curbing illegal migratory flows.

The agreements include clauses governing readmission of these States' own nationals. The EC-Jordan and EC-Egypt Agreements even provide for readmission of nationals of the Contracting Parties, Third States and stateless persons[307]. Likewise the EC-Morocco Agreement contains a Joint declaration relating to readmission which states that –

> The Parties hereby agree to adopt bilaterally the appropriate provisions and measures to cover readmission of their nationals in cases in which the latter have left their countries. For these purposes, in the case of the Member States of the European Union, "nationals" shall be taken to mean Member State nationals as defined for Community purposes.

Readmission is also dealt with in the Cooperation Agreements concluded between the European Union on the one hand and Pakistan and Bangladesh, respectively, on the other.

The Council has adopted

---

301 See *supra* A IV for a detailed assessment on the role the Europe Agreements play for the upcoming enlargement of the European Union.
302 O.J. 1994, L 1/1.
303 O.J. 1997 L 187/3.
304 COM(95)740 final; for the European Parliament's assent see OJ 1996 C 181/15.
305 SEC(95)1719 final; for the European Parliament's assent see OJ 1996 C 78/32.
306 COM(97)554; for the European Parliament's assent see OJ 1998 C 226/26.
307 This information has been supplied by the Secretariat-General of the Council.

- standard clauses to be inserted in future mixed agreements[308], and
- standard statements to be made by the Community and respective third countries that shall form part of final acts of future Community agreements[309].

  The standard clauses stipulate that –

> Article X
>
> The Member States of the European Union and State X agree to cooperate in order to prevent and control illegal immigration. To this end:
>
> – State X agrees to readmit any of its nationals illegally present on the territory of a Member State, upon request by the latter and without further formalities;
>
> – and each Member State agrees to readmit any of its nationals, as defined for Community purposes, illegally present on the territory of State X, upon request by the latter and without further formalities;
>
> The Member States and State X will also provide their nationals with appropriate identity documents for such purposes.
>
> Article Y
>
> State X agrees to conclude bilateral agreements with Member States which so request, regulating specific obligations for readmission including an obligation for the readmission of nationals of other countries and stateless persons who have arrived on the territory of any such Member State from State X or who have arrived on the territory of State X from any such Member State.
>
> Article Z
>
> The Cooperation Council shall examine what other joint efforts can be made to prevent and control illegal immigration.

The standard statements are, for instance, contained in the Final Act of the EC-Pakistan and EC-Bangladesh agreements[310]. The Declarations by the European Community and the Islamic Republic of Pakistan[311] read as follows –

> The European Community recalls the importance attached by its Member States to the effective cooperation with third countries to facilitate the readmission of nationals of the latter who are present illegally in the territory of a Member State.

---

[308] See Council documents 5309/96 (Presse 45) and 4272/96 ASIM 6.

[309] See Council document 12509/95.

[310] EC-Pakistan agreement: COM(98) 357 final, O.J. 1999 C 17/6; EC-Bangladesh agreement: COM(99) 155 final, O.J. 1999 C 143/8.

[311] The declarations contained in the EC-Bangladesh agreement are almost identically in wording and do not deviate in substance.

> The Islamic Republic of Pakistan undertakes to conclude readmission agreements with the Member States of the European Union which so request.

However, third states do not seem to make the conclusion of readmission agreements a primary task. In the EC-Pakistan Agreement one finds a Statement by the Islamic Republic of Pakistan on the Declaration on Readmission Agreements that reads –

> In agreeing to the undertaking 'to conclude readmission agreements with the Member States of the European Union which so request', the Islamic Republic of Pakistan desires to make it clear that the undertaking exclusively represents Pakistan's readiness to enter into negotiations with the objective of concluding mutually acceptable readmission agreements with the Member States of the European Union which so request. At present Pakistan does not have such readmission agreements with any Member State of the European Union. However, on the request of EU Member States, Pakistan is willing to start negotiations or intensify where such negotiations are already underway. Pakistan considers these negotiations as independent of any other bilateral or multi-lateral agreements that we have concluded or are in the process of negotiating with EU Member States or the European Commission. Also, Pakistan does not accept any non-negotiable text for such bilateral readmission agreements.

Many other agreements have been concluded mainly on the basis of Article 132 ECT. Most of these agreements, however, only deal with free movement of goods and trade-related matters. They include mutual commitments to the extent that in the fields covered by respective agreements mutual arrangements shall not give rise to any discrimination between the Member States, their nationals, or their companies or firms on the one hand, and nationals, companies or firms of the associated states on the other. In particular, partnership and cooperation agreements of the kind referred to have been concluded with the Russian Federation[312] and the Newly Independent States, namely with Ukraine[313], Kazakhstan[314], Kyrgyztan[315], Moldavia[316], Belarus[317], Georgia[318], Armenia[319], Azerbejdshan[320] and Uzbekistan[321]. Among these only the Russia Agreement grants workers a personal right of non-discrimination[322].

---

[312] COM(94)257 final
[313] O.J. 1998, L 49/1.
[314] COM(94)411 final
[315] COM(94)412 final
[316] O.J. 1998, L 181/3.
[317] COM(95)44 final
[318] COM(95)135 final
[319] COM(95)136 final
[320] COM(95)137 final
[321] COM(96)254 final
[322] Article 19 of the Agreement

a) Effects of Association Agreements and Council of Association Decisions

The core question with respect to association agreements is related to their effects. The European Court of Justice had to touch upon that issue in several cases, which arose with respect to provisions contained in both association agreements themselves and Council of Association decisions adopted under provisions in respective agreements which empower Councils of Association to either implement the purposes of, or further develop respective agreements. While the Court's jurisdiction over association agreements was not challenged as such there was dispute about the limitations of this jurisdiction. Member States agreed that, as the Court held, from the date of its entry into force, the provisions of an association agreement form an integral part of the Community legal system and that the Court, therefore, has jurisdiction to give preliminary rulings concerning the interpretation of the agreement[323]. However, Germany and the United Kingdom have argued that the jurisdiction thus constituted does not extend to provisions of "mixed" agreements by virtue of which the signatory Member States have entered into commitments relating to the exercise of their own powers, namely access to their territories by nationals of associated states[324]. In *Demirel* the European Court of Justice did not discuss whether this argument was convincing. Rather the Court held that the question posed by Germany and the United Kingdom did not arise because

> Article 238 must necessarily empower the Community to guarantee commitments towards non-member countries in all the fields covered by the Treaty. Since freedom of movement for workers is, by virtue of Article 48 et seq. of the EEC Treaty, one of the fields covered by that Treaty, it follows that commitments regarding freedom of movement fall within the powers conferred on the Community by Article 238.

The Court further observed that its jurisdiction

> cannot be called in question by virtue of the fact that in the field of freedom of movement for workers [...] it its for the Member States to lay down the rules which are necessary to give effect in their territory to the provisions of the Agreement or the decisions to be adopted by the Association Council

because

> in ensuring respect for commitments arising from an agreement concluded by the Community Institutions the Member States fulfil [...] an obligation in relation to the Community.[325]

---

[323] ECJ, judgment of 30 April 1974, case 181/73, *Haegeman v Belgium*, [1974] ECR 449 paras 5+6.

[324] See ECJ, judgment of 30 September 1987, case 12/86, *Demirel v Stadt Schwäbisch Gmünd*, [1987] ECR 3719 para 8.

[325] ECJ, judgment of 30 September 1987, case 12/86, *Demirel v Stadt Schwäbisch Gmünd*, [1987] ECR 3719 para 9-11.

Turning to the issue of the legal quality of Council of Association decisions several judgments given by the European Court of Justice must be considered. In *Greece v. Commission* the Court held that –

> [s]ince it is directly connected with the Association Agreement, [EEC-Turkey Council of Association] Decision No 2/80 forms, from its entry into force, an integral part of the Community legal system.[326]

The Court reaffirmed this jurisprudence in *Sevince*. Since that judgment it can be regarded as a standing principle of Community law that –

> since they are directly connected with the Agreement to which they give effect, the decisions of the Council of Association, in the same way as the Agreement itself, form an integral part, as from their entry into force, of the Community legal system.[327]

Accordingly, the Court may interpret both association agreements and measures of Association Councils in order to ensure uniform application of these elements of Community law under Article 234 ECT.

Additionally, the European Court of Justice had to examine the relation between Association Agreements and Council of Association decisions. Unlike EEC-Turkey Council of Association Decision 1/80 and 2/80, Decision 3/80 of that body does not specify on what date it should enter into force. Therefore, the European Court of Justice had to decide whether such effect can result from the Agreement on which that decision is based. Article 22(1) of the Agreement, provides that –

> [i]n order to attain the objectives of this Agreement the Council of Association shall have the power to take decisions in the cases provided for therein. Each of the Parties shall take the measures necessary to implement the decisions taken...

Taking into account Articles 6, 22(1) and 23 of the EEC-Turkey Association Agreement the Court held, in *Taflan-Met*, that –

> decisions of the EEC-Turkey Association Council are measures adopted by a body provided for by the Agreement and empowered by the Contracting Parties to adopt such measures[328]

and that –

> [i]n so far as they implement the objectives set by the Agreement, such decisions are directly connected with the Agreement and, as a result of the

---

326 ECJ, judgment of 19 November 1989, case 30/88, *Greece v Commission*, [1989] ECR 3711 para 13.

327 ECJ, judgment of 20 September 1990, case C-192/89, *Sevince v Staatssecretaris van Justitie*, 1990 [ECR] I-3461 para 9.

328 ECJ, judgment of 10 September 1996, case C-277/94, *Taflan-Met and others v Bestuur van de Sociale Verzekeringsbank and another*, [ECR] I-4085 para 17.

> second sentence of Article 22(1) thereof, have the effect of binding the Contracting Parties.[329]

The absence of a specified date of entry into force did not render ineffective Decision 3/80 but was interpreted by the European Court of Justice to the extent that this Decision has entered into force on the date of its adoption[330]. Furthermore, France, Greece, Spain and Germany had drawn attention to the fact that the 1983 Commission proposals for implementing Decision 3/80[331] were never adopted. The Court, however, concluded that –

> the binding effect of decisions of the Association Council cannot depend on whether implementing measures have in fact been adopted by the Contracting Parties.[332]

The Court only considered that, provided that implementation of provisions contained in Council of Association decisions is required, non-implementation of such provisions frustrates any claim based thereupon.

The construction applied to association agreements by the European Court of Justice fully underlines the basic assumption that such agreements and related subordinate instruments like Council of Association decisions form an integral part of Community law. It is, therefore, not surprising that the Court attributed direct effects to provisions in both association agreements and Council of Association decisions, provided that such provisions meet the test for direct applicability developed for standard primary and secondary Community law.[333] The Court thus rejected objections to the extent that Council of Association decisions require transformation into national law because they only bind the Contracting Parties of a given association agreement[334].

Under relevant jurisprudence of the European Court of Justice nationals of a Contracting Party of an association agreement can invoke provisions of such an agreement or a Council of Association decision adopted in accordance therewith if, taking into account the wording, the purpose and the nature of the agreement itself, the provision contains a clear and precise obligation which is not subject to the adoption of any subsequent measure of the Contracting Parties[335].

---

[329] ECJ, judgment of 10 September 1996, case C-277/94, *Taflan-Met and others v Bestuur van de Sociale Verzekeringsbank and another*, 1996 [ECR] I-4085 para 18.

[330] ECJ, judgment of 10 September 1996, case C-277/94, *Taflan-Met and others v Bestuur van de Sociale Verzekeringsbank and another*, 1996 [ECR] I-4085 para 21.

[331] O.J. 1983, C 110.

[332] ECJ, judgment of 10 September 1996, case C-277/94, *Taflan-Met and others v Bestuur van de Sociale Verzekeringsbank and another*, 1996 [ECR] I-4085 para 20; cf. Peers 33 CML Rev. (1996), 7, 29.

[333] In *Sevince* the Court has held that Council of Association decisions "must satisfy the same conditions as those applicable to the provisions of the Agreement itself" in order to be recognized as having direct effect: ECJ, judgment of 20 September 1990, case C-192/89, *Sevince v Staatssecretaris van Justitie*, [1990] ECR I-3461 paras 14-15

[334] *Petersmann* ZaöRV 33 (1973) 266, 273; *Hailbronner* EuR 1984, 54, 66

[335] ECJ, judgment of 30 September 1987, case 12/86, *Demirel v Stadt Schwäbisch Gmünd*, [1987] ECR 3719 para 14; case C-192/89, *Sevince v Staatssecretaris van Justitie*, [1990] ECR I-3461 para 15. The Court has consistently reaffirmed this jurisprudence. See ECJ, judgment of 5 October 1994, case C-355/93, *Eroglu* v Land Baden-Württemberg, [1994] ECR I-5113 para 17; judgment of 10

Consequently, interpretation and application of association agreements and Council of Association Decisions follow the same rules as govern standard Community law. The European Court of Justice has argued in favour of this result on a merely technical basis, namely taking into account the method of creation of association agreements and subordinate decisions. This reasoning is reinforced when due regard is had to the substantive content of such agreements and decisions. To the extent that association agreements and Council of Association Decisions do either accord rights to nationals of the associated states or provide for any specific treatment to be accorded, by way of implementation of provisions contained therein, to such nationals, agreements and decisions are modelled upon the market freedoms and related instruments of secondary Community law. In particular –

- Article 12 of the Turkey Agreement provides that the Contracting Parties will be guided by ex-Articles 48, 49 and 50 of the Treaty establishing the European Community in gradually establishing freedom of movement for workers. Similar provisions are found in Article 13 of the Agreement on freedom of establishment, and Article 14 on freedom to provide services. Moreover, Article 9 of the agreement prohibits discrimination as defined by the principles laid down in ex-Article 7 of the EEC Treaty, (Article 12 ECT).
- Article 36 of the Additional Protocol provides that full freedom of movement shall be established in progressive stages, subject to the principles set out in Article 12 of the Agreement, and shall be attained between the end of the 12th and the 22nd year after the entry into force of that Agreement. The Council of Association has been named the competent authority to decide on modifications necessary to achieve this end.
- The EEA Agreement nearly equates the situation of nationals of the Kingdom of Norway, Iceland and the Principality of Liechtenstein ("EEA nationals") to the legal position of EU citizens.
- The Europe Agreements contain detailed provisions related to self-employed economic activity and non-discrimination of CEEC national workers.
- The Maghreb Agreements provide that the treatment accorded to workers employed in the territory of each Member State shall be free from any discrimination based on nationality with regard to working conditions and remuneration[336].

September 1996, case C-277/94, *Taflan-Met and others v. Bestuur van de Sociale Verzekeringsbank and another*, 1996 [ECR] I-4085 paras 24-25; judgment of 23 January 1997, case C-171/95, *Tetik v Land Berlin*, [1997] ECR I-329, para 22; judgment of 17 April 1997, *Kadiman v Freistaat Bayern*, case C-351/95, [1997] ECR I-2133 para 27; judgment of 30 September 1997, case C-36196, *Günaydin v Freistaat Bayern*, [1997] ECR, I-5143 para 24; judgment of 30 September 1997, case C-98/96, *Ertanir v Land Hessen*, [1997] ECR I-5179 para 24; judgment of 19 November 1998, case C-210/97, *Akman v Oberkreisdirektor des Rheinisch-Bergischen Kreises*, [1998] ECR I-7519 para 23; judgment of 26 November 1998, case C-1/97, *Birden v Stadtgemeinde Bremen*, [1998] ECR I-7747 para 19; judgment of 4 May 1999, case C-262/96, *Sürül v Bundesanstalt für Arbeit*, cf. OJ 1999 C-204/12 para 60.

[336] Cf. Article 38 of the Algeria Agreement

- The joint declaration on workers contained in Annex VI of the Final Act of the Fourth Lomé Convention guarantees non-discrimination "as regards working conditions and pay".

It is not surprising, therefore, that the European Court of Justice has applied the same progressive approach to relevant provisions of association agreements as employed when interpreting market freedoms. However, though accepted in principle, this approach has met with severe criticism by Member States, particularly as to the extension of the legal position of Turkish nationals. Moreover, the extremely cautious approach towards according individual rights to CEEC national workers taken by Member States reinforces the view that a majority of Member States wanted to prevent a similar development as in the case of the EEC-Turkey Association Agreement.

To date, the European Court of Justice has attributed direct effects to the following provisions of EEC-Turkey Association Council Decisions:

- Articles 2(1)(b) and 7 of Council of Association Decision 2/76,
- Articles 6(1), 7 and 13 of Council of Association Decision 1/80, and
- Article 3(1) of Council of Association Decision 3/80.
- Conversely, the Court has declined to apply directly –
- Article 12 of Council of Association Decision 2/76,
- Article 29 of Council of Association Decision 1/80, and
- Articles 12 and 13 of Council of Association Decision 3/80.

b) The Powers Conferred upon Councils of Association

Like the EEC-Turkey Association Agreement the Europe Agreements have established Association Councils. Associations Councils consist of members nominated by the respective Contracting Parties. They are charged with implementing the aims defined by the Association Agreements, pursuant to the terms of these agreements.

Associations Agreements bestow certain powers upon Association Councils. The EEC-Turkey Agreement envisages the adoption of decisions which have binding legal force according to the relevant jurisprudence of the European Court of Justice. The Europe Agreements provide for a number of powers enjoyed by Association Councils. In particular, these Councils may adopt decisions aimed at implementing the coordination of social security systems for CEEC workers resident in the EU and for EU citizen workers resident in the CEECs, including detailed rules for administrative cooperation providing the necessary management and control guarantees in that respect[337]. Such decisions shall, however, not affect any rights or obligations arising from bilateral agreements linking the CEECs and the Member States where these agreements grant more favourable treatment[338]. As

---

337 See Article 39 of the Poland Agreement.
338 See Article 40 of the Poland Agreement.

regards establishment, the Association Councils under the Europe Agreements shall take all measures necessary for the mutual recognition of qualification[339].

Association Councils are also empowered to make certain binding decisions. Some authors lend these decisions the legal status of an agreement[340]. To date, however, only the EEC-Turkey Association Council has made binding decisions regulating the legal status of Associated State nationals within the Community. Decisions 2/76 and 1/80 were adopted by the Council of Association to implement Article 12 of the Agreement and Article 36 of the Additional Protocol. Decision 1/80, therefore, prohibits any further restrictions on the conditions governing access to employment for Turkish workers already duly integrated in the labour force of a Member State. In this context, the term "worker" is to be understood as a person who offers services to an employer and places himself under the employer's direction in return for remuneration[341].

2. *The EEA Agreement*

Under the EEA Agreement EEA nationals enjoy freedom of movement, freedom of establishment and freedom to provide services subject to some minor limitations laid down in the Agreement. Articles 28, 31 and 36 of the EEA Agreement on the market freedoms of EEA nationals refer to Annexes V-VIII to the Agreement regulating in detail the scope of application of secondary Community law on freedom of movement including Directive 64/221 and Regulations 1612/68 and 1408/71.

Like EU citizens, EEA nationals' freedom of movement is not dependent on economic activity. Retirees enjoy the rights conferred by Regulation 1251/70[342] and Directives 75/34[343] and 90/365[344], as well as students by Directive 93/96[345]. Moreover, other persons are able to rely on the provisions of Directive 90/364[346].

According to Article 6 of the EEA Agreement the Member States are obliged to comply fully with the existent *acquis communautaire*. Future developments, including judgments of the European Court of Justice, are not included in the *acquis*. For the interpretation of the EEA Agreement, the general rules of public international law as codified in the Vienna Convention on the Law of Treaties apply. The European Court of Justice has held that an identical wording of ECT and EEA Agreement provisions does not necessarily imply an identical meaning.[347] However, the danger of different interpretations should not be over-estimated. The

---

339 See Article 46 of the Poland Agreement.

340 Cf. *Peers* 33 CML Rev. (1996) 7, 8.

341 *Peers* 33 CML Rev. (1996) 7, 21.

342 O.J. 1970, L 142/24.

343 O.J. 1975, L 14/10.

344 O.J. 1990, L 180/28.

345 O.J. 1993, L 317/59.

346 O.J. 1990, L 180/26.

347 ECJ-opinion 1/91 of 14 December 1991, *Draft agreement between the community, on the hand, and the countries of the European Free Trade Association, on the other, relating to the creation of the European Economic Area* [1991] ECR I-6079 para 14.

EEA Agreement expressly aims at the establishment of a uniform legal framework. Article 102(1) of the Agreement stipulates that the EEA Joint Committee shall adhere

> as closely as possible to the adoption by the Community of [...] new Community legislation with a view to permitting a simultaneous application of the latter...

Arguably, therefore, differences in interpreting ECT and EEA provisions do not challenge the conclusion that the concept of freedom of movement of persons is basically identical in both Agreements.

3. *The EEC-Turkey Association Agreement*

The EEC-Turkey Association Agreement accords different categories of rights to Turkish nationals. As far as access to the labour market and related questions of residence status are concerned these rights derive from Council of Association Decision 1/80. According to the European Court of Justice the relevant provisions of Decision 1/80 have direct effect. In turn, the legal bases of Decision 1/80, namely Article 12 of the EEC-Turkey Agreement and Article 36 of the Additional Protocol read together with Article 7 of the Agreement do not have direct effect because they essentially set up a program[348] and promote cooperation between the Contracting Parties in order to achieve the aims of the agreement[349].

a) The Progressive Integration of Turkish Workers

Questions related to entry and sojourn of Turkish nationals have continuously been on the European Court of Justice's agenda. Such questions arose from Articles 6, 7 and 9 of Decision 1/80. These provisions deal with rights of Turkish workers and their family members in relation to the labour market or, as far as children are concerned, education, apprenticeship and vocational training. Decision 1/80 does not deal with first entry and residence in the territories of Member States. The European Court of Justice has observed "that Decision 1/80 does not encroach upon the competence retained by the Member States to regulate ... the entry into their territories of Turkish nationals..."[350]. The Court has applied the same rule to

---

[348] See, with respect to Article 12 of the EEC-Turkey Agreement and Article 36 of the Additional Protocol, ECJ, judgment of 30 September 1987, case 12/86, *Demirel v Stadt Schwäbisch Gmünd*, [1987] ECR 3719 para 23.

[349] See, with respect to Article 7 of the EEC-Turkey Agreement, ECJ, judgment of 30 September 1987, case 12/86, *Demirel v Stadt Schwäbisch Gmünd*, [1987] ECR 3719 para 24.

[350] ECJ, judgment of 16 December 1992, case C-237/91, *Kus v Landeshauptstadt Wiesbaden*, [1997] ECR I-6781 para 25; judgment of 5 October 1994, case C-355/93, *Eroglu v Land Baden-Württemberg*, [1994] ECR I-5113 para 10; judgment of 23 January 1997, case C-171/95, *Tetik v Land Berlin*, [1998] ECR I-329 para 21; judgment of 17 April 1997, case C-351/95, *Kadiman v Freistaat Bayern*, [1997] ECR I-2133 para 31; judgment of 30 September 1997, case C-36/96, *Günaydin v Freistaat Bayern*, [1997] ECR I-5143 para 23; judgment of 30 September 1997, case C-

the question of whether Member States may regulate the entry of family members of Turkish workers[351] because Decision 1/80 does not accord any rights to family reunification to Turkish workers[352]. Admission of Turkish nationals is, therefore, subject to the conditions set at the national level.

However, the European Court of Justice has not reached similar conclusions with respect to Member States' competence regarding the residence status enjoyed by Turkish workers once they have been admitted even temporarily to the territory of a Member State. The Court has construed Article 6(1) of Decision 1/80 as a "system of gradual integration of Turkish workers in the host State's labour force"[353] and has held that –

> by granting to such a worker, after a specified period of legal employment in the Member State, access to any paid employment of his choice, the provisions in question necessarily imply – since otherwise the right granted by them to the Turkish worker would be deprived of any effect – the existence, at least at that time, of a right of residence for the person concerned.[354]

Under the European Court of Justice's jurisprudence Member States are, therefore, free from commitments under Community law only with respect to admission of Turkish nationals to their respective territories and to defining the conditions under which they may take up their first employment.

In later judgments the Court has specified Member States' residual powers more precisely. Member States may authorize Turkish workers to change of employers before completing "one year's legal employment" as referred to in the first indent of Article 6(1) of Decision 1/80. However, *Eker* has made clear that if Turkish workers choose to do so, the period after which they acquire the right to continue employment under Decision 1/80 starts anew[355] because the emergence of this right is conditional on one year's continuous employment by the same employer[356]. Since *Günaydin* the Court stresses that –

98/96, *Ertanir v Land Hessen*, [1997] ECR I-5179 para 23; judgment of 26 November 1998, case C-1197, *Birden v Stadtgemeinde Bremen*, [1998] ECR I-7747 para 37.

[351] ECJ, judgment of 17 April 1997, case C-351/95, *Kadiman v Freistaat Bayern*, [1997] ECR I-2133 para 31.

[352] ECJ, judgment of 30 September 1987, case 12/86, *Demirel v Stadt Schäbisch Gmünd*, [1987] ECR 3719 para 22.

[353] ECJ, judgment of 29 May 1997, case C-386/95, *Eker v Land Baden-Württemberg*, [1997] ECR I-2697 para 23; judgment of 30 September 1997, case C-36/96, *Günaydin v Freistaat Bayern*, [1997] ECR I-5143 para 37. See also the judgment of 30 September 1997, case C-98/96, *Ertanir v Land Hessen*, [1997] ECR I-5179 para 35.

[354] ECJ, judgment of 20 September 1990, case C-192/89, *Sevince v Staatssecretaris van Justitie*, 1990 [ECR] I-3461 para 29. The Court has reaffirmed this jurisprudence in its judgment of 16 December 1992, case C-237/91, *Kus v Landeshauptstadt Wiesbaden*, [1997] ECR I-6781 para 29; judgment of 5 October 1994, case C-355/93, *Eroglu v Land Baden-Württemberg*, [1994] ECR I-5113 para18; judgment of 6 June 1995; case C-434/93; *Bozkurt v Staatssecretaris van Justitie*, [1995] ECR I-1475 para 28.

[355] ECJ, judgment of 29 May 1997, case C-386/95, *Eker v Land Baden-Württemberg*, [1997] ECR I-2697 para 25.

[356] ECJ, judgment of 29 May 1997, case C-386/95, *Eker v Land Baden-Württemberg*, [1997] ECR I-2697 para 22-24.

> Decision 1/80 does not encroach upon the competence of the Member States to refuse Turkish nationals the right of entry into their territories and to take up first employment, nor does it preclude those Member States, in principle, from regulating the conditions under which they work for up to one year as provided for in the first indent of Article 6(1) of that decision.[357]

On the other hand, once admitted, Turkish workers forming part of the regular labour force are no longer subject to national aliens law relating to prolongation of residence permits, temporary residence permits, time limits etc. In *Günaydin*, the Court points out that –

> Article 6(1) cannot be construed as permitting a Member State to modify unilaterally the scope of the system of gradual integration of Turkish workers in the host State's labour force, by denying a worker ... the rights which the three indents of that provision confer on him progressively according to the duration of his employment.[358]

The legal position of persons who are not admitted to the territory of a Member State in their capacity as workers is dependent on whether they are family members of a Turkish worker. The jurisprudence of the European Court of Justice implies that Member States are competent to withhold the status of worker to Turkish nationals on the basis of objective reasons. One such reason is recognized in the first paragraph of Article 7 of Decision 1/80. This provision refers to "members of the family of a Turkish worker... who have been authorized to join him". Thus, Member States may admit Turkish nationals in their capacity as family members, thereby precluding the emergence of rights under Article 6(1) of Decision 1/80. However, family members can derive certain rights from Article 7 of Decision 1/80, including the right to work after three years habitual residence in the host State provided, however, that family members are not admitted to the labour market.

Further objective reasons are inherent in the concept of workers. The Court has consistently applied the Community concept of workers to Turkish nationals benefiting from Decision 1/80[359]. Accordingly, any Member State may admit Turkish nationals who are not family members of Turkish workers as non-workers where such persons seek access to its territory for purposes not covered by the Community concept of worker, thus precluding that any rights under Articles 6 and 7 of Decision 1/80 may arise. In particular, the Court has held, in *Günaydin*, that –

> There is nothing to prevent a Member State from permitting Turkish nationals to enter and reside there only in order to enable them to follow

[357] ECJ, judgment of 30 September 1997, case C-36/96, *Grünaydin v Freistaat Bayern*, [1997] ECR I-5143 para 36. The Court has held almost identically in its judgment of 26 November 1998, case C-1197, *Birden v Stadtgemeinde Bremen*, [1998] ECR I-7747 para 37.

[358] ECJ, judgment of 30 September 1997, case C-36/96, *Günaydin v Freistaat Bayern*, [1997] ECR I-5143 para 37.

[359] This construction must be regarded as the red line underlying the jurisprudence of the European Court of Justice although the Court has expressly held to that extent no earlier than in its judgment of 26 November 1998, case C-1/97, *Birden v Stadtgemeinde Bremen*, [1998] ECR I-7747 paras 24-25.

> within its territory specific vocational training, in particular in the context of a contract of apprenticeship.[360]

It should be noted that the aforesaid is not in conflict with the European Court of Justice's *dictum*, in *Kus*, to the extent that Article 6(1) of Decision 1/80 –

> does not ... make that right dependent on any other condition, such as the circumstances under which the right of entry and residence was obtained[361]

because in *Kus* the Court had to deal with conditions designed to adversely affect the emergence of rights under this provision where the person concerned had been admitted to the host Member State in his capacity as a worker.

b) The Principles Derived from Article 6 of Decision 1/80

Article 6(1) of Council of Association Decision 1/80 provides that –

> [s]ubject to Article 7 on free access to employment for members of his family, a Turkish worker duly registered as belonging to the labour force of a Member State:
>
> – shall be entitled in that Member State, after one year's legal employment, to the renewal of his permit to work for the same employer, if a job is available;
>
> – shall be entitled in that Member State, after three years of legal employment and subject to the priority to be given to workers of Member States of the Community, to respond to another offer of employment, with an employer of his choice, made under normal conditions and registered with the employment services of that State, for the same occupation;
>
> – shall enjoy free access in that Member State to any paid employment of his choice, after four years of legal employment.

According to the European Court of Justice this provision –

> is set out as a series of progressive stages: after one year's employment a Turkish worker acquires the right to continue working for the same employer; after three years' employment he acquires the right to pursue the same occupation, but with an employer of his choice; and after a further year's employment he acquires the right of free access to any paid employment of his choice in the Member State of employment. The purpose of that progressive arrangement is to allow a Turkish worker to acquire more

---

[360] ECJ, judgment of 30 September 1997, case C-36/96, *Günaydin v Freistaat Bayern*, [1997] ECR I-5143 para 32.

[361] ECJ, judgment of 16 December 1992, case C-237/91, *Kus v Landeshauptstadt Wiesbaden*, [1997] ECR I-6781 para 21.

> rights the longer he is employed in a Member State and, accordingly, the greater his degree of integration in that Member State.[362]

The Court further held that it be –

> essential to transpose, so far as possible, the principles enshrined in [Articles 39-41 ECT] to Turkish workers who enjoy the rights conferred by Decision No 1/80[363].

Gradual integration as construed by the European Court of Justice therefore covers two aspects. First, Turkish workers have the right to be issued a work permit provided that they meet the conditions laid down in Article 6(1) of Decision 1/80. Second, similar to Union citizen workers, Turkish workers are entitled to concomitant residence status. Turkish workers are not, however, entitled to move freely within the entire Community but only in the Member State of their residence and employment[364].

c) The Concept of Being Duly Registered as Belonging to the Labour Force

According to the European Court of Justice in order to determine whether a Turkish worker is "duly registered as belonging to the labour force"

> it must be determined ... whether the legal relationship of employment of the person concerned can be located within the territory of a Member State or retains a sufficiently close link with that territory, taking account in particular of the place where the Turkish national was hired, the territory on or from which the paid activity is pursued and the applicable national legislation in the field of employment and social security law.[365]

---

[362] ECJ, judgment of 29 May 1997, case C-386/95, *Eker v Land Baden-Württemberg*, [1997] ECR I-2697 para 19.

[363] ECJ, judgment of 23 January 1997, case C-171/95, *Tetik v Land Berlin*, [1998] ECR I-329 para 20, referencing its judgment of 6 June 1995, case C-434/93; *Bozkurt v Staatssecretaris van Justitie*, [1995] ECR I-1475 para 20. The Court has reaffirmed this jurisprudence in its judgments of 17 April 1997, case C-351/95, *Kadiman v Freistaat Bayern*, [1997] ECR I-2133 para 30; of 30 September 1997, case C-36/96, *Günaydin v Freistaat Bayern*, [1997] ECR I-5143 para 21 and of 30 September 1997, case C-98/96, *Ertanir v Land Hessen*, [1997] ECR I-5179 para 21.

[364] ECJ, judgment of 23 January 1997, case C-171/95, *Tetik v Land Berlin*, [1998] ECR I-329 para 29; judgment of 17 April 1997, case C-351/95, *Kadiman v Freistaat Bayern*, [1997] ECR I-2133 para 30; judgment of 30 September 1997, case C-36/96, *Günaydin v Freistaat Bayern*, [1997] ECR I-5143 para 22; judgment of 30 September 1997, case C-98/96, *Ertanir v Land Hessen*, [1997] ECR I-5179 para 22.

[365] ECJ, judgment of 26 November 1998, case C-1/97, *Birden v Stadtgemeinde Bremen*, [1998] ECR I-7747 para 33; referencing ECJ, judgment of 6 June 1995; case C-434/93; *Bozkurt v Staatssecretaris van Justitie*, [1995] ECR I-1475 paras 22-23; judgment of 30 September 1997, case C-36/96, *Günaydin v Freistaat Bayern*, [1997] ECR I-5143 para 29; judgment of 30 September 1997, case C-98/96, *Ertanir v Land Hessen*, [1997] ECR I-5179 para 39.

It is for the national courts to determine whether the work relationship in question meets these criteria[366]. As regards the character of work relationship the European Court of Justice has held that provisions adopted by Member States which introduce additional criteria run counter to the concept of being duly registered as belonging to the labour force[367]. Any person who "is bound by an employment relationship covering a genuine and effective economic activity" must thus be regarded as being duly registered as belonging to the labour force[368]. Furthermore, the Court has declined to exempt from that concept employment that is dependent on public funding even if its sole purpose is to keep the person concerned from being unemployed[369], provided that respective workers –

> have complied with the requirements laid down by law and regulation in the Member State concerned and are thus entitled to pursue an occupation in its territory.[370]

d) The Concept of Legal Employment

As regards the concept of "legal employment" the European Court of Justice has held that a Turkish worker may only claim for renewal of his work and residence permits if he enjoys a stable and secure situation as a member of a Member State's labour force and if he has an undisputed right of residence[371]. This dictum implies that stability of both residence status and the work relationship must be considered. However, the Court has never touched the issue of whether the employment situation as such, of a Turkish worker, qualifies as stable. In that respect, therefore, no test exists. Turning to the residence status of a Turkish worker, stability cannot be established if the worker in question has been employed under a residence permit which was issued to him as a result of fraudulent conduct which led to his conviction[372]. However, although the Court only referred to a criminal conviction on the basis of the facts before it, administrative fact-finding as to residence fraud must suffice if it respects the due process rights of the person concerned. Further

---

[366] ECJ, judgment of 6 June 1995; case C-434/93; *Bozkurt v Staatssecretaris van Justitie*, [1995] ECR I-1475 para 23.

[367] ECJ, judgment of 30 September 1997, case C-98/96, *Ertanir v Land Hessen*, [1997] ECR I-5179 para 31; judgment of 30 September 1997, case C-36/96, *Günaydin v Freistaat Bayern*, [1997] ECR I-5143 para 33.

[368] Cf. ECJ, judgment of 30 September 1997, case C-98/96, *Ertanir v Land Hessen*, [1997] ECR I-5179 para 43.

[369] ECJ, judgment of 26 November 1998, case C-1/97, *Birden v Stadtgemeinde Bremen*, [1998] ECR I-7747 paras 42-54.

[370] ECJ, judgment of 26 November 1998, case C-1/97, *Birden v Stadtgemeinde Bremen*, [1998] ECR I-7747 para 51.

[371] ECJ, judgment of 20 September 1990, case C-192/89, *Sevince v Staatssecretaris van Justitie*, [1990] ECR I-3461 para 30; ECJ, judgment of 16 December 1992, case C-237/91, *Kus v Landeshauptstadt Wiesbaden*, [1992] ECR I-6781 paras 12 and 22; judgment of 6 June 1995; case C-434/93; *Bozkurt v Staatssecretaris van Justitie*, [1995] ECR I-1475 para 26; judgment of 30 September 1997, case C-98/96, *Ertanir v Land Hessen*, [1997] ECR I-5179 para 47; judgment of 26 November 1998, case C-1/97, *Birden v Stadtgemeinde Bremen*, [1998] ECR I-7747 para 55.

[372] ECJ, judgment of 5 June 1997, case C-285/95, *Kol v Land Berlin*, [1997] ECR I-3069 para 27.

cases of instability relate to cases where Turkish workers benefit from the suspensory effect of an appeal lodged against the refusal of a residence permit[373] or a provisional right of residence granted during the procedure for the grant of a residence permit[374]. However, if relevant procedures lead to recognition of the person in question as having the right of residence this person –

> must be deemed retroactively to have enjoyed, throughout the period in question, a right of residence that was no longer provisional and, accordingly, to have had the benefit of a stable situation as a member of the labour force.[375]

e) Further Assimilation of Status

The European Court of Justice has even gone further in assimilating the legal position of Turkish workers to that of EU citizens. Although the Court accepts that Turkish workers cease to be integrated into the labour force of a Member State if they suffer permanent incapacity to work because "the provisions of Article 6(2) [of Decision 1/80] merely ensure the continuation of the right to employment and necessarily presuppose fitness to continue working"[376] the Court held, in *Tetik*, that a Turkish worker who has been legally employed in a Member State for more than four years has the right to maintain residence in that state for a reasonable period of time for the purpose of seeking new paid employment even if he voluntarily leaves his employment and does not enter into a new employment relationship immediately[377]. The Court held that it is for the national authorities to determine which period is reasonable but that these authorities may not jeopardize the Turkish worker's prospect of finding new employment[378]. The Court considered inadequate a period of a few days but did not determine a minimum period. Taking into account the Court's dictum in *Antonissen* to which reference has been made in *Tetik* this period may extend to up to six months[379]. Arguably the Court would require Member States to grant Turkish workers the same period for seeking employment as granted to EU citizens because Turkish workers are entitled to non-discrimination according to Article 10(1) of Decision 1/80.

---

373 ECJ, judgment of 20 September 1990, case C-192/89, *Sevince v Staatssecretaris van Justitie*, [1990] ECR I-3461 para 31.

374 ECJ, judgment of 16 December 1992, case C-237/91, *Kus v Landeshauptstadt Wiesbaden*, [1992] ECR I-6781 para 13.

375 ECJ, judgment of 16 December 1992, case C-237/91, *Kus v Landeshauptstadt Wiesbaden*, [1992] ECR I-6781 para 17.

376 ECJ, judgment of 6 June 1995; case C-434/93; *Bozkurt v Staatssecretaris van Justitie*, [1995] ECR I-1475 para 38.

377 ECJ, judgment of 23 January 1997, case C-171/95, *Tetik v Land Berlin*, [1997] ECR I-329 paras 27-30.

378 ECJ, judgment of 23 January 1997, case C-171/95, *Tetik v Land Berlin*, [1997] ECR I-329 para 32.

379 Cf. ECJ, judgment of 26 February 1991, case C-292/89, *The Queen v Immigration Appeal Tribunal, ex parte Antonissen*, [1991[ECR I-745 para 21. *Antonissen* has been reaffirmed by the judgment of 20 February 1997, case C-344/95, *Commission v Belgium*, 1997 [ECR] I-1035 paras 15-17.

Moreover, the European Court of Justice has characterized administrative documents issued by Member States as declarative rather than constituent for the status of Turkish workers[380].

Assimilation of status might take additional steps. In *Ergat* and *Nazli*, pending, Advocate General Mischo has proposed that Turkish nationals –

- should be treated similar to EU citizens with respect to the renewal of a residence permit regardless of whether they have not applied for such renewal in sufficient time, thus their residence status being regarded as stable even after expiry of their residence permit[381],
- should not be regarded as having definitely left the labour market if taken into custody and even if convicted though paroled[382],
- may not be expelled and deported on reasons of a general preventive nature in analogy with Article 3(1) and (2) of Directive 64/221/EEC[383].

In particular, the opinion in *Nazli* indicates a new tendency of reasoning. Advocate General Mischo has expressed his view that the rights embodied in Directive 64/221/EEC can be derived directly from Article 39 ECT[384]. That might eventually render irrelevant the fact that, unlike Article 39 ECT, many provisions of Decision 1/80 modelled upon the freedom of movement for workers have not subsequently been implemented.

f) Some Methodological Objections against the Court's Reasoning

Notwithstanding many objections raised by governments of Member States against the Court's constant concept of "*implied* residence rights", while Decision 1/80 only regulates a privileged access to the labour market of those Turkish nationals being part of the regular labour force, the basic principles on the interpretation of the EEC-Turkey Association law have in the meantime become a part of the *acquis communautaire*. Member States have not undertaken any effort to correct the Court's reasoning. Nevertheless, the Court's lack of a convincing methodology should not pass uncommented.

The European Court of Justice consistently holds that without concomitant residence status the rights granted to Turkish workers would be "deprived of any effect"[385], "of all effect"[386], "of any practical effect"[387] or would be "rendered

---

[380] ECJ, judgment of 6 June 1995; case C-434/93; *Bozkurt v Staatssecretaris van Justitie*, [1995] ECR I-1475 paras 29-30; reaffirmed in ECJ, judgment of 30 September 1997, case C-36/96, *Günaydin v Freistaat Bayern*, [1997] ECR I-5143 para 49; judgment of 30 September 1997, case C-98/96, *Ertanir v Land Hessen*, [1997] ECR I-5179 para 55.

[381] Case C-329/97, *Ergat v Stadt Ulm*, Opinion of the Advocate General paras 72-84.

[382] Case C-340/97, *Nazli v Stadt Nürnberg*, Opinion of the Advocate General para 37.

[383] Case C-340/97, *Nazli v Stadt Nürnberg*, Opinion of the Advocate General paras 67-75

[384] Case C-340/97, *Nazli v Stadt Nürnberg*, Opinion of the Advocate General para 75.

[385] ECJ, judgment of 20 September 1990, case C-192/89, *Sevince v Staatssecretaris van Justitie*, [1990] ECR I-3461 para 29; ECJ, judgment of 16 December 1992, case C-237/91, *Kus* v Landeshauptstadt Wiesbaden, [1992] ECR I-6781 para 30; ECJ, judgment of 5 October 1994, case C-355/93, *Eroglu v Land Baden-Württemberg*, [1994] ECR I-5113 para 19.

[386] ECJ, judgment of 6 June 1995; case C-434/93; *Bozkurt v Staatssecretaris van Justitie*, [1995] ECR I-1475 para 28; judgment of 23 January 1997, case C-171/95, *Tetik v Land Berlin*, [1998] ECR I-

totally ineffective"[388]. In addition, the European Court of Justice has derived the alleged necessity to transpose the Community concept of free movement of workers to Turkish workers "so far as possible" from Article 12 of the EEC-Turkey Agreement[389]. This provision stipulates that –

> [t]he Contracting Parties agree to be guided by Articles 48, 49 and 50 of the Treaty establishing the Community for the purpose of progressively securing freedom of movement for workers between them.

However, at the outset of its jurisprudence related to Decision 1/80 the Court had characterized this very provision as a programmatic clause which does not accord any rights to Turkish workers[390]. Nevertheless, the European Court of Justice has employed Article 12 of the EEC-Turkey Agreement as a justification for transposing the Community concept of free movement for workers although this concept was intended to function as a policy guideline rather than as hard law. Thus, the Court has treated Article 12 as a self-fulfilling prophecy. In that course, moreover, the Court has ignored that Article 39(3) ECT distinguishes between four categories of rights, namely –

> (a) to accept offers of employment actually made;
>
> (b) to move freely within the territory of Member States for this purpose;
>
> (c) to stay in a Member State for the purpose of employment ...
>
> (d) to remain in the territory of a Member State after having been employed in that State ...

whereas, in turn, Article 6(1) of Decision 1/80 is modelled upon the right to accept offers of employment only. The lack of entitlements similar to those enshrined in Article 39(3)(b-d) ECT must, therefore, be regarded as a strong indication of Member States' reluctance to give up their competence to control immigration with relation to Turkish workers.

Additionally, Article 6(1) of Decision 1/80 is not rendered ineffective if interpreted on the basis of the assumption that a Turkish worker being integrated into the labour force of a Member State enjoys privileged access to the labour market only without prejudice to a residence right. One year of lawful employment is sufficient to lead in its practical consequence to an implied right to immigrate permanently, although the Court never fails to mention explicitly that the

---

329 para 24; Eker para 19; judgment of 30 September 1997, case C-36/96, *Günaydin v Freistaat Bayern*, [1997] ECR I-5143 para 26; judgment of 30 September 1997, case C-98/96, *Ertanir v Land Hessen*, [1997] ECR I-5179 para 26

[387] ECJ, judgment of 26 November 1998, case C-1/97, *Birden v Stadtgemeinde Bremen*, [1998] ECR I-7747 para 37.

[388] ECJ, judgment of 19 November 1998, case C-210/97, *Akman v Oberkreisdirektor des Rheinisch-Bergischen Kreises*, [1998] ECR I-7519 para 24

[389] See for instance ECJ, judgment of 23 January 1997, case C-171/95, *Tetik v Land Berlin*, [1998] ECR I-329 para 20

[390] ECJ, judgment of 30 September 1987, case 12/86, *Demirel v Stadt Schwäbisch Gmünd*, [1987] ECR 3719 para 12.

competence of Member States to control immigration remains unaffected by its jurisprudence. That this is not true, is clearly shown by the Court's recent judgments in *Günaydin* and *Ertanir*. The German law of issuing temporary residence permits not renewable beyond a certain time limit for temporary purposes like special employment or professional formation becomes inapplicable if employment rights are assimilated to immigration rights. This conclusion is strongly confirmed by the fact that the European Court is gradually dissolving the concept of "belonging to the regular labour force" by using by analogy the freedom of movement privileges granted to EU citizens. The Court has not yet decided what exactly constitutes "belonging to the labour force". Following the recent opinion of Advocate General Mischo relating to employment of a prisoner on parole, one may even be able to acquire a right to immigrate into a Member State regardless of having committed a crime and having been convicted for that crime to a prison sentence involving parole.

Similarly, Article 6(1) of Decision 1/80 could have been interpreted as granting a right to renewal of a work permit provided that respective Turkish workers are eligible for such permit under national legislation which may require a valid residence authorization as a precondition of eligibility. It is true that denial to prolong a residence right may deprive a right of access to the labour market of its practical effect. But this is not logically implying a right to residence. Just as access to self-employed activities hardly means that a state is obliged to grant any other licences and permits, for instance, under environmental law, access to employment cannot be interpreted as implying a right to permits or licences required on the basis of something other than labour market concerns. Thus, the rights granted by Decision 1/80 clearly preclude to undermine the substantive content of a privileged access to the labour market, by refusing a prolongation of a residence permit based upon labour market considerations. This, however, does not mean that other legitimate public policy considerations related to control of immigration are excluded. The Court has failed to examine the substance of the privileges granted in Decision 1/80 on the basis of traditional means of interpreting public international law instruments and taking into account that no consensus had been reached in the Association Council concerning progress in freedom of movement matters. *De lege ferenda*, however, the Court's jurisprudence can hardly be criticised. The Community and the Member States have subscribed to the obligation, laid down in the Association Agreement, to gradually introduce freedom of movement for Turkish workers, taking the freedom of movement for EC-workers as a guideline. What the Court did was, in effect, a partial fulfilment of this obligation, substituting the Association Council.

In its practical effects, the European Court of Justice's jurisprudence is likely to substantially affect immigration policies. Rejected Turkish asylum seekers might eventually qualify for permanent residence status provided that they had been part of the labour force, since the rights under Article 6(1) of Decision 1/80 are according to the Court not conditional on the circumstances under which the right of entry and residence was obtained.

g) Family Members of Turkish Workers

Article 7 of Decision 1/80 provides that –

> [t]he members of the family of a Turkish worker duly registered as belonging to the labour force of a Member State, who have been authorized to join him:
>
> – shall be entitled – subject to the priority to be given to workers of Member States of the Community – to respond to any offer of employment after they have been legally resident for at least three years in that Member State;
>
> – shall enjoy free access to any paid employment of their choice provided that they have been legally resident there for at least five years.
>
> Children of Turkish workers who have completed a course of vocational training in the host country may respond to any offer of employment there, irrespective of the length of time they have been resident in that Member State, provided one of their parents has been legally employed in the Member State concerned for at least three years.

Again, this provision only refers to integration into the labour force of respective host Member States and does not touch the issue of residence status. Nevertheless the European Court of Justice applies the 'concomitant residence status' construction to family members of Turkish workers[391]. On the basis of a more general approach in his opinion in *Ergat* Advocate General Mischo has submitted that the Court treat Articles 6 and 7 of Decision 1/80 similarly as far as residence status is concerned[392]. In turn, the Court defines quite narrowly the residual competence of Member States which only permits the States –

> to authorize any [family member] to join the Turkish worker legally employed there, to regulate their stay until they become entitled to respond to any offer of employment and, if necessary, to allow them, under such conditions as it may specify, to take up employment before the expiry of the initial period of three years laid down by the first indent.[393]

In that respect the Court has emphasized that Member States may introduce necessary conditions such as to prevent fraud or sham marriages[394]. According to the Court such conditions derive justification from the object of Article 7 of Decision 1/80 which is to promote family unity as a means "to favour employment and residence of Turkish workers ... by ensuring that their family links are

---

[391] ECJ, judgment of 5 October 1994, case C-355/93, *Eroglu v Land Baden-Württemberg*, ECR [1994] I-5113 para 23; judgment of 17 April 1997, case C-351/95, *Kadiman v Freistaat Bayern*, [1997] ECR I-2133 para 29.

[392] Case C-329/97, *Ergat v Stadt Ulm*, Opinion of the Advocate General paras 59-60

[393] ECJ, judgment of 17 April 1997, case C-351/95, *Kadiman v Freistaat Bayern*, [1997] ECR I-2133 para 32.

[394] ECJ, judgment of 17 April 1997, case C-351/95, *Kadiman v Freistaat Bayern*, [1997] ECR I-2133 para 38.

maintained ..."[395]. Thus, Member States may impose restrictions of residence aimed at ensuring actual cohabitation of family members of Turkish workers in one household with the worker[396]. Additionally, Article 7 of Decision 1/80 provides for the integration of family members of Turkish workers into the labour force of the Member State of the worker's residence subject to the periods of residence specified therein. The European Court of Justice has held that the precondition of emergence of rights under the first indent of the first paragraph of Article 7 of Decision 1/80 is that family members of Turkish workers reside for three years in the host Member State without voluntary interruption. Conversely, involuntary stays of less than six months in the country of origin do not adversely affect this qualification[397].

Under the second paragraph of Article 7 of Decision 1/80 children are not subject to specified periods of residence provided that they have completed a course of vocational training and one of their parents has been legally employed in the Member State concerned for at least three years. In that respect the Court has held, in *Akman*, that this provision does not require that the respective Turkish worker is still "employed in the host Member State when his child wishes to gain access to the employment market there"[398]. *Akman* did not raise the question of whether children of Turkish workers can also claim a right of return to the Member State where they have completed vocational training and one of their parents has been legally employed. Arguably, children of Turkish workers can waive the right accorded to them by the second paragraph of Article 7 of Decision 1/80 by way of voluntary return to their country of origin.

Moreover, the Court has observed that emergence of rights under Article 7 of Decision 1/80 is dependent on whether respective family members have been authorized to join a Turkish worker resident in a Member State[399]. That seems to imply that entry of a family member of a Turkish worker as an asylum seeker or cases of illegal entry would exclude eligibility for the status of a privileged family member of a Turkish worker, although this conclusion is by no means certain.

Notably, the second paragraph of Article 7 of Decision 1/80 does not impose a nationality requirement. Non-Turkish national family members can, therefore, base a claim on this provision. Additionally, this provision does not include a definition of the term "family member". Some authors propose that a definition can be derived from Community law, especially Regulation 1612/68[400]. Taking into account the reasoning of Advocate General Mischo in *Ergat* this would require that Article 39 ECT implies a certain concept of family ties. However, the freedom of

---

[395] ECJ, judgment of 17 April 1997, case C-351/95, *Kadiman v Freistaat Bayern*, [1997] ECR I-2133 paras 33-34.

[396] ECJ, judgment of 17 April 1997, case C-351/95, *Kadiman v Freistaat Bayern*, [1997] ECR I-2133 para 40.

[397] ECJ, judgment of 17 April 1997, case C-351/95, *Kadiman v Freistaat Bayern*, [1997] ECR I-2133 paras 47-49.

[398] ECJ, judgment of 19 November 1998, case C-210/97, *Akman v Oberkreisdirektor des Rheinisch-Bergischen Kreises*, [1998] ECR I-7519 para 39.

[399] ECJ, judgment of 17 April 1997, case C-351/95, *Kadiman v Freistaat Bayern*, [1997] ECR I-2133 para 39.

[400] Cf. *Peers* 33 CML Rev. (1996) 7, 25.

movement for workers does not imply a Community concept as to the notion of 'family member'[401].

It should be noted, finally, that family members of Turkish workers can qualify as workers regardless of the existence of family ties if they are granted access to the labour market by way of a more favourable treatment than that prescribed by Article 7 of Decision 1/80. Additionally, this qualification might also derive from participation in a family allowance scheme where that scheme is based, pursuant to the law of the Member State concerned, on the premise that compulsory contributions to the social security pension scheme are deemed, in favour of that person, to have been paid in respect of time spent in bringing up a child[402].

h) The Status of other Turkish Nationals

Articles 13 and 14 of the EEC-Turkey Agreement deal with the freedoms of establishment and to provide services. They are said not to be directly applicable for the reason that they are programmatic clauses only[403]. The opposite view has been taken with respect to Article 41 of the Additional Protocol to the Turkey Agreement[404] the first paragraph of which states that –

> [t]he Contracting Parties shall refrain from introducing between themselves any new restrictions on the freedom of establishment and the freedom to provide services.

However, this provision cannot be interpreted as according any unconditional rights to Turkish nationals because Article 41(2) of the Additional Protocol provides that –

> [t]he Council of Association shall, in accordance with the principles set out in Articles 13 and 14 of the Agreement of Association, determine the timetable and rules for the progressive abolition by the Contracting Parties, between themselves, of restrictions on freedom of establishment and on freedom to provide services.

No provisions have thus far been adopted with respect to Turkish students or trainees. Unless such persons qualify as family members of a Turkish worker they may not, therefore, derive any rights from Decision 1/80. However, the European Court of Justice's judgment in *Sürül* indicates that students may qualify as workers under certain conditions[405].

---

401 See *supra* IV 1 b.

402 See ECJ, judgment of 4 May 1999, case C-262/96, *Sürül v Bundesanstalt für Arbeit*, cf. OJ 1999 C204/12 para 95.

403 Cf. *Peers* 33 CML Rev. (1996) 7, 29.

404 Cf. *Peers* 33 CML Rev. (1996) 7, 39.

405 Cf. ECJ, judgment of 4 May 1999, case C-262/96, *Sürül v Bundesanstalt für Arbeit*, cf. OJ 1999 C204/12 paras 81+94.

4. *The Mediterranean Cooperation Agreements*

a) The EEC-Algeria and EEC-Morocco Agreements

The 1978 Maghreb Cooperation Agreements concluded between the European Economic Community and Algeria and Morocco are aimed at

> contributing to the development of Algeria by efforts complementary to those made by Algeria, and of strengthening existing economic links on as broad a basis as possible for the mutual benefit of the Parties.[406]

Part of the measures designed to implement this aim are contained in Title III on co-operation in the field of labour, the basic provision of which accords national treatment for workers who are nationals of the High Contracting Parties:

> The treatment accorded by each Member State to workers of Algerian nationality employed in its territory shall be free from any discrimination based on nationality, as regards working conditions or remuneration, in relation to its own nationals.
>
> Algeria shall accord the same treatment to workers who are nationals of a Member State and employed in its territory.[407]

The European Court of Justice has consistently held that certain provisions contained in the Algeria and Morocco Agreements have direct effect[408]. At the same time, the Algeria and Morocco Agreements constitute no more than a status accorded to nationals of these countries lawfully resident in a Member State. This status extends to certain social rights which will be dealt with in detail *sub specie* Social Rights of Third-Country Nationals. Consequently, the Algeria and Morocco Cooperation Agreements do not impose any limitations on migration control policies as adopted by either the Member States or the Community (under Title IV ECT).

b) The Euro-Mediterranean Agreement with Tunisia

Prior to the entry into force of the Euro-Mediterranean Agreement with Tunisia nationals of Tunisia were subject to the same conditions as nationals of Algeria and Morocco. The Euro-Mediterranean Agreement, however, has widened the scope of cooperation. This more comprehensive approach has also been documented by

---

406 Article 2 of the Algeria Agreement. Article 2 of the Morocco Agreement contains a similar provision.

407 Article 38 of the Algeria Agreement. Article 38 of the Morocco Agreement contains a similar provision.

408 ECJ, judgment of 31 January 1991, case 18/90, *Kziber v Office national d'emploi*, [1991] ECR I-199 paras 15-22; judgment of 20 April 1994, case C-58/93, *Yousfi v Belgium*, [1994] ECR I-1353 paras 16-19; judgment of 5 April 1995, case C-103/94, *Krid v Caisse national d'assurance*, [1995] ECR 719 paras 21-24.

naming the agreement an Association Agreement, and is shown by the aims of the Agreement which are, according to Article 1(2) thereof, to:

- provide an appropriate framework for political dialogue between the Parties, allowing the development of close relations in all areas they consider relevant to such dialogue,
- establish the conditions for the gradual liberalization of trade in goods, services and capital,
- promote trade and the expansion of harmonious economic and social relations between the Parties, notably through dialogue and cooperation, so as to foster the development and prosperity of Tunisia and its people,
- encourage integration of the Maghreb countries by promoting trade and cooperation between Tunisia and other countries of the region,
- promote economic, social, cultural and financial cooperation.

Unlike the EEC-Algeria and Morocco Agreements, the EC-Tunisia Agreement contains a Title dedicated to the right of establishment and services (Title III of the Agreement). The legal status of workers is dealt with in Title IV thereof which governs cooperation in social and cultural matters.

As regards establishment and services, Article 31(1) of the EC-Tunisia Agreement observes that –

> The Parties agree to widen the scope of the Agreement to cover the right of establishment of one Party's firms on the territory of the other and liberalization of the provision of services by one Party's firms to consumers of services in the other.

This provision does not have any direct effects as shown by Article 31(2) of the Agreement which calls upon the Association Council for making recommendations for achieving the objective described in Article 31(1) thereof. However, the EC-Tunisia Agreement binds the Parties to reaffirm its obligations under the GATS, particularly the obligation to grant reciprocal most-favoured-nation treatment in the service sectors covered by that obligation, in terms of its Article 32(1).[409]

Title VI of the EC-Tunisia Agreement on cooperation in social and cultural matters contains detailed provisions related to multiple consequences of mutual migration. Chapter I of this Title focuses on workers. The provisions related to the status of Tunisian workers are modelled upon the former EEC-Tunisia agreement and hence resemble the terms of the EEC-Algeria and Morocco Agreements to a large extent. Inasmuch as the EC-Tunisia Agreement has not resulted in changes of the relevant provisions such provisions must be interpreted in accordance with existing ECJ jurisprudence. According to Article 64(1) of the EC-Tunisia Agreement workers must be accorded national treatment. The same rule applies to temporary workers allowed to undertake paid employment in the territory of a Member State under Article 64(2) of the Agreement; the latter provision has been

[409] Further implications of the GATS will be discussed *infra* 6.

introduced *de novo*. This provision implies that Tunisian workers do not even have a right to be admitted to the labour market of a Member state on a temporary basis. Notably, equality of treatment in the workplace and non-discrimination as regards termination of work relationships is without prejudice to the residence status enjoyed by Tunisian workers. The parties to the EC-Tunisia Agreement have observed, in their Joint declaration relating to Article 64(1) of the Agreement, that –

> With regard to the absence of discrimination as regards redundancy, Article 64(1) may not be invoked to obtain renewal of a residence permit. The granting, renewal or refusal of a residence permit shall be governed by the legislation of each Member State and the bilateral agreements and conventions in force between Tunisia and the Member State.

Moreover, Article 64 of the Agreement does not include any commitments of the EU and its Member States in respect of admission of the family members of Tunisian workers to the labour market of the Member States. Thus, the High Contracting Parties have observed, in a Joint Declaration relating to Article 64 of the Agreement, that –

> Without prejudice to the conditions and procedures applicable in each Member State, the Parties will examine the matter of access to a Member State's labour market of the spouse and children, legally resident under family reunification arrangements, of Tunisian workers legally employed on the territory of a Member State, except for seasonal workers, those on secondment or on placement, for the duration of the worker's authorized stay.

Additionally, the reference by the Joint Declaration to family reunification arrangements, shows that the EC-Tunisia Agreement in itself does not envisage family reunification either. The restrictive approach towards granting access to the territories of the Member States has, however, not been applied to social rights. Indeed, Article 65 of the EC-Tunisia Agreement provides for detailed social rights of Tunisian workers and their family members. Member States, however, retain the power to apply their domestic concept of family according to the Joint declaration relating to Article 65 of the Agreement which states that –

> It is understood that the term 'members of their family' shall be defined according to the national legislation of the host country concerned.

A new sub-paragraph contained in Article 65(1) of the Agreement defines the areas covered by the concept of social security. This provision will be dealt with in detail *sub specie* Social Rights of Third-Country Nationals.

The newly introduced Article 66 of the EC-Tunisia Agreement excludes the application of the chapter on workers to nationals of the parties residing or working illegally in the territory of their host countries. Hence illegal migrants of Tunisian nationality only enjoy social rights as provided for in the national legal orders of the Member States. The provision at issue should, however, not be understood as constitutive for such an exclusion. As a rule, the relevant national legislation and corresponding agreements exclude social welfare benefits for aliens. Accordingly,

Article 66 of the EC-Tunisia Agreement can be interpreted as emphasizing this rule as a principle of European migration law.

Under Chapter II of Title VI of the Agreement the European Union and Tunisia will conduct a regular dialogue on any social matter which is of interest to them. Such dialogue shall be used to find ways to achieve progress in the field of movement of workers and equal treatment and social integration for Tunisian and Community nationals residing legally in the territories of their host countries (see Article 69(1) and (2) of the Agreement), covering, under Article 69(3) of the Agreement:

(a) the living and working conditions of the migrant communities;

(b) migration;

(c) illegal immigration and the conditions governing the return of individuals who are in breach of the legislation dealing with the right to stay and the right of establishment in their host countries;

(d) schemes and programmes to encourage equal treatment between Tunisian and Community nationals, mutual knowledge of cultures and civilizations, the furthering of tolerance and the removal of discrimination.

Three aspects of this provision shall be dealt with in brief.

First, Tunisia seems to be unhappy about the implied prohibition of family reunification under the Agreement as it stands. Tunisia has, therefore, given notice to the European Union and the Member States of a unilateral Declaration concerning Article 69 of the Agreement –

- Considering family reunification as a basic right of Tunisian workers residing abroad,
- bearing in mind that this right is a key factor in maintaining the balance of the family and guaranteeing success at school and the children's social and occupational integration,
- notwithstanding the bilateral agreements concluded between Tunisia and certain Member States of the European Union,

Tunisia wishes the question of family reunification to be the subject of in-depth discussions with the Community with a view to easing and improving the conditions for family reunification.

Second, under the current legal framework any measures taken in the course of implementing the results of the dialogue under Article 69(3)(b) and (c) of the Agreement must be implemented subject to the provisions of Title IV ECT. In that respect the United Kingdom and Ireland might be under an obligation originating from Article 11 ECT which stipulates for loyalty, to participate not only in the dialogue under the EC-Tunisia Agreement but also in the implementation of any prospective results thereof under Title IV ECT.

Finally, implementation of results of the dialogue on anti-discrimination, as provided for in Article 69(3)(d) of the Agreement, will be governed by Article 13 ECT which stipulates for anti-discrimination measures.

The legal status of Tunisians might, furthermore, be influenced by the co-operation in the social field as envisaged by Chapter III of Title VI of the EC-Tunisia Agreement. Article 71 of the Agreement stipulates that cooperation between the Parties in the social field should be consolidated by way of carrying out projects and programmes in any area of interest to them. The same Article focuses on certain issues of migration control in that it states that –

> [p]riority will be afforded to:
>
> (a) reducing migratory pressure, in particular by creating jobs and developing training in areas from which emigrants come;
>
> (b) resettling those repatriated because of their illegal status under the legislation of the state in question;
>
> (c-h) [...].

According to Article 73 of the Agreement a working party as set up by the Association Council shall be responsible for the continuous and regular evaluation of the implementation of Chapters I to III. Chapter IV (i.e. Article 74) of the Agreement provides for lasting cultural dialogue and continuous cultural co-operation between the European Union and Tunisia.

c) Persons under the Sovereignty of the Palestinian Authority of the West Bank and the Gaza Strip

The EC-PLO Agreement does not include provision on the free movement of persons as contemplated in the market freedoms. Rather the third paragraph of Article 58 of the Agreement envisages that –

> [y]outh cooperation, including training of youth workers and youth leaders, youth exchanges and voluntary service activities, could therefore be supported and developed.

However, youth exchange does not open the back door for Palestinian Immigration. Joint Declaration on Article 58 of the Agreement states that –

> [t]he Parties agree that access to employment will not be included in the framework of youth exchange programmes.

5. *The Europe Agreements*

The Europe Agreements accord different treatment to CEEC national workers, self-employed persons and respective family members. Title IV of all Europe Agreements is dedicated to "Movement of Workers, Establishment, Supply of

Services". In employing a language similar to the Treaty establishing the European Community the Europe Agreements are thus modelled upon the market freedoms and the Community concepts embodied therein. Notwithstanding differences with respect to certain details, the Europe Agreements are based upon a uniform approach towards the CEECs and their nationals as regards movement of persons.

The Europe Agreements are association agreements based upon Article 310 ECT (see Article 1(1) of the Agreements). They function, thus, as a first step towards admission of the CEECs. Although agreements concluded under Article 310 ECT do not form a monolithic bloc[410], any interpretation of the Europe Agreements will necessarily be influenced by the jurisprudence of the European Court of Justice related to earlier association agreements. Where the Europe Agreements include provision similar or identical to the terms of the EEC-Turkey Association Agreement or the Cooperation Agreements with the Maghreb countries, these must be applied similarly. In contrast, new methods of interpretation must be developed where the terms of the Europe Agreements delve into new areas of regulation. The construction of individual provisions contained in the Europe Agreements is, however, guided by the core provisions of the agreements themselves, as provided for in their definitions of purpose. The agreements are aimed at –

- providing an appropriate framework for the political dialogue, allowing the development of close political relations between the parties,
- promoting the expansion of trade and the harmonious economic relations between the parties and so to foster the dynamic economic development and prosperity in the associated states,
- providing a basis for the Community's financial and technical assistance to those states,
- providing an appropriate framework for their gradual integration into the Community on the basis that they work towards fulfilling the necessary conditions, and
- promoting cooperation in cultural matters.[411]

By describing the aims of the pre-accession process as such, the Europe Agreements establish a free trade area[412] rather than a common economic area[413] or an internal market[414].

Signatories to the Europe Agreements hope to achieve these objectives in successive stages within a ten years period. This period is divided into two successive stages each of which shall last five years. Although Poland proposed that her Europe Agreement should provide for full freedom of movement after the expiration of the ten year transitional period,[415] and Hungary called for the

---

410 *Maresceau*, in Müller-Graff, East Central European States and the European Communities (1993) 209, 212.

411 See, for instance, Article 1 of the Poland Europe Agreement, O.J. 1993, L 348/2.

412 *Banasinski*, ecolex 1995, 384.

413 *Vörös/Droutsas* ZfV (1998), 2, 6.

414 *Maresceau*, in Müller-Graff, East Central European States and the European Communities (1993) 209, 217-218.

415 Cf. *Pinder*, The European Community and Eastern Europe (1991), 67.

establishment of a modest quota of work permits to be issued for skilled Hungarians willing to work in a Member State for a limited period of time[416], freedom of movement for Eastern European workers is still pending introduction[417].

All Europe Agreements include a Title IV which deals with movement of workers, establishment and supply of services. Differences related to the conditions of the individual CEECs notwithstanding, the provisions of Title IV of all Europe Agreements are generally the same in substance. In particular, the Europe Agreements do not expressly establish a protected residential status for CEEC national workers already present and working in the Member States[418]. The Europe Agreements, thus, grant less favorable treatment than both the EEA Agreement, which extends the freedom of movement to EEA nationals[419], and the EEC-Turkey Association Agreement read together with the Council of Association Decision 1/80. Freedom of establishment has, however, been introduced by the Europe Agreements. This freedom includes an individual right of access to the area comprising Member States' territories for the purpose of pursuing one's economic activities, as well as a right to remain there for this purpose[420]. The CEECs have bound themselves to similar commitments vis-à-vis the Member States[421].

a) The Legal Status of CEEC National Workers

The Europe Agreements provide that, subject to the conditions and modalities applicable in each Member State, CEEC national workers who are legally employed in the territory of a Member State shall be protected from any discrimination based on nationality with regard to working conditions, remuneration or dismissal; according to Joint Declarations it is understood that the concept "conditions and modalities applicable in each Member State" includes appropriate and applicable Community rules. Additionally, "the existing facilities for access to employment for [...] workers accorded by Member States under bilateral agreements ought to be preserved and, if possible improved", taking into account the Member State's labour market situation, national legislation and relevant national policy regarding the mobility of workers[422]. Other Member States are encouraged to conclude similar bilateral agreements[423].

---

[416] Cf. *Pinder*, The European Community and Eastern Europe (1991), 68.

[417] See also *Guild* in *id.* (ed.), The Legal Framework and Social Consequences of Free Movement of Persons in the European Union (1999), 127, 129; *Banasinski*, ecolex 1995, 384, 386; *Maresceau*, in Müller-Graff, East Central European States and the European Communities (1993), 209, 228.

[418] *Guild* in *id.* (ed.), The Legal Framework and Social Consequences of Free Movement of Persons in the European Union (1999), 127, 130.

[419] Cf. *Cremona*, in Maresceau (ed.), Enlarging the European Union (1997), 195,196-197.

[420] *Guild*, in *id.* (ed.), The Legal Framework and Social Consequences of Free Movement of Persons in the European Union (1999), 127, 131.

[421] Cf. *Kuschel*, EuZW (1992), 571-574 for a detailed assessment on the Poland, Hungary and CSFR (as it then was) agreements.

[422] Cf. Article 41(1) of the Poland Agreement

[423] Cf. Article 41(1) of the Poland Agreement

The Europe Agreements cannot be construed as according to workers a right of free entry into the Community. Under the Europe Agreements there is no right to a work permit even if respective CEEC nationals hold a residence permit in a Member State[424]. Moreover, the European Economic Community (as it then was called) in a unilateral Declaration (no. 1) on Chapter I of Title IV of the Europe Agreements which is attached to the Final Acts, has expressed the view that –

> [t]he Community declares that nothing in the provisions of Chapter I 'Movement of Workers' shall be construed as impairing any competence of Member States as to the entry into and stay on their territories of workers and their family members.

Moreover, CEEC workers who reside in a Member State do not enjoy a right to freedom of movement within that Member State or the Community under the Europe Agreements. Conversely, after the CEECs' accession to the European Union freedom of movement will be granted after an interim period. Southern enlargements provide sufficient evidence for both the need for, and the advantages of, transitional arrangements.

Transitional arrangements suspended the full application of the Community provisions on freedom of movement in order to prevent disruption of the labour markets of the existing Member States which could result from immediate and substantial movements of workers following accession[425]. Provisions of the Act concerning the Conditions of Accession of the Hellenic Republic and the Adjustment to the Treaties have apparently been the blueprint upon which the transitional arrangements contained in the Act of Accession of Spain and Portugal have been modelled. The transitional provisions of the second subparagraph of Article 45(1) of the Act of Accession authorized the Member States to maintain national provisions requiring Greek nationals to obtain authorization prior to immigration for the purpose of pursuing an activity as an employed person or seeking and taking up paid employment until 1 January 1988. The same right was conferred upon Greece in its relations with the pre-accession Member States. The provisions concerning Greek nationals constituted, therefore, a derogation from the principle of the free movement of workers. In *Peskeloglou* the Court held that Germany was authorized to maintain existing restrictions during the transitional period, but was prohibited from making more stringent the conditions on the taking up and pursuit of employment through fresh restrictive measures[426]. However, the European Court of Justice held, in *Agegate*, that the provisions governing the transitional arrangements vis-à-vis Spain were to be construed narrowly. In thus deciding the Court applied the long-standing principle of interpretation according to which exceptional clauses, including provisions allowing for derogations from

---

[424] Cf. Article 41(3) of the Poland Agreement.

[425] ECJ, judgment of 23 March 1983, case 77/82, *Peskeloglou v Bundesanstalt für Arbeit*, [1983] ECR 1085 para 12; judgment of 27 September 1989, case 9/88, *Lopes da Veiga v Staatssecretaris van Justitie*, [1989] ECR 2989 para 10.

[426] ECJ, judgment of 23 March 1983, case 77/82, *Peskeloglou v Bundesanstalt für Arbeit*, [1983] ECR 1085 para 13.

the market freedoms, must be narrowly interpreted[427]. Additionally, according to the European Court of Justice, there was no reason to deny equality of treatment to Portuguese workers who were already employed in the territory of one of the pre-accession Member States[428].

The Europe Agreements reflect this jurisprudence in that they stipulate that CEEC workers who have been admitted to the labour market of a Member State shall be accorded national treatment (see Article 37(1), first indent, of the Poland Agreement). Non-discrimination in the working conditions can be considered as directly applicable.

Upon accession of individual CEECs their nationals can only be withheld the freedom of movement by way of transitional arrangements. The need to draft such arrangements in a way which does not render empty the promise of a European Union without internal borders is generally recognized. At the same time, adaptation of the labour markets, in both the present Member States and the CEECs, to the changes caused by CEEC accessions must be considered in the course of the accession negotiations. Instabilities of labour markets might even compromise the idea of eastern enlargement as such. However, to what extent such arrangements should limit, modify or postpone the implementation of the freedom of movement for both workers and EU citizens, is very much a subject of political controversy and must be determined at the policy level.

b) The Legal Position of Family Members

The Europe Agreements deal with the family members of workers only. The legally resident spouse and children of workers who are lawfully employed in the territory of a Member State shall have access to the labour market of that Member State during the entire period of the worker's authorized period of employment, unless the worker is to be classified as a seasonal worker or falls within the scope of bilateral agreements, which are guided by separate provisions[429]. However, respective provisions do not envisage family reunification. The European Economic Community seemingly acted on the basis of the interpretation of the Europe Agreements thus outlined when it gave notice of the unilateral Declaration on Chapter I of Title IV of the Agreements to the respective CEEC plenipotentiaries.

Only spouses and children of a worker lawfully employed in the territory of a Member State shall have access to the labor market of that Member State, and only during the period of that worker's authorized stay of employment (see Article 37(1), second indent, of the Poland Agreement). The status thus created is derivative in nature, as it depends on the work relationship of the lawfully present

---

[427] ECJ, judgment of 14 December 1989, case C-3/87, *The Queen v Ministry of Agriculture, Fisheries and Food, ex parte Agegate*, [1998] ECR 4459 paras 32+39.

[428] ECJ, judgment of 27 September 1989, case 9/88, *Lopes da Veiga v Staatssecretaris van Justitie*, [1989] ECR 2989 para 21.

[429] Cf. Article 37 of the Poland Agreement.

worker[430]. Additionally, the status enjoyed by spouses and children is territorially limited to their Member State of residence[431]. Family reunification is subject to national law[432].

c) Decisions of Association Councils

As far as the status of workers is concerned the Europe Agreements define the role of Association Councils in terms of soft law. In particular, these bodies –

> shall examine granting other improvements including facilities of access for professional training, in conformity with rules and procedures in force in the Member States, and taking account of the labour market situation in the Member States and in the Community.
>
> (Article 41(2) of the Poland Agreement)

Additionally, they "shall examine further ways of improving the movement of workers" during the second stage of the association or earlier if so decided. The Association Councils shall make recommendations to this end. Unlike the EEC-Turkey Association Council, however, they do not have the power to issue binding decisions with respect to movement of persons[433].

d) Freedom of Establishment

A right of entry currently may only be drawn from the provisions on establishment laid down in the Europe Agreements. According to the Europe Agreements, the term "establishment", as used in relation to nationals, is interpreted as the right to take up and pursue economic activities as self-employed persons, as well as to set up and manage undertakings in companies controlled by CEEC nationals.[434] The wording of this provision is not, however, entirely clear. According to the German government the Europe Agreements do not grant a right of entry and sojourn, as suggested by some authors.[435].

However, the right to take up and pursue economic activities may be interpreted as implying a right of access to the territory of the Member States and to reside therein, for the purpose of pursuing one's economic activities. It has been suggested, by analogy to the Court's implied residence right doctrine developed with respect to the EEC-Turkey Association Agreement, that "[t]he right of

---

430 Cf. *Langhammer* Die Assoziierungsabkommen mit der CSFR, Polen und Ungarn: wegweisend oder abweisend (1992), 16; *Gargulla*, Informationsbrief Ausländerrecht (Aliens Law Newsletter) 1995, 181, 186.

431 *Gargulla*, Informationsbrief Ausländerrecht (Aliens Law Newsletter) (1995), 181, 186.

432 *Gargulla*, Informationsbrief Ausländerrecht (Aliens Law Newsletter) (1995), 181, 186.

433 Cf. *Cremona*, in Maresceau (ed.), Enlarging the European Union (1997), 195, 197.

434 See Article 44(1) of the Poland Agreement.

435 Cf. *Cremona* LIEI (1995), 87, 95

residence is a prerequisite of the right of self-employment."[436] On the basis of this understanding the Europe Agreements cannot be read as precluding entry and residence of CEEC nationals pursuing self-employed economic activity.

The same conclusion flows from the unilateral Declaration on Chapter I of Title IV of the Europe Agreements (as quoted *supra*). From this Declaration being limited to movement of workers follows *a contrario* that no national public order reservations can be employed for limiting the scope of establishment as developed by the European Court of Justice. By analogy to the European Court of Justice's dictum in *Antonissen* the suggestion has been made that the Community "concept of establishment must include the preparatory steps to establishment"[437]. Thus, it has been argued that nationals of Associated States have the right to enter the Member States and to establish themselves as self-employed persons[438].

Notwithstanding the construction of establishment as described *supra*, the freedom of self-employed economic activity accorded to CEEC nationals does not either extend to social rights or cover claims for family reunification. Indeed, the Europe Agreements' concept of establishment must not be over-stretched because this concept is different from what would be a mere reiteration of Articles 43-48 ECT. The opposite view[439] does not sufficiently consider the fact that the scope of establishment is defined by the Europe Agreements in a way strictly limited to pursuing economic activity and hence is incapable of being extended any further. Additionally, this view falls short of recognizing that the Europe Agreements, unlike Article 43(1) ECT, do not contain an express prohibition of restrictions on the freedom of establishment, regardless of whether these restrictions adversely affect the free establishment in a direct or an indirect manner. Under this differentiation limitations of social rights and of claims for family reunification qualify as indirect restrictions. Now that the Treaty establishing the European Community shows that indirect restrictions of market freedoms are not *per se* prohibited but only under the concept of equivalent effects, the Europe Agreements could only be read as outlawing limitations of social rights and family reunification in the context of the freedom of establishment by way of clear and non-ambiguous provisions. The language employed by the Europe Agreement is, however, not clear. Consequently, freedom of self-employed economic activity under the Europe Agreements does not include social rights and claims for family reunification.

The same conclusion can be drawn on the basis of the distinction between the Community concepts of "workers" and "self-employed persons". Since CEEC nationals may establish themselves in the European Union under the same conditions as nationals of the Member States in order to "take up and pursue economic activities as self employed persons" or "to set up and manage undertakings"[440], a distinction must be made between employees and self-employed persons. This distinction can be modelled upon the similar delineation of

---

[436] *Guild*, A Guide to the Right of Establishment under the Europe Agreement (1996), 9.

[437] *Guild*, A Guide to the Right of Establishment under the Europe Agreement (1996), 18.

[438] *Peers* 33 CML Rev. (1996), 7, 40.

[439] See *Guild*, A Guide to the Right of Establishment under the Europe Agreement (1996), 24 et seq. for this opposite view.

[440] Cf. Article 44(1) of the Poland Agreement

the scope of the community concepts of dependently employed and self-employed economic activity with respect to Articles 39 and 43 ECT[441]. Since freedom of movement for workers constitutes one of the fundamental principles of the Community, the European Court of Justice has held that the beneficiaries of the term "worker" in Article 39 ECT must be defined uniformly throughout the Community rather than in accordance with the national law of each Member State[442]. The Community concept of the term "worker" must be defined on the basis of objective criteria for rights and duties of worker and employer in an employment relationship. The essential feature of an employment relationship is the performance of services by the worker for and under the direction of an employer over a certain period of time and in return for remuneration[443].

The Europe Agreements guarantee treatment which is no less favourable than that accorded to the states' own companies and nationals in cases involving the establishment of foreign companies and nationals or the operation of such companies and nationals already established on their territory[444].

Article 44(4) of the Poland Agreement provides that –

For the purposes of this Agreement:

(a) 'establishment' shall mean

(i) as regards nationals, the right to take up and pursue economic activities as self-employed persons and to set up and manage undertakings, in particular companies, which they effectively control. Self-employment and business undertakings by nationals shall not extend to seeking or taking employment in the labor market or confer a right of access to the labor market of another Party. The provisions of this chapter do not apply to those who are not exclusively self-employed;

(ii) as regards companies, the right to take up and pursue economic activities by means of the setting up and management of subsidiaries, branches and agencies.

This provision is undoubtedly modeled on the right of establishment provided for in Articles 43-48 ECT. The Europe Agreements must, therefore, be viewed as an initial step in the implementation of the Community concept of the freedom to provide services into the legal and economic relationship between the Community, its Member States and the CEECs. Given the similarity between these concepts, it has been rightly argued that there is no place for national definitions of self-employed economic activity within the ambit of the Europe Agreements[445]. This

---

441 Cf. *Guild*, A Guide to the Right of Establishment under the Europe Agreement (1996), 19.

442 ECJ, judgment of 23 March 1982, case 53/81, Levin v Staatssecretaris van justitie, (1982) ECR 1035 para 11; cf. also the Court's judgment of 19 March 1964, case 75/63, *Unger v Bedrijfsvereniging voor Detailhandel*, [1964] ECR 379.

443 ECJ, judgment of 3 July 1986, case 66/85, *Lawrie-Blum v Land Baden-Württemberg*, (1986) ECR 2121 para 17.

444 Cf. Article 41(1) of the Poland Agreement.

445 *Guild* in *id.* (ed.), The Legal Framework and Social Consequences of Free Movement of Persons in the European Union (1999), 127, 133.

assumption is supported both by the fact that the European Court of Justice has treated self-employment as a Community concept,[446] and by the general aim of the Europe Agreements, i.e. to progressively close the gap between the economic systems of the CEECs and the European Union. The concept of self-employed economic activity under the Europe Agreements is, in principle, the same as the freedom of establishment as provided for by the Treaty establishing the European Community.

The Council has defined self-employed economic activity as all economic activity carried out in person or within the framework of a company, provided that the person carrying out such activity is not dependent on the instructions of an employer[447]. Likewise, the Europe Agreements stipulate that –

> Self-employment and business undertakings by nationals shall not extend to seeking or taking employment in the labor market or confer a right of access to the labor market of another Party (Article 44(4) of the Poland Agreement).

The meaning of establishment under the Europe Agreements seems to match the one provided for in the Treaty establishing the European Community in substance. The legal position of CEEC companies seems, however, to be less clear than the respective position of companies established in one of the Member States. Articles 43-48 ECT must be viewed in connection with Article 3(c) ECT, which prohibits any obstacles to the free movement of goods, persons, services and capital. Although the Europe Agreements contain no provisions to this extent, they do stipulate that CEEC companies and their staff shall be granted, by the Member States and the Community, "a treatment no less favorable than that accorded to its own nationals and companies"[448]. This obligation is reciprocal in nature[449] and resembles international instruments that, in scope and purpose, are confined to creating *inter partes* obligations. Hence serious doubts must be raised as to whether the Europe Agreements create individual rights. The Poland Agreement, viewed as the blueprint of all Europe Agreements in this respect, therefore, speaks of "beneficiaries of the rights of establishment granted by Poland and the Community respectively"[450]. The term "beneficiary" was never used in the Treaty establishing the European Community. Further, the German text of the Agreement applies the term "Begünstigter" – which indicates that respective persons may derive benefits and advantages from a certain provision, but may not invoke the latter in court – instead of "Berechtigter" – which would clearly grant entitlements enforceable by law. The Agreements, therefore, seem to fall short of conferring rights on individuals[451].

---

446 ECJ, judgment of 27 June 1996, *Asscher v Staatssecretaris van Financien*, [1996] ECR I-3089 paras 24-29. In this passage the Court construed self-employment as employment which is not carried out within a relationship of subordination.

447 Cf. *Lange* GewArch 1996, 359, 360 including further reference in n. 9.

448 Article 44(3) of the Poland Agreement.

449 Cf. Article 44(1)(i) of the Poland Agreement.

450 Article 52(1) of the Poland Agreement.

451 This conclusion has also been reached by *Gargulla*, Informationsbrief Ausländerrecht (Aliens Law Newsletter) 1995, 181, 188.

At the same time the treatment of self-employed economic activity must be viewed as non-discriminative[452]. The concept of non-discrimination does not extend as far as the concept of abolition of obstacles in Community law[453]. Whether the European Court of Justice's jurisprudence on the freedom of establishment can be applied unequivocally to establishment as contemplated by the Europe Agreements is, therefore, questionable. Suggestions to this extent[454] seem to be based on a circular argument. They render the Europe Agreements' provisions on establishment subject to the European Court of Justice's construction of the right of establishment as provided for by Articles 34-48 ECT, in order to establish that these provisions generate the same effects for their beneficiaries as primary Community law. The mere fact that certain provisions are triggered by similar actions does not, however, mean that the same legal consequences must be attributed to these actions. In fact, establishment seems to have been regulated more strictly under the Europe Agreements than under Community law. If the intention of the Contracting Parties had been to grant full freedom of establishment to CEEC companies they could, and certainly would have adopted provisions which reiterate the content of primary Community law, as the Community and the Member States did so when concluding the Treaty establishing the European Economic Area. The difference in draftsmanship between the Europe Agreements and the EEA Agreement thus strongly supports the view that the Europe Agreements do not confer individual rights on self-employed CEEC nationals or individual CEEC companies. Beneficiaries of the freedom of establishment are divided into four categories under the Europe Agreements:[455]

- persons carrying out businesses in their own capacity or in a self-employed manner,
- persons who found and run a company,
- CEEC companies that set up and manage subsidiaries, branches and agencies (as provided for in Article 44(4) of the Poland Agreement), and
- key personnel (as provided for in Article 52 of the Poland Agreement)[456].

Freedom of establishment does not extend to sectors such as air, maritime and inland waterways transport (see Article 51(1) of the Poland Agreement). However, the Association Council may make recommendations for improving establishment and operations in these sectors (Article 51(2) of the Poland Agreement). Furthermore, the following kinds of economic activity are excluded from the scope of free establishment, as enshrined in the Europe Agreements:

---

452 See Articles 37(1) and 45 of the Poland Agreement.

453 *Guild* in *id.* (ed.), The Legal Framework and Social Consequences of Free Movement of Persons in the European Union (1999), 127, 134.

454 *Guild* in *id.* (ed.), The Legal Framework and Social Consequences of Free Movement of Persons in the European Union (1999), 127, 135.

455 See Lange GewArch (1996), 359, 365-366.

456 See also the definition given by the Netherlands Department of Justice – Vreemdelingencirculaire of 9 March 1994, Kenmerk 425508/94,/IND, Code TBV 1994/4. A German translation of the *circulaire* has been published in Informationsbrief Ausländerrecht (Aliens Law Newsletter) 1994, 392-393. Attention has been drawn to the fact that the provision governing the right to employ key personnel recalls the European Court of Justice's judgments in *Rush Portugesa* and *Vander Elst*: *Cremona*, in Maresceau (ed.), Enlarging the European Union (1997) 195, 205.

- acquisition and selling of natural resources, agricultural land and forestry (see Article 44(7) of the Poland Agreement)[457],
- legal services not including business consultancy involving relevant legal aspects (see Article 44(7) of the Hungary Agreement read together with Annex XIIc),
- organization of gambling, betting, lotteries and other similar activities (see Article 45(1) of the Romania and Bulgaria Agreements read together with Annexes XVI and XVa, respectively), and
- acquisition of real estates in areas close to the external borders of the Member States (see Article 45(1) of the Romania and Bulgaria Agreements read together with Annexes XVI and XVa, respectively).

Some factual problems do, however, remain. The establishment of a deadline, before which the right to self-employment is to be exercised if there is a lapse of time between the decision to take up self-employed economic activity and the time of economic viability of this activity, will require the guidance of the European Court of Justice [458].

As previously mentioned, the Europe Agreements do not introduce free movement for CEEC workers. Access to the Member States' territories is prohibited, save for CEEC tourists; access to their labour markets is subject to more stringent criteria. Additionally, nationals of certain CEECs must possess a visa when entering the European Union as tourists[459]. CEEC nationals lawfully resident in a Member State are not granted a right to a work permit; Member States are only bound to "examine the possibility of granting work permits to Polish nationals already having residence permits in the Member State concerned" (see Article 41(3) of the Poland Agreement). Arguably, the position of nationals of the other CEECs is even less favorable, as some Europe Agreements do not even include a duty to examine provided for in the Poland Agreement. Moreover, the construction applied to CEEC nationals differs from the legal position enjoyed by Turkish nationals under Article 6(1) of Council of Association Decision 1/80. The European Court of Justice held in *Kus* that the right of a Turkish worker to a work permit carries with it a right of residence[460]. The Europe Agreements, on the contrary, require proof that CEEC nationals are lawful residents before a work permit may be granted.[461].

---

[457] See also Annex XIIc of the Hungary Agreement: "ownership, sale, long-term lease or user right of real property, land and national resources".

[458] See *Guild* in *id.* (ed.), The Legal Framework and Social Consequences of Free Movement of Persons in the European Union (1999) 127, 133-134. The author suggests (id.) that guidance should be taken from the Court's judgment in *Lev*in (case 53/81, [1982] ECR 1035). There the Court held that so long as the activity is genuine and effective, and irrespective of the intention of the individual, it comes within the Community concept of employment under Article 39 ECT.

[459] See Regulation 231/95, O.J. 1995, L 234/1. The Annex of the Regulation includes Bulgaria and Romania.

[460] ECJ, judgment of 16 December 1992 in case C-237/91, *Kus v Landeshauptstadt Wiesbaden*, [1992] ECR I-6781 paras 29, 33.

[461] Cf. *Cremona*, in Maresceau (ed.), Enlarging the European Union (1997) 195, 198.

With regard to admission of CEEC nationals for work immigration, Member States may conclude more favorable agreements on a bilateral basis, pursuant to the aforementioned provision. Germany has concluded several such agreements.[462].

The Europe Agreements do, however, improve the legal position of CEEC workers who reside lawfully in one of the Member States and who are admitted to the latter's labor market. The Europe Agreements have not encroached upon national application "subject to the conditions and modalities applicable in each Member State"[463].

The Agreements grant national treatment to CEEC workers in that their treatment with regard to working conditions, remuneration or dismissal shall be free from any discrimination based on nationality (see Article 37(1), first indent, of the Poland Agreement). As a matter of principle, it is for the Member States to implement non-discrimination in their national legal orders through suitable 'conditions and modalities'[464]. The Joint Declaration to the Final Act links measures implemented to this end to Community principles. This Declaration defines 'conditions and modalities' as relevant pieces of Community law, as applicable in the Member States. Accordingly, the principles developed under the ECT's non-discrimination provisions can be employed when implementing the Europe Agreements vis-à-vis workers. The Europe Agreements provide for the co-ordination of social security systems for CEEC national workers, lawfully employed in the territory of a Member State, as well as for their lawfully resident family members (see Article 38 of the Poland Agreement). Whether a worker is lawfully employed is subject to national law (see Article 58(1) of the Poland Agreement).

With regard to the coordination of social security systems, the Councils of Association "shall by decision adopt the appropriate provisions to implement the objective set out" (see Article 39 of the Poland Agreement). While the social security coordination provisions contained in the Mediterranean Cooperation Agreements take direct effect[465], the need for a Council of Association decision implementing said coordination under the Europe Agreements prohibits them from carrying the same weight[466]. The social security provisions contained in the Europe Agreements have, for this reason, been criticized as regressive[467].

e) Freedom to Provide Services

The Parties to the Europe Agreements undertake to take the necessary steps to allow progressively the supply of services by Community or CEEC companies or nationals who are established in a Party other than that of the person for whom the

[462] See, e.g., the agreement concluded with Poland: BGBl II 1990, 603-604. Cf. Kaligin in NZA (1992), 1111-1116; *Mayer* in Betriebs-Berater 1993, 1428-1431 and *Heyden* in Bundesarbeitsblatt 1993, 26-29 for detailed assessments.

[463] Articles 37(1) and 38(1) of the Poland Agreement; see also Article 41(1) thereof.

[464] Cf. *Gargulla* in Informationsbrief Ausländerrecht (Aliens Law Newsletter) 1995, 181, 183.

[465] Cf. *Cremona* in Maresceau (ed.), Enlarging the European Union (1997), 195, 198.

[466] *Cremona* in Maresceau (ed.), Enlarging the European Union (1997), 195, 199.

[467] *Maresceau*, East Central European States and the European Communities (1993), 209, 228-229.

services are intended, taking into account the development of the services sector in the Parties[468]. In line with that liberalization process, and subject to the national laws and regulations regarding entry and stay, work, labour conditions and establishment of natural persons and supply of services, the Parties shall permit the temporary movement of natural persons providing the service or who are employed by the service provider as key personnel[469], including natural persons who are representatives of a Community or CEEC company or national and are seeking temporary entry for the purpose of negotiating for the sale of services or entering into agreements to sell services for that service provider, where those representatives will not be engaged in making direct sales to the general public or in supplying services themselves.[470]

These provisions do not take direct effect because they require implementation by respective Association Councils which are entrusted with the task to take the necessary measures[471]. Special arrangements govern maritime, air and inland transport[472].

f) The *Ordre Public* and Civil Service Reservations

Article 53 of the Poland Agreement stipulates that –

> 1. The provisions of this chapter shall be applied subject to limitations justified on grounds of public policy, public security or public health.
>
> 2. The provisions of this chapter shall not apply to activities which in the territory of each Party are connected, even occasionally, with the exercise of official authority.

This provision allows Member States to resort to any appropriate measures in situations related to the interests referred to in the first paragraph of the provision quoted above[473]. This reservation is a mere repetition of Article 39(3) ECT and must be interpreted in the same manner[474]. Conversely, the wording of the second paragraph differs form that of Article 39(4) ECT. Article 39(4) ECT states simply from that its "provisions [..] shall not apply to employment in the public service". Hence the construction of the second paragraph may also be different from that of Article 39(3) ECT. Two questions must be addressed. First, is the reservation as stated at all applicable? Second, to what extent does the scope of the 'public service' exception in the Europe Agreements differ from this exception in Article 39(3) ECT?

---

468 Cf. Article 55(1) of the Poland Agreement.
469 The term 'key personnel' is defined for instance in Article 52(2) of the Poland Agreement.
470 Cf. Article 55(2) read together with Articles 58(1) and 52(2) of the Poland Agreement.
471 Cf. Article 55(2) of the Poland Agreement.
472 See Article 56 of the Poland Agreement.
473 *Gargulla* in Informationsbrief Ausländerrecht (Aliens Law Newsletter) 1995, 181, 188-189.
474 The European Court of Justice has thus held in respect of the EEC-Turkey Association Agreement. See ECJ, judgment of 16 December 1992, case C-237/91, *Kus v Landeshauptstadt Wiesbaden*, [1992] ECR I-6781 para 34.

With regard to the first question, the European Court of Justice's judgment in *Lawrie-Blum* provides sufficient authority for the assumption that the 'public service' exception can indeed limit the freedom of establishment. In its judgment on this case, the Court held that –

> [t]o make the application of [ex-] Article 48(3) [ECT] dependent on the legal nature of the relationship between the employee and the administration would enable the Member States to determine at will the posts covered by the exception laid down in that provision.[475]

In other words, economic activity can qualify as involving the exercise of powers conferred by public law and safeguarding the general interests of the state irrespective of the nature of the work relationship. Hence, self-employed economic activity privatized on a contractual basis by the competent body of public law may well fall within the ambit of this reservation.

With regard to the second question, the wording of the 'public service' exception contained in the Europe Agreements seems to be a response to the Court's reasoning in *Lawrie-Blume* where the Court held that –

> 'employment in the public service' within the meaning of [ex-] Article 48(1), (2) and (3) [ECT], must be understood as meaning those posts which involve direct or indirect participation in the exercise of powers conferred by public law [..] and which therefore require a special relationship of allegiance to the state on the part of the persons occupying them..[476]

The exception at issue extends to economic activity merely "*connected* ... with the exercise of official authority" (emphasis added). Evidence of any connection can justify use of the exception under this reservation, while Article 39(4) ECT requires *participation* in the exercise of official authority. Moreover, even if one does not view the phrase "connected ... with the exercise of official authority" as far more extensive than the reservation contained in Article 39(3) ECT, one cannot help but come to this conclusion when having due regard to the phrase extending the scope of the Europe Agreements' reservation to connections of economic activities to the exercise of official authority which are no more than "*occasional*". Consequently, the 'public service' reservation as provided for by the Europe Agreements, may not be viewed as analogous to the similar exception contained in Article 39(4) ECT.

---

[475] ECJ, judgment of 3 July 1986, case C 66/85, *Lawrie-Blum v Land Baden-Bürttemberg*, [1986] ECR 2121 para 26.

[476] ECJ, judgment of 3 July 1986, case C 66/85, *Lawrie-Blum v Land Baden-Bürttemberg*, [1986] ECR 2121 para 27.

g) Further Sources of National Discretion

In a separate Article which does not prejudice the application of the *ordre public* and civil service reservations the Europe Agreements provide that –

> nothing in the Agreement shall prevent the Parties from applying their laws and regulations regarding entry and stay, work, labor conditions and establishment of natural persons, and supply of services, provided that, in so doing, they do not apply them in a manner as to nullify or impair the benefits accruing to any Party under the terms of a specific provision of this Agreement..[477]

In a Joint declaration on that very Article, the Contracting Parties stressed that –

> [t]he sole fact of requiring a visa for natural persons of certain Parties and not for those of others shall not be regarded as nullifying or impairing benefits under a specific commitment.[478]

It has been observed that "[b]oth of these provisions clearly run counter to the intention to create a right of establishment" and that "[a]s any restrictive measure is likely to impair the exercise of a right it is not entirely clear what content this phrase [scil.: 'nullify or impair'] can have"[479]. However, this criticism seems to be unfounded. The wording of the quoted provisions clearly indicates that their scope is limited to the legal relationship established between the parties of the Agreements. They do not therefore affect any rights or benefits which individuals or companies might derive from the Agreements. These provisions seem, rather, to allay any doubts as to the adoption of visa requirements within the context of what used to be the Schengen process, or by individual Member States beyond the scope of the Community's negative list adopted under ex-Article 100c ECT. The provisions mentioned above might well be rendered virtually meaningless when full communitarization of visa policy leads to the adoption of a European positive list. Their remaining scope of application would, therefore, extend solely to the enactment of emergency measures pursuant to Article 64(2) ECT.

6. *The General Agreement on Trade in Services (GATS)*

Globalization might lead to increasing interdependence of economic areas and a substantial growth of the importance of supply of services for the European Union's economy. Both the European Court of Justice and the Commission have taken notice of this development:

> The Commission points out ... that in certain developed countries the services sector has become the dominant sector of the economy and that global

[477] Article 58 of the Poland Agreement.

[478] Declaration on Article 58 of the Poland Agreement.

[479] *Guild* in *id.* (ed.), The Legal Framework and Social Consequences of Free Movement of Persons in the European Union (1999), 127, 136.

> economy is undergoing fundamental structural changes. The trend is for basic industry to be transferred to developing countries, whilst the developed economies have tended to become, in the main, exporters of services and goods with high value-added content. The Court notes that this trend is borne out by the WTO agreement and its annexes ...[480]

The General Agreement on Trade in Services (GATS) will play an important role in administering this process. This agreement aims at world-wide liberalization of provision of services which might influence the rules and conditions governing access to the Member States' territories for the purpose of providing services. Recent association and cooperation agreements concluded by the Community and, where applicable, the Member States of the one part and Third States of the other part envisage the conclusion of agreements aimed at economic integration as provided for in Article 5 of the GATS[481]. This Article provides that the GATS "shall not prevent any of its Members from being a party to or entering into an agreement liberalizing trade in services between or among the parties to such an agreement" provided that such agreement complies with specific terms laid down in the Article in question. Additionally, Article XVI(1) of the GATS provides that –

> With respect to market access through the modes of supply identified in Article I, each Member shall accord services and service suppliers of any other Member treatment no less favourable than that provided for under the terms, limitations and conditions agreed and specified in its Schedule.

Under Article XVII of the GATS Members shall accord national treatment to foreign service providers in the sectors inscribed in respective Schedules by either formally identical treatment or formally different treatment.

Moreover, the Annex on Movement of Natural Persons Supplying Services under the Agreement stipulates that –

> 1. This Annex applies to measures affecting natural persons who are service suppliers of a Member, and natural persons of a Member who are employed by a service supplier of a Member, in respect of the supply of a service.
>
> 2. The Agreement shall not apply to measures affecting natural persons seeking access to the employment market of a Member, nor shall it apply to measures regarding citizenship, residence or employment on a permanent basis.
>
> 3. In accordance with Parts III and IV of the Agreement, Members may negotiate specific commitments applying to the movement of all categories of natural persons supplying services under the Agreement. Natural persons

---

[480] ECJ-Opinion 1/94 of 15 November 1994, *Competence of the Community to Conclude International Agreements Concerning Services and the Protection of Intellectual Property* (GATS and TRIPS), [1994] ECR I-5267 para 40.

[481] See for instance Title III (Articles 31-32) of the EC-Morocco Agreement, COM(95)740 final and Title III (Articles 29-30) of the EC-Israel Agreement, SEC(95)1719 final.

> covered by a specific commitment shall be allowed to supply the service in accordance with the terms of that commitment.
>
> 4. The Agreement shall not prevent a Member from applying measures to regulate the entry of natural persons into, or their temporary stay in, its territory, including those measures necessary to protect the integrity of, and to ensure the orderly movement of natural persons across, its borders, provided that such measures are not applied in such a manner as to nullify or impair the benefits accruing to any Member under the terms of a specific commitment.*
>
> * The sole fact of requiring a visa for natural persons of certain Members and not for those of others shall not be regarded as nullifying or impairing benefits under a specific commitment.[482]

The European Community and its Member States have reserved the competence to introduce or maintain measures limiting market access or national treatment in many sectors and modes of supply[483]. As regards the presence of natural persons they have only taken the commitment to give access to specified categories of persons for temporary stays within a Member State without requiring compliance with an economic needs test. Part of the relevant commitment forms a footnote which states that –

> The duration of "temporary stay" is defined by the Member States and, where they exist, Community laws and regulations regarding entry, stay and work. The precise duration can vary according to the different categories of natural persons mentioned in this schedule.

Given this restrictive approach it is as yet unclear whether the GATS will initiate major change with respect to access of third-country nationals to the territories of the Member States. Nevertheless it must be borne in mind that service provision involves forms of cross-border provision of services which are similar in substance to provision of services as safeguarded by Article 43 ECT[484] and that mutual commitments have been taken by the Community of the one part and respective contracting states of the other part in recent cooperation agreements[485]. Such commitments require implementation by way of Council of Association recommendations in accordance with the GATS[486]. The future framework for provision of services in the European Union by nationals of certain third countries established outside the territories of the Member States might therefore be modelled upon the freedom to provide services under Community law.

---

[482] The note forms part of the Agreement.

[483] See WTO documents GATS/SC/31 of 15 April 1994 and GATS/SC/31/Suppl.2 of 28 July 1995.

[484] Cf. AGIT, Efficient, effective and encompassing approaches to a European Immigration and Asylum Policy, [1999] IJRL [forthcoming] .

[485] Cf. Article 31 of the EC-Tunisia Agreement.

[486] Article 31(2) of the EC-Tunisia Agreement.

7. *The EU-Switzerland Agreement*[487]

Switzerland did not join the European Economic Area because the EEA Agreement did not reach the necessary majority in the respective referendum. In the meantime, however, the European Union and the Swiss Confederation negotiated a series of seven Agreements which were signed on 21 June 1999. These Agreements aim at strengthening the ties between the European Union, its Member States and Switzerland. All seven Agreements shall enter into force on 1 January 2001. One Agreement is dedicated to free movement of persons. The objective of the Agreement on free movement of persons is to gradually arrive at completely free movement of persons between Switzerland and the EU.

a) Swiss Migration Laws

During a transitional period of 12 years Switzerland will retain the competence to control immigration. The transitional period shall consist of two consecutive stages. During the first stage of five years Switzerland will retain her immigration quota system though on the basis of preferential quotas for EU citizens within that system (15,000 residence permits for between one year and up to five years, and 115,500 short-term residence permits)[488]. During the second stage of seven years, Switzerland will in principle grant free movement of persons to EU citizens. The immigration quota for EU citizens shall be abolished. Under a safeguard clause Switzerland will be able to prevent an exceptional inflow of immigrants. If immigration of EU citizens into Switzerland increases by more than ten per cent in excess of the average for the previous three years, Switzerland may limit the number of residence permits to the average of the three preceding years plus five per cent for the following two years[489]. After expiry of the second stage freedom of movement of persons will be fully established. In case of serious difficulties arising from the implementation of the Agreement the Joint Committee may take appropriate measures.

Additionally, the Agreement has been concluded for an initial period of seven years. Switzerland may, thus, decide on renewal for an indefinite period by means of a referendum if necessary[490].

---

[487] EU documents No. 7809/99 to 7815/99.

[488] Article 10(1) and (3) of the Agreement.

[489] Article 10(4) of the Agreement and Chapter VII of Annex 1 – Free Movement of Persons – to the Agreement.

[490] See Article 25(2) of the Agreement. Switzerland has committed herself to "reach a decision on renewal of the agreement during the seventh year of its application, on the basis of the applicable internal procedures" in her Declaration on renewal of the Agreement.

b) Free Movement of Persons

Free Movement of Persons is granted to nationals of the Contracting Parties provided the conditions in Annex 1 to the Agreement are met. Persons who are lawfully resident shall enjoy the right of non-discrimination[491]. While Article 2 of Annex 1 to the Agreement fulfils all requirements for direct applicability, other provisions such as the right to equal treatment with nationals in respect of access to, and the pursuit of, an economic activity, and living, employment and working conditions are formulated in a way aimed at excluding direct applicability[492]. It is, however, rather doubtful whether this wording excludes direct applicability under the conditions applied in the jurisprudence of the European Court of Justice relating to association agreements since the Court's core criterion for direct applicability is that provisions contain a clear and precise obligation which is not subject to the adoption of any implementing measure of the Contracting Parties. Most if not all rights contemplated in Article 7 of the Agreement, and certainly the non-discrimination clauses, meet this criterion.

The Agreement grants free movement to workers, self-employed persons (i.e. the freedoms of establishment and to provide services), and persons not gainfully employed provided that they have sufficient financial means and insurance cover[493]. Generally speaking, the Agreement aims at extending, as far as possible, the rights of status of EU citizens to nationals of the Contracting Parties. To that end Article 16(1) of the Agreement provides that –

> the Contracting Parties shall take all measures necessary to ensure that rights and obligations equivalent to those contained in the legal acts of the European Community to which reference is made are applied in relations between them.

Additionally, under Article 16(2) of the Agreement

> [i]nsofar as the application of this Agreement involves concepts of Community law, account shall be taken of the relevant case-law of the Court of Justice of the European Communities prior to the date of its signature.

Finally, the Agreement is designed to be directly applicable. Article 11(1) of the Agreement stipulates that –

> The persons covered by this Agreement shall have a right of appeal to the competent authorities in respect of the application of the provisions of this Agreement.

Accordingly, Swiss nationals will have access to the European Court of Justice.

Nationals of the Contracting Parties shall enjoy freedom of movement including occupational and geographical mobility. In particular, after a period of two years, nationals of the Contracting Parties shall be accorded equal treatment on the labour

---

491 Article 2 of Annex 1 – Free Movement of Persons – to the Agreement.

492 Article 7 of the Agreement provides that "[t]he Contracting Parties shall make provision ... for the following rights in relation to the free movement of persons".

493 See Article 24 of Annex 1 – Free Movement of Persons – to the Agreement.

market[494]. They enjoy the same tax concessions and welfare benefits, are entitled to vocational training, equal access to housing and must not be discriminated against in the conditions of employment or exercise of union rights. Additionally, nationals of a Contracting Party seeking work in a Member State or Switzerland shall have –

> the right to visit another contracting Party and to remain there after a period of employment of less than one year in order to seek employment and to reside there for a reasonable amount of time, which may be up to six months, to allow them to find out about the employment opportunities corresponding to their professional qualifications and, if necessary, take the appropriate steps to take up employment.[495]

However, persons seeking employment are only entitled to the same assistance as employment agencies in that state grant to its own nationals. They are not entitled to access to social security schemes. Provision of services offered by physical persons for a duration of less than 90 days per year will be liberalized.

The Agreement also contains a commitment of the Contracting Parties to start negotiations at the earliest possible date for general liberalization in the services sector. Furthermore, the Agreement provides for a right to family reunification regardless of the nationality of the family member concerned[496].

Freedom of movement shall comprise

- entry conditions similar to those enjoyed by EU citizens within the European Union, including the abolition of visa requirements[497],
- a right to a renewable residence permit which 'substantiates' the right to reside and pursue an economic activity[498] which includes a right to stay after the termination of economic activity[499],
- the abolition of residence permit requirements for employed and self-employed frontier workers[500] and for providers of cross-border services and their employees authorized to provide services for less than 90 days of actual work per calendar year[501], and
- limitation of termination of residence as enshrined in Directives 64/221/EEC, 72/194/EEC and 75/35/EEC.[502]

Additionally, according to Article 27(3)(b) of the Agreement the "seasonal worker" category is abolished.

---

494 Article 9(1) of Annex 1 – Free Movement of Persons – to the Agreement.

495 Article 2(1) of Annex 1 – Free Movement of Persons – to the Agreement.

496 Article 3.

497 Article 1 of Annex 1 – Free Movement of Persons – to the Agreement.

498 Article 2(1) of Annex 1 – Free Movement of Persons – to the Agreement. See also Article 20(2) of Annex 1 – Free Movement of Persons – to the Agreement with respect to providers of services and their employees authorized to provide a service for a period exceeding 90 days.

499 Article 4(1) of Annex 1 – Free Movement of Persons – to the Agreement. The second paragraph of the mentioned Article references Regulation 1251/70 and Directive 75/34/EEC as in force at the date of signing the Agreement.

500 Articles 7(2), 13(2) of Annex 1 – Free Movement of Persons – to the Agreement.

501 Article 17(b) read together with Article 20(1) of Annex 1 – Free Movement of Persons – to the Agreement.

502 Article 5 of Annex 1 – Free Movement of Persons – to the Agreement. The reference to the mentioned directives covers the *status quo* as in force at the date of signing the Agreement.

c) Institutional Provisions

Article 14 of the Agreement provides that a Joint Committee be established that shall be composed of representatives of the Contracting Parties. According to Article 14(1) the Joint Committee "shall take decisions in the circumstances provided for in the Agreement". There can be no doubt that such decisions will have binding legal force and will form part of the Community legal order. The primary purposes of the Joint Committee are to resolve economic or social difficulties (see Article 14(2) of the Agreement) and to exercise its responsibility for the management and proper application of the Agreement. To that end, the Agreement entrusts the Joint Committee with several tasks as to ensure a parallel development of relevant branches of the law. In particular, the Agreement provides for an exchange of views in the Joint Committee where

- a contracting party initiates the process of adopting a draft amendment to its domestic legislation, or
- a change occurs in the case-law of authorities against whose decisions there is no judicial remedy under domestic law in a field governed by the Agreement.[503]

The Joint Committee may also, under Article 19 of the Agreement, settle disputes regarding the interpretation and application thereof. A similar power of the Joint Committee is provided for in Article 16(2) of the Agreement according to which

> [c]ase-law after that date [scil.: of entry into force] shall be brought to Switzerland's attention. To ensure that the Agreement works properly, the Joint Committee shall, at the request of either Contracting Party, determine the implications of such case-law.

Accordingly, Switzerland will not be bound by ECJ judgments handed down after the entry into force of the Agreement. Switzerland's position is therefore similar to the position of EEA Member States save that the EEA Agreement has established a separate tribunal competent to rule on the interpretation thereof. In the case of Switzerland the Joint Committee's powers come close to judicial powers because 'determination of the implications of ECJ case-law' may involve a decision to the extent that Switzerland makes a commitment to take into account such case-law in her internal legal order.

---

[503] Article 17 of the Agreement.

d) Future EU-Switzerland Cooperation

The Agreement envisages further cooperation in related areas. The Joint declaration on further negotiations states that –

> The European Community and the Swiss Confederation declare their intention of undertaking negotiations to conclude agreements in areas of common interest such as the updating of Protocol 2 to the 1972 Free Trade Agreement and Swiss participation in certain Community training, youth, media, statistical and environmental programs. Preparatory work for these negotiations should proceed rapidly once the current bilateral negotiations have been concluded.

Moreover, Switzerland wishes to cooperate with the European Union and the Member States in asylum matters. The Declaration by Switzerland on migration and asylum policy expresses that

> Switzerland reaffirms its wish to reinforce cooperation with the EU and its Member States in the area of migration and asylum policy. To this end, Switzerland is willing to participate in the EU system for coordinating asylum applications, and it proposes that negotiations be entered into for the conclusion of a convention parallel to the Dublin Convention.

VI. Non-Privileged Third-Country Nationals

1. Survey of Existing Council Resolutions and the Draft Convention of the European Commission

Since 1993 the Council, based upon Article 31 TEU (formerly Article K3), has passed several resolutions on third-country nationals which form an important part of an emerging European Union immigration legislation, although they are expected to undergo substantial changes when submitted in the form of draft regulations or directives under Title IV ECT:

- the Council Resolution of 1 June 1993 on the harmonization of national policies on family reunification[504];
- the Council Resolution of 20 June 1994 on limitation on admission of third-country nationals to the territory of the Member States for employment[505];
- the Council Resolution of 30 November 1994 relating to the limitations on the admission of third-country nationals to the territory of the Member States for the purpose of pursuing activities as self-employed persons[506];
- the Council Resolution of 30 November 1994 on the admission of third-country nationals to the territory of the Member States for study purposes[507], and

[504] SN 2828/1/1993 WGI 1497 (in *Hailbronner*, Kommentar, D.9.1.).
[505] O.J. 1996, C 274/3.
[506] O.J. 1996, C 274/7.

- the Council Resolution of 4 March 1996 on the status of third-country nationals residing on a long-term basis in the territory of the Member States[508].

The structures of the Resolutions on employment, self-employed and students are moulded in a similar pattern. Section A. outlines the general purpose of the Resolution. Section B. lists the group of people to which the Resolution is not applicable, i.e. privileged third-country nationals. Finally, Section C. establishes guiding principles for Member State policies.

Member States endeavour to adapt the principles of the Resolution into their national law until a certain deadline[509]. Although these resolutions are not legally binding,[510] they can be viewed as a common expression of general principles concerning the treatment of third-country nationals in the Member States of the European Union.

The Commission submitted, pursuant to ex-Article K.3(2)(c) TEU, a proposal[511] for a Council Act establishing the Convention on Rules for the Admission of Third-country nationals on July 30, 1997 [512]. The Commission proposal is to serve primarily as a contribution towards the creation of a comprehensive concept of immigration policy in the European Union[513].

Both the existing Council Resolutions and the draft Convention of the Commission differentiate between several categories of third-country nationals pursuing different purposes, in particular the purpose of taking up employment or pursuing self-employed economic activities.

The proposal submitted is based on the view held by all EU Member States that Western Europe cannot be defined as a region of immigration. The draft Convention – in accordance with the immigration policies of Member States – emphasizes as a basic policy guideline that immigration is not encouraged although EU Member States do not generally exclude controlled immigration for employment purposes under specific conditions.

According to Article 2 of the draft Convention, the provisions of the Convention shall apply to nationals of third countries, except where more favourable provisions apply under the following agreements:

(a) bilateral or multilateral agreements concluded between the Community, or the Community and its Member States, of the one part, and third States of the other part, which entered into force before this Convention was signed;

---

507 O.J. 1996, C 274/10.

508 O.J. 1996, C 80/2.

509 See introduction point 5, 3 of the Resolution on family reunion; A. (iv) 3 of the Resolution on employment; A. point 9 3 of the Resolution on self-employed and A. point 6 (2) of the Resolution on students.

510 See introduction point 5 of the Resolution on family reunion; A.(iv) of the Resolution on employment; A. point 9 of the Resolution on self-employed Persons; A. point 6 of the Resolution on students.

511 COM(97)387final.

512 In point 1 of the Draft Legislative Proposal of the Second Report of 28 January 1999 (PE 229.573/final, 19) the European Parliament in principle approves the Commission proposal, subject to numerous amendments introducing not only clarifications and additional legal rights, but also substantial changes.

513 COM(97)387final, 4.

(b) agreements concluded between one or more Member States and third countries which entered into force before this Convention was signed.[514]

The draft Convention shall not apply to:

(a) persons who have applied in a Member State for recognition of refugee status under the terms of the 1951 Geneva Convention;

(b) displaced persons granted admission to stay for temporary protection in a Member State;

(c) persons granted exceptional authorization to stay in the territory of a Member State, particularly on humanitarian grounds.

Similar exceptions to the scope of application can be found in the Council Resolutions.[515]

The regulation proposed by the Commission is somewhat unclear in certain respects[516]. Firstly, it cannot be inferred from its wording whether the exclusion clause applies solely to asylum seekers, or whether it is applicable as well to recognized refugees[517]. According to the explanation of the Commission on Article 2 of the draft Convention, only asylum seekers are to be excluded, whereas recognized refugees fall within the regulations of Chapter VIII on the rights of permanent residents, provided that they meet the conditions of Article 32 of the draft Convention[518].

Secondly, the term "temporary protection" mentioned under paragraph (b) does not exist in some Member States[519]. The European Parliament has called for the creation of a new subparagraph 2a, in order to clarify the fact that exclusion from the area of application shall not affect the right of applicants to a right of family reunification. The Member State of residence may permit them to submit the application on its territory and to remain there while they await a decision[520].

Finally, it remains doubtful to what extent the provisions of Article 2 of the draft Convention leave space, for specific national regulations of Member States[521],

---

514 According to the European Parliament a new subparagraph (ba) is to be included with the following wording: "provisions which Member States apply in favour of their own nationals". See Amendment 2 to the Legislative Proposal of the European Parliament, Second Report, PE 229.573/final, 6.

515 See Section B. of the Council Resolutions on employment, self-employment, on students; II. 3 of the Council Resolution on a long–term basis and point 1 of the general principles of the Council Resolution on family reunion.

516 The German, Belgian and Austrian delegations have commented it in the same way during the discussions on the proposal of the Commission. See the summary of the British presidency on the outcome of the discussions to Chapter III, I and IV, Council Doc. 6488/98, ASIM 63, 16.

517 See the objections of the British, Dutch, French and Swedish delegations, Council Doc. 6488/98, ASIM 63, 18.

518 See COM(97)387final, 9.

519 Stating the objection of the French delegation, see Council Doc. 6488/98, ASIM 63, 17.

520 See Amendment 4 of the Legislative Proposal of the European Parliament, Second Report, PE 229.573/final, 6.

521 The German Bundesrat (Federal Chamber) raised objections against the phrasing of Article 2 arguing that "Spätaussiedler", that do not have the German citizenship when entering the country would be affected by Article 2 of the proposal of the commission. This group of people does have a

especially, whether Article 2 of the draft Convention provides a final regulation by way of replacing national regulations[522], or whether Article 2 solely wants to introduce a minimum standard in the European Union, which would (at least) allow Member States to make further regulations.

2. *Admission on Employment*

a) General Principles

The Council Resolution on employment states as a basic principle: "Member States will refuse entry to their territories of third-country nationals for the purpose of employment."[523] Due to economic, social and political pressure all Member States have limited immigration to exceptional cases. Therefore, even admission for temporary employment is to be avoided in principle[524]. The Council proposal confirms the privileged position of Member State or EEA nationals in job competition. In times of high unemployment the European Employment service (EURES)[525] should be used to improve intra-EU mobility[526].

The Council Resolution on employment does, however, exceptionally allow for admission of workers into the European Union. First, unskilled workers may be recruited seasonally for employment in the agricultural and forestry sectors. Demand for these migrant workers arises primarily from the fact that they are generally willing to perform physically exhausting, hard labour for low wages relative to the standard income of the host country, coupled by the fact that the social system in some EU Member States makes such jobs unattractive for local unemployed persons.

A second exception from the principle of non-admission is made for highly qualified executive personnel[527]. While the recruitment of highly qualified, skilled workers is generally considered as economically profitable, there are also disadvantages resulting from the so-called "brain-drain" problem[528].

---

constitutional right to naturalization. They therefore should be excluded of the application of Article 2. Bundesratsdrucksache (Federal Chamber Document) 788/97, 1 et seq.

522 The Federal Republic of Germany raised questions concerning the right to return according to § 16 of the German Aliens Act (Ausländergesetz), the preferential treatment of German "Spätaussiedler", of Jewish immigrants, of contingent refugees and of persons that shall be granted a residence permit according to § 30 of the German Aliens Act (Ausländergesetz). See Council Doc. 6488/98, ASIM 63, 18..

523 C. (i) of the Resolution.

524 A. (ii) of the Resolution.

525 EURES was initiated by the Commission. It aims for improvement of the employment placement service in the community; see *Haberland*, Zeitschrift für Ausländerrecht und Ausländerpolitik (ZAR) (1996), 3, 8; *Walwei*, ASP (1996), 15, 24; for the function and problems of EURES see *Sladek*, Computergestützte Beratung von Migranten, caritas ´95, Jahrbuch des deutschen Caritasverbandes (1995), 383 et seq.

526 A. (iii) of the Resolution.

527 Cf. *Münz* in Bade (ed.), Das Manifest der 60 (1994), 108.

528 See COM(94)23final., para 59 et seq.

b) Conditions of Admission

According to Article 7 of the draft Convention

> a third-country national may be granted admission to the territory of a Member State for the purpose of paid employment where a job vacancy in a Member State cannot be filled in the short term:
>
> (a) by citizens of the Union; or
>
> (b) by a third-country national who is legally resident in the Member State and already forms part of the regular labour market in that Member State; or
>
> (c) by a third-country national who has been recognized as a long-term resident.

The draft Convention is somewhat more open to migration in comparison to the Council Resolution, which requires Member States to refuse entry for the purpose of employment to third-country nationals[529]. In addition, the Commission proposal does not correspond to national regulations[530] concerning work permits[531]. The wording of Article 7 of the draft Convention does not, however, grant any right to admission to the territory of a Member State; it is phrased, instead, as an optional clause to enable Member States to maintain their restrictive regulations and to deny access to their labour markets, even to third-country nationals who meet the conditions of Article 7 of the draft Convention[532]. Article 7(1) of the draft Convention allows for admission of third-country nationals according to quota policies or other measures established to meet a specific demand for labour[533].

Article 8(1) of the draft Convention provides for admission of third-country nationals who possess a contract of employment valid for at least one year and a labour permit. Since some Member States do not require proof of an existing employment contract for the issue of a residence permit[534], provided that there is a concrete chance of obtaining such contract, i.e. by producing a letter of commitment of a future employer, the proposal has been criticized as overly bureaucratic and too restrictive.

---

529 The German delegation was in favour of such phrasing and expressed this in the discussions. See Council Doc. 6488/98, ASIM 63, 3.

530 The delegations from Germany, Austria and Sweden pointed this out during the discussion. See Council Doc. 6488/98, ASIM 63, 2.

531 Compared to German law on working permits, Article 7 is more restrictive in issuing residence permits without priority examination of employed persons and of the practice of certain activities. On the other hand, the proposed Article renders admission easier than it is according to German Law: A regulation comparable to § 285(3) Code of Social Law (Sozialgesetzbuch) III by which a work permit is not granted to a third-country national residing in a foreign country, but in the case of an ordinance, has not been provided.

532 Nevertheless, the German Bundesrat (Federal Chamber) has disapproved of Article 7 arguing that Article 7 may attract immigration to the European Union of unskilled workers. See Bundesratsdrucksache (Federal Chamber Document) 788/97, 2.

533 See Amendment 12 of the Legislative Proposal of the European Parliament, Second Report, PE 229.573/final, 8.

534 E.g. in Germany and Belgium see Council Doc. 6488/98, ASIM 63, 6.

A residence permit under Article 8 of the draft Convention is to be issued for a period at least equivalent to the duration of the contract of employment to third-country nationals. Some Member States have argued that the validity of the work contract should be the basis for the maximum, rather than the minimum period of validity for a residence permit in order to maintain the temporary character of a residence permit for the purpose of employment in the European Union[535].

Article 8(1), second sentence of the draft Convention limits the first residence authorization to a four-year period. A shorter term of one[536] or two years[537] would more closely correspond to national regulations in order to allow national authorities to grant another title of residence after an appropriate time, conditional upon evidence that the third-country national actually pursued employment[538].

According to Article 8(2) of the draft Convention, a residence authorization granted for the purpose of paid employment may be renewed if the applicant still satisfies the conditions of Article 7(1) of the draft Convention.

Due to the systematic context of Article 8 of the draft Convention one has to conclude that Article 8(1) regulates the first admission/permit to take up an employment (activity) and Article 8(2) only concerns the extension of residence permits for the employment period as stated in the first contract of employment. Only in this case, according to Article 8(2) of the draft Convention, the conditions of Article 7(1) of the draft Convention have to be fulfilled. The wording of Article 8(2) sentence 2 as proposed by the Commission could lead to the wrong assumption that Article 8(2) is also applicable to a second residence permit within (the framework of) the duration of the first contract of employment.

Finally a number of delegations raised problems with the provision on renewal of residence in Article 8(2) of the draft Convention, because they found them generally too absolute and stringent without the possibility for exceptions[539].

c) Admission of Seasonal Workers

According to Article 9(1) of the draft Convention a seasonal worker is a third-country national who retain his legal domicile in a third country but is employed in the territory of a Member State in a sector of activity on the passing of the season under a fixed-term contract for a specific job. This definition is the same as the one in the Council Resolution on employment[540].

According to Article 9(2) of the draft Convention, third-country nationals may be admitted as seasonal workers for a maximum of six months in any calendar year, after which time they must return to their country of origin. The Convention does not confer a right of residence. In cases in which a residence permit has been

---

535 See Council Doc. 6488/98, ASIM 63, 6.

536 By the existing national law in Belgium, Germany, Greece and the Netherlands.

537 By the existing national law in Italy.

538 Many delegations, therefore, were against the 4-year-period and said so during the discussions. See Council Doc. 6488/98, ASIM 63, 7.

539 See Council Doc. 6488/98, ASIM 63, 7.

540 See the Annex of the Resolution.

granted for less than six months, it shall be extended to complete the work for which they were originally granted admission. If the measures applied by the Member States so allow, Article 9(2) of the draft Convention authorizes seasonal workers to remain on Member State territory for a longer period of time in order to work in one or more economic sectors generally in need of seasonal workers[541].

Some Member States consider the grant of admission for a period of up to six months of seasonal work in any calendar year as too generous. According to considerably shorter periods of time, in the national law of some Member States[542] it is argued that a six-months period will gradually lead to immigration[543]. Other Member States, however, consider the period of up to six month too short[544]. Therefore, it might be reasonable to leave the establishment of a time limit to the discretion of each Member State rather than regulating in it a Community instrument[545]. In an amendment to Article 9(2) of the draft Convention, the proposal of the European Parliament provides for the admission of seasonal workers to the territory of a Member State for a longer period in order to take up employment in one or more sectors of seasonal work[546].

Article 9(3) of the draft Convention requires employers to submit the extension request, duly substantiated, at least one month before the initial permit expires.

Article 9(4) of the draft Convention gives preference to persons who have previously performed seasonal work in their host state over other third-country nationals.

d) Admission of Transfrontier Workers

According to Article 10(2) of the draft Convention, transfrontier workers may be admitted for the purpose of paid employment in the frontier zone of a Member State, notwithstanding the principles set out in Article 7 of this draft Convention.

Article 10(1) of the draft Convention defines transfrontier workers as third-country nationals who live in the frontier zone of a third country, but who are employed in the frontier zone of a neighbouring Member State, and who commute between the two countries daily, or at least once a week[547].

The draft Convention and the Council Resolution on employment do not, however, adequately define the term "frontier zone," which may lead to regulatory problems in the future.

---

541 See Amendment 14 of the Legislative Proposal of the European Parliament, Second Report, PE 229.573/final, 9.

542 See Council Doc. 6488/98, ASIM 63, 9.

543 See the Resolution of the German Bundesrat (Federal Chamber), 19 December 1997, Bundesratsdrucksache (Federal Chamber Document) 788/97, 2.

544 E.g. the delegations of Italy, Great Britain, France, whose national laws allow prolongation of 7 to 9 months. See Council Doc. 6488/98, ASIM 63, 9.

545 Proposal of the German delegation during the discussions. Council Doc. 6488/98, ASIM 63, 10.

546 See Amendment 14 of the Legislative Proposal of the European Parliament, Second Report, PE 229.573/final, 9.

547 In the same manner the Council Resolution on employment. See the Annex of the Resolution.

e) Self-employed Persons

While immigration of workers has been strictly limited, the Council Resolution on self-employed does not adopt a restrictive position concerning third-country nationals intending to take-up self-employed activities in a Member State of the European Union [548]. Self-employed persons and entrepreneurial enterprises are generally considered as contributing positively to the economy of the host Member State and are expressly welcomed[549]. If no recognisable economic benefit for the destination state results from the activity of the self-employed person, however, the right to take up the activity will be denied[550].

The Council Resolution on self-employed lays down eleven general principles to be incorporated into national law by January 1, 1996. The Resolution is applicable neither to Union citizens, nor to nationals of bi- or multilaterally associated states[551], e.g. nationals of EEA and EFTA states. The same applies to persons excluded by special agreements such as GATT and GATS, treaties within the OECD or other bilateral treaties. Finally, third-country nationals seeking the right of residence for purposes other than employment are excluded from the application of this Resolution.

The Council Resolution on self-employed refers only to the entry and residence of individuals and does not affect the foundation of enterprises as clarified in point 1 of the general principles. Undertaking "activity as a self-employed person" is defined primarily by the absence of a duty to comply with instructions. In the case of associate partnerships, a right of residence will only be granted if both associates are present and plan to reside permanently in the Member States in question. This provision is to avoid the purchase of a residence right through the acquisition of partnership interests.

The draft Convention similarly states that "admission for the purpose of pursuing an independent economic activity" means the entry into the territory of a Member State of a natural person who is a third-country national in order to pursue in that Member State an economic activity involving no subordinate relationship to an employer." Article 12 of the draft Convention admits third-country nationals wishing to establish themselves in order to pursue an independent economic activity in the territory, provided that they comply with the rules governing the exercise of the activity concerned. They must prove that:

(a) they have sufficient resources to undertake, in the relevant Member State, the activity for which they submit their admission application; and

---

548 The Council Resolution on self-employed relating to the limitations on the admission of third-country nationals to the territory of the Member States for the purpose of pursuing activities as self-employed persons. See O.J. 1996, C 274/7.

549 The following factors are mentioned: investments, innovation, technology transfer and the creation of jobs, see A. 4 of the Resolution; see *Haberland*, Zeitschrift für Ausländerrecht und Ausländerpolitik (ZAR) (1996), 55, 56.

550 Cf. A. point 1. and point 5. of the Resolution.

551 See A. point 1, B. first and third indent of the Resolution.

(b) the business generated by the person admitted will have, during the period of validity of the initial residence authorization, a beneficial effect on employment in the Member State in which he resides.

The Council Resolution on self-employment similarly requires that, in accordance with national law, proof of sufficient resources can be required for the assessment of the conditions under point 2 of the regulation[552].

Since according to Article 12(3) of the draft Convention provisions are made, however, that specific regulations need not be laid down in the draft Convention but solely in implementing regulations according to the Article 36 procedure, objections may be raised, since many detailed regulations of the core provisions of the draft Convention are in effect transferred to the lower level of implementing regulations. This applies particularly to those regulations which are intended to prevent that self-employed (economic) activities serve as a pretext for, in reality, employed work[553] and that persons with permission to take up self-employed work partly work on an employment basis[554].

While the Council Resolution on self-employed only allows for time limitations on admission[555], Article 13(1) of the draft Convention provides that a residence permit shall be issued for at least two years. This period of time appears to be appropriate in order to grant entrepreneurs ample time to establish and develop their activity[556]. The Resolution, however, does not provide for a possibility to subsequently withdraw or limit the residence permit if the activity has not been taken up, or if practice activities undertaken do not comply with the permit issued[557].

At the time of submission of a renewal application, third-country nationals must:

(a) have actually pursued the activity for which admission was authorized;

(b) be able to guarantee that they can continue to pursue that activity lawfully and regularly;

(c) satisfy the condition that the business will have a beneficial effect on employment.

While the Council Resolution on self-employed persons leaves the setting of conditions for the admission of service providers to the Member States[558], Article 14 of the draft Convention on the other hand states that the admission of third-country nationals to the exercise of an activity in the service sector – without prejudice to existing Community law provisions – is regulated according to the Article 36 procedure of the draft Convention. Thus a further important area of the

552 C. point 3 (3), 4 of the Resolution.
553 C. point 2 (2) of the Resolution.
554 C. point 8 (1) of the Resolution.
555 C. point 4 (2) of the Resolution.
556 Most delegations raised objections against the duration of the residence permit considering it too generous and inflexible. See Council Doc. 6488/98, ASIM 63, 22.
557 Most delegations consider it in the same way. Council Doc. 6488/98, ASIM 63, 22.
558 C. point 6 of the Resolution.

scope of the draft Convention is transferred to the level of implementing regulations, even though, according to Article 36 point 3 of the draft Convention the regulations have to be adopted unanimously.

3. Students

The Council Resolution on students provides for the international exchange of young academics[559]. The Resolution is based on the premise that the output of studies must benefit the students' country of origin. Upon course completion, students are expected to return to their home country, in order to make their new knowledge and skills available to this country. Permanent immigration is to be avoided, even if the skills acquired, economically speaking, would be useful for the Member States. Based on this principle, the Resolution aims to support and to promote student exchange, while simultaneously limiting the entry of new labour migrants[560].

The Council Resolution on students elaborates on several basic principles of harmonization, by which Member States should abide in the development and enforcement of national law. These basic principles are not applicable to relatives of EEA states and persons whose right of residence is based on the right to family reunification[561]. Furthermore, these principles are intended to regulate the admission of third-country nationals to a Member State only and do not affect the freedom of movement of students within the territory of the European Union[562].

Chapter V of the draft Convention also deals with the admission for the purposes of study and vocational training. Like the Resolution, the provisions of this Chapter do not apply to pupils in primary and secondary education or to apprentices[563].

The Council Resolution on students applies to four categories of students, who have to be third-country nationals. Admission may be granted to students for the following purposes:[564]

- to take up a course of study,
- study for a doctorate,
- pursue academic activity following a course of higher education within the framework of further study or training, where the earning of income is not the principal aim and
- for participation at (e. g. language) courses in order to be prepared for specific courses of studies.

---

559 O.J. 1996, C 274/10.

560 A. 2-4 of the Resolution; see No. 75 of the Flynn report, which describes the danger of a "brain-drain-effect"; cf. *Haberland*, Zeitschrift für Ausländerrecht und Ausländerpolitik (ZAR) (1996), 3, 9.

561 B. of the Resolution; *Haberland*, Zeitschrift für Ausländerrecht und Ausländerpolitik (ZAR) (1996), 10.

562 A. point 5 of the Resolution.

563 See Article 21.

564 See C. point 1 of the Resolution.

Article 15 of the draft Convention also allows for admission of third-country nationals if they have been admitted to a State or State-recognized establishment of higher education in order to:

(a) attend preparatory courses for a specific course of study in higher education;

(b) pursue a course of study;

(c) prepare a doctoral thesis;

(d) pursue research activity as part of a basic or advanced vocational education after obtaining a degree or higher education diploma, where that activity is not primarily intended to secure an income.

To avoid abuse of this privilege paragraph (a) defines the term "preparatory courses", as courses, including language classes which are intended to prepare third-country nationals to take up studies. Paragraph (b) extends the right of residence to the period of time in which final examinations are taken. Since paragraph (b) deals with final exams the reference to dissertation seems superfluous.

The draft Convention does not provide for a requirement to prove possession of sufficient resources for admission to a course of study in a Member State, contrary to the provisions laid down in the Council Resolution on students[565]. Students from EU Member States, according to Article 1 of the directive 93/96 EEC[566] must provide proof of health insurance coverage, as well as access to resources sufficient to prevent them from becoming dependant on the social security system of the host State. The European Parliament, consequently, has called for the introduction of a new paragraph, allowing Member States to require evidence of health coverage and sufficient resources from third-country nationals[567].

Moreover, it might be reasonable to include into Article 15 of the draft Convention other institutions of professional formation which are comparable to universities. Article 15(b) should also enable to grant admission to students just beginning or continuing their studies[568].

Finally, according to the Council Resolution on students, additional conditions must be fulfilled in order to study in a Member State of the European Union. The admission decision under the Resolution depends on four conditions.

The student must:[569]

- meet the general residence permit conditions for the host state,
- have received a corresponding study offer from the chosen institution,

565 See B. point 2 of the Resolution.

566 O.J. 1993, L 317/59.

567 See Amendment 19 of the Legislative Proposal of the European Parliament, Second Report, PE 229.573/final, 11.

568 Cf. the Resolution by the German Bundesrat (Federal Chamber) of 19 December 1997, Bundesratsdrucksache (Federal Chamber Document) 788/97, 5.

569 See C. point 2 of the Resolution.

- provide proof of sufficient financial means to support the cost of the studies, so that there is no need for social assistance or to take up a full-time job, and
- be covered by a nationally-recognized health insurance scheme.

Article 17 of the draft Convention as well as the Council Resolution on students exclude students from access to the labour market or other economic activities, either in paid employment or in a self-employed capacity. In derogation from this principle subsidiary or short-term work, including seasonal employment, which does not constitute the students' main income and does not interfere with their studies, is allowed[570].

According to the Council Resolution on students, a residence permit for study purposes is to be granted for the (average) length of the course of study. If the period of study is longer than one year, the permit can be initially limited to a one-year period. The authorization may be renewed, if the student fulfils all study requirements by passing tests and examinations. As proof of current enrolment and the residence purpose are necessarily linked, it follows that students must exit the country upon completion or abandonment of the course of study. A change to other fields of study is possible only in the initial phase of the studies. Change at a later date will be considered a change in the purpose of the residence permit[571] and requires a new application for a residence permit.

According to Article 16(1) first sentence of the draft Convention the duration of the residence authorization shall be limited to the length of the course chosen. In the Explanatory Memorandum of the European Commission to Article 16 remarks are made that a certain margin as regards the fixing of the total duration of the residence authorization has to be provided, so as to allow for failures and a right to repeat periods of study[572]. It remains unclear how the term "duration of a course chosen" has to be understood, as a minimum length, ordinary length or any other length given.

Article 16(1), second sentence of the draft Convention suggests that the residence permit is to be issued in relation to the duration of the enrolment at the university. Whether such a regulation is reasonable may be questioned, since most Member States have regulated this issue in detail.

According to Article 16(2) of the draft Convention, residence authorizations may be renewed annually. They shall be renewed if applicants produce evidence that they continue to satisfy the requirements set for the issue of the initial authorization and that they have taken any tests and examinations required by the higher education establishment which they attend. This regulation corresponds to a large degree to the Council Resolution on students[573], which allows for the annual extension of the residence permit. The limitation of the permanent residence permit to a period of one year may, however, keep the student in a state of uncertainty with regard to his right to stay and may create unnecessary administrative work. It

[570] See also C. point 4 of the Resolution.
[571] Cf. C. point 3 of the Resolution.
[572] See COM(97)387final, 16.
[573] C. point 3, 6 of the Resolution.

may be more efficient to provide for the possibility of granting residence permission for a period of two years[574].

Article 16(3) of the draft Convention prohibits students from changing their course of study after completion of their first year. They must submit a fresh application for admission for study purposes if they wish to do so. The need to submit a new application for a residence permit in order to take up studies in case of a change of course after the first year of studies leads to the result that the student first would have to return to his home country, a procedure that would prevent many to take this step[575].

The Council Resolution provides that at the end of the course of study, or if the student abandons his/her studies, authorization to reside expires. Any change in subject will involve a change in the reasons for residence which, as a rule, argues against a fresh authorization or an extension of the existing one if it does not take place within the initial phase of the studies. Similarly, a national of a third country will in principle have to leave the territory of a Member State at the end of a study or if the student abandons his/her studies.

The European Parliament has suggested to admit foreigners interested in preparing their application for studies in the respective State, or those who demonstrate a genuine and realistic plan for completing a course of study. Moreover, these persons should not be required to leave the country in order to extend their residence permit[576].

The Council Resolution on students leaves the regulation of the admission of family members to national legislation. The duration of a residence permit granted to family members of students is to be linked to the residence permit of the student[577]. There is room, however, for further harmonization in this area. The Council Resolution on family reunification is not applicable due to the fact that family members' residence is limited to the duration of the studies[578].

The Council Resolution on students as well as the draft Convention acknowledge that the admission of students from third countries is of great significance to scientific and cultural exchange, as well as to an open university system. The admission of foreign students is essential for the promotion of a global economy and for the improvement of political and social conditions in home countries of students. Conditions for admission, therefore, must not be too rigid, and third-country nationals should be permitted to change their subject of study at least in an early stage. If necessary, residence permit should be extended to allow students to remain in order to pass an examination. Finally, the admission and granting of residence permits to qualified scientists for the purpose of postgraduate studies should be promoted.

---

574 Cf. the Resolution of the German Bundesrat (Federal Chamber), 19 December 1997, Bundesratsdrucksache (Federal Chamber Document) 788/97, 5.

575 Resolution of the German Bundesrat (Federal Chamber), 19 December 1997, Bundesratsdrucksache (Federal Chamber Document) 788/97, 5.

576 See Amendment 22 of the Legislative Proposal of the European Parliament, Second Report, PE 229.573/final, 12.

577 See C. point 5 of the Resolution.

578 The family reunion of third-country nationals, who are family members of Union citizens complies with Article 2 II Directive 90/366/EEC, O.J. 1990, L 180/30.

Article 18 of the draft Convention allows third-country nationals who have completed one of the categories of study specified in Article 15 of the draft Convention, and who wish to continue their studies under another category, to apply for a new authorization without leaving the Member State. Persons who wish to remain in a Member State for another purpose after completing their studies must reapply under the initial admission procedure. According to the exhaustive reference of Article 18 of the draft Convention to the other categories mentioned in Article 15, and according to the Explanatory Memorandum of the Commission.

The right to apply for a new authorisation in the host Member State only applies to students who have successfully completed a course referred to in Article 15 to go on to take a course of the kind referred to under Article 15(b) and Article 15(c). Compelling such students to comply with a renewal procedure would prevent them from re-enrolling from one year to the next, because of the time involved in examining applications. Only in this case they will be allowed to request an extension of their residence authorisation on the spot in order to complete a new course of study. Taking up students at lower level, however, should not be treated similarly. Third-country nationals who want to continue their studies at this level or do subsequent studies under another categories, therefore, must leave the territory of the Member state, in order to be able to apply for a new residence permit.

Chapter V of the draft Convention does not include any regulations which would allow qualified scientists, even after their completion of study and without being enrolled at an institution of higher education/university, to obtain a residence permit. Such a possibility especially should be provided for those scientists not being employed and which therefore do not fall within the scope of the Regulation on employment, because they, e.g., have a scholarship.

4. Trainees

Article 19(1) of the Draft Convention defines trainees as workers residing in the territory of a Member State with the express purpose of improving their skills and qualifications in their chosen occupation in order to pursue it in a third country. They must satisfy the following requirements listed in Article 19(2) of the draft Convention:

(a) they shall hold a training agreement with a host establishment, guaranteeing them sufficient remuneration to support themselves; and

(b) they shall enjoy social security cover for risks that may arise in the host Member State.

Article 19 of the draft Convention, however, does not grant a right to admission, but provides for a discretionary decision[579]. Thus, Member States are allowed to take the current state of the labour market into account when considering

[579] COM(97)387final, 17.

admissions. It is important to remember, however, that educational opportunities of this nature constitute work activities and, as such, usually require a work permit.

Article 19(a) of the draft Convention deals with resources of apprentices. The proposal appears as too rigid since some kind of alimentation paid during the period of apprenticeship cannot be considered as proof of sufficient resources. It might be more reasonable to open up further possibilities, e.g. maintenance paid by third persons, in order to ensure sufficient resources. Moreover, it is unclear what is to be understood by the term "social security cover". While it is clear that social security pension insurance cannot reasonably be required of the persons concerned, the proposal should be amended to require proof of health insurance from all applicants.

The effective exchange of students and scientists in the European Union could be further promoted by extending the right of admission for initial training, as stipulated by Article 19 of the draft Convention, to third-country nationals, if there is a special public interest to grant admission in these cases, or if international training in certain fields is common practice[580].

According to Article 20 of the draft Convention, Member States are to facilitate the admission of third-country nationals as students, trainees or researchers under co-operation programs funded by the Community.

5. *Family Members*

Both the Council Resolution on family reunification, which includes some basic principles, and a separate chapter of the draft Convention deal with admission for the purpose of family reunification.

The principles outlined in Article 24(1) of the draft Convention provide for family reunification, provided that the applicant has been legally resident in, and has furthermore a legal right to reside in a Member State for at least one year.

As outlined in the explanations of the Commission, the proposal is based on the internationally accepted concept of family reunification. This right is derived from the principle of respect towards family life. According to the European Court "it is part of a permanent confirmed jurisprudence of the Court"[581]. The Court also maintains that this principle is recognized by Community Law. The Commission refers to the European Convention on Human Rights and Fundamental Freedoms of November 4, 1950, as well as to the jurisprudence of the European Court for Human Rights.

The conclusion of the European Commission that for the Member a general right on family reunification can be derived from international treaties or general principles of international law seems to be questionable.

The vast majority of international lawyers agrees that general international law recognizes and confirms a minimum standard of human rights, which forms a part

---

[580] See the remarks of the German Bundesrat (Federal Chamber) of 19 December 1997, Bundesratsdrucksache (Federal Chamber Document) 788/97, 4.

[581] See ECJ, judgment of 18 May 1989, case C-249/86, *Commission v Germany*, [1989] ECR 1290 para 10.

of customary international law. The protection of the family in the meantime is principally also regarded as part of this minimum standard. There is general consensus that in this context family reunifications are considered desirable for humanitarian reasons. Yet an individual right of third-country nationals, and therefore a legally binding obligation on states, in the sense that family reunifications in the country chosen to pursue a family life has to be granted, cannot be derived from this principle[582]. The development of a customary right of international law to grant family reunification is not only prevented by permanent state practise to grant no such right but to restrict family reunification and make it dependent on certain additional requirements, but also by the fact that relevant treaties and declarations are clearly reluctant to recognize such a right but are limited to a general undertaking to facilitate family reunification subject to general requirements of immigration policy.

As far as the European Commission made reference to the European Convention on the Protection for the Protection of Human Rights and Fundamental Freedoms from 4 November 1950 one first of all has to conclude that the Convention nowhere contains explicit provisions concerning family reunification. A right to family reunification might, however, be derived from Article 8(1) ECHR, which makes provisions for the protection of everyone's right to respect for his private and family life.

According to the jurisprudence of the European Court of Human Rights, Article 8(1) ECHR generally does not establish a general right to entry and residence in a foreign country[583]; still Article 8(1) ECHR may be violated, if a foreigner is separated from his/her close relatives or spouse[584].

The interpretation of Article 8(1) ECHR has to take into account the effects of immigration measures on existing family relationships. A distinction has to be drawn between measures which terminate an existing title to entry or residence and such measures which terminate resident and thereby affect an existing family relationship. Article 8(1) ECHR in principle applies only in cases in which a administrative measure terminating resident interferes with an existing family relationship. Only exceptionally a refusal to grant entry can be considered as an interference with the private and family life of a person if the private and family life is already clearly established in the territory[585]. If the third country national is refused permission to move to his/her spouse in order to take up family life, Article 8(1) ECHR generally is not affected provided that the spouses can get a residence permit in another state. Only exceptionally Article 8(1) ECHR may be violated if there is no alternative possibility to live together, for instance, if no ties exist between the family and the state in which a legal residence of the whole family

[582] Cf. for example *Scheer*, Der Ehegatten- und Familiennachzug (1994), 7; *Frowein* in Frowein/Stein (eds.), Die Rechtstellung von Ausländern nach staatlichem Recht und Völkerrecht (1987), 2073; *Jahn*, Migration Movement, EPIL Inst. 8, 377 et seq.

[583] Cf. European Commission of Human Rights, decision of 9 June 1958, case 214/56, *X v Belgium*, Yearbook of the European Convention of Human Rights, Vol. 2 (1958/1959), 214 et seq.

[584] Cf. European Commission of Human Rights, decision of 19 May 1977, case 7816/77, *X and Y v the Federal Republic of Germany*, DR 9 (1978), 219 et seq.; European Commission of Human Rights, decision of 8 March 1985, case 10730/84, *Berrehab et al. v Netherlands*, DR 41 (1985), 196 et seq.

[585] Judgment of 14 July 1977, No. 7289/75 and 7349/76, *XY v Switzerland*, EuGRZ 1977, 497, 499.

would be possible. In general, the issue of an interference into an existing family life can only be determined on the basis of a balance of interest. The interests to be assessed do not only include the family life of the third-country national but also the sovereign right of states to control immigration. In this context attention has to be drawn to Article 8(2) ECHR which allows measures "necessary in a democratic society in the interests of national security, public safety or the economic wellbeing of the country, further prevention of disorder or crime, further protection of health or morals, or further protection of the rights and freedoms of others." According to the jurisprudence of the European Court of Human Rights Article 8(1) ECHR does not provide for a general obligation of states to recognise the decision taken by foreigners as to their country of residence. Contracting states, implementing their duty to respect a family life a wide margin of appreciation in assessing the different needs and claims of the community as well as of individuals[586]. Whether a state is in fact obliged to grant entry and residence for the purpose of family reunification thus finally depends on the specific circumstances of the case.

One of the decisive criteria whether a refusal to grant a residence permit for the purpose of family reunion is in accordance with Article 8(1) ECHR is whether it may be reasonably expected that a family member or spouse moves into the country of residence of the family member claiming entry and residence.[587] The absence of close family ties (e.g. due to a long period of separation of the spouses or due to the adulthood of children no obligations to grant a residence permit can be derived from Article 8(1) ECHR[588]. It can also be assumed that a return to a country of origin is acceptable if a separation of parents and children has been established on the basis of a voluntary decision. The residence of minor children therefore, does not imply a right to family reunion for parents and sisters.

Recently the European Court of Human Rights has confirmed these principles in the decision Gül v Switzerland[589]. The Court had to decide on the claim for family reunion of a minor son of Turkish parents who was permitted to live in Switzerland for humanitarian reasons. The Court distinguishes between administrative measures terminating a residence of family members and the issue of immigration for the purpose of family reunification.:

> "The present case concerns not only family life but also immigration, and the extent of a State's obligation to admit to its territory relatives of settled immigrants will vary according to the particular circumstances of the persons involved and the general interest. As a matter of well-established international law and subject to its treaty obligations, a State has the right to control the entry of non-nationals into its territory (see, among other authorities, the Abdulaziz, Cabales and Balkandali v. the United Kingdom judgment of 28 May 1985, Series A No. 94, pp. 33-34, § 67). Moreover,

[586] Cf. *Wildhaber* in Golsong et al. (eds.), Internationaler Kommentar zur EMRK, Article 8 ECHR (1992) para 424 ff.

[587] Cf. for Germany the judgments of the German Bundesverwaltungsgericht (Federal Administrative Court) of 26 March 1982, NJW 1982, 1958, 1960 and of 30 November 1982, NJW 1983, 532, 534.

[588] European Commission for Human Rights, judgment of 6 July 1981, case 9105/80, *Y v Sweden*, EuGRZ 1983, 215.

[589] Judgment of 19 February 1996, *Gül v Switzerland*, RJD 1996-I, 159 et seq.

where immigration is concerned, Article 8 cannot be considered to impose on a State a general obligation to respect the choice by married couples of the country of their matrimonial residence and to authorise family reunification in its territory. In order to establish the scope of the State's obligations, the facts of the case must be considered (see, mutatis mutandis, the Abdulaziz, Cabales and Balkandali judgment previously cited, p. 34, § 68, and the Cruz Varas and Others v. Sweden judgment of 20 March 1991, Series A No. 201, p. 32, § 88).[590]

The Court considers the possibility of a individual right of family reunification only in the case that family reunion can be established in Switzerland. In the case at issue the Court denied this condition since the parents of the child regardless significant economic and humanitarian problems (serious illness of one parent) would have been able to return to Turkey[591]. It follows that Article 8(1) ECHR requires to grant reunification only if the denial of a residence permit would mean the separation of an existing family relationship without a reasonable option to return to the home country[592].

The Geneva Convention of 1951 does not provide a legal basis for a general right to family reunification. The Final Act of the Plenipotentiaries Conference of 28 July 1951, however, contains a Recommendation b) concerning the issue of family unity:

> "CONSIDERING that the unity of the family, the natural and fundamental group unit of society, is an essential right of refugee, and that such unity is constantly threatened and [n]oting with satisfaction that, according to the official commentary of the ad hoc Committee... [t]he rights granted to a refugee are extended to members of his family, RECOMMENDS Governments to take the necessary measures for the protection of the refugee's family, especially with a view to :
>
> Ensuring that the unity of the refugee's family is maintained..."[593]

The Recommendation of the Conference can hardly be interpreted as implying a binding obligation of states to grant family reunification. Notwithstanding the lack of a binding legal force, the Recommendation must be taken into account in the determination-process. In particular the fact that the reunification of a family can only be achieved by granting a residence right has to be considered, since as a rule there will be no alternative country of residence for the family members. In practice recognized refugees are granted family reunification, based on the general principles derived from Article 8(1) ECHR[594]. No conclusions, however, can be drawn from this particular category of persons to the third country generals

---

[590] Cf. ECHR, judgement of 19 February 1996, *Gül v. Switzerland*, RJD 1996-I, 175 et seq.

[591] Cf. ECHR, judgment of 19 February 1996, *Gül v. Switzerland*, RJD 1996-I, 175 et seq.

[592] Cf. ECHR, judgement of 28 May 1985, *Abdulaziz et al. v Great Britain*, Series A no. 94, 33 et seq. and ECHR, judgment of 19 February 1996, *Gül v Switzerland*, RJD 1996-I, 175 et seq.

[593] 189 U.N.T.S. 137.

[594] Cf. *Grahl-Madsen*, The Status of Refugees in International Law, Vol. I (1966), 414 et seq.

regulated by the draft Convention. The draft Convention explicitly excludes refugees under the Geneva Convention from its scope of application[595].

The European Social Charter of 18 October 1961 applies only to family reunification for a commuting employee permitted to reside in the territory of a Member State. Article 19 point 6 only obliges states "to facilitate as far as possible the reunion of the family of a foreign migrant worker permitted to establish himself in the territory". The Committee of Experts established under the Social Charter in its examination of the State Reports has interpreted the wording "as far as possible" as implying a right to regulate the national legislation, which, however, must not be used to deprive the provision of any meaningful content by a too restrictive interpretation. The Committee pointed out that even if family reunification would have to be considered as a rule, would not have to be granted in any case and under any circumstances[596].

Under Article 23(1) and Article 17 of the International Covenant on Civil and Political Rights of 19 December 1966 family is the natural and fundamental group unity of society and is entitled to protection by society and the state (Article 23 (1)). No one shall be subjected to arbitrary or unlawful interference with his privacy, family, home or correspondents (Article 17(1)). These provisions, however, do not necessarily imply a right to be granted a residence permit for the purpose of family reunion. Restrictions based on immigration regulations are admissible as long as such measures are not to be considered as arbitrary. A refusal to grant a residence permit would have to be considered as arbitrary if it is based on unreasonable or inadmissible criteria[597].

The Final Act of the Conference on Security and Co-operation in Europe from 1 August 1975 provides inter alia that "the participating States will deal in a positive and humanitarian spirit with the applications of persons who wish to be reunited with members of their family..."[598] The wording of this passage yet makes clear that this is not regarded as a genuine obligation of international law according to the Vienna Treaty Convention or a rule of customary international law, but merely as a declaration of intent, which – however its legal effect in international law is judged[599] – has no direct legal effect in the domestic legal system[600].

Finally, no general right to family reunification can be derived from the Convention on the Rights of the Child of 1992. According to Article 9 point 1 of the Convention "no child shall not be separated from his or her parents against their will, except when competent authorities subject to judicial review determine, in accordance with applicable law and procedures, that such separation is necessary

---

595 See *infra* Chapter C.VII 1.

596 Cf. *Cholewinski*, Migrant Workers in International Human Rights Law (1997), 137 et seq., 343 et seq. and *Scheer*, Der Ehegatten- und Familiennachzug (1994), S. 83 et seq.

597 Cf. UN-AMR, statement of 9 April 1981, No. 9/35, *Aumeeruddy-Cziffra et al. v Mauritius*, Communication No. 35/1978, Selected Decisions under the Optional Protocol, CCPR/C/OP/1, 67 et seq.

598 Final Act, Chapter Human Contacts (b) "Reunification of families"

599 See *Schweisfurth*, Zeitschrift für ausländisches öffentliches Recht und Völkerrecht (ZaöRV) 36 (1976), 681 et seq.

600 For Germany see the Bundesverwaltungsgericht (Federal Administrative Court), judgment of 26 March 1982, *BVerwGE* 65, 188, 197 and *Hailbronner*, JZ 1983, 574, 576.

for the best interests of the child."[601] From the wording one can conclude that Article 9 point 1 makes provision only for measures terminating a residence right while admission for family reunification is not covered. Furthermore Article 9(4) clearly states that the child's right has no priority over a possible expulsion of even both parents. Provision is made in such cases for a right of information of the parents, or as the case may be, of one parent or the child. Thus the affected persons have no independent individual rights which could prevent measures to terminate the residence. It follows that Article 9 does not have a considerable restrictive impact upon administrative discretion in the area of immigration. [602]

Finally, according to Article 10 of the Convention family reunification shall be dealt with by States Parties in a positive, humane and expeditious manner. Again, the wording of this provision clearly excludes an individual right. The Article can only be interpreted in a way to practise existing domestic regulations, particularly those granting administrative discretion in a manner favourable for family reunification.[603] According to Article 16 of the Convention "no child shall be subjected to arbitrary or unlawful interference with his or her privacy, family.... ". Leaving aside the issue whether a right to family reunification may be concluded from this provision, it has to be noted that interference with family is only prohibited under the Convention in case of an arbitrary refusal of a residence permit[604].

In conclusion it can be said that neither from general international law nor international treaties or conventions provide for a individual right to family reunion by way of granting a residence permit in order to establish a family life[605]. No such right may be derived from the Geneva Convention either, although under particular circumstances the refusal to grant family members of refugees a right of entry and residence may constitute a violation of Article 8 ECHR. In general, international treaties usually provided only for non-binding "endeavour" clauses which may be useful in restricting the scope of administrative discretion in domestic law. Generally speaking, however, states are giving a wide margin of discretion in regulating the issue of family reunification under domestic immigration law. One may regret this from a policy point of view. It does, however, reflect the growing concern of many countries of immigration that family reunification has turned into a major source of immigration which has become very difficult to control.

According to Article 24(1) of the draft Convention, the third-country national must have been legally resident in a Member State for at least one year in order to apply for family reunification. The proposal is more restrictive in this respect than the Resolution concerning family reunification, which leaves the adoption of such waiting periods to the discretion of each Member State. Therefore, it is also more restrictive than national law already in force, which does not require a minimum

---

601 Article 9 point 1 of the Convention on the Rights of the Child

602 Cf. *Göbel-Zimmermann*, Zeitschrift für Ausländerrecht und Ausländerpolitik (ZAR) 1995, 180.

603 See Bundesverwaltungsgericht (Federal Administrative Court), judgment of 11 June 1996, BVerwGE 236, 246 et seq.

604 Cf. *Klos*, Rahmenbedingungen und Gestaltungsmöglichkeiten (1998), 129.

605 In relation to German aliens law see *Hailbronner*, Ausländerrecht, § 17 AuslG (1997) para 10.

time of residence[606]. A flexible regulation would be reasonable considering that obligatory waiting periods could lead to hardship. The residence permit should also be valid for at least one additional year.

According to Article 24(2) of the draft Convention, third-country nationals who want to take up studies in a Member State can only apply for family reunification after a two year's legal stay. Similar requirements concerning the admission to family reunification are not included in the Resolution on students nor in the Resolution on family reunification. The waiting period laid down in Article 24(2), therefore, may be considered as more restrictive as the legal standard in EU Member States which is usually reflected in the resolutions of immigration ministers.

Article 25 of the draft Convention contains a special provision concerning the status of family members of Union citizens not exercising their right to freedom of movement. They are subject to the same conditions as those imposed by Articles 10, 11 and 12 of Regulation No. 1612/68 of October 15, 1968 on freedom of movement for workers within the Community, and to all other relevant provisions of Community law. As family members of European Union citizens are already privileged by Community Law, however, this provision would be more appropriate as a regulation or directive.

The Council Resolution, on the one hand, privileges spouses, children of the resident and his/her spouse, and children adopted in a third country[607]. On the other hand, Article 26 of the draft Convention admits the following persons for the purposes of family reunification, provided that the marriage conforms to the fundamental principles of the law of the Member State:

(a) the resident's spouse;

(b) children of the resident and his or her spouse, including children adopted in accordance with a decision by the authority responsible in the Member State or a decision recognized by that authority;

(c) children, including adopted children, of the resident or his or her spouse, where one or the other of them has the sole parental authority over those children, has been given custody of them, and is de facto responsible for them.[608]

According to Article 26(2) of the draft Convention, unmarried and minor children may be admitted[609]. The Council Resolution sets an upper limit of 16 – 18 years of age[610].

---

606 In the Federal Republic of Germany the duration of residence of third-country nationals is only a factor that has to be taken into account in the discretionary decision.

607 Point 3, 6 and 7 of the Resolution.

608 The European Parliament intends to eliminate the last part of paragraph c. See Amendment 27 of the Legislative Proposal of the European Parliament, Second Report, PE 229.573/final, 13.

609 As to the qualification for admission the time when the application is made shall be decisive. See Amendment 28 of the Legislative Proposal of the European Parliament, Second Report, PE 229.573/final, 14.

610 Point 8 of the basic principles.

Moreover, according to Article 26(3) of the draft Convention, Member States are to look favourably on family reunification involving dependent relatives in the ascending line, as well as other dependent relatives in the descending line, provided that they meet the conditions laid down in Article 28 of the draft Convention.

Article 27 of the draft Convention allows Member States to deny admission to a spouse or a child, and to withdraw the residence permit in cases of fraud or forgery. Moreover, Member States shall refuse to admit a spouse or an adopted child, or may withdraw their residence authorization if it can be proved that the marriage[611] or adoption was carried out solely for purpose of admission[612]. These regulations appear to be indispensable to avoid abuse. Why these principles are contained only in Chapter VII of the draft Convention, however, is a matter of debate. The inclusion of these principles in the general regulations contained in Chapters I and II would strengthen the proposal, and would allow Member States to deny or withdraw a residence permit in the case of fraud, not only in the area of family reunification, but in any area regulated by the draft Convention.

Article 28 requires the submission of an application for family reunification, as well as proof that the applicant possesses sufficient resources to guarantee the living of the joining family[613]. Third-country nationals can apply for family reunification 6 months after entry into the Member State. This regulation should be clarified with a statement to the effect that the support of the joining family and its health insurance coverage will only be deemed as guaranteed if covered by the income of the applicant or by other means possessed by the family as a whole. Such clarification is necessary to prohibit family reunification for third-country nationals supported by social security, as well as for employees with a non renewable contract.

According to Article 29 of the draft Convention, every Member State which has accepted family reunification must grant joining family members residence permits for a period of time equal to that of the applying third-country national's residence permit.

Member States, however, may object this provision since they will consider it necessary in the interest of an effective immigration control to send a foreigner back to his/her home country if after a short stay the reason for which the residence permit had been granted (marriage) has ceased to exist, e.g. due to a divorce. The termination of residence is predominantly regarded as acceptable for a family member at least if no close ties have as yet been established with the country of residence. Considerations of this kind render the regulation of Article 29 of the draft Convention, under which the valid time period for the residence permit of the

---

[611] For fictitious marriages seen the Council Resolution of 4 December 1997 on measures to be adopted on the combating of marriages of convenience, O.J. 1997, C 382/1.

[612] For similar regulations see Council Resolution point 4, 9 and 13. If it is found that the sole purpose of the marriage or adoption is to enable third-country nationals to be admitted to a Member State, the burden of proof shall lie with the Member State. See Amendment 29 of the Legislative Proposal of the European Parliament, Second Report, PE 229.573/final, 14.

[613] Amendment 30 of the Legislative Proposal of the European Parliament, Second Report, PE 229.573/final, 14, provides for the possibility to depart from these conditions in exceptional cases.

third-country national and the joining members of its family must correspond, unsuitable. It should be replaced by a regulation which allows for granting limited residence permits, as well as for an extension of these permits, if the applicant continues to fulfill the requirements established at the time of the initial admission.

Article 30 of the draft Convention contains provisions concerning the employment of persons admitted for the purposes of family reunification. Such persons shall not be authorized to take up employment or pursue an independent economic activity until the expiration of a period of six months from the date of their arrival[614]. Unforeseen changes in the composition or income of the family which create a need for additional income may, in some cases, allow to dispense with the mandatory six-month waiting period[615].

According to Article 31 of the draft Convention, persons admitted for the purpose of family reunification may, under certain conditions, obtain an independent, separate status. Widows, divorced or legally separated spouses or children, who have lost their parents through death, or those who reach the age of majority, may submit an application for residence authorization independent of that under which they were originally admitted[616]. This application must be submitted no later than three months before the expiration of the current residence authorization of the family member[617]. However, if the residence authorization expires earlier than three months after the circumstances justifying admission occur, the application deadline shall be extended to a total of three months. If necessary, the Member State shall issue a provisional residence authorization valid for the period during which their application is being considered and until they are notified of the decision.

6. *Third-Country Nationals Who Want to enter For Other Reasons*

There currently exists no Council Resolution concerning the status of persons who do not fall under one of the above mentioned categories. According to Chapter VI of the draft Convention, however, third-country nationals to whom the provisions of Chapters III, IV, V or VII do not apply may be granted admission to the territory of a Member State if they fulfill the conditions mentioned in Article 22. Chapter VI, therefore, has a subsidiary function and, as such, must be viewed in connection with all the other Chapters granting admission.

Article 22 of the draft Convention requires third-country nationals to fulfill four requirements. First, "(a) they shall have sufficient means to support themselves without engaging in any of the gainful activities referred to in Chapters III and IV".

In addition "(b) they shall enjoy social security cover that is valid in the Member State to which they are seeking admission;". It is not clear, though, whether health insurance coverage is included within the term social security coverage.

---

[614] See Article 30(1).
[615] See Article 30(2).
[616] See Article 31(1).
[617] See Article 31(2).

Furthermore "(c) they shall be able to show the lawful origin of their means of support". How exactly applicants are to prove that their means are of lawful origin, however, is a matter of debate. It is also uncertain whether and how the public authorities responsible for the admission are to verify the lawful origin of these means. Furthermore, a method must be developed to ensure that these practices conform with other activities of the European Union concerning the fight against money laundering.

Finally, "(d) they shall have accommodation in the Member State to which application is made." The term accommodation will have to be stated more precisely in the provisions for the implementation of the proposal, given that the question of whether a hotel accommodation is sufficient has been raised on several occasions.

According to Article 23(1) of the draft Convention, the initial residence authorization shall be issued for a period of at least one year. Article 23(2) of the draft Convention allows for an extension of at least one additional year. It is not clear, however, why these regulations grant a residence permit for a period of at least one year, given that there are a number of purposes which would allow for admission, but do not require a one year long stay. On the other hand, they are considered as far too restrictive and, according to the Legislative Proposal of the European Parliament, ought to be eliminated[618].

7. Long-term Resident Third-Country Nationals

Chapter VIII of the draft Convention privileges persons who are long term residents of a Member State. These persons shall enjoy rights comparable to those of Union citizens in order to ease integration into the society of the host Member State. The proposed provisions are, to some extent, comparable to those of the Council Resolution of March 4, 1996 on the status of third-country nationals residing on a long-term basis in the territory of the Member States[619].

By the definition of Article 32 of the draft Convention, third-country nationals have to be admitted as long-term residents if they have their regular and legal residence in this Member State, and if they are in the possession of a residence permit that allows them to stay for at least 10 years after the initial admission. Article 32, therefore, creates a legal right for a third-country national to a long-term residence status. The admission of a third-country national for the purpose of self-employed or employed work (Article 7), a course of study (Article 15), or for other purposes (Article 22), is left to the discretion of the concerned Member States. Article 32 provides for a minimum time period of five years of residence prior to submission of an application for long-term resident status, on the assumption that a certain degree of integration can be achieved during this time, and that it would give the third-country nationals ample time to prove that he/she

---

[618] See Amendment 26 in the Legislative Proposal of the European Parliament, Second Report, PE 229.573/final, 13, and the Explanatory Statement, Second Report, PE 229.573/final, 23.

[619] O.J. 1996, C 80/2.

wants to remain on a long-term basis[620]. Proof of actual stay in the concerned Member State, as well as the possibility to legally remain in the country for a period of 10 years are, therefore, decisive for granting the status as long-term residing third-country national[621].

Article 32 of the draft Convention does not allow Member States to base the allocation of the long-term residence status on any other criteria. This regulation would extend long-term resident status to third-country nationals condemned to long-term prison sentences in the concerned Member States, and must, therefore, be reconsidered. Whether the proposed five year time period is really sufficient to assume adequate integration of the third-country national is also a matter of debate, especially in the light of the fact that the Council's Resolution on the same subject lays down a period of ten years[622]. It would have been reasonable to make basic knowledge of the Member State's language a condition for proof of an attempt towards integration. The fact that a third-country national granted long-term residence status receives more rights under Article 34 of the draft Convention than those he would otherwise be entitled to under the laws of some Member States is, however, irreconcilable[623].

According to Article 33(1) of the draft Convention, recognition as a long-term resident is to be recorded by a specific entry in the residence authorization document, which will enable the respective person to prove his status more easily[624].

Article 33(2) of the draft Convention entitles long-term residents to a residence permit for the maximum period of time allowed in the Member State after the previously granted authorization expires[625]. Notwithstanding specific regulations of Member States, this authorization must be granted for a minimum of ten years.

Article 34(1) of the draft Convention grants long-term residents access to the entire territory of the Member State in question, authorizes them to exercise all activities referred to in Chapters III, IV and V of the Commission proposal, allows them to reside for all the purposes referred to in Chapters VI and VII, and grants increased protection against expulsion subject to the requirements of law and order and of internal security. Moreover, they shall enjoy the same treatment as Union citizens with regard to access to employment or self-employment, vocational training, trade union rights, the right of association, access to housing, social welfare, and schooling[626].

---

620 See COM(97)387 final, 23. See also the in so far agreeing resolution of the German Bundesrat (Federal Chamber), 19 December 1997, Bundesratsdrucksache (Federal Chamber Document) 788/97, 1.

621 See COM(97)387 final, 23.

622 III. 1 of the Resolution.

623 The rights regulated in Article 34 can for example by German law only be obtained with a residence permit according to § 27 of the German Aliens Act (Ausländergesetz). A residence permit may only be issued in case of 8 years of legal and permanent residence of the third-country national concerned according to § 27(2) point 1(a) of the German Aliens Act (Ausländergesetz).

624 Cf. COM(97)387 final, 23.

625 The proposal of the commission does speak of "expiring" in a misleading way. Cf. COM(97)387 final, 38.

626 Cf. also Part V.2 of the Council's Resolution.

While the Council Resolution on long time residing third-country nationals contains no provisions concerning access to the labour market and professional training in other Member States, Article 35 of the draft Convention provides for a right to:

(a) apply for a vacant job in another Member State in accordance with Article 7;

(b) apply for a permit to study in another Member State as defined in Article 15.

The explanation of the Commission makes clear that the knowledge of a vacant job is sufficient and the reference to a job offer is not binding, but may be used to prove a possibility of knowledge[627].

The express reference of Article 35(1) of the draft Convention to the "keeping of the principles of Article 7", and not to the ones detailed in Article 11, is evidence of the fact that it applies solely to dependent employment, not to independent work in another Member State[628]. The Commission believes that Article 35(1) would not burden national labour markets, as the overall number of immigrants in the Union would not increase[629]. Article 35 has been criticized[630] on the ground that it would induce a social benefits correlated migration movement within the European Union. Migrants, critics maintain, would move to the states with the best economic and social welfare situation. Particularly low paid jobs frequently produce much higher social costs than economic benefits for the host country. Whether such criticism reflects a real concern that social systems which differ substantially within the European Union might be overloaded by third-country nationals using their EU-wide residence right to get access to high standard social welfare systems is a matter of speculation. So far, within the European Union migration movements have not been prompted by different social systems. Whether the situation should be different with relation to third-country nationals, has not yet been demonstrated sufficiently. In addition, the draft regulation solely confers a right to a discretionary decision; Article 7(1) a to c expressly states that an employment may only be filled by a third-country national if the position cannot be filled by a Union citizen on a short time basis, or by a worker currently employed in the labour market in question[631].

According to Article 35(1) b of the draft Convention, long time residing third-country nationals can apply to continue their studies (Article 15) in all Member States. This regulation allows long term resident third-country nationals to study in

[627] The explanations to the draft does explicitly talk about "especially by a job offer". Cf. COM(97)387final, 23.

[628] This also clarifies the explanations to the draft. Cf. COM(97)387 final, 23. After the recognition of a third-country national as long term residing third-country national according to Article 35(2) something else can result though from Article 34(1).

[629] Cf. COM(97)387final, 23.

[630] Decision of the German Bundesrat (Federal Chamber), 19 December 1997, Bundesratsdrucksache (Federal Chamber Document) 788/97, 2.

[631] The delegation of Greece has so far been committed to a more preferential treatment of citizens of the European Union and already employed third-country nationals. See Council Doc. 6488/98, ASIM 63, 4.

one or several of the Member States, given that they are adequately integrated in the European Union. Unequal treatment of Union citizens and third-country nationals in connection with applications for educational programs should be avoided[632]. Third-country nationals settled[633] in a Member State other than the one that recognized them as long term residents shall be recognized as such in their new Member State of residence after a period of two years' residence. The purpose of this regulation is to prevent situations in which a long term residing third-country national according to (1) is granted a right to admittance to work in another Member State, but is, at the same time, seen as a first-time migrant into the Union. This regulation, therefore, enables them to claim the rights to which they are entitled to by their status, even if they reside in another Member State. The two year waiting period required before long term residence status will be recognized in a second Member State, should be viewed as a "trial period," during which the third-country national can determine whether he wants to stay in that Member State on a long-term basis[634].

Once a long-term residing third-country national is recognized as such in a second Member State, Article 35(2) of the Draft Convention eliminates the recognition of this status in the previous Member States of residence. According to Article 32 a third-country national can never, therefore, be simultaneously recognized as a long term residing third-country national by more than one Member State. Recognition is only valid in the Member State in which he has his permanent residence, and he loses the rights connected with that status in his previous Member State of residence. If he wants to return to the first Member State on a long term basis, the long-term residing third-country national in question must fulfill the requirements listed in Article 35(2), and pledge to complete the two-year probatory time period, in order to re-obtain the status of a long term residing third-country national[635].

On the whole, Article 35 of the draft Convention does not come close to granting long-term residing third-country nationals a freedom of movement equal to that of Union citizens. The freedom of movement granted to them applies solely to those seeking employment, or those who want to continue their studies[636]. In addition, admission in these cases is left to a discretionary decision in each Member State. Article 35 partially strengthens the right of a third-country national to travel between Member States, and thus mitigates the existing principle that entry into the European Union is easier than travelling between Member States.

A right to travel into other Member States is granted to family members of long-term residing third-country nationals by several provisions, as well as under the conditions listed in Article 35. This regulation allows long-term residing third-country nationals to reside in the country of the new residence solely for the

---

632 Cf. COM(97)387final, 23 et seq.

633 By the explanations to the draft it is made clear that not one but the permanent residence is meant. Cf. COM(97)387final, 24.

634 Cf. COM(97)387final, 24.

635 Cf. COM(97)387final, 24.

636 But see the Report from the Migration Working Party (Council Doc. 12027/98, ASIM 217, 3) that many Member States had difficulties with this right because of different reasons.

purposes stated in Chapter VII. Although the family members are independently recognized as long term residing third-country nationals, they must still meet the requirements of Article 35(1), if they want to enter another Member State, in order to seek employed work or to continue their studies. Family members will only be recognized as long term residing third-country nationals in the Member State after a two year probatory waiting period as stipulated in the condition stated in paragraph 1[637]. Article 34(1), therefore, does not grant a derived right to family members to enter the country; they only enjoy a right to enter according to Article 35(1).

A right of the family members of a long term residing third-country national to family reunification can be derived from the reference in Article 35(1) of the draft Convention to the principles of Article 7 and Article 15 of the draft Convention. As long as the long term residing third-country national was employed or admitted to a course of studies in accordance with Article 35(1)(a-b), following the principles of Article 7 or of Article 15, rights to family reunification may be granted, as provided for in the provisions of Chapter VII on the admission for purposes of admission to family reunification.

The provisions on the status of long term residing third-country nationals considerably strengthen the rights of foreigners resident in the European Union for a longer period of time. On the other hand, however, the provisions of Chapter VIII on long term residing third-country nationals appear out of place in the proposal of the Commission, given that the rest of the regulation deals solely with the first admission to a Member State of the European Community. These inconsistencies partially contradict the goal of equal treatment of long term residing third-country nationals promoted by the Commission proposal. Whether the provisions on long term residing third-country nationals were necessary within the framework of the proposal has, as a result, been questioned considerably. It may have been more reasonable to regulate the rights of long term residing third-country nationals in a separate act.

The European Parliament has called for the elimination of Chapter VIII[638]. In its Draft Legislative Resolution, the European Parliament challenges the Commission to elaborate on a separate proposal for a statute concerning third-country nationals who lawfully reside in a Member State[639]. The creation of a separate proposal seems necessary, due to the fact that Article 8 of the draft Convention does not fully reflect the complexity of the issue[640].

---

637 Also see the wording of Article 35(2) 1.

638 See Amendment 31 of the Legislative Proposal of the European Parliament, Second Report, PE 229.573/final, 14 et seq.

639 See point 2 of the Draft Legislative Resolution of the European Parliament, Second Report, PE 229.573/final, 20.

640 See the Explanatory Statement of the European Parliament, Second Report, PE 229.573/final, 20.

8. Conclusions

European Community immigration policy is based on the principle that immigration of workers from third countries is not to be encouraged. Exceptions are made, however, for admitting third-country national workers on a temporary basis, as well as for transfrontier workers, who are not considered immigrants in the traditional sense.

Immigration of self-employed persons, on the other hand, is not subject to comparable restrictions. In addition, admission of students from third countries on a temporary basis is to be facilitated; family members of persons already admitted are to enjoy limited rights of immigration. The Commission proposal provides that other third-country nationals may be admitted, provided that they possess sufficient financial means of support. Long-term residents shall enjoy rights equivalent to those of Union citizens.

This is not the case for the right to stay in other Member States. With regard to this right, the proposal only allows for a right of residence for the purpose of employment or for a continuation of studies in another Member State.

The ninth recital of the draft Convention application states that the rules on admission, with the exception of the rules concerning family reunification, and those applying to persons recognized as long-term residents, are not intended to confer a right of residence. The Commission proposal, if adopted, would eventually create individual rights under the general rules developed by the jurisprudence of the European Court of Justice relating to direct applicability of rights granted by Community Law to individuals. The Court has repeatedly pointed out that individuals may rely upon Community Law before national courts, provided that text and provisions are clear and unconditionally quoted. With regard to directives, the Court has stated that Member States who fail to implement these directives in their national law cannot take advantage of this omission. The Court is expected to pursue a similar line of argumentation, regardless of the Member States' opposition to the creation of individual rights.

The conversion of the Commission proposal into a directive or regulation will prohibit Member States from denying a grant of individual rights. In light of this fact, and given the proposal's inconsistencies, it is unlikely that the Commission proposal will be converted into a Community regulation without substantial amendment[641]. It is to be expected, however, that the European Court will play a similar role in developing and expanding the rights of third-country nationals as it did with Union citizen's market freedoms.

---

[641] See the Conclusions of the Report of the Migration Working Party (Council Doc. 12027/3/98, ASIM 217, 4), the Second Report of the European Parliament (PE 229.573/final, 5 et seq.) and *Hailbronner*, CML Rev. 35 (1998), 1050.

VII. Free Movement of Third-Country Nationals within the European Union?

1. *The completion of the internal market and the "right to travel"*

According to Article 14 ECT, the community shall adopt measures to promote the progressive establishment of the inernal market. The internal market comprises an area without internal frontiers, in which the free movement of goods, persons, services and capital is ensured in accordance with the provisions of the Treaty. The completion of the internal market, related market freedoms, and the freedom of movement for EU citizens under Article 18 ECT presuppose the abolition of internal border controls. Additionally, third-country nationals derive, though indirectly, certain benefits from the establishment of the internal market, namely from the freedom of movement for workers and from the freedom to provide services. Since the controversy over the scope of Community competence *vis-à-vis* third-country nationals under the Maastricht Treaty[642] has been overcome by the Amsterdam Treaty, the Community can now proceed, subject to the terms of the new framework established by Title IV ECT, the legislative process initiated by the Commission during the Maastricht era. Relevant Treaty provisions and Commission proposals shall be discussed in the present sub-chapter.

2. *Freedom of Movement under the Amsterdam Treaty*

Article 18 ECT provides that Union citizens have the right to move and reside freely within the territory of the Member States, subject to the limitations and conditions laid down *inter alia* by measures adopted to give it effect. These rights are conferred on them as citizens of the Union and do not depend on the exercise of an economic activity. Thus, the Treaty on European Union legitimizes a state of affairs which had prevailed since the adoption of Directives 90/364/EEC, 90/365/EEC and 90/366/EEC on residence rights by the Council on 28 June 1990.

With regard to entry into, and short stays in, the territory of another Member State, the ECJ has held that "nationals of the Member States of the Community generally have the right to enter the territory of the other Member States in the exercise of the various freedoms recognized by the Treaty and in particular the

[642] The Commission has long taken the view that the internal market logically implies the free movement of all legally resident third-country nationals, arguing that a right of free circulation flows from the requirement to remove internal frontiers as provided for in ex-Article 7a ECT. However, this view has been challenged in particular by some Member States which regard this question as a matter of intergovernmental co-operation. The Amsterdam Treaty has resolved the dispute (see *supra* B XII). For the pre-Amsterdam debate see Alexander, 3 EJIL (1992), 53; *Cremona*, LIEI (1995) 87, 96 et seq.; *Evans*, 5 EJIL (1994), 199; *Hailbronner/Polakiewicz*, 3 Duke J Int'l & Comp. L. (1992), 49; *Hailbronner* in: Duc (ed.) Festschrift für Ulrich Everling (1996), 399 et seq.; *Hoogenboom*, 3 EJIL (1992), 36; *Magiera*, in: Busmeistes (ed.) Verfassungsstaatlickheit, Festschrift für Klaus Stern (1997), 1317, 1332 et seq.; *Oliver*, 5 YEL (1985), 57; *Plender*, 39 ICLQ (1990), 599; *Weber* ZAR 1997, 25 et seq.

freedom to provide services which, according to now settled case-law, is enjoyed both by providers and by recipients of services"[643].

Aside from the public policy exceptions and checks on persons at internal frontiers with the Anglo-Irish Common Travel Area, Union citizens no longer encounter any obstacles to their movements within the Community. Although they may still be subjected to border controls under Article 2 SIC, they have the right to cross with a valid identity card or passport (Article 3 of Directive 73/148/EEC). Union citizens are only required to disclose reasons for which they are staying in that State's territory (furnishing proof, if necessary) if and when they apply for a residence permit, i. e. when they intend to take up residence in the host Member State. If sojourn in another Member State is only temporary, e.g. as a tourist, Union citizens are exempted from such requirements[644].

The position of third-country nationals differs considerably from that of Union citizens. Like Union citizens they are not subject to controls at internal borders. Their right of entry and residence – with the exception of Schengen visa and similar Schengen transit rights – is governed by Member States' domestic laws which are currently neither harmonized nor coordinated. Even those third-country nationals who reside lawfully in the territory of one Member State may enter another Member State only under the conditions of, and in accordance with the procedures laid down by the second Member State.

The Schengen Implementation Convention has considerably improved this situation within the Schengen area by providing for a common Schengen visa valid for the entire territory of the Contracting Parties (Articles 10 and 19 SIC), and a right to move freely for up to three months for aliens not subject to a visa (Article 20 SIC) and for aliens holding a residence permit issued by one of the Contracting Parties (Article 21 SIC).

Union citizens' family members who are not nationals of a Member State enjoy the same right of entry and residence as Union citizens, but this right is derivative in nature; it is restricted to family members from third countries who are related to a citizen exercising his right of free movement. Moreover, in accordance with the Directive 68/360 on the free movement of persons, such family members may, due to their nationality, be subject to a visa requirement.

3. *Freedom of Movement for Third-Country Nationals*

The alleged need to grant third country nationals the right to freedom of movement within the Community has been frequently endorsed by several EU institutions. The ESC discussed it (with special regard to the situation of migrants) in an Opinion of 24 April 1991[645] and in an additional Opinion of 26 September 1991[646]

---

[643] ECJ, judgment of 30 March 1991, case C-68/69, Commission v. Netherlands [1991] ECR I-2637, para. 10.

[644] With the exception, where appropriate, of a declaration of arrival (third sub-para. of Article 4(2) of Directive 73/148/EEC).

[645] O.J. 1991, C 159/12.

on the status of migrant workers from third countries. The European Parliament made a similar request in its Resolution of 14 June 1991 on Union citizenship[647]. The Parliament has since reiterated its recommendations in a number of resolutions. The first concerned the abolition of controls at internal borders and free movement of persons within the European Community, and was adopted on 19 November 1992[648]. A more recent resolution, adopted in September 1995[649], concerned the Commission's Communication on immigration and asylum policies. In the latter Communication, issued on 23 February 1994[650], the Commission stated in point 127, that the logic of the internal market implied the elimination of the condition of nationality for the exercise of certain market freedoms[651]. A first step in this direction would be to allow third-country nationals to move freely within the Union on the basis of their residence permit, which would replace any existing visa requirement. The Schengen Convention provides a limited right of free movement, but is applicable only to Schengen Countries.

On 12 July 1995, the Commission adopted three proposals aimed at abolishing controls on persons at the Union's internal borders[652].

---

646 O.J. 1991, C 339, 82. In its Opinion of 24 March 1994 on the Green Paper on 'European social policy: Options for the Union' (O.J. 1994, C 148/35), the ESC reiterated the recommendations made in its 1991 Opinions.

647 Resolution A3-139/91, O.J. 1991, C 183/473.

648 Resolution A3-0284/92, O.J. 1992 C 337/211.

649 Resolution A4-0169/95, O.J. 1995 C/269/156; para. 40 states that the European Parliament 'deems it of great importance that priority be given to the strengthening of the legal position of citizens of third countries who are legally resident in one of the Member States; confirms its view that the right to free movement in the Union must apply to all persons living legally in the Member States, irrespective of their origin, nationality, religion or colour of skin; calls on the Commission to submit by 1 January 1996 proposals for achieving such aims and to draw up a list of the legal provisions which place such third-country nationals at a disadvantage vis-à-vis Union citizens and of the possibilities for giving them access to European citizenship'.

650 COM(94)23 final. See also the Commission's Communication of 8. 5. 1992 on the abolition of border controls, SEC (92) 877 final, and its Communication on immigration, issued on 23. 10. 1991, SEC (91) 1855 final.

651 SEC (91) 1855 final.

652 These proposals were also made to avoid condemnation for "failure to act", case C-445/93 Parliament v. Commission (O.J. 1994 C 1/12), pending, which will now possibly be withdrawn, see *Peers*, 33 CML Rev (1996), 7, 12, note 12. For a commentary on these measures see *Cremona*, 25 LIEI (1995) 87, 97-99; *Cholewinski*, Migrant Workers in International Human Rights Law (1997), 239 et seq.; *Editorial* comments, Legislating free movement: An over-ambitious Commission package?, 33 CML Rev. (1996), 1-5; *Peers*, ibid., 17.

a) Proposal for a Directive on the elimination of controls on persons crossing internal frontiers – COM(95)347 final and COM(97)106 final[653].

The Commission sought to achieve, by virtue of the draft Directive on the elimination of controls on persons crossing internal frontiers, clarity and legal certainty through the complete abolition of internal border controls. While controls or formalities should no longer be permissible at internal frontiers, the Directive would not have affected the exercise of police powers pursuant to the legislation of each Member State throughout its territory, or the enforcement of obligations to possess and carry documents according to national law (Article 1(2)), as long as such powers are exercised without discrimination between domestic and cross-border traffic, i.e. as long as such controls cannot be regarded as 'disguised' frontier controls. This draft Directive defined 'border control or formality' as any control applied by the public authorities of a Member State or by other persons, under the national legislation of a Member State in connection with, or on the occasion of the crossing of an internal frontier, and any formality imposed on a person in connection with the crossing of an internal frontier, and to be fulfilled on the occasion of such crossing (Article 3(4)). Member States would also have had to abolish any legislation obliging entities such as airlines or shipping companies to carry out controls at internal frontiers.

Article 1(1) of the draft Directive confirmed that all persons, whether or not they are economically active and irrespective of their nationality, would be covered by the abolition of controls at internal frontiers. It follows that internal frontiers might be crossed anywhere not merely at approved crossing points. Article 3(1-3) further specifies the concept of "internal borders", particularly with regard to airports and seaports. The Directive would not entitle third-country nationals lawfully resident in a Member State to take up residence in a second Member State. The free movement of persons in the internal market does not imply rights for third-country nationals which flow directly from the market freedoms (i.e. the taking-up of economic activities as self-employed or employed persons and, hence, the right of residence).

Assurance of a high level of security in a European Union without internal borders and the ability to combat general risks such as illegal immigration require accompanying measures. A Member State, in the event of a serious threat to public policy or public security[654], would be able to reinstate controls at its frontiers within the Community for a maximum period of 30 days by invoking a "safeguard clause" provided for in Article 2. Any Member State taking such action would be bound to notify the Commission and the other Member States immediately, and

---

[653] Proposal for a Council Directive on the elimination of controls on persons crossing internal frontiers (*Commission* original proposal: O.J. 1995, C 289/16; COM(95)347 final; Bull. EU 7-8/95 No. 1.1.2.; COR opinion: O.J. 1996, C 129/46; Bull. EU 1-2/96 No. 1.1.2.; *ESC* opinion: O.J. 1996, C 174/36; Bull. EU 3/96 No. 1.1.1.; *Parliament* opinion, proposing amendments: O.J. 1996 C 347/60; Bull. EU 10/96 No. 1.1.1.; the *Commission*, however, has accepted only some minor changes, see amended proposal, transmitted on 20 March 1997, COM(97)106 final = O.J. 1997, C 140/21).

[654] Clarification is needed of the phrase 'serious threat to public policy or public security', in order to avoid divergences in Member States' interpretations.

supply them with all appropriate information. The extension of controls for a (renewable) additional period of 30 days would be subject to prior consultation of the Commission and the other Member States. Moreover, the elimination of checks would not prevent Member States from adopting measures (including expulsion) on public security grounds, as provided for in Directive 64/221 and in the Draft Directive on the right of third-country nationals to travel in the Community.

b) Draft Directive amending secondary legislation on the free movement of persons – COM(95)348 final[655]

The proposal for a Directive on the free movement of persons affects third-country nationals who are family members of Union Citizens exercising their right of free movement.

The Commission proposes to delete from secondary legislation the requirement that persons produce, when crossing internal frontiers, a valid passport or identity card. Persons who wish to cross an external border must still produce a valid identity card or passport (Article (2)). As stated in the last recital of the proposal, the objective of ex-Article 7a (internal market) is not to allow Union citizens and their family members to travel without possessing requisite travel documents (which is required notably for the issue of a residence permit), nor does it prevent Member States from carrying out checks on individuals in situations other than crossing internal frontiers. Article 1(3) would give Member States the right to require that the persons covered by the Directive possess a valid identity card or passport, and, if necessary, a visa (in the case of a family member who is a national of a third-country for whom a visa is required), when they exercise their right of free movement.

c) Proposal for a Council Directive on the right of third-country nationals to travel within the Community – COM(95)346 final

According to the "right to travel" proposal[656] third-country nationals who are lawfully in the territory of a Member State may travel into the territory of another

[655] Proposal for a European Parliament and Council Directive amending Directive 68/360/EEC on the abolition of restrictions on movement and residence within the Community for workers of Member States and their families and Directive 73/148/EEC on the abolition of restrictions on movement and residence within the Community for nationals of Member States with regard to establishment and the provision of services (*Commission* proposal: O.J. 1995, C 307/18; COM(95)348 final; Bull. EU 7-8/95 No. 1.1.4.; *ESC* opinion: O.J. 1996, C 174/40; *Parliament* opinion (first reading): O.J. 1996, C 347/58; Bull. EU 10/96 No. 1.1.2.; its wishes to amend this proposal, however, have been dismissed by the *Commission*, see reasoning in COM(97)106 final).

[656] Proposal for a Council Directive on the right of third-country nationals to travel in the Community (*Commission* original proposal: O.J. 1995, C 306/5; COM(95)346 final; Bull. EU 7-8/95 No. 1.1.3.; *COR* opinion: O.J. 1996, C 129/46; Bull. EU 1-2/96 No. 1.1.1.; *ESC* opinion: O.J. 1996, C 153/38; Bull. EU 1-2/96 No. 1.1.1.; *Parliament* opinion, proposing amendments: O.J. 1996, C 347/62; Bull. EU 10/96 No. 1.1.3; the *Commission*, however, has dismissed most of the desired changes, see amended proposal, COM(97)106 final = O.J. 1997, C 139/6).

Member State for a short period of time without having to apply for a visa from the Member State they are visiting. The draft directive is considered as a supplement to the proposals put forward by the Commission in December 1993 on the crossing of external frontiers, which provided for equivalence between residence permits issued by Member States and the mutual recognition of visas. On the basis of this proposal an individual could cross an external frontier into a Member State if in possession of a visa or residence permit issued by another Member State, but could not cross an internal frontier. The draft directive would eliminate this anomaly.

The draft directive defines the "right to travel" as the right to cross internal Community borders and to remain in the territory of a Member State for a short stay, or to travel onward, without a visa. It is clear from this definition that the proposal shall not affect conditions of entry at the external borders of Member States, which are covered by other instruments such as Regulation 574/1999[657], the Dublin Convention[658], and communitarized SIC provisions[659]. According to Article 1(2), the Directive shall be without prejudice to rights which Community law confers on third-country nationals who are members of the families of citizens of the Union, or which are granted to third-country nationals and to members of their families, irrespective of nationality if, under an agreement between the Community, its Member States and the relevant third country, they enjoy rights of entry and residence in a Member State identical to those of Union citizens. Furthermore, the Directive shall not affect provisions of Community or domestic law on sojourns other than short stays, or on access to employment, the taking-up of activities as a self-employed person and other lucrative or non-lucrative activities[660] applicable to third-country nationals (Article 1(3)). It does not concern checks at internal borders; the Directive is fully applicable, regardless of whether such checks are retained.

The right to travel granted by the draft Directive would be subject to certain conditions, depending on the residence status of the person in question.

First, according to Article 3 of the draft Directive, Member States shall grant a right of travel to third-country nationals who hold a valid residence permit issued by another Member State. 'Residence permit' is defined as any document or authorization issued by the authorities in a Member State, which permits a person to reside in that Member State for a period of more than six months[661]. For reasons of clarity, Member States would have to provide the Commission and the other Member States with a list of all documents issued for the purposes of this Article that are treated as residence permit equivalents. Any person may travel into the

---

657 Regulation 574/1999 of 12 March 1999 determining the third countries whose nationals must be in possession of visas when crossing the external borders of the Member States, O.J. 1999 L 72/2. Cf. *supra* II 2.

658 Convention determining the State responsible for examining applications for asylum lodged in one of the Member States of the European Communities, signed in Dublin on 15 June 1990 (text reprinted in: O.J. 1997, C 254, 1); the Dublin Convention has entered into force on 1 September 1997(O.J. 1997, C 268/1). For details see *infra* Chapter E.

659 Cf. supra I and II.

660 Last two groups of activities added by the amended proposal, COM(97)106 final = O.J. 1997, C 139.

661 See Article 2 point (2) of the amended proposal, COM(97)106 final = O.J. 1997, C 139.

territories of other Member States for a maximum continuous period of three months, provided that he meets the following requirements: They must possess a valid residence permit and travel document, and they must have sufficient means of subsistence, both to cover the period of the intended stay or transit, and to enable them to return to the Member State which issued the residence permit, or to travel to a third country into which they are certain to be admitted.

Member States shall, in accordance with certain conditions laid down in an Annex to the Directive, readmit any person to whom they have issued a residence permit, and who illegally resides in the territory of another Member State, even if the residence permit is no longer valid. Third-country nationals who hold a residence permit issued by a Member State, and who exercise the right to travel, may be expelled if they do not meet the requirements mentioned above, or if they represent a threat to public order or public security in the Member State in which they exercise the right to travel, or to its international relations.

Second, Member States shall grant the right to travel to third-country nationals who hold a visa which is valid throughout the Community and which is mutually recognized for the purpose of crossing the external frontiers of the Member States. Such persons may travel in the territories of the Member States for the period of stay permitted by the visa, provided that they possess a travel document with a valid visa, and that they have sufficient means of subsistence corresponding to the above mentioned requirements for persons with a valid residence permit (Article 4(1)).

Third, third-country nationals who are exempted from visa requirements by all the Member States shall be allowed to travel in the territories of Member States for a maximum total period of three months within a period of six months from the date of first entry into the territory of one of the Member States, provided that they possess valid travel documents and meet the sufficient means of subsistence requirement (Article 4(2)).

Finally, the latter provisions shall also apply to third-country nationals who are subject to a visa requirement in a number of Member States. In this case, however, the right to travel shall be restricted to the territories of those Member States, that have exempted nationals of the respective third country from the visa requirement, unless the third-country national holds a visa valid throughout the Community, and which is mutually recognized for the purpose of crossing the external frontiers of the Member States. In the latter event, the period of stay in the territories of the Member States which require a visa shall be limited to the period permitted by the visa (Article 4(3)).

These provisions shall not prevent any Member State from extending the authorized stay of a third-country national in its territory beyond the three month period (Article 4(4)).

Third-country nationals in possession of a residence permit issued by a Member State or allowed to enter the Community for a short stay, and who exercise the right to travel, may, as a rule, be expelled if they do not satisfy the relevant conditions, or if they represent a threat to public order[662] or public security in the Member State in which they are exercising the right to travel, or to its international relations (see Article 3(3) and Article 4(5)). According to the new Article 5a, persons who do no longer satisfy the conditions to exercise their right to travel are expressly obliged to leave the 'guest' country without delay[663]. In addition, Article 5 would allow Member States to require persons exercising the right to travel to report their presence in their territories. This registration should not, however, be made subject to more stringent requirements than those applying in comparable situations to EU citizens[664].

The right to travel would be restricted to third-country nationals who are legally in a Member State. By denying this right to persons who entered or are present illegally, and by including provisions for expulsion, the proposal allays concern about the possible impact of the Directive on illegal immigration and provides a further tool for the fight against it.

d) Proposed Amendments to Regulation 16/2/68

In 1998 the Commission has proposed amendments of Regulation 1612/68 on freedom of movement for workers and Directive 68/360 on the abolition of restrictions on movement of residents within the Community for workers of Member States and their families[665]. Although the proposals are primarily directed to modernize the rules governing the freedom of movement of workers of EU Member States[666], the suggested amendments if adopted will also affect third-country nationals.

The Commission proposal aims to improve the situation of legally resident third-country nationals. Such improvements have been frequently requested, based

---

662 Arguably, the concept of 'threat to public order' used when applying this measure should be that of Directive 64/221/EEC of 25. February 1964 (O.J. 1964, 850) as interpreted by the Court of Justice. The Court states that the scope of the concept of public policy 'cannot be determined unilaterally by each Member State without being subject to control by the institutions of the Community'. It also holds that 'the concept of public policy presupposes, in any event, the existence, in addition to the perturbation to the social order which any infringement of the law involves, of a genuine and sufficiently serious threat affecting one of the fundamental interests of society'. The Member States should assess the effectiveness and gravity of the threats according to criteria of reasonableness and proportionality, so that minor infringements cannot have serious consequences such as expulsion (see ECJ, judgment of 4 December 1974, case 41/71, *van Duyn v Home Office*, [1974] ECR 1337; judgment of 26 February 1975, case 67/74, *Bonsignore v Stadt Köln*, [1975] ECR 297; judgment of 28 October 1975, case 36/75, *Rutili v. Minister of the Interior* [1975] ECR 1219; judgment of 27 October 1977, case 30/77, *Regina v Bouchereau*, [1977] ECR 1999). Lacking further definition it is not clear, however, whether the ECJ would take an as restrictive view as it has done with regard to similar clauses in EC legislation (cf. *Peers*, 33 CML Rev. (1996), 7, 47).

663 See Article 5a (End of stay) as introduced by the amended proposal, COM(97)106 final = O.J. 1997, C 139/6.

664 According to a new recital in the amended proposal, COM(97)106 final = O.J. 1997 C 139/6.

665 COM(98)394 final of 22 July 1998.

666 See also Communication from the Commission to the Council and the European Parliament on the follow-up to the recommendations of the High-Level Panel on the Free Movement of Persons (Veil-Report) of 1 July 1998, COM(98)403 final; action plan for free movement of workers, Communication from the Commission of 12 November 1997, COM(97)586 final.

upon the need to adopt a legal framework suitable for a full integration of third-country nationals into the economy and society. The Commission has stated in its Communication of 23 February 1994[667] that "any successful integration policy must of necessity include several components. The first essential elements are the prospect and security of a permanent residence status. Security of stay and permanent residence for all those satisfying stability criteria constitute the fundamental prerequisites for successful integration". In addition, the improvement of the legal situation of third-country nationals is only a logical consequence of the economic and political situation in the European Union, characterized by the concept of the internal market. Notwithstanding requests to afford equal treatment to third-country nationals, the Commission has taken a modest approach based on the Community law as it now stands. The proposal does not change the basic assumption that third-country nationals do not have the right to free movement and the amendments proposed do not create such a right.[668]

Another draft amendment to Regulation 1612/68 aims at making it easier for the members of families from third countries who are already normally and permanently resident in a Member State to obtain visas. For such family members the right to move within the European Union is derived directly from secondary Community law. The Commission proposal does not suggest to totally abolish the visa requirement for the members of the family of Community workers. It suggests a "realistic" approach which takes account of the technical problems connected with the disappearance of visas. Therefore, it is suggested that Member States shall allow family members who are nationals of a third country and who normally reside in a Member State to obtain the necessary visas or equivalent documents in the Member State in which they were residing or in the Member State in which these persons are to take up residence with the worker under the terms of Article 10 of Regulation 1612/68. Thereby, family members would not be obliged to return to their country of origin to obtain a visa for residence purposes when moving with a worker from one Member State to another.

As the Commission has already indicated in its proposal, it would be a logical conclusion to abolish the visa requirement for family members altogether[669]. Since the process of obtaining a visa may be very difficult, the freedom of movement of a Union citizen can be seriously impeded. It would therefore be only a logical consequence to abolish visa requirements for family members. Another proposal concerns the right of residence in the host Member State for divorced spouses. As a result of a divorce, third-country nationals may find themselves deprived of the right to stay in the Member State where they were hitherto resident. That this situation may create extreme difficulties arising from the fact that third-country nationals may have established objective ties whose effects exceed the duration of the marriage. Such is the case in particular when there are common children or where the spouse has exercised a right to pursue a profession.[670] The Commission

---

[667] COM(94)23 final.

[668] COM(98)394 final, 11.

[669] See also the Report of the High-Level Panel on the Free Movement of Persons (Veil-Report) of 18 March 1997.

[670] Veil-Report (1997), 70.

suggests to grant an independent right of residence to family members who have resided with the worker under Article 10 in the event of dissolution of the marriage. The Commission considers this independent right of residence as a necessary corollary to the free movement of workers. Since the decision of going to another country in the exercise of freedom of movement is not just a professional and economic but also a family decision, family members in the view of the Commission cannot be regarded indefinitely as "appendages" of the worker, particularly if the family is broken up as a result of the dissolution of the marriage. Article 4 of the proposal suggests that Member States shall recognize the right of residence on their territory of members of the family of a Community worker who are third-country nationals but who have lived in that Member State for a period of three consecutive years. Where family members are not economically active, the right of residence shall be recognized provided that they can provide evidence that they have sufficient financial resources for themselves and dependants and that they have health insurance covering all risks in the Member State in which they are living. The Commission has taken up another proposal by the Veil-Panel[671] to improve the scope of the right to family reunification and abolishing the age condition for descendants and the dependency condition for ascendants and descendants. Moreover, members of the family who were dependent on or were living under the same roof as the worker in the country whence he comes are granted the right to family reunification. Therefore it is suggested that a certification that family members are dependent on the worker or that they live under his roof in such country is to be considered as sufficient for a right to family reunification. This right is subject to the condition that the family life be already established in the home Member State. Third-country nationals who are children or relatives in the ascending line, who are not dependent on their parents or child and who wish to move directly from a third country to the host Member State to be with their child or parents do not enjoy a Community right under the rules suggested.[672]

The Veil-Panel has suggested to grant third-country nationals a right to pursue a professional activity in the host Member State.[673] Under secondary Community law a third-country national spouse of a Union citizen has a right to take up a professional activity in the Member State where they reside with their spouse. However, where Union citizens pursue a professional activity in the host state (as an employed or self-employed person), their third-country national spouses have a right under existing provisions to pursue a professional activity only as an employed person and not as self-employed. The Panel considers this as a legal gap which is surprising since the right to pursue a self-employed activity was recognized in the 1990 and 1993 Directive for the spouse of a Union citizen who is studying, has retired or is lawfully residing in another Member State. To close that gap third-country national children of Union citizens working in another Member

[671] Veil-Report (1997), 70.
[672] See also Veil-Report (1997), 70.
[673] Veil-Report (1997), 70.

State should be granted the right to pursue an activity not only as an employed but also as self-employed.[674]

The proposals of the Commission for an amendment of the Community provisions on freedom of movement for workers are not intended to establish freedom of movement for third-country nationals or equality of treatment of third-country nationals with Union citizens. Various provisions draw a clear distinction between third-country nationals and Union citizens. With the exception of the general non-discrimination principle on grounds of sex, racial or ethnic origin, religion, belief, disability, age or sexual orientation, the proposals do not extend the equal treatment clauses to third-country nationals. Different treatment by reason of nationality in respect of conditions of employment, enjoyment of financial, fiscal, social, cultural and other advantages is limited to workers who are nationals of a Member State. The general issues of the legal situation of third-country nationals in the European Union as part of a European immigration policy are not dealt with in the proposed amendments.

VIII. Prevention of Discrimination and Racism

1. *The Principle of Non-Discrimination*

Article 12 ECT prohibits discrimination on grounds of nationality provided, however, that discrimination occurs "within the scope of application of this Treaty". The European Court has interpreted this requirement restrictively. In Gravier[675] access to universities (discriminatory student fees) was considered as being within the scope of application of the Treaty, since ex-Article 128 EEC-Treaty envisaged a common policy of professional formation. Similarly, the Court has applied the non-discrimination principle to the payment of law-costs for security reasons[676] or national regulations providing for victims of criminal offences compensation[677] while access to social welfare schemes (the German system to finance the living costs for students enrolled at universities) was decided to be "at the present stage of Community law" not within the scope of application of the Treaty[678]. Recently the Court in Sala[679] has used the concept of European citizenship to apply the non-discrimination laws to access to social benefits intended to compensate for the costs of raising children. The German law excluding aliens without a valid residence permit from such benefits regardless of whether they are *de facto* tolerated was considered a discriminatory treatment,

[674] Veil-Report (1997), 71.

[675] ECJ, judgment of 13 February 1985, case 293/83, *Gravier v City of Lüttich*, [1985] ECR, 593 paras 13-25.

[676] ECJ, judgment of 20 March 1997, case C-323/95, *Hayes v Kronenberger*, [1997] ECR I-1711 para 17.

[677] ECJ, judgment of 17 February 1989 case 186/87 *Cowan*, [1989] ECR 195 para 17.

[678] ECJ, judgment of 21 June 1988, case 39/86, *Lair v University of Hannover*, [1988] ECR 3161 para 15.

[679] ECJ, judgment of 12 May 1998, case C-85/96, *Sala v Freistaat Bayern*, [1998] ECR I-2691 para 63.

since German nationals were entitled to such benefits on the mere basis of their habitual residence within Germany.

Article 12 ECT does not explicitly restrict the application of the non-discrimination clause to EU citizens. The practice of Member States, however, has always drawn a clear distinction between third-country nationals and EU citizens and different treatment of third-country nationals on grounds of nationality has always been considered as being in accordance with Community law.[680]

In contrast to the general discrimination prohibition on grounds of nationality, equal treatment for male and female workers for equal work (Article 141(1) ECT) has always been seen as a human right valid for all workers regardless of their nationality.[681] Although ex-Article 119 ECT did not explicitly make provision for legislation on equal opportunities and access to employment, Council adopted several directives for that purpose[682], even before Article 141(3) has explicitly authorized the Council to adopt measures to ensure the application of the principle of equal opportunities, including the right to ensure full equality in practice by compensatory measures (Article 141(4)).

Under the Maastricht Treaty the Community had not been entrusted with a competence to ensure non-discriminatory treatment on reasons prohibited in the national constitutions of EU Member States as being contrary to general recognized human rights perceptions, i.e. discrimination on grounds of race, religion, sex etc. In order to ensure non-discriminatory treatment of all human beings this has generally been considered as a matter lying within the exclusive competence of the Member States. The principle of non-discrimination on the grounds specified in Article 13 ECT as such, however, may well be considered as part of the general principles of law, recognized in the constitutions of the Member States and therefore constituting an integral part of Community law according to established jurisprudence of the European Court.

Article 13 ECT has not only codified the principle of non-discrimination based on sex, racial or ethnic origin, religion or belief, disability, age or sexual orientation as part of Community law, but has empowered the Council to take appropriate action to combat discrimination. By providing an explicit power to adopt positive measures, Article 13 ECT has implicitly made a substantial political decision in favour of a political concept which has been very controversial among EU Member States. The right to non-discrimination has generally been understood as an individual right against the state not to be discriminated; there is, however, no consensus as to what extent non-discrimination embraces a comprehensive concept including positive action to combat discrimination wherever and by whomever it is exercised. This explains why Article 13 ECT has been drafted in very careful and

---

[680] Von *Bogdandy*, in Grabitz/Hilf (eds.), Kommentar zur Europäischen Union, Article 6 ECT para 33 with reference to the jurisprudence of the European Court; *Smit/Herzog*, Commentary on the EEC Treaty Article 6 ECT para 7.06.

[681] Cf. ECJ, judgment of 8 April 1976, case 43/75, *Gabrielle Defrenne v Société anonyme belge de navigation aérienne Sabena* [1976] ECR 455 paras 61+64.

[682] E.g., directive 76/207/EEC on the implementation of the principle of equal treatment for men and women as regards access to employment, vocational training and promotion and working conditions, O.J. 1976 L 39/1.

restrictive terms. Measures based on Article 13 ECT are permanently subject to a unanimity requirement and to a mere consultation procedure by the Parliament.

Among EU Member States there is hardly any consensus as to what extent Article 13 can and should be used for an anti-discrimination legislation within the framework of a European Policy to integrate foreigners and to abolish discriminatory treatment at all levels of society and economy. The European Commission as a first measure based upon Article 13 ECT has proposed an action plan designed to counter racism by legislative measures.[683] Before the Amsterdam Treaty various non-legislative measures to fight racism and xenophobia were adopted in the form of parliamentary reports, joint declarations, recommendations and establishment of monitoring agencies.

The Joint Declaration against Racism and Xenophobia of 1986[684], recommended in the Evrigenis report[685] as a basis for EC policy against racism and xenophobia, was designed to be merely a non-binding declaration of intent. As an alternative to binding legislation in the absence of a Community competence, it proposed that the Council adopt a resolution on racism. This text, however, was rejected by some members of the Council. The ensuing division within the Council resulted in a delay of two years until a declaration text was finally agreed upon by all members. The new text was considerably less specific than the original proposal.[686] As far as legal measures were concerned, the Council requested that the Member States adopted measures which they deemed suitable. The declaration did not, however, contain any specific proposals for special anti-discrimination legislation. At the time, the national governments represented in the Council were of the opinion that legal measures against racism and xenophobia should be taken only by the Member States. This opinion was shared by the Commission, which could not find an appropriate legal basis. Activities which took place on the European level at that time were, thus, mostly symbolic in nature[687].

Council and Parliament subsequently adopted various declarations, *inter alia* the

- Resolution on the fight against Racism and Xenophobia in the Fields of Employment an Social Affairs[688]
- Resolution on the Response of Educational Systems to the Problems of Racism and Xenophobia[689]
- Resolution on Racism, Xenophobia and Anti-Semitism[690]
- Resolution of the Council and the Representatives of the Governments of the Member States, meeting within the Council, concerning the European Year against Racism[691],

and finally, based upon Article 235,

---

683 COM(1998), 183, p.12 et seq.
684 O.J. 1986, C 158/1.
685 European Parliament (1985), Committee of Inquiry into the raise of fascism and racism in Europe, EP Doc A2 160/85.
686 Resolution by the Council 29. may 1990, O.J. 1990, C 157/1.
687 Cf. *Bell*, EU Anti-discrimination policy, EP working document, Lib 102 EN, 02, 1998, p 14.
688 O.J. 1995, C 296/13.
689 O.J. 1995, C 312/1.
690 O.J. 1995, C 308/140.
691 O.J. 1996, C 237/1.

- the Resolution of the European Monitoring Centre for Racism and Xenophobia in Vienna.[692]

The European Monitoring Centre is charged with the task of providing objective, reliable and comparable information on the occurrence of racism, anti-semitism, and xenophobia at the European level. The Centre is to examine these occurrences and analyse the causes, consequences and recent remedies. In order to meet these objectives, the Centre is to establish a European information network on racism and xenophobia (RAXEN). Further activities of the Centre include the organization of round table meetings, the formulation of conclusions or expert opinions for the Community or for Member States, the promotion of research in racism and xenophobia, and the publication of an annual report.[693] The Centre is a legal subject in its own right, and has extensive legal authority in each Member States.[694] It co-operates[695] with other countries or international organizations, especially with the European Council, which, in turn, is represented by one member on the Management Board.[696]

Constant efforts by human rights organizations and the European Parliament finally led to an agreement on a Community competence for binding measures, as suggested already in 1995 by the Kahn Commission[697].

2. *Article 13 ECT and Immigration and Asylum Policy*

Article 13 ECT provides for a legislative power to adopt anti-discrimination legislation. The Commission has relied upon the new competence to submit a proposal for regulations against racial discrimination before the end of 1999[698]. In addition, before the entry into force of the Amsterdam Treaty the Commission has relied upon the market freedoms in order to suggest an amendment to the Freedom of Movement Regulation No. 1612/69.[699] The proposal prohibits discrimination on grounds of sex, race or ethnic origin, religion of conviction, disability, age or sexual orientation since, according to the European Commission, such discrimination constitutes a barrier to the free movement of workers and their families and impairs the integration of migrant workers exercising their right to freedom of movement and that of their families. It may be expected that proposals put forward on the basis of Article 13 ECT will be controversial. The unanimity requirement, however, will constitute a barrier to the establishment of a anti-discrimination policy which is not generally accepted among the EU Member States.[700]

---

692 Cf. Regulation 1035/97establishing a European-Monitoring Centre on Racism, O.J. 1997, L 151/1.
693 See Article 2 reg. 1035/97.
694 See Article 6 reg. 1035/97.
695 See Article 7 reg. 1035/97.
696 See Article 8(1) reg. 1035/97.
697 See *Bell*, EU Anti-Discrimination Policy, EP working document, Lib 102 EN, 02, 1998, 11.
698 Commission, An Action-Plan against Racism, COM (19)183, fin. 12.
699 O.J. 1998, C 344/9.
700 *Langrish,* 23 E.L. Rev 1998, 3, 15; *Lecheler*, JuS 1998, 392, 396.

Notwithstanding the difficulty to reach consensus on a common European policy against discrimination and racism, there are several international and national legal instruments and principles which may constitute a basis for further Community action.

Generally speaking, racial discrimination is banned by law in all Member States. Some Member State constitutions expressly prohibit racial discrimination.[701] Article 14 of the European Convention on Human Rights, in addition, guarantees the prohibition of racial discrimination in every State.

Frequently, compensatory legislative measures are considered necessary to overcome the discrepancy between law and social reality, which has given rise, in particular, to discussions on gender equality, but which may also be important in the context of racial discrimination or protection of ethnic minorities.[702] Measures and remedies implemented by Member States vary greatly. Some states, for instance, have established specialized equality agencies. Great Britain created the Commission for Racial Equality, the Netherlands established the Equal Treatment Commission, Sweden appointed an Ombudsman of Ethnic Discrimination, and Belgium started the Centre pour l'Egalité des Chances et la Lutte contre le Racisme. The German Federal Government's Commissioner for Affairs relating to Foreigners is a similar institution, and advises both the government and individuals. All these institutions support or assist individual complaints, provide general information and advice, and, in doing so, seek to promote the effectiveness of anti-discrimination provisions in these countries.[703]

Furthermore, some countries have instituted positive measures to combat structural discrimination. In the Netherlands and the UK, several local authorities practice contract compliance. Firms competing for public-sector contracts must submit a detailled report on their equal opportunity policies, and even on the ethnic composition of their labour force. In the Netherlands, for example, the Act for the Promotion of Proportional Labour Participation of Non-Nationals requires all companies with more than 35 employees to monitor the ethnicity of their employees, and to draw up plans for the creation of a proportional workforce. This law, however, was not wholly successful; only a quarter of all enterprises actually disclosed the required information. The 1994 act originally required that the number of foreigners employed reflect the ethnic and racial composition of the area in which the firm was established. This provision was abolished in 1997.[704] The

---

[701] See Art 11 of the Belgian Constitution, Sec. 5(2) of Finnish Constitution, Art 3(3) of the German Basic Law, Art 3(2) of the Italian Constitution, Art 1(1) of the Constitution of the Netherlands, Art 13(2) of the Portugal Constitution, and Art 14 of the Spanish Constitution.

[702] Cf. for European Legislation: "European Commission, Proposal for a Council Directive on the Burden of Proof in Cases of Discrimination based on Sex" COM(96) 340 fin., p. 3; The same debate exists on the national level, cf. for example in Germany: Federal Diet Doc. 8/4461 (Report); *Heun* in: Dreier, Grundgesetz-Kommentar, Vol. 1 Art 3, para 87, with further evidence. For racial discrimination in the European Union, see *Bell*, EU Anti-Discrimination Policy, EP working document, Lib 102 EN, 02, 1998, p 26 et seq.

[703] Cf. *Bell*, EU Anti-discrimination Policy, EP working document, Lib 102 EN, 02, 1998, p 27.

[704] Cf. *Bell*, EU Anti-discrimination Policy, EP working document, Lib 102 EN, 02, 1998, p 31 et seq; see further *Forbes & Mead*, Measure for Measure: a Comparative Analysis of Measures to Combat Racial Discrimination in the Member Countries of the European Community, 1992.

Netherlands thus ranks among the experienced in the implementation of different forms of affirmative action legislation. The other Member States - with the exception of the UK[705]- have not adopted any similar legislation to combat racism.

For a future European legislation framework, different regulatory actions are available according to Member States' experience with anti-discrimination legislation. Several EU Member States have introduced special laws to penalize racism, racist speech or incitement to racial hatred. Article 13 ECT does not include a competence to prescribe criminal offences or sanctions.[706] This does not mean, however, that the Community cannot specify certain sanctions for infringement or abuse within its own area of legislative competence, so long as these sanctions be regarded as sufficiently effective, proportionate and dissuasive,[707] and are implemented on a clear and unambiguous legal basis.[708] In general, the Community will leave the prescription and imposition of sanctions as a means to ensure the effective application of anti-discrimination law to the Member States.[709]

In a case on gender discrimination prohibited by the EC-directive on equal access to employment, the Court ruled that Member States must adopt sanctions which are suitable to guarantee effective legal protection, and that the sanction must possess a deterrent effect.[710] Criminal sanctions are often criticised as ineffective due to the burden of proof, a lack of sufficient confidence in law enforcement authorities, and a lack of direct compensation for the victim.[711] This criticism is not fully convincing. Penalizing of racially motivated discrimination has a strong symbolic effect; it demonstrates that the society takes such violations seriously. Another advantage provided by criminal law is the resulting political protection.[712]

Another regulatory option are civil law suits. In employment discrimination cases, which is an area in which the EC can use the power conferred upon it by Article 13 ECT,[713] the law can award damages to a person who has been a victim of discrimination. The amount of compensation, in order to satisfy the requirement of efficiency must be substantial.[714] Whether this jurisprudence covers punitive

---

705 Specially Northern Ireland, see Fair Employment Act 1989, cf.: *Bell*, EU-Anti discrimination policy, EP working document, Lib 102 en, 02, 1998, p 32.

706 Cf. ECJ, judgment of 25 September 1984, case 117/83 *Karl Könnecke GmbH v BALM* [1984] ECR 3291. The Amsterdam Amendment now proscribes in Art 31 TEU a EU-competence to harmonize statutory definitions of offences in the area of terrorism, trade of drugs and organized crime.

707 Advocate General *Jacobs* in ECJ, judgement of 72 October 1992, case C-240/90, *Germany v Commission* [1992] ECR 5383, 5410 et seq.

708 Cf. Advocate-General *Verloren van Themat* in ECJ, judgment of 25 September 1984, case 117/83, *Karl Könecke GmbH v BALM*, [1984] ECR 3291, 3315.

709 This is the Community practice in the vast majority of cases: Cf. European Union and Criminal Law in: *Hood*, Policing the European Union, Oxford 1995, p. 181, 183 et seq.

710 Cf. ECJ, judgment of 22 April 1997, case C-180/95, *Draehmpaehl v Urania Immobilienservice,* [1997] ECR I-2195, para 25.

711 Cf. *Bell*, EU Anti-Discrimination Policy, EP working document, Lib 102 en, 02, 1998, p 31.

712 Cf. *Beer*, Würde oder Gleichheit (1995) p. 318 et seq.

713 See supra a).

714 Cf. ECJ, judgment of 22 April 1997, case C-180/95, *Draehmpaehl v Urania Immobilienservice* [1997], ECR I-2195, para 25; Adomeit, NJW 1997, 2295, 2296; *Volmer*, BB 1997, 1582, 1584.

damages – considered by German courts as unlawful and possibly even unconstitutional[715] – may, however, be doubtful considering the reluctance of some Member States against such concepts.[716] Nevertheless, damages in non-discrimination cases may be difficult to prove.

Further legal remedies, including contract compliance, ethnic monitoring, and positive action, are currently being discussed to combat racial discrimination.[717]

First, contract compliance means that an employer found guilty of discrimination may be disqualified from future public procurement contracts. Another form of contract compliance requires firms competing for public sector contracts to submit details of their equal opportunity policies, as well as data on the ethnic composition of their labour force.[718] The Community adopted certain forms of contract compliance in the 1993 reform of the Structural Funds. Article 7 of the new regulation states that, *inter alia*, actions founded by the Structural Funds or the EIB must conform to the content of the Treaties, including compliance with the principle of equal opportunity for men and women.[719]

Second, ethnic monitoring requires firms to monitor the ethnic profile of their workforce as a whole, as well as of individual applicants. If participation is not ethnically balanced, employers must carry out an affirmative action plan to rectify the situation. [720] This form of countermeasure against racism will, however, be difficult to carry out in practice at the European level. An enterprise can not recruit a workforce which accurately represents each minority in a given society. It might be possible if monitoring were limited to one or two groups; on the other hand, however, monitoring implemented in a limited form would discriminate against groups which do not benefit from ethnic monitoring in a particular sector. These limitations notwithstanding, ethnic monitoring has been successful in increasing the awareness of ethnic groups.

Affirmative action usually entails programs designed to favour or promote the interests of disadvantaged groups.[721] A number of affirmative action measures are already in practice in the area of equal opportunity for men and women. Some Member States have implemented employment quota, which reserve a specific number of positions for women or men if they are not represented with 50 % in the workforce.[722] The ECJ ruled that automatic quota schemes contradict the principle

---

715 Cf. Bundesgerichtshof (Federal Supreme Court), judgment of 4 June 1992, case IX ZR 149/91 [1992], BGHR vol. 118, 312, 343 et seq.

716 The commitment of the German government on the Fundamental law acting in the Council is a matter of controversy. It is uncontroversial that the German government will have to strive for a solution which is compatible with the Basic Law. Cf. Bundesverfassungsgericht (Federal Constitutional Court), judgment of 28 January 1987, BVerfGE 92, 203, 236 f.; *Rojahn* in: *v* Münch/Kunig, Grundgesetz-Kommentar, vol. 2, third ed, Art 23, para 54.

717 See *Bell*, EU-Anti discrimination policy, EP working document, Lib 102 en, 02, 1998, p 32.

718 *Bell*, EU Anti-Discrimination Policy, EP working document, Lib 102 en, 02, 1998, p 32.

719 Cf. Regulation 2081/93, O.J. 1993, L 193.

720 Cf. *Bell*, EU Anti-Discrimination Policy, EP working document, Lib 102 en, 02, 1998, p 34.

721 This is a synonym for reverse discrimination. See the definition provided by *Harris/O'Boyle/Warbrick*, Law of the European Convention on Human Rights (1995), p. 485.

722 In 11 of 15 Länder within Germany, a quota for public services is prescribed by law, cf. *Laubinger*, H.W. 87, (1996), 305, 315 et seq.

of gender equality.[723] The *Marshall* decision indicates, however, that quotas are acceptable under EU law if the law allows consideration of all facts in the actual case.[724] This decision is interpreted as an acceptance of affirmative action programs to curb racism.[725] Whether this interpretation is correct however, is doubtful. Affirmative action in gender discrimination cases is explicitly authorized by Article 141 ECT and previously Article 2(4) of Directive 76/207 EEC[726]. The Treaty does not provide otherwise for an exception from the equal treatment principle. Article 14 ECHR does not authorize contracting states to adopt positive measures against racism or engage in affirmative action to reduce existing discrimination[727]. The legal situation is similar in some EU Member States. In Germany, Article 3(3) of the Basic Law prohibits measures of positive discrimination, provided these are not justified by reasons other than race, by an exception within the Constitution or, finally, within the nature of the matter itself.[728] In *Kalanke* the European Court of Justice confirmed that discrimination under positive action is only admissible under the conditions of a strictly limited legal exception.[729] This is the legal basis limiting all activities in the area of racial discrimination. Affirmative action which results in granting preferential treatment to ethnic minorities or special categories of migrant workers is discriminating against other groups. As a result, measures taken to combat racism under Article 13 ECT may not imply affirmative action or reverse discrimination.

Efforts to combat racism must respect such limitations. This does not mean, however, that positive action is wholly excluded.[730] If a measure promotes ethnic minorities without discriminating other individuals or groups, it may be adopted. Legal remedies thus are not generally limited to civil or penal law measures. Success rates are highest with measures which aim at integrating ethnic minorities into society privileges to an ethnic minority. Law can only provide a framework for society. The most important task in the fight against racism and xenophobia is integration of foreigners into society.

---

723 ECJ, judgment of 17 October 1995, case C-440/93, *Kalanke v Freie Hansestadt Bremen* [1995] ECR I-3051, paras 19-22.

724 ECJ, judgment of 11 November 1997, case C-409/95, *Marschall v Land Nordrhein-Westfalen* [1997], ECR I-6363, para 33.

725 *Bell*, EU Anti-Discrimination Policy, EP working document, Lib 102 en, 02, 1998, 35 et seq.

726 O.J. 1976, L 39/40.

727 Cf. *Fawcett*, The Application of the European Convention on Human Rights (1987), 305.

728 Cf. Bundesverfassungsgericht (Federal Constitutional Court), judgment of 8 November 1994, BVerfGE 74, 163, (181); *Suerbaum*, Der Staat, 1989, 419, 440.

729 Cf. ECJ, judgment of 17 October 1995, case C-440/93, *Kalanke v Freie Hansestadt Bremen* [1995] ECR I-3051 para 21.

730 Cf. some proposals by *Bell*, EU Anti-Discrimination Policy, EP working document, Lib 102 en, 02, 1998, p 35.

D

Social Rights of Third-Country Nationals

I. The Relevance of Human and Social Rights within the Treaties and the Concept of a Charter of Fundamental Human Rights

1. Third-Country Nationals within Community Law and Human Rights Instruments

As to the 13 million third-country nationals living within the European Union, there are several different regimes and provisions applicable. First, there is Community law which is quite ambiguous as to the incorporation of third-country nationals. On the one hand, the personal scope of application of some social provisions, e.g. those which are work place related (safety, gender equality at work), apply to both EU citizens and legally resident third-country nationals[1]. Freedom of movement in Articles 39 and 40 (ex-Articles 48 and 49) ECT is applicable to "workers". But even if one might deduct from this wording and an examination of the travaux préparatoires[2] that third-country nationals should have been included in the personal scope of application of those provisions, the European Court of Justice has consistently held that the notion of "worker" means a worker who is a national of a Member State. Therefore, secondary legislation on the basis of Article 42 (ex-Article 51) ECT, for instance Regulation 1408/71, is in principle only applicable to EU citizens. Argument has been raised that "[i]t is hardly overstating the case to say that citizens of non-Member States (third-country nationals) have been virtually invisible as far as the EC Treaty is concerned"[3]. Moreover, according to the specific group of third-country nationals to which the individual belongs, different rules apply as to social benefits, public assistance, the aggregation of periods, the export of pensions, the consideration of family members living abroad when assessing family benefits, and to equal treatment in general.

Nevertheless, in the Maastricht Treaty, issues relating to third-country nationals were defined as matters for intergovernmental cooperation in the third pillar with the focus primarily on governing and restricting immigration into the European Union. In March 1996 the Council of Ministers adopted a resolution on the status

---

1 Cf. Communication from the Commission on the social situation and employment of migrant women, COM(88)743 final; joined cases 281, 283, 284, 285 and 287/85, judgment of 9 July 1987, *Germany and others v Commission*, [1987] ECR 3203; see furthermore Article 137(3) ECT which provides that the Council may adopt rules on the "conditions of employment for third-country nationals legally residing in Community territory." Cf. furthermore as to the situation of third-country nationals *Cremona*, 1995 LIEI, 87; *Evans*, 5 EJIL 1994, 199.

2 Cf. *Plender*, 39 International and Comparative Law Quarterly (1990), 599, 605; *Jacobs* (ed.), European Law and the Individual (1976), 39.

3 *Cremona*, 1995 LIEI 87; cf. as to the European Union and the status of third-country nationals also Council of European Committee on Migration (CDMG), The Legal Status of Long-Term Migrants in Europe, paper by *Groenendijk*, CDMG (96) 27, 16-17.

of third-country nationals residing on a long-term basis in the territory of a Member State[4]. This resolution is not legally binding; Member States are only requested to take the principles of the resolution into account for their policy on integration of immigrants (Article I). Furthermore, they are requested to report on those policies to the Council before 1997 (Article VII). The preamble states that the aim of the resolution is to facilitate the integration of the settled migrants into the host society and to contribute to the security and stability both in daily life and work and to the social peace in the Member States. According to Article III, third-country nationals should be recognized as long-term residents if they have lawfully resided without interruption in the territory of the state for a specified period not exceeding ten years. Furthermore, the settled migrants and the family members are entitled to equal treatment with the nationals of the host country as regards working conditions, membership of trade unions, public housing, social security, emergent health care and compulsory schooling; the status can be refused on grounds of public policy and lack of stable income.

With the Amsterdam Treaty, the Schengen acquis has been incorporated into Title IV of the Treaty enabling "other measures in the fields of asylum, immigration and safeguarding the rights of nationals of third countries, in accordance with the provisions of Article 63" (Article 61(b) ECT).

Nevertheless, to a large extent, some groups of third-country nationals may refer to Regulation 1408/71, e.g. family members of EU citizens or refugees and stateless persons. For the remaining group of third-country nationals, social rights depend on whether there is a special treaty, e.g. an association agreement, and whether there are bilateral or multilateral treaties covering the issue at stake; if not, there is no entitlement as to coordination or equal treatment and different national regimes in each Member State[5] are applicable[6]. Assessing the situation of third-country nationals in social security therefore seems rather difficult. Therefore, several attempts to achieve equal treatment between EU citizens and third-country nationals have been made. Some of those are based on human rights instruments and the principle of equality such as the decision of the European Court of Human Rights in *Gaygusuz* where the Court considered social security benefits as "possession" and granted equal treatment to a Turkish national. Others argue that since some groups like refugees and stateless persons or persons falling within the scope of application of an association agreement already have a defined status in social security law, other third-country nationals should be treated equally. The Commission itself submitted not only a proposal as to the extension of the existing Regulation 1408/71 in 1997, but also elaborated a new proposal on social security being applicable to all persons being insured in a social security scheme, which has been submitted in 1999.

---

4 O.J. 1996 C 80/2

5 As to the different treatment of third-country nationals within the EU-Member States see *von Maydell/Schulte* (eds.), Treatment of Third-Country Nationals in the EU and EEA Member States in Terms of Social Security (1995) *passim*.

6 An overview on the different regimes is to be found in the contributions by *Onslaw-Cole*, *van Amersfoort*, *Eicke*, *Apap*, *Guild*, *Stola* and *Peers*, in Guild (ed.), The Legal Framework and Social Consequences of Free Movement of Persons in the European Union (1999) *passim*.

This chapter therefore examines, after a short overview on the gradual incorporation of human rights in Community law, the existing provisions in the ECT which are already applicable to third-country nationals within working conditions and gender equality. Second, a short survey of Regulation 1408/71 and the new proposals submitted by the Commission is given, followed by an analysis of the principle of equal treatment and the implications of *Gaygusuz* for Community Law. At the end, an overview of the regulations within the field of social security law under human rights instruments can be found.

2. *Human and Social Rights within Community Law*[7]

In addition to the provisions relating mainly to economic issues, a constant development in the human rights area within the Community has taken place. In the 1970s the incorporation of human rights into Community Law was mostly due to the case-law of the European Court of Justice which examined gradually the validity of Community Acts against human rights' standards[8]. The European Court of Justice referred in several cases to the European Convention of Human Rights[9] and other human rights treaties[10].

Besides the introduction of Union citizenship for EU nationals, a Comité des Sages chaired by *Maria de Lourdes Pintassilgo* submitted a Final Report entitled "For a Europe of Civic and Social Rights" in 1996[11], which was followed by a Report of a High Level Panel on Free Movement chaired by *Simone Veil* in 1997 in which third-country nationals were included as well[12].

---

7 Cf. *supra* Chapter B II for a detailed discussion of the binding force of human rights upon the legislative powers of the Community.

8 Cf. *Hartley*, The Foundations of European Community Law, 3rd ed. (1994), 132 et seq; *Jacobs*, in: Curtin/Henkel (eds.), Institutional Dynamics of European Integration (1994), vol. II, 561 et seq; *Lenaerts*, 16 EL Rev. (1991) 367; *Pipkorn*, Revue trimestrielle des droits de l'homme (1993), 221; *Schermers*, 27 CML Rev. (1990) 249 et seq.

9 ECJ, judgment of 28 October 1975, case 36/75, *Rutili v Minister of the Interior*, [1975] ECR 1219; ECJ, judgment of 13 December 1979, case 44/79, *Hauer v Land Rheinland-Pfalz*, [1979] ECR 3727; ECJ, judgment of 5 March 1980, case 98/79, para. 15, *Pecastaing v Belgian State*, [1980] ECR, 691; ECJ, judgment of 15 May 1986, case 222/84, *Johnston* v *Chief Constable of the Royal Ulster Contabulary*, [1986] ECJ 1651, judgment of 30 September 1987, case 12/86, *Demirel v Stadt Schwäbisch Gmünd*, [1987] ECR 3719.

10 Cf. for the European Social Charter and Convention No. 111 of the ILO ECJ, judgment of 15 June 1978, case 149/77, *Defrenne v Société anonyme belge de navigation aérienne Sabena*, [1978] ECR 1365; as to the UN Covenant on Civil and Political Rights ECJ, judgment of 18 October 1989, case 374/87, *Orkem v Commission*, [1989] ECR 3283; ECJ, judgment of 18 October 1990, case C-297/88, *Dzodzi v Belgian State*, [1990] ECR I-3763.

11 This report is also to be found in Annex IV, in *Betten/Mac Devitt*, The Protection of Fundamental Social Rights in the European Union (1996), 241 et seq.

12 Report of the High Level Panel on the free movement of persons chaired by *Simone Veil*, presented to the Commission on 18 March 1997, Council Document 7035/97 of 8 April 1998; see also the Communication from the Commission to the Council and the European Parliament on the follow-up to the recommendations of the High-Level Panel on the Free Movement of Persons, COM(98)403 final. Cf. for the development and the increasing importance of human rights *Alston/Weiler*, The European Union and Human Rights: Final Project on an Agenda for the Year 2000. Cf. as to the

The Amsterdam Treaty proclaims that the Union is founded on the principles of liberty, democracy, respect for human rights and fundamental freedoms and the rule of law. The respect for the fundamental rights guaranteed by the Human Rights Convention of 1950 is emphasized in Article 6(2) TEU[13], as well as in the third recital of the preamble. Article 46 includes Article 6(2)TEU when defining the areas of law which fall within the competence of the Court. Article 7 TEU imposes penalties on Member States who fail to respect fundamental rights.

Social rights[14] and the Social Charter of 1961[15], as well as the Community Charter of 1989 in which third-country nationals are mentioned in the preamble, are mentioned in both the fourth recital of the preamble and in Article 136 ECT, which provides that the rights embodied in those instruments are to be considered guidelines for both Community and Member State activities (Article 136(2) ECT). Programs conceived and implemented by either party should promote employment, improve living and working conditions with a view towards harmonization, ensure proper social protection, promote dialogue between management and labor, develop human resources with the aim of achieving lasting high employment and eliminate social exclusion[16].

In addition, Article 13 ECT empowers the Council to take appropriate action to combat discrimination based on sex[17], racial or ethnic origin, religion or belief, disability[18], age or sexual orientation –

> Without prejudice to the other provisions of this Treaty and within the limits of the powers conferred by it upon the Community, the Council, acting unanimously on a proposal from the Commission and after consulting the European Parliament, may take appropriate action to combat discrimination

---

setting up of a single coordinating structure within the EU Commission responsible for human rights and democratization the "Lenz-Report", A4-393/97, 14.

13 Ex-article F.

14 Cf. as to fundamental social rights within the EU *Betten/Mac Devitt*, The Protection of Fundamental social Rights in the European Union (1996).

15 Cf. for the convergence of European social policy *Sciarra*, in Alston/Harris (eds.), The European Union and Human Rights (1999), 473 (forthcoming). As to the relation between the ESC and social rights within the EU see *Harris*, in: Betten/Mac Devitt, The Protection of Fundamental Social Rights in the European Union (1996), 107 et seq.

16 Cf. for an overview of the existing situation the report of the expert group on fundamental rights chaired by *Spiros Simitis* "Affirming Fundamental Rights in the European Union Time to Act", Brussels, February 1999, 6. Cf. furthermore European Commission, European Social Policy Forum 1998 – Summary Report (1999).

17 As to the scope of application and content of Article 13 cf. Article 13, Anti-discrimination: the way forward, Conference Documentation, 3/4 December 1998, Vienna; and for related questions the report of the European Commission (Employment and Social Affairs) by *Prechal/Senden*, Monitoring Implementation and Application of Community Equality Law (1996), General Report 1996 of the Legal Experts Grout on Equal Treatment of Men and Women, Brussels (1997); 4 Equality Quarterly News (1998), Newsletter of the expert legal group on the application of European law on equal treatment between men and women, Brussels 1998. As for equality law cf. *Hervey/O'Keeffe* (eds.), Sex Equality Law in the European Union (1996); *Hervey*, 4 European Law Journal (1998), 196 et seq; *Bell*, The new Article 13 EC Treaty: a sound basis for European anti-discrimination law?", Maastricht Journal of European and Comparative Law 6 (1999), 5.

18 Cf. *Whittle*, Disability Discrimination and the Amsterdam Treaty, 23 European Law Review (1998), 50 et seq.

based on sex, racial, ethnic origin, religion or belief, disability, age or sexual orientation.[19]

The non-discrimination clause, however, does not take direct effect, and secondary legislation based upon it must be adopted by unanimous vote. Nevertheless, given that the European Court of Justice ruled in *Grant v South-West Trains Ltd.* that the equal pay and equal treatment directives prohibiting gender based discrimination could not be extended to two lesbian women, the insertion of Article 13 could be of great importance[20] and may alter future decisions on this issue[21].

3. *A Charter of Fundamental Rights in the European Union*

Nevertheless, there is no catalogue of human and social rights, and the role of some conventions within the field of social rights, e.g the ILO-Conventions, remains rather vague[22]. As a result of this deficit, the Expert Group on Fundamental Rights chaired by *Spiros Simitis* submitted a report called "Affirming Fundamental Rights in the European Union Time to Act " in February 1999. The report explicitly names several human and social rights, and suggests that these rights be incorporated into a Fundamental Charter and into the Treaties. In spite of this suggestion and several conferences on this issue, it remains uncertain whether these rights would apply only in cases in which there is a link to Community law, e.g. on the basis of the right to freedom of movement and cross-border elements, as well as whether the personal scope of application should be limited to European citizens, or whether it should be extended to third-country nationals.

II. SOCIAL RIGHTS IN ARTICLES 138, 139 AND 141 ECT

Social rights enshrined in Article 138, 139 and 141 ECT are not confined to EU-nationals, but are applicable to both EU citizens and third-country nationals. According to a communication by the Commission, Article 141 ECT, as well as other legislation relating to sexual discrimination, is applicable to EU citizens and third-country nationals[23]. Before the incorporation of Article 137(3) ECT,

---

19 Cf. for Article 14 ECHR which has no independent existence for instance *Gomien/Harries/Zwaak*, Law and practice of the European Convention on Human Rights and the European Social Charter (1996), 349 et seq.

20 Cf. for the importance of this provision the Starting Line Group, in *Chopin/Niessen*: Proposals for Legislative Measures to Combat Racism and to Promote Equal Rights in the European Union (1998), 16; Comité des Sages, in Academy of European Law, European University Institute, Leading by Example; A Human Rights Agenda for the European Union for the Year 2000 (1998).

21 ECJ, judgment of 17 February 1998, case C-249/96, *Lisa Jacqueline Grant v South-West Trains Ltd.*, [1998] ECR I-621, para 48. Cf. to the importance of Article 13 also *Allen*, Article 13, Anti-discrimination: the way forward, Conference Documentation, December (1998), 7, 10; *Bell*, 5 ELJ (1999) 63 et seq.

22 Cf. as to the suggestion of a Community Catalogue *Lenaerts*, 1991 ELR 367, at 373-390 with further references.

23 Commission, Communication from the Commission on the social situation and employment of migrant women, COM(88)743 final.

providing that the Council may adopt rules on the "conditions of employment for third-country nationals legally residing in Community territory"[24], the European Court of Justice ruled in *Germany and others v Commission*[25] that ex-Article 118 ECT was concerned with the living and working conditions of all workers resident in the Community. The Court found in particular that the situation of third-country nationals working in the Community was within the scope of ex-Article 118 in so far as this had an impact on the Community employment market and on working conditions. On the other hand, the Court denied any powers of the Community as to cultural integration –

> The promotion of the integration into the workforce of workers from non-member countries must be held to be within the social field within the meaning of Article 118, in so far as it is closely linked to employment. This also applies to their integration into society, having regard to the objectives pursued by the contested decision, inasmuch as the draft measures in question are those connected with problems relating to employment and working conditions, and there is no reason to consider that the decision intended to give a different meaning to that concept. As regards the cultural integration of immigrant communities from non-member countries, whilst this may be linked, to an extent, with the effects of migration policy, it is aimed at immigrant communities in general without distinction between migrant workers and other foreigners, and its link with problems relating to employment and working conditions is therefore extremely tenuous. Moreover, migration policy capable of falling within the social field within the meaning of Article 118 only to the extent to which it concerns the situation of workers from non-member countries as regards their impact on the Community employment market and on working conditions.[26]

1. Fields covered by Social Security Provisions in the Treaty

Besides Article 42 (ex-Article 51) ECT, social security measures were mainly adopted after the Single European Act on the basis of ex-Article 118a ECT[27].

---

[24] Before the incorporation in the Treaty the legal basis for action within this field existed in the Agreement on Social Policy annexed to Protocol 14 TEU allowing the Council to take decisions on conditions on employment for third-country nationals.

[25] ECJ, judgment of 9 July 1987, joined cases 281, 283, 284, 285 and 287/85, *Germany and others v Commission*, [1987] ECR 3203.

[26] Judgement of 9 July 1987, *Germany and others v Commission*, joined cases 281, 283, 284, 285, 287/85, [1987] ECR 3202. Cf. annotations by *Constantinesco/Simon*, Journal du droit international (1988), 493; *Decaux*, Revue trimestrielle de droit européen (1987), 707; *Desolre*, Cahiers de droit européen (1990), 453; *Hartley*, 23 EL Rev. (1988) 122; *O'Keeffe*, International Labour Law Reports (1987), 346; *Simmonds*, 34 CML Rev. (1988) 177; *Traversa*, Rivista di diritto europeo (1988), 5.

[27] Cf. for the social competences and policy for instance *Arl*, Sozialpolitik nach Maastricht (1997): *Balze*, Die sozialpolitische Kompetenz der Europäischen Union (1994); *Blanpain/Schmidt/Schweibert*, Europäisches Arbeitsrecht, 2nd ed. (1996), para 115; *Kessler/Meyer*, Revue internationale de droit économique 1992, 129; *Kliemann*, Die europäische Sozialintegration nach Maastricht (1997); *Kuhn*, Die soziale Dimension in der Europäischen Gemeinschaft (1996); *Ringler*,

Community competence in the field of social rights is currently found in Articles 136–145 ECT[28]. Article 137 ECT covers a wide range of fields. The most significant among these are: improvement of the working environment to protect workers' health and safety, working conditions, information exchange and worker consultation; the integration of persons excluded from the labor market, without prejudice to Article 150 ECT; gender equality with regard to labor market opportunities and treatment at the workplace (para. (1)). Furthermore, para. (3), which enforces the policy of decision-making by unanimous vote of the Council, addresses social security and social protection of workers; protection of workers upon termination of the employment contract; representation and collective defence of the interests of workers and employers, including co-determination, subject to para. (6)[29]; conditions of employment for third-country nationals legally resident in Community territory and financial contributions to promote employment and job-creation, without prejudice to the provisions relating to the Social Fund. In contrast to the emphasis on the mere coordination of social policy and regulations relating thereto[30], Title XI ECT may point towards a tendency to promote harmonization[31]. A proposal submitted by *Danny Pieters* in 1991 on creation of a European Social Security System for migrant workers has not been realized[32].

2. *Provisions Relating to Workplace Health and Safety*

As previously mentioned, most of the directives within the field of social security speak to the issue of safety in the workplace. [33] Four of these directives were created prior to the incorporation of ex-Article 118a ECT[34]. Given that ex-Article

---

Die Europäische Sozialunion (1997); *Schmähl*, in Europäische Sozialpolitik (1997), 9; *Schulz*, Maastricht und die Grundlagen einer Europäischen Sozialpolitik, (1996).

28 Cf. as to the amendments by the Amsterdam Treaty *Langer*, in Bergmann/Lenz (eds.), Der Amsterdamer Vertrag (1998), 93, 95.

29 According to para 6 the provisions do not apply to pay, the right of association, the right to strike or the right to impose lock-outs.

30 Cf. for instance to the 1989 Action Programme relating to the implementation of the Community Charter of Basic Social Rights of Workers, COM(89)568 final. "The social security schemes vary greatly in nature from one Member State of the Community to another. This reflects the history, traditions and social and cultural practices proper to each Member State, which cannot be called into question. There can therefore be no question of harmonizing the systems existing in this fields."

31 Cf. as to the question of harmonization *Majone*, The European Community between Social Policy and Social Regulation, EUI Working Paper, SPS No. 92/97.

32 *Pieters*, ZIAS 1991, 72 et seq.

33 Cf. *Baldwin/Daintith*, Harmonization and hazard. Regulating workplace health and safety in the European Community (1992); *Banks*, in CDE 1993, 537; *Beglinger*, Die Haromonisierungsbestrebungen der EG auf dem Gebiet des technischen Arbeitsschutzes (1991); *Koll/Wirmer*, Zeitschrift für Sozialhilfe und Sozialgesetzbuch (1993), 236; *Wank*, in von Maydell/Schnapp (eds.), Die Auswirkungen des EG-Rechts auf das Arbeits- und Sozialrecht der Bundesrepublik Deutschland (1992), 63 et seq.; *id./Börgmann*, Deutsches und europäisches Arbeitsschutzrecht (1992); *Willms*, in Groeben/Thiesing/Ehlermann (eds.), Kommentar zum EU-/EG-Vertrag, Article 102a – 136a EGV, 5th edition (1999), 3/3116.

34 These are Council Directive 77/576/EEC of 25 July on the approximation of the laws, regulations and administrative provisions of the Member States relating to the provision of safety, signs at

118a ECT was applicable to all persons employed within Community territory, regulations based on this provision also apply to third-country nationals[35].

3. Gender Equality in Work

Article 141 (ex-Article 119) ECT, like Article 13 ECT, relates to gender discrimination, and contains in its third paragraph an authorization for measures that aim at safeguarding the application of the principle of equality and equal treatment for men and women[36]. Article 141 ECT should, thus, be regarded as a special provision to Article 13 ECT in this area[37]. Article 141 ECT replaces the former Article 119 ECT[38], which was the only provision in Title VIII of the Treaty having direct effect within the Member States without any further implementation[39] requiring that men and women are to be treated equally in employment by the Member States –

---

places of work (O.J. 1977 L 229/12); Council Directive 78/610/EEC of 29 June 1978 on the approximation of the laws, regulations and administrative provisions of the Member States on the protection of the health of workers exposed to vinyl chloride monomer (O.J. 1978 L 197/12); Council Directive 80/1107/EEC of 27 November 1980 on the protection of workers from the risks related to exposure to chemical, physical and biological agents at work (O.J. 1980 L 327/8); Council Directive 82/501/EEC of 24 June 1982 on the major-accidental hazards of certain industrial activities (O.J. 1982 L 230/1).

35 Numerous directives have been based upon Art. 118a ECT.

36 Cf. for the case-law as regards equal treatment and the situation in different EU-Member States European Commission, Directorate General V, Employment, Industrial Relations and Social Affairs, Recueil sur l'égalité de traitement entre les hommes et les femmes dans la Communauté européenne (1997); Newsletter of the expert legal group on the application of European law on equal treatment between women, Equality Quarterly News, Autumn (1998); *Lenaerts*, CDE 1991, 39.

37 Cf. as to the relation between Article 13 and Article 141 ECT *Zuleeg*, Article 13, Anti-discrimination: the way forward, Conference Documentation 3/4 December 1998, 28: *Bell*, 6 Maastricht Journal of European and Comparative Law (1999) 5, 9.

38 Cf. as to Article 119 ECT and gender equality *Barlett*, Gender and Law, 1993; *Bouchard*, 31 Osgoode Hall Law Journal (1993), 31 et seq.; *Colneric*, in Däubler, Festschrift Gnade (1992), 627 et seq.; *Currall*, in Groeben/Thiesing/Ehlermann (eds.), Kommentar zum EU-/EG-Vertrag, Article 102a-136a EGV, 5th edition (1999), 3/1192; *Peters*, 2 ELJ (1996) 177 et seq.; *Ebsen*, Recht der Arbeit 1993, 11 et seq.; *Ellis*, European Community Sex Equality Law, 1991; *Fenwick/Hervey*, 2 EMLR (1995) 443 et seq.; *Fuchsloch*, Das Verbot der mittelbaren Geschlechtsdiskriminierung, (1995); *Kyriazis*, Die Sozialpolitik der Europäischen Wirtschaftsgemeinschaft in bezug auf die Gleichberechtigung männlicher und weiblicher Erwerbstätiger, (1990); *Langenfeld*, Die Gleichbehandlung von Mann und Frau im Europäischen Gemeinschaftsrecht (1990). *McCrudden*, 13 Oxford J Leg Stud (1993) 320 et seq.; *Prechal/Burrows*, Gender Discrimination Law of the European Community (1990); *Rating*, Mittelbare Diskriminierung der Frau im Erwerbsleben nach europäischen Gemeinschaftsrecht (1994).

39 Cf. ECJ – *Defrenne v Sabena* (Defrenne No. 2), ECJ, judgment of 8 April 1976, case C-43/75, [1976] ECR 455: "The principle that men and women should receive equal pay, which is laid down by Article 119, may be relied on before the national courts. These courts have a duty to ensure the protection of the rights which that provisions vests in individuals, in particular in the case of those forms of discrimination which have their origin in legislative provisions or collective labour agreements, as well as where men and women receive unequal pay for equal work which is carried out in the same establishment or service, whether private or public." Cf. annnotations by *Crisham*, CML Rev. 1977, 108; *Philip*, Revue trimestrielle de droit européen 1976, 529; *Schwarze*, EuR 1977, 44; *Wyatt*, EL Rev. (1976) 399 and 414.

> The principle that men and women should receive equal pay, which is laid down by Article 119, may be relied on before the national courts. These courts have a duty to ensure the protection of the rights which that provision vests in individuals, in particular in the ECJ, (...) case of those forms of discrimination which have their origin in legislative provisions or collective labor agreements, as well as where men and women receive unequal pay for equal work which is carried out in the same establishment or service, whether in private or public.[40]

The European Court of Justice has emphasized the importance of gender equality on several occasions, and stated that the elimination of discrimination based on sex forms part of the fundamental rights[41]. Several directives relating to the principle of equal pay and gender equality are currently in force[42].

Besides the interpretation of Article 119 ECT by case-law, Protocol No. 2 to the TEU clarified its scope of application with regard to the notion of "pay"[43], and some issues might have been the subject of social cooperation and agreements according to Protocol No. 14. While the first two paragraphs of Article 6 of Protocol No. 14 are quite similar to ex-Article 119 ECT, the last paragraph allowed for the implementation of positive measures in favor of women. A similar provision allowing for positive measures[44] on behalf of both sexes is now found in Article 141(4) ECT –

---

40 Cf. ECJ – *Defrenne v Sabena* (Defrenne No. 2), ECJ, judgment of 8 April 1976, case 43/75, [1976] ECR 455. Cf. annnotations by *Crisham*, CML Rev. (1977), 108; *Philip*, Revue trimestrielle de droit européen (1976), 529; *Schwarze*, EuR (1977), 44; *Wyatt*, 2 EL Rev. (1976), 399 and 414.

41 Defrenne No. 3, ECJ, judgment of 15 June 1978, case 149/77, [1978] ECR 1365, para 27; cf. annotations by *Imbrechts*, Revue trimestrielle de droit européen 1986, 231; *Pernice*, EuR 1979, 410; *Wyatt*, 3 EL Rev. (1978), 483.

42 Council Directive 75/117/EEC of 10 February 1975 on the approximation of the laws of the Member States relating to the application of the principle of equal pay for men and women (O.J. 1975 L 45/19); Council Directive 76/207/EEC of 9 February 1976 on the implementation of the principle of equal treatment for men and women as regards access to employment, vocational training and promotion, and working conditions (O.J. 1976 L 39/42); Council Directive 79/7/EEC of 19 December 1978 on the progressive implementation of the principle of equal treatment for men and women in matters of social security (O.J. 1979 L 6/24); Council Directive 86/378/EEC of 24 July 1986 on the implementation of the principle of equal treatment for men and women in occupational social security schemes (O.J. 1986 L 225/40); Council Directive 86/613/EEC of 11 December 1986 on the application of the principle of equal treatment between men and women engaged in an activity, including agriculture, in a self-employed capacity, and on the protection of self-employed women during pregnancy and motherhood (O.J. 1986 L 359/56); Council Directive 92/85/EEC of 19 October 1992 on the introduction of measures to encourage improvements in the safety and health at work of pregnant workers and workers who have recently given birth or are breastfeeding (O.J. 1992 L 348/1); Council Directive 93/104/EC of 23 November 1993 concerning certain aspects of the organization of working time (O.J. 1993 L 1993/18); Council Directive 96/34/EC of 3 June 1996 on the framework agreement on parental leave concluded by UNICE, CEEP and the ETUC (O.J. 1996 L 145/4).

43 Cf. ECJ, judgment of 17 May 1990, case 262/88, *Barber v Guardian Royal Exchange Assurance*, [1990] ECR I-1889.

44 Cf. as to positive measures *Benda*, Notwendigkeit und Möglichkeit positiver Aktionen zugunsten von Frauen im öffentlichen Dienst, Rechtsgutachten im Auftrag der Senatskanzlei (1986); *Goldman*, Justice and Reverse Discrimination (1979); *Gräfrath*, Wie gerecht ist die Frauenquote? (1992); *Greenawalt*, Discrimination and Reverse Discrimination (1983); *Maidowski*, Umgekehrte

With a view to ensuring full equality in practice between men and women in working life, the principle of equal treatment shall not prevent any Member State from maintaining or adopting measures providing for specific advantages in order to make it easier for the underrepresented sex to pursue a vocational activity or to prevent or compensate for disadvantages in professional careers.

III. Third-Country Nationals under the Current EC Provisions and the Proposed Extension of the Personal Scope of Application of Social Security Regulations

1. Survey

The right to freedom of movement confers on every citizen of the Union the right to move and reside freely within the territory of the Member States, subject to the conditions laid down in the Treaty[45]. Article 39 (ex-Article 48) ECT enhances for EU citizens the right to freedom of movement for workers. Therefore, any national of an EU Member State has the right to stay in every other Member State mainly for the purpose of employment and to remain there indefinitely. Furthermore, freedom of movement signifies the abolition of any discrimination based on nationality between workers of different EU Member States as regards employment, remuneration and other conditions of work. Since freedom of movement could not fully be attained without binding measures affording social protection, the EEC Treaty entrusted the Council of Ministers to adopt measures within this field based on Article 42 ECT (ex-Article 51). The Council thus has the power, in conformity with the provisions of the Treaty, to lay down detailed rules for the exercise of the rights to social benefits which the persons concerned derive from the Treaty[46]. Currently social security is mainly coordinated by Regulation (EEC) No. 1408/71 and the implementing Regulation 547/72; both regulations have been amended on several occasions[47]. The Court consistently held that Regulation 1408/71 in particular is intended to prevent a worker who, "by exercising his right of free movement, has been employed in more than one Member State from being placed in a worse positions than one who has completed

Diskriminierung (1989); *Peters*, 2 ELJ (1996) 177 et seq., at 178 and 181-183; *Shaw*, in Hepple/Szyczak (eds.), Discrimination: The Limits of Law (1992), 386 et seq.

45 Article 17 (ex-Article 8a) ECT.

46 ECJ, judgment of 21 October 1975, case 24/75, *Teresa et Silvana Petroni v Office National des pensions pour travailleurs salariés (ONPTS),* Bruxelles, [1975] ECR 1149, at 1160 (cf. also annotation by *Gosseries*, Journal des tribunaux du travail 1977, 26

47 Cf. also Council Regulation (EC) No. 1399/1999 of 29 April amending Regulation (EEC) No. 1408/71 on the application of social security schemes to employed persons, to self-employed persons and to members of their families moving within the Community and Regulation (EEC) No. 547/72 laying down the procedure for implementing Regulation (EEC) No. 1408/71. O.J. 1999 L 164/1.

his entire career in only one Member State"[48]. Community regulations overrule in a wide range of situations the principle of territoriality[49].

Third-country nationals residing in the European Union are partially covered by Community law, e.g. family members of EU citizens may in several cases be entitled to benefits on the basis of Regulation 1408/71; the same applies for refugees, stateless persons and citizens of the European Economic Area. Nationals of third countries might also be covered by the Association, Europe or Mediterranean Agreements; furthermore, there might be multilateral or bilateral agreements of some Member States with third states, e.g. the Interim Agreements elaborated by the Council of Europe. If none of these special rules apply, third-country nationals have no express entitlement as to any coordination or equal treatment compared with EU citizens.

Facing the difficult and unequal status of third-country nationals and the privileged treatment[50] of some of them, the issue of an inclusion of third-country nationals within Regulations No. 1408/71 and 54/72 had already been debated at the Porto Conference[51]. One of the major issues when discussing the extension of the personal scope was whether the Community had the legal competence in this field[52]; such extension was favored on the basis of ex-Articles 51 and 235 ECT that the notion of "worker" did not have to be interpreted in the strict sense of EU citizens, since the rationale underlying Article 51 seemed to be that of an independent yet supporting article in the sense that there should be coordination for anyone who has been legally subject as an employee to the social security systems of various Member States –

> The extension of the scope of application of the coordination regulations to third country nationals legally resident and/or working in a Member State is possible legally speaking; as a matter of fact, it may even be imperative.[53]

Although not all participants adopted this view, there was a broad consensus that Community law at least did not prevent an extension of the personal scope of application of Regulation 1408/71[54].

---

[48] ECJ, judgment of 5 May 1977, case 104/76, *Jansen v Landesversicherungsanstalt Rheinprovinz*, [1977] ECR 829; ECJ, judgment of 10 March 1983, case 232/82, *Baccini v ONEM*, [1983] ECR 583.

[49] As to the principle of territoriality and the Community Regulations on social security cf. *Hailbronner*, EuZW 1991, 171 et seq.; *Cornelissen*, 33 CML Rev (1996), 439.

[50] Cf. as to the privileged third-country nationals *Hailbronner*, in Due (ed.), Festschrift für Ulrich Everling (1995), 399.

[51] Cf. for instance the contributions by *Altmaier/Verschueren, Gouloussis, Lyon-Caen, Muus, Pieters, Pizarro, Zuleeg*, in: Commission of the European Communities/Departamento de Relacoes Internacionais e Convencoes de Seguranca Socia (eds.), Social Security in Europe. Equality between Nationals and Non-Nationals, European Conference, Porto, November 1994 (1995).

[52] *Schulte*, in Jorens/Schulte (eds.), European Social Security Law and Third Country Nationals (1998), 155, at 176.

[53] *Pieters*, in Commission of the European Communities/Departamento de Relacoes Internacionais e Convencois de seguranca Social (eds.), Social security in Europe. Equality between Nationals and Non-Nationals, European Conference Porto November 1994, 189, 236.

[54] *Altmaier/Verschueren*, in: Commission of the European Communities/Departamento de Relacoes Internacionais e Convencois de Seguranca Social (eds.), Social Security in Europe. Equality between Nationals and Non-Nationals, European Conference Porto November 1994, 245.

In 1994 the Commission submitted a proposal to extend Article 22(1)(a) of Regulation 1408/71 ensuring the right to immediate and emergency health care to people insured in one Member State who stay for a short time in another Member State to third-country nationals[55]. The Council, however, did not accept the Commission's view when adopting Regulation 3095/95 later in 1995[56]. In 1995 the Commission suggested the issuing of a Council directive on the rights of third-country nationals to travel in the Community[57]. At a later stage, the Commission submitted the proposal for a Convention (now possibly a directive) under Article 63 ECT, as revised by the Amsterdam Treaty on rules for the admission of third-country nationals which deals with the admission as well as the right to seek employment in other EU-Member States[58]. In 1997 the Commission suggested an extension of the personal scope of application of Regulation 1408/71 to third-country nationals[59] and in 1999 the Commission submitted a proposal as to social security as a whole being applicable also to third-country nationals[60].

2. *The Existing Regulation 1408/71*

a) The Personal Scope of Application

The right to freedom of movement is limited to EU citizens and their families[61]. Regulation 1408/71 is therefore currently applicable to the following groups[62] –

- employed or self-employed persons who are or have been subject to the legislation of one or more Member States and who are nationals of one of the

---

55 Amended proposal for a Council Regulation (EC) amending Regulation (EEC) No. 1408/71 on the application of social security schemes to employed persons, to self-employed persons and to members of their families moving within the Community, Regulation (EEC) No. 574/72 laying down the procedure for implementing Regulation (EEC) No. 1408/71 and Regulation (EEC) No. 1945/93 amending Regulation (EEC) No. 1247/92, O.J. 1995 C 242/7.

56 O.J. 1995 L 335/1.

57 See for instance the proposal for a Council Directive on the rights of third-country nationals to travel in the Community, COM(95)346 final, O.J. 1995 C 306/5.

58 Proposal for a Council Act establishing the Convention on rules for the admission of third-country nationals to the Member States, COM(97)387 final, O.J. 1997 C 337/9.

59 Proposal for a Council Regulation (EC) amending Regulation (EEC) No. 1408/71 as regards its extension to nationals of third countries, O.J. 1998 C 6/15; and cf. also the proposal for a Council directive extending the freedom to provide cross-border services to third-country nationals established within the Community, COM(99)3 final; O.J. 1999 C 1996/179.

60 Cf. as to the social perspectives *Schulte/Mäder* (eds.), Die Regierungskonferenz Maastricht II (1996).

61 Cf. as to the situation of third-country nationals *inter alia* Report on the High Level Panel on the Free Movement of persons chaired by Mrs. *Simone Veil*, presented to the Commission on 18 March 1997, 7, 73 et seq., and 78; *Schulte*, in von Maydell/Schulte (eds.), Treatment of Third Country Nationals in the EU and EEA Member States in Terms of Social Security Law (1995), 105; *Eichenhofer*, ZAR 1996, 62.

62 See also *Schulte*, in: Jorens/Schulte (eds.), European Social Security Law and Third-Country Nationals (1998), 155, at 168.

Member States[63] or who are stateless persons or refugees residing within the territory of one of the Member States;

- the members of the family[64] and the survivors of the persons referred to above;
- the survivors of employed or self-employed persons who have been subject to the legislation of one or more Member States, irrespective of the nationality of such employed or self-employed persons, where their survivors are nationals of one of the Member States, or stateless persons or refugees residing within the territory of one of the Member States;
- civil servants[65] and persons who, in accordance with the legislation applicable, are treated as such, where they are or have been subject to the legislation of a Member State to which this Regulation applies.

The concept of an "employed or self-employed" person is defined in Article 1 as any person who is insured by a social security scheme applying to employed or self-employed persons. It is therefore possible that a person who cannot be considered as a worker under Article 48 ECT is to be regarded as falling under Article 51 ECT and Regulation 1408/71[66].

b) The Substantive Scope of Application

Benefits covered by social security regulations and especially Regulation 1408/71[67] are, irrespective of whether they are general or special, contributory or non-contributory[68], the following: sickness and maternity benefits, invalidity benefits,

---

[63] In *Belhouab* the ECJ decided that the condition of nationality is to be interpreted in the sense that the status of being a national of one of the Member States refers to the time of the employment, or the payment of contributions relating to the insurance periods and of the acquisition of the corresponding rights (ECJ, judgment of 12 October 1978, case 10/78, [1978] ECR 1915).

[64] Cf. as to family members D.I.1; as to the doctrine of "derived rights" which has hot been upheld cf. ECJ, judgment of 30 April 1996, case C-308/93, *Bestuur van de Sociale Verzekeringsbank v J.M. Cabanis-Issarte*, [1996] ECR I-2097, and *Schulte*, in: Jorens/Schulte (eds.), European Social Security Law and Third Country Nationals (1998), 155, at 169.

[65] Cf. as to the extension of the personal scope of application Council Regulation (EC) No. 1608/98 of 29 June 1998 amending Regulation (EEC) No. 1408/71 on the application of social security schemes to employed persons, to self-employed persons and to members of their families moving within the Community and Regulation (EEC) No. 574/72 laying down the procedure for implementing Regulation (EEC) No. 1408/71 with a view to extending them to cover special schemes for civil servants, O.J. 1998 L 209/1.

[66] As to the notion of "worker" see *Sidéris*, 441 Schweizerische Zeitschrift für Sozialversicherung und berufliche Vorsorge (1997) 257, 263; *Verschueren*, in: Jorens/Schulte (eds.), European Social Security Law and Third Country Nationals (1998), 187, at 194.

[67] The most recent amendment dates of 29 April 1999 (Council Regulation (EC) No. 1399/1999 amending Regulation (EEC) No. 1408/71 on the application of social security schemes to employed persons, to self-employed persons and to members of their families moving within the Community and Regulation (EEC) No. 574/72 laying down the procedure for implementing Regulation (EEC) No. 1408/71, O.J. 1999 L 164/1. Cf. as to the inclusion of supplementary pensions the Proposal for a Council Directive on safeguarding the supplementary pension rights for employed and self-employed persons moving within the European Union, O.J. 1998 C 5/4.

[68] According to Regulation 1247 of 30 April 1992 non-contributory benefits are included under certain conditions set out in Article 4(2) of Regulation 1408/71 which includes special non-contributory benefits which are provided under a legislation or schemes other than those referred to in para. 1 or

including those intended for the maintenance or improvement of earning capacity, old-age benefits, survivors' benefits, benefits in respect of accidents at work and occupational diseases, death grants, unemployment benefits, family benefits[69].

Social security regulations and especially Regulations No. 1408/71 and 574/72 aim at a coordination of social security systems[70]. Due to the different national social security schemes, a harmonization has not been envisaged[71]. Therefore, Community law does not affect the substantive and procedural differences; Member States remain free to decide who is to be insured, which benefits should be granted and under what conditions, how many contributions should be paid, how benefits should be calculated and for how long they should be granted, provided that this system does not constitute any discrimination on the basis of nationality[72]. The coordination is purely "internal"[73]. Countries which are not members of the Community or the EEA are therefore generally not included.

The Court held on several occasions that freedom of movement could not be attained if, as a consequence of the exercise of the right to freedom of movement, migrant workers were to lose the advantages in the field of social security guaranteed to them by the laws of a single Member State since such a consequence could deter Community workers from exercising their right to freedom of movement and would therefore constitute an obstacle to that freedom[74] According to Article 39(2) (ex-Article 48(2)) ECT freedom of movement of workers is to "entail the abolition of any discrimination based on nationality between workers of the Member States as regards employment, remuneration and other conditions of work and employment." The principle of equality is furthermore contained in Article 3(1) of Regulation 1408/71 providing that subject to the special provisions

---

excluded by virtue of para. 4 where such benefits are intended either to provide supplementary, substitute or ancillary cover against the risks covered by the branches of social security referred to in para. 1(a) to (h) or solely as specific protection for the disabled. Cf. also *Schulte*, Sozialhilfe- und sozialhilfeähnliche Leistungen und Europäisches Gemeinschaftsrecht, legal expertise on behalf of the Federal Ministry for the Family and the Elderly, Bundesmnisterium für Familie und Senioren, Bonn 1994.

69 Cf. as to the ECJ's jurisprudence in social security cases *Moore*, 35 CML Rev (1998), 409.

70 Cf. as to social security legislation in the Community Commission, Social Security for Workers, Social Europe 3/92, 1993; *Schulte*, in Jorens/Schulte (eds.), European social Security Law and Third Country Nationals (1998), 155 et seq.; *Schulte* (ed.), Soziale Sicherheit in der EG. Verordnung (EWG) Nr. 1408/71 und sonstige Bestimmungen, 3rd edition (1997); *Pennings*, Introduction to European Social Security Law, Social Security in the European Union (1994).

71 *Cammilleri*, La protection sociale en Europe (1993), 19; 41 *Sidéris*, Schweizerische Zeitschrift für Sozialversicherung und berufliche Vorsorge (1997) 257, 261; *Pieters*, Introduction into the Social Security Law of the Member States of the European Community (1990); *Lippert*, Soziale Vergünstigungen und Arbeitnehmerfreizügigkeit in Europa (1995).

72 ECJ, judgment of 15 January 1986, case 41/84, *Pinna v Caisse d'Allocation familiales de la Savoie*, [1986] ECR 1; ECJ, judgment of 7 February 1991, case C-227/89, *Rönfeld v Bundesversicherungs-anstalt für Angestellte*, [1991] ECR I-323; ECJ, judgment of 30 January 1997, case C-340/94, *de Jaeck v Staatssecretaris von Financien*, [1997] ECR I-461; ECJ, judgment of 4 October 1991, case C-349/87, *Parashi v Landesversicherungsanstalt Württemberg*, [1991] ECR I-4501.

73 Cf. *Verschueren*, in: Jorens/Schulte (eds.), European Social Security Law and Third Country Nationals (1990), 187, at 190.

74 ECJ, judgment of 22 February 1990, case C-228/88, *Bronzino v Kindergeldkasse*, [1990] ECR I-531; ECJ, judgment of 22 February 1990, case C-12/89, *Gatto v Bundesanstalt für Arbeit*, [1990] ECR I-557.

of this Regulation, persons resident in the territory of one of the Member States to whom this Regulation applies shall be subject to the same obligations and enjoy the same benefits as nationals of that State". Article 7(2) provides that a migrant worker is also to enjoy the same social and tax advantages as national workers in the state of employment[75]. The European Court of Justice ruled in 1974 that the rule regarding equality of treatment forbids not only overt discrimination, but also treatment, which by the application of other criteria of differentiation, leads in fact to the same result[76]. Member States are therefore not allowed to reserve any social security benefits solely for its nationals and are not permitted to require qualifying conditions that are harder for nationals of other Member States to achieve[77].

Another main objective of Community legislation in this field is the determination of the legislation applicable and to ensure that workers moving within the Community are subject to the social security scheme of one Member State only. Thus, Article 13(1) enshrines the principle that persons to whom the Regulation applies are subject to the legislation of one single Member State only. The point of departure is the principle that a person employed in the territory of one Member State shall be subject to the legislation of that state; Article 13(2) refers to the principle *lex locis laboris*. The principle itself is specified in Title II of the Regulation, also with exceptions expressly provided for in the Regulation.

Another principle in Regulation 1408/71 is the retention of rights and the export of benefits, not only applicable to the payment, but also to the acquisition of benefits[78]. Therefore, Article 10(1) provides that in cases of invalidity, old-age and survivors' benefits, pensions for accidents at work or occupational diseases and death grants Member States are legally precluded from withdrawing or reducing benefits on the ground that the recipient resides in the territory of Member State other than that in which the institution responsible for payment is situated. This provision, however, does not apply to sickness, unemployment and family benefits, for which Title III of the said Regulation lays down special provisions.

With Regulation 1247/92 of 30 April 1992[79], the Council limited the export of the special non-contributory benefits. Provided that they are listed in Annex II(a) to the Regulation, these benefits are paid exclusively to persons residing in the territory of the Member State concerned, where necessary through aggregation of

---

[75] The principle of equality is also to be found in Article 7 of Regulation 1612/68 prescribing that a worker who is a national of a Member State may not be treated differently in the territory of other Member States from national workers in respect of employment and working conditions.

[76] ECJ, judgment of 12 February 1974, case 152/73, *Giovanni Maria Sotgiu v Deutsche Bundespost*, [1974] ECR 153, 164; cf. also annotation by *Tizzano*, Il Foro italiano 1974 IV, Col. 210; *Pacteau*, Recueil Dalloz Sirey 1975, Jur. P. 606; *Wyatt*, 1 EL Rev. 1975, 62. As to direct and indirect discrimination cf. also *Sidéris*, 41 Schweizerische Zeitschrift für Sozialversicherung und berufliche Vorsorge (1997), 257, 272.

[77] ECJ, judgment of 7 March 1991, case C-10/90, *Masgio v Bundesknappschaft*, [1991] ECR I-1119, at 1139; ECJ, judgment of 4 October 1991, case C-349/87, *Parashi v Landesversicherungsanstalt Württemberg*, [1991] ECR I-4501, 4524.

[78] ECJ, judgment of 10 June 1982, case 92/81, *Camera v Institut national d'assurance maladie-invalidité*, [1982] ECR 2213, at 2224; ECJ, judgment of 23 October 1986, case 300/84, *van Roosmalen v Bestur van de Bedrijfsvereniging voor de Gezondheid, Geestelijke en Maatschappelijke Belangen*, [1986] ECR 3097, at 3122.

[79] O.J. 1992 L 136/1.

the residence periods completed in the territory of any other Member State, without any discrimination on grounds of nationality[80]. According to Article 19(1)(b) of Regulation 1408/71, payments have to be made by the social security institution with which the beneficiary is affiliated or by the social security institution of his place of residence at the former's expense. A worker entitled to unemployment benefits in one Member State seeking work in another can retain his right to benefit during his stay in the latter for a maximum period of three months. Benefits in such cases are provided by the social security authorities of the State in which he seeks work at the expense of the institution with which the worker is affiliated (Article 69).

Furthermore, the Regulation assures for a continuous contribution record by means of aggregation[81] taking into account the entire "European career" of a migrant worker. In the case of sickness and maternity benefits, for instance, Regulation 1408/71 requires that the authorities of a Member State, whose legislation provides that the acquisition, retention or recovery of the right to benefit is conditional upon the completion of insurance periods, take into account insurance periods completed under the legislation of any other Member State as if they were periods completed under its own legislation (Article 18). Similar provisions relate to the aggregation in the case of invalidity, old-age and death pensions, death grants, unemployment benefits and family benefits (Articles 38, 45, 64, 67 and 72). In cases in which the amount of the benefits under national law depends on whether the family members reside in the same country as the migrant worker, Regulation 1408/71 provides that the national authorities take into account the family members of the person concerned who are resident in the territory of another Member State as if they were resident in the territory of the competent state.

80 The compatibility of this regulation with the ECT was debated and decided in the affirmative in ECJ, judgment of 4 November 1997, case C-20/96, *Kelvin Albert Snares v Adjudication Officer*, [1997] ECR I-6057; cf. also the annotations by *Keunen*, Rechtspraak sociale verzekering 1998, n° 185; *Lhernould*, Revue belge de sécurité sociale 1998, 797.

81 Cf. inter alia ECJ, judgment of 5 October 1994, case C-165/91, *van Munster v Rijksdienst voor Pensioenen*, [1994] ECR I-4661; ECJ, judgment of 26 October 1995, case C-481/93, *R. Moscato v Bestuur van de Nieuwe Algemene Bedijfsvereniging*, [1995] ECR I-3525; ECJ, judgment of 26 October 1995, case C-482/93, *S.E. Klaus v Bestuur van de Nieuwe Algemene Bedrijfsvereniging*, [1995] ECR I-3551.

3. *The Proposal for an Extended Personal Scope of Application and for a Council Regulation (EC) on Coordination of Social Security Systems*

In 1998 the Commission proposed to extend the personal scope of application of Regulation 1408/71 to third-country nationals[82]. The proposal is based on several considerations relating to equality of treatment, human rights and the fact that Regulation 1408/71 already applies to workers moving within the Union even where they have not exercised their right to freedom of movement as migrant workers. Furthermore the large number of legal instruments governing problems encountered by nationals of third countries in connection with the coordination of Member States' social security schemes and the significant legal and administrative complexity are mentioned, as well as the possible creation of problems such as double levying of contributions in the case of service providers employing workers who are nationals of third countries. Any entitlement to enter, to stay or reside in a Member State or to have access to its labor market is expressly excluded. The Economic and Social Committee welcomed this proposed extension to third-country nationals legally resident in the Community and shared the opinion of the Commission that the Regulation would help in the fight against illegal and undeclared work. In addition, the proposal would cover internal coordinating provisions and should therefore considerably simplify the legal and administrative situation, given that the coordination of Member States' social security rules regarding third country nationals is currently governed by a number of bilateral and multilateral agreements. As to the financial implications the Committee points out that those might be only modest since the persons concerned are already affiliated to a Member State social security system. Besides those general comments the Committee suggested in particular an amendment of some of the provisions of Regulation 1408/71 by deleting references to the nationality of the persons concerned and to categories of persons who are not EU citizens[83].

In 1999 a Proposal for a Council Regulation (EC) on coordination of social security systems was submitted[84]. As to the personal scope of application, the draft regulation should apply to persons who are or have been subject to the social security legislation of one or more Member States, as well as to the members of their family and to their survivors; there is no limitation as to EU citizens, refugees or stateless persons. Equality of treatment is enshrined in Article 3 of the proposal. The matters covered resemble Article 4 of the existing regulation, namely sickness, maternity, invalidity, old age, accidents at work, survival, death, unemployment, pre-retirement and the family; it should not apply to social assistance and should not affect the legislative provisions of any Member State concerning a shipowner's

---

[82] O.J. 1998 C 6/15; The German Government, in principle, supported this extension already in 1995(BT-Drs. 13/1348, 37: "Gleichwohl ist hier eine generelle unterschiedliche Behandlung von Drittstaatsangehörigen gegenüber den Staatsangehörigen aus den Mitgliedstaaten und den Staatenlosen und Flüchtlingen auf Dauer sozialpolitisch nicht mehr zu vertreten. (...)").

[83] Opinion of the Economic and Social Committee on the 'Proposal for a Council Regulation (EC) amending Regulation (EEC) No 1408/71 as regards its extension to nationals of third countries' (98/C 157/08), O.J. 1998 C 157/30.

[84] COM(98)779 final., O.J. 1999 C 38/10.

obligations. The same applies to the principles governing the coordination of social security schemes. Article 4 names the aggregation of periods, Article 5 the waiving of residence rules and Article 8 provides for one legislation of a single Member State to be applicable. Special rules in the event of posting are contained in Article 9. Rules concerning voluntary insurance or option continued insurance may be found in Article 11 and special rules regarding personnel employed by diplomatic missions and consular posts and auxiliary staff of the European Communities are contained in Article 12.

4. *Equal Treatment under Community Law*

a) Equal Treatment and EU citizens

Community law offers a wide range of provisions relating mainly to equal treatment of citizens of EU Member States[85]. This is due to the fact that the European Community primarily focuses on the realization of the four fundamental freedoms which are economy-related: the free movement of goods and capital, the freedom of workers, the freedom of establishment and to provide services. In social security issues equality of treatment is enshrined in Article 3 of Regulation 1408/71[86] and Articles 7-9 of Regulation 1612/68. Article 7 (2) of Regulation 1612/68, for instance, imposes on the Member States the same obligations as to rendering social advantages to migrant workers[87]. The Commission proposed an amendment to Regulation 1612/68 on 14 October 1998 which aims at strengthening equal treatment of EU citizen workers. Thus, paragraphs (1) to (3) of Article 7 of Regulation 1612/68 shall be replaced and a fifth paragraph shall be added. The proposed provisions read –

> 1. A worker who is a national of a Member State may not, in the territory of another Member State, be treated differently from national workers by reason of his nationality in respect of any conditions of employment and work, particularly as regards health, safety and hygiene, remuneration and dismissal or occupational rehabilitation, reinstatement or re-employment, should he become unemployed or fully or partially unfit for work.
>
> 2. A worker who is a national of a Member State shall enjoy the same financial, fiscal, social, cultural and other advantages as national workers.
>
> 3. A worker who is a national of a Member State shall, by virtue of the same right and under the same conditions as national workers, have access to all levels of education and university or other vocational training and to vocational rehabilitation, retraining and other training.

---

85 Cf. for instance to the principle of equal treatment *Schulte*, in Jorens/Schulte (eds.), European Social Security Law and Third Country Nationals (1998), 155, at 178.

86 Cf. for the equality of treatment of EU citizens *Verschueren*, in: Jorens/Schulte (eds.), European Social Law and Third Country Nationals (1998), 187, at 191.

87 Cf. as to the jurisprudence relating to equal treatment *Eichenhofer*, 30 CML Rev (1993) 1021, at 1022-1025.

[...]

5. Where working conditions, professional advancement or certain advantages accorded to workers depend, in a Member State, on the occurrence of certain facts or events, any comparable facts or events which have occurred in any other Member State shall entail the same consequences or confer the same advantages accorded.[88]

The Court held that equality of treatment does not only relate to overt discrimination by reason of nationality, but that other forms of discrimination which – by the application of other criteria – lead de facto to the same results, are contrary to Community law[89]. Member States are therefore not allowed to reserve any social security benefits for its nationals only and are not permitted to impose qualifying conditions that are harder to meet for nationals of other Member States, including those relating to place of origin, place of birth, place of ordinary residence, etc[90].

b) Equal Treatment and Third-Country Nationals in General

Third-county nationals on the other hand are generally excluded from Community guarantees, except in those cases in which a special regime is applicable. Therefore, equal treatment was deemed necessary and incorporated in several documents of Community bodies[91].

The 1989 Social Charter stated that legally resident workers from non-member countries and members of their families should be able to enjoy "comparable" treatment to Community workers as regards living and working conditions although the responsibility for those measures was left with the Member States. In 1994 the Commission published a Communication to the Council and the European Parliament on Immigration and Asylum Policies which is also based on the approach that the integration of legal immigrants including the assimilation of their rights with those of Member State citizens should be strengthened[92]. The Council and the Member States recognized in their resolution of 5 October 1995 on the fight against racism and xenophobia in the fields of employment and social affairs "the great importance of implementing, in the field of social policy, policies based on the principle of non-discrimination and equal opportunities at Union and

---

88 O.J. 1998 C 344/9.

89 ECJ, judgment of 12 February 1974, case 152/73, *Sotgiu v Deutsche Bundespost*, [1974] ECR 153, 164, para 11.

90 As to the importance of equal treatment cf. to ECJ, judgment of 30 April 1996, case C-308/93, (*Cabanis-Issarte*), [1996] ECR I-2097; ECJ, judgment of 21 October 1975, case 24/75 (*Petroni*), [1975] ECR 1149; ECJ, judgment of 7 March 1991, case C-10/90 (*Masgio v Bundesknappschaft*), [1991] ECR I-1119, at 1139; ECJ, judgment of 4 October 1991, case C-349/87 (*Paraschi v Landesversicherungsanstalt Württemberg*), [1991] ECR I-4501, at 4524.

91 Cf. for instance the Green Paper submitted by the Commission, COM(93)551 final of 17 November 1993; White Paper, COM(94)333 final of 27 July 1994.

92 COM(94)23 final dated 23 February 1994; Green Paper on European Social Policy Options for the Union, Summary of responses dated 30 June 1994; para. 65; COM(94)333 final /2.

Member State level, within the framework of their respective powers, as a contribution to the common fight against racism and xenophobia." The European Parliament called for equal treatment to be given to Community nationals and nationals of third countries in the social sphere[93]. The principle of equal treatment of third-country nationals in comparison with EU citizens is also incorporated in Article 34(1)(e) of the "Proposal for a Council Act establishing the Convention on rules for the admission of third-country nationals to the Member States", submitted by the Commission in 1997[94], with regard to access to employment or self-employment, vocational training, trade union rights, the right of association, access to housing, whether in the private, public or para-state sector, social welfare and schooling, provided that the third-country national is a long-term resident. Article 32 defines a long-term resident as a national of a third country who has had his ordinary and lawful residence in one Member State, and who possesses a residence title authorizing residence for at least ten years after the first issue. On 28 January 1999, however, the Parliament approved the Commission proposal, but decided that Chapter VIII should be deleted[95] pointing to the fact that the Treaty distinguishes in a more detailed manner between admission (Article 62(2) ECT), immigration, long-term visas and residence permits (Article 63(3) ECT) and the rights of third-country nationals legally resident in a Member State (Article 63(4) ECT).

With the Amsterdam Treaty, Article 13 ECT was incorporated, stating that "without prejudice to the other provisions of this Treaty and within the limits of the powers conferred by it upon the Community, the Council, acting unanimously on a proposal from the Commission and after consulting the European Parliament, may take appropriate action to combat discrimination based on sex, racial or ethnic origin, religion or belief, disability, age or sexual orientation." A clear statement as to the position of third-country nationals was never adopted[96] although the *Kahn* Commission identified that the main victims of racism are "foreigners from outside or inside Europe", and that to effectively combat racism, measures must be targeted towards the protection and integration of those persons –

> The Union has an imperative obligation to combat racism and racial discrimination. Indeed, as long as immigrants from non-EU countries are

---

93 Cf. for instance resolution dated 30 January 1997 on racism, xenophobia and anti-semitism and the European Year against Racism, 1997.

94 COM(97)387 final, O.J. 1997 C 337/9.

95 Second Report on the proposal for a Council Act establishing the Convention on rules for the admission of third-country nationals to Member States and a draft Convention on rules for the admission of third-country nationals to the Member States on the European Union, A4-0045/99, PE 229.573/final.

96 Cf. as to the various provisions under discussion *Winn*, Staatsangehörige von Drittländern in der Europäischen Union. The Right to Equal Treatment (1995); Free Movement for non-EC-workers within the European Community (1997).

denied Community residential status, the process of their integration will be retarded and their segregation prolonged.[97]

The Commission also took the view that an amendment of the Treaty should be directed towards the elimination of all forms of discrimination against persons, or groups of persons, whether citizens of the European Union or not[98].

c) Equal Treatment under Community Agreements

Equal treatment of third-country nationals is partially given on the basis of Community Agreements[99]. Article 4 of the EEA Agreement[100], for instance, is identical to ex-Article 6 ECT when providing that "within the scope of application of this Agreement, and without prejudice to any special provisions contained therein, any discrimination on grounds of nationality shall be prohibited." Furthermore, as to social security, Annex VI to the EEA Agreement, for instance, refers to Article 29 of the EEA Agreement which is similar to ex-Article 51 ECT: secondary legislation in social security is extended to the entire EEA[101]. As to Switzerland, equal treatment as regards conditions of employment and working conditions, especially pay, dismissal, or reinstatement or re-employment is enshrined in Article 9 of Annex 1 to the Agreement between the European Community and its Member States, on the one part, and the Swiss Confederation, of the other, on the Free Movement of Persons, which has been signed on 21 June 1999 and which shall enter into force on 1 January 2001. Negotiation on social security systems led to Annex II which refers to Regulations 1408/71 and 574/72. [102] Of major importance is the evolution under the Association Agreements with

---

97 European Council Consultative Commission on Racism and Xenophobia, Final Report, Ref. 6906/1/95 Rev. 1 Limite RAXEN 24, General Secretariat of the Council of the European Union (1995), at 44.

98 At 59. Cf. also *Bell*, 9 Maastricht Journal of European and Comparative Law (1999) 5, 19.

99 As to equality of treatment, the legal status of third-country nationals and the ECJ case-law cf. *Zuleeg*, in Barwig et al. (eds.), Festschrift für Fritz Franz und Gert Müller (1994), 448 et seq.; *Eichenhofer* (ed.), Social Security of Migrants in the European Union Tomorrow (1997); *Peers*, 33 CML Rev (1996) 7 et seq.; *Peers*, ELR 1997, 342 et seq.; *Stahlberg*, EuroAS 1997, 119; *Schieffer*, in: Hailbronner (ed.), 30 Jahre Freizügigkeit in Europa (1998), 183 et seq. An overview on social rights of third-country nationals under the different agreements is offered by *Stahlberg*, EuroAS 1997, 119, at 123.

100 O.J. 1994 L 1/1.

101 *Sakslin*, in Jorens/Schulte (eds.), European Social Security Law and Third-Country Nationals (1998), 398; as to the EEA and Austria see *Siedl*, in Jorens/Schulte (eds.), European Social Security Law and Third-Country Nationals (1998), 419 et seq.

102 Cf. as to difficulties during the negotiations, especially with regard to the health systen, the right to unemloyment benefit and the right to reside as an unemployed person in Switzerland *Langer*, in Jorens/Schulte (eds.), European Social Security Law and Third-Country Nationals (1998), 431, at 468; *Schumacher*, in: Barwig et al. (eds.), Sozialer Schutz von Ausländern in Deutschland (1997), 135, at 150; the implications especially for the different social security and health care schemes are mentioned in the "Botschaft des Schweizerischen Bundesrates and das Parlament betreffend die sieben sektoriellen Abkommen EU-Schweiz", 26 et seq.

Turkey and the Maghreb countries[103]. The Association Agreement with Turkey was signed on 12 September 1963[104]. Article 6 sets up an Association Council in order to ensure the implementation and progressive development of the Association. Article 9 prohibits any discrimination on the grounds of nationality. The Additional Protocol dated 23 November 1970 provides for freedom of movement. Article 39 states that social security measures should be adopted. Those measures must for instance enable workers to aggregate their periods of employment or insurance spent in different EU-Member States for retirement, invalidity and death benefits and health care; furthermore, export of several benefits to Turkey should be possible.

Pursuing this aim, the Association Council adopted Decision No. 3/80[105] on 19 September 1980; this decision also provides for equal treatment and coordination of benefits for the nationals of the Contracting Parties moving within the Community and between the Community and Turkey. As to the personal scope of application, Decision No. 3/80 is applicable to workers who are or have been subject to the legislation of one or more Member States, who are Turkish nationals, to family members residing in the Community and survivors. Article 3 provides that "subject to the special provisions of this Decision, persons resident in the territory of one of the Member States to whom this Decision applies shall be subject to the same obligations and enjoy the same benefits under the legislation of any Member State as the nationals of that State" with regard to sickness and maternity benefits, invalidity benefits including those intended for the maintenance or improvement of earning capacity, old age and survivors' benefits, benefits for accidents at work and occupational diseases, death grants, unemployment benefits and family benefits". The Decision is applicable to all general and special social security schemes whether contributory or non-contributory, but not to social and medical assistance or the consequences of war. In February 1983 the Commission submitted a proposal for a Council Regulation implementing this decision[106]. This

---

[103] Cf. for the treatment of third-country nationals under those agreements *Brinkmann*, in Jorens/Schulte (eds.), European Social Security Law and Third-Country Nationals (1998), 258 et seq.; *Centel*, in Jorens/Schulte (eds.), European Social Security Law and Third-Country Nationals (1998), 281 et seq.; *Eicke*, in Guild (ed.), The Legal Framework and Social Consequences of Free Movement of Persons in the European Union (1999), 89 et seq.; *Roberts*, in: Jorens/Schulte (eds.), European Social Security Law and Third-Country Nationals (1998), 209 et seq.; *Sieveking*, in: Jorens/Schulte (eds.), European Social Security Law and Third-Country Nationals (1998), 235 et seq.; *Sieveking*, ZIAS 1995, 227 et seq.

[104] For the legal status of Turkish nationals see Chapter C V.

[105] Decision No. 3/80 of the Association Council of 19 September 1980 on the Application of the Social Security Schemes of the Member States of the European Communities to Turkish workers and members of their families, O.J. 1983 C 110/60.

[106] O.J. 1983 C 110/19. Cf. as to social security of Turkish workers in the EU and Decision No. 3 for instance *Centel*, in Jorens/Schulte (eds.), European Social Security Law and Third-Country Nationals (1998), 281, at 289; *Delbrück/Tietje*, ZAR 1995, 29; *Hänlein*, ZAR 1998, 21; *Hänlein*, in Jorens/Schulte (eds.), European Social Security Law and Third-Country Nationals (1998), 300 et seq.; *Schumacher*, in: Barwig et al. (eds.), Sozialer Schutz von Ausländern in Deutschland (1997), 135, at 152; *Schuler*, EuroAS 1995, 167 et seq.; *Sieveking*, NZS 1994, 213 et seq.; the issue of social security including the German-Turkish social security agreement is offered by *Eichenhofer*, ZIAS 1997, 136 et seq.

regulation, resembling Regulation 574/72 implementing Regulation 1408/71, has not, however, been adopted as yet[107].

In two cases relating especially to social security issues, the European Court of Justice had to decide upon the direct effect of Decision No. 3/80 of the Association Council[108]. In *Taflan-Met*[109] the European Court of Justice decided that despite the lack of a special provision the aforementioned decision entered into force on the date of adoption (19 September 1980). Furthermore, the European Court of Justice stated that as long as supplementary measures being necessary for implementing the Decision have not been adopted, Articles 12 and 13 of the Decision do not have direct effect in the territory of the Member States. Individuals therefore can not rely upon those provisions before the national courts. In contrast to this decision, the plaintiff in *Sürül*[110] relied solely on the principle of non-discrimination on grounds of nationality and invoked Article 9 of the Association Agreement and Article 3(1) in order to be entitled to a social security benefit[111]; in the case submitted, German authorities refused to grant child care allowance because the husband of Mrs. Sürül only possessed – as a student – a limited residence permit, but no regular residence permit ("Aufenthaltsberechtigung" or "Aufenthalts-erlaubnis"). The European Court of Justice referred to its case-law as to direct applicability and stated –

> It follows from the foregoing considerations that Article 3(1) of Decision No. 3/80 establishes in the area in which that decision applies, a precise and unconditional principle such as is capable of being applied by a national court and, therefore, of governing the legal situation of individuals. The direct effect which must therefore be accorded to that provision means that the persons to whom it applies are entitled to rely on it before the courts of the Member States.[112]

---

107 Cf. as to the lack of adoption *Barwig*, in Sieveking et al. (eds.), Sozialer Schutz von Ausländern (1997), 113, at 123; *Hänlein*, EuroAS 1997, 21, at 23; *Zuleeg*, ZAR 1997, 170, at 172.

108 Cf. as to the discussion on this issue *Brinkmann*, in Jorens/Schulte (eds.), European Social Security Law and Third-Country Nationals (1998), 258, at 269; *Delbrück/Tietje*, ZAR 1995, 29 et seq.; *Schuler*, EuroAS 1995, 167 et seq.; *Schulte*, EuroAS 1995, 167 et seq.; *Schumacher*, DRV 1995, 681 et seq.; *Sieveking*, NZS 1994, 213 et seq.

109 ECJ, Case C-277/94, judgment of 10 September 1996, *Taflan-Met and others v Bestuur van de Sociale Verzekeringsbank*, [1996] ECR I-4085; cf. annotations by *Gümrükcü/Neumann/Fleisch* (eds.), Bikulturalität-staatliches Handeln-Mensch (1997), 69; *Hänlein*, EuroAS 1997, 21 et seq.; *Hänlein*, ZAR 1998, 21 et seq.; *Langer*, in Jorens/Schulte (eds.), European Social Security Law and Third-Country Nationals, 1998, 441, at 457; *Sieveking*, in: ITES Jahrbuch 1997-1998; *Zuleeg*, ZAR 1997, 170.

110 ECJ, judgment of 4 May 1999, case C-262/96, [1999] ECR.

111 The question as whether "Landeserziehungsgeld" should be granted according to the principle of non-discrimination is treated by *Sieveking*, NZW 1994, 213, at 218, and – with a view to the Gaygusuz-judgment including the export of pensions– by *Schumacher*, in: Barwig et al. (eds.), Sozialer Schutz von Ausländern in Deutschland (1997), 135, at 146 and 154; cf. to the principle of equality and the export of "Arbeitsmarktrenten" *Hänlein*, ZAR 1998, 21, at 27; *Wißmeyer*, Mitteilungen der LVA Oberfranken und Mittelfranken 1987, 129, 157.

112 ECJ, judgment of 30 September 1987, case 12/86, *Demirel v Stadt Schwäbisch Gmünd*, [1987] ECR 3719; judgment of 20 September 1990, case C-192/89, *Sevince v Staatssecretaris van Justitie*, 1990 [ECR] I-3461; judgment of 31 January 1991, case C-18/90, *Office national de l'emploi v Kziber*,

The Cooperation Agreements with the Maghreb States[113] as well as the new Euro-Mediterranean Partnership Agreements also contain non-discrimination clauses with regard to working conditions and remuneration for those being legally employed within the Community. Equality provisions are to be found in Article 40 of the EEC-Morocco Agreement, in Article 39(1) of the Agreement with Algeria[114] and in Article 64 of the Euro-Mediterranean Partnership Agreement with Tunisia.[115]

In *Kziber*, for instance, the European Court of Justice held that Article 41(1) of the Agreement with Morocco[116] lays down in a clear, precise and unconditional way a prohibition of discrimination based on nationality against Moroccan nationals and their family members living with them in the field of social security and that this provision is directly applicable in the Member States.[117] The European Court of Justice furthermore considered the material and personal scope of application and decided that the concept of social security in Article 41(1) of the Agreement must be interpreted in analogy with Regulation 1408/71 and referred explicitly to the unemployment benefits mentioned in Article 4 of Regulation 1408/71. As to the personal scope of application, the European Court of Justice held that Article 41(1) of the Agreement includes both active workers and those who have left the labour market, either through retirement or by way of one of the other contingencies covered by social security. The European Court of Justice pointed out that paragraphs 2 and 4 of Article 41 refer explicitly to the aggregation of periods and the possibility of transferring benefits to Morocco in respect of old-age and invalidity pensions and annuities enjoyed by retired workers. The European Court of Justice decided furthermore that the principle of non-discrimination based on nationality means that a person who satisfies all the conditions laid down by national legislation may not be refused unemployment allowances for the benefit of young persons in search of employment on the grounds of nationality.

[1991] ECR I-199; case C-58/93, *Yousfi v Belgian State*, [1994] ECR I-1353; judgment 5 April 1995, case C-103/94, *Krid v CNAVTS*, [1995] ECR I-719; judgment of 3 October 1996 case C-126/95, *Hallouzi-Choho v Bestuur van de Sociale Verzekeringsbank*, [1996] ECR I-4807; judgment of 16 January 1998, case C-113/97, *Henia Bebahenini* v Belgian State, [1998] ECR I-183.

113 Cf. as to the cooperation agreements *Gacon-Estrada*, in Jorens/Schulte (eds.), European Social Security Law and Third-Country Nationals (1998), 323.

114 Similar ton Articles 40 and 41 of the Agreement with Morocco, Articles 39 and 40 relate to social security; decisions implementing the principles governing social security are to be adopted by the Association Council.

115 A joint declaration to Article 64(1) of the Agreement relates to the principle of non-discrimination and the issue of a residence permit: "With regard to the absence of discrimination as regards redundancy, Article 64(1) may not be invoked to obtain renewal of a residence permit. The grating, renewal or refusal of a residence permit shall be governed by the legislation of each Member State and the bilateral agreements and conventions in force between Tunisia and the Member State."

116 Cooperation Agreement between the European Economic Community and the Kingdom of Morocco signed in Rabat on 27 April 1976, O.J. 1978 L 264; a new agreement has been signed on 26 February 1996 (see Chapter C V); as to the legal status under those Agreements cf. *Nadifi*, Revue du Marché commun 1989, 289 et seq.

117 Cf. as to the application of Article 41 (1) in the case of a family member who has acquired Belgian citizenship opinion of Advocate General *Alber* in case C-179/98, *Belgium v Fatna Mesbah*.

In *Yousfi* the European Court of Justice confirmed this view and stated that the term "social security" in Article 41(1) has to be interpreted in the same way as Regulation 1408/71; therefore disability allowances are included.[118] The scope of application was then extended to transitional benefits under the Netherlands Algemene Ouderdomswet. *Hallouzi-Choho* referred to the spouse of a Moroccan worker and the question as to whether stricter requirements for third-country nationals are compatible with Article 41 of the Morocco Agreement –

> The principle laid down in Article 41(1) of the Agreement, of freedom from any discrimination based on nationality in the field of social security against Moroccan and members of their family living with them in relation to nationals of the Member States in which they are employed means that the person referred to by that provision must be treated as if they were nationals of the Member State concerned ... so that the national legislation at issue cannot impose upon those persons more or stricter conditions than those applicable to nationals of that Member State.[119]

In *Krid*[120] the concept of direct applicability of the principle of equality in Article 39(1) was extended by analogy to the Agreement with Algeria, being applicable also to members of workers' families continuing to live in the Member State in which the worker was employed[121]. The substantive scope of application was interpreted in accordance with the existing case-law in analogy with Regulation 1408/71 and the European Court of Justice pointed out that since Regulation 1247/92 had entered into force, benefits such as the supplementary allowance from the National Solidarity Fund are covered as well. In *Babahenini* the European Court of Justice ruled in favor of the spouse of a Algerian worker who had been living in Belgium with her husband who then received a disabled person's allowance without having worked in Belgium herself, being of the opinion that the stricter requirement for the applicant was not compatible with the principle of non-discrimination.[122]

---

[118] ECJ, Case C-58/93, *Zoubir Yousfi v Belgian State*, judgment of 20 April 1994, [1994] ECR I-1353.

[119] ECJ, Case C-126/95 para 35 und 36, *A. Hallouzi-Choho v Bestuur van de Sociale Verzekeringsbank*, judgment of 3 October 1996, [1996] ECR I-4087; cf. annotations by *Burrows*, ELR 1997, 166; *Coustet*, Revue du marché commun unique européen 1996, n° 4, 202; *Eicke*, in Guild (ed.), The Legal Framework and Social Consequences of Free Movement of Persons in the European Union (1999), 89, at 101; *Luby*, Journal du droit international 1997, 575; *Minderhoud*, Rechtspraak Vreemdelingenrecht 1996, 1997, n° 86; *Simon*, Journal du droit international 1997, 511; *Schumacher*, in: Barwig et al. (eds.), Sozialer Schutz von Ausländern in Deutschland (1997), 135 et seq.

[120] Case C-103/94, *Zoulika Krid v Caisse nationale d'assurance vieilesse des travailleurs salariés (CNAVTS)*, judgment of 5 April 1995, [1995] ECR I-719. Cf. annotations by *Bonnet*, Droit du travail et de la sécurité sociale 1995, 248; *Chavrier/Honorat/Pouzoulet*, L'actualité juridique, droit administratif (1995), 714; *Luby*, Journal du droit international 1997, 573; *Restelli*, Les petites affiches 1995, n°107, 6; *van der Steen*, Nederlands tijdschrift voor Europees recht 1995, 78; *Weber*, ZAR 1996, 37.

[121] Cooperation Agreement concluded between the European Communities and the Algerian Republic signed on 26 April 1976 in Algier, entered into force on 1 November 1978, O.J. 1978 L 263.

[122] Case C-113/97, judgment of 15 January 1998, *Henia Babahenini v Belgian State*, [1998] ECR I-183

Since the European Court of Justice referred several times to Regulation 1408/71 when deciding upon the substantive scope of application and the notion of "social security" in the association agreements, the question arose as to whether amendments to Regulation 1408/71 should be incorporated automatically e.g. in Decision 3/80 of the EEC-Turkey Association Council. On the one hand, it has been argued that the Contracting Parties wanted the updated version to be incorporated, except for those "adaptations qui modifient fondamentalement le contenue des dispositions ou (...) adaptations qui ont des conséquences financières importantes"[123]. On the other hand, the view has been expressed that on the basis of the judgment in *Taflan-Met* and an examination of *Babahenini* it "is the Council's turn to adjust the provisions if necessary"[124]. According to the judgment of the European Court of Justice in *El-Yassini*[125] the case-law of the European Court of Justice as to the right to an extension of a residence permit cannot – on grounds of the substantial differences between the wording, the object and the purpose of the rules of the EEC-Turkey Association Agreement and the EEC-Morocco Agreement – be applied by analogy to Article 40(1) of the EEC-Morocco Agreement –

> The first paragraph of Article 40 of the Cooperation Agreement between the European Economic Community and the Kingdom of Morocco, (...) is to be interpreted as not precluding in principle a host Member State from refusing to extend the residence permit of a Moroccon national whom it has authorised to enter its territory and to take up gainful employment there, for the entire period during which he has that employment there, where the initial reason for the grant of his leave to stay no longer exists by the time that his residence permit expires. The situation would be different only, if, in the absence of grounds relating to the protection of a legitimate national interest, such as public policy, public security or public health, that refusal were to affect the right actually to engage in employment conferred on the person concerned by a work permit duly granted by the competent national authorities for a period exceeding that of his residence permit. It is for the national court to determine whether that is the case.

In the Euro-Mediterranean Agreements the principle of non-discrimination is enshrined, for instance, in Article 64 of the Agreement with Tunisia[126] which provides that "the treatment accorded by each Member State to workers of

---

123 *Jorens*, Tijdschrift voor Sociaal Recht, Revue de Droit Social 1997, 183.

124 *Hänlein*, in Jorens/Schulte (eds.), European Social Security Law and Third-Country Nationals (1998), 300, at 308.

125 ECJ, judgment of 2 March 1999, case C-416/96, *El-Yassini v Secretary of State for Home Department*, [1999] ECR, with annotations by *Blazquez Rodriguez*, La ley – Unión europea 1999 n° 4807, 7; *Idot*, Europe 1999 Mai Comm. N° 182, 17 and Comm. N° 173, 12, *Novak*, ELR 1999, 131; see furthermore *Eicke* in Guild (ed.), The Legal Framework and Social Consequences of Persons in the European Union (1999), 89, at 103; *Guild*, in Guild (ed.), The Legal Framework and Social Consequences of Persons in the European Union (1999), 127, at 129.

126 Euro-Mediterranean Partnership Agreement establishing an association between the European Communities and their Member States, of the one part, and the Republic of Tunisia, of the other part, O.J. 1998 L 97/2. This Agreement replaces the Cooperation Agreement of 25 April 1976.

Tunisian nationality employed in its territory shall be free from any distinction based on nationality, as regards working conditions, remuneration and dismissal, relative to its own nationals". Article 64(3) prescribes the same treatment in Tunisia to workers being nationals of a Member State and being employed in its territory. Illegal immigrants are excluded from the personal scope of application (Article 66). Non-discrimination in social security is contained in Article 65(1). According to Article 67(1) the Association Council shall adopt provisions to implement the principles set out in Article 65. As to the direct applicability, a decision by the European Court of Justice has yet to be issued.[127] Subjects covered by the Agreement are sickness and maternity benefits, invalidity, old-age and survivors' benefits, industrial accident and occupational disease benefits and death grants, unemployment and family benefits. Article 65(2) states that periods of insurance, employment or residence completed by such a worker in various Member States shall be added for the purpose of pensions and annuities, that the workers in question shall receive family allowances for members of their families who are resident in the Community, and that workers in question shall be able to transfer freely to Tunisia, at the rates applied by virtue of the legislation of a Member State, any pensions or annuities in respect of the named social security benefits; special non-contributory benefits, however, are exempted.

As to the Europe Agreements with ten states of central and Eastern Europe[128], equal treatment provisions refer to working conditions, remuneration or dismissal for legally employed workers, e.g. Article 37 of the Agreement with Poland.[129] Provisions here are linked to the conditions and modalities applicable in each Member State. Comparing the principle of non-discrimination in the Europe Agreements with Community provisions and the jurisprudence of the European Court of Justice, especially in *Meyers*[130] *Guild* therefore concludes as to the applicability of this provision to social security benefits –

> This would then mean that benefits such as a separation allowance for inconvenience to a migrant worker or family benefits related to employment must be accorded to Polish workers legally employed on the territory of a Member State on a non-discriminatory basis with own nationals. This right of non-discrimination would not of course deal with the issue of aggregation and export of social security contributions and benefits.[131]

---

[127] As to Article 40 of the former Agreement with Tunisia, *Brinkmann* points out that this provision is identical to the clauses in the Algerian and Morocco Agreement; therefore, this provision should have direct effect (in Jorens/Schulte (eds.), European Social Security Law and Third-Country Nationals (1998), 258, at 270).

[128] See *supra* Chapter A IV 2 and Chapter C V 5.

[129] Cf. as to the Europe Agreements *Gargulla*, InfAuslR 1995, 181 et seq.; *Guild*, in Guild (ed.), The Legal Framework and Social Consequences of Free Movement of Persons in the European Union (1999), 127; *Husmann*, in Jorens/Schulte (eds.), European Social Security Law and Third-Country Nationals (1998), 361; *Husmann*, Zeitschrift für Sozialreform 1998, 100; *Maresceau*, in Müller-Graff (ed.), East Central European States and the European Communities: Legal Adaptation to the Market Economy (1993), 209; *Peers*, 32 CML Rev (1995), 187; *Schumacher*, DRV 1993, 681.

[130] ECJ, Case C-116/94, *Meyers*, [1995] ECR I-2131.

[131] *Guild*, in Jorens/Schulte (eds.), European Social Security Law and Third-Country Nationals (1998), 342, at 343.

In addition, *Guild* is of the opinion that the non-discrimination clause in the Agreement with Poland may be capable of having direct effect,[132] in accordance with *Taflan-Met*. However, this effect is deemed unlikely for the social security provision of Article 38 which contains no general provision as to equal treatment.[133] Article 38 of the Agreement with Poland refers to workers of Polish nationality, legally employed in the territory of a Member State and to members of their families legally resident there and provided that all periods of insurance, employment and residence completed by such workers in the various Member States shall be added together for the purpose of pensions and annuities in respect of old age, invalidity and death and for the purpose of medical care for such workers and such family members. Article 38 provides furthermore that any pensions and annuities in respect of old age, death, industrial accident or occupational disease, or of invalidity resulting therefrom, with the exception of non-contributory benefits, shall be freely transferable at the rate applied by virtue of the law of the debtor, Member State or States. Article 39 provides for an implementation by decision of the Association Council.[134]

In the Partnership and Cooperation Agreements with many of the states of the former Soviet Union equal treatment clauses are inserted as well. Article 23 of the Agreement with Russia prescribes equal treatment being applicable to Russian nationals legally employed in the territory of a Member State. Nevertheless, the wording of the provision is different from other Agreements since the Community and the Member States "shall ensure" this aim;[135] moreover, the Cooperation Council shall issue recommendation for its implementation. Article 24 relates to social security; implementation within this field will take place by further agreement between the parties following a recommendation by the Cooperation Council (Article 27). Article 27 also refers to the Cooperation Council the task of examining those improvements which can be made in working conditions for businessmen, but the Council itself is limited to recommendations.

In contrast to the Association Agreements mentioned above, it is unlikely that Annex IV to the Lomé IV Agreement between the ACP countries and the Community should have direct effect and confer individual rights, since according to the wording, workers "shall", as regards social security benefits linked to employment, enjoy treatment free from any discrimination based on nationality.[136]

---

132 *Guild*, in: Jorens/Schulte (eds.), European Social Security Law and Third-Country Nationals (1998), 342, 359.

133 *Guild*, in: Jorens/Schulte (eds.), European Social Security Law and Third-Country Nationals (1998), 342, at 352; in *Guild* in Guild (ed.), The Legal Framework and Social Consequences of Free Movement of Persons in the European Union (1999), 127, at 130, she considers a suggestion of direct applicability as premature.

134 As to the Agreement with Poland see *Husmann*, in Jorens/Schulte (eds.), European Social Security Law and Third-Country Nationals (1998), 361, at 381; *Florek*, ZIAS 1995, 101; *Florek/Uscinska*, in Jorens/Schulte (eds.), European Social Security Law and Third-Country Nationals (1998), 387; Komentarz do Ukladu Europejskiego (Europe Agreement Commentary), 1994; *Soltysinski*, Uklad o stowarzyszeniu miedzy Polska a Wspolnotami europejskimi (Europe Agreement establishing an Association between Poland and the European Communities), Panstwo i Prawo 1992, 13.

135 In Article 19 of the Agreement with the Ukraine the wording is "endeavour to ensure".

136 *Martin and Guild*, however, point out that Annex IV may create direct effect (Free Movement of Persons in the European Union (1996), 293)

d) Equal Treatment after the Gaygusuz Judgment

The judgment of the European Court of Human Rights in *Gaygusuz v. Austria*[137] led to a renewed discussion on equal treatment of third-country nationals[138] since equality of treatment of third-country nationals exists presently only in those cases in which the benefit is not linked to the nationality of the applicant, but is based on contributions, insurance payments, residence requirements, etc. The principle of equal treatment is to be found in the opinion of the Commission as follows –

> If foreign citizens are permitted to enter and to work in a country, and if they make payments into the prevailing system of insurance on the same basis as nationals, the difference in treatment [based on nationality] does not appear to have objective and reasonable justification.[139]

In the *Gayusuz* judgment the Court considered the Austrian emergency assistance as a pecuniary right falling within the scope of "possession" in Article 1 of Protocol No. 1 to the European Convention of Human Rights and could not see any objective and reasonable justification as to the different treatment between Austrians and non-Austrians. The question arose as to whether this judgment might entail any consequences for the existing Community provisions governing social security.

As mentioned above, even if the Community itself did not accede to the Convention, human rights are respected and mentioned in the treaties and the case-law of the European Court of Justice. Nevertheless, Advocate-General *Darmon* stated in *Orkem* that the Court is not bound by the case-law of the European Court of Human Rights[140]. The European Commission on Human Rights, on the other hand, recalled in its decision of 9 February 1990 "that if a State contracts treaty obligations and subsequently concludes another international agreement which disables it from performing its obligations under the first treaty, it will be answerable for any resulting breach of its obligations under the earlier treaty."[141] In principle, the European Court of Justice would therefore be free to consider whether entitlement to benefits based on contributions constitutes "possessions."[142] As to the principle of equal treatment, it is argued that this principle is part of the constitutions of the Member States, of international instruments and Community

---

[137] European Court of Human Rights, judgment of 16 September 1996, *Gaygusuz v Austria*, application no. 39/1995/545/631, RJD 1996-IV 1129.

[138] Cf. as to the decision of the European Court of Human Rights *van den Bogaert* (ed.), Social Security, Non-Discrimination And Property (1997); *Brinkmann*, in Jorens/Schulte (eds.), European Social Security Law and Third-Country Nationals (1998), 257, 278; *Hailbronner*, JZ 1997, 397 et seq.; *Peers*, 22 ELR (1997) 342, at 350; *Sieveking*, in Jorens/Schulte (eds.), European Social Security Law and Third-Country Nationals (1998), 235, at 255; *Verschueren*, 34 CML Rev. (1997) 991 et seq.; *Verschueren*, in van den Bogaert (ed.), Social Security, Non-Discrimination and Property (1997), 99 et seq.

[139] *Gaygusuz v Austria* RJD 1996-IV 1129 para. 50.

[140] Opinion of the Advocate-General, case 374/87, *Orkem v Commission*, [1989] ECR 3283,

[141] European Commission of Human Rights, decision of 9 February 1990, No. 13258/87, *M & Co. v Germany*, 64 DR 138-146 (1990).

[142] *Brinkmann*, in Jorens/Schulte (eds.), European Social Security Law and Third-Country Nationals (1998), 257, at 278/279.

law and is therefore to be applied[143] on the basis of references to the European Court of Justice's judgment in *Weiser*[144] where this principle was applied to pension rights and a Communication of the UN Human Rights Committee[145]. The question as to whether this should result in the extension of provisions to third-country nationals is left undecided –

> With regard to the analysis made above and to the delicate position of the final judge in this matter, the Court of Justice, it does not seem possible to give a final answer on the question of whether the exclusion of third-country nationals from the scope of Regulation 1408/71 is compatible with fundamental rights. Even if it appears that the answer should be negative.[146]

It is even suggested that the proposed extension of the Regulation 1408/71 might entail an infringement of human rights in cases in which nationals of Member States of the Council of Europe who are Contracting Parties to the European Convention on Social Security or the Interim Agreements – together with bilateral agreements – are treated more favorably than under Community law[147]. As to the situation of Turkish nationals within the Community, Decision No. 3/80 of the Association Council guarantees equal treatment to Turkish nationals within most social security schemes, although different treatment still persists when exporting child allowance or unemployment benefits. Referring to this Decision, the European Court of Justice decided on 10 September 1996[148] that Decision No. 3/80 is legally binding on the Member States, but that it shall not take direct effect or be directly applicable prior to the implementing of appropriate measures in the Member States. In the light of *Gaygusuz*, however, this might change.

As to the distinction between contributory and non-contributory security schemes it should be mentioned that – even if the judgment of the ECHR is not particularly clear – the link between the payment of contributions and the grant of benefits seems to be of some importance; as to the application of Regulation 1408/71 *Verschueren* points to the European Court of Justice case-law holding that a benefit is to be regarded as a social security benefit if it is granted to recipients without any individual and discretionary assessment of personal needs on the basis of a legally defined position and if it concerns one of the risks expressly listed in Article 4(1) of Regulation 1408/71[149] and states –

---

143 *Verschueren*, 34 CML Rev. (1997) 991, at 1009.

144 ECJ, judgment of 14 June 1989, Case C-37/89; *Weiser v Caisse nationale des barraux francais*, [1990] ECR I-2395.

145 Communication of CCPR No. 196/1985, *Gueye and others v France*, 11 HRLJ (1990), 150.

146 *Verschueren*, in van den Bogaert (ed.), Social Security, Non-Discrimination and Property (1997), 99, 119. Cf. as to the risk of a double standard according to which the outcome would depend on whether the state is a member of the European Union or not *Aksay*, in van den Bogaert (ed.), Social Security, Non-Discrimination And Property (1997), 45, at 49.

147 *Van der Steen*, in van den Bogaert (ed.), Social Security, Non-Discrimination and Property (1997), 121, at 122.

148 ECJ, judgment of 10 September 1996, case C-277/94, *Taflan-Met v Bestuur van de Sociale Verzekeringsbank and another*, [1996] ECR I-4085.

149 ECJ, judgment of 10 October 1996, cases C-24/94 and C-312/94, *Ingrid Hoever and Iris Zachow v Land Nordrhein-Westfalen*, [1996] ECR I-4895. Cf. also *Becker*, Die Sozialgerichtsbarkeit 1998, 553; *Eichenhofer*, Europäische Zeitschrift für Wirtschaftsrecht 1996, 716; *Eichenhofer*, Die

> Therefore, it seems difficult to advocate the extension of the personal scope of Regulation 1408/71 to third-country nationals on the basis of the reasoning of the European Human Rights Court in the Gaygusuz case. Apparently, in this case the Court criticized discrimination based on nationality in social security because there was a link tocontri butions paid by the beneficiary. (...) However, if the Gaygusuz judgment has to be interpreted as meaning that social security rights are to be considered as property rights because of their pecuniary nature, without any link to the payment of taxes or contributions, then the rights following from Regulation 1408/71 would also come under the notion of property rights of Article 1 of Protocol No. 1. In that case, the non-discrimination provision of Article 14 ECHR should also be applied to Regulation 1408/71.[150]

IV. Social Rights within the Council of Europe

In addition to the protection of social rights within the Community legislation, particularly measures to coordinate, and possibly harmonize, different social security schemes, social rights are also protected under the European Convention of Human Rights and in the European Social Charter. On the occasion of the second Summit of Heads of State and Government of the Council of Europe's Member States in Strasbourg on 10-11 October 1997, the Heads of State declared *inter alia* "that social cohesion is one of the foremost needs of the wider Europe and should be pursued as an essential complement to the promotion of human rights and dignity". The Action Plan appended to the declaration also related to social rights –

> Promotion of social rights: the Heads of State and Government undertake to promote social standards as embodied in the Social Charter and in other Council of Europe instruments, and call for the widest possible adherence to these instruments; they resolve to improve the exchange of good practice and information between Member States and to intensify their cooperation in this field. (...) New strategy for social cohesion: the Heads of State and Government instruct the Committee of Ministers to define a social strategy to respond to the challenges in society and to carry out the appropriate structural reforms within the Council of Europe, including the setting up of a specialised unit for monitoring, comparing and handling issues linked to social cohesion.

Sozialgerichtsbarkeit 1997, 449; *Hopkins*, The Journal of Social Welfare & Family Law 1997, 513; *Novak*, St. Galler Europarechtsbriefe 1996, 398; *Verschueren*, 34 CML Rev. (1997) 991, at 1011.

150 *Verschueren*, 34 CML Rev (1997) 991, at 1012, and 1013; similarly *Sieveking*, in Jorens/Schulte (eds.), European Social Security Law and Third-Country Nationals (1998), 235, at 255.

1. Social Rights according to the European Convention on Human Rights

Despite the fact that the European Convention on Human Rights[151] protects classic fundamental rights, which primarily regulate infringements on the rights of the individual by the state[152], it may also be applied to issues concerning social benefits[153], e.g. if the applicant refers to Article 6 or Article 14 of the Convention, which provide for equal treatment ("the enjoyment of the rights and freedoms set forth in the Convention shall be secured without discrimination on any ground such as national ... or social origin"), or Article 1 of Protocol No. 1[154] to the Convention securing the peaceful enjoyment of possessions[155]. The Parliamentary Assembly being aware of this lack of social rights within the European Convention Human Rights therefore adopted on 23 June 1999 Resolution No. 1415 relating to additional protocols in the field of social rights[156].

Before the judgment in *Gaygusuz v Austria*, it was mainly the Commission[157] that decided as to whether social benefits fall within the scope of application of the term "possessions" in the First Protocol[158].

---

151 Cf. as to Protocol No. 11 and the revised supervisory system *Drzemczewski*, 1997 EJIL 59 et seq.; *Eissen*, Bulletin des droits de l'homme 1995, 3 et seq.; *Golsong*, Human Rights Law Journal 1992, 265 et seq.; *Malinverni*, Schweizerisches Zentralblatt für Staats- und Verwaltungsrecht 1997, 289 et seq.; *Schlette*, ZaöRV 1996, 905 et seq.

152 *Villiger*, Handbuch der Europäischen Menschenrechtskonvention (EMRK) (1993), 86, 384.

153 Cf. for the control mechanisms and the merger of the Commission and the European Court of Human Rights after Protocol No. 11 (ETS No. 155) Council of Europe, Short Guide to the European Convention on Human Rights, 1998, 137; *Drzemczewski*, 143 New Law Journal (1993) 125 et seq.; *Golsong*, 13 HRLJ (1992) 265 et seq.; *Drzemcewski*, Revista IIDH 1995, 47 et seq.; *Gomien/Harris/*Zwaak, Law and Practice of the European Convention on Human Rights and the European Social Charter (1996), 31; *Malanczuk*, Akehurst's Modern Introduction to International Law, 7th revised edition, (1997), 218.

154 Cf. as to the protection of property *Condorelli*, in Pettiti et al. (eds.), La Convention Européenne des droits de l'homme (1995), 971 et seq.; Council of Europe, Short guide to the European Convention on Human Rights (1998); *Jacobs/White*, The European Convention on Human Rights, 2nd ed. (1996), 248 et seq.; *Gelinsky*, Der Schutz des Eigentums gemäß Article 1 des Ersten Zusatzprotokolls zur Europäischen Menschenrechtskonvention (1996), 29 et seq.; *Gomien/Harris/ Zwaak*, Law and practice of the European Convention on Human Rights and the European Social Charter (1996), 311 et seq.; *Lemmens*, in van den Bogaert (ed.), Social Security, Non-Discrimination and Property (1997), 25, 26; *Peukert*, in *Frowein/Peukert* (eds.), Europäische Menschenrechts-konvention, EMRK-Kommentar, 2nd edition, (1996), 772 et seq.; Villiger Handbuch der Europäischen Menschenrechtskonvention (EMRK), (1993), 384 et seq.; *Scheinin/Krause*, in van den Bogaert (ed.), Social Security, Non-Discrimination And Property (1997), 59 et seq.. As to social rights and property in different countries cf. *Kjonstad*, in van den Bogaert (ed.), Social Security, Non-Discrimination and Property (1997), 75 et seq.; as to discrimination in domestic social security systems *von Maydell*, in van den Bogaert (ed.), Social Security, Non-Discrimination and Property (1997), 89 et seq.

155 "Every natural or legal person is entitled to the peaceful enjoyment of his possessions. No one shall be deprived of his possessions except in the public interest and subject to the conditions provided for by law and by general principles of international law. (...)"

156 EuroAS 1999, 135.

157 Cf. as to the case-law of the Court and the Commission *Enrich i Mas*, Revue trim. Des droit de l'homme 1992, 147 et seq.

158 *Lemmens*, in van den Bogaert (ed.), Social Security, Non-Discrimination and Property (1997), 25, at 30.

The Commission has maintained that social security benefits such as the right to a pension[159] might be considered as "possessions" within the meaning of Article 1 of Protocol No. 1. In *Stigson v. Sweden* the Commission stated –

> However, the Commission has considered that the right to a pension which is based on employment can in certain circumstances be assimilated to a property right. This may be the case where special contributions have been paid or the employer as in the present case, has given a more general undertaking to pay a pension on conditions which can be considered to be part of the employment contract. (...)[160]

The Commission considers Article 1 as applicable if the beneficiary (or a third person on his behalf) contributes to these payments[161], and if there is a direct link between the amount of the contribution and the amount of the benefit such that the beneficiary has an "identifiable and claimable share in the fund" –

> The Commission has next examined the applicant's complaints under Article 1 of Protocol No. 1, and notes that the social security legislation concerned, (...) is set up as a general insurance (Volksverzekering) based on the principle of social solidarity. No direct link exists between the level of contributions and the benefits awarded. Consequently, a person does not have, at any given moment, an identifiable and claimable share in the fund. [162]
>
> Therefore, the Commission is of the opinion that, under the circumstances presented above, the right to benefits cannot be considered a property right and be described as 'possessions' within the meaning of Article 1 of Protocol No. 1 to the Convention. Accordingly, the applicant's complaints under Article 1 of Protocol No. 1 to the Convention must be rejected under Article 27 para. 2 of the Convention as *rationae materiae* incompatible with the provisions of the Convention.[163]

With regard to the amount of the benefit to be awarded, the Commission held in *Müller v Austria* that evidence that the applicant paid contributions to the social

---

[159] Cf. case of *Anna Claes v Belgium*, 44 DR (1997) 88, 94. The Commission pointed out that the right to unemployment benefits cannot itself be considered a right of property, but, that "when, as in Belgium, the body responsible for paying unemployment benefits is partly financed by the National Security Office, to which the applicant paid contributions as a worker, the question may arise whether unemployment benefits could be considered 'possessions' within the meaning of Article 1 of Protocol 1."

[160] 43 DR (1986) 131, 132; cf. furthermore *J.W. and E.W. v United Kingdom*, 40 DR (1983) 153, 154, and *Peukert*, in Frowein/Peukert (eds.), Europäische Menschenrechtskonvention, EMRK-Kommentar, 2nd ed. (1996), 772.

[161] There is no established case-law as to the qualification of the so-called "mixed benefits"; in *G. v Austria*, 38 DR (1984) 84, the Commission ruled that a claim of entitlement to a survivor's pension for civil servant does not constitute a possession attracting the protection of this provision where, as in Austria, these pensions are based on the principle of maintenance and are not entirely founded by prior contributions.

[162] Cf. case of *X. v The Netherlands*, 28 CD (1987) 224, 244.

[163] *F.P.J.M. Kleine Staarmann v The Netherlands*, 42 DR (1985) 162, 166; cf. *Hendrika Sophia Vos v The Netherlands* (1985), 191.

insurance scheme does not necessarily entitle him to an award of a particular amount –

> Now, whereas it is conceivable that the right of a beneficiary to an old age insurance system to which one has paid contributions is a right of ownership guaranteed by Article 1 of the First Protocol, the same is not necessarily true where the exact amount of the pension is concerned. The Commission considers that even if it is assumed that Article 1 of the First Protocol guaranteed persons who have paid contributions to a social insurance system the right to derive benefits from the system, it cannot be interpreted as entitling that person to a pension of a particular amount.[164]

The Commission argues that the operation of a social security system is fundamentally different from the management of a private life insurance company. It points to the fact that, because of its public importance, the social security system must take political decisions into account, especially those relating to financial policy. According to the Commission, it should be conceivable that a deflationary trend may oblige States to reduce the nominal amount of pensions[165].

The minority opinion of the Commission in *Feldbrugge*[166], which addressed the issues of health insurance and sickness allowances, did not reflect this distinction[167]. They draw attention to the fact that particularly in the area of sickness and accident insurance, benefits are financed by contributions directly or indirectly deducted from the workers' remuneration, and that individual deductions are calculated based on a pecuniary estimate of foreseeable risk using the same method as that employed by private insurance companies to calculate premiums[168]. The Commission concluded as follows –

> 17. The position is not fundamentally different in the Deumeland case where the scheme is funded by an appropriation in the Land's budget. In substance, it may be considered that this appropriation constitutes a part of the remuneration for the services performed by the workers.
>
> The fact that in certain cases the scheme is also funded by State contributions in addition to those of the employers and workers does not substantially alter the nature of the scheme involved which remains an insurance scheme. The State's role might be compared to that of a 'reinsurer' in private insurance.
>
> It follows that in substance there is no difference in nature between a public insurance scheme and a private insurance scheme as regards the technique for covering the risks.[169]

---

[164] 32 DR (1975) 25, 31; cf. furthermore *J.W. and E.W. v United Kingdom*, 40 DR (1983) 153, 154.

[165] Cf. *van den Broek*, Legal Issues of European Integration, (1986), 52, 68: *Gelinsky*, Der Schutz des Eigentums gemäß Article 1 des Ersten Zusatzprotokolls zur Europäischen Menschenrechtskonvention, (1996), 41, who favours equal treatment of both private and public insurance schemes.

[166] Cf. for the Report of the Commission Decisions of the European Court of Human Rights of 27 February 1985, Series A, No. 99, 32.

[167] Decision of the European Court of Human Rights of 29 May 1986, Series A, No. 99, 41.

[168] P. 42, para 16 of the Commission's Minority Opinion.

[169] P. 43.

The Commission dealt with the issue of export of social security benefits in *J.W. and E.W. v United Kingdom*, in which the applicants had moved to Australia[170]. In its decision, the Commission held that "even if the right to benefit from a scheme will normally also apply to an increase in regular cases, this is not necessarily the case where a person leaves the country where the specific schemes operates."[171] The Commission offered the following opinions on whether this differential treatment could amount to a discrimination according to Article 14 of the Convention: "it is almost inevitable that, where a person in effect changes from one social security system to another, he may find that his entitlements differ from those of persons in other countries", and that "the applicants will only lose the benefit of future increases in their pensions, whose purpose broadly speaking is to compensate for rises in the cost of living in the United Kingdom." There is an objective and reasonable justification for restricting the scope of their entitlement under the United Kingdom system; such restrictions, therefore, do not violate Article 14 of the Convention.

In *Gaygusuz v Austria*[172], the European Court of Human Rights took a slightly different approach as to the existing case-law of the Commission when interpreting the notion of "possession" in Protocol No. 1 to the European Convention. The case related to the questions of whether emergency assistance paid in Austria falls within the meaning of "possessions" in Article 1 of the First Protocol and whether equal treatment for the applicant, a third-country national, should be granted. The question arose when the applicant, a Turkish national who had worked in Austria for several years, applied for an advance on his pension in the form of emergency assistance (Notstandshilfe). Emergency assistance is paid to persons who are no longer entitled to unemployment benefit in order to guarantee them a minimum income; it is funded by contributions, as well as by additional state aid. The minimum amount granted is 75 per cent of the previously granted unemployment benefit. The competent Employment Agency rejected the application on the grounds that the applicant was not an Austrian national or EU citizen, which was one of the conditions laid down in Section 33(2) of Austria's 1977 Unemployment Insurance Act for entitlement to an allowance of that type.

When addressing the meaning of "possession" in Article 1 of Protocol No. 1, the Court pointed to the fact that emergency assistance was granted to persons who had exhausted their entitlement to unemployment benefits and who satisfied the statutory conditions. Entitlement to the benefits was thus linked to the payment of unemployment contributions to the unemployment fund. Therefore, no entitlement takes place in cases in which such contributions have not been made. The

---

170 40 DR (1983) 153; cf. for further case-law of the Commission within the field of social security Peukert, in *Frowein/Peukert* (eds.), Europäische Menschenrechtskonvention, EMRK-Kommentar (1996), 773.

171 40 CD (1983) 153, 154.

172 Decision of 16 September 1996, No. 39/1995/545/631, Reports of Judgments and Decisons 1996-IV; cf. *van den Bogaert* (ed.), Social Security, Non-Discrimination and Property (1997); *Hailbronner*, JZ 1997, 397 et seq.; *Verschueren*, 34 CML Rev. (1997) 991 et seq.; *Schumacher*, in: Barwig et al. (eds.), Sozialer Schutz von Ausländern in Deutschland (1997), 135, at 144-148; *Verschueren*, in van den Bogaert (ed.), Social Security, Non-Discrimination and Property (1997), 99 et seq.

European Court of Human Rights then stated – in a different approach to the Commission when requiring a "direct link"- that it was not necessary to rely solely on the link between an entitlement to emergency assistance and the obligations to pay taxes or other contributions, but that the right to emergency assistance as provided for in the applicable legislation was of pecuniary nature[173]. Taking into account that the applicant would have had a right according the existing legislation, provided that he was in possession of Austrian nationality, this conclusion seems to correspond to the Court's approach under the "legitimate expectations" doctrine[174]. The consequences of this judgment are not yet absolutely clear. It has been concluded from the fact that the Court qualified the benefits in question (the so called "follow-up benefits") as social security and not social assistance benefits, that the result might be that many benefits which are regarded as social assistance benefits under national legislation and which are intended to provide a minimum means of subsistence will now fall under the scope of the right of possession[175]. Nevertheless, the Court is not very clear as to which benefits should be regarded as a pecuniary right. Nevertheless, the view prevails that "benefits which are not financed by individual contributions and which are not linked to other social security benefits or which do not supplement an insufficient amount of social security benefit, do not fall under the protection of the right of possession within the meaning of the European Convention of Human Rights."[176]

As to the principle of equal treatment, the Court did not follow the reasoning of the Austrian government, which argued that differential treatment was based on the idea that the state has special responsibilities towards its own nationals, and must take care of them and provide for their essential needs[177]. The Court viewed this argument as unpersuasive and ruled that, as the applicant was legally resident in Austria and had contributed to the unemployment fund in the same capacity and on the same basis as Austrian nationals, the difference in treatment between Austrians and non-Austrians regarding entitlement to emergency assistance was not based on any "objective and reasonable justification" since the applicant was legally resident in Austria and had worked there at certain times, had paid contributions to the unemployment insurance fund in the same capacity and on the same basis as Austrian nationals, had satisfied the conditions for the award of the social benefits in question and was therefore in the same situation as an Austrian national. Furthermore, the applicant did not fall into any of the relevant statutory categories

---

173 Para 41.

174 ECHR 29 November 1991, *Pine Valley Developments*, Publ. Court., Series A, no. 222, 23, § 51; ECHR, 20 November 1995, *Pressos Compania naviera*, Publ, Court. Series A, no. 332, 21, § 31. Cf. *van den Bogaert*, in van den Bogaert (ed.), Social Security, Non-Discrimination and Property (1997), 123, at 126; *Lemmens*, in van den Bogaert (ed.), Social Security, Non-Discrimination and Property (1997), 25, at 31.

175 *Jorens*, in van den Bogaert (ed.), Social Security, Non-Discrimination and Property (1997), 15, at 19.

176 *Jorens*, in van den Bogaert (ed.), Social Security, Non-Discrimination and Property (1997), 15, 19.

177 Para 50.

excluding the grant of those benefits. Subsequently, the European Court of Human Rights awarded the applicant the sum of ATS 200,000 (~ €14,500)[178].

In terms of the impact of this decision, not only the consequences for Community law are discussed, but it has even been suggested as a consequence of *Gaygusuz* that existing differentiations in the allocation of social security or social assistance, based on citizenship, nationality or EU citizenship, need to be abolished. Differentiation based on the duration of stay or work in the country, or on lawfully determined residence permit classifications, should probably be acceptable as long as such criteria are applied in an objective and reasonable way[179]. It is even asked whether *Gaygusuz* might be the starting point for the drafting of a whole new code of social security law[180].

2. *The European Interim Agreements on Social Security Schemes*

Two Interim Agreements[181] on social security schemes have been ratified (or signed) by several Western and European states. Both Agreements were signed on 11 December 1953[182]. They are in force in 17 Member States[183] and have been signed by the Czech Republic and Lithuania. A protocol to each agreement extends the personal scope of application to refugees[184]. Since most of the Contracting Parties are now Members of the European Union (or the EEA), where Regulation 1408/71 is applicable, the Interim Agreements are of particular importance for Turkish and Cypriot nationals[185], as well as for nationals of Eastern and Central European states. An explanatory report was drawn up in 1998 in order to facilitate their signature and ratification[186]. Despite the fact that there are special agreements for the central and Eastern European States, the compliance with the Interim Agreements might provide for further rights, since, for instance, in contrast to Article 2 of the Interim Agreements containing the principle of equal treatment, no

---

[178] Cf. as to the amount of damages awarded the dissenting opinion by judge *Matscher* as to the Austrian background and the consequences of this judgment for Austria *Mazal*, in van den Bogaert (ed.), Social Security, Non-Discrimination and Property (1997), 51 et seq.

[179] *Scheinin/Krause*, in van den Bogaert (ed.), Social Security, Non-Discrimination and Property (1997), 59, at 73.

[180] *Lemmens*, in van den Bogaert (ed.), Social Security, Non-Discrimination and Property (1997), 25, 33; cf. as to the possible consequences also *Stahlberg*, EuroAS 1997, 119, at 121.

[181] Cf. *Remmert*, in Jorens/Schulte (eds.), European Social Security Law and Third-Country Nationals (1998), 468, 473-477; *Schumacher*, in: Barwig et al. (eds.), Sozialer Schutz von Ausländern in Deutschland (1997), 135, at 138-143.

[182] ETS Nos. 12 and 13.

[183] These are Belgium, Cyprus, Denmark, France, Germany, Greece, Iceland, Ireland, Italy, Luxembourg, the Netherlands, Norway, Portugal, Spain, Sweden, Turkey and the United Kingdom.

[184] ETS No. 12 A and No. 13 A.

[185] *Schumacher*, in: Barwig et al. (eds.), Sozialer Schutz von Ausländern in Deutschland (1997), 135, at 139.

[186] SS-AC-Committee (sub-committee to the CDSS); cf. *Remmert*, The Contribution of the Council of Europe to European Coordination Law, in *Jorens/Schulte* (eds.), European Social Law and Third Country Nationals (1998), 467, 476.

such provision has been enshrined in the Agreements with Eastern and Central European States[187].

The first Agreement focuses on social security schemes relating to old age, invalidity and survivors, and entitles nationals of any of the Parties to receive the benefit of the laws and regulations of any other Party under the same conditions as nationals of the latter Party, assuming that they fulfil certain residence requirements. The second Interim Agreement covers all remaining social security schemes and contains similar provisions for those fields. Despite efforts at the Community level to this purpose, schemes for civil servants are not included in these Agreements. The residence requirement is not defined within the convention. Nevertheless, during the drafting of the Agreements, the Contracting Parties held that temporary or occasional residence did not constitute ordinary residence[188]. Residence requirements differ from one Agreement to the other and are to be reduced in cases of occupational injury benefits.

The Interim Agreements are applicable solely to nationals of the Contracting Parties. Therefore, other third-country nationals are not covered by those provisions. On the other hand, the agreements have been partially supplemented by bilateral conventions which offer the same scope of protection for the insured person. It is suggested that third-country nationals covered by such agreements fall within the scope of application of Regulation 1408/71, on the grounds that Article 3 provides for the application of "any agreement relating to the laws and regulations referred to in Article 1 which has been or may be concluded by any two or more of the Contracting Parties". Nevertheless, it should be noted that Regulation 1408/71 does not constitute a treaty under public international law. This view was rejected by the CDSS in 1993[189]. The same applies for the Association Agreements (including the Europe Agreements with Central and Eastern European States) since they – according to the case-law of the European Court of Justice – also form a part of Community law[190].

3. *The European Convention on Social Security*

The European Convention on Social Security[191] is supplemented by an Agreement for the Application of the European Convention on Social Security[192]. This Convention was designed to replace the two Interim Agreements (Article 76).

---

187 Cf. *Remmert*, The Contribution of the Council of Europe to European Coordination Law, in Jorens/Schulte (eds.), European Social Law and Third Country Nationals (1998), 467, 477; as to the principle of equal treatment in the Interim Agreements cf. *Schumacher*, in: Barwig et al. (eds.), Sozialer Schutz von Ausländern in Deutschland (1997), 135, at 141.

188 Cf. *Remmert*, The Contribution of the Council of Europe to European Coordination Law, in Jorens/Schulte (eds.), European Social Law and Third Country Nationals (1998), 467, 475.

189 CDSS (93) 6, The European Interim Agreements on Social Security: Legal aspects and possibilities for ratification by Central and Eastern European States, 5.

190 ECJ, judgment of 31 January 1991, case 18/90, *Kziber v Office national d'emploi* , [1991] ECR I-199.

191 ETS No. 78. Cf. *Remmert*, The Contribution of the Council of Europe to European Coordination Law, in Jorens/Schulte (eds.), European Social Law and Third Country Nationals (1998), 467, 478.

192 ETS No. 154.

Convention No. 118 of the ILO on equality of treatment (social security), Regulation 3 of the Council of the European Community on Social Security for Migrant Workers and revisions on the latter instrument were also taken into account[193]. Principles governing this instrument are: equality of treatment, unity of applicable legislation, maintenance of acquired rights or rights in the process of being acquired and the export of benefits. The Convention does not effect obligations under ILO conventions or Community law. On the other hand, in cases in which Community law is not applicable and the person concerned is a non-privileged third-country national, this Convention on Social Security could be applicable.

Some of the provisions of the Convention are directly applicable, such as the general provisions and the rules for determining the applicable legislation as well as for the opening of rights and calculation of benefits. Other provisions which are not directly applicable serve as a model for subsequent bilateral and multilateral agreements[194].

According to Article 2, the Convention applies to all legislation governing the following branches of social security: sickness and maternity benefits, invalidity benefits, old-age benefits, survivors` benefits, benefits for occupational injuries and disease, death grants, unemployment benefits and family benefits. The application of the Convention does not depend on whether the social security scheme is a general or a special one, or whether it is contributory or non-contributory[195].

As to the personal scope of application, the Convention is applicable for all nationals of the Contracting Parties, for refugees and stateless persons residing in the territory of a Contracting State, as well as for the survivors of third-country nationals who were subject to the legislation of one or more of the Contracting Parties, provided that the survivors themselves are nationals of the Contracting Party (Article 4). The personal scope of application is broadened, however, by a Protocol which provides that the provisions of the Convention are to apply to all persons who are or have been subject to the legislation of one or more of the Contracting Parties as well as to the members of their families and their survivors[196]. Nevertheless, the Protocol allows the Contracting Parties to make a declaration that they apply Article 8 and/or Article 11 of the Convention which deal with equal treatment of persons to whom the Convention applies and with the export of benefits payable in the territory of a Contracting Party, respectively, only to persons originally covered by the Convention.

---

193 Cf. also *Remmert*, in The Contribution of the Council of Europe to European Coordination Law, in Jorens/Schulte (eds.), European Social Law and Third Country Nationals (1998), 467, 478.

194 *Remmert*, The Contribution of the Council of Europe to European Coordination Law, in Jorens/Schulte (eds.), European Social Law and Third Country Nationals (1998), 467, 478/479.

195 It is not applicable to social or medical assistance schemes, to benefit schemes for victims of war or its consequences, or to special schemes for civil servants or persons treated as such.

196 ETS No. 154. The Protocol was opened for signature on 11 May 1994 and has so far been signed by Austria, Greece and Luxembourg.

4. *The European Social Charter and the Revised Social Charter*

The European Social Charter of 1961 being in force in 22 Member States of the Council of Europe[197] is the sister treaty to the European Convention on Human Rights. Despite the similarities between some provisions and Community law, an adhesion to the European Social Charter has not been realized[198].

The European Social Charter names 19 fundamental rights grouped in Part I and Part II of the Charter[199]. Part I is a declaration of the aims which the Contracting Parties will pursue by all appropriate means (Article 20 (1) (a)), whereas Part II contains detailed articles. According to Part III of the Charter, the Contracting Parties consider themselves bound by at least five of the most important articles[200] and by not less than ten articles or numbered paragraphs of Part II of the Charter which they may select themselves. The right to social security is enshrined in Article 12 –

> With a view to ensuring the effective exercise of the right to social security, the Contracting Parties undertake
>
> 1. to establish or maintain a system of social security;
>
> 2. to maintain the social security system at a satisfactory level at least equal to that required for ratification of International Labour Convention (No. 102) Concerning Minimum Standards of Social Security;
>
> 3. to endeavour to raise progressively the system of social security to a higher level;
>
> 4. to take steps, by the conclusion of appropriate bilateral and multilateral agreements, or by other means, and subject to the conditions laid down in such agreements, in order to ensure –
>
> > (a) equal treatment with their own nationals of the nationals of other Contracting Parties in respect of social security rights, including the retention of benefits arising out of social security legislation, whatever

---

197 ETS No. 35; The ESC is in force for: Austria, Belgium, Cyprus, Denmark, Finland, France, Germany, Greece, Iceland, Ireland, Italy, Luxembourg, Malta, the Netherlands, Norway, Poland, Portugal, Slovakia, Spain, Sweden, Turkey, the United Kingdom. It has been signed by the Czech Republic, Hungary, Latvia, Liechtenstein, Romania, Slovakia, Switzerland, the "Former Yugoslav Republic of Macedonia" and the Ukraine.

198 Cf. *Fonteneau*, in Council of Europe (ed.), The Social Charter of the 21st Century (1997), 80, at 81, and *de Schutter*, in Council of Europe (ed.), The Social Charter of the 21st Century (1997), 154, at 161 and 164, he states that an adhesion could be possible since the supervisory systems of both treaties are not comparable and the rules elaborated by the ECJ in its opinion of 28 May 1996 thus are not applicable to the ESC. The two systems, especially cases relating to gender equality and positive measures aiming at removing *de facto* inequalities are discussed by *de Schutter* on p. 163.

199 Cf. as to the European Social Charter *Harris*, The Eurpean Social Charter, 19874; *Wiebringhaus* in Baer-Kaupert (ed.), Die Sozialcharta des Europarates Essays in honour of C.H. Aubin (1979), 265; for the ESC and ILO instruments *Kahn-Freud*, in: Jacobs (ed.), European Law and the Individual (1976), 181 et seq.; *Lidal*, in: Council of Europe (ed.), The Social Charter of the 21st Century (1997), 70, at 73.

200 Articles 1, 5, 6, 12, 13, 16 and 19.

movements the persons protected may undertake between the territories of the Contracting Parties;

(b) the granting, maintenance and resumption of social security rights by such means as the accumulation of insurance or employment periods completed under the legislation of each of the Contracting Parties.[201]

Four more rights are to be found in an Additional Protocol of 1988:[202]

- the right to equal opportunities and equal treatment in matters of employment;
- the right to be informed and to be consulted within the undertaking;
- the right to take part in the determination and improvement of the working conditions and working environment in the undertaking[203]; and
- the right of every elderly person to social protection[204].

The general application of the Charter and the Additional Protocol is subject to the principle that the enjoyment of the social rights laid down must be guaranteed "without discrimination on grounds of race, color, sex, religion, political opinion, national extraction or social origin"[205]. According to the appendix, which forms an integral part of the Charter (Article 38), "without prejudice to Article 12, para. 4, and Article 13, para. 4, the persons covered by Articles 1 to 17 include foreigners only insofar as they are nationals of other Contracting Parties lawfully resident or working regularly within the territory of the Contracting Party concerned (...)." A treatment as favorable as possible should be granted to refugees as defined in the Geneva Convention staying lawfully in the territory of a Contracting State. A similar provision as to stateless person may be found in the Appendix to the Revised Social Charter.

As to the personal scope of application, the Charter itself uses terms like "everyone", "all workers and their dependants" and "all workers and employers." However, the Appendix, being an integral part of the Charter, defines the personal scope in a narrow sense since foreigners are included in Articles 1 to 17 only "insofar as they are nationals of the Contracting Parties lawfully resident or working regularly within the territory of the Contracting Parties concerned, subject to the understanding that these articles are to be interpreted in the light of the provisions of Articles 18 and 19." The above-mentioned provisions of the Charter are therefore not applicable if the citizen of a state who has not ratified the Charter

---

201 With regard to social security provisions in Community law and other international instruments, *Vandamme*, for instance, points out that "social security has not figured prominently in the jurisprudence of the Charter (...)." (133 ILR (1994) 635, at 639).

202 ETS No. 128; it has been ratified by Denmark, Finland, Greece, Italy, the Netherlands, Norway, Slovakia and Sweden, and signed by Austria, Belgium, Cyprus, the Czech Republic, France, Germany, Iceland, Latvia, Luxembourg, Slovenia, Spain, the former Yugoslav Republic of Macedonia and Turkey.

203 Cf. as to safe and healthy working conditions under Community legislation *supra* II 1. *Vandamme* therefore considers the protection of the right to safe an healthy working conditions as appearing outdated in the States of the European Union in the light of its extensive legislation this subject (133 ILR (1994) 635, at 637).

204 Cf. as to the reforms of the Charter since 1989 and proposals for further improvements *Pucci di Benisichi*, in Council of Europe (ed.), The Social Charter of the 21st Century (1997), 43 et seq.; *Lidal*, in Council of Europe (ed.), The Social Charter of the 21st Century (1997), 70 et seq.

205 Cf. the preamble of the Charter.

is lawfully employed in a state who has done so[206]. Despite the fact that the Committee on the European Social Charter[207] pointed out during its reform debate that it was of great importance to extend the protection guaranteed in the Charter to all people within the territories of the Parties, the Committee of Ministers decided not to change the wording of the Appendix, a fact which was criticized by some members of the Charte-Rel Committee[208].

Despite the fact that the rights in the ESC are formulated as subjective rights, they cannot be enforced by an individual. This fact is often cited in favor of the opinion that the social rights of the Charter are to be regarded as principles which have to be observed in legislation and the practices dealing with the persons concerned[209]. It has been argued that the Contracting Parties themselves did not have the intention to give any direct effect to those provisions. Mention is made of the Annex to Part III, according to which, "the Charter contains legal obligations of an international character, the application of which is submitted solely to the supervision provided in part IV thereof" and our attention is drawn to the fact that this Appendix forms an integral part of the Charter[210]. One deduction from this provision is the prohibition of any direct application by national courts in favour of individuals[211]; another view is that there might be a distinction between provisions in which the Contracting Parties "undertake" to promote a special right and those – which can be considered as binding – in which the Contracting Parties "recognize" a special right[212]. Additionally, it has been suggested that some of the rights of the ESC which are sufficiently precise might be directly applicable[213].

Nevertheless, it should be noted that most of the provisions of the ESC are far too vague as to give them any direct effect. Article 33 ESC leads to the conclusion that normally the Charter is to be implemented by national legislation[214]. In special

[206] *Wiebringhaus* points out that the scope of application might be enlarged "indirectly" when social security benefits to family members of a national of a Contracting State or family reunion questions re at issue (in Baer-Kaupert (ed.), Die Sozialcharta des Europarates Essays in honour of C.H. Aubin (1979), 263, 270).

[207] Cf. as to the activities of the Charte-Rel Committee Council of Europe, Secretariat, Activities of the Council of Europe in the Migration Field, 20 May 1996, CDMG(96)15 E, p. 37.

[208] Cf. *Libal*, in Council of Europe (ed.), The Social Charter of the 21st Century, Colloquy organised by the Secretariat of the Council of Europe (1997), 70, at 76: "This, I think, is a missed opportunity to make a major improvement to the Charter which should find some sort of compensation. It may be true that parties in most instances do not exclude from legislation (...) foreigners from non-Contracting Parties, but I would consider it an act of solidarity with those who often are least protected, namely migrant workers and their families, if future ratifications of the Charter were accompanied by a declaration that all people lawfully resident or working regularly within the territory of the party were to be protected"

[209] *Delpérée*, Revue des droit de l'homme 1968, 549, at 575; *Lerche*, Verfassungsrechtliche Zentralfragen des Arbeitskampfes (1968), 82; *Strasser*, 8 EPIL (1985) 211, at 212 with further references; *Wengler*, Die Unanwendbarkeit der Europäischen Sozialcharta im Staat (1969), 10.

[210] Cf. Article 38 ESC. Cf. for the German view *Isele*, Die Europäische Sozialcharta (1967), 65, at 71.

[211] *Tennfjord*, Annuaire Européen IX (1962), 79: "It should be noted, however, that the Charter cannot be invoked by individuals in national courts (...)." Cf. for further references *Wengler*, Die Unanwendbarkeit der Europäischen Sozialcharta im Staat (1969), 12.

[212] *Zuleeg*, ZaöRV 35 (1975), 341, 342.

[213] *Bleckmann*, Europäischer Sozialraum (1993), 55, at 57, and in: Cahiers de droit européen, 1967, 388.

[214] *Strasser*, 8 EPIL (1985) 211, 212.

cases an implementation by collective agreement might be possible. Article 33 provides –

> 1. In Member States where the provisions of paragraphs 1, 2, 3, 4, and 5 of Article 2, paragraphs 4, 6, and 7 of Article 7 and paragraphs 1, 2, 3 and 4 of Article 10 of Part II of this Charter are matters normally left to agreements between employers or employers' organizations and workers' organizations, or are normally carried out otherwise than by law, the undertakings of those paragraphs may be given and compliance with them shall be treated as effective.

As to the implementation of the economic and social rights of the Charter, the Contracting Parties are required to submit regular reports on the implementation. A Protocol amending the Charter of 1991 bore important consequences with regard to a more effective functioning of the Committee of Ministers and to the sanctions to be applied in cases of non-compliance[215]. The 1995 Protocol on collective complaints empowers NGOs, international and national organizations of workers, and employers to issue direct complaints[216].

A revised European Social Charter was adopted in May 1996 and entered into force on 1 July 1999[217]. The Council of Europe Parliamentary Assembly has expressed a strong commitment towards expediting the process of ratification and introducing a distinct European Court of Social Rights to guarantee observance of obligations under the Charter[218].

The revised Charter is a comprehensive instrument bringing together the already existing rights in the ESC of 1961 and the additional protocols. In addition, new rights are included as to the right to protection against poverty and social exclusion, the right to housing, to protection in case of termination of employment, the right to protection against sexual harassment and victimization, the right of workers with family responsibilities to equal opportunities and equal treatment and the rights of workers' representatives. Amendments are to be found in the

---

[215] ETS No. 142. The Protocol has been ratified by Austria, Cyprus, Finland, France, Greece, Ireland, Italy, Malta, the Netherlands, Norway, Poland, Portugal, Slovakia and Sweden. Signatory states are Belgium, the Czech Republic, Hungary, Latvia, Luxembourg, Slovenia, Spain, the former Yugoslav Republic of Macedonia and the United Kingdom.

[216] ETS No. 158; It has been ratified by Cyprus, Finland, Italy, Norway, Portugal and Sweden, and entered into force on 1 July 1998; signatory states are Belgium, Denmark, France and Slovenia. Cf. as to the Additional Protocol inter alia *Brillat*, European Human Rights Law Revue 1996, 53; *Harris*, in Council of Europe (ed.), The Social Charter of the 21st Century (1997), 100 et seq.; *Jaeger*, 10 Leiden Journal of International Law (1997) 69 et seq.; *Lörcher*, in Council of Europe (ed.), The Social Charter of the 21st Century (1997), 130 et seq.; *Prouvez*, in Council of Europe (ed.), The Social Charter of the 21st Century (1997), 140 et seq.; *Sudre*, Revue générale de droit international public 1996, 715.

[217] ETS No. 163; an overview is offered in EuroAS 1999, 121 et seq. The revised Charter has been signed by Albania, Austria, Belgium, Bulgaria, Cyprus, Denmark, Estonia, Finland, Greece, Iceland, Lithuania, Luxembourg, Moldova, Portugal, Slovakia, Ukraine and the United Kingdom and has been ratified by France, Italy, Romania, Slovenia and Sweden.

[218] Council of Europe Parliamentary Assembly, Future of the European Social Charter, Doc. 7980, 1998.

reinforcement of the principle of non-discrimination[219], an increased equality between women and men in all fields covered by the treaty[220], better maternity protection and social protection for mothers, an increased social, legal and economic protection for children at work[221] and outside and for disabled persons[222]. As to social security, the Convention refers to a "satisfactory level" instead of ILO's minimum standards[223].

As to the personal scope of application, the wording is similar to the existing Charter of 1961; a treatment as favorable as possible and in any case not less favorable than under the obligations accepted by the Party under the said Convention and under any other existing international instrument applicable will be granted by each party to refugees as defined in the Convention relating to the Status of Refugees of 1951 and the Convention on the Status of Stateless Persons of 1954. As to this remaining narrow scope of application, some authors questioned the requirement of a legal residence in the country or the lack of any equal treatment provision as regards third-country nationals –

> The fact is that with regard to rights which are as fundamental as for example the right to protection of health (Article 11) or the right to social and medical assistance (Article 13), it is a very questionable practice to restrict entitlement to persons lawfully resident in the state where they are located: one might also question the usefulness of excluding persons not legally resident from the guarantees enshrined in the revised European Social Charter particularly as, firstly, a whole series of the provisions of the Charter cannot in principle be applied to such individuals since they refer to the exercise of a job to which they have no access and, secondly, the difference between the situation of a foreigner lawfully resident in the territory of a state party and that of a foreigner not lawfully resident there is sufficiently objective to justify, where appropriate, differentiated treatment between the two situations, provided that it is reasonably justified.[224]

---

[219] The clause of non-discrimination being based on Article 14 of the European Convention on Human Rights reads that benefits of all the rights of the Charter should be ensured without any discrimination on any ground such as "race, colour, sex, language, religion, political or other opinion, national extraction or social origin, health, association with a national minority, birth or other status" (Appendix Part V, Article E); as to the difference in the wording (in the ECHR there is the notion of "national origin"), the Explanatory Report notes in para. 136: "Whereas national extraction is not an acceptable ground for discrimination, the requirement of a specific citizenship might be acceptable under certain circumstances, for example for the right to employment in the defense forces or in the civil service."

[220] Cf. as to the right of men and women to equal pay also the ILO's Equal Remuneration Convention of 1951 (No. 100) and European Union legislation and case-Law as mentioned *supra* I 3.

[221] Cf. as to the importance of the incorporation of the provision relating to the employment of children and Article 7: *Vandamme*, 133 ILR (1994) 635, at 637-638.

[222] Cf. as to the Revised Social Charter *Pucci di Benisichi*, in: Council of Europe (ed.), The Social Charter of the 21st Century (1997), 43, 55-58; *Vandamme*, 133 ILR (1994) 635.

[223] ILO Convention No. 102 of 1952.

[224] *De Schutte*, in: Council of Europe (ed.), The Social Charter of the 21st Century (1997), 154, at 160; an extension to third-country nationals legally resident in the country concerned is also favoured by *Fonteneau*, in Council of Europe (ed.), The Social Charter of the 21st Century (1997), 80, at 86.

Furthermore, it is argued, that this practice is not consistent with Article 14 of the European Convention on Human Rights and the case-law, especially in the *Gaygusuz* or expulsion cases –

> Consequently, it is certain that at least in cases where the same right of freedom is recognized by the case-law both of the European Social Charter and the European Convention on Human Rights, restricting protection of such a right to nationals of the other states parties cannot be accepted. Consideration should also be given, even in other fields, to the relevance of differentiated treatment based merely on the nationality of the potential beneficiary of a right; either this difference in treatment can be justified, and in that case it must be so within the limits imposed by the rule of non-discrimination – and it should be recalled that this rule does not prohibit differentiated treatment based on an objective and reasonable justification; or it cannot be justified and in that case why should the authors of the revised Social Charter have codified it?[225]

5. *Other Instruments relating to Social Rights*

Other treaties relate solely to specific groups of social benefits or have a limited personal scope of application. Included among these are the European Convention on Social and Medical Assistance[226], the European Agreement on "Au-Pair"-Placement[227] and the European Convention on the Social Protection of Farmers[228]. The European Code of Social Security defines norms for social security coverage and establishes minimum levels of protection[229]. One convention focuses on the legal status of migrant workers[230]. Provisions relating to equal treatment might be found, for instance, in Article 1 of the European Convention on Social and Medical Assistance and Protocol Related Thereto[231], and in Article 18 and 19 of the European Convention on the legal status of migrant workers[232] with regard to

---

225 *De Schutte*, in: Council of Europe (ed.), The Social Charter of the 21st Century (1997), 154, at 166. Cf. as to the ECHR also *Fonteneau*, in: Council of Europe (ed.), The Social Charter of the 21st Century (1997), 80, at 81; *Cahen*, in: Council of Europe (ed.), The Social Charter of the 21st Century (1997), 154, at 160.

226 ETS No. 14. Cf. as to this Convention Council of Europe, Secretariat, Activities of the Council of Europe in the Migration Field, 20 May 1996, CDMG (96) 15 E, 47/48.

227 ETS No. 68.

228 ETS No. 83.

229 ETS No. 139.

230 European Convention on the Legal Status of Migrant Workers, ETS No. 193.

231 "...shall be entitled equally with its own nationals and under the same conditions to social and medical assistance provided by the legislation."

232 This Convention applies to nationals of the Contracting Parties and not to seasonal and frontier workers; the provisions relate to the main aspects of the legal status of migrant workers, especially to recruitment, medical examinations and vocational tests, travel, residence and work permits, family reunion, housing, conditions of work, the transfer of savings, social security, social and medical assistance, expiry of the contract of employment, dismissal and re-employment, and preparation of return to the country of origin.

matters of social security and social and medical assistance[233]. In addition, the Committee of Ministers has adopted a large number of Resolutions and Recommendations for the benefit of migrant workers and members of their families[234].

---

[233] ETS No. 93; Article 18 provides: "1. Each Contracting Party undertakes to grant within its territory, to migrant workers and members of their families, equality of treatment with its own nationals, in the matter of social security, subject to conditions required by national legislation and by bilateral or multilateral agreements already concluded or to be concluded between the Contracting Parties concerned.
2. The Contracting Parties shall moreover endeavour to secure to migrant workers and members of their families the conservation of rights in course of acquisitions and acquired rights, as well a provision of benefits abroad, through bilateral and multilateral agreements."

[234] The most important of these are listed in Council of Europe, Secretariat, Activities of the Council of Europe in the Migration Field (20.5.1996), CDMG (96)15 E. p. 9 and 49 and *Kattau*, Romanian Journal of International Affairs 1995, 72, at 75.

E

Refugees and Asylum Seekers

I. Introduction

1. Factors and Agents of a European Refugee Policy

a) The Role of UNHCR

In light of its complexity, single states cannot deal adequately with the asylum and refugee problem; the issue must be addressed at the international level. International cooperation in asylum and refugee matters has traditionally taken place within the United Nations system, under the aegis and within the framework of UNHCR. Two main methods in the development of international law on refugees and asylum within this setting have prevailed. First, through the conclusion of international conventions, which is often a long and burdensome path. Second, by the adoption of non-binding resolutions and recommendations.

Although the Executive Committee of the High Commissioner's Programme was originally created to, upon request, merely advise the High Commissioner on questions dealing with the exercise of the Office's statutory functions, as well as on the appropriateness of providing international assistance through the Office in order to solve specific refugee problems, it has recently taken on an increasingly important role[1]. The Executive Committee has gradually become more influential in the everyday management of UNHCR, including, among other tasks, policy development in relevant fields[2]. In its annual general and specific conclusions, the Executive Committee has repeatedly emphasized the basic character of the principle of non-refoulement[3], holding that the principle "was progressively acquiring the character of a peremptory rule of international law"[4]. In addition, it has reported violations of the principle in particular instances[5], made statements on the applicability of the norm to certain cases[6], and exhorted states to abide by the

---

1 Established in 1958 through UNGA Res. 1166 (XII) of 26 November 1957 and ECOSOC Res. 672 (XXV) of 30 April 1958. The Executive Committee of the High Commissioner's Programme is a subsidiary organ of the United Nations General Assembly pursuant to Article 22 UN-Charter and at the same time an internal governing body of UNHCR (cf. *Türk*, Das Flüchtlingshochkommissariat der Vereinten Nationen (UNHCR) (1992), 100, especially note 298).

2 Cf. *Morris*, 2 IJRL (1990), 38.

3 See only Conclusion No. 6 (1977); Conclusion No. 65 (1991), Report of the 42nd Sess.: UN doc. A/AC.96/783 (21 October 1991).

4 Report of the 33rd Sess.: UN doc. A/AC.96/614, para 70.

5 See e.g. Conclusion No. 46 (1987), Report of the 39th Sess.: UN doc. A/AC.96/702, para 204; Conclusion No. 50 (1988), Report of the 39th Sess.: UN doc. A/AC.96/721, para 23; Conclusion No. 55, Report of the 40th Sess.: UN doc. A/AC.96/737 (19 October 1989), para 22 (d).

6 See Conclusion No. 58(1989), paras (f), (g).

fundamental principle of non-refoulement even in situations of mass influx[7]. However, the conclusions of the Executive Committee do not create legally binding obligations. No express power of authentic interpretation of the Geneva Convention has been conferred upon the Executive Committee[8]. Furthermore, the value of Executive Committee conclusions as an expression of state practice must be regarded with caution. The Executive Committee consists of only fifty member states[9]. Even though the United Nations General Assembly regularly takes note of the reports of the Executive Committee[10], it does not adopt them in a strict sense, but adopts its own annual resolution on the work of UNHCR. United Nations General Assembly resolutions usually draw heavily on the text of the Executive Committee conclusions, notably those on international protection. The extent of correspondence must, however, be examined carefully in each individual case. Reports of the Executive Committee and the conclusions contained therein can, therefore, not be attributed to the United Nations General Assembly as such[11]. Executive Committee conclusions can be considered as the expression of a legal opinion of a UNHCR-organ as to the present or future state of refugee law[12]. While Excom conclusions may contribute to the formation of *opinio iuris*, their actual legal content must be scrutinized carefully. They do not necessarily reflect an expression of a uniform state practice nor can they be considered as a subsequent agreement of contracting states on the interpretation of the Geneva Convention. For the purposes of formation of customary international law as well as for the conclusion of international agreements a clear distinction must be drawn between states in their capacity as autonomous subjects of international law and states as members of an organ of international organization. The formation of international law within the framework of an international organization is subject to the powers granted to the international organization by the treaty establishing the organization.

---

7 See e.g. Conclusion No. 15 (XXX) (1979) (Refugees without an Asylum Country), UN doc. A/AC.96/572, 15; Conclusion No. 19 (XXXI) (1980) (Temporary Refugee), UN doc. A/AC.96/588, 14; Conclusion No. 22 (XXXII) (1981) (Protection of Asylum-Seekers in Situations of Large-Scale Influx), UN doc. A/AC.96/601, 15; Conclusion on Former Yugoslavia, e.g. October 1994, reprinted in 7 IJRL (1995), 142, 160; Conclusion No. 74 (XLV) (1994) (General Conclusion on International Protection), paras (h), (k), and (l). On Executive Committee Conclusions see also *Goodwin-Gill*, The Refugee in International Law, 2nd ed. (1998), 127 et seq.

8 See the terms of reference of the Executive Committee laid down in UNGA Res. 1166 (XII) of 26 November 1957 and ECOSOC Res. 672 (XXV) of 30 April 1958, which do not provide for such a power of interpretation.

9 See GA Res. 49/171 of 23 December 1994, UN GAOR, 49th Sess., Suppl. No. 49, (A/49/49). Twelve Member States are members of the Executive Committee (see *ECRE*, Note from the European Council on Refugees and Exiles on the Harmonization of the Interpretation of Article 1 of the 1951 Geneva Convention, para 4).

10 See e.g. GA Res. 3454 (XXX) of 9 December 1975, UN GAOR 30th Sess., Suppl. No. 34 (A/10034); GA Res. 36/125 of 14 December 1981, UN GAOR 36th Sess., Suppl. No. 51 (A/36/51); GA Res. 49/169 of 23 December 1994, UN GAOR 49th Sess., Suppl. No. 49 (A/49/49).

11 Even then it would have to be carefully examined if the respective conclusion has a legal content and which state has approved of it; see *Brownlie*, Principles of Public International Law, 4th ed. (1990), 4th ed. (1990), 630, 699; see also *Türk*, Das Flüchtlingshochkommissariat der Vereinten Nationen (UNHCR) (1992), 78, note 215.

12 For a different view see *Brill*, The 1951 Convention Definition of Refugee Status and the Issue of Agents of Persecution (1992), 11.

Therefore, UNHCR-Excom conclusions can be considered as part of international law only insofar as UNHCR has been granted corresponding powers. Therefore, Excom-conclusions must be reviewed in the context of states' expressed opinion and in light of the actual state practice[13].

During the crisis in the former Yugoslavia during July 1992, UNHCR convened an International Meeting on Victims of the Humanitarian Crisis and presented the so-called Comprehensive Response to the Humanitarian Crisis in the former Yugoslavia (CRHC)[14] at the conclusion of this meeting. Members of the Humanitarian Issues Working Group also dealt with problems of temporary protection in their regular meetings[15]. State cooperation under the auspices of UNHCR was, however, confined to meetings for the purpose of consultations and the exchange of views[16]. Scepticism and reluctance towards formal harmonization, and even towards the adoption of non-binding guidelines prevailed. No agreement on the creation of such an instrument could be reached[17]. Parties to the meeting stressed instead the value of regional cooperation and coordination[18].

Due to the complexity and length of the procedures required, the conclusion of further international treaties on refugee and asylum law is currently not a viable option. It is also doubtful whether a consensus on possible new treaties could be reached among States at a universal level. The legal effect of Executive Committee conclusions and recommendations, as well as of General Assembly resolutions on the harmonization and development of international refugee and asylum law is limited. Tangible results in the development within the framework of the United Nations are, as a result, likely to prove difficult to attain in the foreseeable future. Nevertheless, endeavours to negotiate guidelines and principles at the universal level must be continued in order to achieve a broader consensus in the future.

---

13 See also *Goodwin-Gill*, The Refugee in International Law, 2nd ed. (1998), 128 et seq.

14 UN doc. HCR/IMFY/1992/2 of 24 July 1992, reprinted in *IGC*, Report on Temporary Protection, 252; see also the working document for the second meeting of the CRHC follow-up committee, ibid., 25.

15 See the informal meetings on temporary protection of 30 September 1992, of 21 January 1993, of 25 March 1993, of 23 March 1994, of 30 June 1994 and of 20 April 1995 *IGC*, Report on Temporary Protection, 24 et seq., 252 et seq.

16 See Executive Committee Conclusion No. 74 (XLV) 1994 (General Conclusion on International Protection), paras (h), (k) and (l); Conclusion No. 77 (XLV) (1995) (General Conclusion on International Protection), UN doc. A/AC.96/860, para 19 (f); Conclusion No 79 (XLVII) (1996) (General Conclusion on International Protection), UN doc. A/AC.96/878, para 21 (m).

17 Report of the Sub-Committee of the Whole on International Protection 46th Sess., UN doc. A/AC.96/858 of 17 October 1995, para III. 12. Recently, slight progress can be observed in the field of temporary protection. Three various informal meetings have been organized by UNHCR in Geneva, bringing together a limited number of Government and academic experts for informal exchanges of views on aspects of the subject of temporary protection for persons who are not covered by the application of the 1951 Convention and the 1967 Protocol relating to the Status of Refugees, but who are nevertheless in need of international protection. The goal was to explore the development of guiding principles in this field (see the Progress Report on Informal Consultations on the Provision of International Protection to All Who Need it, Standing Committee of the Executive Committee, UN doc. EC/47/SC/CRP.27 of 30 May 1997).

18 See Executive Committee Conclusion No. 74 (XLV) 1994, para (o); Conclusion No. 80 (XLVII) (1996) (Comprehensive and Regional Approaches within a Protection Framework). For a discussion of possibilities of a closer cooperation within the UN-system see *Beyer*, Improving International Responses to Humanitarian Situations (1989) , 9, 12, 25-29.

These attempts must, however, be accompanied and supplemented by efforts at the level of smaller – regional – organizations with stronger possibilities of *legal* action[19].

b) The Need for a European Approach

Refugee problems in Africa, Asia, the Americas and Europe vary widely, and justify a distinct treatment of the particularly "European" situation[20]. These differences result from the variations in the economic, social and legal cultures of each area. The refugee situation in Europe generally can be characterized by the following factor. First, refugee flows in Europe are predominantly economically motivated, rather than ethnically or politically[21], while in Africa they are often created by artificial borders and ethnic conflicts. Second, forced migration to Europe has increasingly led to immigration with resulting integration problems. Third, for economic reasons, as well as diverging human rights traditions, reception standards in Europe are generally higher than in other continents. It is European practice, for example, to give permanent residence status to recognized refugees in spite of the fact that the Geneva Convention does not oblige contracting states to grant permanent asylum, but contains a cessation clause in Article 1 C. Consequently, there is a particular need to develop more flexible additional instruments to provide for temporary protection of persons fleeing from general violence. Furthermore, in contrast to Africa and Asia, European legal and administrative traditions have generally supported the practice of adjudicating asylum claims on a case-by-case basis. Confronted with the post-World War II mass influx of refugees fleeing war-torn countries or situations of general violence or danger, however, these asylum procedures often proved inadequate for practical and financial reasons. Europe has been confronted with a similar situation at the end of the Cold War and the collapse of Communism. A large number of people fled to Europe after the opening of the Eastern European borders. These Eastern European refugees are no longer regarded as a foreign policy asset and have contributed to making Europe sensitive to mass refugee and migratory flows considered as uncontrollable by traditional techniques[22].

The most important steps in the harmonization of European national refugee and asylum policies to date have been taken in the framework of the European Union. The Treaty of Amsterdam confirmed the will of the Member States to advance the process of harmonization through the introduction of far-reaching EC-competencies in the field of asylum and refugee law. Within the structure of the EU, Member States asylum and refugee policy harmonization is recognized as an indispensable requirement for the achievement of the goals of the EC-Treaty. The establishment of unimpeded freedom of movement for persons through the

19 See also UNHCR, Note on International Protection of 7 September 1994, UN doc. A/AC.96/830, para 54, reprinted in 6 IJRL (1994), 679, 706.
20 Cf. *Kälin*, Towards a Concept of Temporary Protection (1996), 9 et seq.
21 The flight movements due to the war in the former Yugoslavia must be seen as an exception.
22 See *Dacyl* in Korella/Twomey (eds.), Towards a European Immigration Policy, (1993), 85, 92+93.

abolition of border controls calls for supporting measures, such as the harmonization of measures to combat crime, and a common European immigration and asylum policy[23]. In an area of free movement without border controls, in which third-country nationals can move freely from one Member State to the other, uniform standards for the admission of refugees and asylum seekers must be adopted to ensure equal chances of an alien seeking protection regardless of the country in which an application for protection is filed. Flight into a European Union of open borders is no longer flight into one single Member State, but flight into a common area of justice and social security. Differences in the legislation of Member States concerning the admission of asylum seekers, recognition rates of similar categories of refugees, and the legal status of Convention refugees and civil war refugees may cause unequal and unjust distribution of asylum seekers and refugees among Member States. The fact that only a few "frontier states " must carry the burden of receiving war refugees contradicts the idea of solidarity between Member States belonging to a common area of economy, law and policy. In light of Europe's traditional adherence to principles of social justice and respect for human rights, a common approach governing the admission of refugees and asylum seekers will have to be elaborated. A common policy of control and reception will be an indispensable step towards the establishment of a common European concept of asylum and refugee policy. An integral part of a European refugee policy is the concept of "safe third countries", a strategy to prevent the emergence, and to abolish the root causes of refugee flows, and a common position on regional protection. Finally, from a foreign policy point of view, the EU must adopt a uniform policy concerning the prevention of refugee generating economic or political conditions and towards refugee generating countries and their responsibility to cooperate in repatriation and resettlement of refugees.

Member States' policy on *de facto* refugees and temporary protection must also be included in harmonization efforts. The number of persons seeking refuge in the Union who are not covered by the Geneva Convention far exceeds the number of Convention refugees. Any European system of asylum law and policy which aims for a minimum of comprehensiveness and effectiveness must address the issues of *de facto* refugees and temporary protection[24]. *De facto* refugees cannot be separated from asylum seekers in practice, as they are often merely rejected asylum applicants[25]. Another aspect of a common European protection regime relates to the guaranty of a standard level of minimum protection in order to remedy the existing differences in social welfare in the absence of binding rules of public

---

[23] Cf. the Report from the Ministers responsible for immigration to the European Council meeting in Maastricht on immigration and asylum policy of 3 December 1991, reprinted in *Guild/Niessen*, The Developing Immigration and Asylum Policies of the European Union, (1996), 449 at 450 and 457. See also *supra* Chapter A.

[24] Communication from the Commission to the Council and the European Parliament on the right of asylum, 11 October 1991, SEC(91) 1857 final, 7; *Fitzpatrick*, 35 Va. J. Int'l L. (1994),13, 68; *Dacyl* in Korella/Twomey (eds.), Towards a European Immigration Policy (1993), 85, 86; *Thorburn*, 7 IJRL (1995), et seq. Cf. also the Commission in its Communication to the Council and the European Parliament on Immigration and Asylum Policies of 23 February 1994, COM(94)23 final, 16 and 27 et seq.

[25] *Hailbronner*, Die Rechtsstellung der de-facto-Flüchtlinge in den EG-Staaten (1993), 124.

international law as to social protection of asylum seekers and temporarily protected persons[26]. Additionally, if policies concerning temporary protection were more clear and transparent, the pull effect created by complicated legal systems might be diminished, as the probability of being granted or denied protection could be calculated more easily[27].

The Austrian presidency of the EU recently presented a strategy paper for a future common policy in immigration and asylum[28]. Although this paper does not contain concrete legal measures and has not received the support of the Council, its contribution in the creation of an entire strategy of a future legislation in asylum and refugee matters must be recognized. The paper suggests a policy of agreements with states of origin of refugees, development aid and intervention in conflict regions as part of a comprehensive concept of a European asylum and immigration policy[29].

c) Cooperation in the Area of Asylum and Refugee Policies in the Framework of the Council of Europe and the OSCE

Activities in the field of asylum and refugee policy have also been incorporated into the framework of the Council of Europe. The Parliamentary Assembly of the Council of Europe regularly releases reports, recommendations and resolutions on asylum and refugee matters[30]. Only rarely, however, have these non-binding instruments been followed by a recommendation of the Committee of Ministers[31]. Recently, the Parliamentary Assembly launched an attempt to design a Council of Europe Convention on minimum rights in asylum procedures[32].

Important work is additionally carried out by the Ad Hoc Committee of Experts on the Legal Aspects of Territorial Asylum, Refugees and Stateless Persons

---

26 Cf. also *Julien-Lafferrière*, AWR-Bull. 3(1979) 30, 32; *Hofmann*, in European Commission, Law in humanitarian crises, Vol. I, 249, 259; for social rights of aliens see generally part D.

27 *Hailbronner*, Die Rechtsstellung der de-facto-Flüchtlinge in den EG-Staaten (1993), 132.

28 Cf. Council doc. 9809/98.

29 Cf. Council doc. 9809/98.

30 See e.g. Report on the situation of *de facto* refugees, 5 August 1975 (Rapporteurs: MM. Dankert and Forni), doc. 3642; Recommendation 773 (1976) on the situation of *de facto* refugees; Recommendation 787(1976) on harmonization of eligibility practice under the 1951 Geneva Convention on the Status of Refugees and the 1967 Protocol; Recommendation 1068 (1988) on the right to territorial asylum; Recommendation 1149 (1991) on Europe of 1992 and refugee policies; Report on the crisis in Yugoslavia: displaced populations, 27 January 1992 (Rapporteur: Sir John Hunt, United Kingdom Conservative), doc. 6554; Recommendation 1176 (1992) on the crisis in Yugoslavia: displaced populations; Report on the situation of refugees and displaced persons in the former Yugoslavia, 19 January 1993 (Rapporteur: Mr. Flückiger, Switzerland, Radical Democrat), doc. 6740; Recommendation 1316 (1997) on the state of emergency in Albania, para 5. iii. Cf. also rec. 1374/98 on the Situation of refugee women in Europe. For a list of recent recommendations and resolutions see Council of Europe, Activities of the Council of Europe in the migration field, (1996), CDMG (96) 15 E, 60 et seq.

31 See e.g. Recommendation R(81) 16, of 5 November 1981 on the harmonization of national procedures relating to asylum; Recommendation R(84) 1, of 25 January 1984 on the protection of persons satisfying the criteria in the Geneva Convention who are not formally recognized as refugees.

32 See Süddeutsche Zeitung of 25 April 1997, 2.

(CAHAR). According to its terms of reference, the CAHAR follows developments in the field of asylum, refugees and stateless persons in particular in member states of the Council of Europe, but also at the level of the United Nations and other international organizations. It promotes regular information sharing in order to obtain a common position among the member states. The concept of a safe third country from the perspective of third countries, the right of rejected asylum seekers to appeal, and the return of rejected asylum seekers have all been matters of recent debate[33]. The CAHAR is working on the harmonization of asylum and refugee policies in the member states of the Council of Europe. Its primary task is to draw up legal instruments – conventions and recommendations – for discussion and adoption by the Committee of Ministers. The Committee plays a significant role as a forum for consultation and discussion of asylum and refugee affairs beyond the European Union. It also allows Eastern European states to participate in a wider European cooperation.

As a forum for cooperation in asylum and refugee matters, the Council of Europe offers the advantage of a tried and tested European system of human rights protection with a judicial review mechanism. The geographical scope of the Council of Europe is remarkably larger than that of the EU. However, the large number of member states of the Council of Europe makes harmonization within its framework more burdensome than within the European Union. In addition, the fact that the European Convention on Human Rights has granted far-reaching rights of judicial complaint to individuals, which have been strengthened recently[34], does not necessarily increase the probability of an agreement on asylum and refugee questions among the member states of the Council of Europe. The Council of Europe organs do not have the authority to adopt legally binding instruments. International treaties are the main instrument of action in the Council of Europe; drafting these treaties is often difficult and time consuming. Cooperation in the framework of the Council of Europe can, therefore, only supplement, but not substitute harmonization within the European Union.

Another framework for harmonization is the *Organization for Security and Cooperation in Europe (OSCE)*[35]. Several arguments, especially those concerning the temporary protection policies of the Member States, speak in favour of the OSCE as a framework for harmonization. The OSCE is currently the largest organization at the European level. Both refugee-generating-countries, as well as their immediate neighbours and western host-states are included among its 53 member states[36]. Furthermore, it possesses a developed mechanism of early

---

[33] Cf. CAHAR(96) 11; CAHAR(96) 12; see also CAHAR, 42nd Meeting, Meeting Report, CAHAR(96) 18.

[34] By virtue of the eleventh additional protocol to the European Convention on Human Rights; see ETS 155.

[35] It is sometimes regarded as the "most suitable inter-governmental structure" to respond to situations of mass-influx. See *Marx*, Temporary Protection (1994), 15.

[36] The OSCE (not only through its renaming) has developed into an international organisation, cf. *Bortloff*, Die Organisation für Sicherheit und Zusammenarbeit in Europa (1986), 400; *Seidl-Hohenveldern/Loibl*, Das Recht der Internationalen Organisationen, 6th ed. (1996) para 248 et seq., para 2217.

warning, conflict prevention and conflict solution[37], along with permanent decision-making structures[38]. Its recently established High Commissioner for National Minorities has a mandate for many possible conflict scenarios. His main task is to observe human rights situations and to initiate an early warning system[39]. Finally, the OSCE is recognized as a regional organization of the UN, pursuant to Chapter VIII of the UN Charter[40]. On the other hand, however, pragmatic considerations disqualify the OSCE as the proper forum for harmonization. While its large membership, like that of the Council of Europe, can be viewed as an advantage, it also hampers agreements. This is especially true for the OSCE, as the Helsinki Final Act of 8 June 1973 requires that all decisions be made by general consensus[41]. In addition, presumably due to a lack of political will on the part of OSCE member states, no steps towards a formalized harmonization of asylum and refugee policies within the OSCE are currently under way within the OSCE human rights office (ODHIR)[42].

2. *Development and Status Quo of a European Refugee Policy*

The lack of a legislative Community competence notwithstanding, Member States have advanced the harmonization of asylum and refugee law since the beginning of the 1980s through the conclusion of agreements and conventions, as well as the adoption of non-legally binding instruments and the creation of numerous committees to deal with the problems of a European asylum and refugee policy. The goal of a harmonization of Member State asylum policy based on the Geneva Convention was first mentioned in 1989, when the European Council adopted the "PALMA-document"[43], which established the so-called group of co-ordinators. The "PALMA document" expressed the hope, within a fixed time period, to deal with the subjects, and to realize measures in the areas listed below –

1. Uniform international obligations in the area of asylum law. This goal was attained when Italy abolished its geographical limitation to the Geneva Convention.

2. Establishment of a European system of responsibilities for the adjudication of asylum claims (under the Dublin Convention).

---

37 See *Fastenrath*, KSZE, A.6 III. For the limits of the dispute settlement mechanism which became apparent in the course of the Yugoslavia conflict however, see *Wenig*, Möglichkeiten und Grenzen der Streitbeilegung ethnischer Konflikte durch die OSZE (1996), 259.

38 Ibid. A.6 I; Further *Bortloff*, Die Organisation für Sicherheit und Zusammenarbeit in Europa (1986), 370 et seq.

39 *Fastenrath*, KSZE, A.6 II; Cf. also *Bortloff*, Die Organisation für Sicherheit und Zusammenarbeit in Europa (1986), 383 et seq.

40 *Marx*, Temporary Protection (1994), 15; see also *Thorburn*, 7 IJRL (1995), 459, 478.

41 See the Final Recommendations of the Helsinki-consultations, 6. para (69), reprinted in *Fastenrath*, KSZE A. 0, 6.

42 *Thorburn*, 7 IJRL (1995), 459, 478.

43 Reprinted in *Guild/Niessen*, The Developing Immigration and Asylum Policies of the European Union, (1996), 443.

3. Simplified procedures for manifestly unfounded asylum applications.
4. Rules on the freedom of movement of asylum seekers between the Member States.

A first step in the realization of these aims was taken when the Member States signed the Dublin Convention. The Convention's main features are the creation of a system of exclusive competences for the adjudication of asylum claims, the imposition of a duty on the Member States to readmit asylum seekers who have illegally moved from the territory of one Member State to another, and the coordination of expulsion measures after the final rejection of an asylum claim. As opposed to the Schengen Implementation Convention, the Dublin Convention was signed and ratified by all Member States and entered into force on 1 September 1997. The terms of the treaty do not allow for a formal accession of non-Member States[44]. The inclusion of other states, in particular Eastern European states, Switzerland, Canada and the Northern European, into the system of cooperation has, however, occasionally been proposed but never achieved. As the ratification process for the Dublin Convention has proven more time consuming than expected, the Council has decided to postpone the decision on parallel agreements until the Dublin Convention is functioning in its original signatory States[45].

The Schengen Implementation Convention, originally signed on 19 June 1990 by the Benelux countries, Germany and Italy, and to which all Member States except for the United Kingdom and Ireland have meanwhile acceded, is an attempt to further promote the harmonization of legal provisions on entry and asylum among a smaller group of states. The SIC section on asylum law mainly corresponds with the Dublin Convention and is no longer applied after the Dublin Convention entered into force on 1 September 1997[46]. However, the SIC goes beyond the Dublin Convention, insofar as it allows for the harmonization of entry and visa provisions, including a uniform visa stamp and uniform control procedures. All Schengen-visa holders enjoy the right to move freely within "Schengenland" for a short-term stay. Furthermore, the SIC regulates police cooperation, uniform registration duties and mutual assistance in law enforcement in the field of criminal law[47].

The Member States, the Council and the Commission released a number of political action programmes concerned with the development of a European asylum and refugee policy soon thereafter. Although these programmes are not legally binding, they have fostered the advancement of the harmonization process through the formulation and shaping of certain goals to be reached. In its Communication of 11 October 1991[48], the Commission emphasized the necessity to accelerate the procedures for the adjudication of asylum claims. In addition, a number of more general measures were mentioned, e.g. harmonization of the conditions for rejection of entry at the external borders of the Union, the provisions

---

44 See Article 21(1) of the Dublin Convention.
45 For further details see part III.
46 See Article 1 of the protocol of Bonn of 26 April 1994, BGBl. II 1997, 739.
47 For further details see *infra* part III.
48 SEC(91) 1857.

and practices relating to *de facto* refugees, the conditions of entry for asylum seekers, as well as the creation of mechanisms for mutual information exchange and a common system of legal remedies. These objectives have partially been realized through the adoption of several non-legally binding resolutions and recommendations.

The ministers responsible for immigration adopted a report for the European Council meeting in Maastricht on immigration and asylum policy dealing with the harmonization of the asylum and immigration policies of the Member States on 3 December 1991[49]. A work-programme contained therein established six main areas for harmonization –

1. The application and implementation of the Dublin Convention,
2. the harmonization of substantive asylum law (including the establishment of unambiguous conditions for the determination of manifestly unfounded asylum applications, the creation of a unified definition and harmonized application of the principle of first host country, the common assessment of the situation in countries of origin with regard to both admission and expulsion, the harmonized application of the definition of a refugee as given in Article 1A of the Geneva Convention),
3. the harmonization of expulsion policies,
4. the establishment of a clearing house,
5. legal examination (examination of the problem of guaranteeing harmonized application of asylum policy), and
6. conditions for receiving applicants for asylum.[50]

The Council laid down the priorities of immigration policy in an additional action plan of 2 December 1993[51]. The Council announced a Joint Action plan to achieve a harmonized application of the Geneva Convention refugee definition and to establish a uniform set of minimum guarantees in asylum procedures. Asylum applications were to be decided upon according to harmonized substantive and procedural standards. In order to incorporate the aims of immigration and asylum policies into the external relations of the EU, principles were to be included in bi- or multilateral readmission agreements, which should lead to a connection between the Europe agreements, association agreements and cooperation agreements concluded by the EU and the Member States on the one side, and the practice of third states concerning the readmission of their own and foreign nationals on the other.

The Commission released a new Communication to the Council and the European Parliament on 23 February 1994 in response to the general debate on

---

49 Document WGI 930, reprinted in *Guild/Niessen*, The Developing Immigration and Asylum Policies of the European Union, (1996), 449 et seq.

50 WGI 930, 8, 9.

51 Quoted in *Hailbronner*, ZAR 1995, 3, 7.

harmonization of Member State asylum and refugee policies[52]. Asylum and immigration policy was now placed in the more general context of the problem of managing migratory movements. Tackling the root causes of migration movements through foreign and economic policy created and implemented at the European level was declared as an integral part of the concept. In its Communication, the Commission suggested several steps going beyond its work programme of 1991 –

1. Take action to reduce migration pressure (through the improvement of accurate information collection and exchange on migratory flows into the Union and their causes, as well as through the establishment of an "observatory" for migration, the creation of a definition of actions to be taken in order to tackle root causes of various types of migratory movements (human rights policies, humanitarian assistance, security policy, etc.)),
2. develop a set of minimum standards for fair and efficient asylum procedures,
3. elaborate on a convention on manifestly unfounded asylum applications and the implementation of the third host country principle,
4. harmonize policies regulating the status of those who cannot be admitted as refugees, but whom, in light of the general situation prevailing in that country, Member States would not require to return to their country of origin,
5. harmonize schemes on temporary protection, and
6. develop a system to monitor absorption capacities, and to create a mechanism which would provide support to Member States who are willing to assist other Member States faced with situations of mass influx; similarly, to support projects of Member States of third transit countries unexpectedly faced with new pressures.

Community immigration ministers adopted four instruments on asylum procedure at their meeting in London on 30 November to 1 December 1992. They agreed on the Resolution on manifestly unfounded applications for asylum[53], the Resolution on a harmonized approach to questions concerning third host countries[54], the Conclusions on countries in which there is generally no serious risk of persecution[55] and on the foundation of a Centre on Information, Reflection and Exchange on asylum questions (CIREA)[56]. The Justice and Home Affairs Council adopted four further acts on 20 June 1994: first, the Guidelines for joint reports on third countries[57], second, the Circulation and confidentiality of joint reports on the

---

52 COM(94) 23 final.
53 Reprinted in *Guild*, op. cit., 141 et seq.; *Hailbronner*, Ausländerrecht, D 12.1.
54 Reprinted in *Guild*, op. cit., 161 et seq.; *Hailbronner*, op. cit., D 12.2.
55 Reprinted in *Guild*, op. cit., 177 et seq.; *Hailbronner*, op. cit., D 12.3.
56 Reprinted in *Guild*, op. cit., 191 et seq.; *Hailbronner*, op. cit., D 12.4.
57 O.J. 1996 C 274/52.

situation in certain third countries[58], third, Conclusions concerning procedures for drawing up joint reports on the situation in third countries[59], and fourth, the Second activity report on the Centre for Information, Discussion and Exchange on Asylum (CIREA)[60]. On 20 June 1995 the Council adopted the Resolution on minimum guarantees for asylum procedures[61] and on 22 December 1995 it adopted the Council Recommendation on concerted action and cooperation in carrying out expulsion measures[62].

The joint position on the harmonized application of the definition of the term 'refugee' in Article 1 of the Geneva Convention of 28 July 1951 relating to the status of refugees[63], defined by the Council on the basis of ex-Article K.3 of the Treaty on European Union, was adopted on 4 March 1996. It represents a major step in the course of harmonizing the substantive asylum rules of the Member States.

One disadvantage of the Dublin Convention and the SIC is the limit of their respective scopes of application to asylum seekers who apply for refugee status under the Geneva Convention, while the large majority of persons seeking protection in the EU, and, in particular, those fleeing general violence, e.g. civil wars and natural disasters, are not covered by the Geneva Convention for various reasons[64]. Most Member State legal systems allow for the possibility of granting different types of humanitarian permission to remain in their territory for a limited period of time. The laws of the Member States concerning this category of persons vary to a considerable degree, especially with regard to admission criteria, and rights and benefits to be granted. Harmonization of these rules is an important part of a comprehensive European asylum and refugee policy[65]. A number of instruments have already been agreed upon with regard to *de facto* refugees and burden-sharing. Community immigration ministers acted for the first time in this area with the adoption of the Resolution on people displaced by the conflict in the former Yugoslavia at their meeting in London of 30 November to 1 December 1992[66]. At their Copenhagen meeting of 1 to 2 June 1993, the Resolution on certain common guidelines as regards the admission of particularly vulnerable groups of distressed persons from the former Yugoslavia was adopted by the ministers for

58 O.J. 1996 C 274/43.

59 Quoted in *De Jong*, unpublished conference paper, 4 (on file with the author).

60 O.J. 1996 C 274/55.

61 O.J. 1996 C 274/13.

62 O.J. 1996 C 5/3.

63 O.J. 1996 L 63/2.

64 This group of persons is often called "*de facto* refugees". The term was apparently used for the first time by *Fragomen*, 3 Case W. Res. L. Rev. (1970), 45, 58. It was later made widely known by Recommendation No. 773 (1976) of the Parliamentary Assembly of the Council of Europe and is still being used by legal writers (see only *Goodwin-Gill*, The Refugee in International Law, 1st ed. (1983), 17; *Hailbronner*, Die Rechtsstellung der de-facto-Flüchtlinge in den EG-Staaten (1993), e.g. 12; *Kälin*, Grundriss des Asylverfahrens (1990), 26; *Marugg*, Völkerrechtliche Definitionen des Ausdruckes "Flüchtling" (1990), 181; *Lambert*, Seeking Asylum (1995), 126).

65 See already the Commission in its Communication to the Council and the EP of 23 February 1994, COM(94) 23 final; and the new Article 63(2) ECT after entering into force of the Treaty of Amsterdam.

66 Unpublished, on file with the author. Cited in O.J. 1995 C 262/1.

immigration[67]. A further step was taken with the Council's resolution of 25 September 1995 on burden-sharing with regard to the admission and residence of displaced persons on a temporary basis[68]. This resolution was later supplemented by the Council decision of 4 March 1996 on an alert and emergency procedure for burden-sharing with regard to the admission and residence of displaced persons on a temporary basis[69]. The Commission has submitted a proposal to the Council for a Joint Action based on ex-Article K.3(2)(b) of the TEU concerning temporary protection of displaced persons as of 5 March 1997 and 24 June 1998[70].

The Treaty of Amsterdam will now bring a new quality of harmonization through the integration of the asylum and refugee policy in the framework of the ECT. In anticipation of the new legal framework, the Council did not pass many measures based on the Maastricht Treaty in 1998. The Council adopted a Joint Action on the basis of Article K.3 of the TEU on 19 March 1998, introducing a programme of training, exchanges and cooperation in the field of asylum, immigration and crossing of external borders, the so-called ODYSSEUS-programme[71]. The general objective of the ODYSSEUS-programme is to extend and strengthen existing cooperation between Member States and States applying for accession in matters of asylum, immigration and crossing external borders (Article 1(3)). In order to achieve this objective, the European Union will finance training and exchange measures, as well as studies and research on these matters[72]. In the field of asylum, measures are to focus primarily on a coordinated application of the Dublin Convention, especially with regard to the application of procedures, time limits and evidence. The projects should also promote a future close cooperation between national administrations, in particular, *inter alia,* in systems of documentation on countries of origin[73]. In the field of immigration, measures should be concerned with the admission of third country nationals, residence rules, family reunification and with combating illegal immigration and illegal entry[74]. The ODYSSEUS-programme will by financed by the Community with a budget of ECU 12 million for a four year period.

Further, the Council has adopted several Joint Actions concerning the financing of specific projects in favor of asylum seekers and refugees on the basis of Article K.3 TEU. Among these are the Joint Action of 22 July 1997 concerning the financing of specific projects in favor of displaced persons who have found temporary protection in the Member States and asylum seekers[75], the Joint Action of 22 July 1997 concerning the financing of specific projects in favor of asylum seekers and refugees[76], the Joint Action of 27 April 1998 concerning the financing

---

67 Reprinted in *Guild/Niessen*, The Developing Immigration and Asylum Policies of the European Union, (1996), 293 et seq.
68 O.J. 1995 C 262/1.
69 O.J. 1996 L 63/10.
70 COM(97) 93 final; COM (98) 372 final.
71 O.J. 1998 L 99/2.
72 See Article 2-6.
73 Cf. Article 7 with further areas of cooperation.
74 Cf. Article 8 with further areas of cooperation.
75 O.J. 1997 L 205/3.
76 O.J. 1997 L 205/5.

of specific projects in favour of displaced persons who have found temporary protection in the Member States and asylum seekers[77], the Joint Action of 27 April 1998 concerning the financing of specific projects in favour of asylum seekers and refugees[78], and recently the Joint Action of 26 April 1999 establishing projects and measures to provide practical support in relation to the reception and voluntary repatriation of refugees, displaced persons and asylum seekers, including emergency assistance to persons who have fled as a result of recent events in Kosovo[79]. These Joint Actions were adopted in order to improve facilities for the admission of asylum seekers and refugees, to improve the conditions under which such persons are voluntarily repatriated and to encourage the sharing of responsibility between the Member States. They are also the result of a call to undertake specific projects on an experimental basis, with a view to the future establishment of appropriate legal instruments in these areas. Finally, on 13 January 1999 the Commission submitted a proposal for a Council Decision establishing a Community action programme to promote the integration of refugees[80].

3. The Legal Framework for a Community Policy on Visas, Asylum, Immigration and other Matters Related to Free Movement of Persons after Entry into Force of the Treaty of Amsterdam

The fact that, pursuant to Article 2, No. 15 of the Treaty of Amsterdam, a new Title IV "Visas, asylum, immigration and other policies related to free movement of persons" (Articles 61-69 ECT) has been inserted in Part Three of the Treaty establishing the European Community is particularly relevant to the harmonization of Member States asylum and refugee policy. Subject areas previously included in the Third Pillar of the Union, in which solely intergovernmental cooperation within the framework of the Union took (and still takes) place, have been transferred to the First Pillar, thus shaping new genuine Community competencies[81].

In order to progressively establish an area of freedom, security and justice, Article 61 ECT obliges the Council to adopt, *inter alia* –

- within a period of five years after entry into force of the Treaty of Amsterdam, measures aimed at ensuring the free movement of persons in accordance with Article 7a (Article 14 ECT), in conjunction with directly related compensatory

---

77 O.J. 1998 L 138/6.
78 O.J. 1998 L 138/8.
79 O.J. 1999 L 114/2.
80 COM(98) 731 final, O.J. 1999 C 36/20.
81 For the implications of this shift for the legal instruments available, voting methods, the role of EC organs in the legislative process, and judicial review see *supra* Chapter B. The United Kingdom, Ireland and Denmark in principle do not take part in the adoption by the Council of measures pursuant to Title IV ECT (cf. Article 69 ECT read together with Article 1 of the Protocol on the Position of the United Kingdom and Ireland and the Protocol on the Position of Denmark respectively). Concerning the lack of legal effect and applicability of the provisions of Title IV ECT, measures adopted pursuant to that Title, and other acts, see also Article 2 of the respective Protocol. However, both the United Kingdom and Ireland (see Article 3, 4, 6 und 8 of the Protocol) as well as Denmark (see Articles 4, 5 und 7 of the Protocol) have reserved different "opting-in" possibilities.

measures with respect to external border controls, asylum and immigration, in accordance with the provisions of Article 62(2) and(3) ECT and Article 63(1)(a) and(2)(a) ECT

- other measures in the fields of asylum, immigration and safeguarding the rights of nationals of third countries, in accordance with the provisions of Article 63.

As the phrasing of the new provisions shows ("the Council shall adopt")[82], they do not only contain competences, but also oblige the Council to act in support of further harmonization. This is especially true for those norms which foresee the adoption of measures within a five-year time period[83].

a) Asylum

Article 63(1) ECT prescribes that measures on asylum must be taken in accordance with the Geneva Convention of 1951. It is questionable whether this reference to the Geneva Convention has the effect of incorporation of the Geneva Convention into Community law. On the one hand, Article 63(1) ECT must be interpreted as an affirmation of Member States' clear commitment to their obligations under the Geneva Convention. On the other hand, however, the reference to the Geneva Convention has a limited scope. Article 63(1) ECT prescribes requirements for Community action only. Hence the Geneva Convention has not been communitarized. Rather the reference to the Convention must be interpreted as a self-imposed limitation of the Community's competence under Article 63(1) ECT. The European Court may define whether Community institutions have transgressed the limits imposed by the Geneva Convention for the treatment of refugees. To that extent, Member States' practice under the Convention will influence the interpretation of Article 63(1) ECT.

Article 63(1) ECT enumerates detailed measures on asylum, which the Council, acting in accordance with the procedure referred to in Article 67, shall adopt within a period of five years after the entry into force of the Treaty of Amsterdam. Included among these are –

- criteria and mechanisms for determining which Member State is responsible for considering an application for asylum submitted by a national of a third country in one of the Member States,
- minimum standards on the reception of asylum seekers in Member States,
- minimum standards with respect to the qualification of nationals of third countries as refugees,
- minimum standards on procedures in Member States for granting or withdrawing refugee status.

The list of competencies is exhaustive, i.e. there is no comprehensive Community competency for an asylum policy as a whole. Rather, the Council has been authorized to adopt only the measures listed in Article 63(1)(a-d) ECT, which are the following.

---

[82] See Articles 61, 62 and 63 ECT.

[83] See Articles 63(1)(a-d), (2)(a) and (3)(b) ECT.

The Dublin Convention already contains such criteria and mechanisms for determining which Member State is responsible for considering an application for asylum submitted by a third-country national in one of the Member States (Article 63(1)(a) ECT). Chapter VII (Articles 28-38) SIC equally contained provisions establishing a responsibility system for asylum requests. However, since the entry into force of the Dublin Convention on 1 September 1997 these provisions no longer apply (see Article 1 of the Protocol of Bonn of 26 April 1994[84]). Moreover, Chapter VII SIC has not been attributed to an EU legal basis by virtue of Council Decision 1999/436/EC determining the legal basis for each of the provisions or decisions which constitute the Schengen acquis[85]. Whether Member States will extend the responsibility system of the Dublin Convention, or opt for that of the Schengen Implementation Convention in the long run, is a question that has not yet been finally resolved. However, suggestions made point at adoption of Community legislation under Article 63(1)(a) ECT with the revised content of the Dublin Convention rather than at a "revival" of Chapter VII SIC[86]. This would certainly be a preferable solution if the United Kingdom and Ireland decided to take part in this measure. If the United Kingdom and Ireland choose not to opt in, the question of whether the responsibility system under the Dublin Convention should be continued as a treaty under international law would have to be carefully reconsidered. This would be advantageous, in that it would include the United Kingdom and Ireland, and would, therefore, promote EU-wide cooperation.

The Council shall adopt minimum standards on the reception of asylum seekers in Member States within five years of the entry into force of the Treaty of Amsterdam (Article 63(1)(b) ECT). This provision aims at assimilating the legal position of asylum seekers in the Member States during the asylum procedure, including everything but the procedure itself[87]. Questions such as the right to work, access to education, family reunion, social assistance, free movement and identity and travel documents can be addressed. Whilst the Council may merely establish "minimum" standards, Member States may always grant a more favourable legal status to asylum seekers, uninhibited by the Council.

Article 63(1)(c) ECT calls upon the Council to adopt standards with respect to the qualification of nationals of third countries as refugees within five years after the entry into force of the Treaty of Amsterdam. In light of the Joint Position defined by the Council on the basis of Article K.3 TEU on 4 March 1996 which concerns the harmonized application of the definition of the term 'refugee' in Article 1 of the Geneva Convention of 28 July 1951 relating to the status of refugees[88], the new Community competency makes it possible to improve this instrument and tackle its weak points. A legally-binding directive, for example,

---

84 BGBl. II 1995, 739.

85 O.J. 1999 L 176/17.

86 Cf. point 36(b)(i) of the Action Plan of the Council and the Commission on how best to implement the provisions of the Treaty of Amsterdam on an area of freedom, security and justice, O.J. 1999 C 19/1.

87 Harmonization of procedures for granting or withdrawing refugee status will follow Article 63(1)(d) ECT.

88 O.J. 1996 L 63/2.

could be adopted. It must be emphasized, however, that the Council has no competence to establish binding comprehensive standards. It cannot forbid a Member State to interpret the Geneva Convention more generously than determined by the Council.

Finally, under Article 63(1)(d) ECT the Council shall adopt minimum standards on procedures in Member States for granting or withdrawing refugee status within five years after the entry into force of the Treaty of Amsterdam. This provision, in particular, foresees improvement and further development of numerous Council acts which were adopted either before or after the entry into force of the TEU in the field of asylum procedures. The Council does not have the competence to issue final and comprehensive regulations on all details of asylum procedures; it may only adopt minimum standards.

The Council Resolution of 18 December 1997[89] lays down the priorities for cooperation in the field of justice and home affairs for the period from 1 January 1998 to the date of entry into force of the Treaty of Amsterdam. Cooperation with regard to immigration and asylum should be improved, *inter alia,* by the following measures: the implementation of the Dublin Convention and a study of the possibility of concluding conventions parallel to Dublin, the harmonization of national procedures for granting the right to asylum and of the conditions for the reception of asylum applicants, the development of the EURODAC system and the improvement of exchanges of information and cooperation with countries of origin.

The Council and the Commission submitted an action plan on how best to implement the provisions of the Treaty of Amsterdam in an area of freedom, security and justice on 3 December 1998 [90]. The following measures in the field of asylum are to be taken within two years after the entry into force of the Treaty: continued examination of the criteria and conditions for improving the implementation of the Dublin Convention and of the possibility of transforming the legal basis to the Amsterdam system(Article 63(1)(a) ECT), the implementation of EURODAC[91], the adoption of minimum standards in Member State procedures for granting or withdrawing refugee status (Article 63(1)(d) ECT), the limitation of "secondary movements" by asylum seekers between Member States, agreement on a unified definition of minimum standards for the reception of asylum seekers, with a particular attention to the situation of children (Article 63(1)(b) ECT), and the undertaking of a study of the merits of a single European asylum procedure. The adoption of minimum standards with respect to the qualification of nationals of third countries as refugees and the definition of minimum standards for subsidiarity protection granted to persons in need of international protection (Article 63(2)(a) second part) are to be realized within five years of the entry into force of the Treaty of Amsterdam.

---

89 O.J. 1998 C 11/1.

90 O.J. 1999 C 19/1.

91 See also the Proposal for a Council Regulation concerning the establishment of EURODAC for the comparison of the fingerprints of applicants for asylum and certain other aliens of 26 May 1999 (COM(99) 260 final). For further details see *infra* III.8.

On 28 October 1998 the Commission submitted a work programme for 1999 which outlines the policy priorities[92]. Consequently, in 1999, the Commission will concentrate its efforts on actively promoting the action plan requested by the Council on how best to implement the provisions of the Treaty of Amsterdam. This will involve, in addition to fulfilling present commitments and any new initiatives, initiating the process of recasting a number of draft legislative instruments currently under negotiation, in order to make them compatible with the institutional and other provisions of the Treaty of Amsterdam. This will be particularly important in areas transferred to the Community "pillar", namely measures related to immigration, asylum, external frontier-crossing and judicial cooperation. Further, the Commission submitted a work programme for 1999 which contains the new legislative proposals that the Commission plans to present in 1999[93]. It intends to submit, *inter alia*, legislative proposals on the application of the new provisions of the Treaty of Amsterdam on the fields of immigration, asylum, crossing of external frontiers and judicial cooperation.

b) Refugees and Displaced Persons

According to Article 63(2) ECT, the Council, acting in accordance with the procedure referred to in Article 67 ECT[94], shall adopt measures on refugees and displaced persons in the following areas –

> (a) minimum standards for giving temporary protection to displaced persons from third countries who cannot return to their country of origin and for persons who otherwise need international protection[95],
>
> (b) promoting a balance of effort between Member States in receiving and bearing the consequences of receiving refugees and displaced persons[96].

Although Title IV ECT does not expressly define the term "refugee", a systematic interpretation of Article 63(2) of the Geneva Convention views "refugees" as persons who fulfil the conditions of Article 1A(2) of the Geneva Convention. "Displaced persons", conversely, are persons who do not fulfil the requirements of this provision. Article 63(1) ECT calls on the Council to adopt measures on asylum in accordance with the Convention of 28 July 1951 and the Protocol of 31 January 1967 relating to the status of refugees, as well as with other relevant treaties. As a result, the qualification of nationals of third countries as "refugees" mentioned in Article 63(1)(c) ECT means qualification as a "refugee" under the 1951 Convention. The same understanding must apply when interpreting Article 63(2) ECT.

---

[92] COM(98) 0604 final, O.J. 1998 C 366/1.

[93] COM(98) 0609 final, O.J. 1998 C 366/11.

[94] For further details on the procedure see *supra* Chapter B.

[95] Measures under this subparagraph are subject to the five year period referred to in Article 63 ECT.

[96] Measures under this subparagraph, pursuant to Article 63(4) subparagraph 3 ECT, are not subject to the five year period referred to above.

What is meant by "persons who otherwise need international protection" in Article 63(2)(a) ECT is not exactly clear. Several acts adopted by the Council under ex-Article K.3(2)(a) TEU – the burden-sharing resolution of 25 September 1995[97], the decision on an alert and emergency procedure of 4 March 1996[98] and, in particular, the resolution of 14 October 1996 laying down the priorities for cooperation in the field of justice and home affairs for the period from 1 July 1996 to 30 June 1998[99] – indicate that the first clause mentioned in Article 63(2)(a) ECT (temporary protection to displaced persons) refers to situations of mass-influx of refugees, while the second clause ("persons who otherwise need international protection") covers persons granted temporary protection for reasons of public international law, or for humanitarian reasons on an individual basis, rather than as a member of a group of refugees[100].

The Community competency laid down in Article 63(2)(a) ECT allows, first, for the establishment of minimum rights for temporarily protected persons and persons who otherwise need international protection. This concerns, for example, issues such as the right to work, access to education, the right to family reunion, social assistance, free movement, and identity and travel papers. The term "minimum standards" is broad enough to further include provisions on the scope of application (the beneficiaries) of rules on temporary protection and humanitarian residence permits, the procedure of establishing temporary protection and the relationship to the asylum procedure.

Article 63(2)(b) ECT gives the Council a competence to adopt measures with the aim of promoting burden-sharing with regard to Convention refugees and displaced persons. Whether the "promotion" of a balance of effort may result in a final and binding imposition of criteria and mechanisms for burden-sharing has deliberately been left open. The word "promotion" is vague in comparison with other possible terminology; a restrictive interpretation of this provision, therefore, seems to be justified.

Article 64(2) ECT contains a very important new innovation, which allows the Council to adopt provisional measures for a maximum duration of six months to benefit an affected Member State in the event of one or more Member States being confronted with an emergency situation characterized by a sudden inflow of nationals of third countries, without prejudice to paragraph 1[101] and accepted by a qualified majority on a proposal from the Commission. In cases of emergency, this Article allows for a simplified voting procedure[102], as this will promote timely decision-making and action.

---

97 O.J. 1995 C 262/1.

98 O.J. 1996 L 63/10.

99 O.J. 1996 C 319/1. In this resolution the examination of the problems of temporary protection and burden-sharing (para 4 (f)) and the examination of forms of alternative protection (*de facto* protection and humanitarian residence permit (para 4 (g)) represent two completely separate issues.

100 For instance after rejection of an asylum claim.

101 Pursuant to Article 64(1) ECT Title IV ECT shall not affect the exercise of the responsibilities incumbent upon Member States with regard to the maintenance of law and order and the safeguarding of internal security.

102 On the voting procedure according to Article 67 ECT see *supra* Chapter B.

c) Visas, External Borders and the Return of Illegal Residents

The Treaty of Amsterdam has also created new Community competencies in the field of visas, external borders and the return of illegal residents (Articles 62(2), 63(3)(a) ECT)[103]. With the incorporation of the Schengen *acquis* into the framework of the Union, secondary acts of harmonization in the area of visa policy and return policy will also take immediate effect upon the entry into force of the Treaty of Amsterdam[104]. Issues surrounding the imposition of visa requirements and the establishment of conditions for the granting of visas, as well as return policies, are integral factors in asylum and refugee policy, and affect the beneficiaries of protection measures in particular.

II. Harmonization of the Criteria for Recognition as a Political Refugee

All Member States of the Union are bound by the Geneva Convention relating to the Status of Refugees. Even though the majority of refugees coming to Europe are not covered by the Geneva Convention[105], the Convention remains the most important instrument of refugee protection, as well as virtually the only treaty establishing obligations for the Member States under public international law in this field[106]. The Convention allows the Contacting Parties a large margin of interpretation, which often results in interpretative divergences among the Member States[107]. These disparities in interpretation, in turn, may serve as an incentive for refugees to search for the highest level of protection available in Europe, achieved, if necessary, through migration from one European State to another. The Dublin system's policy of delegating exclusive responsibility to single State for examining an asylum application[108] favours the establishment of uniform principles on recognition, and makes the harmonization of the criteria for recognition as a political refugee a primary goal in the harmonization process[109]. The Council of the EU adopted the joint position on the harmonized application of the definition of the term 'refugee' in Article 1 of the Geneva Convention of 28 July 1951 relating to

---

103 For further details see *supra* Chapter C.

104 Or, if upon entry into force of the Treaty of Amsterdam the Council has not yet determined the legal basis for the provisions or decisions which constitute the Schengen *acquis* (see Article 2(1), 2nd indent of the Protocol Integrating the Schengen *Acquis* into the Framework of the European Union) acts based on Title VI of the Treaty on European Union (see Article 2(1), 4th indent of the Protocol). For further details see *supra* part C.

105 See *UNHCR*, Refugees and Others of Concern to UNHCR (1996) Statistical Overview, Table 13; see also *supra* part A.

106 For other treaties touching on refugee issues see e.g. *Goodwin-Gill*, The Refugee in International Law, 2nd ed. (1998), 311 et seq.

107 For the European Parliament's opinion see the Resolution on the harmonization of forms of protection complementing refugee status in the European Union of 10 February 1999, O.J. 1999 C 150/203.

108 See Chapter E III.

109 See the Report from the Ministers responsible for immigration to the European Council meeting in Maastricht on immigration and asylum policy, above note 23.

the status of refugees on 4 March 1996[110]. The following sections will deal first with the problems related to the use of the Geneva Convention as a basis for refugee protection in Europe(1), as well as with an evaluation of the progress made through the joint position(2) and, finally, with the prospects of harmonization after entry into force of the Treaty of Amsterdam(3).

1. The Geneva Convention as a Starting Point for a Common European Asylum and Refugee Policy

a) Interpretation of the Geneva Convention

The most important provision in the Geneva Convention is the "non-refoulement principle", which reads as follows –

> "No Contracting State shall expel or return ("refouler") a refugee in any manner whatsoever to the frontiers of territories where his life or freedom would be threatened on account of his race, religion, nationality, membership of a particular social group or political opinion."

The term "refugee" is defined in Article 1A(2) of the Geneva Convention and applies to any person who –

> "As a result of events occurring before 1 January 1951[111] and owing to well-founded fear of being persecuted for reasons of race, religion, nationality, membership of a particular social group or political opinion, is outside the country of his nationality and is unable or, owing to such fear, is unwilling to avail himself of the protection of that country; or who, not having a nationality and being outside the country of his former habitual residence as a result of such events, is unable or, owing to such fear, is unwilling to return to it."

As a treaty under public international law, the Geneva Convention may be authentically interpreted by the Contracting States[112]. States, therefore, play a decisive role in the shaping of the actual content of the norms of the treaty. Statements on the interpretation of a treaty made by organs of an international organization, such as the Office of UNHCR and the Executive Committee of the High Commissioner's Programme[113], may serve as auxiliary means of interpretation but cannot replace the predominant importance of state practice. Resolutions of international bodies have binding force for the Contracting States only if, and insofar as the treaty grants express or implied powers of interpretation

---

[110] In the following "the joint position" or "the Council's joint position", O.J. 1996 L 63/2 et seq.

[111] This time limit has been abolished through the Protocol Relating to the Status of Refugees of 10.1.1967, 606 UNTS 267, ("additional protocol of 1967"); reprinted in *Plender*, Basic Documents on International Migration Law (1997), 102 et seq. The additional protocol of 1967 has been ratified by all Member States.

[112] Cf. *Brownlie*, Principles of Public International Law, 4th ed. (1990), 626; *Nguyen Quoc Dinh*, Droit International Public (1984), 249, para 166.

[113] See *supra* note 1.

to that organ[114]. No power of authentic interpretation has been conferred upon the Office of UNHCR[115]. Notwithstanding the fact that UNHCR has the duty of supervising the application of the provisions of the Convention according to Articles 35(1) of the Geneva Convention and 8a of UNHCR-Statute, no express competence to adopt binding statements on the interpretation of the Geneva Convention has been included, nor has such a competence been implied. There is no need to deduce competence from UNHCR capacity to fulfil its tasks efficiently[116]. Other supervisory organs of international organizations, such as the European Commission, similarly lack the power to give binding interpretations of the establishing treaty[117].

Pursuant to Articles 38 of the Geneva Convention, 94(1) UN-Charter, the International Court of Justice may rule on disputes between parties to the Geneva Convention over its interpretation or application which cannot be settled by other means. However, no references have been made to the International Court of Justice at the request of a party to a dispute to date. Member States interpret the Geneva Convention's definition of refugee to some extent quite differently.

b) Persecution by Non-State Agents

The question whether persecution carried out by non-state entities amounts to persecution particularly, has been subject to widely divergent interpretations. The wording of Article 1A(2) of the Geneva Convention is not clear as to the requirement of state accountability. No further conclusions as to the interpretation of Article 1A(2) of the Geneva Convention can be drawn from either the context of the provision[118], from other pertinent norms of international treaties applicable in the relations between the parties[119], or from the purpose and objective of the Convention[120].

While the courts of all Member States seem to require that actions of "state-like" entities and actions of private entities may, in the absence of sufficient protection by the state, qualify as political persecution[121], by way of attributing acts

---

[114] See *Ipsen*, Völkerrecht, 4th ed. (1999), 121, para 3.

[115] See also *Masing* in Grawert et al (eds.), Offene Staatlichkeit, Essays in Honour of Ernst-Wolfgang Böckenförde (1995), 51, 79; *Grahl-Madsen*, The Status of Refugees in International Law (1966), Vol. I, 333; *Holborn*, Refugees: A Problem of our Time, Vol. I (1975), 161 et seq.; *Lentini*, Boston College Third World Journal 2 (1985), 183, 197. For a different view see *Türk*, Das Flüchtlingshochkommissariat der Vereinten Nationen (UNHCR) (1992), 165.

[116] For a different view see *Türk*, Das Flüchtlingshochkommissariat der Vereinten Nationen (UNHCR) (1992), 167; *Brill*, The 1951 Convention Definition of Refugee Status and the Issue of Agents of Persecution, (1992), 9, 10.

[117] See *v.d. Groeben/Thiesing/Ehlermann*, Kommentar zum EWG-Vertrag, 4th ed. (1991), Article 155, note 8 et seq.

[118] See Article 31(2) of the Vienna Convention on the Law of Treaties.

[119] See Article 31(3)(c) of the Vienna Convention on the Law of Treaties.

[120] See Article 31(1) of the Vienna Convention on the Law of Treaties.

[121] See judgments of French courts (Dankha judgement, cf. *Julien-Lafferrière*, J.D.I. 1 (1984), 119, Danish courts (cf. *Carlier* et al. (eds.), Who is a Refugee? (1997), 326, para 67), Dutch courts (ibid., 512, para 48), British courts (ibid. 598, para 51) and Austrian courts (ibid., 45, para 75).

carried out by private individuals to state authorities[122], there are contradictory views and practices as to the circumstances under which purely private acts amount to persecution. A restrictive theory maintains that private acts amount to persecution if the state tolerates, supports or approves of the private acts (so-called "state-complicity" standard)[123]. According to a more extensive theory, evidence of the factual inability of the state to protect its citizens from attacks of private individuals or entities is sufficient to establish persecution (so-called "incapacity" or "incapability" standard)[124]. According to the latter position, persecutory acts carried out by private individuals or entities, which occur in the course of an internal armed conflict may be considered persecution in the sense of Article 1A(2) of the Geneva Convention, even if the state has completely or partly lost its territorial sovereignty.

c) Military Actions and Punishment of Deserters

Member States also have different opinions on the question of whether "neutral" actions, such as criminal laws of general applicability punishing objectors to military service or deserters for reasons of conscience, can amount to persecution. The wording of Article 1A(2) of the Geneva Convention "(...) persecuted for reasons of (...)" shows that the term "persecution" implies evidence of deliberate intent. The wording does not, however, exclude the situations described above from fulfilling this requirement.

State practice in general does not require evidence of persecutory intent in a subjective sense from either the persecutor or the persecuted. The establishment of persecutory intent in the sense of an objectively discernible aim of an action, however, is sometimes required[125]. While prosecution for conscientious objection to military service as such is recognized as persecution in several EU-Member States[126], other courts deny the validity of this argument, arguing that it is up to every State to admit exceptions to military service[127]. With regard to military

[122] See German courts, e.g. BVerfGE 80, 315, 336.

[123] See e.g. Austrian courts (judgment of the Verwaltungsgerichtshof of 27.7.1995, Zl 95/19/0048, quoted in *Holeschofsky*, in Barwig/Brill, Aktuelle asylrechtliche Probleme der gerichtlichen Entscheidungspraxis in Deutschland, Österreich und der Schweiz (1996), 73, 79), French courts (Conseil d'Etat of 27.5.1983, judgment Dankha, Recueil des Décisions du Conseil d'Etat 1983, 220; Commission des Recours de Réfugiés, Contentieux des Réfugiés (1999), 106 et seq.), Belgian courts (see *Carlier* et al. (eds.), Who is a Refugee? (1997), 95, para 76; *d'Aoust*, Jurisprudence, Observations, Rev. Dr. D'étr. 1993, 338, 339) and German courts (see e.g. BVerfGE 80, 315; BVerwG, NVwZ 1996, 85).

[124] See Danish courts (*Carlier* et al. (eds.), Who is a Refugee? (1997), 326, para 67), Dutch courts (ibid., 512, para 48; see also *van der Veen*, NYIL 11 (1980), 167, 171) and British courts (cf. ibid., 598, para 51).

[125] See the German Bundesverfassungsgericht, (Federal Constitutional Court) BVerfGE 80, 315, 335 and the Bundesverwaltungsgericht, (Federal Administrative Court) BVerwGE 87, 152.

[126] See Dutch and French courts, *Bodart*, 7 IJRL (1995), 39, 48, note 34.

[127] German courts (e.g. BVerwG, EZAR 201 No. 10; BVerwGE 81, 41, 42; BVerwGE 69, 320, 321), Austrian courts (e.g. Verwaltungsgerichtshof, VwGH of 17.2.1993, No. 92/01/0784; VwGH of 6.5.1992, No. 92/01/0408, ZfVB 1993/4/1042; VwGH of 8.4.1992, No. 92/01/0243, ZfVB

measures taken in a civil war, the objectively discernible aim can exist in cases when state forces conduct military actions in a manner directed towards the physical destruction of persons belonging, or attributed to the adversary based on one of the characteristics listed in Article 1A(2) of the Geneva Convention, regardless of whether these persons resist or take part in the military activities. The same is true for actions of the state forces which aim at the deliberate extermination of the ethnic, cultural or religious identity of the entire insurgent part of the population[128].

d) Internal Flight Alternative

Finally, there are different views on whether the fear of persecution must be established for the entire territory of the refugee's home state, i.e., whether an internal flight alternative rules out acknowledgement of refugee status. The wording of Article 1A(2) of the Geneva Convention supports the view that fear of persecution must prevail in the entire territory of the state of origin of the claimant, based on the argument that if persecution merely takes place in a part of the respective territory, persons seeking protection may avail themselves of the protection of their country of origin. This interpretation is supported by a closer reading of the context of Article 1A(2) of the Geneva Convention, in particular Article D of the Geneva Convention. Pursuant to this provision, the Convention shall not apply to persons who are at present receiving protection or assistance from organs or agencies of the United Nations other than the United Nations High Commissioner for Refugees. This stipulation is an expression of the general principle of subsidiarity in international protection.

State practice related to questions of when, and under which conditions the exclusion ground of an internal flight alternative applies, however, is not unequivocal. Several national courts do examine the existence of an internal flight alternative[129]. If one exists, the condition of "(...) is unable or, owing to such fear, is unwilling to avail himself of the protection of that country" is rejected and refugee status denied. In some states, the flight alternative must be both "reasonable" and safe[130], and some take social and economic factors into account to a varying degree[131]. However, established conditions and modalities of an internal flight alternative are not uniform.

1993/3/745), British courts (Immigration Appeal Tribunal of the United Kingdom, Dountes v. Secretary of State; Atibo v. Immigration Officer, London (Heathrow) Airport (1978) Imm AR 93).

128 See the German Bundesverfassungsgericht, (Federal Constitutional Court) BVerfGE 80, 315 340.

129 See United Kingdom courts, R. v. Immigration Appeal Tribunal, ex p. Jonah (1985) Imm AR 7; R. v. Secretary for the Home Department, ex p. Yurekli (1990) Imm AR 334; German courts BVerfGE 80, 315, 342; BVerfG, IJRL 4 (1992), 94, 95; and the Dutch Council of State, Judicial Division, 18.8.1978, Rechtspraak Vreemdelingenrecht 1978 No. 30 and AB 1979 No. 159; id., Judicial Division, 21.6.1979, Rechtspraak Vreemdelingenrecht 1979 No. 8 and AB 1980 No. 9.

130 See for example Austrian courts (see *Carlier* et al. (eds.), Who is a Refugee? (1997), 31, para 41), Danish courts (*ibid.*, 313, paras 37-38), British courts (*ibid.*, 579, para 23).

131 See the Swiss jurisdiction (see *Carlier* et al. (eds.), Who is a Refugee? (1997), 132, para 39; 156, para 86) and German decisions (BVerwG v. 14.12.1993, DVBl. 1994, 524, 526; see also the detailed

2. *The Joint Position of the Council on the Harmonized Application of the Definition of the Term 'Refugee' of 4 March 1996*

While the aim of the joint position was to settle controversies concerning the interpretation of the Geneva Convention; its final form represents a formal compromise on diverse opinions on the interpretation of the treaty[132]. The instrument remains vague in many areas and open to interpretation by authorities of the Member States.

a) Content

The joint position relates exclusively to the examination of the criteria as defined in Article 1 of the Geneva Convention. It does not deal with the grant of temporary protection to displaced persons permitted to remain in the territory of a Member State on the basis of domestic law for humanitarian reasons[133].

The joint position generally views persecution as either an act carried out by a state organ, be it the central state or federal states, regional or local authorities, and regardless of its status in international law, or an act of parties or organizations controlling the State[134]. Persecution by third parties is considered to fall within the scope of the Geneva Convention in cases in which it is based on one of the grounds listed in Article 1 A of that Convention, is individual in nature, and is encouraged or permitted by the authorities. The joint position holds that, if official authorities fail to act, such persecution should give rise to individual examination of each application for refugee status, in accordance with national judicial practice and with special regard to whether or not the failure to act was deliberate. The persons concerned may be eligible for appropriate forms of protection under national law in either case. [135] Official state authorities may be considered to have failed to act in situations where a State is gradually losing its power, finds itself in a situation of open civil war, guerrilla war, or has collapsed into complete anarchy[136]. In cases in which a State is undeliberately unable to protect its citizens or has ceased to exist, Member States are free to judge acts as persecutory under Article 1A(2) of the Geneva Convention. In summary, the joint position supports, in principle, the "state-complicity" standard mentioned above. However, it leaves room for a more generous interpretation of the Convention by the Member States. Even these Member States generally in favor of a more generous approach with regard to non-state persecution, however, have acknowledged the "state accountability" theory as an acceptable interpretation of the term refugee under Article 1A of the Geneva

---

explications in *Hailbronner*, Ausländerrecht, Article 16a of the Basic Law (1998), para 222 et seq.; further *Carlier* et al. (eds.), Who is a Refugee? (1997), 251, para 34; 268, para 65).

[132] Examples of diverging opinions on the interpretation of Article 1A(2) of the Geneva Convention can be found above on II.1.a.

[133] See O.J. 1996 L 63/2, para 1.

[134] O.J. 1996 L 63/2/3, para 5.1.

[135] O.J. 1996 L 63/5, para 5.2.

[136] Concerning the question under which conditions there may exceptionally be persecution in such situations see *infra* the following paragraph.

Convention. Therefore, the joint position supports the assumption that the Geneva Convention leaves to contracting states a considerable margin of appreciation in defining the term refugee.

In the context of European asylum law, a harmonization on the issue of non-state persecution would be desirable. The issue, however, is clearly connected with the question as to under what conditions temporary protection should be granted to victims of civil war, war or political unrest. Many factors speak in favor of including the issue of protection in case of non-state persecution in the framework of temporary protection schemes rather than in the framework of the Geneva Convention.

With regard to the related question of whether the dangers of an internal armed conflict constitute persecution, the joint position holds in para. 6[137] that reference to a civil war or an internal or generalized armed conflict, and its inherent dangers, is not in itself sufficient to warrant the grant of refugee status. Fear of persecution must be established based on one of the grounds in Article 1A of the Geneva Convention, and must be individual in nature. In such situations, persecution may stem either from legal authorities or any third parties encouraged or tolerated by them, or from *de facto* authorities in control of part of the territory in which the State has lost its power to protect. The term "*de facto* authorities in control of part of the territory" is vague and leaves wide scope for interpretation. Some conclusions as to the meaning of the phrase can be taken from pronouncements made by the German Federal Administrative Court on the meaning of the similar term of "quasi-state entities"[138]. According to the Court, a territorial sovereignty is only state-like if it is based on an effective and stable power, organized in a durable and effective way in the form of a State[139]. Effectiveness and stability require a certain continuity and durability, embodied primarily in the permanence of the power structure, as well as in its ability to assert itself[140].

Furthermore, according to the joint position, the use of armed forces does not, in principle, constitute persecution if it is in accordance with international rules of war and internationally recognized practice. Such actions are to be considered persecution, however, if, for instance, authority is established over a particular area and attacks on political opponents or on the population fulfil the criteria in para. 4 of the joint position[141], i.e. if they are, roughly speaking, sufficiently serious in nature or by fact of their repetition, and are based on one of the grounds mentioned in Article 1 A[142].

The fear of punishment for conscientious objection, absence without leave or desertion is, pursuant to para. 10 of the joint position, to be investigated on a case-by-case basis. It cannot be used as the sole justification for a grant of refugee status. The penalty must be assessed in accordance with the principles set out in

---

137 See O.J. 1996 L 63/2/5, para 6.

138 Quasi-staatliche Gebietsgewalt, see e.g. the judgment of the Federal Administrative Court of 6 August 1996, Buchholz 402.25 § 1 AsylVfG No. 190.

139 *Ibid.*

140 *Ibid.*

141 O.J. 1996 L 63/5, para 6.

142 For further details see O.J. 1996 L 63/2/3, para 4.

para. 5 of the joint position, which specifies principles on the origins of persecution. In cases of absence without leave or desertion, the person concerned must be afforded refugee status if the conditions under which military duties are performed alone constitute persecution. Similarly, in the light of the remaining requirements laid down in the definition, refugee status may be granted in cases of punishment of conscientious objection, deliberate absence without leave and desertion on grounds of conscience if the performance of military duties would have lead the person concerned to participate in acts which fall under the exclusion clauses in Article 1F of the Geneva Convention[143]. This clause raises problems of interpretation. First, the specific significance of the reference to Article 1F of the Geneva Convention is unclear, due to the fact that the examination of refugee status must still be undertaken "in the light of all other requirements of the definition". Second, the exclusion clauses in Article 1F of the Geneva Convention are open to interpretation. Third, war crimes never constitute an exclusion ground under Article 1F of the Geneva Convention. Rather, responsibility for war crimes under international criminal law follows from individual acts[144]. Therefore, it may appear difficult though not impossible to predict whether a particular asylum seeker is facing a serious risk of persecution for failure to perform military duties as a result of being forced to participate in illegal acts pursuant to Article 1F of the Geneva Convention. There must have been at least a serious risk of involvement in violations of humanitarian laws of war. As a consequence, the reference to Article 1F of the Geneva Convention may prove to be unsuitable in the context of the assessment of refugee status. In summary, the joint position generally takes a conservative position on this matter. It follows from the clause "in the light of all the other requirements of the definition", that the punishment or prosecution of conscientious objection, absence without leave or desertion, as such, do not constitute persecution. All conditions of Article 1A(2) of the Geneva Convention must be fulfilled, regardless of the circumstances.

The joint position regulates the subject of internal flight alternatives in the following manner: Where it appears that persecution is clearly confined to a specific part of a country's territory, it may be necessary to ascertain whether the person concerned is unable to find effective protection in another part of his own country (to which he then may reasonably be expected to move) in order to fulfil the condition laid down in Article 1A of the Geneva Convention, i.e. that the person concerned "is unable or, owing to such fear (of persecution), is unwilling to avail himself of the protection of that country"[145]. When protection in another part of a country is to be judged as "effective" and when a person may "reasonably be expected to move" to another part of his country of origin, however, remains unsolved. Therefore, the joint position allows for different interpretations by national authorities and courts as to when there exists an internal flight alternative, and when the right to protection must be upheld.

---

143 O.J. 1996 L 63/6/7, para 10.

144 See Article 20 and 2 of the International Law Commission Draft Code of Crimes against the Peace and Security of Mankind, Report of the International Law Commission on the work of its forty-eighth session, 6 May – 26 July 1996, UN GAOR, 51st Sess., Suppl. No. 10 (A/51/10), 110 and 18.

145 O.J. 1996 L 63/6, para 8.

b) The Significance of the Joint Position for the Interpretation of the Geneva Convention

The impact of the joint position on the interpretation of the Geneva Convention is limited due to its legal nature. As a "subsequent agreement between the parties of the Convention regarding the interpretation of the treaty" according to Article 31(3)(a) of the Vienna Convention on the Law of Treaties[146], the joint position is only binding on Member States[147]. The limited extent of the legal effect of the joint position is acknowledged in the preamble, and reads as follows –

> – These guidelines shall be notified to the administrative bodies responsible for recognition of refugee status, which are hereby requested to take them as a basis, without prejudice to Member States' case-law on asylum matters and their relevant constitutional positions.
>
> – This joint position is adopted within the limits of the constitutional powers of the Governments of the Member States; it shall not bind the legislative authorities or affect decisions of the judicial authorities of the Member States.[148]

The joint position is, however, valuable as an expression of state practice[149]. Article 31(3)(b) of the Vienna Convention on the Law of Treaties stipulates that parties to a treaty may engage in "subsequent practice in the application of the treaty which establishes the understanding of the parties regarding its interpretation" for a treaty to have binding effect on all contracting states of an international convention[150]. Accordingly, the joint position can be viewed as an expression of standard practice in EU-Member States. There is currently no evidence of universal acceptance of the "complicity standard" supported by the joint position or any other standard and a recognition of the margin of appreciation left by the Convention in defining the term refugee. At the level of the European Union, the joint position – despite the fact that it is only a singular act – promotes the emergence of a state practice which will correspond to the "complicity standard"[151] and, as such, embodies a unified statement on the interpretation of the Geneva Convention refugee definition by governments of the Member States. There are, however, two exceptions. First, both the Danish and Swedish delegations made a declaration to the protocol stating that, in their opinion,

---

146 In the following "of the Vienna Convention on the Law of Treaties".

147 See *Nguyen Quoc Dinh*, Droit International Public (1984), § 168; *Yasseen*, RCADI (1976) (III), 3 at 46 both generally about subsequent agreements pursuant to Article 31(3)(a) of the Vienna Convention on the Law of Treaties.

148 See also *De Jong*, Conference paper, 7. For general explications on the legal effects of joint positions adopted under Article K.3(2)(a) TEU see *Hailbronner* in Hailbronner/Klein/Magiera/Müller-Graff, Handkommentar zum EUV/EGV, Article K EUV (1996) para 76 et seq., 86. See *supra* Chapter B for further details.

149 See Article 31(3)(b) of the Vienna Convention on the Law of Treaties.

150 See Commentary of the International Law Commission on the Draft Articles on the Law of Treaties, 61 AJIL (1967), 357.

151 Singular acts do contribute to the emergence of state practice, see *Karl*, Vertrag und spätere Praxis im Völkerrecht (1983), 114.

persecution by private agents justifies a grant of refugee status according to Article 1A(2) of the Geneva Convention beyond those cases where the state tolerates or supports these actions. Both delegations held that the Convention should also apply when state authorities were simply unable to afford its citizens the necessary protection against private attacks[152]. Second, the joint position does not bind legislative authorities or affect decisions of the judicial authorities of the Member States. As a whole, the joint position represents an important statement of *opinio iuris* of Member State governments. If future practice corresponds to the principles laid down in the joint position, it may develop into regional European law. Whether, and to what extent national courts and/or parliaments will adapt their practice to conform to the principles of the joint position, however, remains to be seen[153].

3. *Prospects of Harmonization after Entry into Force of the Treaty of Amsterdam*

The main weakness of the joint position lies in the fact that it lacks a legally binding effect for the legislature and the judiciary of the Member States. As long as this deficit remains, it will not be possible to tackle the major critical point, namely the absence of judicial supervisory mechanisms. Even if the joint position was binding, an efficient implementation could only be assured through judicial enforcement mechanisms[154].

The Amsterdam Treaty has changed the legal framework. According to Article 63(1)(c) ECT the Council will be able to adopt binding rules on the interpretation of the Geneva Convention. The competence laid down in Article 63(1)(c) ECT is, however, limited to the creation of "minimum standards". This prohibits the Council from adopting a legally binding *restrictive* interpretation of the Geneva Convention. The Member States, on the other hand, remain free to interpret the Convention in a more generous manner than proposed by the Council.

Title IV ECT, as well as any acts adopted pursuant to it – including interpretative statements on the Geneva Convention – will be subject to judicial review by the European Court of Justice according to Articles 220 et seq. ECT. Only the preliminary rulings procedure under Article 234 ECT is modified pursuant to Article 68 ECT[155]. Member State courts or tribunals, against whose decisions there is no judicial remedy under national law, are the sole entities empowered to request a ruling from the Court of Justice on questions of interpretation of Title IV ECT, e.g. on the scope of the new EC-competencies, or on the validity or interpretation of secondary acts based on that Title, which are

---

[152] See Annex II to the joint position.

[153] See also the Council Decision of 26 June 1997 on monitoring the implementation of instruments adopted concerning asylum, O.J. 1997 L 178/6 et seq. According to this decision the presidency of the Council every year forwards a questionnaire to the Member States designed to show how they have implemented the instruments concerning asylum adopted by the Council and by the Ministers responsible for immigration.

[154] See *Hailbronner*, ZAR 1995, 3, 8.

[155] For further details see Chapter B.

raised in a pending case and which are considered necessary to render a judgement. Further, pursuant to Article 68(3) ECT, the Council, the Commission or a Member State may ask the Court of Justice to rule on a question of interpretation of Title IV ECT, or of acts of Community institutions based on that Title[156]. Requests for an abstract ruling on the interpretation of the ECT, or on a secondary act are not provided for in the ECT.

III. ASYLUM PROCEDURE UNDER THE DUBLIN AND SCHENGEN CONVENTIONS

1. Introduction

The Schengen Implementation Convention[157] was declared operative for Belgium, Germany, France, Luxembourg, the Netherlands, Portugal and Spain on 26 March 1995. The SIC chapter on responsibility for the processing of applications for asylum (Articles 28-38 SIC) has, thus, been applicable in the mentioned Member States between this date and 1 September 1997 (the entry into force of the Dublin Convention). Belgium has only participated in asylum cooperation as from 1 January 1997. Belgium's participation was delayed due to the fact that an Aliens Act had to be introduced before the asylum law chapter of the SIC could be applied. The entire Schengen Convention became applicable in Italy, Greece and Austria after 1 April 1998. Finally, it should be mentioned that the protocols and agreements for the accession of Denmark, Finland and Sweden were signed together with the cooperation agreement with Norway and Iceland on 19 December 1996[158]. Thus, by the year 2000, at the latest, the whole of western Europe will represent an area without internal border controls, with the exception of Switzerland, the United Kingdom and Ireland.

The Dublin Convention determining the State responsible for examining applications for asylum lodged in one of the Member States of the European Communities[159] contains roughly the same regulations as the corresponding chapter of the SIC. The Dublin Convention was established by an *ad hoc* immigration group, set up at an informal meeting of the Community immigration ministers in London on 10 October 1986. The Convention was signed in Dublin on 15 June 1990 by the (at that time) twelve Member States – with the exception of Denmark, which signed the agreement on 13 June 1991. Austria, Sweden and Finland accepted the Dublin Convention as a part of the EU *acquis* upon accession to the EU[160]. The Dublin Convention entered into force for the twelve original Contracting Parties on 1 September 1997[161], and for Austria and Sweden on 1

---

[156] Rulings given by the Court of Justice in response to such requests, however, do not apply to judgments of courts or tribunals of the Member States which have become *res iudicata* (see Article 68(3) ECT).

[157] See supra Chapter B III 3.

[158] See Europe – No. 6880, 4. This Agreement has been replaced by the 1999 Association Agreement; cf. *supra* Chapter B VII 5.

[159] An English version of the Dublin Convention is reproduced in O.J. 1997 C 254/1.

[160] Austria and Finland: 1 October 1997; Sweden: 1 December 1997.

[161] O.J. 1997 C 268/1; BGBl. II 1997, 1452.

October 1997[162]. Since the entry into force of the Amsterdam Treaty the communitarized parts of the Schengen *acquis* apply to the thirteen Member States participating in Schengen Protocol closer co-operation (see Article 2(1) of the Schengen Protocol).

2. *Concept of Exclusive Competence*

The general objective of both agreements is to ensure that only one Contracting Party is held responsible for processing an asylum application submitted by a third-country national (the so-called "one-chance-only principle")[163]. The aim of this regulation is, on the one hand, to prevent asylum seekers from being passed from one country to another without any one country accepting responsibility for processing the asylum application ("refugee-in-orbit" phenomenon). On the other hand, it should also work to minimize uncontrolled further migration of the asylum seeker within the treaty area, particularly through the initiation of parallel or successive asylum applications ("asylum-shopping").

The Schengen/Dublin concept is based on exclusivity. In principle, the Member State responsible for examining and taking a decision on an asylum application also has a duty to ensure that the asylum seeker leaves the Schengen/Dublin territory if his application is rejected. The application for asylum is processed according to the relevant provisions of the national law of the country[164]. The two asylum law treaties therefore harmonize neither substantive asylum law nor procedure. The establishment of a system for attributing exclusive responsibility for the examination of an asylum application at the European level has, however, made it necessary to recognize on an optional basis a negative decision by another contracting party ("optional negative binding effect)". Courts are only likely to recognize such decisions made by authorities of other Contracting Parties if they can be reasonably assured that procedural and substantive standards of national asylum law, even if they differ, fulfil minimum requirements under the Geneva Convention and general principles of law. Each Member State has signed the 1957 Geneva Convention on Refugees (as amended by the New York Protocol of 31 January 1967), as well as the European Convention on Human Rights[165]. Efforts on the part of Member States to harmonize European asylum laws have contributed considerably to the concept of a European asylum law. The Council Resolution of June 20 1995 on minimum guarantees for asylum procedures[166] and the Joint Position of 4 March 1996 on the harmonized application of the definition of the

---

[162] BGBl. II 1997, 1731.

[163] Cf. preamble to the Dublin Convention; Article 3(2) of the Dublin Convention, Article 29(3) SIC.

[164] Cf. Article 3(3) of the Dublin Convention.

[165] The preamble and Article 2 of the Dublin Convention strengthens the obligations of the Member States under the Geneva Convention. In contrast, neither SIC or of the Dublin Convention refer at any point to the European Convention on Human Rights, a point criticized by *Bolten*, in Meijers, (ed.), Schengen: Internationalisation of Central chapters of the Law on Aliens, Refugees, Security and Police (1991), 22.

[166] Cf. O.J. 1996 C 274/13.

term "refugee" in Article 1 of the Geneva Convention, defined by the Council on the basis of ex-Article K.3 TEU[167], are evidence of these efforts.

The Schengen/Dublin concept of responsibility creates an opportunity for, rather than imposing an obligation on, Member States to recognize a foreign decision on an asylum application. The exception clauses provided for in both treaties allow, in special circumstances, for the investigation of an asylum application in cases where another state has or had responsibility for examination and reached a negative decision. Exercising this right shifts responsibility away from the previously responsible State[168]. This salvation clause was included in the treaties, on the one hand, in light of the interest held by Member States in maintaining sovereignty in the sensitive area of asylum law. On the other hand, however, it also takes account of the legal situation in those countries in which a constitutional right to asylum is recognized. Both France and Germany, for example, were bound by their respective constitutions to re-investigate an asylum application under certain circumstances. This requirement applied even if another Member State had already rejected the application, and thus rendered the objective of the Schengen/Dublin system (the prevention of so-called "asylum-shopping") unobtainable. The constitutions of both countries have since been amended in an effort to prevent the emergence of "reserve" asylum destinations[169].

In Germany, Article 16a(5) of the Basic Law now explicitly permits the mutual recognition of decisions in asylum cases. In principle, entry from a Member State of the European Community is covered by the "safe third-country concept" (Article 16a(2) of the Basic Law), which prohibits persons entering from another Member State from invoking the right to asylum in Article 16a(1) of the Basic Law. The "safe third-country concept" ,however, is not applicable if Germany is responsible for processing an asylum application under the Dublin Convention[170]. Since the entry into force of the Dublin Convention, the "safe third-country concept" of the Schengen Implementation Convention is no longer applicable to asylum seekers coming from Schengen States/EU Member States[171]. The Federal Office for the Recognition of Foreign Refugees (*Bundesamt für die Anerkennung ausländischer Flüchtlinge* – BAFl) examines whether the criteria laid down in the Schengen/Dublin Convention on allocation of responsibility to another contracting state are met. A deportation order under § 34a(1) of the Asylum Procedure Act (Asylverfahrensgesetz – AsylVfG) will only be issued once the State involved has agreed to accept the asylum seeker[172]. The salvation clause contained in the SIC will, in practice, only be exercised by German officials if a given case can be dealt with within a period of two weeks and if past experience shows that an expeditious return to the country of origin or third country is possible. In such cases, an

167 Cf. O.J. 1996 L 63/2; on the question of the legal standing of Council Resolutions and the binding effect of Joint Positions, see *supra* Chapter B.

168 Cf. Article 3(4) of the Dublin Convention; Article 29(4) / Article 30(2) SIC.

169 An article 53-1 was inserted into Part VI of the French Constitution of 4 October 1958 by an Act of 25/11/93; cf. *Rossetto*, RMC 1994, 315, 321.

170 Bundesverfassungsgericht (Federal Constitutional Court), judgement of 14 May 1996, Vol. 94, 49.

171 Report of the Federal Ministry of the Interior, 20 June 1995, Asylerfahrungsbericht 1994.

172 For more details see 6.a).

unsuccessful asylum seeker will be returned to his country of origin or to a safe third state according to normal procedures, without making the "detour" through the SIC/Dublin Agreement.

3. *Criteria for the Determination of the Competent State under the Dublin Convention*

Objective criteria are used to determine the state responsible for dealing with an asylum application. The principle common to both treaties in this regard is that the State which takes the greatest share of responsibility for the presence of the asylum seeker in the treaty area should be the one to process the application[173]. A hierarchically ordered catalogue[174], which contains six basic criteria and several modifications and exceptions, has grown out of this principle. Included among these criteria are the following: a family-bond-criterion[175]; the issuing of a residence permit[176]; the possession of a valid visa[177]; illegal entry[178]; the permission to enter without a visa[179] and, as a criterion of last resort, the first application for asylum[180]. In addition to the system of these six basic criteria, the Dublin Convention provides detailed rules for cases in which, for example, the asylum applicant is in possession of one of the following –

- a visa issued on the written authorization of another Contracting Party[181],
- a transit visa[182],
- multiple valid or expired residence permits and visas issued by different Member States[183].

These criteria highlight the fact that the Dublin system does not allow the asylum seeker the freedom to choose the State in which to lodge an asylum application[184]. Furthermore, it must be viewed in close connection with the common visa and external border policy systems. These policy areas were previously covered by the Schengen Convention and for all Member States by the Draft Convention on the Crossing of External Frontiers. This Convention has been

---

173 See also *O'Keeffe*, YEL 1991, 185, 198; *Schraml*, AWR – Bulletin 1991, 65, 69; *Bolten*, in *Meijers*, (ed.), Schengen: Internationalisation of Central chapters of the Law on Aliens, Refugees, Security and Police (1991), 12.

174 Cf. Article 3(2) of the Dublin Convention; such an explicit regulation does not appear in Schengen II.

175 Cf. Article 4 of the Dublin Convention; Article 35 SIC. The term family member is restricted to spouses, children who are minors, or parents where the asylum seeker is a child.

176 Article 5(1) of the Dublin Convention; Article 30(1)(a) SIC.

177 Article 5(2) of the Dublin Convention; Article 30(1)(a) SIC.

178 Article 6 of the Dublin Convention; Article 30(1)(e) SIC.

179 Article 7(1) of the Dublin Convention; Article 30(1)(d) SIC.

180 Article 8 of the Dublin Convention; Article 30(3) SIC.

181 See Article 5(2)(a) of the Dublin Convention.

182 See Article 5(2)(b) and (c) of the Dublin Convention.

183 Article 5(3) and(4) of the Dublin Convention.

184 Criticised by *Achermann*, Das Schengener Übereinkommen als Ausgangspunkt der Harmonisierung europäischer Asylpolitik, in *Achermann* et al. (eds.), Schengen und die Folgen (1995), 79, 101 et seq.

awaiting signature since 1991, but has been blocked due to the dispute between Britain and Spain over the territorial effect of the agreement in Gibraltar, and, more recently, on the question of whether the interpretation of this convention falls within the jurisdiction of the ECJ[185].

The Committee established by Article 18 of the Dublin Convention took a decision on provisions for the implementation of the Dublin Convention on 9 September 1997. Chapter IV of this decision contains regulations on the means of proof to be used and on the procedures to determine the state responsible for examining an asylum application. Two lists of means of proof were established and laid down in Annex III to the decision[186]. List A establishes the means of probative evidence used to conclusively prove responsibility under the Dublin Convention, save where they are rebutted by evidence to the contrary, i.e. with proof that the document is not genuine[187]. List B details means of proof indicating responsibility dependent on an evaluation of all facts of the case. Evidence under List B is by nature rebuttable and the means of proof listed are not exhaustive. Member States are to provide examples of the various types of administrative documents, based on a version contained in List A. Examples of various documents are reproduced in a joint handbook assisting authorities in the identification of false documents produced by asylum seekers. Finally, Article 26 of the Decision No 1/97 of 9 September 1997 contains several regulations on the consequences of the determination of responsibility of the Member States.

The Decision No 1/98 of June 30 1998 of the Committee set up by Article 18 of the Dublin Convention[188] regulates the use of information on ways and means by which asylum seekers enter the European Union, including provisions on the exchange of fingerprint data under Article 15 of the Dublin Convention vital to identify asylum seekers and their travel route within the EU[189].

4. *Personal Scope of Application*

Article 1 of the Dublin Convention defines an application for asylum as a request whereby an alien seeks protection from a Member State under the Geneva Convention by claiming refugee status within the meaning of Article 1 of the Geneva Convention, as amended by the New York Protocol[190]. It is not, therefore, necessary to file a formal application for asylum according to the usual national

---

185 For details on the common visa regime and external border policies of the communitarized SIC provisions see *supra* Chapter C I-II.

186 Article 24(1) of Decision No. 1/97.

187 Article 24(2) of Decision No. 1/97.

188 O.J. 1998 L 196/49.

189 Article 4 of Decision No. 1/98.

190 Although the wording of the application for asylum definition in Article 1 SIC is slightly different in that it makes additional reference to a right of residence, the personal scope of the application of the two conventions does not differ. Protection under the Geneva Convention is also granted if a refugee is enjoying a temporary right of residence until he can voluntarily return or be forcibly deported to a safe third country. Thus, the SIC was applicable irrespective of whether a residence right was obtained in the proper national sense.

procedures. It is sufficient that the refugee asserts in a general way that he has been the subject of political persecution. Whether this claim stands up under subsequent investigation is not relevant to the question of the applicability of the Dublin system for determining responsibility. Equally important, however, is the fact that the Dublin Convention, like the Schengen Implementation Convention, applies solely to asylum applicants, while humanitarian refugees, civil war refugees or persons enjoying protection against refoulement under international human rights treaties, like Article 3 of the European Convention on Human Rights or Article 3 of the United Nations Anti-Torture Convention are not covered as such. A mere assertion on any other grounds for humanitarian protection (e.g. inhumane treatment or torture with no political implications), not aimed at obtaining refugee status under the Geneva Convention, does not fall under the criteria of the Dublin Convention[191].

Although it is quite clear, in theory, that political persecution and inhuman treatment are not identical, it has become increasingly difficult to draw a clear line in practice, particularly in situations like war, civil war or a total collapse of the authority as happened in Somalia or former Yugoslavia. Asylum applicants frequently do not distinguish clearly between political persecution within the meaning of Article 1 of the Geneva Convention, and other forms of persecution, such as inhuman treatment, torture or risks in a general situation of violence or war. They seek whatever protection may be granted. During asylum proceedings, asylum seekers may well change their arguments, implicitly or explicitly withdraw an asylum application directed towards recognition as a convention refugee, and switch to any other form of protection against refoulement available under international or national law. National asylum law, in some cases, does not even clearly distinguish between forms of protection for political persecution and protections against other risks like the death penalty, inhuman treatment or endangerment of life and health.

In Germany, therefore, while a claim to protection from deportation under § 51(1) of the German Aliens Act (Ausländergesetz)[192] will be covered by the Dublin rules, a claim under § 53 of the German Aliens Act (Ausländergesetz)[193] to prevent

---

[191] See also *van der Klaauw*, The Dublin Convention, the Schengen asylum chapter and the treatment of asylum applications, in Het Akkord van Schengen en vreemdelingen; een ongecontroleerde grens tussen recht en beleid?, Verslag studiedag OSR 31 Oktober (1996), 37 (45).

[192] § 51(1) AuslG reads as follows: "An alien may not be expelled to a State in which his life or freedom is threatened on account of his race, religion, nationality, membership of a particular social group or political opinion."

[193] § 53 AuslG – Grounds for refusing to expel –

(1) An alien may not be expelled to a State in which there is actual danger of his being subjected to torture,

(2) An alien may not be expelled to a State in which he is being sought for a criminal act and there is a risk of capital punishment. In such cases, the provisions on extradition will apply.

(3) Where another State has made a formal request for extradition, or for arrest in connection with notification of a request for extradition, the alien may not be expelled to that State until a decision has been made on the extradition.

deportation cannot be upheld under Dublin/Schengen. In any case, seeking protection under § 53 of the German Aliens Act (Ausländergesetz) does not protect foreigners from deportation to other Member States. The "Concept of Normative-Guarantee" of safety (Parliament has declared Member States as "safe third countries") laid down in Article 16a of the Basic Law applies in EU countries since any third-county national who reaches these States is guaranteed protection under the European Convention on Human Rights[194]. In cases in which a foreigner is returned or deported to another EU country, an investigation of potential grounds preventing deportation based on the Convention, as provided for in § 53 of the German Aliens Act (Ausländergesetz), is therefore unfounded[195].

Problems may arise when an asylum application is withdrawn, or when statements are changed in order to ensure some kind of protection. Sometimes claims for protection are changed to inhibit a transfer of responsibility under Dublin. If an asylum applicant withdraws a claim, the Dublin concept becomes inapplicable in principle. Whether a humanitarian refugee seeking protection can be returned or deported to a third state or a Dublin Member State is a matter of national law and bilateral agreements

One could ask, however, whether this principle applies if a request to take responsibility for an asylum application has been formally submitted by a State under the Dublin Convention. A successful request to take over a withdrawal of the asylum claim or a change of arguments clearly does not prevent a transfer of responsibility which has already taken place.

Based on the criteria laid down in the Dublin Convention, one could argue, however, that responsibility for examining an asylum application arises as soon as an asylum application is filed in one Dublin Member State, even if it is later withdrawn. The competent State would then be responsible for examining whether there is still an asylum claim pending in the sense of the Dublin Convention, or whether that application has been effectively withdrawn. While a number of practical reasons support this interpretation, it may prove extremely difficult to verify the existence of a previous asylum claim, and thus allocate exclusive

---

(4) An alien may not be expelled if the expulsion is inadmissible under the Convention on the Protection of Human Rights and Fundamental Freedoms, of 4 November 1950 (BGBl. II 1952, 686).

(5) A general risk that an alien may be threatened with criminal prosecution and punishment in another State and, unless otherwise determined by paragraphs 1 to 4, a specific risk of a statutory penalty pursuant to the laws of another State, will not constitute a bar to expulsion.

(6) The expulsion of an alien to another State may be waived if there is considerable actual risk to the person, the life or the freedom of the alien in that State. Risks in that State to which the population or population group to which the alien belongs are in general exposed, will be taken into account when decisions are made under § 54 AuslG.

[194] Article 16a(2) of the Basic Law provides that asylum should not be granted to someone who enters Germany from a member state of the European Communities or another third country where the application of the Convention relating to the Status of Refugees and the Convention for the Protection of Human Rights and Fundamental Freedom is assured.

[195] See decision of the Federal Constitutional Court (Bundesverfassungsgericht) of 14 May 1996, Vol. 94,49.

responsibility to a State other than the one in which the original asylum claim was submitted.

The answer to this question depends on the interpretation of the legal definitions in Article 1 of the Dublin Convention of the terms "application for asylum" and "examination of an application for asylum," as well as on the determination of the "decisive" moment in the transfer of the third-country national, which then determines if the Dublin Convention is applicable. The government of the Netherlands has suggested that the ultimate classification of an asylum application cannot be decided until responsibility under the Dublin system has been allocated[196]. Responsibility after withdrawal of an application can therefore only be transferred if, at the time of the withdrawal, the request to take over responsibility has already been accepted, since the procedure for determining which country is competent has already been completed.

Demarcation between different categories of refugees is difficult, and highlights the need for further progress in the establishment of an effective mechanism for European burden-sharing with regard to persons admitted on a temporary basis for humanitarian reasons. The Council Resolution of 25 September 1995 on burden-sharing with regard to the admission and residence of displaced persons on a temporary basis[197], as well as the Council Decision of 4 March 1996 on an alert and emergency procedure[198] do not yet present a satisfactory legal basis for coping efficiently with a growing problem of mass influx of "humanitarian refugees"[199].

5. *Obligations of the Contracting Parties and Individual Rights*

The responsible Contracting Party must take charge of the asylum seeker from a non-responsible Member State and must allow him/her to return in the case of movement to another Member State during the course of the proceedings[200]. The Member State responsible for examining an application for asylum according to the criteria described above is obliged to complete the examination of the application for asylum[201]. Article 1(1)(d) of the Dublin Convention defines the term "examination of an application for asylum" in a wide sense, embracing all measures of examination, decisions or rulings given by the competent authorities on an application for asylum, except for procedures used to determine the State responsible for examining the application for asylum pursuant to the Dublin Convention[202]. The procedure for determining the competent State under Article 4

---

[196] Cf. Sch/II-As(96) 39 Rev.

[197] O.J. 1995 C 262/1.

[198] O.J. 1996 L 63/10.

[199] Cf. also *Kerber*, Temporary Protection: An Assessment of the Harmonization policies of European Member States, 9 IJRL (1997), 453 – 471.

[200] Cf. Article 10(1)(a) /Article 11 of the Dublin Convention; Article 31(2) and(3) SIC; on the duty to take back during a current process, see Article 10(1)(c) /Article 13 of the Dublin Convention; Article 33 SIC.

[201] Article 10(1)(b) of the Dublin Convention; similar Article 29(3) SIC.

[202] An identical definition is to be found in Article 1 SIC (processing of an application for asylum).

et seq of the Dublin Convention must, therefore, be carried out separately from the asylum application examination[203].

To ensure adherence to the one-chance-only principle, and to prevent the refugee-in-orbit phenomenon, the Dublin concept of responsibility obliges Member States to examine an application for asylum lodged by an alien, i.e. any person other than a national of a Member State of the European Communities[204], within the territory of any of them[205]. This obligation is, however, restricted in two ways.

First, the obligation is only applicable with regard to third-country nationals. A third-country national is defined as any person other than a national of a Member State of the European Communities[206]. The system for determining responsibility is, therefore, not applicable in cases involving EU citizens[207].

Second, any Member State is free at any time to refer an asylum seeker to a third country[208]. It must, however, observe all obligations under international law, in particular the refoulement prohibition in Article 33 of the Geneva Convention and Article 3 of the European Convention on Human Rights. An asylum seeker may be sent back to a non-EU country regardless of whether the State has responsibility for the asylum application under the Dublin Convention[209]. The Dublin Convention refers to the obligations of the Contracting Parties under the Geneva Convention and calls for cooperation with UNHCR officials in the implementation of the Convention. Every asylum seeker is, therefore, guaranteed the right to have his application dealt with by one of the Member States. The preamble to the Dublin Convention expressly states that the agreement is intended to prevent an asylum seeker being passed from one State to another without any one accepting responsibility for the examination of his application. However, this formulation does not mean that in every case a Member State will be responsible for examining an application for asylum in substance. The Dublin Convention (Article 3(5)) explicitly preserves the right of each Contracting Party to refer an asylum seeker to a third state in accordance with its own national law and

---

203 See also *Huber* in Neue Zeitschrift für Verwaltungsrecht (NVwZ) 1996, 1069, 1073.

204 See definition of Article 1 SIC; Article 1(1)(a) of the Dublin Convention.

205 Cf. Article 29(1) SIC; Article 3(1) of the Dublin Convention extends the duty to investigate to applications made at the border. Whether this formulation actually leads to a materially wider duty to investigate is doubtful, as border controls in general occur within the territory of a country's jurisdiction. In any case, each country is obliged under Article 33 of the Geneva Convention not to send asylum seekers who seek protection at their borders back to the country of persecution; see *Classen*, DVBl. 1993, 700, 703; for diss. view *Achermann*, Das Schengener Übereinkommen als Ausgangspunkt der Harmonisierung europäischer Asylpolitik in *Achermann* et al. (eds.), Schengen und die Folgen (1995), 79, 92.

206 Cf. Article 1(1)(a) of the Dublin Convention; Article 1 SIC. The definition of the term Alien deserves special attention in the context of the Schengen Convention: although not all Member States are included in the Schengen Convention, only citizens of non-EU countries are counted as Aliens for the purposes of realizing an area without internal borders (Article 7 a ECT).

207 Criticised by *Achermann*, Das Schengener Übereinkommen als Ausgangspunkt der Harmonisierung europäischer Asylpolitik, in *Achermann* et al. (eds.), Schengen und die Folgen (1995), 79, 113.

208 Cf. Article 29(2) SIC; Article 3(5) of the Dublin Convention. A third country is any country which is not a party to the Schengen/Dublin Conventions, see Article 1 SIC.

209 Cf. No. 3 of the Resolution on a harmonized approach to questions concerning host third countries, passed by Immigration Ministers in London, 30/11 and 1/12/92, reproduced in *Hailbronner*, Ausländerrecht, D 9.3.

international commitments. If a rejection, expulsion or deportation to a third country is not possible or suitable, a contracting state may request that the country responsible under the Dublin system takes responsibility for the application. That State may then investigate, following the transfer of the asylum seeker, the possibility of sending the asylum seeker to a safe third country. Decisions of this nature may be reached exclusively in accordance with national law, although such decisions must conform with the refoulement prohibition in the Geneva Convention. A duty to examine the application for asylum only arises if transfer to a safe third country proves impossible.

These provisions have been the subject of heavy criticism[210]. It has been argued that lack of a guarantee to have an asylum claim examined in substance by one of the Contracting States, as well as the reference to the third-country concept, is contrary to the purpose of the Dublin Convention as laid down in the preamble, i.e. to guarantee that every application for asylum will be examined by one of the Member States. Other authors hold, in addition, that these provisions violate the Geneva Convention, if not in substance, then "at least in its spirit", by permitting a return or rejection to a third state which may not provide sufficient access to an asylum procedure.

While it is true that the Convention does not guarantee that every asylum application will be examined in substance by one of the Contracting States, this critique fails to take the basic legal prerequisites for a general obligation to process asylum claims in account. The Dublin Convention was not intended to provide a legal basis for obligations which extend beyond those already established under the Geneva Convention. Signatories to the Geneva Convention are not obliged to grant refugee status, or even to admit asylum seekers to an asylum procedure, in order to determine whether they qualify as a Convention refugee. The Geneva Convention only provides for access to a procedure in order to determine whether an applicant would face a serious risk of persecution in case of return, rejection or deportation. Neither the Schengen Convention nor Dublin were created to change the basic rules on the obligation of States towards asylum seekers. Furthermore, as a matter of legal policy, there seems to be little point in establishing a general right to examine an asylum application without regard to the possibility of receiving sufficient protection in third states. A guarantee to have the asylum claim examined in one of the Member States of the Union would hardly promote the development of further cooperation with third countries in the area of asylum law, whether through bi- or multilateral agreements. This does not mean that the concept of a safe third country, which itself is a major component of the co-ordination of European asylum policy, is not without deficiencies. Further European cooperation is needed with regard to a common procedure of evaluating the relative safety of third countries, as well as with regard to a procedure for the rejection or return to safe third countries in connection with adequate precautions to guarantee that *bona fide* asylum seekers do, indeed, have a fair chance of

---

[210] See *Bolten* in Meijers (ed.), Schengen: Internationalisation of Central chapters of the Law on Aliens, Refugees, Security and Police (1991), 22; *Gerlach*, Zeitschrift für Rechtspolitik (ZRP) 1993, 164, 166; *Ulmer*, Asylrecht und Menschenwürde (1996), 92 et seq.

gaining access to an asylum procedure. Establishment of the area comprising Member States' territories as a guaranteed asylum resort, however, does not seem appropriate, particularly in the light of the progress made in the establishment of an international regime of refugee protection.

Furthermore, it is also important to remember that, even in cases in which there is no alternative protection available, the obligation to examine an application for asylum does not imply a right of entry or residence[211], or an individual right to asylum. Neither the wording nor the spirit of the Dublin Convention create an individual right of asylum. The determination of criteria of exclusive responsibility does not restrict each Contracting State's right to determine each application in accordance with its national provisions. Whether, and under what conditions an entitlement to asylum exists is dependent on relevant provisions in national legislation, independent of the provisions establishing responsibility under the Dublin Convention. Contracting Parties are simply obliged to observe the terms of the Geneva Convention. As no right to asylum can be derived from the Geneva Convention, it follows that none can be derived from the Dublin Convention, which merely refers to the Geneva Convention on this issue[212]. The history of the Convention confirms this argument: the concept of an individual right to asylum has never received support at the international level and was never a subject of serious intergovernmental negotiations[213].

An evaluation of the extent to which certain provisions of the Dublin Convention are directly applicable and may imply individual rights for asylum seekers must be dealt with separately. Direct applicability of international treaties in the municipal law of every Contracting State is to be determined by national law. The emergence of individual rights generally requires that treaty provisions are sufficiently precise, as well as designed in their international context to create individual rights. In response to a corresponding question from the Austrian delegation on the interpretation of the Dublin Convention, the Council General Secretariat stated in its reply of March 1995[214] that an examination of the principles, structure and provisions of the Convention led to the conclusion that it was only addressed to the Member States. No provision in the Convention could, therefore, be interpreted as giving an asylum seeker the right to demand that his application is dealt with by a particular Member State. Nor do the provisions of the Dublin Convention which require the agreement of the asylum seeker create any such right[215]; they merely entitle the asylum seeker to prevent the application of these provisions and, hence, indirectly reduce the number of applicable criteria for determining responsibility, which would then be restricted to those contained in

---

211 Cf. Article 29(2)(1) SIC; the Dublin Convention has no provision on this point.

212 See also *Huber*, Neue Zeitschrift für Verwaltungsrecht (NVwZ) 1996, 1060, 1073; on the Refoulement prohibition see *Kälin*, Das Prinzip des Non-Refoulement, (1982) *passim*; *Gornig*, das Refoulement-Verbot im Völkerrecht (1987) *passim*; *Stenberg*, Non-Expulsion und Non-Refoulement (1989) *passim*.

213 Cf. the reply of the German government on 1 August 1994 to a question to Parliament, Bundestags-Drucksache (Parliament Document) 12/8342; on the right to asylum cf. *Tomuschat*, Europäische Grundrechte-Zeitschrift (EuGRZ) 1992, 257.

214 Doc. 5118/95 ASIM 52.

215 Cf. Article 9, 3(4) of the Dublin Convention.

Articles 4-8 of the Dublin Convention. Accordingly, an asylum seeker cannot be a party to a dispute in a procedure between Member States on determination of responsibility. This does not, however, exclude Member States taking the interests of asylum seekers or special links with a particular Member State into account[216].

Whether this interpretation proves correct will depend largely on the practice in Member States. Generally speaking, the Council Secretariat rightly emphasizes the interstate-character of the obligations established by the Dublin Convention. The formulation of Article 3(1) of the Dublin Convention "Member States undertake to examine" points to a restricted meaning of the obligations placed on Member States by the Convention. All rhetoric aside, it is clear that the basic purpose of the obligation is to process an application for asylum. Similarly, the purpose of the Dublin Convention as a whole is to establish a system of allocation of responsibility, primarily in the public interest. Conversely, the preamble of the Dublin Convention states that the agreement is to avoid any situation in which applicants for asylum are left in indefinite doubt with regard to the likely outcome of their application. It obliges all Contracting Parties to "provide all applicants with a guarantee that their applications will be examined by one of the Dublin States." As previously mentioned, however, this motive is not sufficiently reflected in the substantive provisions of the Convention. Each Member State has the right to deal with an application for asylum outside the framework of the agreement. Furthermore, all Member States reserve the right to send an asylum seeker to a third state in accordance with national law and international commitments. It seems clear, therefore, that the system established by the Dublin Convention does not, and is not intended to establish individual rights beyond the national legal framework of the Member States. The final judgement, however, will be made by national courts. National courts may very well argue that the Convention does, in fact, establish individual rights, especially with regard to Article 3(4) and Article 9 of the Dublin Convention.

Divergent interpretations of the Dublin Convention may lead to an undesirable variance in practice. A certain level of harmonization in the interpretation of the Dublin provisions is, therefore, clearly needed. Article 68(1) ECT stipulates that the ECJ may be requested to give a ruling if a question on the interpretation of the new ECT Title on the validity or interpretation of acts of Community institutions based on Title IV ECT is raised in a case pending before a court or tribunal against whose decisions there is no judicial remedy under national law[217]. In addition, pursuant to Article 68(3) ECT, the European Court of Justice has jurisdiction on the above mentioned matters if the Council, the Commission or a Member State so requests.

---

[216] Cf. Article 4 of the Dublin Convention.

[217] The ECJ shall not have jurisdiction to rule on any measure or decision taken pursuant to the proviso concerning the maintenance of law and order and the safeguarding of internal security, cf. Article 68(2) of Title in the ECT. On the question of who is to decide on the limits of the ECJ`s jurisdiction, see supra Chapter B XI 3.

6. *Transfer Procedure*

a) Transfer Requests to Signatory States

When a person seeking asylum in one of the Member States submits an application, the official responsible is to examine whether the asylum claim falls within the scope of application of the Dublin Agreement. If the official cannot prove that responsibility should be allocated to another Signatory State, or decides that the application fulfils the conditions for the use of the safeguard clause, an asylum procedure will be initiated. If there is sufficient evidence to prove that the case should be assigned to another Signatory State, the case will be passed to the agency responsible for the Dublin-coordination.

Dublin rules also apply if an asylum seeker enters a Member State via a third country which is also a Contracting Party of the Schengen Implementation Convention[218]. Even if a Member State has enacted safe third country rules, e.g. Germany, these rules are replaced by Dublin rules on responsibility. The Co-ordinating Agency examines whether the requirements for a transferral of responsibility to another Signatory State are met.

If a Member State decides that another Signatory State is responsible for processing an asylum claim, a "standard form for determining the State responsible for an application for asylum"[219] is completed. A written request is filed, asking for a transferral, and is sent to the agency responsible for such matters in the state in question. The request must be made no later than six months after the application for asylum; if this limit is not observed, the state to which the application was initially directed retains responsibility for the case[220]. If a requested state denies responsibility within a period of three months after the request for transferral, the requesting Member State has the right of rejoinder. If the requested country refuses to accept the case even after a renewed application, the co-ordinating Agency of the requesting country will usually pass the case on to the appropriate branch of the competent authority for the recognition of foreign refugees and the application will be processed. If the requested State agrees to accept responsibility, or if it does not respond to the request within a period of three months – which is viewed as implicit acceptance of the request[221] – the asylum seeker's case will be dealt with according to national law.

Germany applies the following procedure: If an asylum seeker arrives from a Signatory State which approved the transfer, it must first be proven that the asylum seeker has no right to asylum in Germany by virtue of his arrival from a Signatory State. Second, his deportation to the Signatory State of origin will be arranged[222]. Objections to deportation raised during the examination process on the grounds of

---

[218] See Federal Ministry of the Interior BMI, Asylerfahrungsbericht 1994 (20/6/1995); Bundesverfassungsgericht (Federal Constitutional Court), 14 May 1996, Neue Zeitschrift für Verwaltungsrecht (NVwZ) 1996, 702.

[219] Cf. annex 4 Schengen Document.

[220] Article 11(1) of the Dublin Convention.

[221] Article 11(4) of the Dublin Convention.

[222] See § 29(3) read together with §§ 26a, 34a of the German Asylum Procedure Act (Asylverfahrensgesetz).

alleged danger of political persecution or inhuman treatment are not taken into consideration[223]. The asylum seeker may lodge an objection to the order for deportation within two weeks after the order has been issued[224]. This objection, however, does not automatically suspend the order[225]. In addition, it is not possible to stop a deportation by claiming a temporary legal protection provided under the regulations governing administrative courts[226]. The deportation order takes immediate effect and, in practice, is to be carried out as soon as the order for deportation is issued.

If the asylum seeker did not arrive via a Signatory State which approved the transferral, the application will be dismissed and the applicant will be required to leave the Federal Republic of Germany within a week of notification of the decision[227]. If the applicant refuses to leave the country, deportation to the responsible Signatory State will be announced[228]. Objections to deportation raised during the examination process may also be disregarded[229]. Legal action against an order to leave the country within a given time limit, as well as against the announcement of deportation, may be taken within a week[230]. The action has no suspensory effect[231]. The asylum seeker may, however, apply for temporary legal protection[232].

In practice, the three month limit on responses to requests to take over responsibility has proven too long to achieve a workable application of the system of allocation of responsibility. Due to the fact that Signatory States are limited in their right to detain asylum seekers, asylum seekers frequently disappear during the three month investigation period. Two recommendations have been adopted within the Schengen Agreement in order to solve this problem. The first reduces the length of the response period to one month[233]. The second restricts the implementation of a period of investigation to include urgent transferral requests only.

The Dublin Convention, in contrast, provides for a time limit of three months without flexibility[234]. Given the practical need to incorporate the shortened Schengen time limits into the Dublin Convention, a Committee decision

---

223 § 31(3) of the German Asylum Procedure Act (Asylverfahrensgesetz). In different circumstances according to § 53 of the German Aliens Act (Ausländergesetz) such objections must be considered.

224 See § 74(1) of the German Asylum Procedure Act (Asylverfahrensgesetz), § 42(1) Administrative Courts Act (VwGO).

225 § 75 of the German Asylum Procedure Act (Asylverfahrensgesetz).

226 § 34a(2) of the German Asylum Procedure Act (Asylverfahrensgesetz). This provision is consistent with the Basic Law: See Federal Constitutional Court (BVerfG), 14/5/96, Neue Zeitschrift für Verwaltungsrecht (NVwZ) 1996, 708.

227 § 36(1) of the German Asylum Procedure Act (Asylverfahrensgesetz); see § 29(3)(1) of the German Asylum Procedure Act (Asylverfahrensgesetz).

228 See § 35(2) of the German Asylum Procedure Act (Asylverfahrensgesetz).

229 § 31(3)(3) of the German Asylum Procedure Act (Asylverfahrensgesetz).

230 See § 74(1) of the German Asylum Procedure Act (Asylverfahrensgesetz), § 42(1) Administrative Courts Act (VwGO).

231 § 75 of the German Asylum Procedure Act (Asylverfahrensgesetz)

232 See § 36(3) and(4) of the German Asylum Procedure Act (Asylverfahrensgesetz).

233 11/683/96 ASIM 159.

234 Article 11(4) of the Dublin Convention.

established a different time limit in Article 11(6) of the Dublin Convention than that required under Article 18 of the Dublin Convention. According to Article 4 of the Committee's Decision No 1/97 of 9 September 1997[235], the Member State responsible for an applicant is to make every effort to reply to the request within a period not exceeding one month from the date on which the request was received. In particularly difficult cases, the requested Member State may also, before the one-month time limit expires, produce a temporary reply indicating the period within which it will be possible to give a definite reply. The period of extension should be as short as possible and may not exceed the period of three months from the date on which the request was received under any circumstances, as regulated in Article 11(4) of the Dublin Convention[236]. The Committee will assess the effects of this provision in practice after one year. It will be decided at that time whether a period of one month will be implemented as a maximum time limit[237].

The process of transferral is to be initiated upon agreement of the requested State. Transfer of the asylum seeker must take place no later than one month after the acceptance of the transferral request[238]. The fact that it is frequently impossible in practice to execute a transfer within this time limit, despite all reasonable efforts on the part of the requesting State, however, could place the legal nature of this time limit in question. If it is to be seen as an exclusive time limit, failure to complete the transfer in a timely manner would make the State requesting a transferral responsible for the asylum application. An asylum seeker could evade, e.g. by hiding, transfer and render the agreement ineffective. In a decision related to the purpose of Schengen II, the Executive Committee[239] held that the Signatory State which accepts the transferral is to remain responsible for the applicant if the transfer cannot be executed within a period of one month due to the actions of the asylum seeker (e.g.: disappearance, illness, pregnancy, imprisonment). It retains responsibility until it can be proven that the asylum seeker has left the Schengen territory. If, however, the failure to transfer within the time limit cannot be attributed to the actions of the asylum seeker, the requesting State is to be held responsible for the asylum claim[240].

Regulations on the transfer of asylum applicants are found in Decision No. 1/97 of 9 September 1997 of the Committee set up by Article 18 of the Dublin Convention[241]. Where it is agreed that the applicant should be transferred to a second Member State, the first Member State is bound to ensure as far as possible that the applicant does not evade transfer. For this purpose, the first Member State will determine, in the light of the circumstances of each case, and in accordance with national laws and procedures, how the transfer of the applicant should take

---

[235] O.J. 1997 L 281/1.

[236] Article 4(2) of the Committee's Decision No. 1/97 of 9 September 1997.

[237] Article 4(4) of the Committee's Decision No. 1/97 of 9 September 1997.

[238] Article 11(5) of the Dublin Convention.

[239] Cf. annex 4 Sch/II-As(96) 36.

[240] Cf. of Article 11(5) of the Dublin Convention providing that a transfer of the applicant must take place not later than one month after acceptance of the request to take over; see also Conclusions of the Immigration Ministers relating to the transfer of asylum applicants pursuant to the Dublin Convention, 4464/1/95 CIREA 3 rev. 1 sec. I, H.

[241] O.J. 1997 L 281/1.

place[242]. Article 21 of Decision No. 1/97 establishes several deadlines for the transfer of asylum applicants. A specimen *laissez-passer* for transfer of applicants for asylum is provided for in Annex II hereto[243].

b) Transferral Requests from Signatory States

All applications by other States to take over responsibility are processed and examined on the basis of the files provided by the SIC (e.g.: visa, residence permit) and other evidence. Evidence provided by the Schengen Document, as well as a coherent, extensively detailed, and verifiable statement made by the applicant are taken into consideration[244]. If the requested State decides that the case should remain within the jurisdiction of the requesting State, it must submit a written justification for this decision. The answer to a request for transfer of responsibility must be given within a period of one month, if possible, and within a maximum period of three months (failure to answer to be taken as acceptance, see above). If the requested State comes to the conclusion that it is responsible for a case, then the request to take over responsibility is accepted. While the method of transfer is being deliberated, the competent agency in the Signatory State is informed of the intended final destination of the applicant[245], and is asked whether the applicant will be travelling voluntarily or whether he will be accompanied. In order to ensure that the asylum seeker is not denied entry, the border agencies concerned are notified of the impending transfer[246]. The Member State transferring the asylum seeker receives a receipt upon arrival of the applicant – this document completes the transfer process.

7. *Problems of Application*

a) Retroactive Application

Neither the Schengen Implementation Convention nor the Dublin Convention are applicable retroactively. Asylum applications submitted prior to the entry into force of the Dublin Agreement do not fall into the scope of application of the Convention. Whether evidence used to determine the allocation of responsibility which took place before 26 March 1995 (such as the issue of visa, residence permits etc.) are to be taken into account, however, is still a matter of debate. Although the Schengen States have not reached agreement on this issue, a pragmatic consensus has been reached, which allows that visa and residence

---

[242] Article 20(1) of Decision No. 1/97.
[243] Article 22 of Decision No. 1/97.
[244] Cf. Recommendations of the Central Group for the Harmonization of the requirements for determining the responsible State, Sch/II-As(96) 36 App 2.
[245] This is usually the institution which lies nearest to the place of transferral on the border, cf. § 18(1) of the German Asylum Procedure Act (Asylverfahrensgesetz).
[246] Cf. § 18(4) No 1 of the German Asylum Procedure Act (Asylverfahrensgesetz).

permits issued before Schengen entered into force are to be taken into account for asylum proceedings still pending at that time. In addition, recognition as a refugee and the granting of a right of residence[247] are relevant for the determination of responsibility, even if this recognition was granted prior to 26 March 1995.

No agreement, however, could be reached on the determination of responsibility in cases in which an asylum seeker was rejected before Schengen entered into force. The majority of the Contracting States refuse responsibility on the basis of previous rejections of asylum applications, with the argument that consideration of such applications would, in effect, amount to a retroactive application of the Convention.

b) The Dublin Convention and the Visa Regime of the Draft External Borders Convention

A number of other problems may affect the application of the Dublin Convention. One problem may result from the link between the Dublin Convention and the visa regime for the EU, as established in the EU Draft External Borders Convention, and for the Schengen States in the Schengen Implementation Convention. It was originally assumed that the External Border Convention would enter into force more or less simultaneously with the Dublin Convention. Due to the ongoing dispute between the United Kingdom and Spain over the status of Gibraltar and, more importantly, the recent signature of the Amsterdam Treaty which covers the same area of regulation, however, it seems as if the External Border Convention will never be ratified[248]. As a result, the rules on the crossing of external borders and on a common visa regime will remain applicable for the Schengen Contracting States, but not for the non-Schengen Dublin States. Although the two sets of rules are technically quite different, they are linked in a number of ways, as shown by the decision of the Schengen Executive Committee on 27 June 1996 on the issuance of visa issued on the authorisation of another Contracting State. Under the Schengen system, such a visa, if issued in accordance with the common rules laid down in Articles 9 and 17 SIC, allocates responsibility to the represented State[249]. Similar rules apply under the Dublin Convention[250]. The Dublin Convention, however, requires the written authorization of another Member State. This may not always be reasonable or possible among Schengen States, or in light of the prospective European visa policy. Divergence in the application of the Dublin Convention may arise as a result due to varying regulation of the visa regime.

---

247 Article 35(1) SIC.
248 See above III.
249 Article 30 SIC.
250 Article 5 of the Dublin Convention.

c) Family Reunification

Use of the consultation procedure established in Article 9 of the Dublin Convention becomes a matter of consideration if visas are issued to spouses by different Dublin Member States. Under this provision, a Contracting Party other than the one responsible under the above mentioned criteria can be asked to accept responsibility at the request of the asylum seeker, if the request can be justified by "*humanitarian reasons based in particular on family or cultural grounds.*" [251] Adjudication of this request is, in principle, left to the Member State to which it is submitted. A duty to bring families together exists under Article 4 of the Dublin Convention only when a Member State has already granted refugee status to one member of the family. In principle, both agreements operate on the basis that asylum applications from members of the same family may be dealt with in different countries. Deviation from the rules for determining responsibility is only allowed for in cases in which special humanitarian and family grounds exist. The Dublin Agreement does not establish criteria to determine what constitutes a special humanitarian ground. Examples of special humanitarian and family grounds could conceivably include serious illness or other particular need for care of a family member, as well as minority, pregnancy or birth. The above-mentioned principle notwithstanding, it remains questionable whether, under the conditions in Article 9 of the Dublin Convention, a Contracting Party may be obliged to accept responsibility under Article 8 of the European Convention on Human Rights[252]. It could be argued that Article 8 of the Convention is breached if the asylum procedure takes longer for reasons beyond the control of the asylum seeker, thus separating an existing family, or if it can be shown that the separation of a family member from the rest of the family should be deemed intolerable. The same argument could be used in relation to children who are dependent on the care of one or both parents. State responsibility in cases in which different Member States are responsible for different family members could be determined according to the "majority principle", whereby responsibility would be attributed to the Member State with the greatest number of family members.

d) Practical Problems and Experiences

The implementation of the Dublin Concept has not yet proven significant in the effort to reduce the number of manifestly unfounded or abusive asylum claims.

In 1996 Germany was asked to take over responsibility for 2,641 cases. 1,505 requests came from the Netherlands, of which 78 per cent were successful. 856 requests were from France, with a success rate of 39 per cent. 769 asylum seekers were actually sent to Germany.

In comparison, Germany made transfer requests for 1,330 cases; 69 per cent of these requests were granted. The bulk of the requests (89 per cent) was addressed

---

[251] Cf. Article 9(2) of the Dublin Convention; Article 36 SIC.

[252] See *Frowein/Zimmermann*, Der völkerrechtliche Rahmen für die Reform des deutschen Asylrechts, Bundesanzeiger No. 42a (1993), 50 et seq.

to France (566) and to the Netherlands (435). By 31 December 1996, 713 asylum seekers had been handed over to the responsible State.

Differing rates of acceptance for transfer requests may result from varying interpretations of the Schengen requirements relating to proof. Both conventions contain provisions on the information or proof necessary to determine responsibility. Requests for transfer of responsibility have been unsuccessful in many cases partly due to differing application of the requirements of the Schengen Convention, particularly in cases in which requests have been based on the statement of an asylum applicant without any further evidence.

With regard to this problem, the Central Group adopted a recommendation providing that requests based on the statement of an asylum applicant are, in principle, admissible provided that the applicant's statement is consistent, sufficiently detailed and verifiable[253].

A similar conclusion is to be expected for the Dublin Convention. There is, however, no explicit legal basis for simply transferring recommendations and resolutions of the Schengen Executive Committee to the Dublin Convention. On the other hand, from a practical perspective, it is difficult to see how the Non-Schengen States could prevent a recourse to previous practices under the Schengen Implementation Convention. The problem could be solved through a reference to the practical application of the Schengen rules in a common declaration of the Dublin States upon the entry into force of the Dublin Convention.

A comparative survey shows that Schengen cases accounted for 1.2 per cent of all German, 16 per cent of all French, 7 per cent of all Dutch, 36.2 per cent of all Portuguese and 3.63 per cent of all Spanish asylum applications[254].

One may speculate about the relatively small number of Schengen cases, particularly taking into consideration the number of cases in which an asylum seeker is transferred to the responsible state, as well as the significant administrative efforts still necessary for transfer. Even after a request to take over responsibility has been granted, a high percentage of asylum seekers disappear before they can be transferred, in order to prevent their return or deportation to the responsible state[255]. If national authorities have to wait for the outcome of national judicial procedures against a deportation order, the four-week time limit for a transfer of responsibility is likely to frequently prove insufficient.

In addition, it has become increasingly difficult to obtain information about the travel route of an asylum applicant. Since the entry into force of the Schengen Implementation Convention/Dublin Agreement, asylum seekers have rapidly been trying to avoid return or transfer to the responsible State. Obligatory and comprehensive finger-printing, which would also require corresponding national legislative measures, seems to be crucial to the effort to reduce the number of multiple asylum claims within the European Union.

---

[253] Recommendations of the Central Group regarding Harmonization of the Conditions Required for Establishing the Responsibility of a State, adopted in March 7, 1996, SCH/II-AS(96) 36, Annex II; 11638/96 ASIM 159.

[254] The numbers refer to the date of entry-into-force of the Schengen Convention, 26 March 1995 until 1 January 1996, Sch/II-As(96) 36 App 6.

[255] Approx. 30 percent of all asylum seekers in Germany disappear before a transfer can be effected.

The number of Schengen cases does not, however, indicate definite success or failure of the Dublin system as such. A well-functioning system would reduce "asylum shopping" through the very existence of rules on the allocation of exclusive responsibility. Even a highly organized system of refugee movements is, however, sensitive to legal and administrative loopholes. In addition, the psychological impacts of the implementation of these systems must also be considered. It is difficult to estimate exactly how many asylum seekers would have tried their luck in another Schengen State, had the Schengen Convention not entered into force. In any case, there is no alternative to the fundamental philosophy behind the Dublin concept of attributing responsibility to only one Member State of the European Union.

The Schengen and Dublin Convention have established a special type of burden-shifting rather than a burden-sharing. Under the Dublin Convention, besides States who may rightly be held responsible for carrying the burden of asylum proceedings by issuing a visa or residence permit, there are also states which have to carry the main burden of a massive influx of illegal migrants due to their geographical location. In the absence of an effective system to identify asylum seekers and travel routes, the Dublin system works to the disadvantage of those states in which asylum seekers actually file an asylum claim, primarily those Member States in the proximity of regions producing mass refugee movements. The Dublin system therefore in its present form can hardly be considered as a model of burden-sharing.

8. *EURODAC*

a) The History of Eurodac[256]

One of the most important problems in the practical application of the Dublin rules is to establish a person's identity and travel route. Frequently asylum applicants have either no documents or fake documents. The effective operation of the Dublin mechanism depends on the possibility to identify asylum seekers and to establish their travel route into the EU. In 1991 it was agreed that a feasibility study for a Community-wide fingerprint system for asylum applicants should be undertaken. The result was the decision to establish a system for the computerized comparison of fingerprints in order to facilitate the application of the relevant rules for determining which Member State is responsible for considering an application for asylum.

In March 1996 Member States began negotiations on a convention to establish an identification system based on the comparison of the fingerprints of asylum seekers. In December 1998 they agreed upon a draft "Convention drawn upon the basis of Article K.3 of the Treaty of European Union concerning the establishment of "Eurodac" for the comparison of fingerprints of applicants for asylum." The

[256] Cf. explanatory memorandum of a Proposal for a Council Regulation (EC) concerning the establishment of "Eurodac" for the comparison of the fingerprints of applicants for asylum and certain other aliens, para 1, COM(99) 260 final – CNS 99/0116.

Eurodac system consists of a computerized central database equipped with a fingerprint recognition system. The system would function through the collection of fingerprint data by Member States and its transmission to this Central Unit. The Member States are legally obliged to take fingerprints of every non-EU (third-country) national aged 14 or over who applies for asylum. The Central Unit would compare individual sets of fingerprints against the data retained in the system at the request of a Member State. The fingerprint data should be stored for ten years if there are no exceptions requiring an earlier deletion.

The arrival of a large number of migrants from the Middle East, especially from Iraq in 1997, promoted the European Council in Luxembourg to call for a response to the "massive influx." In January 1998 the foreign ministers agreed to examine whether Eurodac should be extended to illegal immigrants. The result was the submission of a draft Protocol in February 1999, which was intended to further facilitate the application of the Dublin Convention by providing for the collection of fingerprint data relating to persons apprehended in connection with the irregular crossing of an external border. This data would be available for the purposes of comparison with the fingerprints of aliens who subsequently claim asylum in one of the Member States. In addition, the Protocol provided for the possibility of Member States to check with Eurodac data in order to determine whether a person found illegally present within a Member State had previously claimed asylum in another Member State.

The original intention to adopt the Eurodac Convention and the Additional Protocol as intergovernmental instruments under Title VI of the Treaty on European Union has been outdated by the entry into force of the Amsterdam Treaty which has conferred, upon the Community, the competence to enact binding rules in asylum and immigration matters.

The Council (Justice and Home Affairs) decided at its meetings on 3-4 December 1998 and 12 March 1999 to "freeze" the texts of the Convention and the Protocol and invited the Commission to put forward a proposal for a Community legal instrument incorporating the frozen texts. In July 1999 the Commission submitted a proposal for a Council Regulation (EC) concerning the establishment of "Eurodac" for the comparison of the fingerprints of applicants for asylum and certain other aliens[257] as its first legislative proposal under Title IV ECT.

b) The Proposal for a Council Regulation (EC) Concerning the Establishment of "Eurodac"

The draft regulation is based in substance on the draft Convention and the draft Protocol[258]. Provisions which would be incompatible with the nature of the proposed legal instrument and its legal framework have been omitted[259] –

---

[257] Cf. COM(99) 260 final – CNS 99/0116.

[258] Both drafts are reprinted in the Annex of the Proposal for a Council Regulation (EC) concerning the establishment of "Eurodac" for the comparison of the fingerprints of applicants for asylum and certain other aliens. COM(99) 260 final – CNS 99/0116.

- In contrast to the draft Convention the draft Regulation does not need to confer jurisdiction on the Court of Justice.
- There is no need for implementation provisions because the ECT grants sufficient power to the Commission.
- A major change concerns the adaptation of Eurodac to the data protection regime established under the ECT, in particular to Directive 95/46/EC on the protection of individuals with regard to the processing of personal data and on the free movement of such data.

The Commission has argued that "since the Eurodac system is set up on the basis of Title IV of the Treaty (Visa, asylum, immigration and other policies related to free movement of persons), the processing of personal data carried out by the Member States within the context of the Eurodac system is subject to the principles laid down by Directive 95/46/EC". Consequently, the Commission states that –

> the national data protection supervisory authorities established under the Directive are responsible for monitoring the processing of personal data by the Member States in the framework of Eurodac. By virtue of Article 286 of the Treaty, Directive 95/46/EC also applies to the processing of personal data by the Central Unit, since the Central Unit will be established within the Commission. The Central Unit will be subject to the Regulation which the Commission will propose under Article 286 of the Treaty, and to supervision by the independent supervisory body referred to in Article 286. Articles 13 to 20 of this Regulation clarify and specify some of the principles laid down in Directive 95/46/EC in relation to the specific situation of Eurodac. Amendments have been made to the frozen Convention text to ensure that the Regulation is consistent with the requirements laid down in Directive 95/46/EC. Article 6 of the frozen Protocol text, which restricted the right of access of persons apprehended in connection with the irregular crossing of an external border, has not been incorporated in the Regulation, since it is incompatible with Directive 95/46/EC.

c) General Provisions

Article 1[260] of the draft regulation determines the purpose of the Eurodac system. The system may only be used to determine which Member State is responsible under the Dublin Convention for examining an application for asylum lodged in a Member State, and to facilitate the application of the Dublin Convention under the conditions set out in this Regulation (Article 1(1)) while any other purposes are excluded. Data cannot be used or requested for criminal investigations or

---

[259] Cf. explanatory memorandum of a Proposal for a Council Regulation (EC) concerning the establishment of "Eurodac" for the comparison of the fingerprints of applicants for asylum and certain other aliens, para 4.2, COM(99)260 final – CNS 99/0116.

[260] The following description of the contents of the proposal widely follows the explanatory memorandum of the Commission proposal, para 4.5, COM(99)260 final – CNS 99/0116.

administrative control purposes. In accordance with Article 1(2) Eurodac shall consist of a Central Unit (para (a)), a computerized central database in which the data is processed for the purpose of comparing the fingerprints of applicants for asylum and certain other aliens (para (b)) and means of data transmission between the Member States and the central database (para (c)). Article 1 also provides that the rules governing Eurodac shall apply to operations effected by the Member States as from the transmission of data to the Central Unit until use is made of the results of the comparison (Article 1(2)) and that without prejudice to the use of data intended for Eurodac by the Member State of origin in databases set up under the latter's national law, fingerprints and other personal data may be processed in Eurodac only for the purposes set out in Article 15(1) of the Dublin Convention (Article 1(3)). This means that fingerprints which a Member State takes and communicates to the Eurodac Central Unit may also be used in databases set up under that Member State's national law for another purpose[261]. The Central Unit will be located within the Commission. Article 3 also concerns the compilation of statistical data, a new addition since the draft Convention but necessary for an effective monitoring of performance and utility of Eurodac.

The terms used in the Regulation generally have the same meaning as in the draft Convention. A difference is made concerning the definition of "applicant for asylum". For the purpose of Eurodac, Article 2 specifies that it covers persons on whose behalf an asylum application has been made. This is designed in particular to cover minors aged between 14 and 18 years, on whose behalf an application may be lodged by a guardian or legal representative[262].

d) Data on Applicants for Asylum

According to Article 4(1) every Member State is obliged to fingerprint every asylum applicant aged at least 14 years of age and to transmit the fingerprint data together with other data specified in Article 5 to the Central Unit. The Central Unit records this data immediately (para 2). Article 4(3) provides that the Central Unit has to compare each received new set of fingerprints of an asylum applicant with the fingerprint data on asylum applicants which has been supplied by other Member States and has been stored in the central database. Thereby multiple asylum applications within the territory of the Member States shall be identified. According to Article 4(4), a Member State may also request that fingerprints of an asylum applicant transmitted to the Central Unit are also compared with fingerprint data on asylum applicants previously transmitted to the Central Unit.

The Central Unit communicates the results to the Member State of origin. In the case of an apparent match the Member State of origin has to check the comparison as well. If the checking confirms the results of the Central Unit the Member State and the other Member States concerned have to apply the procedures set out in the

---

[261] So expressly the explanatory memorandum of the proposal for an EURODAC-Regulation, COM(99)260 final – CNS 99/0116, para 4.5.

[262] Cf. for this and other slight differences: explanatory memorandum of the proposal for an EURODAC-Regulation, COM(99)260 final – CNS 99/0116, para 4.5.

Dublin Convention. If verification at the national level shows that the apparent match detected by the Central Unit is not in fact a genuine match or that the data is otherwise unreliable, the Member State of origin shall erase the data as soon as this is established. Para 7 provides for the adoption of implementing rules setting out the detailed procedures necessary for the application of this Article. The procedures for taking the fingerprints are left to the Member States concerned, acting in accordance with the obligations under the European Convention for the Protection of Human Rights and Fundamental Freedoms.

Article 5 provides an exhaustive list of the data which must be recorded in the central database (para 1). Media used for transmitting fingerprint data to the Central Unit will be destroyed, in the interests of data protection and security, unless the Member State of origin has requested their return.

Data on asylum applicants may be stored in Eurodac for a maximum period of 10 years from the date on which the fingerprints were taken. In its explanatory memorandum the Commission points out that this provision may be in contrast to the principle laid down in Article 6(1)(e) of Directive 95/46/EC, that data should be kept in a form which permits identification of data subjects for no longer than is necessary for the purposes for which the data was collected or for which it is further processed. The Commission therefore "strongly" recommends that the Council should examine again whether it is necessary to conserve data relating to asylum applicants for a ten-year period. An exception to the ten-year rule is made in cases where the person concerned acquires citizenship of the Union (Article 7).

e) Illegal Immigrants

In accordance with the Additional Protocol the draft regulation obliges the Member States to take fingerprints from illegal immigrants and send such data to the Central Unit (Article 8). The use of this data is clearly limited. It may be compared only with data on asylum applicants which is subsequently transmitted to the Central Unit. A comparison with data on persons apprehended in connection with the irregular crossing of the external border which is previously or subsequently transmitted to the Central Unit, is excluded (Article 9). The data may be stored only for a maximum of two years. It must be erased when the person concerned has been issued with a residence permit, when the person has left the territory of the Member States or when the person in question acquires citizenship of the Union (Article 10), since the data consequently loses its relevance in determining responsibility for a claim for asylum.

Chapter IV concerns aliens found illegally present in a Member State. There is no obligation or right under Community law to fingerprint persons found illegally present within its territory. It depends on the national law whether Member States use Eurodac in order to find out whether a person found illegally present on its territory has previously claimed asylum in another Member State. Therefore the Central Unit may use the data transmitted by a Member State only to compare it with data on applicants for asylum which has previously been transmitted to the Central Unit by other Member States and recorded in the central database. Data of aliens found illegally present in a Member State is not recorded in the Central Database.

f) Individual Rights, Liability and Supervision

Within the context of the Eurodac system, the Member States act as controllers, i.e. the entities which determine the purposes and the means of the processing of personal data. The Central Unit processes personal data on behalf of the Member States (see Article 3) and as such is a processor. Most obligations of Directive 95/46/EC are addressed to the controller. The responsibilities of the processor are more specific and it must act on instructions from the controller. Article 13(1-3) specifies the responsibilities of the Member State of origin, acting as a controller at the moment of collection, transmission and reception of personal data. Paragraph (4) specifies the requirements for the processor with regard to confidentiality and security. Article 14 concerns the data security in application of Article 17 of the data protection Directive 95/43/EC. A number of provisions deal with data security and access to and correction or erasure of personal data recorded in the central database. The competence to request a correction is reserved to the Member State of origin, except in cases where the Central Unit is required to erase data automatically at a certain point or is instructed to amend or erase data by the Member State of origin. Article 16 is designed to ensure that the Central Unit keeps complete records of data processing operations within the Central Unit for the purpose of data protection monitoring and security. For these purposes, records may be kept for a maximum period of one year.

The liability for damages follows in principle the responsibility of the processor. The Member States as controller of the processing are liable for damages. They may be exempted if they can prove that they are not responsible for the event giving rise to the damage.

The rights of the alien follow the data protection directive, in particular Article 10, 12, 22 and 28(4) of Directive 95/46/EC. Article 18 contains a list of items that the alien must be informed about and also states when the information had been provided. He may require correction and erasure in any Member State. He has the right to receive written reactions to a request without excessive delay. Further, the Article grants the right to apply to a supervisory authority or a court if he is refused the access or if he wants to have his data corrected or erased.

Articles 19 et seq envisage joint supervisory and national authorities. Article 19 makes an explicit reference to Article 28 of Directive 95/46/EC, leaving no doubt that the national supervisory authorities have the competence to review the legality of all processing operations carried out by the Member States. Article 20 make provision for an independent joint supervisory authority to be established on an interim basis to monitor the processing of personal data by the Central Unit until the supervisory body referred to in Article 286 of the Treaty has been established.

Finally, the proposal includes provisions concerning costs (Article 21), annual monitoring and evaluation (Article 23) and penalties to be applied in cases of abuse of data recorded in the central database (Article 24). The territorial scope of the draft regulation is adjusted to the scope of the Dublin Convention of 15 June 1990.[263]

g) Legal Problems: Clarity and Conformity with Human Rights

Eurodac has, as yet, attracted little attention from the legal community. The Eurodac Draft Convention and the Draft Protocol extending the Eurodac Convention have been the subject of a thorough scrutiny in the House of Lords Select Committee's Report "Fingerprinting Illegal Immigrants: Extending the Eurodac Convention"[264]. The report discusses some basic legal issues which will have to be considered in the Commission's work on the draft regulation.

One issue relates to legal certainty being one of the fundamental principles of Community law[265]. Article 8, which corresponds to Article 3 of the draft Eurodac Protocol, requires the fingerprinting of all third-country nationals aged 14 or over "apprehended in connection with an irregular border crossing". While fingerprinting of illegal immigrants does not meet basic objections under human rights aspects, it must be reasonably clear who is subject to fingerprinting and for what purpose. Article 6 of the Dublin Convention makes a Member State responsible when it can be proved that an applicant for asylum has "irregularly crossed the border into a Member State by land, sea or air, having come from a non-Member State of the European Communities".

Article 8 of the draft regulation must be seen in context with Article 6 of the Dublin Convention and its other provisions attributing responsibility. It follows that fingerprinting requirements only apply if data can be used to identify the responsible Dublin State.

The wording of Article 8 is clear in so far as fingerprints are not be taken from third-country nationals who attempt to enter from another Member State or from those arriving from outside the EU who are turned back at the border. There is less clarity with regard to the meaning of "apprehended ... in connection with the irregular crossing of the border". The Council has agreed on the following statement for the Council minutes –

> The Member States declare that the obligation to take fingerprints of aliens apprehended "in connection with the irregular crossing of an external border" is not limited to the situation where an alien is apprehended at or close to the external border itself. This provision also covers cases where an alien is apprehended beyond the external border, where he is still en route and there is no doubt that he crossed the external border irregularly. This could be the

263 The normal territorial scope of the Treaty is broader than that set out in Article 19 of the Dublin Convention.

264 Cf. Report of the select Committee on European Communities of the House of Lords, HL Paper 69, 1998 – 1999, 10th Report of 8 June 1999.

265 Cf. ECJ, judgment of 18 March 1975, case 78/74, *Deuka v Einfuhrstelle für Getreide und Futtermittel*, [1975] ECR 421 para 12; ECJ, judgment of 10 July 1980, case 32/79, *Commission v UK*, [1980] ECR 2403, para 46; ECJ, judgment of 5 March 1980, case 265/78, *Ferwerda v Produktshap voor Vee en Vlees*, [1980] ECR 617 para 14 et seq.

> case, for example, where, subsequently to the crossing of the external border, an alien on board a (high speed) train is detected during on board checks, or where an alien transported in a sealed commercial vehicle is apprehended at the moment of disembarkation from the vehicle.[266]

Leaving aside the problem of whether Council minutes are an adequate instrument to clarify uncertainties in the text of a Community instrument affecting human rights, problems of determining the scope of application of Article 8 remain. Restricting fingerprinting to cases where there is "no doubt" of an irregular border crossing as opposed to mere "suspicion" places a heavy burden on immigration or police officials and may be difficult to implement in practice. In addition there is a considerable risk of conflicting rules arising from the application of Article 11. According to Article 8, fingerprints of illegal immigrants must be taken and will be stored for up to two years. Article 11 leaves the decision whether to fingerprint an alien found to be illegally present to each Member State, wishing to find out whether the alien has previously lodged an asylum application in another Member State. The prints may not be stored in the Central Unit. The distinction between the two categories of illegal immigrants may be practically difficult and potentially injust. An illegal immigrant apprehended in the Member State is illegally present and may have crossed the border illegally before.

There are no criteria determining with sufficient clarity whether a person has been apprehended in connection with illegal border crossing or has simply been found to be illegally present within the territory of a Member State. One possible solution would be to enlarge the scope of application of Eurodac altogether. At present, Eurodac is limited to the purposes of Dublin. This may soon turn out to be too restrictive. There is a need to exchange data on illegal immigration beyond the scope of the Dublin Convention for purposes of an effective control of immigration, illegal employment, illegal access to social benefits etc. Rather than elaborating separate data collection systems (Schengen Information System, Eurodac) with different procedural rules, different principles on data storing and access to data, it would be preferable to think about the establishment of a European Aliens Registry System. It is, however, evident that such collection of data about asylum applicants and illegal immigrants will give raise to human rights issues relating to the right of privacy (Article 8 of the European Convention on Human Rights) and, as to fingerprinting of children, relating to the United Nations Convention on the Rights of the Child (1989).

The European Court of Human Rights has decided that storing and release of data relating to an individual's private life is an interference with the right to respect for private live in Article 8(1) of the European Convention on Human Rights[267]. Therefore there can be little doubt that compulsory fingerprinting interferes in principle with the right to respect private life in Article 8(1) of the European Convention on Human Rights. The question is whether this interference

---

[266] This minutes statement is taken over by the Commission in the Explantory memorandum of the proposal of the EURODAC- regulation, Cf. COM(99)260 final – CNS 99/0116, para 4.5.

[267] Cf. ECHR, jugdment of 25. March 1987, *Leander v. Sweden*, Series A 116, para 48; ECHR jugdment of 31. January 1995, *Friedl v. Austria*, Series A 305 B, para 47.

can be justified on one or more of the grounds set out in Article 8(2) of the Convention. This requires that fingerprints are taken "in accordance with the law" and are "necessary in a democratic society". Like the Convention and the Protocol, the draft regulation is intended to facilitate the application of the Dublin Convention. Fingerprinting is believed to be a necessary means of determining responsibility. Establishing the immigration history of an individual asylum applicant is essential to attribute responsibility under Dublin. In addition, fingerprinting is necessary to prevent crimes frequently committed in connection with illegal immigration.[268]

The aim of the Dublin Convention to establish an exclusive system of responsibility in order to avoid "asylum shopping" and prevent a waste of limited resources for processing asylum seekers is clearly a legitimate aim which justifies interference in the right of privacy in a democratic society. It must be taken into account that asylum seekers are applying for a status implying a bundle of rights and privileges. Determination of an asylum seeker's identity and his way into the EU are indispensable requirements for the functioning of a distributory system. It can hardly be considered as an excessive burden for an asylum seeker to cooperate in the process of examining whether the conditions for recognition are met. Fingerprinting, as a means of physical identification of a person's visible appearance, does not differ substantially from taking pictures or identifying other physical characteristics, like the colour of eyes etc.

Questions have been raised concerning the mandatory fingerprinting of child asylum seekers and illegal immigrants. Article 16 of the United Nations Convention on the Rights of the Child provides that "No child shall be subjected to arbitrary or unlawful interference with his privacy". The purpose of this provision is to recognize the specific protection needs of children. Even if the fingerprinting of adult asylum seekers or illegal immigrants is generally justified under Article 8(2) of the European Convention on Human Rights, the United Nations Convention can be interpreted as requiring a higher level of protection of minor children subject to an interference into privacy. On the other hand, concerns about the special protection needs of minor children seem to be largely exaggerated in the case of fingerprinting. There are no indications that minor children are particularly affected by any attempts to capture their physical characteristics in order to determine their identity.

In conclusion, human rights concerns related to the taking of fingerprints seem to be based upon a largely exaggerated concept of privacy. It is obvious that in Member States that have traditionally been reluctant to introduce any kind of residence registry fingerprinting is automatically assimilated to criminal procedure. This, however, is not the case in continental legal thinking. Fingerprinting of asylum seekers has become a common feature in most national asylum systems as a precondition of any efficient asylum system. There is no convincing reason why it should not be adopted for a European asylum system. Sufficient precautions, however, have to be taken to ensure the security of such data and to enable asylum seekers access to the information stored and a possibility to challenge the

---

[268] Cf. for this propose *supra* Chapter C III.

correctness of their data. By reference to the EC Directive on the protection of data the draft regulation has taken care of this problem.

IV. HARMONIZATION OF MINIMUM STANDARDS ON THE RECEPTION OF ASYLUM SEEKERS[269]

The Commission has repeatedly stressed the necessity to harmonize the Member States' reception standards for asylum seekers[270]. The ministers responsible for immigration created a work-programme in their report for the European Council meeting in Maastricht on immigration and asylum policy of 3 December 1991[271], which marked the conditions for receiving applicants for asylum, among others, as targets of harmonization[272]. The primary reason for harmonizing the reception standards for asylum seekers is to avoid, within the limits of the Dublin responsibility system, an influx of large groups of asylum seekers into the Member States with the most favourable system[273].

According to Article 63(1)(b) ECT, the Council, acting in conformity with the procedure referred to in Article 67 ECT[274], shall adopt measures on asylum in accordance with the Geneva Convention of 28 July 1951 and the Protocol of 31 January 1967 relating to the status of refugees and other relevant treaties, within the area of minimum standards on the reception of asylum seekers in Member States within a period of five years after entry into force of the Treaty of Amsterdam. As previously mentioned, this provision confers a competence to assimilate the legal position of asylum seekers in the Member States during the asylum procedure upon the EU, including everything but the procedure itself. On the one hand, the provision increases the potential for harmonization considerably, as the creation of a Community competence will allow the Council to adopt genuine Community legislation, as regulated in Article 249 (ex-Article 189) ECT. This legislation could take the form of a directive, with all its legal implications. The Council is also obliged to take action within five years following the entry into force of the Treaty of Amsterdam. On the other hand, the fact that the Council,

[269] This chapter only deals with the substantial rights of asylum seekers. For the harmonization of asylum procedures see *infra* part V.

[270] See the Communication to the Council and the European Parliament concerning the right of asylum of 11 October 1991 (SEC(91) 1857 final, 7) and the Communication of 23 February 1994 (COM(94)23 final, 26, para 89).

[271] Document WGI 930, reprinted in *Guild/Niessen*, The Developing Immigration and Asylum Policies of the European Union, (1996), 449 et seq.

[272] WGI 930, 8, 9.

[273] See already SEC(91) 1857 final, 7. The numbers of asylum seekers in the Member States are highly unequal. In 1985, about 44 percent of all asylum applicants in Western Europe sought refuge in the Federal Republic of Germany. In 1990, this share was 45 percent, in 1992, 65 percent. Germany's share of all new asylum seekers in the EU was 43 percent in 1987, 89 percent in 1991, 79 percent in 1992, 49 percent in 1995, and 53 percent in 1996 (see *Reermann*, Costs of Caring for Foreigners: An EU Comparison, conference paper (1997), 1).

[274] I.e. during a transitional period of five years following the entry into force of the Treaty of Amsterdam unanimously on a proposal from the Commission or on the initiative of a Member State and after consulting the European Parliament.

pursuant to Article 67 ECT, will act unanimously within these first five years, reduces the chances of progress in harmonization. Further, the fact that the Council may only adopt "minimum standards" takes account of the fact that Member States were not willing to go beyond a minimum standard of rights, leaving it to every Contracting State to provide for additional rights.

There is no obligation under public international law to admit asylum seekers to the territory of a state. The principle of non-refoulement, as enshrined in various international treaty provisions, such as Article 33 of the Geneva Convention, Article 3 of the European Convention on Human Rights and Article 7 of the Covenant on Civil and Political Rights must, however, be observed[275]. In principle, there are no standards imposed by public international law on the arrangement of economic, social and political rights of asylum seekers[276]. As a result, the rights granted to asylum applicants vary considerably among Member States[277].

Accommodation is provided for all asylum seekers requiring protection in the Central and North European states, such as Denmark, Finland, Germany, the Netherlands and Sweden. The same is true for France, Luxembourg and, with certain restrictions, for Spain[278]. Belgium and Austria also belong to this group of states. Accommodation for refugees, even though stipulated by law, is not always guaranteed in practice for administrative reasons (Belgium), or depending on the local and regional situation (Austria), due to lack of sufficient housing[279]. In other states, e.g. Greece, Ireland and Portugal, the provision of accommodation is left to UNHCR, municipalities and non-governmental organizations, such as the Red Cross and churches[280].

With regard to welfare aid, some Member States, such as Austria, Denmark, Ireland, Germany, Luxembourg, the Netherlands and Sweden, have a separate welfare system for asylum seekers, which offers benefits at a lower level than that of general social assistance schemes. Benefits in this system are often granted in kind, and for a limited period of time only. In Germany, asylum seekers have a legal claim to benefits, while comparable benefits in the United Kingdom are granted through subordinate legislation and subject to a wide margin of discretion. In France, the highest benefits are paid in the first month and decrease thereafter; in other countries, such as Germany, Finland and the Netherlands, benefits increase with the duration of the stay. The Southern European states afford the lowest level of benefits[281]. Italy, Portugal and Spain grant only limited financial assistance for a

---

[275] Concerning the safe third country principle and the responsibility system of the Dublin Convention see *infra* VI. 2.

[276] See also *Maaßen*, Die Rechtsstellung des Asylbewerbers im Völkerrecht (1997), 379.

[277] For an overview see *Liebaut/Hughes*, Legal and Social Conditions for Asylum Seekers and Refugees in Western European Countries (1997); further *Reermann*, Costs of Caring for Foreigners: An EU Comparison, conference paper (1997), 3 et seq.

[278] In Spain reception centres are partly run directly by state agency and partly through NGOs (see *Liebaut/Hughes*, Legal and Social Conditions for Asylum Seekers and Refugees in Western European Countries (1997), 208).

[279] See *Liebaut/Hughes*, Legal and Social Conditions for Asylum Seekers and Refugees in Western European Countries (1997), 18.

[280] See *Liebaut/Hughes*, Legal and Social Conditions for Asylum Seekers and Refugees in Western European Countries (1997), 109, 122, 191.

[281] See also *Reermann*, Costs of Caring for Foreigners: An EU Comparison, conference paper (1997), 3.

restricted amount of time. Greece does not provide any financial assistance[282]. In the Southern European states, asylum seekers are predominantly helped by voluntary and charitable organizations. This is the case in Greece in particular, but also holds true for Italy and Portugal. In Spain, the work of these organizations is supported by government funds.

The provision of aid for medical care is restricted to the minimum level of medical care in most Member States, such as Austria, Denmark, Finland, France, Germany, Greece, Italy, Luxembourg, the Netherlands and Sweden. Full access to medical care is afforded in Ireland, Portugal and, in principle, in the United Kingdom. Negotiations on new legal regulations concerning the restriction of medical care are, however, currently underway in Great Britain[283].

Many Member States prohibit asylum seekers from taking up gainful employment during the entire period of the asylum procedure. Germany, Finland, the Netherlands, Austria, Portugal, Sweden, Spain and the United Kingdom, however, allow for employment in a limited capacity; such employment is subject to permission from the competent authorities. In Finland, the United Kingdom and Sweden, a work permit can be granted for a minimum stay of 3 – 6 months. In Germany, such permits were previously made available after asylum seekers left the initial reception centre, where they were obliged to live for a minimum of 3 months. The Federal Ministry for Labour and Social Affairs issued an order on 30 May 1997 refusing work permits for asylum seekers who entered Germany after 15 May 1997[284].

Several points must be made in summary. First, Member States' systems of granting social rights to asylum seekers vary widely with respect to the amount of benefits granted, the period during which benefits are granted, the provision of specific assistance in specific situations, eligibility criteria and the exclusion of certain benefits[285]. Nevertheless, several common principles can be discerned. The Central and North European states traditionally provide accommodation and other subsistence benefits, often granted in kind. Several states, such as Belgium, Luxembourg, France, Austria and the United Kingdom, provide limited housing and financial assistance. Second, there is often a considerable difference between the social benefits legally provided for and those actually granted, especially in Belgium and Austria. Administrative obstacles often complicate access to benefits (Belgium), and sometimes even exclude a large part of asylum seekers from benefits. Finally, while there is a general willingness to offer work permits, increasing economic problems in the Union have resulted in a certain hesitation to grant such permission. Southern European countries such as Greece, Italy, Portugal and Spain, are in a special situation. The overall level of benefits in these Member States is lower than in other Member States in several respects, especially with

---

282 See *Liebaut/Hughes*, Legal and Social Conditions for Asylum Seekers and Refugees in Western European Countries (1997), 109.

283 See *Reermann*, Costs of Caring for Foreigners: An EU Comparison, conference paper (1997), 3.

284 See also *Hailbronner*, Ausländerrecht, § 2 AsylVfG (1998) para 31.

285 See also *Reermann*, Costs of Caring for Foreigners: An EU Comparison, conference paper (1997), 4; *Liebaut/Hughes*, Legal and Social Conditions for Asylum Seekers and Refugees in Western European Countries, January (1997).

regard to housing, subsistence benefits, medical care and access to the labour market. In Germany, foreign refugees are granted benefits for the entire duration of their lawful stay in the territory and benefits increase with the length of the sojourn for certain categories of persons.

V. Harmonization of the Rules of the Member States on Temporary Protection, De Facto Protection and Humanitarian Residence Permits; Burden-Sharing

1. Introduction

Legal protection of refugees and asylum seekers arises partially from the fulfilment of the duties of a state under international treaties. Large categories of persons, e.g. those fleeing from general dangers resulting from international or internal armed conflicts, drought, famine, natural or environmental disasters, etc., however, are not covered by international conventions. In the framework of Article 1A(2) of the Geneva Convention, for instance, evidence of *general* dangers does not per se suffice to establish a fear of persecution[286], even though persecution may exist in these situations under certain conditions[287]. In addition, at least some Member States hold the view that they are not bound by the Geneva Convention to grant treatment guaranteed by the Convention to persons "persecuted" by non-state actors if the state of origin is unable to afford effective protection, to victims of typical military actions in civil wars, to persons fearing punishment for desertion or objection to military service for reasons of conscience, or if an internal flight alternative exists.

A substantial number of persons not protected by the Geneva Convention deserve, nevertheless, international protection. They are protected through provisions of the domestic legislation of the Member States in various ways, predominantly on a temporary basis[288]. Although there is general agreement on the

---

[286] See also e.g. *Jahn* in *Bernhardt*, (ed.), Encyclopedia of Public International Law, Refugees, Inst. 8 (1985), 453; *Perluss/Hartmann*, 26 Va. J. Int'l L. (1986), 551, 597; *Hailbronner*, 26 Va. J. Int'l L. (1986), 857, 859; *Hyndman*, 9 Hum. Rts. Q. (1987), 49, 51; *Hofmann* in Office for Official Publications of the European Communities, Law in humanitarian crises, Vol. I, 249, 251; *Butcher*, 5 Geo. Immigr. L. J. (1991), 435, 437; *Heyman*, 24 San Diego L. Rev. (1987), 449, 456; *Kälin*, 3 IJRL (1991), 435, 442.

[287] Cf. e.g. *Goodwin-Gill*, The Refugee in International Law, 2nd ed. (1998), 75; *Hathaway*, The Law of Refugee Status (1991), 188; *Coles* in Defense of the Alien VII (1985), 78, 97; *Arboleda/Hoy*, 5 IJRL (1993), 66, 85; *Kälin*, Towards a Concept of Temporary Protection (1996). No unanimity exists with regard to the question of how far persecution has to be individualized.

[288] For a survey of the legislation of the Member States on temporary protection see *Hailbronner*, Die Rechtsstellung der De-facto-Flüchtlinge in den EG-Staaten (1993), further see *Lambert*, Seeking Asylum (1995), 126 et seq.; *Humanitarian Issues Working Group of the International Conference on the Former Yugoslavia*, Survey on the Implementation of Temporary Protection, 8 March 1995 (*HIWG*, Survey on the Implementation of Temporary Protection); *Secretariat of the Intergovernmental Consultations on Asylum, Refugee and Migration Policies in Europe, North America and Australia*, Report on Temporary Protection in States in Europe, North America and Australia, August 1995 (*IGC*, Report on Temporary Protection); *Liebaut/Hughes*, Legal and Social Conditions for Asylum Seekers and Refugees in Western European Countries (1997).

basic fact that protection extending beyond the scope of application of international treaties should be granted to certain categories of persons, the practice of states differs considerably. Temporary protection is generally granted on the basis of varying legal foundations. In addition, there is no consensus on the kind of persons entitled to temporary protection. During the conflict in former Yugoslavia, some Member States admitted all citizens of former Yugoslav States without distinction;[289] others accepted only persons from certain regions of origin[290]. Some actions favoured only wounded and sick persons, or persons who had been held in a prisoner-of-war or internment camp, deserters and/or the aged[291]. Others actions provided for admission based on the date of entry into a receiving country[292]. While all Member States grant access to primary and secondary schooling, access to universities is often restricted and rarely available[293]. Most Member States grant equal access to employment[294] subject to a work permit. A work permit is sometimes granted automatically in connection with a residence permit;[295] other states require a waiting period[296]. Social assistance is granted either on terms equal to those afforded recognized refugee status[297], or frequently reduced welfare benefits are given. It is often granted in kind[298]. Large differences also exist among Member States concerning admission of family reunion. Some prohibit it entirely[299], while others allow for it on extraordinary humanitarian reasons[300]. Some only admit the nuclear family[301], while others extend the right to family reunion to include extended family[302]. Identity or travel documents are granted in a small number of states[303].

---

[289] See e.g. Italy (*Nascimbene*, Riv. Int'l Dir. dell' Uome 6 (1993), 419, 423); the Netherlands (*IGC*, Report on Temporary Protection, 141).

[290] Austria (*Taucher*, AJPIL/ÖZöRV 49 (1995), 227, 233); Denmark (*ECRE*, Biannual Meeting 1996, 6, 7); Belgium (*IGC*, Report on Temporary Protection, 54; *HIWG*, Survey on the Implementation of Temporary Protection, 13); France (*IGC*, Report on Temporary Protection, 103); Luxembourg (*HIWG*, Survey on the Implementation of Temporary Protection, 53).

[291] Denmark (*IGC*, Report on Temporary Protection, 72, 77, 78); Italy (*Nascimbene*, ibid.); Germany (*IGC*, Report on Temporary Protection, 117); Greece (*HIWG*, Survey on the Implementation of Temporary Protection, 42); United Kingdom (*HIWG*, ibid., 81).

[292] Austria (*Taucher*, AJPIL/ÖZöRV 49(1995), 227, 233).

[293] See the table on education in *IGC*, Report on Temporary Protection, 242.

[294] Denmark, however, only exceptionally grants work permits, see *IGC*, Report on Temporary Protection, 82.

[295] Belgium, Finland, Italy, Netherlands, Sweden, United Kingdom, see the table on employment in *IGC*, Report on Temporary Protection, 243.

[296] Germany and Switzerland (*IGC*, Report on Temporary Protection, 121; 210).

[297] Finland (*IGC*, Report on Temporary Protection, 96); Belgium (ibid., 62); partly in Germany (in case of an "Aufenthaltsbefugnis" pursuant to § 30(1) Ausländergesetz (Aliens Law), see § 120 Bundessozialhilfegesetz (Federal Law on Social Assistance)); Sweden (*HIWG*, Survey on the Implementation of Temporary Protection, 75).

[298] Austria, Belgium, Denmark, Germany, Italy, Netherlands, Norway, partly Sweden, Switzerland (see the table on social assistance in *IGC*, Report on Temporary Protection, 245).

[299] In Germany with regard to persons with a "Duldung."

[300] Denmark (*IGC*, Report on Temporary Protection, 62).

[301] Italy (*IGC*, Report on Temporary Protection, 132); Finland (ibid., 97); Belgium (ibid., 62).

[302] Austria (*HIWG*, Survey on the Implementation of Temporary Protection, 9).

[303] See e.g. § 32 a(7) and § 39(2) of the German Aliens Act (Ausländergesetz); Sweden (*HIWG*, Survey on the Implementation of Temporary Protection, 75); Spain (*IGC*, Report on Temporary Protection, 181).

The procedures on temporary protection vary depending on the respective legal basis and there is disagreement on the question of the relationship between temporary protection and regular asylum procedures. While regulations in some Member States make the grant of temporary protection dependent on a renunciation or withdrawal of an asylum application[304], others allow the applicant to choose[305]. In the case of an option, however, asylum procedures are usually suspended during temporary protection[306]. Access to the asylum procedure is sometimes restricted by a time limit[307]. Finally, some countries terminate temporary protection regimes after a certain period of time and automatically start asylum procedures[308].

These legislative disparities, as well as a number of other factors[309], may create wide divergences in the number of people seeking refuge in the different Member States[310].

2. *Harmonization Efforts*

Especially during, and in the aftermath of the war in the former Yugoslavia, it became increasingly clear that Member State rules protecting persons who are not recognized as Convention refugees, but who still deserve protection, must be harmonized[311]. Immigration ministers released two resolutions concerning the protection of people displaced by the conflict in the former Yugoslavia[312]. The impact of the two resolutions on the harmonization process has, however, been negligible, partially as a result of their concrete and definite scope of application being restricted to the Yugoslavian conflict.

---

304 See e.g. § 32a(2) of the German Aliens Act (Ausländergesetz).

305 Italy (*IGC*, Report on Temporary Protection, 129); Spain (ibid., 177).

306 Finland (*IGC*, Report on Temporary Protection, 89); Belgium (ibid., 58); United Kingdom (ibid., 218).

307 Austria (see § 7(1) Asylgesetz (Asylum Law)).

308 Denmark (*HIWG*, Survey on the Implementation of Temporary Protection, 24); France (ibid., 104).

309 Besides this, for example, the geographical situation of the receiving country and historical ties play an important role.

310 This has been shown again during the conflict in former Yugoslavia. See *supra* part A.

311 See the priority work programme adopted by the Council on 30 November 1993, which makes provision for a detailed examination of the question of burden-sharing with respect to the admission and residence of refugees in western Europe; the resolution adopted by the European Parliament on 19 January 1994 on the general principles of a European refugee policy, O.J. 1994, C 44/106 et seq.; the Communication from the Commission to the Council and the European Parliament of 23 February 1994, COM(94), 23 final, para 92; according to O.J. 1995, C 262/1 the European Council meeting in Essen on 9 and 10 December 1994 called upon the Council (Justice and Home Affairs) to study the problems caused by an influx of refugees with a view to finding an effective arrangement for future sharing of the burden of humanitarian assistance as soon as possible.

312 See the resolution on people displaced by the conflict in the former Yugoslavia, adopted by the ministers for immigration at their meeting in London on 30 November and 1 December 1992, unpublished; and the resolution on certain common guidelines as regards the admission of particularly vulnerable groups of distressed persons from the former Yugoslavia, adopted by the ministers with responsibility for immigration at their meeting in Copenhagen on 1 and 2 June 1993, unpublished, both cited in O.J. 1995, C 262/1.

The Council adopted a resolution on burden-sharing with regard to the admission and residence of displaced persons on a temporary basis on 25 September 1995[313]. It was supplemented by the decision on an alert and emergency procedure for burden-sharing with regard to the admission and residence of displaced persons on a temporary basis of 4 March 1996[314]. The Commission submitted a proposal for a Joint Action based on Article K.3(2)(b) TEU concerning temporary protection of displaced persons to the Council on March 5 1997[315].

On 24 June 1998 the Commission submitted an amended proposal for a Joint Action on temporary protection of displaced persons[316]. The basic outlines of the proposal submitted on 5 March 1997 have not been altered, but some regulations have been supplied and put in more precise terms. The main amendments proposed by the Commission are the following –

- Article 3(2): The duration of the temporary protection regime established by a decision of the Council shall not exceed five years on aggregate.
- Article 4(3): The principles governing the return shall be coordinated by the Council.
- Article 5: The report provided for by Article 4(1) shall also refer to all future means for implementing solidarity in the application of the temporary protection scheme. Such solidarity shall be implemented in accordance with the provisions of the Joint Action on solidarity in the admission and residence of beneficiaries of the temporary protection of displaced persons.

On 24 June 1998 the Commission submitted, pursuant to Article K.3(2)(b) TEU, a proposal for a Joint Action concerning solidarity in the admission and residence of beneficiaries of the temporary protection of displaced persons[317] which must enter into force on the same date as the Joint Action concerning temporary protection. The Commission proposed the following principles –

- When temporary protection regimes are adopted, or on the basis of the report referred to in Article 4 of the Joint Action on temporary protection, the Council may, acting unanimously on the initiative of a Member State or of the Commission, adopt decisions implementing solidarity mechanisms providing for assistance to the Member States particularly affected by the admission of beneficiaries of temporary protection (Article 2(1)).
- The decision provided for by Article 2(1) of this Joint Action principally involves the granting of financial assistance from the Community budget designed to cover certain costs generated by the admission of beneficiaries of temporary protection (Article 3).
- The decision provided for by Article 2(1) may also, as a secondary measure, define the rules allowing the beneficiaries of temporary protection to be distributed between Member States, before or on arrival in the territory of the Member States. This potential distribution shall not affect the rules of the

---

313 O.J. 1995, C 262/1.
314 O.J. 1996, L 63/10.
315 COM(97) 93 final, O.J. 1997, C 106/13.
316 COM(98) 0372 final – CNS(97) 0081, O.J. 1998, C 268/13.
317 COM(98) 0372 final – CNS(98) 0222, O.J. 1998, C 268/22.

Dublin Convention of 15 June 1990, unless the Member States decide to suspend the examination of such applications for asylum under the conditions set out by the second subparagraph of Article 10(1) of the Joint Action on temporary protection (Article 4).

The Commission has focussed on the protection of persons fleeing from their country of origin *en masse* as a result of a situation of generalized violence, and has deemed a coordinated approach with regard to persons requiring humanitarian protection by virtue of their individual situations unnecessary[318]. It may be reasonable to restrict the issue of coordination to mass influx situations. In a long term perspective, however, individual applications for humanitarian temporary protection cannot be excluded from a European asylum law. Divergent Member State interpretations of Article 3 of the European Convention on Human Rights, as well as differences in the prerequisites for a grant of humanitarian status may not only significantly influence mass refugee movements, but may also be important factors in terms of numbers. The necessity to harmonize the criteria for recognition as a Convention refugee has never been questioned, due to the concept of the EU as a European legal space affording protection on the same legal basis. Basically the same reasons apply with regard to admission on the basis of Article 3 of the Convention and on similar humanitarian grounds.

Hitherto, Article 3 of the European Convention on Human Rights has been considered only as an obstacle for expulsion. However, in recent years Article 3 of the Convention has been given a broad interpretation[319]. Therefore the question arises if Article 3 of the Convention could also be regarded as a basis for granting admission. The European Court of Human Rights has not yet granted a right of entry based upon Article 3 of the Convention emphasizing that there is no right of asylum under the European Convention on Human Rights[320]. Consequently, it is conceivable as yet only in exceptional cases that a claim to admission may result from Article 3 of the Convention.

3. *Burden-Sharing*

The idea that burdens arising from the admission of, and care for considerable numbers of refugees should be shared between the admitting states is not a new one. It has already found expression in the fourth consideration of the Preamble to the Geneva Convention. Even prior to the ratification of this Convention, in the inter-war period, it has often been cited as a problem to be dealt with in the context of discussions in search for solutions to the refugee problem[321].

---

[318] Commission of the European Communities, Draft Working document of the departments of the Commission of the European Communities, 1.2.1993, Humanitarian Protection of *De Facto* Refugees in the European Community, Summary V. 2; cf. further the proposal for a Joint Action of 5 March 1997, which solely relates to mass influx situations, "where there is a risk of distortionary effect on a significant scale", COM(97) 93 final, 5, para 12(2).

[319] For details see *infra* part F.

[320] *Jacobs/White*, The European Convention on Human Rights, 2nd ed. (1996), 60 et seq., including further references.

[321] See *Skran*, Refugees in Inter-War Europe (1998), 68, 70.

The notion of burden-sharing, as such, should not be misunderstood as a strategy supported by over-burdened states to rid themselves of an excessively large number of refugees and asylum seekers. It should be viewed, instead, as a means to maintain and restore admission capacities in the long term in a wide variety of countries. The limited capacity of "frontier states" to absorb foreigners has been recognized frequently[322]. In a close union of states such as the EU, a unified, collective cooperation approach should prevail, which may also prevent states from resorting to violations of the principle of non-refoulement in case of a mass influx of refugees exceeding the administrative capacity[323].

According to Article 63(2)b ECT, the Council may adopt measures to promote burden-sharing with regard to Convention refugees and displaced persons. The term "promotion of a balance of effort" indicates that the competence of the Community is limited[324]. Additionally, pursuant to the third indent of Article 63(4) ECT, measures adopted under Article 63(2)(b) ECT are not subject to the five year period. In light of the unanimity requirement set down in Article 67(1) ECT for the five years following the entry into force of the Treaty of Amsterdam, it seems that the field of burden-sharing will still remain for some time an area of basic disagreement.

Any legal instrument on burden-sharing must include, first, consensus on the criteria used in the calculation of the shares of the "refugee burden" for each state, and, second, a detailed description of the procedure to be used in the implementation of these burden-sharing measures.

a) Criteria for Burden-Sharing

Several proposals establish criteria for the distribution of responsibility among Member States. The Council Resolution of 1995 evaluates the contribution made by each Member State to the prevention or resolution of the crisis, in particular through the allocation of military resources to support United Nations Security Council or OSCE operations and missions, as well as the measures taken by each Member State to afford local protection to people in danger, or to provide humanitarian assistance in the affected region. It also takes into account all economic, social and political factors which may affect the capacity of a Member State to admit a certain number of displaced persons under satisfactory conditions[325]. Some authors, however, are critical of the use of criteria such as a country's gross domestic product and its contribution to military or humanitarian

---

[322] See also *Walzer*, Spheres of Justice (1983), 31 et seq.

[323] Cf. also *Thorburn*, 7 IJRL (1995), 459, 474; *Adelmann*, 4 IJRL (1992), 4; *Kirisci*, Provide Comfort and Turkey: Decision Making for Humanitarian Intervention, Kent Papers in Politics and International Relations, Series 3 No. 3, University of Kent at Canterbury (1993); *Hailbronner*, Zeitschrift für Ausländerrecht und Ausländerpolitik 1995, 3, 10; *id.*, Die Rechtsstellung der De-facto-Flüchtlinge in den EG-Staaten, 142 et seq.; *ECRE*, Position of the European Council on Refugees and Exiles on Sharing the Responsibility: Protecting Refugees and Displaced Persons in the Context of Large Scale Arrivals, para 1.

[324] See ibid.

[325] See the Council resolution on burden-sharing of 25 September 1995, O.J. 1995, C 262/1/3.

missions, as these factors do not reflect a country's true absorption capacities. Contribution in areas not directly connected with the reception of refugees, it is argued, should not be considered when calculating each country's share of refugees. In addition to a country's infrastructure for reception and assistance of refugees, the cultural, linguistic and family bonds of the refugees and displaced persons should be included as criteria[326].

Other writers suggest the use of the size of the population of a Member State, the size of its territory and the amount of the GP as criteria for burden-sharing. Each State's financial contribution to the EU would be used as an indicative figure to determine its share of the responsibility. The indicative figures could be modified based on the contribution of a Member State to peace-keeping operations and its use of foreign and security policy measures in the country of origin[327]. Another concept considers the population size of the host state, the number of refugees accepted on prior occasions, the ethnic composition of the admitting country and the economic strength of the receiving country as appropriate criteria[328].

It is doubtful whether the frequent reference to military operations should be taken into account. Member States "shall support the Union's external and security policy actively and unreservedly in a spirit of loyalty and mutual solidarity" pursuant to Article 11(2) TEU. " Contributions to the supply of military resources made by each Member States in fulfilment of its duties under Article 11(2) TEU should not be mixed with refugee issues, and, in particular, not with the question of burden-sharing with regard to the admission of refugees. Indices of a state's economic strength and admission capacities should be the sole criteria for the creation of a system of burden-sharing[329]. Included among these factors could be: the geographical size of the state, the size of its population and the gross domestic product.

b) The Legal Nature of the Resolution on Burden-Sharing and the Decision on an Alert and Emergency Procedure

The Council Resolution of 25 September 1995 on burden-sharing with regard to the admission and residence of displaced persons on a temporary basis has been based on Article K.1. TEU, while the Decision of 4 March 1996 cites Article K.3(2)(a) TEU as its legal basis.

No explicit answer is given in the wording of the provision to the question of whether the acts adopted under the second alternative of Article K.3(2)(a) TEU are binding or not. Nor can a clear answer be drawn from the system of Article K.3

---

326 *ECRE*, Comments from the European Council on Refugees and Exiles on the 1995 "burden-sharing" resolution and decision adopted by the Council of the European Union, para 6.

327 *Thorburn*, 7 IJRL (1995), 459, 475, 476.

328 *Dacyl* in Korella/Twomey (eds.), Towards a European Immigration Policy (1993), 85, 104.

329 The rules applicable in the field of economic and social cohesion (new Article 158 et seq. ECT) could serve as a model.

and the TEU as a whole[330]. The Member States have informally agreed to define the legal effect of each individual joint position in the act itself[331]. However, no such agreement exists with respect to the cooperation under the second alternative of ex-Article K.3(2)(a) TEU. Whether the Member States will bind themselves to a regulation will, therefore, be determined anew for each individual act[332]. An examination of the texts of the two acts with regard to both formal characteristics and substance shows the general unwillingness on the part of Member States to enter into strict legal obligations. The Resolution has been published in series C of the Official Journal, which is devoted to the publication of non-normative communications and information[333]. Furthermore, according to paragraph 1(a), the Resolution applies solely to persons, "whom the Member States are prepared to admit". This formulation is evidence of the fact that it was not intended to create new obligations to recognize additional categories of persons pursuant to this Resolution. In addition, paragraph 2 of the Resolution holds that harmonized action "may" be required under certain circumstances. Neither harmonized action, nor acceptance of the criteria for burden-sharing set down in paragraph 4 of the Resolution are mandatory. It is stated in this provision that the burden "could be shared (...) taking account of the following criteria". In general, the Resolution does not contain any phrase which would make it binding, either in individual parts, or as a whole.

The Council Decision on an alert and emergency procedure of 4 March 1996 was published in series L of the Official Journal (which contains secondary legislation). It is called a "decision"[334], and, in the same formal language, "introduces" an alert and emergency procedure. It does not, however, create legally binding obligations. An urgent meeting of the Co-ordinating Committee referred to in Article K.4 "may" be convened, pursuant to paragraph 1 of the Decision. According to paragraph 1(a), "harmonized action" will be implemented when "envisaged", i.e. if, and when the Member States are willing to do so. Under paragraph 2, clause 5, the Member States only indicate the numbers of persons who "will" be admitted and when they shall be admitted. The Decision does not oblige Member States to admit persons or to make compensatory payments.

c) The Scope of Application of the Resolution on Burden-Sharing

The scope of application of the burden-sharing Resolution is set down in paragraph 1(a). The instrument applies to –

---

330 *Hailbronner* in Hailbronner/Klein/Magiera/Müller-Graff, Handkommentar zum EUV/EGV, Article K (1996) para 85 takes into account Article K.3(2)(c), Article K.5, Article J.2, and Article L TEU.

331 Op. cit., para 87.

332 See Article 2 (a) and (f) of the Vienna Convention on the Law of Treaties.

333 For the argument that publication in series L of the Official Journal could indicate the willingness to be bound by an act see *König/Pechstein*, Die Europäische Union, Tübingen (1995), 91. See also *supra* Chapter B.

334 In the framework of the first pillar of the European Union decisions are binding upon those to whom they are addressed. See Article 189 para 4 ECT.

persons whom Member States are prepared to admit on a temporary basis under appropriate conditions in the event of armed conflict or civil war, including where such persons have already left their region of origin to go to one of the Member States. The persons concerned are in particular –

- those who have been held in a prisoner-of-war or internment camp and who cannot otherwise be saved from a threat to life or limb,
- those who are injured or seriously ill and for whom medical treatment cannot be obtained locally,
- those who are, or have been, under a direct threat to life or limb and whose protection in their region of origin can not otherwise be secured,
- those who have been subjected to sexual assault provided that there is no suitable means for assisting them in safe areas situated as close as possible to their homes,
- those who, having come directly from combat zones, are within the borders of their countries and cannot return to their homes because of the conflict and human rights abuses.

According to paragraph 1(b), the Resolution does not apply –

to any person with respect to whom there are serious reasons for considering that he has –

- committed a crime against peace, a war crime or a crime against humanity, as defined in the international instruments drawn up to make provision in respect of such crimes,
- committed a serious non-political crime prior to being admitted by one of the Member States on a temporary basis.

Persons already admitted to a Member State's territory at the time of the adoption of the Resolution are not included in the scope of its application, pursuant to paragraph 7.

The Resolution is intended to cover persons in need of protection regardless of their potential qualification as refugees under Article 1A(2) of the Geneva Convention[335]. Both instruments apply in situations of mass influx, as well as for individuals temporarily admitted to the territory of a Member State on humanitarian grounds[336]. Paragraph 1 (a) of the Resolution allows for request for temporary protection in a limited number of cases: exclusive coverage exists for situations of armed conflict or civil war. However, the need for temporary protection might result from numerous other factors, such as floods, droughts, epidemics, earthquakes, other environmental catastrophes, or other extraordinary

[335] *Kälin*, Towards a Concept of Temporary Protection (1996), 30, 31 considers this critically in regard to the persons mentioned in the 4th and 5th indent of para 1 a) of the resolution.

[336] According to para 1 a) and para 2 of the resolution a harmonized action may be required, "for instance", in case of a mass influx of displaced persons into the territory of a Member State or where there exists a strong probability that a Member State may soon have to cope with such an influx.

and temporary conditions in a state that prevent aliens who are nationals of that state from safely returning to their state of origin[337].

One may argue that such other causes for a mass flight, however, ought to have been included in a EU-burden sharing mechanism. Otherwise, in a mass influx situation resulting from, for example, a natural disaster, or one of the other events listed above, Member States could reject their common responsibility on the ground that co-operation had only been agreed upon in case of mass influx resulting from armed conflict or civil war. A blanket clause would have been preferable, providing for co-operation and burden-sharing in all cases of mass influx. Furthermore, the scope of application of the two instruments has been criticized as being overly restrictive even in cases of armed conflict or civil war by the listing of exemplary cases[338]. This list is not, however, final or exhaustive. To that extent, the criticizm seems to be unfounded.

d) Criteria and Implementation

Member States state in paragraph 4 of the Resolution that they will share the burdens of a harmonized admission action equally. The following factors have been listed as possible criteria for the distribution of burden resulting from the admission and residence of displaced persons on a temporary basis in crisis situations –

- the contribution which each Member State is making to prevention or resolution of the crisis, in particular by the supply of military resources in operations and missions ordered by the United Nations Security Council or the Organization for Security and Cooperation in Europe and by the measures taken by each Member State to afford local protection to people under threat or to provide humanitarian assistance,

- all economic, social and political factors which may affect the capacity of a Member State to admit an increased number of displaced persons under satisfactory conditions.

First, the optional character of these criteria – according to paragraph 4 the burden "could" be allocated based on the criteria listed – must be viewed as a major weakness in the Resolution. Second, the criteria listed are so general that they will have to be further specified if they are to provide an effective basis for burden-sharing measures.

Together with the decision on an alert and emergency procedure, the Resolution establishes a procedure for "harmonized action" to reach decisions on burden-sharing. Paragraph 2 of the Resolution requires harmonized action if, for example, there is a mass influx of displaced persons into the territory of the Member States, or if there are reliable signs of an impending influx. An action of this kind will be especially envisaged for situations in which help and adequate protection is not

---

337 See e.g. Section 244 A (b)(1)(B) and (C) of the U.S. American Immigration and Nationality Act.

338 See *Kälin*, Towards a Concept of Temporary Protection (1996), p. 30.

available in the region of origin, or if the region is so geographically close to the EU that it could itself be considered as belonging to the region of origin. The opinion of UNHCR is obtained before decisions are made.

The emergency rules laid down in Articles 1(1), 8(1), 10(1), and 19(1) of the Council's Rules of Procedure[339], may be applied if necessary in order to ensure prompt action. Both the exact course of "harmonized action" and the content of such action, e.g. a decision on admission, etc., however, remains unclear. The term "concerted action by the European Union for the admission and residence of displaced persons on a temporary basis" is repeated in the Decision of 4 March 1996. The instrument is incorporated into a detailed set of procedural rules[340]. The content of a "harmonized action" is not specified further, rendering the Decision in reality void of independent meaning.

In the Resolution of 25 September 1995, the Member States describe the distribution of persons from the crisis regions as a "matter of priority which will enable fairness to be best achieved in the interests of the persons concerned"[341]. Apart from this definition, the Resolution does not further regulate a burden-sharing procedure. The general considerations seem to envisage burden-sharing solely in the form of financial compensation. The Council Decision of 4 March 1996 does, however, regulate the burden-sharing procedure in greater detail. It introduces an alert and emergency procedure in order to implement the principles laid down in the burden-sharing Resolution in cases of emergency. An urgent meeting of the Co-ordinating Committee referred to in Article K.4 TEU may be convened at the initiative of the Presidency of the Council, a Member State or the Commission[342]. The following topics might, among others, be put on the agenda of this urgent meeting –

- a study of the situation and an assessment of the extent of population movement,
- an appraisal of the expediency of urgent intervention at European Union level,
- a study of other possibilities, including any local action,
- the drawing up of a timetable and a progressive plan for anticipated admission requirements,
- an indication by each Member State of the number of persons who will be admitted and when they will be admitted, pursuant to paragraph 4 of the Council Resolution of 25 September 1995,

---

339 O.J. 1993, L 304/1.

340 See para 1 of the decision of 4 March 1996.

341 See para 5 of the resolution. Curiously, the German text has a different meaning. It lays down that the allocation of the persons has to be arranged primarily in the conflict region itself, in order to achieve the greatest possible fairness in the interest of the persons concerned. It reads: "Es besteht Einvernehmen darüber, daß die Aufteilung der Personen vorrangig schon in den Krisengebieten geregelt werden muß, so daß die größtmögliche Ausgewogenheit im Interesse der betroffenen Personen ermöglicht wird" (see O.J. 1995, C 262/3).

342 See para 1.

- coordination with the Commission's actions in the area of humanitarian aid,
- exchange of information with the United Nations High Commissioner for Refugees and coordination of the admission plan,
- coordination with third countries.[343]

The main purpose of the urgent meeting is to decide whether a situation exists which requires concerted action by the European Union with regard to the admission and residence of displaced persons[344]. Committee members shall be advised by those responsible for asylum and immigration affairs in the Member States. A report on the situation is to be prepared periodically and, in any event, prior to the aforementioned meeting by the Presidency of the Council in collaboration with the Commission. The report is to be drafted by the Presidency and the Commission, with the support of the General Secretariat of the Council. The opinion of UNHCR must also be taken into account. This report will eventually be forwarded to all Member States.

The procedure concludes with a "decision on burden-sharing"[345]. Depending on the outcome of the proceedings of the aforementioned Co-ordinating Committee, a proposal will be prepared for submission to the Council for approval. The provisions laid down by the Council's Rules of Procedure for urgent cases[346] may be applied if a month elapses without agreement within the Co-ordinating Committee. Pursuant to paragraph 4 of the Resolution, the detailed arrangements for admitting displaced persons are to be decided upon by each Member State.

The procedure seems to be overly complicated; closer examination, in fact, reveals a lack of contour and a number of shortcomings. The ultimate effects of this "harmonized action" concluded by a "decision on burden-sharing"[347] are highly questionable, especially given the fact that the content of the "harmonized action," as well as the legal character of the "decision on burden-sharing" under paragraph 3 of the Decision remain vague. Even though "the drawing up of a timetable and a progressive plan for anticipated admission requirements" is on the agenda of the urgent meeting[348], the Resolution does not allow for an actual common decision on burden-sharing. Instead, the Member States, pursuant to paragraph 4 of the Resolution, are left to determine "the number of persons who will be admitted and when they will be admitted. [349] Finally, "the detailed

---

[343] Pursuant to paragraph 4 of the decision the Co-ordinating Committee may, while the crisis lasts, hold frequent meetings at intervals to be decided on by the Committee itself and on the basis of paragraph 2 of the decision (i.e. with the agenda described above).

[344] In order for a situation requiring concerted action to exist, the conditions of paragraphs 1 and 2 of the Council resolution of 25 September 1995 have to be fulfilled.

[345] See para 3 of the decision.

[346] See *supra* note 339.

[347] See para 3 of the decision of 4 March, 1996.

[348] See para 2 clause 4 of the decision of 4 March 1996.

[349] Para 2, 2nd indent of the decision.

arrangements for admitting displaced persons shall be decided on by each Member State"[350].

e) Admission and Return, Rights Granted, Relationship to the Asylum Procedure

Neither instrument creates rules relating to a uniform admission and return of persons benefiting from a temporary protection regime, nor do they speak to the question of which rights, e.g. residence permits, the duration of the stay, the right to work, housing, education, social assistance, family reunion, etc., are to be granted to persons receiving a temporary protected status. The detailed arrangements for the admission of displaced persons shall, instead, be decided by each Member State[351].

The general considerations of the Resolution declare that the instrument does not interfere with the rules laid down in the Dublin Convention of 15 June 1990 in cases in which a person applies for refugee status under the Geneva Convention. In addition, according to paragraph 6, the Resolution does not affect practices followed by individual Member States, or by all Member States under bilateral or multilateral agreements relating to admission on humanitarian grounds. To what extent the Resolution allows for a change from a temporary protection scheme to the asylum procedure and vice versa is still a matter of debate. The problem has, however, been dealt with in the proposal of the Commission for a Joint Action on temporary protection[352].

Neither the Council Resolution of 25 September 1995, nor the Council Decision of 4 March 1996 created a comprehensive legal system on temporary protection of displaced persons. Their major fault lies in the fact that they are not legally binding. Their content cannot, however, be left free of criticizm. These shortcomings notwithstanding, the two instruments represent, at the very least, a first step towards a closer international cooperation in the field of displaced persons within the framework of the European Union on the way towards the establishment of legally binding instruments with a more clearly shaped content[353].

---

[350] Para 4 of the decision.

[351] Cf. para 4 of the decision of 4 March 1996.

[352] See the explanations *infra* V.4.b. et seq.

[353] Similar judgments on the value of the two resolution and the decision have rendered by the following authors: *ECRE*, Comments from the European Council on Refugees and Exiles on the 1995 "burden-sharing" resolution and decision adopted by the Council of the European Union, 1; *Kälin*, Towards a Concept of Temporary Protection (1996), 6; *De Jong*, conference paper, 9.

4. Temporary Protection

a) The Concept of Temporary Protection

Temporary protection is not an established part of public international law but a political instrument developed to cope with specific situations[354]. It is granted by the national authorities as an autonomous act in reaction to a specific crisis situation of mass influx based upon a special decision to admit a specific group of persons and for a specific duration of time and can therefore not be legally claimed before a judiciary body[355]. Nevertheless, temporary protection must be framed and evaluated in the light of international obligations of states[356].

The concept of temporary protection is designed to be applied to groups of persons as a spontaneous reaction to their urgent needs in situations of mass flight as an emergency situation[357]. It has the advantage of offering immediate and flexible protection to individuals in need[358]. Though temporary protection schemes are not meant to replace the institution of asylum, they can, nonetheless, offer immediate humanitarian protection to larger groups of people who have been forced to flee from their homes and country[359]. Temporary protection is, by definition, limited to the time during which the conditions in the country of origin do not allow a safe and dignified return of the individuals involved[360].

The wording of the concept suggests its two key elements[361]. On the one hand, *temporary* protection is not designed to be a durable – and thus permanent – solution for a refugee crisis. Displaced persons must return to their country of origin after the situation has improved to a extent that international protection is no longer needed, and their return in safety and dignity is possible. On the other hand, the concept embodies the idea of international *protection*, comprising, *inter alia*, admission to a host country, the granting of basic rights during residence and compliance with the principle of non-refoulement[362].

b) The Commission Proposal for a Joint Action on Temporary Protection

On 5 March 1997 the Commission submitted a proposal to the Council for a Joint Action based on ex-Article K.3(2)(b) of the Treaty on European Union concerning temporary protection of displaced persons[363]. The Member States discussed the

---

[354] *Kälin*, Towards a Concept of Temporary Protection (1996), 11.
[355] Cf. *International Centre for Migration Policy Development*, Final Report, Registration for TPS, 16.
[356] Cf. *Kälin*, Towards a Concept of Temporary Protection (1996), 11.
[357] *International Centre for Migration Policy Development*, Final Report, Registration for TPS, 18.
[358] See the Commission's amended proposal for a joint action on temporary protection of displaced persons of 26 June 1998, explanatory memorandum, 4/2.
[359] See ibid.
[360] See ibid, 4/3.
[361] Cf. *International Centre for Migration Policy Development*, Final Report, Registration for TPS, 17.
[362] Cf. *International Centre for Migration Policy Development*, Final Report, Registration for TPS, 17; for the principle of non-refoulement as a basis of temporary protection see *Kälin*, Towards a Concept of Temporary Protection (1996), 12 et seq.
[363] COM(97) 93 final.

proposal during an informal meeting on 9-10 October 1997[364]. The Co-ordinating Committee established under ex-Article K.4 TEU examined the proposal on 3 November 1997 and released a report on the state of the discussions[365]. Finally, the European Parliament gave its opinion on the proposal on 6 November 1997[366].

c) The Legal Nature of the Proposed Joint Action

The proposed Joint Action is to be legally binding[367], but will not create individual rights or be self-executing[368]. Most of the proposal's provisions leave decisions to the discretion of the Member States, as indicated by the wording that "Member States shall ensure ..." or "... should". Only a few articles contain a clear obligation to implementation on the legislative level in the Member States. [369] If a Joint Action under the Maastricht Treaty requires changes in the laws of the Member States, the obligation is generally assumed to be limited to the submission of the text of the respective Joint Action to the competent constitutional organs within a certain period of time[370]. In an explanatory memorandum concerning the proposal for a Joint Action on temporary protection, the Commission stressed that the purpose of the proposed Joint Action is not to create a new right to seek temporary protection, which would in any way supplement the existing right to seek asylum[371].

The Joint Action does not entirely prevent Member States from acting autonomously in situations of mass influx. As long as no temporary protection regime has been established by the Council, Member States are allowed to independently adopt adequate measures for persons in need of international protection[372]. Furthermore, the Joint Action does not mitigate the prerogative of Member States to grant more favourable conditions to persons in need of international protection[373].

d) The Scope of Application

According to Article 1(b), the Joint Action is applicable to "persons in need of international protection". "Any third-country national or stateless person who has

[364] See EU doc. 12391/97 ASIM 223 of 19 November 1997.
[365] See EU doc. 12391/97 ASIM 223.
[366] See EU doc. 12038/97 ASIM 216 of 19 November 1997.
[367] See the explanatory memorandum of the Commission, COM(97) 93 final, 4, para 9.
[368] COM(97) 93, final, 8, para 23. For explications about the legal effects of Joint Actions in general see *Hailbronner* in Hailbronner/Klein/Magiera/Müller-Graff, Handkommentar zum EUV/EGV, Article K EUV (1996) para 88.
[369] See e.g. Article 6 ("Member States shall deliver a residence authorisation") and Article 8 para 2 ("There shall be equality of treatment between beneficiaries of a temporary protection regime and recognised refugees regarding remuneration, social security and other working conditions").
[370] Ibid., para 94.
[371] COM(97) 93 final, 4, para 8.
[372] COM(97) 93 final, 4, para 9.
[373] Cf. Article 2(3).

left his or her country of residence and whose safe return under humane conditions is impossible in view of the situation prevailing in that country" belongs to this category. A 1994 UNHCR proposal lists examples of persons covered by this definition, in particular:[374]

- persons who have fled from areas affected by armed conflict and persistent violence;
- persons who have been or are under a serious risk of exposure to systematic or widespread human rights abuses, including those belonging to groups compelled to leave their homes by campaigns of ethnic or religious persecution; and
- persons who for other reasons specific to their personal situation are presumed to be in need of international protection.

The formulation "persons in need of international protection" includes all persons, regardless of whether or not they are covered by the Geneva Convention[375]. The proposal, however, speaks exclusively to situations of mass influx, a policy field in which there is a risk of disparate effects on a significant scale[376]. The purpose of this proposal is not to harmonize Member State laws on humanitarian residence permits granted on an individual basis. Mass influx is defined in Article 1 (c) of the proposal as "the arrival within the Union of a significant number of persons who claim to be in need of international protection or a strong probability that such a situation may soon arise." The Presidency of the Council[377] proposed to amend this definition to read "*the sudden arrival (...)*". The European Parliament shares the view of the Council and has added that a mass influx only occurs in situations of a sudden arrival of persons *from one particular country or region*[378].

Restricting the term "mass influx" to situations of sudden arrival of a significant number of persons seems reasonable. An amendment to the effect that they must come from one particular country or region, however, does not seem justified, given that only the *number* of persons arriving is of importance to the receiving countries; their country or region of origin is irrelevant. The European Parliament has proposed the insertion of an Article 2(3a) into the Joint Action, which would emphasize that the Joint Action is to supplement the Geneva Convention relating to the Status of Refugees, and is only applicable in cases of a sudden mass influx of persons in need of international protection into the EU. This amendment, however, seems unnecessary. The text of the proposed Joint Action is clear in its statement of purpose to the effect that the instrument refers exclusively to situations of mass influx[379]. The scope of application of the proposed Joint Action extends beyond

---

[374] Note on International Protection of 7 September 1994, UN doc. A/AC.96/830, para 47, reprinted in IJRL 6(1994), 679, 703.

[375] Even though the primary goal of temporary protection is to protect persons not falling under the Geneva Convention, cf. COM(97) 93 final, 4, 5, para 10.

[376] COM(97) 93 final, 5, para 12.

[377] See EU doc. 12391/97 ASIM 223 of 19 November 1997.

[378] See EU doc. 12038/97 ASIM 216 of 6 November 1997, 3.

[379] Apart from this, harmonization of rights is also necessary for beneficiaries of humanitarian residence permits granted on an individual basis.

that of the Resolution and Decision described above[380]. All persons from areas affected by armed conflict are to benefit from it, not only particular groups[381]. Finally, the scope of application of the Joint Action is concluded by a blanket clause, which includes cases not listed among the examples. The inclusion of this blanket clause was deemed necessary due to the fact that mass influx situations arise from situations other than armed conflict[382].

Pursuant to Article 2(1), the proposed Joint Action does not apply to persons admitted by Member States under national temporary protection regimes established prior to the entry into force of the instrument. Furthermore,

> the benefit of a temporary protection regime shall not apply to any person with respect to whom there are serious reasons for considering that he or she has
>
> – committed a crime against peace, a war crime, or a crime against humanity, as defined in the international instruments drawn up to make provision in respect of such crimes;
>
> – committed a serious non-political crime outside the country of refuge prior to his or her arrival on the territory of one of the Member States;
>
> – been guilty of acts contrary to the purposes and principles of the United Nations.[383]

A Member State may also deny the grant of a temporary protection regime to any person, if there are reasonable grounds to believe that he poses a threat to the national security of that State, or if, having been convicted of a particularly serious crime by a final judgment, he constitutes a danger to the community of that Member State.

e) The Procedure to Establish a Temporary Protection Regime

Article 3(1) of the Commission proposal for a Joint Action provides for a procedure governing the establishment of a Council decision on a Union-wide temporary protection regime. In cases of mass influx of persons in need of international protection[384], the Council decides to establish a temporary protection regime and must judge whether adequate protection can be found in the region of origin[385]. The decision will specifically list the groups of persons to which the temporary protection regime applies, as well as the duration of the regime. The European Parliament is of the opinion that a clause should be added to Article 3(2) of the Commission proposal, thus limiting the duration of a temporary protection

---

380 See *supra* V.3.b.

381 See the examples listed in the resolution of 25.9.1995, O.J. 1995, C 262/1/2.

382 See *supra*.

383 Article 11.

384 Those are the persons listed in Article 1 (b) of the Commission proposal, cf. also the remarks on the scope of application, *supra* V.4.d.

385 The term "region of origin" relates to the neighbour states, COM(97) 93 final, 5 para 13.

regime to a maximum of five years[386]. This limitation seems inappropriate, given the fact that it may be necessary to grant temporary protection which extends beyond the five year period. It may not, on the other hand, always be advisable to grant permanent residence titles after a five year period[387].

A substantial number of war refugees from former Yugoslavia received temporarily in Germany have been staying in Germany for several years. An automatic change into a permanent residence status after a specified period of time would probably not increase the inclination to return. Everything depends of course on the special circumstances of each case. A decision is to be made by the Council at the initiative of any Member State or the Commission. Either party may ask UNHCR for an opinion. The European Parliament has proposed[388] mandatory UNHCR consultation.

The European Parliament takes part in the legislative process by commenting upon the Commission report on the situation in the country of origin and making recommendations according to Article 4(1) of the proposal. The Parliament has suggested a stronger role for itself in the decision-making process[389] which has been favorably received by the Commission[390].

Every year, and at least six months before the end of a temporary protection regime, the Commission shall submit a report to the European Parliament and the Council on the situation in the country of origin and on the application of the temporary protection regime by the Member States, as well as on its financial implications[391]. In the light of this report, and at least three months before the end of a temporary protection regime, the Council shall take a second decision either to revise the decision taken in accordance with Article 3 or, if the situation in the country of origin allows safe return under humane conditions, to phase out the regime and to return the persons concerned[392]. The European Parliament has suggested an alternative phrasing of Article 4(2) of the Joint Action. Instead of the term "the Council shall (...) decide to revise (...)" the EP proposes the formulation "the Council shall (...) decide to extend the decision taken in accordance with Article 3 with the necessary adaptations". This change suggested by the EP might indeed render Article 4(2) of the Joint Action more clear.

f) Rights Granted

The Commission proposal addresses the issue of rights to be granted to the beneficiaries of a temporary protection regime. The rights set down in the

---

386 See EU doc. 12038/97 ASIM 216 of 6 November 1997, 4.
387 See also *infra* V.4.f.
388 See EU doc. 12038/97 ASIM 216 of 6 November 1997, 9.
389 See EU doc. 12038/97 ASIM 216 of 6 November 1997, 9.
390 Ibid.
391 In the drafting of the report the Commission will rely on a number of external sources for help, in particular the Member States, but also international organisations and non-governmental organisations (cf. ibid., para 16).
392 Article 4(2), first and second indent.

Commission proposal for a Joint Action are minimum rights[393]. The deliverance of a residence permit to the beneficiaries of the temporary protection regime for the duration of the regime is prescribed by Article 6. The provision is not self-executing and does not create an individual right to receive temporary protection or a residence permit[394]. The Presidency of the Council has suggested in the discussion proceedings on the Commission proposal to change the word "residence permit" to the term "a document, by virtue of which they can stay in the territory of the Member States according to the national laws during the temporary protection regime." This phrase is preferable to the one proposed by the Commission since it leaves more discretion to the Member States as to the type of residence title they wish to grant and therefore guarantees more flexibility. The European Parliament has proposed to include in the residence permit a right to freedom of movement in the country of residence[395]. An unlimited right to freedom of movement seems, however, problematic in view of the provisional nature of temporary protection. Receiving countries might under certain circumstances have reasonable grounds for restricting the freedom of movement of temporarily protected persons.

According to Article 13 of the Commission proposal for a Joint Action, Member States should examine whether long-term measures should be introduced for beneficiaries of temporary protection in cases where the Council has not adopted a decision to phase out the temporary protection regime after five years. One possibility would be the conversion of the temporary residence titles into unlimited ones. However, there is no obligation to effect such a transition. The European Parliament is of the opinion that any temporary protection regime should not exceed the period of five years, after which the Council has to decide on more permanent measures failing which the temporary residence titles are automatically transformed into unlimited ones[396]. In order to harmonize the Member States' rules on temporary protection it would indeed be useful for the Council to decide on more permanent measures of any kind instead of leaving this decision up to the Member States' authorities. However, a mandatory period of five years is hardly acceptable. In order to enable a flexible reaction to different kinds of situations of mass influx of persons, the time at which more permanent measures ought to be envisaged should be left open. Furthermore, an automatic transition of temporary residence titles into permanent ones in case of inactivity of the Council endangers the very concept of temporary protection and return.

According to the proposal of the Commission, the Member States shall further ensure that the beneficiaries of a temporary protection regime have the right to reunion with their spouses and their minor and dependent children[397]. This provision raises doubts. It is questionable whether there should be an immediate

---

[393] See Article 2(3).

[394] See the explanations of the Commission in its explanatory memorandum, COM(97) 93 final, 8, para 23. Ibid., 4 para 8; 6, para 14.

[395] See EU doc. 12038/97 ASIM 216 of 6 November 1997, 6.

[396] See EU doc. 12038/97 ASIM 216 of 6 November 1997, 10.

[397] Article 7(1) of the proposal. For purposes of proof the absence of marriage or filiation documents itself should not be considered an impediment (Article 7(2)). Instead, all the relevant facts and circumstances should be taken into account in order to assess the validity of any evidence and the credibility of the claimant's statements.

and general right of family reunion for temporarily protected persons. The characteristic feature of temporary protection is its provisional nature designed in view of a return. This speaks against family reunion which usually is attributed as a tendency to intensify a person's bonds to a country and therefore prevents return. Whether this assumption is true, however, may be subject to closer scrutiny. The majority of Member States is not prepared however to grant a general right to family reunification to temporarily protected persons[398], without regard to the particular circumstances of each case. The use of waiting periods cannot generally be used as a suitable alternative means to prevent unwanted permanent immigration. A proposal by the European Parliament[399] that "the Member States will enable as far as possible the reunification (...)" may pave the way for a political solution, without, however, solving the issue in substance.

The issue is whether the separation of a family for the time of temporary protection can be considered as an acceptable and suitable part of a European temporary protection scheme. Unlike migrant workers in general, refugees admitted under temporary protection schemes frequently have no other flight alternative. The fundamental right to have a family life would clearly be affected if separation, even temporarily, disrupts existing family relations. Minor children who are dependent on the care of a parent should therefore be entitled to live with one or both parents who are admitted temporarily under a temporary protection scheme. A separation of spouses may appear as an acceptable measure to ensure the temporary nature of protection, provided that neither of the spouses is dependent on the other's permanent assistance and that separation does not last for such a long time that it leads to a disruption of existing family relations. An assessment of the special circumstances of each case would seem to be necessary to accommodate properly the humanitarian needs of temporarily protected persons on the one side and legitimate public interests to maintain the temporary nature of protection and to ensure return once the circumstances giving rise to protection have changed on the other side. Generally speaking, however, temporary protection should be considered under the perspective of granting protection to an existing family rather than to a group of isolated individuals, every one of whom is evaluated on his specific merits regardless of existing family relations.

The Commission's proposal provides that temporarily protected persons will be granted permission to engage in gainful activity and enjoy equal treatment as recognized refugees as far as remuneration, social security and other working conditions are concerned[400]. After a period of one year, during which provisional measures are allowed, the Member States shall endeavor to provide housing facilities similar to those granted to recognized refugees (Article 9(1)). Similarly, temporarily protected persons shall receive social assistance, particularly with regard to means of subsistence and medical care. Where a person holds a work permit, his ability to provide for himself is to be taken into consideration. Access to public education will be ensured under the same conditions as apply to recognized

---

398 See *supra*.

399 See EU doc. 12038/97 ASIM 216 of 6 November 1997, 7.

400 Article 8.

refugees. No provisions are made for the granting of identity and travel documents or for freedom of movement in the state of reception. The Joint Action does not support the creation of new rights under public international law superseding those already derived from the Geneva Convention and the ECHR, but to harmonize such rights in order to prevent undesirable pull-effects caused by the fact that people would otherwise seek refuge where most rights seem to be available[401].

It is doubtful whether equal treatment of temporarily protected persons with recognized refugees should be granted. In practice, temporarily protected persons frequently have been treated on an equal level with asylum seekers rather than recognized refugees. This distinction is supported by a reasonable and objective criterion: the provisional and exceptional character of the admission for humanitarian reasons of temporarily protected persons. The rights granted to recognized refugees under the Geneva Convention are based on the implicit assumption that protection in principle is of an unlimited time and geared to permanent integration into the social and political life of the host country. Temporary protection schemes on the other hand are destined to enable a provisional stay in the host country, with a view to return when conditions have changed.

g) The Relationship of the Temporary Protection Regime to the Asylum Procedure

Article 10 of the Commission proposal for Joint Action allows for the postponement of an asylum claim examination, filed by a beneficiary of a temporary protection regime under the Geneva Convention, until the Council has adopted a decision on the phasing out of the temporary protection regime for a period of up to five years. The proposal, however, does not deal with the withdrawal of an asylum application as a condition for granting temporary protection.

Four different models are currently used to determine the relationship of temporary protection to individual asylum procedures in cases of mass influx. The first allows prospective beneficiaries to choose between two procedures at any point during their sojourn in a Member State. The second allows for the suspension of asylum procedures during temporary protection, as well as for their resumption after the termination of the temporary protection regime. Temporary protection is rendered conditional on the final renunciation or withdrawal of an asylum claim in a third model, which effectively rules out the freedom of choice between the two procedures. Finally, a fourth model allows for termination of temporary protection after a certain period of time and for the transformation of temporary residence titles into permanent ones without further examination.

Allowing the beneficiaries of a temporary protection regime free access to the asylum procedure at any given time would be beyond Member States' duties under the Geneva Convention. Affording free access could also jeopardize one of the

[401] COM(97) 93 final, 4, para 8.

goals of temporary protection – the simplification of procedures and the reduction of individual examination of claims in cases of mass influx.

Preventing or suspending requests for an examination of a claim for protection under the Geneva Convention in case of temporary protection, however, does not conflict with the duties imposed on the Member States by the Geneva Convention. The Geneva Convention does not oblige states to grant political asylum to everybody fulfilling the requirements of the refugee definition under Article 1A of the Convention. Member States, however, are obliged to examine any claim for protection against return, expulsion, extradition or deportation in a country of alleged persecution and to grant protection if the examination proves that there is in fact a serious risk of persecution. The Geneva Convention therefore does not provide for a specific status as a recognized refugee. The substantive rights of refugees laid down in the Convention generally apply only in the case where a Member State has chosen to grant the status of a recognized refugee. Neither admission for the purpose of seeking protection nor the granting of temporary protection for victims of war or political violence trigger the entitlement to all rights of recognized political refugees under the Convention. Temporary protection therefore does not conflict with the Member States' obligations as long as the prohibition of non-refoulement is complied with. It follows that any model must allow for an examination as to whether there is a risk of persecution once the temporary protection regime has been terminated. This examination must not, however, be carried out by way of formal asylum procedure. [402] Nor does it necessarily have to result in the grant of a permanent residence permit[403].

The wording of Article 10 of the Commission proposal has been challenged by several Member States. Some Member States oppose the exclusion of asylum seekers from the temporary protection regime. Even those who favour this exclusion, however, disagree on the legal status of rejected asylum applicants. Furthermore, not all delegations are satisfied with the suspension of the examination of asylum claims during a temporary protection regime[404]. An alternative version of Article 10 has been formulated in response to these criticisms[405], whereby the Joint Action does not infringe upon rights guaranteed by the Geneva Convention relating to the status of a refugee. Furthermore, the suspension of asylum claim examinations, according to Article 10(3), would not exceed three years, and would not last longer than the temporary protection regime.

---

402 UNHCR is of the opinion that upon termination of temporary protection, the presumption exists that a return is possible. In case of individuals claiming that they continue to be in need of protection in spite of the improvement of the situation in the country of origin, such claims could be dealt with in summary procedures involving basic safeguards and, in particular, the right to appeal with suspensory effect against a negative decision; see UNHCR background note, Informal Meeting on Temporary Protection, 20 April 1995, 6, para 22, reprinted in: *IGC*, Report on Temporary Protection, 258 et seq.

403 Since the Geneva Convention does not require the granting of a permanent residence permit, see e.g. Article 1 C(5) of the Geneva Convention.

404 See EU doc. 12391/97 ASIM 223 of 19 November 1997, 2.

405 See op. cit., 6.

The European Parliament has presented another version of Article 10[406] providing for a maximum suspension period of three years.

h) Termination of the Regime and Return of the Persons Concerned

If the situation in the country of origin allows for a safe return under humane conditions, Article 4(2) of the Commission proposal calls on the Council to evaluate the possibility of phasing out the temporary protection regime and returning the persons concerned. Both decisions must be justified in a Commission report on the situation in the country of origin. In its explanatory memorandum, the Commission states that the term "safe return under humane conditions" corresponds with similar expressions used in this context[407]. Safe return under humane conditions means –

- the *right to return*[408] freely to the homes of origin;
- *safety*, including physical and legal safety;
- *non-discrimination and respect for other fundamental human rights*, as for example freedom of movement, respect for family life, freedom of opinion and religion, property rights, etc.;
- in order to provide for the basic needs of returnees and to enable them to reintegrate, *assistance and shelter* may also be a necessary element, often requiring international aid;
- repatriation may also require an effective system for *monitoring* the reintegration process, through the establishment and functioning of domestic and international mechanisms for the protection of returnees' human rights.[409]

Prior agreement between the parties involved is considered as essential to the resolution of these issues[410]. The European Parliament has suggested that the first three conditions for return in safety and dignity be expressly incorporated into the text of the Joint Action[411]. When organizing the return of the affected persons, priority will be given to the promotion of voluntary repatriation. The proposal calls for close cooperation with the responsible international organizations, and, in particular, with UNHCR[412]. The Commission views the policy of voluntary return as "by far the least complicated and most humane option". It releases national

---

[406] See EU doc. 12038/97 ASIM 216 of 6 November 1997, 8.

[407] The Commission names "safe, dignified and humane return" or "return in safety and dignity" (see *UNHCR*, Handbook on Voluntary Repatriation: International Protection, 11; see further *Kälin/ Achermann*, Rückkehr von Gewaltflüchtlingen in Sicherheit und Würde: Ein neues Instrument der Flüchtlingsaussenpolitik?, Bern (1992).

[408] The italicised style of this sentence and the following is contained in the original text.

[409] COM(97) 93 final, 7, 8, para 19.

[410] Op. cit.

[411] See EU doc. 12038/97 ASIM 216 of 6 November 1997, 5.

[412] Article 4(3) of the Commission proposal.

administrations from having to deal with numerous "last-minute" asylum applications and grants the persons concerned a wide margin of freedom to create their own return plan[413].

A regime of return must fulfil two basic requirements. First, return must promote the concept of temporary protection. Temporary protection is not intended as a privileged access to immigration but as an exceptional and provisional measure to provide protection against specific dangers arising from the very situation which has given rise to a temporary protection scheme. Once those conditions in the home country have changed, there is no basic reason to treat temporarily protected persons differently from any other person faced with the general economic, political and social conditions in his home country. Therefore, return must primarily be orientated towards a change of those conditions that have in the first place induced temporary protection. Additional conditions such as decent economic living conditions, a possibility of obtaining employment, stable political conditions etc. are beyond the concept of temporary protection and mean basically a privileged treatment of temporarily protected persons.

From a humanitarian perspective, a second basic requirement of any return scheme is that temporarily protected persons must obviously enjoy shelter against forced return in inhuman conditions. Humanitarian expectations, however, cannot be guaranteed according to the economic and social conditions in host countries. There is no right to maintain a living standard acquired during the time of temporary protection. On the other hand, it must not be ignored that temporarily protected persons frequently have no alternative than to give up their home and personal property. The specific fate of being expelled will have to be taken into consideration when evaluating the conditions of return. This again, however, cannot mean that return, including forced return, is only envisaged if the general economic, political and social conditions have improved to such an extent that living conditions are comparable with the conditions in the country of temporary protection. The criteria must be whether persons having received temporary protection are upon return in a fundamentally weaker situation than the local population which is expected to remain in the country and contribute to the re-establishment of economic and political order of the home country.

i) Burden-Sharing

The Commission proposal establishes no new substantive criteria or factors for burden-sharing and does not elaborate on the old criteria. The amendment concerning the procedural implementation of burden-sharing contained in the Commission proposal must be considered modest at best. Under Article 4(1) the Commission will have to submit a report on the situation in the country of origin, as well as on the financial implications of a temporary protection regime for the Member States. According to Article 5, the Council is to take this report into account when examining how best to assist Member States particularly affected by

[413] COM(97) 93 final, 8, para 20.

a mass influx of persons in need of international protection. Both the legal requirements, and the consequences in case of failure are so vague that they seem to leave the creation of supportive measures to chance[414]. This weakness notwithstanding, the driving purpose of the Joint Action is the creation of conditions for an effective sharing of responsibility with regard to mass influxes of persons in need of international protection[415]. Indeed, the standardization of rights during temporary protection represents a necessary condition for an equitable sharing of the responsibilities resulting from a mass influx situation.

Discussion of the Commission proposal shows profound disagreement among Member States[416]. Some Member States are fundamentally opposed to more concrete and binding instruments on burden-sharing than the existing ones[417]. To overcome the existing deadlock in the negotiations it has been suggested the issue of burden-sharing should be separated from the issue of temporary protection although there is obviously an inseparable connection between the two issues. The Commission has taken up this suggestion in its proposal on temporary protection. The European Parliament has suggested that the Council should be granted the power to enact *ad hoc* burden-sharing decisions with binding force[418]. According to Article 5(1) of the EP proposal the Council would be given the power to decide to establish, on the basis of the report to the Commission referred to in Article 4, measures to assist Member States particularly affected by the mass influx of persons in need of international protection including financial compensation and a distribution of persons in need of international protection. Whether Member States will be able to agree *ad hoc* on burden-sharing criteria and a formula for distribution in a situation of mass influx of refugees appears doubtful. A legal instrument which is generally applicable in case of mass influx of refugees should therefore be agreed upon.

VI. Asylum Procedure

1. *Minimum Standards of Procedure*

a) Geneva Convention and the European Human Rights Convention

Every Member State is a Contracting State of the Geneva Convention on Refugees and the European Convention on Human Rights. Despite the different national laws concerning asylum and asylum procedure laws, common principles apply in Member States that follow from the commitment to the Geneva Convention of

---

[414] The Commission's explications in its explanatory memorandum stating that the measures allowed for in Article 5 may for example take the form of financial compensation and/or, if that is not sufficient, a fair allocation of the persons who are fleeing from the crisis regions (COM(97) 93 final, 8, para 21) do not alter this impression because no details are given about how to proceed.

[415] Ibid., para 21.

[416] See EU doc. 12391/97 ASIM 223 of 19 November 1997.

[417] See the resolution on burden-sharing and the decision on an alert and emergency procedure, *supra* V.3.

[418] See EU doc. 12038/97 ASIM 216 of 6 November 1997, 6.

1951 and the European Convention on Human Rights. International treaties like the United Nations Convention against Torture and other Cruel, Inhuman or Degrading Treatment or Punishment of 10 December 1984[419] or the Convention on the Rights of the Child of 20 November 1989[420] may be neglected for the examination of procedural standards. On the one hand, they regulate only marginal aspects of asylum or asylum procedure law. On the other hand, no conclusions may be drawn from these instruments which are different from those drawn from the European Convention on Human Rights or the Geneva Convention.

Additionally, all Member States participate in the decision-making process of the Committee of Ministers of the Council of Europe concerning questions of asylum and asylum procedure laws[421]. Even though such decisions and resolutions of the UNHCR Executive Committee are only of a recommendatory nature they may be used as guidelines for developing a European asylum law.

According to Article 63 ECT the European Community has the power to adopt legislation in asylum and immigration matters. Although the Community has not acceded to either the Geneva Convention or the European Convention on Human Rights it must adhere to the standards laid down in these instruments under Article 6(2) TEU and Article 63(1) ECT[422].

As regards the Geneva Convention, Article 63(1) ECT must be interpreted as a self-imposed obligation of the Community which has the character of Community law. This provision does not, however, entrust the European Court of Justice with jurisdiction over Member States' conduct with a view to compliance with the obligations laid down in the Geneva Convention. The Court's jurisdiction is limited to deciding whether Community institutions have disregarded the standards set in the Geneva Convention in terms of treatment of refugees.

Based on the common commitment of the Member States and the Community to the Geneva Convention, a number of legal restrictions arise, concerning the scope of political action in the field of asylum procedures. The Geneva Convention itself does not contain any provisions as to the asylum procedure. In addition, there is no obligation of the contracting states to grant the Convention status to those who meet the refugee definition of Article 1A of the Geneva Convention[423]. Any subsequent attempt to provide for an individual right of asylum on the level of international law and a corresponding obligation of states has failed[424]. The United Nations Declaration on Territorial Asylum of 1967[425] confirms the right of every state to grant asylum in the exercise of its sovereignty[426].

---

[419] Cf. UNHCR, Collection of International Instruments and Other Legal Texts Concerning Refugees and Displaced Persons, vol. 1, Universal Instruments, Geneva 1995, 223.

[420] Ibid. 331.

[421] Cf. CAHAR a(99) 6, Selected Texts concerning territorial asylum and refugees adopted within the Council of Europe, Strasbourg, June 1999.

[422] Cf. *supra* Chapter B II for a detailed discussion of the binding force of human rights upon the legislative powers of the Community.

[423] *Goodwin-Gill*, The Refugee in International Law, 2nd ed. 1996, 174 et seq.

[424] *Goodwin-Gill*, op. cit., 176.

[425] UNGA RES 2312 (XXII) of 14 December 1967.

[426] "Asylum granted by a state, in the exercise of its sovereignty, to persons entitled to invoke Article 14 of the Universal Declaration of Human Rights, including persons struggling against colonialism,

Even though the Geneva Convention does not contain an obligation to grant asylum, it is still accepted that certain principles of procedural law can be deduced from the principle of non-refoulement laid down in Article 33 of the Geneva Convention. There are considerable differences of opinion among the contracting states as well as between UNHCR and certain contracting states concerning the substantive content of the principle of non-refoulement in terms of its procedural consequences, particularly in situations of large-scale refugee movements. In order to concretize the Geneva Convention, UNHCR frequently refers to decisions of the UNHCR Executive Committee and the Handbook about procedures and criteria for assessing refugee status, edited by UNHCR[427]. Relevant decisions and recommendations of the EU Immigration Ministers as well as bodies of the EU also refer to these decisions on a regular basis[428]. However, it must be noted that the Member States or bodies of the EU do not make use of these recommendations and decisions as legally binding provisions for the interpretation of Community instruments concerning asylum procedures.

Notwithstanding a large number of unsolved issues of interpretation, some conclusions which have been widely accepted can be derived from the principle of non-refoulement which are essential for the scope of political action in the European Union. The following rules are based on the accepted practice of interpretations of Article 33 of the Geneva Convention as laid down in decisions, regulations and legal practice of Member States –

- In addition to expulsion, deportation and extradition, the prohibition of non-refoulement excludes every other form of return at the border to a persecuting country or a country that itself may return a refugee to a persecuting state (Prohibition of chain expulsion).
- Contracting States have to provide for a fair procedure to examine the danger of political persecution within the meaning of Article 1A of the Geneva Convention since only by the establishment of a formal procedure of some kind can the risk of becoming a victim of persecution can be properly ascertained[429].
- The obligation to examine a danger of persecution as a result of enforced return applies also in cases of manifestly unfounded or abusive asylum applications. Neither illegal entry nor the lack of valid travel or passport documents constitute sufficient grounds to justify residence terminating measures without examining whether there is a serious risk of persecution[430].

Article 3 of the European Convention on Human Rights, prohibiting torture, inhuman or degrading treatment or punishment is interpreted by the European Court of Human Rights as a prohibition not to expel, deport or extradite a foreigner to a country when substantial grounds have been shown for believing that the person concerned faces a real risk of being subjected to torture or inhuman or

---

shall be respected by all other states" (Article 1(1)); cf. UNHCR, Collection of International Instruments and Legal Texts Concerning Refugees and Displaced Persons, vol. 1, 1995,74.

427 Geneva, September 1979.

428 Cf. e.g. the Resolution of the Council on miminum guarantees for asylum procedures which globally refers to the conclusions of the UNHCR Executive Comittee and the Recommendation No. R 81.

429 Correspondingly the German Federal Constitutional Court, vol. 94, 49, 91 et seq.

430 Cf. *Kälin*, Asyl 1998.

degrading treatment or punishment in the country to which he is to be returned[431]. The European Court of Human Rights has originally set high standards of proof of this risk due to the fact that the European Convention on Human Rights does not contain a right to asylum. " Substantial grounds" or a "real risk" is required while a considerable margin of appreciation is granted to immigration authorities[432]. The Court has noted in *Vilvarajah*[433] that general dangers for the population in the situation of a civil war or violent clashes are not sufficient to substantiate a risk in terms of Article 3 of the European Convention on Human Rights.

Article 13 of the Convention on Human Rights contains another procedural requirement relating to judicial protection. It guarantees a right to appeal to an independent instance to a person who claims that his rights laid down in the Convention on Human Rights are violated. The European Court of Human Rights did not interpret Article 13 as requiring a right to appeal every time a person claims a violation of his rights. An "arguable claim"[434] is required. It is a matter of controversy under which circumstances an "arguable claim" is to be considered. To date, the Court has not explicitly defined the conditions for an "arguable claim" but has stated that the requirements under Article 13 have to be examined individually[435]. According to a prevailing view in the literature, the requirements are fulfilled if there are substantial grounds to believe that there is a concrete danger of torture and inhuman treatment in the state of origin, provided the claim has not been seriously examined at the first instance and denied on general considerations[436].

The Committee of Ministers of the Council of Europe in a recent recommendation[437] has suggested that governments of Member States ensure that the following guarantees are complied with in their legislative practice –

1. the authority is judicial; or, if it is a quasi-judicial or administrative authority, it is clearly identified and composed of members who are impartial and who enjoy safeguards of independence;
2. the authority has competence both to decide on the existence of the conditions provided for by Article 3 of the Convention and to grant appropriate relief;
3. the remedy is accessible for the rejected asylum seeker; and
4. the execution of the expulsion order is suspended until a decision under 2. is taken.

The explanatory memorandum[438] makes clear that expulsion in the context of the Recommendation means "any measure of removing an alien forcibly, e.g. refusal of entry or deportation". The Recommendation, however, applies only to a

---

431 Cf. *Cruz-Varas v Sweden*, Series A 201.

432 Cf. *Goodwin-Gill*, The Refugee in International Law, 2nd ed. (1998), 316.

433 ECHR, judgment of 20 October 1991, *Vilvarajah and Others v United Kingdom*, Series A 215.

434 Cf. ECHR, judgment of 27 April 1988, *Boyle and Rice*, No. 117/165-6, Series A 131; cf. *Hampson*, The Concept of an Arguable Claim under Article 13 of the European Convention on Human Rights, 39, ICLQ (1990) 891.

435 Cf. ECHR, judgment of 27 April 1988, *Boyle and Rice*, No. 117/165-6, Series A 131.

436 Asyl 1998, 31.

437 No. R (98), 13, see CAHAR (99/6), Selected Texts Concerning Territorial Asylum and Refugees adopted within the Council of Europe, vol. 1, Strasbourg, June 1999, 108.

438 Op. cit. at p. 110.

claim based on Article 3 of the European Convention on Human Rights while the exercise of rights by rejected asylum seekers to appeal against a negative decision on the asylum request is not covered.

b) Problems of Harmonization and the Council Decision of 1995 on Minimum Standards of Asylum Procedure

Until now, the emphasis of European efforts to harmonize asylum law has been on border controls, common visa rules and efforts to prevent asylum-shopping rather than on procedures. Conflicting national traditions as to administrative decision-making and judicial protection made it difficult for Member States to participate in the development of a common European asylum procedure. Most decisions and legal instruments were devoted to the fight against illegal immigration and abusive asylum claims. With the emergence of large networks of illegal trafficking of refugees, closely connected with organized crime, the question of common visa rules and principles on controlling external frontiers became dominant in the process of abolishing internal border controls. The Dublin Convention of 1990, primarily designed to devise a legal framework for exclusive competence to deal with asylum seekers also limited itself to establishing rules on determination of competence and transfer of asylum seekers to the competent state. Procedural issues were deferred to a later stage of European immigration and asylum law harmonization, although the concept has obviously been based on the implicit assumption of an equivalence of asylum procedures and substantive asylum law.

In the context of growing criticism against a "one sided" attempt of harmonizing the European right of asylum by human rights organizations ("Fortress Europe") and internal objections against referring asylum seekers to other Member States with considerably divergent rules on asylum procedures, the need to include asylum procedure in the agenda of the European harmonization of asylum legislation became apparent. Minimum standards for asylum procedures have for the first time been laid down by the Council in the Resolution of 20 June 1995[439] which were to be applied for the examination of asylum applications within the meaning of Article 3 of the Dublin Convention.

The competence of the Community under Article 63 (1)(d) ECT is restricted to the determination of minimum standards for procedures of granting or withdrawing the status of refugees in Member States. The wording "minimum standards" shows that it was not intended to create a EU law of asylum procedures that would replace national laws by a comprehensive European law. Only minimum standards are to be established, which do not prevent Member States from maintaining their procedural law provided, however, that it is in compliance with such minimum standards.

The purpose of common procedural rules is to establish the prerequisite for the effective application of the Dublin Convention and particularly for the implementation of the rules on exclusive competence that allow the referral of an

[439] *Guild*, The Developing Immigration and Asylum Policies of the European Union (1996), 413.

asylum seeker to the competent contracting state without the need for a previous individual assessment of safety by the contracting state.

Beyond the need to have common rules on asylum procedure to make Dublin work, there is, however, also a more basic consideration requiring a European harmonization of asylum procedures. Immigration of asylum seekers being an integral part of a general migration movement towards western Europe, procedures on dealing with asylum seekers may have a substantial influence upon the decision-making process, regardless of whether an application for asylum comes from an individual or from a trafficking organization. Since illegal immigration into any Member State necessarily affects any other Member States as a result of the abolition of border controls, the length of procedures, as well as the procedural rights and possibilities, may have a substantial influence upon the immigration situation, beyond the realm of a single EU State's asylum law.

In its Action Plan of 3 December 1998 on how best to implement the provisions of the Treaty of Amsterdam[440], the Council has given priority to the fixing of minimum standards of asylum procedures noting the necessity of accelerated procedures. Besides a higher efficiency of the Dublin Convention, the implementation of EURODAC, the prevention of irregular migration within the EU and the fixing of minimum standards for the reception of asylum seekers by the Member States within a two year period, minimum standards on procedure are also to be established as an integral part of a European asylum law.

The European Commission has identified two possible approaches to a first-pillar instrument on asylum procedures:[441]

- to establish a certain level of procedural safeguards and guarantees which all Member States would have to provide, in the interests of procedural fairness, whilst allowing Member States some degree of flexibility to determine the details of the administrative arrangements necessary for implementing these guarantees and to decide whether they wished to apply all the measures for speeding up procedures; or
- to adopt a more prescriptive approach, which would require all Member States to apply exactly the same procedure, so that full harmonization would be achieved.

The Commission has already indicated that it will bring forward a proposal in line with approach a) in view of the structure of the Action Plan on how best to implement the provisions of the Treaty of Amsterdam establishing an area of freedom, security and justice. The Action Plan envisages an instrument on asylum procedures within two years of the entry into force of the Amsterdam Treaty. In addition, it makes provision for a study with a view to establishing the merits of a single European asylum procedure. This – according to the European Commission – seems to imply that the European Union should first aim to put in place a binding instrument on asylum procedures, and then, in the longer term, on the basis of the study which the Action Plan called for, should consider the merits of the single

---

440 O.J. 1999 C 19/1.

441 Commission Working Document, Towards Common Standards on Asylum Procedures, Sec. (1999) 271 fin. of 3 March 1999, 7.

asylum system which would presumably also cover issues such as reception and the refugee definition[442]. The Commission has also taken up the suggestion of the Action Plan to reduce the duration of asylum procedures[443]. Although the Commission agrees to ensure that asylum procedures should be accelerated it emphasizes that asylum procedures contain the necessary safeguards to ensure that all those in need of protection are correctly identified. The Commission does not consider that the level of guarantees envisaged in the Resolution on minimum guarantees for asylum procedures in relation to such basic safeguards as appeal rights, legal advice and interpretation facilities can be reduced. It indicates, however, that it might be necessary to revisit some of the derogations and exceptions contained in paragraph 10 of the Resolution on minimum guarantees. The problem of duration of asylum procedures, however, is clearly approached from the point of increasing efficiency rather than weakening existing safeguards[444].

To speed up the procedure an approach is proposed which would envisage a simple structure for the asylum system. The Community legal instrument would not, therefore, require Member States to introduce or maintain multi-tiered appeal systems. The Working Document refers to the existing national judicial systems and constitutional requirements which determine to what extent Member States will be able to simplify appeal arrangements. The starting point of the Commission proposal is that provided the necessary safeguards are in place to ensure a good standard of decision-making by asylum determination bodies, a single appeal or review of the substance of the decision will normally be sufficient (without prejudice to the power of higher courts to rule on points of law)[445].

2. *The Safe Third-Country Concept in the European Union*

a) The 1992 Resolution of the Community Immigration Ministers

The Resolution of Immigration Ministers of 30 November/1 December 1992[446] intends to restrain irregular migration from safe first countries of reception to western European states for economic and other reasons. The Resolution points to the problem of refugees and asylum seekers unlawfully leaving countries where they have already been granted protection or have had a genuine opportunity to seek such protection. Reference to a possibility to seek protection means in effect a deviation from the previous concept based upon the idea that an asylum seeker has a right to choose his country of asylum.

The Resolution of the EC-Ministers of Immigration concerning host third countries does not affect the application of the Dublin Agreement. In case of an application of the Dublin Agreement the Member State basically considers the

---

442 Commission Working Document, Towards Common Standards on Asylum Procedures at No. 9.
443 Action Plan § 36 b O.J. C 19, 23 January 1999.
444 Commission Working Document, Towards Common Standards on Asylum Procedures at No. 15.
445 Op. cit. at. No. 16.
446 *Guild*, The Developing Immigration and Asylum Policies of the European Union, 1996, 161.

possibility of applying the principles of the host third country. It is therefore possible that instead of transferring an asylum seeker to a competent Dublin State, the person is sent back to the safe third country. The Dublin Agreement is applicable if an asylum seeker can in fact not be sent back or expelled to a safe third country. A Member State can furthermore not refuse its competence for reviewing an application for asylum according to the Dublin Agreement with the argument that the requesting Member State could have applied a safe third country rule and transferred an asylum seeker to a safe third state.

The Resolution does not provide explicitly for a particular procedure in case of an asylum seeker arriving from a safe third country. It refers to the Resolution by the Immigration Ministers about manifestly unfounded applications for asylum of 30 November /1 December 1992[447]. Under No. 1 b) of this Resolution an application for asylum may not be subject to determination by a Member State of refugee status under the terms of the Geneva Convention on the status of refugees when it falls within the provisions of the Resolution on host third countries. As a procedural basis for applying the concept of host third countries the Resolution mentions the following criteria –

1. The formal identification of a host third country in principle precedes the substantive examination of the application for asylum and its justification.
2. The principle of the host third country is to be applied to all applicants for asylum irrespective of whether or not they may be regarded as refugees.
3. Thus, if there is a host third country, the application for refugee status may not be examined and the asylum applicant may be sent to that country.
4. Any Member State retains the right, for humanitarian reasons, not to remove the asylum applicant to a host third country.

Cases falling within this concept may be considered under the accelerated procedures provided for in the Resolution on manifestly unfounded asylum claims.

No. 2 of the Resolution provides that fulfilment of a number of requirements laid down in the Resolution determines a host third country and should be assessed by the Member State in each individual case. These requirements are –

1. In those third countries, the life or freedom of the asylum applicant must not be threatened, within the meaning of Article 33 of the Geneva Convention.
2. The asylum applicant must not be exposed to torture or inhuman or degrading treatment in the third country.
3. It must *either* be the case that the asylum applicant has already been granted protection in the third country or has had an opportunity, at the border or within the territory of the third country, to make contact with that country's authorities in order to seek their protection, before approaching the Member State in which he is applying for asylum, *or* that there is clear evidence of his admissibility to a third country.
4. The asylum applicant must be afforded effective protection in the host third country against refoulement, within the meaning of the Geneva Convention.

The interpretation of this clause is controversial. Most Member States of the European Union apply the safe third country concept as a rebuttable presumption

---

[447] *Guild*, op. cit., 241.

which means that notwithstanding a presumption in favour of safety there has to be an individual examination. In favour of this interpretation one may point to the wording of the Resolution whereby fulfilment of the requirements should be assessed in "each individual case". It is not absolutely clear, however, whether this applies to the procedural rules or whether it applies only to the procedure to determine a country as a safe third country.

There is no mechanism which would ensure a common interpretation of the safety requirements laid down in the Resolution. The Resolution does envisage an exchange of information and a consultation with UNHCR; there is, however, no procedure for a common assessment of safety. Member States will take into account, on the basis in particular of the information available from the UNHCR, known practice in the third country, especially with regard to the principle of non-refoulement before considering sending asylum applicants to them. It remains, however, within the discretion of Member States to decide by which procedure a determination of safety is made. Practice differs widely. Some Member States have introduced a formal procedure by way of legislation or administrative regulation to determine a list of safe third countries. Other Member States have not introduced a list of safe third countries but proceed on the basis of administrative *ad hoc* decisions on safety.

The divergent application of the Resolution in the Member States makes clear that the Resolution leaves a wide margin of interpretation. It is clear that the Resolution does not support a concept which has until now dominated the legislation of a number of western European countries whereby only applicants could be excluded from access to the asylum procedure who have been resident for some time in a safe third country and therefore have already "found protection" in a host third country. A similar concept is contained in No. 85 of the UNHCR Executive Committee Resolution to which the Resolution of Immigration Ministers refers. The text of the 1992 Resolution, however, makes clear that the mere possibility of finding protection elsewhere must be considered as sufficient. Similarly, a recently adopted recommendation of the Committee of Ministers of the Council of Europe about guidelines on the application of the safe third concept[448] has stated as a guideline, in order to assess whether a country is a safe third country to which an asylum seeker can be sent, that the following criteria should be met in each individual case –

- observance by the third country of international human rights standards relevant to asylum as established in universal and regional instruments including compliance with the prohibition of torture, inhuman or degrading treatment or punishment;
- observance by the third country of international principles relating to the protection of refugees as embodied in the 1951 Convention and the 1967 Protocol relating to the Status of Refugees, with special regard to the principle of non-refoulement;

[448] Recommendation No. R (97) 22, CAHAR (99) 6, Selected Texts Concerning Territorial Asylum and Refugees adopted within the Council of Europe, Vol. 1, Strasbourg, June 1999, 97.

- the third country will provide effective protection against refoulement and the possibility to seek and enjoy asylum;
- the asylum seeker has already been granted effective protection in the third country or has had the opportunity, at the border or within the territory of the third country, to make contact with that country's authorities in order to seek protection there before moving on to the Member State where the asylum request is lodged or, that as a result of personal circumstances of the asylum-seeker, including his or her prior relations with the third country, there is clear evidence of the admissibility of the asylum seeker to the third country.

The last point makes clear that the mere opportunity to make contact is considered as sufficient to exclude an asylum seeker from access to procedure.

The European Commission in its Working Document of March 1999 identifies a number of issues relating to the 1992 Resolution on a harmonized approach to questions concerning host third countries[449]. The Commission emphasizes that the application of the safe third country concept must be subject to stringent safeguards in order to ensure that the principle of non-refoulement is given effect. Since No. 4 of the Resolution envisages that the procedures on determining the safety of a third country should be reviewed from time to time and that consideration should be given to whether any additional measures are necessary, a comparison of national practices has been undertaken by the Commission in accordance with the Council decision on monitoring the implementation of instruments adopted concerning asylum[450]. The Commission noted that some areas have been identified where Member States' practices vary significantly. The Commission identifies the following issues which could usefully be reviewed with a view to adopting additional measures in order to clarify existing measures –

- the need for contacts with the third country and the provision of documentation to ensure that the asylum applicant will be readmitted and that the third country is aware that the substance of the applicant's asylum claim has not been examined;
- whether the requirement currently set out in paragraph 2(d) of the Resolution that the applicant must be afforded effective protection in the host third country against refoulement should be amended to state that effective protection must include the availability of an effective remedy in the third country;
- clarification of the obligation to assess in each individual case that the fundamental requirements for the determination of a host third country are fulfilled;
- the scope for common assessments of third countries, for the purpose of assessing whether an applicant's life or freedom would be threatened in the third country (paragraph 2(a) of the Resolution) and whether an applicant would be exposed to torture or inhuman or degrading treatment in the third country (paragraph 2(b) of the Resolution), and the role of safe third country lists;
- the application of the concept in situations of "mere transit".

---

[449] Op. cit. at p. 9.

[450] O.J. 1997 L 178/6.

The list of issues identified shows clearly that notwithstanding the principles laid down in the Resolution there are different views among the Member States relating to the application of the safe third country concept. The scope of possible application of the concept reaches from the German concept whereby an irrebuttable presumption has been introduced based on a list of safe third countries determined by the Basic Law (Member States) or legislative provision (other third states). This concept leaves no administrative discretion for an individual evaluation of the situation in third countries declared as safe. Other Member States apply the safe third country concept as a rebuttable presumption requiring the asylum seeker to present facts or evidence suitable to refute the presumption of safety in order to have access to the asylum procedure. Some other Member States apply the concept only as one of several criteria which have to be considered when reviewing an asylum application.

The German concept has provoked heavy criticism from UNHCR and human rights associations which derive the obligation to provide an individual case by case-evaluation of safety from the Geneva Convention. An exception would be allowed only if there is an international agreement providing for the exclusive competence of another safe contracting state and ensuring that state's jurisdiction for reviewing a request for asylum[451].

b) International Law Objections

It has frequently been argued that safe third country clauses are not in accordance with the Geneva Convention on Refugees and the European Convention on Human Rights. EU Member States as contracting parties to both Conventions are obliged to examine whether a serious risk of political persecution, inhuman or degrading treatment or punishment exists if a person is to be expelled, extradited, deported or returned to a country of origin or third country. In case of a return to a third country it is recognized that every contracting state under the Geneva Convention is obliged to refrain from returning a refugee or asylum seeker to a third country which may deport or return that person to a persecuting state. The non-refoulement prohibition is generally considered as being of an absolute nature; it therefore applies also in cases of illegal entry, intentional destruction of travel documents or disguising of the true identity[452].

The major objection against the safe third country concept is based upon the danger of persecution which cannot be sufficiently excluded even in the case of a "safe" third country. It is argued that implicit standards of fairness of procedure require that safety has to be examined in every individual case according to the special circumstances of each case. UNHCR was originally opposed to any kind of safe third country concept but has changed its view by accepting the application of a safe third country concept under certain conditions; that adequate provisions are

---

[451] Cf. AGIT, Efficient, Effective and Encompassing Approaches to a European Immigration and Asylum Policy, 9 June 1999, 7; ECRE, ENAR, MPG, Guarding Standards – Shaping the Agenda, April 1999, E 9.

[452] See e.g. *Kälin* in Asyl 1988, 23, 28 et seq.

made, that the state in which the asylum seeker is returned can be regarded as safe on the basis of a careful and fair examination of the criteria determining the safety of a country and always subject to the special circumstances of a case. Therefore, a general assumption of safety of a third country must in any case be rebuttable and a refugee must have a fair chance of submitting evidence that in his particular case a country generally considered as a safe country does not provide sufficient protection, with the result that access to asylum procedure must be guaranteed in any case. An irrebuttable presumption of safety based upon a fixed list of safe third countries either determined by law or by administrative regulation must be considered as unacceptable[453].

In its judgment on the 1993 Asylum Reform of 14 May 1996, the German Federal Constitutional Court did not share these objections. In its view it is within the legislative power of Parliament to determine on the basis of criteria set by the Basic Law the safety of a third country by stating an irrebuttable presumption of safety. The Constitutional Court emphasizes, however, that safety of a third country requires that the asylum seeker had been granted access to a procedure and that a decision may be obtained by the competent authorities on an application for protection under the Geneva Convention. Although the Court admits that the Geneva Convention does not require a specific type of procedure, it follows from the general obligation of contracting parties of a treaty to co-operate in good faith in the fulfilment of the aims of the treaty. Contracting states, therefore, cannot evade their obligations arising from the Geneva Convention by the absence of any kind of procedure suitable to determine whether a person fulfils the requirement of a refugee under Article 1A of the Geneva Convention. The Court has observed that only by way of some kind of a formal procedure it is possible to determine whether the prohibition of refoulement would be affected by return or deportation[454].

Although there is no general consensus among Member States on the irrebuttable presumption model, it must be mentioned that at least within the Dublin Convention the concept of attribution of exclusive responsibility, the safety of another contracting state being responsible under the terms of the Dublin system may be generally presumed, provided always that Member States adhere to the common standards laid down in the Immigration Ministers' Resolution of 1992 and the Minimum Guarantees Resolution of 1995.

There are other objections of a more political nature challenging the reasonableness and practicability of the whole concept. These objections are based on the correct assumption that any kind of safe third country concept means a shifting of responsibility to the first safe host country. A fully efficient safe third country concept may exclude the entry of asylum seekers into most Member States unless they have common borders with a potential country of origin, with exception of those asylum seekers who enter the state directly from their home state, by way of air or sea transport. In the context of enlarging the European Union this would mean that shift the major burden of receiving asylum seekers will

---

[453] Statement of UNHCR to the Federal Constitutional Court in joined cases 1938/95, 2315/95 (1993 Asylum Reform); not reproduced in BVerfGE 94, 49 et seq.; on file with the author.

[454] Op. cit. at p. 91 et seq.

be shifted to the newly acceding Eastern European countries and to Spain and Portugal, concerning influxes from the Maghreb-states. It must be mentioned, however, that a safe third country concept of whatever kind cannot be looked upon as an isolated national instrument to get rid of unwanted asylum seekers. It requires a concerted effort to establish a mechanism providing for a provisional protection in the region, assistance to first host countries and joint action to prevent the emergence of conditions causing a mass flow of refugees. Finally, safe third country concepts as well as the attribution of exclusive responsibility require common procedural and substantive asylum law standards. To refer an asylum seeker to a "safe" third country which applies substantially different standards in defining a refugee or relating to the standard of proof required would seem to be difficult. One has to keep in mind, however, that even within one EU Member State there are frequently different interpretations, particularly in states with a elaborate federal system. To establish a European system of exclusive responsibility does not require uniform procedural and substantive asylum law standards. Provided that all state parties participating in the system fulfil minimum standards of fairness of procedure and compliance with the Geneva Convention and the European Convention on Human Rights, differences in interpreting these Conventions do not as such justify a claim of unjust or unfair treatment.

c) Inherent Difficulties of the Safe Third Country Concept

Most Member States practising a safe third country concept do not use the concept as much as one might expect. Although Germany is surrounded by third countries which are either by constitutional law or by Parliamentary legislation declared as safe third countries it still registered 98,644 asylum seekers in 1999[455]. Except for persons legally entering Germany with a visitors visa, only asylum seekers arriving at German airports or seaports do not fall under the Dublin Convention's safe third country concept. Only a relatively small number of asylum seekers arriving from safe third countries, however, are sent back to that country according to the asylum procedure law, i.e. without further examination of the substance of the claim. In 1996 32,100 foreigners were deported from Germany, 4,484 due to a negative outcome of their asylum procedure[456].

One of the primary reasons for the rare application of the safe third country concept of the Dublin Convention lies in the fact that return to a safe third country where he or she may claim protection under the Geneva Convention, whether return is based on bilateral readmission agreements or informal agreements, requires as a rule proof that an asylum seeker in fact illegally entered Germany from a specific third country of a Dublin State. Asylum seekers, who are normally well informed about the legal consequences of having travelled to a safe third country, usually evade return proceedings by hiding the travel route and destroying

---

455 Bundesamt für die Anerkennung Ausländischer Flüchtlinge, Asylpraxis, 3rd ed. (1999), 23.

456 These figures are based on information of the Interior Ministry in Lower Saxony, see 3. Migrationspolitisches Forum, 11.5.1998, Bonn; attention has to be paid that the number of deportations does not relate to the number of asylum seekers in a given period of time.

all travel documents and other evidence which could hint at a previous transit through a safe third country. A substantial increase in the number of criminal proceedings for using falsified documents also indicates a general strategy of covering the travel route and/or identity thereby making the application of readmission agreements and return arrangements impossible. In the absence of any other country which might be willing to grant entry and residence, an asylum seeker's claim to be facing political persecution or inhuman or degrading treatment has to be examined unless a state decides to grant a humanitarian residence permit or any other kind of protection. Frequently, in such cases it may be more time-consuming to look for a third country willing to take back an asylum seeker than to examine an asylum claim in substance. The complex nature of return proceedings, the bureaucratic nature of the procedure, the high level of evidence required and time limits frequently preclude the operation of safe third country concepts, even if a safe third country is in principle willing to apply the agreement. Therefore, on balance, the institution of return proceedings to a safe third country frequently faces more difficulties than examining an asylum claim in substance.

Notwithstanding the fact that the safe third country concept has not been implemented with a large degree of success in most Member States, the evaluation frequently made that the safe third country concept has proven to be useless and will soon be abolished altogether seems to be premature. First of all, its possibilities in connection with a Dublin type system of attribution of responsibility is underestimated. Once there are efficient data systems established tracing the travel route of asylum seekers and other persons, who have illegally entered a Member State, it can be expected that irregular migration in general and subsequent asylum applications in particular lose much of their present attractiveness. In addition, the safe third country concept must also be evaluated on its psychological merits. Experience has shown that in Germany as in other states the introduction of the safe third country concept has resulted in a significant decrease in the number of asylum seekers. Obviously, the general threshold to be returned without access to the asylum procedure has been taken into general consideration when deciding which country to choose as a final destination.

In its judgment of 14 May 1996, the German Federal Constitutional Court disagreed with Mr. Kälin's objection concerning the German third country concept[457]. According to the Court's view the legislators, while amending the German Basic Law, could, on the basis of the criteria set by law, irrefutably take for granted that asylum seekers in Member States and other safe third countries are safe from persecution. However, the Court emphasized the possibility that petitions for protection are in fact possible in this third-country and decisions concerning these petitions can be obtained by the responsible authority[458]. Apart from that, however, neither the Geneva Convention on Refugees prescribes a uniform

[457] Statement of *W. Kälin* before the Federal Constitutional Court 21/22 November 1995; summarized by the court in its judgment of 14 May 1996, BVerfGE 94, 49, 81 et seq.; see also *Kälin*, Asyl 1996, 73.

[458] See the judgment of the German Bundesverfassungsgericht (Federal Constitutional Court) of 14 May 1996, joined cases 2 BvR 1938/93; 2 BvR 2315/93 (1993 Asylum Reform), BVerfGE 94, 49, 91.

procedure for the determining of the refugee status, nor has a certain state practice evolved as yet.

A conclusion to be drawn from these considerations is that no objections based on international and European law exist against a third-country concept, which presumes safety in cases of entry to the territory from a safe third country (mere transit through the safe third country is sufficient). The introduction of a irrefutable statement that a certain third country has to be regarded as safe remains an option for future action, as an opposing uniform practice of European states has not emerged yet, and both the Geneva Convention on Refugees and the European Convention on Human Rights prescribe no specific procedure for the examination, if the refoulement prohibition is observed. Nor would it be possible, within the framework of agreements concerning competence between states which agreed on uniform principles concerning asylum procedure law, which correspond with the Geneva Convention and the European Convention on Human Rights, to raise objections against a system of refoulement or transfer of applicants to the competent contracting state without the necessity of a further examination of the safety of this state in a particular case. The Dublin Convention, which implicitly is based on this presumption, one the one hand allows Member States to grant asylum seekers access to an asylum determination procedure in specific cases, in deviation from the distribution of competence established by the Convention. On the other hand, however, the Dublin Convention refers asylum seekers, without any examination of the content of the asylum application or the safety of the other contracting state, to the state competent according to the Convention.

The main objections from a legal policy perspective against any kind of third country concept are, however, directed against the implied transfer of responsibility for the reception and examination of refugees seeking protection. A fully functioning third country concept would, with the exception of asylum seekers who entered the state directly from their home state, exclude almost all other applicants. Such a third country concept would still keep the way open for an asylum procedure for those applicants, to whom such a procedure is applicable as the result of a European competence regulation (e.g. based on the issuing of a visa), or where entry and residence are explicitly granted. In contrast, asylum seekers who illegally entered the territory would be excluded from asylum procedures as far as the entry via a neighbouring state can be proved.

These objections were to a certain extent supported by the German Federal Constitutional Court by pointing at the establishment of a European asylum law space which would be emerging within the framework of the European Union. From this perspective the third country concept is not conceived as the final stage of an asylum law system, in which the responsibility concerning asylum law is continuously further and further transferred to those states which have a direct border with persecuting countries and which are often economically and technically overcharged by a mass immigration of refugees seeking protection. The third country concept has to be seen rather as part of a developing concept which includes help for the most affected countries and, in the long term, a European distribution of the burden. In this context, however, it is important that, in derogation of the previously applied system of asylum law, help should primarily be provided for adjacent regions and that at the same time, through the exclusion of a right to free choice of asylum country, claims for asylum as a means to immigrate shall be prevented.

3. Manifestly Unfounded or Abusive Asylum Claims

a) Fast-Track Procedures

The Resolution of the Ministers responsible for Immigration on Manifestly Unfounded Applications for Asylum[459] provides for the possibility to apply in cases of manifestly unfounded asylum applications as defined in the Resolution, a fast-track procedure. Member States may introduce an accelerated procedure which need not include full examination of an asylum claim at every level of the procedure. Manifestly unfounded claims as defined by the Resolution would fall in the scope of application of such a procedure although the Resolution makes clear that an asylum application need not necessarily be included within an accelerated procedure if there are national policies providing for its acceptance on other grounds. In addition, the possibility to introduce accelerated procedures does not exclude that Member States may operate admissibility procedures as distinct from accelerated procedures under which application may be rejected very quickly "on objective grounds".

The Resolution defines an application as manifestly unfounded if it clearly raises no substantive issues under the Geneva Convention and the New York Protocol for one of the following reasons –

- there is clearly no substance to the applicant's claim to fear persecution in his own country; or
- the claim is based on deliberate deception or is an abuse of asylum procedures.

Both reasons are further defined in the Resolution. No. 6 defines those applications in which there is no question of refugee status within the terms of the Geneva Convention. This may be because –

- the grounds of the application are outside the scope of the Geneva Convention: the applicant does not invoke fear of persecution based on his belonging to a race, a religion, a nationality, a social group, or on his political opinions, but reasons such as the search for a job or better living conditions;
- the application is totally lacking in substance: the applicant provides no indications that he would be exposed to fear of persecution or his story contains no circumstantial or personal details;
- the application is manifestly lacking in any credibility: the story is inconsistent, contradictory or fundamentally improbable.

Under Point 7 the Resolution also mentions the possibility of an internal flight alternative. Accelerated procedure may be applied to an application which is clearly limited to a specific geographic area where effective protection is readily available for that individual in another part of his own country to which it would be

---

[459] Reproduced in *Guild/Niessen*, The Developing Immigration and Asylum Policies (1996), 141.

reasonable to expect him to go[460]. For the second alternative, the Resolution mentions cases in which the applicant has, without reasonable explication:

- based his application on a false identity or on forged or counterfeit documents which he has maintained are genuine when questioned about them;
- deliberately made false representations about his claim, either orally or in writing, after applying for asylum;
- in bad faith destroyed, damaged or disposed of any passport, other document or ticket relevant to his claim, either in order to establish a false identity for the purpose of his asylum application or to make the consideration of his application more difficult;
- deliberately failed to reveal that he has previously lodged an application in one or more countries, particularly when false identities are used;
- having had ample earlier opportunity to submit an asylum application, submitted the application in order to forestall an impending expulsion measure;
- flagrantly failed to comply with substantive obligations imposed by national rules relating to asylum procedures;
- submitted an application in one of the Member States, having had his application previously rejected in another country following an examination comprising adequate procedural guarantees and in accordance with the Geneva Convention on the Status of Refugees. To this effect, contacts between Member States and third countries would, when necessary, be made through UNHCR.

The criteria listed above, however, are considered by the Resolution only as indications of bad faith which justify consideration of a case in the accelerated procedure, in the absence of a satisfactory explanation for the applicant's behaviour. Therefore, Member States remain free to admit an asylum seeker in spite of one of the circumstances generally justifying the assumption of an abusive asylum claim. The use of forged documents, therefore, does not in all cases lead to an application of an accelerated procedure if an applicant can show a sufficient explanation for his behaviour.

The Resolution adds another important qualification for the application of an accelerated procedure. The existence of factors indicating an abusive or manifestly unfounded asylum procedure does not change the need to examine a well founded fear of persecution under Article 1A of the Geneva Convention. This is made clear by the formulation that the factors listed under Point 9 (deliberate deception or

---

[460] For a thoughtful summary of the circumstances under which refugee protection may lawfully denied on the ground that an asylum seeker is able to avail himself or herself to an internal protection alternative see *J. C. Hathaway*, Michigan Guidelines on the Internal Protection Alternative, The University of Michigan Law School, 9-11 April 1999.

abuse of asylum procedure) cannot in themselves outweigh a well founded fear of persecution under Article 1 of the Geneva Convention and none of them carries any greater weight than any other. It is not absolutely clear what is meant by this formulation. Obviously, in case of a danger of persecution, abuse of an asylum claim does not justify a denial of protection under the Geneva Convention. On the other hand, the Resolution does not exclude that factors indicating the abuse of an asylum application may not be taken into consideration in the determination of an asylum claim. Thus, it follows that deliberate deception or abuse of asylum procedure does not trigger the application of a different set of procedural rules without changing applicable standards as to proof of a claim for protection.

Finally, the Resolution specifies that it does not affect national provisions of Member States for considering under accelerated procedures, where such procedures exist, other cases "where an urgent resolution of the claim is necessary, if it is established that the applicant has committed a serious offence in the territory of the Member States, if a case manifestly falls within the situations mentioned in Article 1F of the 1951 Geneva Convention, or for serious reasons of public security, even where the cases are not manifestly unfounded."

The Resolution is not applicable if a state wishes to apply a safe third country concept to asylum seekers entering from a third country. Point 1(b) explicitly authorises Member States, without prejudice to the Dublin Convention, to exclude an application for asylum from a determination process when it falls within the host country's resolution.

The Resolution on Minimum Guarantees for Asylum Procedures of 20 June 1995[461] refers largely to the 1992 Resolution. While the 1992 Resolution did not contain any procedural rules, the 1995 Resolution focuses upon general standards applicable for all kinds of asylum determinations. The general guarantees are, in principle, also applicable to manifestly unfounded asylum applications subject, however, to some restrictions and limitations laid down in the Resolution of 1992 and some specific provisions in the Resolution on Minimum Guarantees of 1995.

The general guarantees concerning the examination of asylum applications include:

- Asylum application shall be examined by any authority, fully qualified in the field of asylum and refugee matters;
- Decisions shall be taken independently in the sense that all asylum applications will be examined and decided upon individually, objectively and impartially;
- When examining an application for asylum the competent authority must, of its own initiative, take into consideration and seek to establish all the relevant facts and give the applicant the opportunity to present a substantial description of the circumstances of the case and to prove them;
- Competent authorities are to be adequately provided with staff and equipment;
- As long as the asylum application has not been decided on, the applicant is to be allowed to remain in the territory of the State in which his application has been lodged or is being examined;

---

461 OJ 1996 C 274/13.

- Asylum seekers must be informed of the procedure and their rights and obligations during the procedure, in a language which they can understand;
- Before a final decision is taken on the asylum application, the asylum seeker must be given the opportunity of a personal interview with an official qualified under national law;
- The decision on the asylum application must be communicated to the asylum seeker in writing and he must be informed of the reasons if applicable.

The particular provisions applicable in the case of manifestly unfounded or abusive asylum claims concern primarily appeal or review procedures which may be more simplified than those generally available in the case of other rejected asylum applications. The Minimum Guarantees Resolution of 1995 states that there should be no *de facto* or *de jure* grounds for granting refugee status to an asylum applicant who is a national of another Member State. This clause has become obsolete as a result of the special Protocol on Asylum Claims by a national of a EU Member State.

b) The Right to Appeal and Suspensory Effect

The Resolution of 1995 on Minimum Guarantees has stated several principles concerning appeal procedures and suspensory effect. According to Point 16 an asylum seeker shall be given an adequate period of time within which to appeal and to prepare his case when requesting review of the decision. Time limits must be communicated to the asylum seeker in good time. Until a decision has been taken on the appeal, the general principle will apply that the asylum seeker may remain in the territory of the Member State concerned. Where the national law of a Member State permits a derogation from this principle in certain cases, an asylum seeker should at least be able to apply to a court or independent review authority for leave to remain in the territory of the Member State temporarily during procedures before those bodies, on the grounds of the particular circumstances of his case; no expulsion may take place until a decision has been taken on this application (Point 17).

In cases of manifestly unfounded asylum applications a Member State may derogate from the general principle that provision shall be made for an appeal to a court or a review authority which gives an independent ruling on individual cases. Member States in derogation from this principle may exclude the possibility of lodging an appeal against a decision to reject an application if, instead, an independent body which is distinct from the examining authority, has already confirmed the decision. This clause dates back to a previous practice of Member States providing for an internal review procedure rather than an appeal to a court.

Whether this clause has any justification may well be doubted. The principle of judicial protection has in the meantime been almost universally recognized, even in cases of manifestly unfounded asylum applications.

In addition, Member States may provide for exceptions from the principle that until a decision has been taken on the appeal, asylum seekers may remain in the territory of the Member State concerned. The Resolution restricts such exceptions to limited cases when, in consideration of objective criteria extraneous to the application itself, an application is manifestly unfounded on the basis of No. 9 and 10 of the 1992 Resolution on Manifestly Unfounded Applications for Asylum. This reference concerns only deliberate deception or abuse of asylum procedure while other cases of manifestly unfounded asylum applications do not fall under this clause. If a state opts for an exception from the general principle that an asylum seeker may remain, it must be guaranteed that the decision on the application is taken at a high level and that additional sufficient safeguards (e.g. review before the execution of the decision by another authority, which must be of a central nature and have the necessary knowledge and experience in the field of asylum and refugee law) ensure the correctness of the decision. It follows that even in this case a decision must not be executed before it is reviewed by that authority. The Minimum Guarantees Resolution does not determine the conditions under which Member States may provide for exceptions under these clauses.

The Commission in its Working Document of March 1999 has envisaged that its proposal for a Community legal instrument will maintain the general concept laid down in the 1992 Resolution on Manifestly Unfounded Asylum Applications. It intends, however, to describe more specifically the procedural consequences which the application of the manifestly unfounded concept could have. In addition, the Commission considers that the arguments for applying the concept on the grounds that the applicant lacks credibility or that an internal flight alternative is available, or that the "exclusion clauses" in Article 1F of the Geneva Convention apply, deserve to be re-examined. Finally, the Commission thinks it would be necessary to spell out more clearly the distinction between cases which are "manifestly unfounded" because the safe third country concept can be applied and those "manifestly unfounded" cases where the substance of the asylum claim is examined.

Whether an agreement on more substantive procedural rules on manifestly unfounded asylum claims can be achieved, remains to be seen. Member States' practice differs widely. One may find national laws about the treatment of manifestly unfounded asylum applications in almost every Member State which are more or less based on the Immigration Ministers' Resolution of 1992. It is, however, difficult to determine a harmonized concept of the treatment of manifestly unfounded asylum applications. Some Member States include the factors indicating the abusiveness of asylum applications in the determination procedure, while other Member States will apply certain procedural rules only in cases of a rejection of asylum claims as manifestly unfounded.

Human rights organizations frequently criticize the whole concept of manifestly unfounded or abusive asylum claims as a potential violation of fundamental standards of a fair asylum procedure. Particularly the Resolution of 1995 on Minimum Guarantees is heavily criticized as not adequately ensuring what kind of cases fall under an accelerated procedure nor containing any guarantee that asylum seekers are in fact given adequate procedural minimum standards. It is argued that a new legal instrument to be adopted by the European Community would have to determine a set of individual rights including a right to appeal to an independent court with suspensory effect. Otherwise, basic protection needs of asylum seekers would not be adequately taken care of and the prohibition of refoulement would not be properly respected[462].

In Germany, a restriction of judicial review and suspensory effect in cases of manifestly unfounded applications has been introduced by a constitutional amendment of 1993. The Basic Law provides in Article 16a(2) that in cases of application of the safe third country concept, terminating measures are to be executed independently of a remedy. In implementing this provision, the asylum procedure law[463] states that a deportation may be ordered as soon as it can be executed. In the case of a deportation to a safe third country no judicial order is admissible suspending such execution.

In case of manifestly unfounded asylum applications Article 16a(4) of the German Basic Law provides that the implementation of measures terminating a person's sojourn shall, in the case of asylum seekers from safe countries of origin and in other cases that are manifestly unfounded or considered to be manifestly ill-founded, be suspended by the court only where "serious doubt exists as to the legality of the measure"; the scope of the investigation may be restricted and objections submitted after the prescribed time limit may be disregarded. Details are laid down in the Asylum Procedure Act[464]. Sections 30 and 36 deal with the procedure in cases of manifestly unfounded asylum applications. In such cases the alien shall be set a time limit of one week in order to leave the country. Complaints against the notification announcing deportation following a rejection of an asylum claim as manifestly unfounded must be filed within a period of one week. Any deportation prior to a court decision is not admissible if the complaint has been lodged in due time. An order to suspend deportation may only be issued if there are serious doubts as to the legality of the administrative act against which a complaint has been filed.

The Federal Constitutional Court ruling on the constitutionality of these provisions has not shared objections based on constitutional and international law[465]. According to the Court's view, the restriction of the power of the judge to suspend deportation does not interfere with the right of a refugee to an efficient judicial review. Considering the difficult problems relating to the high number of asylum seekers the restriction of judicial powers is considered as being based on a just balance of interests. It must be taken into account that the restriction of the power to suspend execution of a decision only takes place under circumstances which already ensure to a very high degree that an asylum seeker's rights are not violated[466].

To what extent the Minimum Guarantees Resolution is implemented in other Member States may be difficult to examine. The United Kingdom basically

---

[462] See ECRE, ENAR, MPG Guarding Standards – Shaping the Agenda, 14.

[463] § 34a of the German Asylum Procedure Act (Asylverfahrensgesetz).

[464] German Asylum Procedure Act (Asylverfahrensgesetz) as amended of 29 October 1997, see *Hailbronner*, Ausländerrecht, B 2. An English translation provided by the German Bundesinnenministerium (Federal Ministry of the Interior) has been published by Inter Nationes, Bonn.

[465] See the judgment of the German Bundesverfassungsgericht (Federal Constitutional Court) of 14 May 1996, BVerfGE 94, 49.

[466] See the judgment of the German Bundesverfassungsgericht (Federal Constitutional Court) of 14 May 1996, BVerfGE 94, 49, 91.

provides under the rules in force, even in cases of manifestly unfounded asylum applications, for a right of appeal with suspensory effect. However, asylum seekers may be excluded who are returned to another country on the basis of an arrangement of the United Kingdom on attribution of competence. The law basically provides that a rejection of an asylum claim may be repealed only for persons who have left the United Kingdom. It seems, however, that there is an alternative possibility of legal protection concerning the compatibility of a deportation with the Geneva Convention that is increasingly made use of by applicants for asylum. The United Kingdom Government has suggested in a draft of a new immigration and asylum bill that this type of appeal should be abolished. The government has emphasized that it considered it vital for the operation of the Dublin Convention that rapid return to the state taking responsibility under the Dublin system would be effected. Therefore, a restriction of remedies has to be considered as indispensable "both as a deterrent to abusive or unfounded applicants and to ensure that those in need of protection have their claim considered as soon as possible[467]. It seems that there are no special rules in France for the limitation of judicial protection in cases of manifestly unfounded or abusive asylum applications. In principle, however, remedies against an order to leave the country have no suspensory effect. It is reported that expulsions are frequently executed before the applicant has had an opportunity to state his objections with a administrative judge[468]. In France, according to the *Ordonnance of 2 November 1945 relative aux conditions de l'entrée et séjour des étrangers en France* there is a right to appeal against an *arrêt de reconduite à la frontière*. In this case an act must not be executed within a 48 hour period following notification. The President of the Administrative Court has to decide on the appeal within 48 hours[469].

It has been reported that in other Member States there is frequently a legal remedy against a rejection of an asylum claim but it is frequently not considered as having a suspensory effect with the result that the possibility of filing an appeal can be criticized as irrelevant[470]. Some countries such as Finland seem to exclude the right to appeal against a decision on rejection of an application for asylum as manifestly unfounded[471]. This procedure seems to be particularly applicable in the case of an applicant entering from a safe third country. Most Member States, however, grant a right of appeal to an independent court in case of a rejection of an asylum application as inadmissible or manifestly unfounded. Under the Dutch law an applicant for asylum may request an interim order against expulsion from the

---

[467] For a survey see the chapter on the United Kingdom in *Liebaut/Hughes*, Legal and Social Conditions for Asylum Seekers and Refugees in Western European Countries (1997).

[468] *Ibid.*

[469] Cf. Article 22 bis. I and II in the version of the Alien and Asylum Reform 1998; Lois no. 98-349 of 11 May 1999 relative à l'entrée et au sejour des étrangers en France et droit d'asile, Journal officielle of 12 May 1998, 7087, Article 15.

[470] Cf. Safe Third Country Policies in European Countries: Sweden, op. cit.; Summary Descriptions of Asylum Procedures of States in Europe, North America and Australia, IGC, 1995 Sweden, 7.

[471] Safe Third Country Policies in European countries: Finland.

President of the Court. Generally, an applicant is not expelled before a decision on his request for interim protection has been passed[472].

c) Asylum Application at the Border

Point 23 of the Minimum Guarantees Resolution of 1995 provides that Member States may apply special procedures to establish, prior to the decision on admission, whether or not the application for asylum is manifestly unfounded. No expulsion measure will be carried out during this procedure. However, any asylum seeker arriving at their frontiers must be afforded an opportunity to lodge an asylum application.

Under Point 24 of the Resolution an asylum seeker may be refused admission at the border where an application for asylum is manifestly unfounded. In such cases, the national law of a Member State may permit an exception to the general principle of the suspensory effect of the appeal. This means that an asylum seeker may be refused admission; an applicant cannot enforce provisional admission to the territory of a state by filing an appeal. In order to exclude the risk of being returned to a country in which an asylum seeker may face a danger of persecution, it is provided that the decision on the refusal of admission must be taken in such a case by a Ministry or comparable central authority and that additional safeguards (i.e. prior examination by another central authority) ensure the correctness of the decision. Such authorities must be fully qualified in asylum and refugee matters.

It may be doubtful whether a concept of internal review by administrative authorities meets the standard of an effective review. Although in the absence of an "arguable claim" Article 13 ECHR is not applicable, there should be a possibility of reviewing a decision by border authorities by a court if an asylum seeker is to be returned to a country in which he claims a serious risk of political persecution. On the other hand, there is a legitimate concern by states that the mere filing of an asylum claim should not result in an obligation to grant entry and residence. Therefore, the concept of examining a claim before entry is granted or refused has been taken up by some Member States in special airport or border procedures.

In line with Point 25 of the Minimum Guarantees Resolution, the German Asylum Procedure Act has introduced a specific procedure in case of entry by air. This procedure, however, does not apply to every alien filing an asylum application at the airport but only to aliens arriving from a safe country of origin or aliens who apply for asylum with the border authority at an airport and who do not prove their identity by way of a valid passport. In such cases the asylum procedure is conducted prior to the decision on entry, in so far as the alien can be accommodated on the airport premises during the procedure or cannot be accommodated on the airport premises merely because of a necessary hospital stay. The alien is immediately given the opportunity to lodge an asylum application with a branch office of the Federal Office for the Recognition of Asylum Seekers. The

---

[472] Cf. Safe Third Country Policies in European Countries: The Netherlands; Summary Decsriptions of Asylum Procedures, The Netherlands, 12.

Federal Office will immediately hear the alien in person. Subsequently, the alien is given the opportunity to contact a person of his own choice authorized to practise law. If the Federal Office turns down an asylum application as being manifestly unfounded, the Federal Office will notify the alien of the fact that he will be deported should he enter the country. If the alien's asylum application is turned down as being manifestly unfounded, the alien is refused leave to enter. The decision of the Federal Office is served on the asylum seeker by the competent border authority. The alien is given three days to file an application for the grant of temporary relief with an administrative court. In such cases the refusal of leave to enter shall not be enforced prior to the court decision. The court may suspend the deportation only if there are serious doubts as to the legality of the administrative act against which a complaint has been filed. It has to decide within a period of two weeks. Otherwise the alien shall be permitted to enter the country.

Similar procedures have been introduced in other Member States such as France and the Netherlands through the concept of "waiting zones". The Commission does not mention such procedures in its Working Document. There is, however, a need to adopt a legal instrument governing the filing of asylum applications at the border. Although in general, asylum applications at the borders are insignificant in terms of numbers, with the exception of asylum applications at airports, the situation may change with the introduction of a EURODAC system reducing the attractiveness of illegal immigration.

Finally, the procedural guarantees applicable to filing asylum applications at the border do not apply to cases where an asylum seeker arrives from a safe third country. In such cases Member States may refuse admission without granting a right to provisionally remain in the territory of the Member State. Member States may also provide that the decision rejecting the application, its underlying reasons and any possibility of appeal, if there is under national law such a possibility, may be communicated to the asylum seeker orally instead of in writing.

4. *Safe Country of Origin Concept*

a) Conclusions on Safe Countries of Origin of 1992

The conclusions on countries in which there is generally no serious risk of persecution[473] adopted by the Ministers responsible for immigration on 30 November and 1 December 1992 for the first time try to specify the "safe country of origin principle". The conclusions aim to establish a harmonized approach to applications for asylum from countries which generally produce a high proportion of clearly unfounded asylum applications and to reduce pressure on the competent authorities that are at present overburdened with such applications. The conclusions refer to the procedural provision in the Resolution on Manifestly Unfounded Applications for Asylum. The case of an asylum seeker from a safe

[473] *Guild*, The Developing Immigration and Asylum Policies, 177; see also European Parliament, Asylum in the European Union: The "Safe Country of Origin Principle", Working Document W-7, 2-97.

country of origin is treated as a manifestly unfounded application if "there is clearly no substance to the applicant's claim to fear persecution in his own country."[474] It is open to an individual Member State to decide that a country is one in which there is in general terms no serious risk of persecution. In deciding whether a country is safe the Member States, in accordance with the Resolution on Manifestly Unfounded Applications, will take into account the criteria which are set out in the conclusions of Ministers.

The conclusions state that a safe country of origin is a country which can be clearly shown normally not to generate refugees or where it can be clearly shown in an objective and verifiable way that circumstances which might in the past have justified recourse to the 1951 Geneva Convention have ceased to exist. An assessment by an individual Member State of a country as one in which there is generally no serious risk of persecution should not automatically result in the refusal of all asylum applications from its nationals or their exclusion from individualized determination procedure. The Member State will consider the individual claims of all applicants from such countries and any specific indications presented by the applicant which might outweigh a general assumption of third country safety. In this context Member States may opt to have this decision taken by an accelerated procedure. Whether a state wants to apply this procedure is within his own discretion.

The conclusions cite a number of criteria for the designation of a country as safe. These are the following –

- previous numbers of refugees and recognition rates in a country with a low recognition rate and in the absence of major changes it is reasonable to assume that low recognition rates will continue and that the country tends not to produce refugees;
- observance of human rights by examining whether a country has undertaken formal obligations and whether in its domestic law and practice it meets those obligations. The conclusions refer to the situation whereby a pattern of breaches of human rights may be exclusively linked to a particular group within a country's population or to a particular area of that country. This should be recognized in determining a safe country of origin. In addition, the readiness of the country concerned to allow monitoring is considered as relevant in judging how seriously a country takes its human rights obligations;
- democratic institutions; consideration should be given to democratic processes, elections, political pluralism and availability and effectiveness of judicial protection;
- stability; an assessment must be made of the prospect of dramatic change in the immediate future.

The conclusions make clear that this is not an exhaustive list of criteria. Member States may take into consideration other criteria of assessment than those previously mentioned, which will be reviewed from time to time[475]. Furthermore,

---

[474] See Resolution on manifestly unfounded applications for asylum, No. 1. (a) in connection with No. 8.

[475] See No. 6 of the Conclusions on countries in which there is generally no serious risk of persecution.

assessments of the risk of persecution in individual countries should be based upon as wide a range of sources of information as possible, including advice and reports from diplomatic missions, international and non-governmental organizations and press reports. Information from UNHCR has a specific place in this framework. Member States have the goal of reaching common assessment of certain countries. To this end, Member States will exchange information on any national decision taken in this context. This exchange is mainly facilitated by the Centre for Information, Discussion and Exchange on Asylum (CIREA). As early as 1988 the Council of Ministers decided to cooperate in assessing the situation in certain countries of origin. It was agreed that to this end joint country reports should be drawn up on the basis of information received from the local diplomatic missions and representatives of the countries of the Union. Based on this agreement a "clearing house" was established, to act as a database for Member States. It is charged with the collection, exchange and dissemination of information and with the documentation on all matters relating to asylum. This clearing house is also charged with developing greater informal consultation, information exchange and harmonization of statistical information on asylum seekers[476]. On 20 June 1994 the Council of Ministers responsible for immigration agreed on guidelines concerning the content of these joint reports concerning the situation of countries from which asylum seekers arrive. At the same time a procedure for the drawing up and dissemination of these reports within the framework of CIREA was worked out.

Both the country reports and the consultations and documents of CIREA are confidential. The European Parliament, along with other organizations, has criticized the fact that the country reports are not checked and has demanded that the clearing house should be given an independent status and must be monitored by the Parliament[477].

In its Working Document of 3 March 1999 on asylum procedures the Commission envisaged a revision of the safe country of origin concept. The Conclusions on countries in which there is generally no serious risk of persecution indicate several assessment criteria. An examination of the application of these Conclusions[478], however, shows – according to the Commission – that Member States in practice apply this principle in a very different way. Furthermore, the safe country of origin principle would be the only case in which an accelerated asylum procedure on the basis of a general assessment instead of individual circumstances is applied. Therefore, in the Commission's view, the suitability of the concept must be revised. The Commission envisages three options for proceeding –

- to abandon the safe country of origin concept. In looking at this option, the considerations might be: whether it is procedurally fair to apply a mechanism which does not take account of the individual circumstances of the case; whether, in the light of experience, the concept has genuinely

---

[476] See European Parliament, Asylum in the European Union: The "Safe Country of Origin Principle", Working Document W-7, November 1996.

[477] See Resolution A 3 – 0337/92; see also EP report A 4 – 0315/96.

[478] See the Council Decision of 26 June 1997 on monitoring the implementation of instruments adopted concerning asylum, OJ EC L 178 from 7 July 1997, page 6.

been useful to Member States in enabling them to speed up the processing of individual cases; and whether the Member States have noted a sustained decrease in the number of unfounded claims.

- to retain the concept, but by providing for a central determination of safe countries within the framework of the Council. Such an approach would be justified, if there was a consensus that the safe country concept was useful and justifiable, but that it was procedurally unfair for one Member State to apply the safe country concept in relation to a country which no other Member State regards as "safe".
- to retain the concept in its present form, and to allow for the adoption of implementing measures, so that each Member State would still decide independently to which countries of origin it would apply the concept, if indeed it chose to make use of the concept at all[479].

The Commission in 1999 also stated that based on the "Conclusions on countries in which there is generally no serious risk of persecution" of the EU Ministers responsible for immigration, concerning the safe country of origin concept, hardly a uniform legal situation or practice in the Member States has emerged. Some Member States do not apply the safe country concept at all, while other Member States apply the concept in principle but have no list of safe countries, while a third group of countries regards such lists as an important instrument for restricting the abuse of the right to asylum[480]. The survey concerning the practice of the "safe country of origin principle", commissioned by the European Parliament in 1996, shows great differences[481] in lists of safe countries of origin. Next to certain Central Eastern European states, such as Poland, the Czech Republic, Hungary, Romania and Bulgaria which are generally considered as safe countries of origin, one may also think of states like Russia, Benin, Ghana, Niger, Senegal, and Tanzania whose qualification as a safe country of origin is questioned by some Member States or not recognized in other Member States. There is a strong argument in favour of a binding list of safe countries of origin which must be drawn up by a common EU-definition procedure, if the concept is to become part of the European Community asylum law.

5. *Asylum Application From Nationals of EU-Member States*

The Asylum Protocol adopts a modified safe country of origin concept in intra-Community relations[482]. The concept reflects the present state of European integration, i.e. the European Union is not, and does not yet resemble, a single

[479] See SEC (1999), 271 final, page 13.
[480] See European Parliament, Asylum in the European Union: The "Safe Country of Origin Principle", Working Document W-7, page 5 et seq. (EP report: Safe Countries of Origin).
[481] EP Report: Safe Countries of Origin, page 5.
[482] *Hailbronner/Thiery* EuR 1998, 583, 590.

(federalist) state[483]. Member States are, therefore, still bound by the non-refoulement principle, as contemplated by Article 33 of the Geneva Convention[484].

The Asylum Protocol obliges Member States to regard one another as safe countries of origin. This construction, however, presumes the right of rebuttal, which is dealt with in paragraphs (a) – (d) of the Sole Article of the Asylum Protocol. These paragraphs regulate the grounds for rebuttal in general (paragraphs (a) – (c)), as well as in individual cases (paragraph (d))[485]

The Asylum Protocol has been criticized as an instrument which, through its *de facto* abolition of the individual examination of asylum applications lodged by EU citizens, allows Member States to disregard their duty to treat all refugees equally, as provided for in Article 3 of the Geneva Convention[486]. This criticism is, however, unfounded for several reasons. It is true that Article 3 calls for equal treatment, without regard to a refugee's country of origin. Yet the differentiation between countries (including the Member States) which qualify as safe countries of origin and those which do not, is justified by the different political conditions with regard to the observance of human rights obligations, in particular the Geneva Convention and the European Convention for the Protection of Human Rights. Inherent in the idea of discrimination is the notion of arbitrariness or unfairness. The differentiation made in the Asylum Protocol does not violate a refugee's due process rights under the Geneva Convention, as it places the burden of proof solely on refugees whose country of origin has been determined according to objective criteria to be "safe". In addition, the 'safe country' definition can be rebutted, not only in individual cases, but may also be challenged under paragraphs (a) – (c) of the Sole Article of the Asylum Protocol. In particular, if a Member State invokes Article 15 of the European Convention for the Protection of Human Rights and Fundamental Freedoms, it may no longer be regarded as a safe country of origin[487].

The controversy between Spain and Belgium over the treatment of ETA terrorist suspects gave rise to serious disputes, *inter alia,* during the drafting process of the Asylum Protocol. These conflicts are reflected in the following pieces of Community legislation –

- the Declaration relating to the Protocol on asylum for nationals of Member States of the European Union, and
- the Declaration by Belgium on the Protocol on asylum for nationals of Member States of the European Union.

The Declaration adopted by the Intergovernmental Conference protects the right of Member States to implement the necessary procedures, in order to fulfill their

---

483 *Hailbronner/Thiery* EuR 1998, 583, 592.

484 A slightly different view has been taken by *Zimmermann* NVwZ 1998, 450, 454. He argues that the closer the EU comes to a state the less binding is the non-refoulement principle. Obviously, common democratic standards having been established all over the EU there will not be any persecution of EU citizens by their home countries which triggers the refugee definition of the Geneva Convention. However, such development does not affect the independent statehood of the Member States which is the decisive criterion for the relevance of the non-refoulement principle. See *Hailbronner/Thiery* EuR 1998, 583, 590; cf. *Marschang* KJ 1998, 69, 78.

485 *Hailbronner/Thiery* EuR 1998, 583, 591.

486 *Marschang* KJ 1998, 69, 78.

487 *Zimmermann* NVwZ 1998, 450, 453.

obligations under the Geneva Convention. Belgium has declared that it will "carry out an individual examination of any asylum request made by a national of another Member State". Under the Belgian Declaration, this examination is subject to paragraph (d) of the Sole Article of that Protocol, and thus ensures Belgium's compliance with its obligations under the Asylum Protocol. While the Protocol does not prohibit individual examinations of asylum applications lodged by EU citizens, it regards them as manifestly unfounded. Even unfounded asylum applications, however, must be processed in a fast-track procedure. Paragraph 29a (1) of the German Asylum Procedure Act, for example, stipulates that applications "shall be turned down as being manifestly unfounded, unless the facts or evidence produced by the alien pose a reason for the presumption that he faces political persecution in his country of origin in spite of the general situation there"[488]. This provision conforms to the wording and spirit of paragraph 20 of the Council Resolution of 20 June 1995 on minimum guarantees for asylum procedures[489], which is referred to in the Declaration relating to subparagraph (d) of the Sole Article of the Protocol on asylum for nationals of Member States of the European Union.

---

[488] Translation of the Asylum Procedure Act by the Federal Ministry of the Interior as published by Inter Nations (1998).

[489] O.J. 1996, C 274/13.

F

Termination of Residence, Expulsion, Deportation and Return

I. DESCRIPTION OF THE PROBLEM

Faced with an increase in both legal and illegal immigration, Member States of the European Union have been striving for measures to ensure better control of their external borders, and to prevent illegal presence of foreign nationals. Problems relating to expulsion and deportation have become more complex in the course of the development of a European visa policy and with the establishment of permits allowing third-country nationals to make short-term visits, *inter alia*, to other Member States.

The abolition of border-controls between the Schengen States has further complicated the situation. It must be deemed a core principle inherent in the concept that the European Union is to be an area of justice and that every Member State must ensure that illegally present third-country nationals leave the area comprising Member States' territories (unless a special permission is granted to enter and remain in another Member State)[1]. The Schengen Implementation Convention therefore provides for an obligation to ensure that a third-country national leaves the territory of the Schengen States. National administrative and judicial orders and decisions to ensure the termination of residence, expulsion, deportation and return remain, however, strictly limited in their legal effects to the territory of the country of residence. Unlike judgments of civil courts, deportation orders cannot be enforced beyond the borders of the Member State whose authorities have issued the order. With the abolition of internal border controls the European Union has already grown into a region of de facto free movement, although in strict legal terms third-country nationals may not be allowed to move from one Member State to another. By doing so, however, they may, according to national law, fulfill their obligation to leave the Member State in the absence of a residence permit, regardless of the fact that they enter another Member State illegally.

Under the aspect of a common European immigration policy the change of jurisdiction as a consequence of illegal migration within the EU is even more important. Currently enforceability of national deportation orders is confined to the territory of the issuing Member State. National administrative and judicial remedies against an order to leave may have a suspensive effect and will have to be

---

1 As a consequence, under the German Aliens' Act of 1990 a third-country national who has to leave the Federal Republic fulfills that obligation by entering another EU-Member State only if his presence there is lawful (§ 42(4) of the German Aliens Act (Ausländergesetz); see Bundestags-drucksache (Parliament Document). 11/6321, p. 71, and *Häußer* in Verwaltungsarchiv (VerwArch) 17 (1996) 241, 253 et seq.

commenced anew in the new State of residence to achieve legal residence, again with limited territorial effect.

According to Article 63 ECT the European Community has the competency to regulate matters of illegal immigration, as well as the presence of illegal third-country nationals including the repatriation of such persons. It is generally recognized that such measures must comply with the Treaty establishing the European Union, the European Convention for the Protection of Human Rights and Fundamental Freedoms of 4 November 1950 (in particular, Articles 3, 8 and 14 thereof), as well as with the Geneva Convention of 28 July 1951 relating to the Status of Refugees, and other conventions.

Since the attribution of the Schengen *acquis* to EU legal bases the SIC provisions related to termination of residence form the cornerstone of expulsion and deportation regimes at the European level. Additionally, relevant Council Decisions and Joint Actions adopted during the Maastricht era continue to bind on all Member States under international law. Finally, relevant Council Recommendations and Resolutions must be considered guiding both interpretation of legally binding instruments and prospective Community legislation under Title IV ECT. Currently, the framework of the European regime governing termination of residence comprises –

- Article 23 SIC
- related provisions of the
  - Joint Action of 22 July 1997 adopted by the Council on the basis of ex-Article K.3 of the Treaty on European Union, concerning the financing of specific projects in favour of displaced persons who have found temporary protection in the Member States and asylum-seekers[2],
  - Joint Action of 27 April 1998 adopted by the Council on the basis of ex-Article K.3 of the Treaty on European Union, concerning the financing of specific projects in favour of displaced persons who have found temporary protection in the Member States and asylum-seekers[3],
  - Council Decision of 26 May 1997 on the exchange of information concerning assistance for the voluntary repatriation of third-country nationals[4],
  - Council Decision of 16 December 1996 on monitoring the implementation of instruments adopted by the Council concerning illegal immigration, readmission, the unlawful employment of third-country nationals and cooperation in the implementation of expulsion orders[5],
- the Recommendations
  - of 30 November 1992 regarding common practices on expulsion in the Member States, adopted by the Ad-hoc-group Immigration[6],

[2] O.J. 1997 L 205/3.
[3] O.J. 1998 L 138/8.
[4] O.J. 1997 L 147/3.
[5] O.J. 1996 L 342/5.
[6] Recommendation of the Ministers of the Member States of the European Communities with responsibility for immigration of 30 November 1992 regarding practices followed by Member States on expulsion (not officially published; an English version is reprinted in *Meijers et al.*, A new immigration law for Europe? The 1992 London and 1993 Copenhagen Rules on Immigration,

- of 30 November 1994 concerning a specimen bilateral readmission agreement between a Member State of the European Union and a third country, adopted by the Council[7],
- of 1 June 1993 concerning checks on, and expulsion of, third-country nationals residing or working without authorization, adopted by the Ministers of the Member States of the European Communities with responsibility for immigration[8],
- Recommendation concerning transit for the purposes of expulsion, adopted by the Ministers the Member States of the European Communities with responsibility for immigration on 30 November 1992[9],
- the addendum of 1 and 2 June 1993, to the recommendation concerning transit for the purposes of expulsion, adopted by the Ministers the Member States of the European Communities with responsibility for immigration[10],
- of 30 November 1994 concerning a specimen bilateral readmission agreement between a Member State and a third country, adopted by the Council[11],
- of 24 July 1995 on the guiding principles to be followed in drawing up protocols on the implementation of readmission agreements, adopted by the Council[12],
- of 30 November 1994 concerning the adoption of a standard travel document for the expulsion of third-country nationals, adopted by the Council[13],

• the Council Resolutions
  - of 4 March 1996 on the status of third-country nationals residing on a long-term basis in the territory of the Member States[14],
  - of 26 June 1997 on unaccompanied minors who are nationals of third countries[15],
  - Council Resolution of 20 June 1995 on minimum guarantees for asylum procedures[16].

Utrecht (1993), 83-88. For a commentary on this recommendation see, for example, *de Roos/Steenbergen/Swart*, in Meijers et al., op. cit., 35-39.

7 O.J. 1996, C 274/20.
8 Not officially published.
9 Published in O.J. 1996 C 5/5.
10 Published in O.J. 1996 C 5/7.
11 O.J. 1996 C 274/20.
12 O.J. 1996 C 274/25.
13 O.J. 1996 C 274/18.
14 O.J. 1996 C 80/2.
15 O.J. 1997 C 221/23.
16 O.J. 1996 C 274/13.

II. Common Principles on Expulsion

1. General policy

a) The Communitarized SIC Provisions

The Schengen Signatory States also expressed a general policy for combating the unlawful presence of third-country nationals in the Community in the Schengen Implementation Convention. According to Article 23(1) SIC, third-country nationals who do not fulfill, or who no longer fulfill the short visit conditions applicable within the territory of a Schengen State must, as a matter of principle, leave the territories of all Schengen States immediately. Only if he holds a valid residence permit issued by another Schengen State he is entitled to enter the territory of that Schengen State (Article 23(2) SIC). If the third-country national in question does not leave voluntarily, if it can be assumed that he does not intend to do so, or if his immediate departure is required for reasons of national security or public policy, he must be expelled from the territory of the Schengen State within which he was arrested under the national law of that Schengen State. The Schengen State in question may only allow the person concerned to remain within its territory if the application of that law does not permit expulsion (Article 23(3) SIC). Upon expulsion third-country nationals may be sent to their country of origin, or to any other State to which they may be permitted entry, particularly under the relevant provisions of the readmission agreements concluded by Schengen States (Article 23(4) SIC). The latter provision, however, shall not preclude the application of the relevant provisions on the right of asylum or the Geneva Convention (Article 23(5)). Article 3(5) of the Dublin Agreement deals with the expulsion of asylum seekers, and allows every Member State to expel asylum seekers according to national law and the Geneva Convention.

The expulsion provisions of the Schengen Convention raise several questions. First, since their communitarization, the provisions of Article 23(1) and (2) SIC cannot be deemed to impose directly applicable obligations on third-country nationals who are no longer in possession of a valid residence permit to exit[17]. Accordingly, Article 23(1) SIC obliges Schengen States to harmonize national laws on expulsion, though leaving them a certain margin of implementation. Implementation covers both substance and procedure[18]. Article 23(4) SIC obliges Schengen States to terminate the residence of third-country nationals who no longer fulfill the conditions of legal residence. However, the Schengen Convention does not restrict the power of States to make deportation dependent on procedural requirements[19]. Hence Schengen States must consider relevant national provisions when carrying out their obligation under Article 23(4) SIC.

Second, various types of cases of termination of residence must be considered separately. As a matter of principle, however, third-country nationals not

---

[17] The issue of direct effect of obligations has been discussed in detail *supra* C II 3 f.

[18] Cf. *Westphal* in Huber, Handbuch des Ausländerrechts, Article 23 SIC paras 2-4 with respect to procedure.

[19] Cf. *Westphal* in Huber, Handbuch des Ausländerrechts, Article 23 SIC para 5.

authorized to stay in their respective country of residence, or in any other Schengen State, must be expelled and deported to their countries of origin unless they voluntarily leave the country they stay in[20]. The very concept of Schengen as an area of free movement of persons without internal border controls is contrary to exclusively national perceptions of illegal entry and residence. Communitarization of this concept significantly contributes to implementing the Community concept of an area of freedom, security and justice which requires a common European regime of termination of illegal residence.

Third-country nationals in possession of a long-term residence permit are permitted to stay in other Member States for a period of up to three months. In case of an overstay, such third-country nationals may be forced to return to the State that issued their regular residence permits rather than to the State of origin. The obligation to expel to the Schengen State that has issued the relevant residence permit is construed by analogy to the obligation created under Article 23(2) SIC.[21]

The Schengen Convention does not contain provisions on expulsion and deportation for reasons of national security or public order. This type of expulsion has not been co-ordinated within the Schengen system. Hence a number of particular questions arise. First, it is somewhat controversial whether a residence permit issued by another Schengen State may be withdrawn by the State of actual residence. It seems fairly obvious that the communitarized SIC provisions do not generally authorize Schengen States to annul or restrict the validity of administrative permits granted by any other Schengen State. To the extent, however, that Schengen authorizes Schengen States to issue a visa with supranational effect, every Schengen State has a corresponding right to annul such permits with effect to the other Schengen States. The legal situation is only different with respect to national residence permits. Where such a visa is in question, Schengen States may issue an order of expulsion or deportation, however, the effect of which must be limited to the territory of the issuing State. In such cases, all national provisions relating to the effect of expulsion or deportation remain applicable, including legal barriers to re-entry and renewal of applications for a residence permit. Unless the State of regular residence decides to revoke or withdraw a third-country national's residence permit or authorize such withdrawal by another Schengen State, the third-country national may be deported to the State of regular residence rather than to his home State. This may prove unsatisfactory in terms of internal security due to the abolition of internal border controls. However, this is the logical consequence of a system of national residence permits in an area of uncontrolled movement of persons. As every Member State retains the right to issue a national permit for entry and residence – though limited in its effects to national territory – regardless of a third-country national's having been reported for denial of entry on the national list of another Schengen State, it must be assumed that national decisions to the opposite effect, relating to a third-country national's residence or movement must also be accepted as part of the system notwithstanding the fact that after the abolition of internal border controls

---

[20] Cf. *Nanz* in Zeitschrift für Ausländerrecht und Ausländerpolitik (ZAR) 1994, 99, 104.

[21] Cf. *Westphal* in Huber, Handbuch des Ausländerrechts, Article 23 SIC para 42.

restrictions to move within the area comprising Schengen States' territories can hardly be enforced.

With regard to titles of entry and residence issued according to communitarized SIC provisions or prospective Community regulations or directives, each Member State acts as a trustee of the other Member States. Schengen visas are issued according to common requirements laid down in the Schengen Convention. Every Schengen State may issue – representing to that extent any other Schengen State – a Schengen visa and revoke this visa provided that the requirements under the Schengen Convention are not fulfilled at the time of entry or at any later stage. The problem arises with regard to reasons for withdrawal or revocation not provided for in the Schengen Convention. It cannot be assumed that the Schengen Convention does contain an exhaustive list of requirements for granting (or withdrawal) of a Schengen visa. Therefore, national reasons for expulsion may actuate termination of a Schengen visa. Furthermore, Member States may determine the State into which the deportee must be returned on a discretionary basis.

Communitarized SIC provisions do not expressly deal with the withdrawal of a residence title issued by another State. An Executive Committee decision regulating the procedure for the withdrawal or revocation of a Schengen visa[22] does not establish a legal basis for administrative decisions, but provides for a common administrative practice of co-operation based on the assumption of mutual agreement on the withdrawal of a Schengen visa between the Schengen States concerned[23]. With regard to refusal of entry, the decision has been implemented without major difficulties. However, some authors have criticized that withdrawal of a visa by an other State than the issuing one can be an impermissible infringement of the competence of the issuing State[24]. This objection may be overcome, however, where the State of actual residence intending to withdraw the visa consults the issuing State within the framework of the Schengen Information System before revocation. Such conduct may be justified by analogy to Article 25 SIC. Agreement of the issuing State, however, is dispensable if one accepts the basic premise that Schengen States issuing or withdrawing a Schengen visa are acting on an authorization by the Schengen Convention in representation of the other Schengen States.

The situation is somewhat different when a third country national who possesses a national residence title, which is valid for a period of more than 3 months in another Schengen State (Article 18 SIC), must be deported for reasons of national security. In this case, it is common practice is that such a title cannot be withdrawn by another Schengen State[25]. Instead, consultation is used in accordance with Article 25 SIC before expulsion. The issuing State has to check whether the third-country national fulfills the conditions for a withdrawal of the title. If it decides to withdraw the title, an announcement of the denial of entry and residence must be

---

[22] Decision of 14 December 1993, SCH/Com-ex(93) 24. The resolution has been attributed to Article 62(2)(b) ECT.

[23] Cf. for Germany No. 4.1.2.2. Allgemeine Anwendungshinweise zum Schengener Durchführungsübereinkommen (AAH-SDÜ).

[24] Cf. *Huber* in Neue Zeitschrift für Verwaltungsrecht (NVwZ)1996, 1059, 1073.

[25] Cf. *Huber* in Neue Zeitschrift für Verwaltungsrecht (NVwZ)1996, 1059, 1072 et seq.

filed in the SIS. If it decides otherwise, the third-country national is deported to the issuing State and can then be reported on the national file for the purpose of being denied entry[26]. It is still a matter of debate whether withdrawal of residence permits in cases, in which the issuing State consents to the withdrawal, may also be carried out by the State of residence. A common practice to that effect could simplify and accelerate the administrative procedure without jeopardizing the competence of the issuing State.

Deportation following the withdrawal of a residence permit may also raise problems of co-ordination. First, it must be determined whether Article 23(3) SIC allows for deportation under national law. In the absence of a European deportation regime, there is hardly any alternative to divergent national practices and laws. Member States therefore retain the right to grant a national residence title, or deport the third-country national to another Schengen State, for which he holds a valid residence title. This follows by analogy to Article 23(2) SIC. If all requirements for expulsion are met, a third-country national may also be deported to his country of origin, or to another State ready to admit the third-country national in accordance with of a treaty between the parties. Expulsion to another Schengen State can only be carried out on the basis of an agreement, in order to protect third-country nationals from being pushed back and forth within the Schengen area.[27]

After deportation, re-entry into the Schengen area is ruled out if the concerned third-country national has been filed in the SIS for a denial of entry to the Schengen area. If third-country nationals are reported on the national list for denials of entry of one Schengen State only, further questions arise. If the file contains a note relevant for the whole Schengen area, i.e. if the registration fulfills the requirements of Article 96(2) and (3) SIC[28] third-country nationals may not move freely in the Schengen area (Article 21 SIC), even if in possession of a Schengen visa or another residence title. Third-country nationals are then excluded from entry into the territory of the Schengen State on the national list of which they are registered. Entry into that State regardless of the mentioned restriction is illegal.

b) Joint Actions, Council Decisions, Recommendations, and Resolutions

In its Recommendation of 30 November 1992 regarding common practices on expulsion in the Member States[29] the Ad-hoc-group Immigration formulated a general policy guideline at the European level for the first time. According to the Recommendation persons found –

---

[26] Cf. *Westphal* in Huber, Handbuch des Ausländerrechts, Article 23 SIC para 27.

[27] Cf. *Nanz* in Zeitschrift für Ausländerrecht und Ausländerpolitik (ZAR) 1994, 99, 104.

[28] Cf. *Westphal* in Huber, Handbuch des Ausländerrechts, Article 23 SIC para 40: That means, that the reasons for writing out of this third-country national must fullfill the criterias, which are prescribed in this article. Otherwise the writing out does not have relevance in the Schengen system.

[29] Recommendation of the Ministers of the Member States of the European Communities with responsibility for immigration of 30 November 1992 regarding practices followed by Member States on expulsion.

(A) to have entered or remained unlawfully in Member States (where their stay has not been regularized);

(B) to be liable to expulsion on grounds of public policy or national security; or

(C) to have failed definitely in an application for asylum and to have no other claim to remain, should be expelled, unless there are compelling reasons, normally of a humanitarian nature, for allowing them to remain.

The Recommendation was drafted by the Ad-hoc-group Immigration, and received full support even before the Maastricht Treaty defined this issue as a matter of common interest.

As a rule, expulsion should take place to the country of origin or to any other country to which the individual may be admitted. Persons expelled on public policy or national security grounds should not be sent to another Member State unless they have a right of residence in that State. The recommendation contains several procedural guidelines, which deal, in particular with legal protection. Several provisions have been presented which propose, under appropriate circumstances, to restrict the personal liberty of people awaiting expulsion, i.e. to keep the persons concerned in custody, and to allow fingerprinting of those to be expelled, in order to ease the process of identification. The Recommendation states/rules that expulsion should be executed as soon as possible after the decision to expel an individual has been made, and stresses the need to make arrangements with the authorities of the State to which expulsion must be effected, and/or through which transit will be necessary. If no readmission agreements exist, consideration should be given to their establishment with the appropriate States, preferably on a multilateral and standardized basis, and, if possible, using the 29 March 1991 Agreement between Poland and the Schengen States[30]. In the meantime the Council has adopted a standard readmission agreement[31] and has included readmission policy in the policy guidelines for the Community's external or trade relations[32].

The Recommendation further calls for, *inter alia*, the introduction (insofar as legislation does not already exist) of laws providing for the prosecution of people who knowingly facilitate, or attempt to facilitate the entry or transit of illegal entrants, and, subject to appropriate safeguards, the prosecution of those who knowingly harbour individuals who have entered or remained unlawfully. Special attention must be paid to people who commit such acts in return for reward, or as a member of a criminal organization. The Ad-hoc-group has also recommended that appropriate measures are to be taken to prohibit the employment of those third-country nationals known to have entered into, or remained in a Member State in breach of immigration or third-country nationals provisions, or of those who are

---

30 BGBl. II 1993, 1099; II 1994, 3537. For details about the developing common European return policy see infra, point IV.

31 Council Recommendation of 30 November 1994 concerning a specimen bilateral readmission agreement between a Member State of the European Union and a third country, O.J. 1996, C 274/20.

32 Cf. *supra* Chapter C V 1 for the relevant standard clauses and standard statements.

not authorized to work under immigration or aliens law, or related provisions. Finally, the appendix of the decision details several principles, which Member States have been encouraged to use as guidelines for the exchange of information in order to combat the unlawful trafficking of illegal immigrants.

Combating illegal immigration requires the implementation of effective means of identification, and of apprehension of those to be expelled. Consequently, in another recommendation "concerning checks on and expulsion of third-country nationals residing or working without authorisation"[33], Member States have reaffirmed the need to introduce a system of checks with a view to ensuring that third-country nationals continue to fulfill the relevant conditions of sojourn. The exchange of information between Member States relating to the types of checks and control procedures, together with related legislation, should be carried out within the framework of the CIREFI. Any checks on persons suspected of residing or working illegally in Member States must be carried out in conformity with national legislation, and should seek to reinforce all common efforts to combat illegal immigration into the Community.

c) Voluntary repatriation

Enforcement of expulsion measures is unnecessary where third-country nationals are persuaded to return voluntarily. After some Member States established programs to support the voluntary return of legally, as well as illegally resident third-country nationals, the Council (under the Maastricht Treaty) adopted a decision on exchange of information in the field of assistance for voluntary repatriation of third-country nationals[34]. Two months later, the Council adopted a Joint Action to finance specific projects intended to facilitate the voluntary repatriation of displaced persons enjoying temporary protection in the Member States, and of asylum seekers. This financial aid program was launched on an experimental basis in 1997, and funded from the general budget of the European Union. The aggregate costs of this aid were not to exceed 10 million ECU[35]. The program was extended in 1998, and the budget for this year was 13 million ECU in total. Further development of action in this area will be based on the evaluation of this experiment[36]. If measures undertaken in the field of law prove to have a substantial and positive effect on the situation, the Council is inclined to adopt a

---

[33] Recommendation of the Ministers of the Member States of the European Communities with responsibility for immigration of 1 June 1993 concerning checks on and expulsion of third-country nationals residing or working without authorization – not officially published.

[34] Council Decision of 26 May 1997 on the exchange of information concerning assistance for the voluntary repatriation of third-country nationals, O.J. 1997 L 147/3.

[35] See Joint Action of 22 July 1997 adopted by the Council on the basis of ex-Article K.3 of the Treaty on European Union, concerning the financing of specific projects in favour of displaced persons who have found temporary protection in the Member States and asylum-seekers, O.J. 1997 L 205/3.

[36] Joint Action of 27 April 1998 adopted by the Council on the basis of ex-Article K.3 of the Treaty on European Union, concerning the financing of specific projects in favour of displaced persons who have found temporary protection in the Member States and asylum-seekers, O.J. 1998 L 138/8.

legal basis for the development of programs for voluntary repatriation within the framework of the Amsterdam Treaty.

d) Special Groups of Third-Country Nationals

Execution of deportation orders may raise particular problems with regard to special groups of persons. The Council has adopted particular resolutions concerning the status of long-term residents and of unaccompanied minors.

No definition of long-term residents currently exists in Community law. The definition contained in Article 32 of the draft convention on rules for the admission of third-country nationals to the Member States[37], which holds that a long term resident is a person who has been legally resident in a Member State on a regular basis for at least five years, and who is authorized to reside in that State for a total period of at least 10 years, may be used as a starting point. In order to facilitate the integration of third-country nationals who are settled in the territory of a Member State as long-term residents, the Council has established a number of principles to ensure that the length of residence is duly taken into account[38].

In its Resolution the Council calls upon Member States to ensure that –

> It should be possible for a residence authorization granted to a long-term resident to be cancelled or not renewed on one of the following grounds:
>
> – the fact that an expulsion measure has been issued against the long-term resident in accordance with the provisions of the legislation of the Member State concerned, on the understanding that such resident enjoys, with respect to the expulsion measure taken concerning him, the maximum legal protection provided for in the legislation of the said Member State, in accordance with procedures guaranteeing that due account is taken of the length of his period of legal residence.
>
> Where the expulsion measure was adopted for reasons of public policy, these should be based on the personal behaviour of the long-term resident involving a sufficiently serious threat to public policy, or to national security;
>
> – the long-term resident has definitively left the territory of the Member State concerned,
>
> – the long-term resident has been absent from the territory of the Member State concerned for a period to be determined by that Member State's legislation, which should in no case be less than six consecutive months,
>
> – the residence authorization has proved to have been obtained by means of fraud.[39]

---

37 O.J. 1997 C 337/9.

38 Council resolution of 4 March 1996 on the status of third-country nationals residing on a long-term basis in the territory of the Member States (96/C80/02), O.J. 1996 C 80/2.

39 Point VI of the Resolutuion.

The Commission proposal for a Council Act establishing the Convention on rules for the admission of third-country nationals to the Member States shadowed the intention to confirm the privileged position of long term residents[40]. This proposal for a convention, based on ex-Article K.3(2) TEU, envisaged some of the rights guaranteed to long term residents in Point VIII of the Resolution. Article 34(1)(d) of the proposed convention affords long term residents increased protection against expulsion, subject to the requirement of law and order and internal security. This provision only formulates a principle, however, and must be supplemented by implementation regulations. The Council has not yet adopted this proposal. In light of the fact that the Treaty of Amsterdam establishes a new legal basis, it is unlikely that the draft convention will ever enter into force. Promotion of integration of long term residents into Member States' societies will, however, and regardless of the limited Community competence in this respect[41], most likely continue to be an underlying concept of prospective Community legislation. One may, therefore, reasonably assume that the principle of increased protection against expulsion will be included in future legislation on expulsion matters.

In recent years, an increasing number of unaccompanied third-country national minors has entered and remained illegally in the territory of Member States The situation of unaccompanied third-country national minors is generally vulnerable, and they often require special safeguards and care. In light of this fact Member States have agreed upon a Council Resolution in June 1997[42] establishing guidelines for the treatment of unaccompanied minors, especially with regard to the conditions for their reception, stay and return and, in the case of asylum seekers, the decisions on asylum procedures[43].

The Resolution defines, in Article 1, that unaccompanied minors are

> third-country nationals below the age of eighteen, who arrive on the territory of the Member States unaccompanied by an adult responsible for them whether by law or custom, and for as long as they are not effectively in the care of such a person

and

---

[40] O.J. 1997 C 337/9.

[41] Cf. *supra* Chapter B X 5.

[42] Council Resolution of 26 June 1997 on unaccompanied minors who are nationals of third countries, O.J. 1997 C 221/23. That Resolution is without prejudice to the international commitments entered into by Member States, in particular pursuant to the United Nations Convention on the Rights of the Child, 1989. Under Article 2 of that Convention –

> States Parties shall respect and ensure the rights set forth in the present Convention to each child within their jurisdiction without discrimination of any kind, irrespective of the child's or his or her parent's or legal guardian's race, colour, sex, language, religion, political or other opinion, national, ethnic or social origin, property, disability, birth or other status.

In addition, Article 3 of the Children's Rights Convention stipulates that "[i]n all actions concerning children ... the best interests of the child shall be a primary consideration". Finally, Article 22 of the Convention aims at protecting and assisting minors who seek refugee status or who are regarded as refugees.

[43] As for the latter see also Council Resolution of 20 June 1995 on minimum guarantees for asylum procedures, O.J. 1996 C 274/13.

> minors who are nationals of third countries and who are left unaccompanied after they have entered the territory of the Member States

unless the persons concerned are family members of an EU citizen, EEA nationals or members of an EEA national's family, whatever the latter's nationality may be where, respectively, rights to freedom of movement are being exercised (Article 1(2) of the Resolution).

As a rule, Article 2(1) of the Resolution suggests that –

> Member States should take appropriate measures, in accordance with their national legislation, to prevent the unauthorized entry of unaccompanied minors and should cooperate to prevent illegal entry and illegal residence of unaccompanied minors on their territory.

Accordingly, the resolution aims at limiting the unauthorized presence of unaccompanied minors in the area comprising Member States' territories solely on a temporary basis unless the minors concerned have been granted refugee status.

Article 5 of the Resolution specifically deals with return of unaccompanied minors. The basic principle Member States should implement in their national legislation and administrative practice is that return be conditional on the availability of adequate reception and care on arrival in the country of return (Article 5(1) of the Resolution). Adequacy has been defined to the extent that reception and care "can be provided by parents or other adults who take care of the child, or by governmental or non-governmental bodies". The Resolution expressly states that Member States may return minors not allowed to prolong their stay, to their country of origin or a third country prepared to accept them "only" if the adequacy requirement is met. Additionally, Article 5(4) of the Resolution expresses that –

> In any case, a minor may not be returned to a third country where this return would be contrary to the Convention relating to the status of refugees, the European Convention on Human Rights and Fundamental Freedoms or the Convention against Torture and other Cruel, Inhuman or Degrading treatment or Punishment or the Convention on the Rights of the Child, without prejudice to any reservations which Member States may have tabled when ratifying it, or the Protocols to these Conventions.

With respect to return regimes Article 5(3) of the Resolution is obviously based uponthe principle enshrined in Article 3(1) of the Children's Rights Convention according to which "[i]n all actions concerning children ... the best interests of the child shall be a primary consideration". The Resolution suggests, therefore, that Member States cooperate –

> (a) in re-uniting unaccompanied minors with other members of their family, either in the minor's country of origin or in the country where those family members are staying;
>
> (b) with the authorities of the minor's country of origin or with those of another country, with a view to finding an appropriate durable solution;

(c) with international organizations such as UNHCR or UNICEF, which already take an active part in advising governments on guidelines for dealing with unaccompanied minors, in particular asylum-seekers;

(d) where appropriate, with non-governmental organizations in order to ascertain the availability of reception and care facilities in the country to which the minor will be returned.

With a view to implementing, inter alia, the Resolution on unaccompanied minors, the Council has decided that "[s]pecific projects intended to improve admission facilities for asylum-seekers and refugees in the Member States shall be undertaken on an experimental basis during 1998"[44]. Such projects involve financial aid for return programmes in favour of unaccompanied minors.

e) The Prospective Common Policy under the Amsterdam Treaty

Under the Amsterdam Treaty the European Community has been granted powers in the area of illegal immigration and the repatriation of illegal immigrants. Under Article 63(3) ECT the Council shall adopt –

measures on immigration policy within following areas:

(b) illegal immigration and illegal residence, including repatriation of illegal residents.

With respect to expulsion and deportation both the scope of application of this provision and its inherent limitations require detailed examination. The definition of repatriation includes both voluntary and involuntary repatriation, i.e. expulsion and deportation. Article 63(3) ECT refers solely to illegal residents, which seems to restrict Community competence to cases of repatriation of resident third-country nationals excluding illegal immigrants apprehended at the border.

Such interpretation would, however, be overly restrictive since no real difference can be made between "illegal residence" and "illegal immigrants". Moreover, Article 63 ECT must be seen in its systematic context as a whole. Article 63(3) ECT deals with measures on immigration policy while Article 63(1) ECT focuses on measures on asylum, and Article 63(2) ECT envisages measures on refugees and displaced persons. Proposals related to reception and protection of refugees and asylum-seekers within the European Union generally also deal with entry of these persons. Provisions on entry of immigrants who are not refugees or asylum-seekers may be based on Article 63(3)(a) ECT which allows for the adoption of measures with regard to conditions of entry and residence. The term "illegal" in Article 63 ECT will, therefore, be supplemented by regulations based on the competencies conferred upon the Community in Article 63(1), (2) and (3)(a) ECT. Accordingly, Article 63(3)(b) establishes a comprehensive competence to

---

[44] see Article 1(1) of the Joint Action of 27 April 1998 adopted by Council on the basis of ex-Article K.3 TEU, concerning the financing of specific projects in favour of asylum-seekers and refugees, O.J. 1998 L 138/8.

regulate termination of residence, as well as repatriation of all illegal immigrants (not only those who have become residents). Expulsion and deportation are covered by this competency. After all, to be effective[45] the prospective common immigration policy requires the competency in the area of repatriation to be comprehensive.

Community competence with respect to termination of residence is not, however, exclusive. The second paragraph of Article 63 ECT states that "measures adopted by the Council pursuant to points 3 and 4 shall not prevent any Member States from maintaining or introducing in the areas concerned national provisions which are compatible with this Treaty and with international agreements". Hence Member States and the Community share responsibility for both adoption and implementation of immigration policy. Member States may introduce or maintain national provisions, so long as these are compatible with the common immigration policy. If a measure implemented at the national level contradicts a Community instrument, the latter enjoys priority – this is the primary consequence of the requirement of compatibility with the Treaty. Article 10 ECT prohibits Member States from endangering the aims of the Treaty, and consequently, obliges them to avoid contradictions between Community and national law[46].

2. *Responsibility for Deportation*

Cooperation between Member States will be necessary in order to facilitate the transport of an expellee to his designated country. The Recommendation concerning transit for the purposes of expulsion, approved by the Ministers on 30 November 1992[47], provides, in Section II, that in principle –

> A Member State which has decided to expel a third-country national
>
> – to a third country should in principle do so without the person transiting through the territory of another Member State,
>
> – to another Member State should in principle do so without the person transiting through the territory of a third Member State.

However, under Section III, "[w]here there are special reasons to justify this and, in particular, in the interests of efficiency, speed and economy, Member States may ask another Member State to authorize entry into its territory or transit through its territory of third-country nationals who are the subject of an expulsion measure". The Member State requesting the transit must provide all necessary

---

45 Effectiveness is an acknowledged interpretation principle of the Treaty establishing the European Community. Cf. ECJ, judgment of 15 July 1960, case 20/59, *Italy v High Authority*, [1960] ECR 683(708); ECJ, judgment of 10 January 1980 case 792/79, *Camera Care v Commission*, [1980] ECR 119, para 16; *Chevallier*, R.M: Methods and Reasoning of the European Court in its Interpretation of Community Law, CMLR 2 (1964/65), 21, 32 et seq.

46 ECJ, judgment of 21 September 1983, case 205-215/82, *Deutsche Milchkontor v Germany,* [1983] ECR 2633, para 17.

47 Published in O.J. 1996 C 5/5.

information, and, in particular, the expellee's final destination (Section V). The transit State may then authorize the expelling State to provide the escort or decide to provide the escort itself in cooperation with the expelling State (Section IV). According to Section VI transit may be refused –

- where the third-country national who is the subject of a request for overland transit constitutes a threat to public order, national security or the international relations
- of the transit State,
- where the information referred to in Section V(3) is not considered satisfactory.

If the expulsion measure cannot be carried out, the State through which transit must take place may return the expellee, without any formalities, to the territory of the requesting State (Section VII).

If expulsion cannot be carried out at the expense of the third-country national, or of a third party, the requesting State shall be liable for the costs involved (Section VIII). Member States should strive for a bilateral agreement on the conditions under which it may be possible to forego cost refunds paid for individual cases, and replace it with an annual settlement of expenses incurred by expulsion operations at either party's request.

The addendum to the recommendation concerning transit for the purposes of expulsion, approved by the Ministers responsible for Immigration on 1-2 June 1993 provides for further measures to facilitate expulsion, in particular, in cases involving air transit[48]. In case of expulsion by air, accompanied by transit through the transit zone of an airport, the requirements of entry and transit authorization are dispensed with, provided that the country of transit is properly notified. Denial of permission by the transit State must be communicated to the requesting State within 24 hours of the notification of transit. In addition, Member States must draw up a joint list of contact authorities, in order to facilitate the transfer of relevant information. Member States have also agreed on concerted efforts to exchange information on seats available on flights[49], in an effort to promote closer cooperation in the implementation of expulsion measures.

III. Common European Return Policy

Expulsion and deportation of third-country nationals frequently prove to be difficult, due to the absence of travel or identity documents. Certain countries of origin are reluctant to identify their nationals, and to provide them with the necessary travel documents. Such obstacles may only be overcome by common European efforts towards an integrated return and foreign development policy.

---

[48] Published in O.J. 1996 C 5/7.

[49] See Council Recommendation of 22 December 1995 on concerted action and cooperation in carrying out expulsion measures (O.J. 1996 C 5/3).

In principle, States are obliged under customary international law to readmit their own nationals, as well as third-country nationals who have illegally migrated through their respective territories to a neighbouring State. Most Member States have concluded readmission agreements with some third countries, which lay down readmission obligations and procedures. In 1996 the European Council adopted a model readmission agreement to be used by the Member States as a basis for negotiation with third countries on the conclusion of further readmission agreements. In addition, standard texts to be included in mixed agreements or Community agreements with third countries aim at the conclusion of readmission agreements between Member States and third countries involved in economic cooperation or an association with the European Community. Moreover, Member States have adopted a standard travel document, in an effort to improve the efficiency of expulsion measures. The development of a common repatriation policy with respect to the countries of origin is, however, imperative.

1. Obligations of States under Public International Law to Readmit their Own and Foreign Nationals

The principle of readmission of one's own nationals is generally recognized in treaties under international law. Due to the uniform *opinio iuris* on this topic, as well as consistent State practice, it is also viewed as a principle of customary international law[50]. States of origin, as a result, must not make the readmission of their own nationals dependent on mere formal requirements, like presentation of valid documents, provided that the nationality of a person to be returned can be established by other evidence. Moreover, according to principles of good faith, home States are obliged to cooperate in the execution of their own nationals' readmission, and must issue, in the absence of valid travel documents, any necessary substitute papers within reasonable time[51].

Recent readmission agreements reflect a tendency toward an obligation on States to readmit nationals of third States and stateless persons who have continued their journey to a neighbouring State, even if they did not fulfil entry and residence requirements of the State first entered. However, due to lack of a long-standing common European practice and *opinio iuris* there is no evidence to date of a strict obligation, derived from customary international law, of neighboring States to readmit 'illegal' third-country nationals and stateless persons. Principles of good neighbourly conduct do, however, provide an element of emerging customary law with regard to the development of a common European responsibility for dealing with uncontrolled migration movements.[52]

---

[50] Cf. *Lehnguth/Maaßen/Schieffer*, ZFSH/SGB 1998, 387, 390; ECJ, judgment of 4 December 1974, case 41/74, *van Duyn v Home Office*, [1974] ECR 1337, paras 21+23.

[51] See *Hailbronner* in ZaöRV 57 (1997) 1, 45 et seq.

[52] According to the general principles of international law a State, however, does have an obligation to a neighbouring State to readmit nationals of third States if the manner in which the first State supported or tolerated illegal migration of third State nationals is considered reproachable. Additionally, States are committed to repatriate refugees having fled from violence or persecution once the conditions causing that flight have changed. Those States which granted temporary

2. *Model Return Agreements*

Bilateral readmission agreements between Member State and third countries have provided an important starting point to overcome some of the difficulties with regard to States' obligations to readmit their own and certain foreign nationals. Member States began work in 1993 on a set of common principles to be included in bilateral and multilateral readmission agreements. These efforts led to the adoption of a specimen bilateral readmission agreement, which was approved by a Council Recommendation of 30 November 1994[53]. These guidelines of the Recommendation must be used by the Member States as a basis for negotiation with third countries on the conclusion of readmission agreements, though it has been recognized that they must be used in a flexible way by the Member States and may, therefore, be adapted to the particular needs of the respective Contracting Parties.

In order to facilitate the readmission of persons staying illegally on the territory of the other Contracting Party, i.e. persons who do not, or who no longer, fulfil the conditions for entry or residence, and to facilitate the transit of persons in a spirit of cooperation, and on the basis of reciprocity, Member States have focussed their attention on the following principles: Pursuant to Article 1 of the specimen agreement, which deals with the readmission of own nationals, each Contracting Party shall, at the request of the other Contracting Party, and without any formality, readmit persons staying illegally on the territory of the other Contracting Party, provided that it has been proved, or may be validly assumed, that they possess the nationality of the requested Contracting Party. The same shall apply to persons who have been deprived of the nationality of the requested Contracting Party since entering the territory of the requesting Contracting Party without having been promised naturalization by the requesting Contracting Party. Upon application by the requesting Contracting Party, the requested Contracting Party shall, without delay, issue the travel documents required for their repatriation to the persons to be readmitted. The requesting Contracting Party shall readmit such persons under the same conditions, as long as examinations reveal that they where not in possession of the nationality of the requested Contracting Party when they departed from the territory of the requesting Contracting Party. This shall not apply if the readmission obligation is based on the fact that the requested Contracting Party deprived the person in question of its nationality after that person entered the territory of the requesting Contracting Party without a promise of naturalization by the requesting Contracting Party.

Third-country nationals shall be readmitted without formalities in two cases. First, if it can be proved, or validly assumed, that the person entered the territory of the requesting State via the requested State. The Contracting Parties, however,

---

protection to these refugees are entitled to demand that the home State repatriate them. The obligation to repatriate does not only cover one's own nationals but also extends to persons who, preceding the circumstances which caused them to flee, had their permanent residence in that State from which repatriation is now requested. The obligation to repatriate lies upon the State of residence and is not dependent upon the willingness of the individual to return.

[53] O.J. 1996 C 274/20.

shall make every effort to give priority to the deportation of nationals to a State adjacent to their country of origin (Article 2). Second, if that person possesses a valid visa, or a valid residence permit issued by the requested party. If both Contracting Parties issued a visa or a residence permit, responsibility shall reside with the Contracting Party whose visa or residence permit expires last (Article 3).

Any application for readmission must be submitted within a maximum of one year after the Contracting Party noted the illegal entry and presence of the said national of a third country on its territory. The obligation for admission lapses after the expiration of the one year period (Article 6). With regard to transit, the Contracting Parties shall allow third-country nationals to pass through their territory in transit at the request of another Contracting Party, and if admission to other possible States of transit and to the State of destination is assured (Article 7).

Readmission agreements are often accompanied by protocols laying down certain technical details for their implementation. Member States also adopted a series of guiding principles to be used as a basis for negotiating such protocols in a Council Recommendation adopted on 24 July 1995[54]. The Recommendation contains several detailed proposals concerning readmission and transit procedures and – in particular – approved means of identifying persons to be readmitted. The purpose of a protocol must outline acceptable means of proving or establishing a presumption of nationality and of entry via the territory of the requested party.

One must bear in mind, however, that the existing system is based on the principle of bilateralism and is shaped by considerable legal uncertainties in the implementation of treaties, as well as of customary law obligations on a State's or foreign nationals. These factors make the creation of European standards more difficult. In spite of some progress achieved through the adoption of the above-mentioned instruments, Member States are still facing substantial legal and practical difficulties in the operation of bilateral readmission agreements. A multilateral treaty approach may be better suited to achieve effective cooperation from the part of countries of origin[55]. On the other hand, bilateral agreements are often favored, due to the fact that they allow for greater flexibility. Procedures can be adapted to reflect the special relationship between two contracting parties; bilateral provisions are, as a result, generally more specific than those contained in multilateral agreements. Bilateral agreements avoid ponderous and frequently time-consuming negotiations involving several contracting parties to reach a frequently vague compromise. These advantages could be important, especially with respect to the readmission of foreign nationals, given that regional peculiarities and relations between neighboring States often favor a "made to measure" solution. On the other hand, multilateral agreements, provided that they are enforced effectively by common European action, may be more advantageous in the long run, in that they can prevent a fragmentation of contractual practice and increase the risks of violating international law obligations and use readmission obligations as a "bargaining position". Finally, principles established in multilateral negotiations related to the readmission of a State's or foreign nationals

---

54 O.J. 1996 C 274/25.

55 For this view see already *Hailbronner*, ZaöRV 57 (1997) 1, 48.

can often be implemented with greater political and economic force on, and with more serious consequences for the State concerned. In the long run, multilateral treaties based on uniform principles can offer considerable advantages, particularly since specific issues may be dealt within additional protocols. Further, the questionable practice of blackmailing by making readmission of citizens dependent on *per capita* payments, could be more easily encountered by common European action.

3. *Standard Travel Document*

Third-country nationals frequently try to prevent execution of expulsion or deportation by destroying the necessary travel documents. Additionally, authorities of countries of destination are often unwilling to provide assistance. The Council suggested the adoption of a standard travel document for the expulsion of third-country nationals in a Recommendation of 30 November 1994 as a remedy to this problem[56]. The standard travel document was introduced on 1 January 1995 and is valid for a single journey. All Member States must use this document to facilitate the expulsion of third-country nationals from the area comprising Member States' territories.

Member States expressed their willingness to implement specific mechanisms to improve the procurement of the necessary documentation from the consular authorities of the third State to which third-country nationals must be expelled when they lack travel or identity documents in the Council Recommendation of 22 December 1995 on concerted action and cooperation in carrying out expulsion measures[57]. The provisions on presumption of nationality of the standard readmission agreement adopted by the Council on 30 November 1994 must be used as guiding principles. If it proves impossible to obtain the necessary travel documents through these means, the standard travel document adopted by the Council on 30 November 1994 should be issued.

4. *Common Policy with Respect to Countries of Origin*

There is almost universal agreement among the Member States that issues of return and repatriation should be included in a comprehensive immigration policy concept of the EU including the relations with countries of origin[58].

However, financial concessions and economic aid to ease burdens on a State requested to repatriate persons should not be combined with readmission obligations in a reciprocal sense, but should be granted independently under separate agreements, preferably in combination with questions of economic development with respect to European solidarity. The success of such agreements

---

[56] O.J. 1996 C 274/18.

[57] O.J. 1996 C 5/3.

[58] See Parlamentarischer Staatssekretär *Edurard Lintner*, answer of 23 September 1997 to a parliamentary question, Bundestagsdrucksache (Parliament Document) 13/8596, 12 (no. 20).

depends, however, on prior coordination among the countries required to repatriate, primarily in an effort to avoid the misuse of economic aid as a compensation for the performance of executing obligations under international law. An inappropriate linking of financial aid to the execution of readmission obligations could be avoided if, for example, the recognition of readmission obligations, or adherence to corresponding multilateral readmission agreements was made a precondition for entry into negotiations on economic aid for reconstruction. One should, in addition, consider whether a contractual clause could be included in cooperation agreements to demonstrate that economic cooperation is dependent on the adherence to existing readmission obligations[59].

Indeed, such clauses have been included in recent cooperation and association agreements concluded by the European Community with third States. More direct and specific support of the requirement that general readmission principles must be respected by all States concerned, regardless of whether they have been concluded on a bi- or multilateral basis, however, is desirable. In addition, readmission of illegal immigrants must be emphasized as a precondition for the initiation of accession to the European Union, of the Central Eastern European Countries[60]. To date, however, only the EU-Slovenia Agreement provides for

> cooperation designed to prevent illegal activities such as ... clandestine immigration and the illegal presence of either party's nationals on the other's territory, with due allowance for the principles and practices of readmission.[61]

IV. The International Law Framework

1. *Protection against Expulsion by International Law -The Legal Framework of Prospective European Legislation*

a) General remarks

Termination of residence, expulsion and return of immigrants are subject to requirements under customary international law and international treaties. At the UN level, the 1966 International Covenant on Civil and Political Rights (CCPR)[62] and the 1951 Geneva Convention include regulations which protect against expulsion. Selected ILO Conventions contain similar provisions[63]. Both the Covenant and the Convention provide essential benchmarks of a European return policy and future immigration legislation under the Amsterdam Treaty, as both have been ratified by all Member States of the European Union. The European

59 For this view see already *Hailbronner* in ZaöRV 57 (1997) 1, 49.

60 Cf. i.e. Communication from the Commission – Romania: Accession Partnership, O.J. 1998 C 202, annex para 3.7.

61 Article 98(1) of the EU-Slovenia Agreement.

62 Text: 6. ILM (1967) 368; ratified by all Member States of the EC.

63 See for Example Article 8 of the Convention No. 97 concerning Migration for Employment (120 U.N.T.S. 71) and Articles 8 and 9 of the ILO Convention No. 143 concerning Migrant Workers.

Convention on Human Rights is perhaps the most important legal instrument at the European level in the context of a future European legislation. Further, the European Convention on Establishment of 1955 and the European Convention on the Legal Status of Migrant Workers may, although not binding for most Member States, also be mentioned[64]. They constitute the international legal framework relevant for the national and future EC legislation, subject, however, always to a specific analysis of whether the EC is restricted by such norms in its law making.

b) The Covenant on Civil and Political Rights

National law and equally prospective Community law must be compatible with the provisions of the Covenant on Civil and Political Rights. Due regard must be had to Articles 13 and 17 CCPR with respect to expulsions and, in particular, the effects thereof for family life. Additionally, legislation must comply with the prohibition of discrimination in Articles 2, 3 and 26 CCPR.[65]

The Covenant on Civil and Political Rights does not contain a general prohibition of expulsion. However, it sets some limits and certain procedural guarantees in its Article 13[66] which provides that –

> An alien lawfully in the territory of a State Party to the present Convenant may be expelled therefrom only in pursuance of a decision reached in accordance with law and shall, except where compelling reasons of national security otherwise require, be allowed to submit the reasons against his expulsion and to have his case reviewed by, and be represented for the purpose before, the competent authority or a person or persons especially designated by the competent authority.

At first glance this provision does not seem relevant for a European legislation because Article 13 CCPR merely contains procedural requirements rather than establishing substantial limitations for expulsion. Article 13 CCPR seems to require primarily a statutory procedural basis for an expulsion order. However, the UN Human Rights Commission has extended the scope of application of Article 13 CCPR by declaring legal authorization of collective expulsions of third-country nationals to be in violation of Article 13 CCPR[67]. In addition, expulsions carried out on manifestly arbitrary grounds are also considered contrary to Article 13 CCPR even if based on national law[68]. Accordingly, prohibition of arbitrary expulsions is one major purpose of the procedural rights enshrined in Article 13 CCPR. This limitation of national competence with respect to expulsion must also guide prospective Community legislation.

---

[64] The Migrant Workers Convention has entered into force in 6 of 15 Member States (Sweden, Spain, Portugal, The Netherlands, Italy and France). The Convention of Establishment has entered into force in 8 of 15 Member States. (Belgium, Denmark, Germany, Greece, Ireland, Italy Luxembourg, The Netherlands, United Kingdom).

[65] Cf. *Jagerskiold*, in Henkin (ed.), The International Bill of Rights (1981), 168, 183 et seq.

[66] Cf. *Nowak*, CCPR Commentary (1993), (1993), Article 13 CCPR para 2.

[67] General comment 15/27, § 10, reproduced in *Nowak*, CCPR Commentary (1993), 863.

[68] Cf. *Maroufidou v Sweden*, No 58/1979, § 9.3.

Legislation and practice must also meet the standards of Article 17(1) CCPR which corresponds to Article 12 of the Universal Declaration of Human Rights and prohibits arbitrary and unlawful interference with, *inter alia*, the family. However, expulsions authorized under national legislation cannot be considered unlawful within the meaning of Article 17(1) CCPR[69] since the notion of "unlawful" is understood as contrary to the national legal system[70]. Similarly the term "arbitrary" refers to reasons justified by national law. Every act of a State organ, including national legislation, must conform to the provisions of the Covenant.[71]

c) The 1951 Convention Relating to the Status of Refugees

Articles 32 and 33 of the 1951 Geneva Convention protect against expulsion and termination of residence for refugees. The Convention's guiding principle with regard to expulsion is expressed in Article 33(1), the principle of "non-refoulement"[72]. Article 33(1) prohibits the expulsion, or the return of a refugee

> in any manner whatsoever to the frontiers of territories where his life or freedom would be threatened on account of his race, religion, nationality, membership of a particular social group or political opinion.

This prohibition is limited by Article 33(2), which states that a refugee may not claim the benefit of non-refoulement if there is reason to believe that he represents a danger to the security of the country in which he currently resides, or if he has been convicted by a final judgment of a particularly serious crime, and, therefore, constitutes a danger to the community of that country.

The gravity of the offence may be used as a yardstick to balance interests; social and economic conditions awaiting the refugee upon return may also be taken into account. Both the offence in question and the perceived threat to the community would need to be extremely grave in order to justify a disregard for danger to the life of the refugee. A less serious offence and a less serious threat may justify the return of an individual likely to face less serious harassment or discrimination.[73]

Article 32(1) of the Geneva Convention protects refugees legally resident in the territory of a Signatory State from expulsion, except on grounds of national security or public order, and Article 32(2) affords the refugee some procedural rights in the case of expulsion[74]. These rights correspond to the rights granted in

69 Cf. *Mauritan-women case*, No 35/1978, § 9.2(b)2(i)4.

70 *Nowak*, CCPR Commentary (1993), Article 17 CCPR para 11 cf. general comment 16/32, § 3, reproduced in *Nowak*, CCPR Commentary (1993), 864.

71 Cf. *Mauritian-women case*, No 35/1978, § 9.2(b)2(i)8; further *Nowak*, CCPR Commentary (1993), Article 17 CCPR para 12, 14.

72 The term derives from the French "refouler", which means "repulse" or "drive back" of an invader or enemy (Le Robert & Collins dictionary). Cf. further *Goodwin-Gill*, The refugee in international law, 2nd ed., 1996, 117 et seq. A detailed analysis of the principle of non-refoulement has been provided by *Kälin*, Das Prinzip des Refoulements (1982), *passim*.

73 *Goodwin-Gill*, The Refugee in International law, 1996, 140.

74 Cf. Bundesverwaltungsgericht (Federal Administrative Court), judgment of 25 November 1959, BVerwGE 7, 333 *Yugoslav Refugee Case*, summary in 26 ILR 496; Bundesverwaltungsgericht (Federal Administrative Court) decision of 30. September 1959, BVerfGE 7, 231; *Homeless third-*

Article 13 of the CCPR. The principle of non-refoulement may prevent a deportation, even if the third-country national has been lawfully expelled. If the third-country national is in danger of torture or death in the country of origin, deportation is prohibited.[75]

2. *Protection against Expulsion by the European Convention on Human Rights*

As indicated by Article 6(2) TEU and pursuant to consistent jurisprudence of the European Court of Justice the fundamental rights guaranteed by the European Convention on Human Rights contribute to the European Union's constitutional order[76]. At the same time, however, individuals can directly invoke their rights granted by the Convention by bringing a complaint against a Member State before the European Court of Human Rights.

The European Convention on Human Rights itself does not expressly deal with expulsion. In turn, some rights enshrined therein such as the prohibition of torture (Article 3 of the Convention)[77] and the right of privacy and family (Article 8 of the Convention)[78] have been interpreted as according to third-country nationals concerned, certain safeguards against expulsion. In addition, Article 4 of the Fourth Protocol and Article 1 of the Seventh Protocol to the Convention provide express protection against expulsion. The relevance of these rights is, however, rather small since not all Member States have ratified these protocols[79].

a) Protection against expulsion by the Fourth and Seventh Protocol to the Convention

Article 4 of the Fourth Protocol provides that "[c]ollective expulsion of aliens is prohibited". Collective expulsion is defined as any measure of the competent authority compelling third-country nationals as a group to leave the country, except where such measure is taken after and on the basis of a reasonable and objective examination of the particular case of each individual member of the group[80]. A number of cases involving the expulsion of a multitude of third-country nationals based on similar reasons does not qualify as a collective expulsion. Aliens expelled

---

country national Case, summary in 26 ILR 503; cf. further examples for decisions and national provisions at *Goodwin-Gill*, The Refugee in international law, 1996, 151.

75 Executive Committee Conclusion No. 7 (1977), cf. *Goodwin-Gill*, The Refugee in international law, 1996, 152.

76 See *supra* Chapter B II.

77 See *infra* b).

78 See *infra* c).

79 Protocol No. 4 has not been ratified by Greece, Spain and the UK. Protocol No 7 has not entered into force in the UK, Spain, Portugal, the Netherlands, Ireland, Germany and Belgium.

80 European Commission of Human Rights, decision of 3 October 1975, No 7011/ 75, *Becker v Denmark*, 4 DR 215,(235).

on the basis of an individual reasoned decision cannot, therefore, raise a claim of unlawful collective expulsion.[81]

With respect to cases of expulsion of individual third-country nationals, Article 1(1) of the Seventh Protocol guarantees that –

> An alien lawfully resident in the territory of a State shall not be expelled therefrom except in pursuance of a decision reached in accordance with law and shall be allowed:
>
> (a) to submit reasons against his expulsion,
>
> (b) to have his case reviewed, and
>
> (c) to be represented for these purposes before the competent authority or a person or persons designated by that authority.

Unlike Article 4 of the Fourth Additional Protocol, however, this Article only requires compliance with the rule of law; it does not generally prohibit expulsion[82]. The procedural rights granted by Article 1 of the Seventh Additional Protocol are similar to those accorded by Article 13 CCPR. The exercise of these procedural rights, however, is limited by Article 1(2) of the Seventh Additional Protocol according to which –

> An alien may be expelled before the exercise of his rights under paragraph 1.a, b and c of this Article, when such expulsion is necessary in the interests of public order or is grounded on reasons of national security.

Signatory States of the Protocol offered suggestions on the interpretation of the clause in an Explanatory Memorandum[83]. The Memorandum asks Member States to apply the principle of proportionality when expelling a person under the exception clause.

Both protocols establish only minimum standards for expulsion. The ban on collective expulsion and the guarantee of certain procedural rights do not grant more than a right of an individual decision under the rule of law.

b) The protection against expulsion in case of inhuman treatment (Article 3 ECHR)[84]

Article 3 ECHR provides that –

> No one shall be subjected to torture or to inhuman or degrading treatment or punishment.

---

[81] European Commission of Human Rights, decision of 16 December 1988, No. 14209/88, *A v Netherlands*, 59 DR 274.

[82] *Harris/O'Boyle/Warbrick*, Law of the European Convention on Human Rights (1995), 565.

[83] Explanatory Memorandum on the Seventh Protocol, CE Doc. H(83) 3.

[84] Cf. *Alleweldt*, Protection Against Expulsion Under Article 3 of the European Convention on Human Rights, EJIL 4 (1993) 360 et seq.

Article 3 of the European Convention on Human Rights may accord protection against expulsion or deportation in cases where expulsion or deportation as such constitute inhuman treatment. Strasbourg jurisprudence has thus far identified examples such as the expulsion or deportation of an ill person, or deportations causing grave suffering[85]. In particular cases the anguish likely to be caused by the anticipation of impending violence may be considered as inhuman treatment[86]. This may be the case with regard to torture victims suffering trauma when confronted with the possibility of forced return to the land in which they were tortured[87]. Accordingly, the circumstances of a deportation (or extradition) may *eo ipso* constitute inhuman or degrading treatment.

In addition, the European Court of Human Rights has applied Article 3 of the European Convention on Human Rights to situations where third-country nationals are returned, expelled or deported to a State in which they are liable to face inhuman or degrading treatment. The application of Article 3 of the Convention to these cases is based on the idea that deportation (or extradition) does constitute in itself inhuman or degrading treatment since the deporting State treats a person inhumanly by admitting that the deportee is facing inhuman or degrading treatment upon return in his home country. This concept has been elaborated already by the European Commission for Human Rights. In a decision of 1983 the Commission pointed out that –

> according to established case law, extradition may under exceptional circumstances constitute treatment prohibited by Article 3 of the Convention. This is the case, for example, where the person concerned is in danger of being subjected, in the State to which he must be extradited, to torture or any treatment contrary to Article 3.[88]

The European Court of Human Rights has delivered a number of judgments on the relevance of Article 3 ECHR for decisions of extradition, expulsion and deportation. In its famous judgment in the 1989 Soering case, the Court stated for the first time that:

> the decision by a Member State to extradite a fugitive may give rise to an issue under Article 3, and hence engage the responsibility of that State under the Convention, where substantial grounds have been shown for believing that the person concerned, if extradited, faces a real risk of being subjected to torture or inhuman or degrading treatment or punishment in the requesting country.[89]

---

85 Cf. ECHR, judgment of 18. January 1978, *Ireland v United Kingdom*, Series A 25, para 162; European Commission of Human Rights, decision of 19 January 1984, No 9330/81, *Bulus v Sweden*, 35 DR, 57, 62; cf. further *Harris/O'Boyle/Warbrick*, Law of the European Convention on Human Rights (1995), 73.

86 Cf., ECHR, judgment 7 July 1989, *Soering v United Kingdom*, Series A 161, para 100.

87 Cf. ECHR, judgment 7 March 1991, *Crus Varas et al. v Sweden*, Series A 201, para 83/84.

88 Cf. European Commission of Human Rights, decision of 3 May 1983, *Altun v Germany*, No. 10308/83, DR 36, 231 et seq.

89 See the judgment of the European Court of Human Rights of 7 July 1989, *Soering v United Kingdom*, Series A No. 161 para 91.

This line of reasoning was later extended to apply to decisions to expel a third-country national.[90]

The Court has been careful not to extend the scope of application of Article 3 of the European Convention on Human Rights beyond the case of an individual and clearly foreseeable risk as a result of an expulsion (or extradition). In *Vilvarajah* the Court held that a mere possibility of ill-treatment in a situation of internal disturbances was not, in itself, sufficient to justify a claim for a breach of Article 3, if the personal position of the person in question is not substantially worse than that of the majority of members of the same population group returning to their country of origin[91]. In a more recent case involving a Colombian drug smuggler who had cooperated with the French authorities and, as a result, feared revenge upon return to Columbia, the Court noted the general situation of violence in the country of destination. It ruled, however, that this circumstance alone could not render deportation a violation of Article 3 of the Convention[92]. The applicant's deportation was thus carried out in accordance with Article 3 of the Convention, given the lack of relevant evidence to prove the existence of a real risk in this particular case. In particular, the Court pointed at the fact that there were "no documents to support the claim that the applicant's personal situation would be any worse than that of other Colombians, were he to be deported."[93]

It follows that general dangers affecting the entire population of a country as a result of internal upheaval or armed conflict, drought, famine, or a generally poor human rights situation are not sufficient to establish a real risk of inhuman treatment pursuant to Article 3 of the European Convention on Human Rights[94]. The Court's judgment in *Chahal* may, however, lead to the conclusion that a real risk could result from a risk affecting an entire group of persons. Existence of a real risk was proved in this case, based on the fact that the applicant was a well-

---

[90] See judgments of the European Court of Human Rights of 20 March 1991, *Cruz Varaz v Sweden*, Series A No. 201; of 20 October 1991, *Vilvarajah and Others v United Kingdom*, Series A No. 215; see also the judgment of 15 November 1996, *Chahal v United Kingdom*, RJD 1996-V, 1831.

[91] See the judgment of 30 October 1991 in *Vilvarajah v United Kingdom*, Series A No. 215, paras 111 and 112.

[92] See ECHR, judgment of 29 April 1997 *H.L.R. v France*, RJD 1997-III, 745, para 41.

[93] Id., para 42.

[94] See also *Hailbronner*, Ausländerrecht, (1997), A1, § 53 para 47, 52a. The judgment of the Court of Human Rights in the case Vilvarajah is, however, interpreted differently by several authors who see the Statement of the Court made in para 111 of the Vilvarajah judgment in its context, and in particular with findings made in para 110. In this paragraph the Court had found that UNHCR voluntary repatriation programme which, had begun to operate at the end of December 1987, provided a strong indication that by February 1988 the situation had improved sufficiently to enable large numbers of Tamils to be repatriated to Sri Lanka, notwithstanding the continued existence of civil disturbance. Authors argue that because of this improvement of the general situation in Sri Lanka, the Court considered the level of general danger as relatively low, and that it was not sure whether the Court would not admit a violation of Article 3 ECHR in situations of extremely high general danger (see e.g. *Trechsel* in Barwig/Brill, Aktuelle asylrechtliche Probleme der gerichtlichen Entscheidungspraxis in Deutschland, Österreich und der Schweiz, 1996, 97; *Egelund* in UNHCR (ed.), The European Convention on Human Rights and the Protection of Refugees, Asylum Seekers and Displaced Persons (1996), 7, 8; *Alleweldt*, Schutz vor Abschiebung bei drohender Folter oder unmenschlicher oder erniedrigender Behandlung oder Strafe, 1996, 47).

known supporter of Sikh separatism[95], and because the Court was persuaded that elements in the Punjab police were accustomed to act without regard to the human rights of suspected Sikh militants[96].

Another issue of interpretation, on which the European Court of Human Rights has pronounced, relates to the question of whether actions carried out by non-State actors may qualify as "inhuman or degrading treatment", or whether Article 3 of the European Convention on Human Rights refers only to acts of the State or attributable to the State. While the Court stated in *Cruz Varas* that the conditions in the requesting country must be assessed against the standards of Article 3 of the Convention, in order to establish responsibility thereunder, it also emphasized that there was "no question of adjudicating on or establishing the responsibility of the receiving country, whether under general international law, under the Convention or otherwise."[97] More recently, in *Ahmed*, the Court agreed with the Commission's view that the deportation of the applicant to Somalia constituted a violation of Article 3 of the Convention. It repeated, further, that the current lack of State authority in Somalia did not exclude the fact of a violation of Article 3 of the Convention, due to the "absolute nature" of the provision[98]. Finally, the Court expressly stated in *H.L.R v France* that it –

> does not rule out the possibility that Article 3 of the Convention may also apply where the danger emanates from persons or groups of persons who are not public officials.[99]

In such cases, however, it must be proved that the risk is real, and that receiving State authorities are unable to grant appropriate protection.[100]

In its recent jurisprudence the Court has considerably expanded the notion of inhuman treatment beyond those acts traditionally associated with that concept. In *Soering* and similar cases the Court developed its concept of Article 3 ECHR as a protection against expulsion and deportation on the basis that no State would be allowed to assist in delivering anybody to a State in which he or she would be facing inhuman treatment in the sense of intentional deprivation of life and personal integrity under inhuman circumstances, the extraditing or expelling State itself having commited an inhuman act.

In *D v United Kingdom* (St. Kitts case) the "accomplice" concept was considered. The applicant, suffering from AIDS, maintained that his removal to St. Kitts would violate Article 3 of the European Convention on Human Rights since he had no close relatives or friends, no financial resources or access to any means

---

95 See the judgment of the European Court of Human Rights of 15 November 1996, *Chahal v United Kingdom*, No. 70/1995/576/662, paras 98 and 106.

96 Id., paras 100 and 105. See also *Hailbronner,* Ausländerrecht, § 51 (1998) para 52; for a dissenting view, however before release of the said judgment, *Villiger*, Handbuch der Europäischen Menschenrechtskonvention (1993) 185 para 304.

97 See ECHR, judgment of 20 March 1991 in *Cruz Varaz and Others v Sweden*, Series A No. 201, para 69.

98 See ECHR, judgment of 17 December 1996 in *Ahmed v Austria*, RJD 1996-VI, 2195, para 46.

99 ECHR, judgment of 29 April 1997 in *H.L.R. v France*, RJD 1997-III, 745 para 40.

100 *Ibid.* Corroborated in the judgment of the European Court of Human Rights of 2 May 1997, *D. v United Kingdom*, RJD 1997-III, 777, para 49.

of social support there. He argued, further, that there was no medical treatment available comparable to that in the United Kingdom. His death would, as a result, not only be accelerated, but would occur under inhuman and degrading conditions although clearly nobody could be held responsible for the general medical circumstances in St. Kitts. The Court held that the implementation of the decision to remove the applicant would violate Article 3 of the Convention, and observed that –

> Aside from these situations and given the fundamental importance of Article 3 in the Convention system, the Court must reserve to itself sufficient flexibility to address the application of that Article in other contexts which might arise. It is not therefore prevented from scrutinizing an applicant's claim under Article 3 where the source of the risk of proscribed treatment in the receiving country stems from factors which cannot engage either directly or indirectly the responsibility of the public authorities of that country, or which, taken alone, do not in themselves infringe the standards of that Article. To limit the application of Article 3 in this manner would be to undermine the absolute character of its protection. In any such context, however, the Court must subject all the circumstances surrounding the case to a rigorous scrutiny, especially the applicant's personal situation in the expelling State.[101]

In addition, the Court has repeatedly argued that Article 3 of the European Convention on Human Rights provides an absolute protection. In *Chahal v United Kingdom*[102] the Court declared a deportation of a Indian national, considered by the British authorities as a terrorist, as a violation of Article 3 of the European Convention on Human Rights with the argument that –

> Article 3 enshrines one of the most fundamental values of democratic society ... The court is well aware of the immense difficulties faced by States in modern times in protecting their communities from terrorist violence. However, even in these circumstances, the Convention prohibits in absolute terms torture or inhuman or degrading treatment or punishment irrespective of the victim's conduct. ... The prohibition provided by Art. 3 against ill-treatment is equally absolute in expulsion cases.[103]

According to the jurisprudence of the European Court of Human Rights the limits of protection contained in Article 33(2) of the Geneva Convention do not apply in cases involving a risk of inhuman or degrading treatment. The protection under Article 3 ECHR being granted as "absolute" and not subject to restriction even in case of war or national emergency, therefore means that the protection applies even in cases of a serious and imminent threat to public order or national

---

[101] ECHR, judgment of 2 May 1997, *D. v United Kingdom*, RJD 1997-III, 777, para 49.
[102] Cf. ECHR, judgment of 15 November 1996, *Chahal v United Kingdom*, RJD 1996-V, 1831, paras 98-105.
[103] ECHR, judgment of 15 November 1996, *Chahal v United Kingdom*, RJD 1996-V, 1831, para 79.

security[104]. The methodological basis of this jurisprudence, however, seems to be weak and insufficiently founded in the international legal order on the rights of third-country nationals.

Although the Court itself has repeatedly emphasized that Article 3 of the European Convention on Human Rights does not contain in itself a right of residence or asylum and Contracting States may provide for the expulsion of third-country nationals according to generally recognized principles of international law and subject to treaty restrictions[105], it has concluded from Article 3 of the Convention an absolute protection against expulsion. To expand the concept of the absolute character of Article 3 of the European Convention on Human Rights, that is, nobody may be tortured or treated inhumanly even in case of war or emergency (see Article 15(2) of the Convention), to a duty to afford absolute protection against dangers resulting from the home State or as a consequence of the general living conditions in the home State, misses the systematic context of international refugee law. There is in fact no absolute protection against expulsion under customary international law or treaty law. Neither Article 31(2) of the Geneva Convention nor Article 13 CCPR provide such absolute protection. This is also confirmed by Article 1 of the United Nations Declaration on Territorial Asylum:

> The right to seek or to enjoy asylum may not be invoked by any person with respect to whom there are serious reasons for considering that he has committed a crime against peace, a war crime or a crime against humanity, as defined in the international instruments drawn up to make provision in respect of such crimes.[106]

The assumption that Article 3 of the European Convention on Human Rights affords absolute protection against expulsion or extradition becomes even more doubtful in the light of the recent jurisprudence of the Court expanding the concept of inhuman treatment to cases of insufficient medical supply in the country of origin.[107]

The extensive interpretation of Article 3 of the European Convention on Human Rights by the European Court of Human Rights has been applauded by many authors[108] while others have criticized it[109]. Among the more prominent critics is the German Federal Administrative Court which has refused the application of Article 3 of the European Convention on Human Rights to cases of non-State persecution[110]. The Federal Administrative Court argues that the Court's

---

[104] ECHR, judgment of 15 November 1996, *Chahal v United Kingdom*, RJD 1996-V, 1831, para 49 et seq.

[105] ECHR judgment of 15 November 1996, *Chahal v United Kingdom*, RJD 1996-V, 1831, para 73 et seq.

[106] UNCHR, Collection of International Instruments and Other Legal Texts, Vol. I (1999), 73.

[107] Cf. ECHR, judgment of 2 May 1997, *D v United Kingdom*, Reports 1997-III, 777, para 49 et seq; see further *infra* 4b.

[108] Cf. *Kälin* in Hailbronner/Klein (ed.), Einwanderungskontrolle und Menschenrechte – Immigration Control and Human Rights, 1999, 51 et seq; *Zimmer*, ZAR 1998, 115.

[109] Cf. *Hailbronner* in Die Öffentliche Verwaltung (DÖV) 1999, 617 et seq.

[110] Cf. Bundesverwaltungsgericht (Federal Administrative Court), judgment of 15 April 1997, NVwZ 1997, 1127, (1129).

jurisprudence may well lead to a very vague duty to grant admission and protection to victims of civil war, natural disasters and adverse living conditions.

From a methodological point of view the European Court of Human Rights jurisprudence does not satisfy basic methodological requirements. It seems to be based more or less on a rather arbitrary case-by-case approach rather than on a systematic interpretation of the Convention's provisions. Although one can agree basically with the thesis that the European Convention on Human Rights must be interpreted in a dynamic way, taking into account the changing environment of different forms of persecution, extension of the scope of application of the Convention's provisions must be in line with a common basic conviction of Contracting States and with the need to provide for sufficiently clear and foreseeable guidelines as to the future scope of application of the Convention. In particular it is impossible to draw a precise borderline between persons facing a serious threat to life and personal integrity by insufficient medical treatment and persons suffering serious illness or death as a result of intolerable economic conditions in many parts of the world on the basis of the judgment in *D. v United Kingdom*. By deriving from Article 3 of the European Convention on Human Rights a right of entry, as the logic of the humanitarian character of this Article would seem to imply (although the European Court has not yet gone so far), it would become apparent that Article 3 of the Convention has developed into a general right contrary to its clear wording, legislative history and purpose.

Moreover, unlike the prohibition of refoulement derived from Article 3 of the European Convention on Human Rights, Article 33 of the Geneva Convention is not of an absolute character, as indicated by its second paragraph. The jurisprudence of the European Court of Human Rights as to the absolute character of Article 3 ECHR raises difficult problems of distinguishing between the danger of political persecution and the danger of inhuman or degrading treatment. Frequently no distinction will be possible, particularly in the light of the most recent jurisprudence of the Strasbourg Court to extend the concept of inhuman treatment far beyond its original meaning. The limitations contained in the Geneva Convention relating to a danger to the security of the State or the public order may become obsolete, contrary to the clear wording and system of international refugee law.

c) Protection against expulsion by Article 8 ECHR (family life and privacy)

Article 8 of the European Convention on Human Rights has acquired major importance with respect to protection against expulsion or deportation of third-country nationals. This provision stipulates that -

> (1) Everyone has the right to respect for his private and family life, his home and his correspondence.
>
> (2) There shall be no interference by a public authority with the excercise of this right except as is in accordance with the law and is necessary in a democratic society in the interests of national security, public safety or the economic well-being of the country, for the prevention of disorder or crime for the protection of health or morals, for the rights and freedoms of others.

The European Court of Human Rights has repeatedly decided that Article 8 of the Convention does not provide for an absolute protection against expulsion or deportation of an third-country national, interfering with his private and family life. Article 8 of the Convention obliges Member States to evaluate and balance public interests in favor of a deportation or expulsion against private interests for the protection of private and family life.[111]

Family life in the sense of Article 8 of the European Convention on Human Rights has been interpreted extensively. The Court has relied upon the actual circumstances of a case, determining the relationship rather than formal categories of the respective national law[112]. Members of a family protected by Article 8 of the Convention are not only parents and minor children[113] but also close relatives such as grandparents and aunts[114]. However, it is not sufficient to demonstrate a legal relationship in order to claim the protection of family life. Rather it must be established that unity of the family actually exists[115].

It is not necessary, however, that family members are living together under one roof. In *Berrehab* the Court held that a legal as well as actual relationship between a divorced father and his daughter constitutes a family in the sense of Article 8 of the European Convention on Human Rights[116]. On the other hand mere social ties are insufficient to demonstrate evidence of a family link. Homosexual couples or the relationship between a prison inmate and his fiancée are protected by the rights of privacy while they have not been considered by the Court as family life[117]. However, a legalized relationship is not required for protection as a family where an unmarried couple has common children[118]. The Strasbourg Court thus seems to apply alternative criteria relating to either a legal relationship or the existence of common children.

Where a family in the sense of Article 8 of the European Convention on Human Rights exists, expulsion or deportation interfering with family life can only be justified on the grounds laid down in paragraph (2) of this Article. The Convention, however, does not provide for a right to choose the country of residence in which to lead one's family life[119]. The existence of a family as such is not sufficient to grant protection against expulsion or deportation[120]. Two requirements must first

---

[111] *Wildhaber* in The Modern World of Human Rights, Essays in Honour of Thomas Burgenthal, 1996, 103 et seq; Id., in Internationaler Kommentar zur EMRK, Article 8 EMRK; V*illiger*, Handbuch der EMRK, 1993, 327 et seq.

[112] ECHR, judgment of 18 December 1986, *Johnston et al v Ireland*, Series A 112, para 55 et seq.

[113] ECHR, judgment of 13 June 1979, *Marckx v Belgium*, Series A 31, para 14;

[114] ECHR, judgment of 13 June 1979, *Marckx v Belgium*, Series A 31, para 21.

[115] Cf. *Hobe*, Aufenthaltsbeendende Maßnahmen und Menschenrechte, in Hailbronner/Klein (ed.), Einwanderungskontrolle und Menschenrechte – Immigration Control and Human Rights, 1999, 197, 198 et seq.; *Groenendijk/Guild/Dogan*, Security of residence of long term migrants, 1998, 8 et seq.

[116] ECHR, judgment of 21 June 1988, *Berrehab v Netherlands*, Series A 138, para 21.

[117] Cf. *Jacobs/White*, The European Convention on Human Rights, 1996, 176.

[118] Cf. ECHR, judgment of 18 December 1986, *Johnston and others v Ireland*, Series A 112 para 25.

[119] ECHR, judgment of 18 May 1985, *Abdulaziz and others v UK*, EuGRZ 1985, 567; *Jacobs/White,* The European Convention on Human Rights, 1996, 181.

[120] Cf. European Commission of Human Rights, decision of 19 May 1977, No. 7816/77, *X and Y v Germany*, DR 9, 219, 220; European Commission of Human Rights, decision of 14.7.1977, No. 7289/75, 7349/76, *X and Y v Switzerland*, DR 9, 57, 74.

be met. First, there must be an actual link to the State of residence[121] and, second, it must be demonstrated that, based on a balance of interests in the concrete case the enforced return of the third-country national is not "necessary" in a democratic society. Removal of a third-country national is necessary if the State can provide evidence that there is a pressing social need for an expulsion and that expulsion is proportional to a legitimate public interest[122]. In the course of a balancing process, the effect of the expulsion upon the family as a whole and the individual to be expelled, the nature of the actual existing family ties and the length of residence have to be balanced against the public interest, in particular the gravity of criminal offences and the danger of future disturbances of public interest[123].

Save for a few exceptions[124], the Court has had to deal with cases of expulsion or deportation based on criminal offences. In *Moustaquim*[125] it had to decide on the expulsion of a Moroccan national living in Belgium since the age of two and having practically no ties with Morocco. The Court held that the expulsion interfered to an unproportional extent with family life taking into account that the third-country national concerned had committed the criminal offences referred to as justification of expulsion when he was still a juvenile. In its more recent jurisprudence the Court has maintained that even the committing of a large number of serious criminal offences does not justify expulsion if there are very strong ties to the country of actual residence while the ties to the original home country are weak or practically non-existent. In *Beldjoudi v France*[126] the third-country national concerned had been entitled to French citizenship and had been married to a French woman for twenty years. In *Narsi*[127] the Court concluded that expulsion was unproportional regardless of a series of grave offences and a considerable danger to the public order since the third-country national concerned was deaf and dumb since his birth and had no actual possibility of living an ordinary life in his home country. Again in *Mehemi*[128] the complainant had no actual ties to his home country Algeria, since he could not speak the language, nor had he ever lived in Algeria. On the other hand, the very fact that a third-country national was born or has grown up in the country of actual residence does not necessarily preclude expulsion notwithstanding strong family ties. In *Boujlifa*[129] and *Bouchelika*[130] expulsion was declared as permissible, taking account of the gravity of criminal offences that had been committed and of the possibility of return to the third-country national's home country. In *Bouchelika* the Court pointed to the fact that

---

121 Cf. *Groenendijk/Guild/Dogan*, Security of residence of long term migrants, 1998, 9.

122 Cf. *Sherlock*, E.L.Rev 23 (1998) HR/62, 64.

123 Cf. *Hobe* in Hailbronner/Klein (eds), Einwanderungskontrolle und Menschenrechte – Immigration Control and Human Rights (1999), 197 (202).

124 In *Berrehab* (ECHR, judgment of 21 June 1988, *Berrehab v Netherlands*, Series A 138) expulsion was justified by the need to protect the economic wellbeing of the country. The Court did in principle acknowledge this as a legitimate aim; the expulsion, however, was declared unproportional.

125 Cf. ECHR, judgment of 18 February 1991, *Moustaquim v Belgium*, Series A 193.

126 Cf. ECHR, judgment of 26 March 1992, *Beljoudi v France*, Series A 234.

127 Cf. ECHR, judgment of 13 July 1995, *Narsi v France*, Series A 320, B,. 11.

128 Cf. ECHR, judgment of 26 September 1997, *Mehemi v France*, Reports 1997-VI, 1959.

129 Cf. ECHR, judgment of 21 October 1997, *Boujlifa v France*, Reports 1997-VI, 2250.

130 Cf. ECHR, judgment of 27 January 1997, *Bouchelkia v France*, Reports 1997-I, 47.

the complainant was unmarried at the time of the expulsion and still had some ties to his country of nationality, i.e. Algeria.

There has been a debate within the Court on the legal situation of long-term residents who have been born or grown up in the country of actual residence. According to the majority of the Court, birth or growing up in one's country of actual residence forms one criterion in the balancing of interests. In turn, the minority, supported by some authors[131], believes that expulsion ought to be considered under these circumstances as generally inadmissible. Judge Petitti states in a dissenting vote that –

> ... this line of decisions does not provide a solution to the general problem, which is a matter for the Member States of the Council of Europe, if they have the will to harmonize their policies in this field and cooperate, so as to take account of immigration and differences in the rules adopted with regard to integration and family reunion by certain States with a view to strengthening protection of families.[132]

Protection against expulsion or deportation by Article 8 of the European Convention on Human Rights should remain the result of a balancing of interests in each individual case. The jurisprudence of the Court will constitute the legal framework to be implemented by the national administrations. It would be possible, however, to draft some guidelines based on the jurisprudence of the Court taking into account the criteria developed by the Court.[133]

The question arises as to whether the right of family life should be extended to new forms of "family" which do not match traditional concepts according to national law. The European Commission of Human Rights has decided that homosexual couples may rely upon the right of privacy as a protection against expulsion of one of the partners of such a relationship. The Commission has rightly pointed out that the right of privacy does not automatically protect against expulsion. There is no breach of Article 8 of the Convention on Human Rights unless it is established that the couple cannot live elsewhere[134].

3. *Other Council of Europe Conventions*

Within the framework of the Council of Europe several other legal instruments may restrict the right of Schengen States to expulsion or deportation. Particularly important among these are the European Social Charter (ESC), the European Convention on Establishment (ECE) and the European Convention on the Legal Status of Migrant Workers (ECMW). These Conventions grant procedural rights

---

[131] Cf. *Cholewinski*, Netherlands Quarterly of Human rights, 1994, 287 et seq.

[132] Cf. ECHR, judgment of 13 July 1995, *Narsi v France*, Series A 320, B, 28.

[133] Cf. the criteria catalogue in *Groenendijk/Guild/Dogan*, Security of residence of long term migrants, 1998, 15.

[134] Cf. European Commission of Human Rights, decision of 3 May 1983, No. 9369/81, *X and Y v UK*, 32 DR 220, 221 et seq; cf. also Hessischer Verwaltungsgerichtshof (Administrative Appeal Court), judgment of 1. August 1997, Zeitschrift für Ausländerrecht und Ausländerpolitik (ZAR) 1998, 183.

which are as a rule not directly applicable. Article 9(4) ECMW, for example, permits migrant workers to remain in their country of residence in the case of involuntary unemployment, for a limited period of time, and provided that they are entitled to unemployment benefit[135]. These legal instruments are generally less important, however, than the European Convention on Human Rights or the Geneva Convention, primarily due to the fact that they apply exclusively to third-country nationals who are nationals of other Signatory States[136]. In addition, the ECE and the ECMW have not been ratified by all Member States of the European Union[137]. The ESC, though having been ratified by all Member States, does not necessarily provide for a common European standard since its provisions are subject to a variety of opt-out clauses which have been used by several Member States to a varying degree[138]. Article 19 (point 8) ESC provides protection against expulsion, except in cases involving a danger to national security, or an offence against public interest or morality in accordance with Article 20(1)(b). This provision, however, is not binding for Austria, Denmark and Sweden.

V. OUTLOOK

The means of ensuring that foreign nationals fulfil the conditions applicable for entry, residence, and employment must be further harmonized, if the Community intends to maintain control over increasing migration flows. The Council has already expressed its willingness to give priority to, *inter alia*, the improvement of cooperation between Member States on expulsion of illegal immigrants and to the solution of problems of readmission and cooperation with the countries of origin[139]. In an attempt to evaluate the practical effect of the Council's progress in these fields of law, as well as to provide useful lessons for future work, Member States have agreed on an annual questionnaire, designed to show how they have implemented the instruments adopted by the Council concerning illegal immigration, readmission, the unlawful employment of third-country nationals and cooperation in the implementation of expulsion orders[140]. In addition, the Council shall adopt measures on illegal immigration and illegal residence, including repatriation of illegal residents, within a period of five years after the entry into force of the Treaty of Amsterdam under Article 63(3)(b) ECT.

---

[135] Cf. *Cholewinski*, Migrant workers in International Human Rights law, 1997, 401 et seq.

[136] Cf. *Cholewinski*, Migrant workers in International Human Rights law, 1997, 400.

[137] The Migrant Workers Convention has entered into force in 6 of 15 Member States (Sweden, Spain, Portugal, The Netherlands, Italy and France). The Convention of Establishment has entered into force in 8 of 15 Member States. (Belgium, Denmark, Germany, Greece, Ireland, Italy Luxembourg, The Netherlands, United Kingdom).

[138] According to Article 20 ESC, the signatory States can declare, which parts of the Charter they regard as binding . Only the Member States Italy and Belgium accepted all provisions of the Charter.

[139] See Council Resolution of 14 October 1996 laying down the priorities for cooperation in the field of justice and home affairs for the period from 1 July 1996 to 30 June 1998, O.J. 1996 C 319/1, point I (4)(i) and (j).

[140] Council Decision of 16 December 1996 on monitoring the implementation of instruments adopted by the Council concerning illegal immigration, readmission, the unlawful employment of third-country nationals and cooperation in the implementation of expulsion orders, O.J. 1996 L 342/5.

Matters of expulsion, termination of residence and return will be an integral part of an integrated concept of a European immigration policy[141]. The Austrian presidency proposed, *inter alia,* a junction between economic aid or cooperation and return guarantees in bilateral negotiations between the EU and third States[142]. The presidency also demanded that future policy on these matters ensure that asylum-seekers, or other third-country nationals who have been denied the right to immigration or sojourn, are denied a right of access to the labor market or integration not only based on the duration of their stay as asylum-seeker[143]. Further, the Council paper calls for agreements between States of transit and States of origin to inform the people in the country of origin about the illegality of immigration and return procedures in case of illegal entry. This information should be distributed by the immigration country and the State of origin[144]. The agreements should be guided by the principle of immediate and unconditional readmission of every illegal immigrant in his previous State of residence[145]. In order to solve the problem of refusal of readmission in the absence of valid documents, the establishing of a new agency verifying nationality by a variety of objective criteria has been suggested. The verification of the nationality according to this new instrument should also impose an obligation on States to readmit their own verified nationals.[146]

The Austrian paper has influenced in a general manner the Action Plan of the Council and the Commission on how best to implement the provisions of the Treaty of Amsterdam on an area of freedom, security and justice of 3 December 1998[147]. The Action Plan points out that overall migration strategies should be established (Point 34), which include the establishment of a coherent EU policy on readmission and return within a two year period. This includes the combatting of illegal immigration through, *inter alia*, information campaigns in transit countries and in the countries of origin (Point 36 (c)(ii) and (iii)). Within five years of the entry into force of the Amsterdam Treaty an improvement of the possibilities for the removal of persons who have been refused the right to stay should be followed through improved EU coordination, implementation or readmission clauses, and development of European official (Embassy) reports on the situation in countries of origin (Point 38(c)(i)). These general aims were concretized in guidelines for a European migration strategy issued by the German presidency of the EU Council in May 1999[148]. In this paper the Council emphasizes the importance of expulsion. Expulsion measures should be quickly and consistently applied in accordance with international agreements. Taking into account the reluctance of third countries to enter into formal commitments with respect to readmission[149] the Presidency has re-emphasized that respective clauses should be incorporated in association and

---

[141] Council Document 9809/98 of 28 September 1998.
[142] Cf. Council Document 9809/98 of 28 September 1998, para 61.
[143] Cf. Council Document 9809/98 of 28 September 1998, para 69.
[144] Cf. Council Document 9809/98 of 28 September 1998, para 110.
[145] Cf. Council Document 9809/98 of 28 September 1998, para 111.
[146] Council Document 9809/98 of 28 September 1998, para 112.
[147] O.J. 1999 C 19/1.
[148] Cf. Council Doc 8815/99 of 28. May 1999).
[149] Cf. the Declarations by Pakistan and Bangladesh as reproduced *supra* in Chapter C V 1.

cooperation agreements concluded by the Community with third countries (para 28).

The mentioned documents show the general direction of the European policy concerning illegal third-country nationals. This policy must be integrated in a comprehensive strategy of migration including cooperation with the countries of origin and transit and a harmonization of rules of entry, sojourn, and return. Illegal migration must be considered in close connection with return policy. There can be no convincing European immigration and asylum policy without a strict policy of returning those third-country nationals who do not possess a valid residence permit or any other title authorizing temporary or permanent admission to the area comprising Member States' territories.

G

Bibliography

I. Articles and Books

Achermann, Alberto, Das Erstasylabkommen von Dublin, Schweizerische Zeitschrift für Asylrecht und -praxis (1990), p. 12 et seq.

Achermann, Alberto/Gattiker, Mario, Safe Third Countries: European Developments, International Journal of Refugee Law 7 (1995), p. 19 et seq.

Achermann, Alberto/Bieber, Roland/Epiney, Astrid/Wehner, Ruth (eds.), Schengen und die Folgen – Der Abbau der Grenzkontrollen in Europa, Bern, München, Wien (1995)

Akcay, Deniz, The consequences of the Gaygusuz judgement in the national legal order and the Community legal order, in Van den Bogaert, Stefaan (ed.), Social Security, Non-Discrimination and Property, Antwerpen-Apeldoorn (1997), p. 45 et seq.

Akmann, Torsten, Die Zusammenarbeit in den Bereichen Justiz und Inneres als "3. Säule" des Maastrichter Unionsvertrages, Juristische Arbeitsblätter (1994), p. 49 et seq.

Albors-Llorens, Albertina, Changes in the Jurisdiction of the European Court of Justice under the Treaty of Amsterdam, Common Market Law Review 35 (1999), p. 1273 et seq.

Alexander, Willy, Free Movement of Non-EC Nationals: A Review of the Case-Law of the Court of Justice, European Journal of International Law 3 (1992), p. 53 et seq.

Altmaier, Peter/Verschueren, Herwig, Consequences and Options with regard to the Extension of the Scope of Regulation 1408/71 to Nationals of Non-Member Countries, in Commission of the European Communities (ed.), Social Security in Europe: Equality between Nationals and Non-Nationals, European Conference Oporto November 1994, Lisbon (1995), p. 247 et seq.

Appleyard, Reginald (ed.), International migration today, Volume I: Trends and prospects, Unesco Paris (1988)

Arboleda, Eduardo/Hoy, Ian, The Convention Refugee Definition in the West: Disharmony of Interpretation and Application, International Journal of Refugee Law 5 (1993), p. 66 et seq.

Ardittis, Solon (ed.), The Politics of East-West Migration, New York (1994)

Arl, Thorsten Günther, Sozialpolitik nach Maastricht: Kompetenzgefüge und Rechtssetzung unter EWG/EG-Vertrag und Sozialabkommen, Frankfurt (1997)

Axt, Heinz-Jürgen, Zypern: EU-Beitrittsverhandlungen mit offenem Ausgang, integration 22 (1999), p. 127 et seq.

Bade, Klaus J., Deutsche im Ausland – Fremde in Deutschland. Migration in Geschichte und Gegenwart, München (1992)

Bade, Klaus J., Das Manifest der 60. Deutschland und die Einwanderung, München (1994)

Bade, Klaus J./Weiner, Myron (eds.), Migrations Past, Migrations Future, Oxford (1997)

Bäumler, Helmut, Schengener Abkommen und Wirtschaftskriminalität – Informationelle Zusammenarbeit der Sicherheitsbehörden, Computer und Recht (1994), p. 487 et seq.

Baldwin, Robert/Daintith, Terence, Harmonization and hazard: Regulating workplace health and safety in the European Community, London (1992)

Balze, Wolfgang, Die sozialpolitischen Kompetenzen der Europäischen Union, Baden-Baden (1994)

Banasinski, Cezary, Assoziierung Polens mit den Europäischen Gemeinschaften, ecolex (1995), p. 384 et seq.

Bank, Roland, The Emergent EU Policy on Asylum and Refugees – The New Framework Set by the Treaty of Amsterdam: Landmark or Standstill?, Nordic Journal of International Law 68 (1999), p. 1 et seq.

Banks, Karen, L'Article 118 A. Element dynamique de la politique sociale communautaire, Cahiers de Droit Européen (1993), p. 537 et seq.

Barta, Vit/Richter, Sander, Die Osterweiterung der Europäischen Union aus westlicher und östlicher Sicht. Europa 1996. Auswirkungen einer EU-Osterweiterung. Schriftenreihe Europa des Bundeskanzleramts, Wien (1995), p. 23 et seq.

Bartlett, Katherine T., Gender and Law: Theory, Doctrine, Commentary, Boston (1993)

Barwig, Klaus/Lörcher, Klaus/Schumacher, Christoph (eds.), Familiennachzug von Ausländern auf dem Hintergrund völkerrechtlicher Verträge, Baden-Baden (1985)

Barwig, Klaus/Lörcher, Klaus/Schumacher, Christoph (eds.), Asylrecht im Binnenmarkt. Die europäische Dimension des Rechts auf Asyl, Baden-Baden (1989)

Barwig, Klaus/Brill, Wolfgang, Aktuelle asylrechtliche Probleme der gerichtlichen Entscheidungspraxis in Deutschland, Österreich und der Schweiz, Baden-Baden (1996)

Becker, Ulrich, EU-Erweiterung und differenzierte Integration, Baden-Baden (1999)

Beglinger, Michael, Die Harmonisierungsbestrebungen der EG auf dem Gebiet des technischen Arbeitsschutzes, Chur (1991)

Behlke, Karsten, Das Mindesheitenrecht der Republik Lettland (1996)

Beinhofer, Paul, Europäischer Abbau der Grenzkontrollen und polizeiliche Aufgabenerfüllung, Bayerische Verwaltungsblätter (1995), p. 193 et seq.

Bell, Mark, Schifting Conceptions of Sexual Discrimination at the Court of Justice: From *P v S to Grant v SWT*, European Law Journal 5 (1999), p. 63 et seq.

Bell, Mark, The New Article 13 EC Treaty: A Sound Basis for European Anti-Discrimination Law?, Maastricht Journal of European and Comparative Law 6 (1999), p. 5 et seq.

Benda, Ernst, Notwendigkeit und Möglichkeit positiver Aktionen zugunsten von Frauen im öffentlichen Dienst. Rechtsgutachten erstattet im Auftrag der Senatskanzlei – Leitstelle Gleichstellung der Frau – der Freien und Hansestadt Hamburg, Freiburg (1986)

Bercusson, Brian, Maastricht: a fundamental change in European labour law, European Journal of Industrial Relations 1 (1992), p. 177 et seq.

Bercusson, Brian, European Labour Law, London (1996)

Bergmann, Jan, Der Amsterdamer Vertrag. Eine Kommentierung der Neuerungen des EU- und EG-Vertrages, Köln (1998)

Berksü, Sengül, The impact of the Gaygusuz judgement on the rights of Turkish workers legally and permanently residing in the Community, in Van den Bogaert, Stefaan (ed.), Social Security, Non-Discrimination and Property, Antwerpen-Apeldoorn (1997), p. 35 et seq.

Bernhardt, Rudolf/Geck, Wilhelm Karl/Jaenicke, Günther/Steinberger, Helmut (eds.), Völkerrecht als Rechtsordnung, Internationale Gerichtsbarkeit, Menschenrechte. Festschrift für Hermann Mosler, Berlin, Heidelberg, New York (1983)

Betten, Lammigje/MacDevitt, Delma (eds.), The Protection of Fundamental Social Rights in the European Union, The Hague, London, Boston (1996)

Betten, Lammigje, The Role of Social Partners in the Community's Social Policy Law-Making: Participatory Democracy or Furthering the Interests of Small Elites, in Engels, Chris/Blanpain, Roger (eds.), Labour Law and Industrial Relations at the Turn of the Century, Liber Amicorum in honour of Roger Blanpain, The Hague (1998), p. 239 et seq.

Beyer, G.A., Improving International Responses to Humanitarian Situations, Refugee Policy Group, Washington, D.C., December (1989)

Bieber, Roland, Die Abkommen von Schengen über den Abbau der Grenzkontrollen, Neue Juristische Wochenschrift (1994), p. 294 et seq.

Bieber, Roland/Monar, Joerg (eds.), Justice and Home Affairs in the European Union: The Development of the Third Pillar, Brussels (1995)

Birg, Herwig, World Population Projections for the 21st Century, Frankfurt, New York (1995)

Birk, Rolf, Die Umsetzung von Vereinbarungen der Sozialpartner im Rahmen des sozialen Dialogs, in Zentrum für Europäisches Wirtschaftsrecht, 6. Bonner Europa-Symposium: Der soziale Dialog in Europa – Entwicklung und Perspektiven, Bonn (1996), p. 73 et seq.

Birk, Rolf, Vereinbarungen der Sozialpartner im Rahmen des Sozialen Dialogs und ihre Durchführung, Europäische Zeitschrift für Wirtschaftsrecht (1997), p. 453 et seq.

Blank, Michael, Europäische Kollektivverträge und Sozialer Dialog, in Däubler, Wolfgang/Bobke, Manfred/Kehrmann, Karl (eds.), Festschrift für Albert Gnade, Köln (1992), p. 649 et seq.

Blanpain, Roger/Windey, Paul, European Works Councils: The European Directive (94/95 EEC) of September 22, 1994, Information and Consultations of Employees in Multinational Enterprises in Europe, Leuven (1994)

Blanpain, Roger/Schmidt, Marlene/Schweibert, Ulrike, Europäisches Arbeitsrecht, Baden-Baden (1996)

Blaschke, Jochen, Internationale Migration: Ein Problemaufriß, in Knapp, Manfred (ed.), Migration im neuen Europa, Stuttgart (1994), p. 23 et seq.

Bleckmann, Albert, Die Sozialrechts-Charta des Europarates und die allgemeinen sozialen Rechtsgrundsätze der EG, Schriften des Europainstituts der Universität des Saarlandes 7 (1993)

Bleckmann, Albert, Interpretation et application en droit interne de la Charte Sociale Européenne, notamment du droit de grève, Cahiers de Droit Européen (1967), p. 388 et seq.
Blüm, Norbert, Europäische Sozialpolitik nach Maastricht, in Kirchhoff, Paul/Offerhaus, Klaus/Schöberle, Horst (eds.), Festschrift für Franz Klein, Köln (1993), p. 43 et seq.
Bodart, Serge, Les réfugiés apolitiques: guerre civile et persécution de groupe au regard de la Convention de Genève, International Journal of Refugee Law 7 (1995), p. 39 et seq.
Böcker, Anita/Groenendijk, Kees/Havinga, Tetty/Minderhoud, Paul (eds.), Regulation of Migration, Amsterdam (1998)
Bödding, Benedikt, Die gemeinschaftsrechtlichen Instrumentarien der Sozialpartner, Diss. Münster (1996)
Bödding, Benedikt, Die europarechtlichen Instrumentarien der Sozialpartner, Baden-Baden (1996)
Bookmann, Bonhard, Das Verhandlungsverfahren nach dem Maastrichter Sozialpolitischen Abkommen, in Oberender, Peter/Streit, Manfred (eds.), Europas Arbeitsmärkte im Integrationsprozeß, Baden-Baden (1995), p. 193 et seq.
Bookmann, Bonhard, Agenda Control by Interior Groups in EU Social Policy, Journal of Theoretical Politics 10 (1998), p. 215 et seq.
Borgmann, Bernd, Entsendung drittstaatsangehöriger Arbeitnehmer durch EU-Unternehmen nach Deutschland, Zeitschrift für Ausländerrecht und Ausländerpolitik (1996), p. 119 et seq.
Bortloff, Jens, Die Organisation für Sicherheit und Zusammenarbeit in Europa – Eine völkerrechtliche Bestandsaufnahme, Berlin (1996)
Braun, Wilfried, Asylpolitik in der Europäischen Union, in Müller-Graff (ed.), Europäische Zusammenarbeit in den Bereichen Justiz und Inneres – Der Dritte Pfeiler der Europäischen Union, Baden-Baden (1996), p. 75 et seq.
Breuss, Fritz, Cost and Benefits of EU's Eastern European Enlargement. WIFO Working Paper No. 78, Vienna (1995)
Breuss, Fritz/Tesche, Jean, A General Equilibrium Analysis of East-West Migration: The Case of Austria-Hungary. IEF Working Paper No. 14, Research Institute for European Affairs, University of Economics and Business Administration, Vienna (1996)
Bribosia, Emmanuelle/Weyembergh, Anne, Extradition et Asile: Vers un espace judiciaire européen?, Revue Belge de Droit International 30 (1997), p. 69 et seq.
Brill, Walter L., The 1951 Convention Definition of Refugee Status and the Issue of Agents of Persecution: A Comparative and Human Rights Based Analysis. Unpublished manuscript, University of Geneva (1992)
Brillat, Regis, A New Protocol to the European Social Charter Providing for Collective Complaints, European Human Rights Law Review (1996), p. 53 et seq.
Britz, Gabriele/Schmidt, Marlene, Die institutionalisierte Mitwirkung der Sozialpartner an der Rechtsetzung der Europäischen Gemeinschaft – Herausforderung des gemeinschaftsrechtlichen Demokratieprinzips, Europarecht 1999, p. 22 et seq.
Brownlie, Ian, Principles of Public International Law, 4th ed. Oxford (1990)
Brübach, Thomas, Die Zusammenarbeit der Mitgliedstaaten der Europäischen Union auf dem Gebiet Inneres und Justiz, unter besonderer Berücksichtigung der Asyl- und Einwanderungspolitik sowie der polizeilichen Zusammenarbeit, Aachen (1997)
Buchner, Herbert, Die sozialpolitische Entwicklung der Europäischen Gemeinschaft im Spannungsfeld von hoheitlicher Regelung und tarifautonomer Gestaltung, Recht der Arbeit (1993), p. 193 et seq.
Bunz, Axel/Neuenfeld, Caroline, Europäische Asyl- und Zuwanderungspolitik, Aus Politik und Zeitgeschichte, Beilage zu "Das Parlament", 44 (1994), B 48, p. 37 et seq.
Calavita, Kitty, Italy and the New Immigration, in Cornelius, Wayne A. et al. (eds.), Controlling Immigration: A Global Perspective, Stanford (1994), p. 304 et seq.
Cammilleri, Anne-Francois, La protection sociale en Europe, Paris (1993)
Carlier, Jean-Yves/Vanheule, Dirk (eds.), Europe and Refugees: A Challenge, The Hague, London, Boston (1997)
Carlier, Jean-Yves/Vanheule, Dirk/Hullmann, Klaus and Pena Galiano, Carlos (eds.), Who is a Refugee? A Comparative Case Law Study, The Hague, London, Boston (1997)
Centel, Tankut, The Social Security of the Turkish Workers in Europe within the Framework of the Association Agreement, in Jorens, Yves/Schulte, Bernd (eds.), European Social Security Law and Third-Country Nationals, Brussels (1998), p. 281 et seq.
Cesarani, David/Fulbrook, Mary, Citizenship, Nationality and Migration in Europe, London (1996)

Charpentier, Jean, Les conditions d'accès des étrangers dans l'espace de Schengen, in Institut Européen d'Administration Publique (Edité par Alexis Pauly), Les accords de Schengen: Abolition des frontières intérieures ou menace pour les libertés publiques?, Maastricht (1993), p. 65 et seq.
Charpentier, Louis, L'arrêt "Kalanke", expression du discours dualiste de l'égalité, Revue Trimestrielle de Droit Européen (1996), p. 281 et seq.
Chiodi-Ferro, Ilda, Migration. Eine erweiterte ökonomische Analyse unter Berücksichtigung außerökonomischer Erkenntnisse, Winterthur (1994)
Cholewinski, Ryszard, The Protection of the Right of Economic Migrants to Family Reunion in Europe, International and Comparative Law Quarterly 43 (1994), p. 568 et seq.
Cholewinski, Ryszard, Migrant Workers in International Human Rights Law: Their Protection in Countries of Employment, Oxford (1997)
Chopin, Isabelle, The Starting Line Group: A Harmonised Approach to Fight Racism and to Promote Equal Treatment, European Journal of Migration and Law 1 (1999), p. 111 et seq.
Chopin, Isabelle/Niessen, Jan, Proposals for Legislative Measures to Combat Racism and to Promote Equal Rights in the European Union, Brussels (1998)
Cicekli, Bülent, The Legal Position of Turkish Immigrants in the European Union, Ankara (1998)
Classen, Claus Dieter, Der Verweis auf Drittstaaten – eine offene Flanke der europäischen Asylrechtsabkommen?, Archiv des Völkerrechts 33 (1995), p. 219 et seq.
Clever, Peter, Sozialer Dialog – ein Mittel europäischer Sozialpolitik, Zeitschrift für Sozialhilfe und Sozialgesetzbuch (1996), p. 188 et seq.
Coen, Martin, Abgestufte soziale Integration nach Maastricht, Europäische Zeitschrift für Wirtschaftsrecht (1995), p. 50 et seq.
Coen, Martin, Drittstaatsangehörige im EG-Sozialrecht, Europäisches Arbeits- und Sozialrecht (1997), p. 119 et seq.
Coffey, Peter, Europe: Toward 2001. International Studies in Economics and Econometrics, Dordrecht, London, Boston (1996)
Cohen, Robin, The Cambridge Survey of World Migration, Cambridge (1995)
Coleman, David A., Does Europe Need Immigrants? Population and Work Force Projections, International Migration Review 26 (1992), p. 413 et seq.
Coles, G.J.L., Some Reflections on the Protection of Refugees from Armed Conflict Situations, in Defense of the Alien VII (1985), p. 78 et seq.
Collinson, Sarah, Beyond Borders: West European Migration Policy towards the 21st Century, London (1993)
Collinson, Sarah, Europe and International Migration, London (1994)
Colneric, Ninon, Verbot der Frauendiskriminierung im EG-Recht – Bilanz und Perspektiven, in Däubler, Wolfgang/Bobke, Manfred/Kehrmann, Karl (eds.), Arbeit und Recht, Festschrift für Albert Gnade zum 65. Geburtstag, Köln (1992), p. 627 et seq.
Commission des Recours des Réfugiés, Contentieux des Réfugiés. Jurisprudence du Conseil d'Etat et de la Commission des recours des réfugiés. Année 1998, Fontenay (1999)
Cornelissen, Rob, The Principle of Territoriality and the Community Regulations on Social Security (Regulations 1408/71 and 574/72), Common Market Law Review 33 (1996), p. 439 et seq.
Cornelius, Wayne A./Martin, Philip L. (eds.), Controlling Immigration: A Global Perspective, Stanford (1994)
Council of Europe, Explanatory report on the European Convention on the legal status of migrant workers, Strasbourg (1978)
Council of Europe (ed.), Migrant Workers and their Families: Protection within the European Social Charter, Strasbourg (1996)
Council of Europe (ed.), Social Charter of the 21st Century. Colloquy organised by the Secretariat of the Council of Europe, Human Rights Building 14-16 May 1997, Strasbourg (1997)
Council of Europe (ed.), Short Guide to the Convention on Human Rights, Strasbourg (1998)
Cremona, Marise, Citizens of Third Countries: Movement and Employment of Migrant Workers within the European Union, Legal Issues of European Integration 21 (1995), p. 87 et seq.
Cremona, Marise, Movement of Persons, Establishment and Services, in Maresceau, Marc (ed.), Enlarging the European Union: Relations between the EU and Central and Eastern Europe, London and New York (1997), p. 195 et seq.
Curtin, Deirdre, The Constitutional Structure of the Union: A Europe of Bits and Pieces, Common Market Law Review 30 (1993), p. 17 et seq.

Curtin, Deirdre, Fundamental Social Rights and the Notion of European Citizenship, in Betten, Lammigje/MacDevitt, Delma (eds.), The Protection of Fundamental Social Rights in the European Union (1996), p. 53 et seq.

Curtin, Deirdre/Meijers, Herman, The Principle of Open Government in Schengen and the European Union: Democratic Retrogression, Common Market Law Review 32 (1995), p. 391 et seq.

Czaplinski, Wladyslaw, Energing Regional Refugee Law in Europe, AWR-Bulletin 35 (1997), p. 79 et seq.

Däubler, Wolfgang, Europäische Tarifverträge nach Maastricht, Europäische Zeitschrift für Wirtschaftsrecht (1992), p. 329 et seq.

Dacyl, J.W., A Protection System for Non-Convention Refugees in Europe, in Korella, G.D./Twomey, P.M. (eds.), Towards a European Immigration Policy, Brussels (1993), p. 85 et seq.

De Jong, Cornelius, Towards a European Immigration Policy under the Treaty on European Union, in Korella/Twomey (eds.), Towards a European Immigration Policy, Brussels (1993), p. 45 et seq.

De Jong, Cornelius, Is there a need for a European asylum policy in the absence of an asylum crisis?, unpublished conference paper presented at the Conference on Refugee Rights and Realities, University of Nottingham, 30 November 1996

Delbrück, Jost/Tietje, Christian, Die Frage der unmittelbaren Anwendbarkeit des Assoziationsratsbeschlusses EWG/Türkei Nr. 3/80, Zeitschrift für Ausländerrecht und Ausländerpolitik (ZAR) 1995, p. 29 et seq.

Delpérée, Francis, Les droits sociaux et la Charte Sociale Européenne, Revue des Droits de l'Homme (1968), p. 549 et seq.

Desolre, Guy, La politique migratoire de la communauté, Cahiers de Droit Européen (1990), p. 443 et seq.

Deubner, Christian, Harnessing Differentiation in the EU: Flexibility after Amsterdam, Ebenhausen (1999)

Deubner, Christian, Enhanced Cooperation of EU Member States after Amsterdam, Ebenhausen (1999)

Di Fabio, Udo, Die "Dritte Säule" der Union – Rechtsgrundlagen und Perspektiven der europäischen Polizei und Justizzusammenarbeit, Die Öffentliche Verwaltung (DÖV) 1997, p. 89 et seq.

Dinkel, Reiner Hans/Lebok, Uwe, Demographische Aspekte der vergangenen und zukünftigen Zuwanderung nach Deutschland, Aus Politik und Zeitgeschichte, Beilage zu "Das Parlament", 44 (1994), B 48, p. 27 et seq.

Döring, Diether, Zur Alterssicherung von Zuwanderern in den Ländern der Europäischen Union, Sozialer Fortschritt 43 (1994), p. 239 et seq.

Dörr, Oliver, Das Schengener Durchführungsübereinkommen – ein Fall des Art. 24 Abs. 1 GG, Die Öffentliche Verwaltung (DÖV) 1993, p. 696 et seq.

Dötsch, Jochen, Vereinbarungen der europäischen Sozialpartner, Arbeit und Arbeitsrecht (1998), p. 262 et seq.

Dolvik, John, Europeanisation of Trade Unions-Dynamics and Constraints. Paper presented at the IREC Conference, Copenhagen (1996)

Donges, Jürgen B., Einwanderungspolitik – Möglichkeiten und Grenzen, Bad Homburg (1994)

Donner, J.P.H., Abolition of Border Controls, in Schermers, Henry G. et al., Free Movement of Persons in Europe: Legal Problems and Experiences, Dordrecht, Boston, London (1993), p. 5 et seq.

Doomernik, Jeroen/Penninx, Rinus/Amersfoort, Hans van, A Migration Policy for the Future, Brussels (1997)

Drüke, Luise, Refugee Protection in the Post Cold War Europe, in Institut Européen d'Administration Publique (Edité par Alexis Pauly), Les Accords de Schengen: Abolition des frontières intérieures ou menace pour les libertés publiques?, Maastricht (1993), p. 105 et seq.

Drüke, Luise, Harmonization of Asylum Law and Judicial Control under the Third Pillar, in Bieber/Monar (eds.), Justice and Home Affairs in the European Union: The Development of the Third Pillar, Brussels (1995), p. 167 et seq.

Drzemczewski, Andrew, The Need for a Radical Overhaul, New Law Journal 143 (1993), 125 et seq.

Drzemczewski, Andrew, A Single Court of Human Rights in Strasbourg, Revista Istituto Interamericano de Derechos Humanos (1995), p. 47 et seq.

Drzewicki, Krystof/Krause, Catarina/Rosas, Allan, Social Rights as Human Rights: A European Challenge, Turku (1994)

Duvigneau, Johan Ludwig, From Advisory Opinion 2/94 to the Amsterdam Treaty: Human Rights Protection in the European Union, Legal Issues of European Integration 25 (1999), p. 61 et seq.

Ebsen, Ingwer, Zur Koordinierung der Rechtsdogmatik beim Gebot der Gleichberechtigung von Männern und Frauen zwischen Europäischem Gemeinschaftsrecht und innerstaatlichem Verfassungsrecht, Recht der Arbeit 46 (1993), p. 11 et seq.

Ehlermann, Claus Dieter, Differentiation, Flexibility, Closer Cooperation: The New Provisions of the Amsterdam Treaty, European Law Journal 4 (1998), p. 246 et seq.

Eichengreen, Barry, Thinking about Migration: Notes on European Migration Pressures at the Dawn of the Next Millenium. University of California at Berkeley, Department of Economics, Center for International and Development Economics Research, Working Paper No. C 93-019, Berkeley (1993)

Eichenhofer, Eberhard, Co-ordination of Social Security and Equal Treatment of Men and Women in Employment: Recent Social Security Judgments of the Court of Justice, Common Market Law Review 30 (1993), p. 1021 et seq.

Eichenhofer, Eberhard, Die sozialrechtliche Stellung von Ausländern aus Nicht-EWR- und Nicht-Abkommensstaaten, Zeitschrift für Ausländerrecht und Ausländerpolitik (ZAR) 1996, p. 62 et seq.

Eichenhofer, Eberhard, Das dem Vertrag über die Europäische Union angefügte "Protokoll über die Sozialpolitik", in Ahrens, Hans-Jürgen/Rengeling, Hans-Werner (eds.), Europäisierung des Rechts, Köln, Berlin, Bonn, München (1996), p. 151 et seq.

Eichenhofer, Eberhard, Deutsch-Türkische Sozialrechtsbeziehungen, Zeitschrift für ausländisches und internationales Arbeits- und Sozialrecht (1997), p. 136 et seq.

Eicke, Tim, The Third Country Agreements: The Right to Work and Reside in the First Generation Agreements, in Guild, Elspeth (ed.), The Legal Framework and Social Consequences of Free Movement of Persons in the European Union, The Hague, London, Boston (1999), p. 89 et seq.

Eijsbouts, Willem Thomas, Borders and Democracy: The Schengen Treaties, Yearbook of European Studies (1993), p. 57 et seq.

Einarsen, Terje, The European Convention on Human Rights and the Notion of an Implied Right to de facto Asylum, International Journal of Refugee Law 2 (1990), p. 361 et seq.

Eissen, Marc-André, L'Aspect Institutionnel du Protocole No. 11 à la Convention, Bulletin des droits de l'Homme (1995), p. 3 et seq.

Ellis, Evelyn, Recent Case Law of the Court of Justice on the Equal Treatment of Women and Men, Common Market Law Review 31 (1994), p. 43 et seq.

Ellis, Evelyn, European Community Sex Equality Law, Oxford (1991)

Ellis, Evelyn, Recent Developments in European Community Sex Equality Law, Common Market Law Review 35 (1998), p. 379 et seq.

Elsen, Charles, Schengen et la coopération dans les domaines de la justice et des affaires intérieures: Besoins actuels et options futures, in European Institute of Public Administration (edited by Monica den Boer), The Implementation of Schengen: First the Widening, Now the Deepening, Maastricht (1997), p. 3 et seq.

Enrich Mas, Montserrat, Les droits sociaux dans la jurisprudence de la Cour et de la Commission Européennes des Droits de l'Homme, Revue Trimestrielle des Droits de l'Homme (1992), p. 147 et seq.

Epiney, Astrid, Rechte und Pflichten der Drittausländer, in Heckmann/Tomei (ed.), Freizügigkeit in Europa, Bamberg (1996), p. 56 et seq.

European Council on Refugees and Exiles (ECRE) (eds.), Asylum in Europe: Review of refugee and asylum laws and procedures in selected European countries (II), London (1994)

European Council on Refugees and Exiles (ECRE) (eds.), Comments from the European Council on Refugees and Exiles on the 1995 "burden-sharing" resolution and decision adopted by the Council of the European Union, London (1996)

European Council on Refugees and Exiles (ECRE) (eds.), Position of the European Council on Refugees and Exiles on Temporary Protection in the context of the need for a supplementary refugee definition, International Journal of Refugee Law 9 (1997), p. 534 et seq.

Evans, Andrew, Third-Country Nationals and the Treaty on European Union, European Journal of International Law 5 (1994), p. 199 et seq.

Faist, Thomas, Migration in transnationalen Arbeitsmärkten. Zur Kollektivierung und Fragmentierung sozialer Rechte in Europa, Zeitschrift für Sozialreform 41 (1995), p. 36 et seq.

Falkner, Gerda, The Maastricht Protocol on Social Policy: Theory and Practice, Journal of European Social Policy 6 (1996), p. 1 et seq.

Fassmann, Heinz/Münz, Rainer, Europäische Migration und die Internationalisierung des Arbeitsmarktes, in Innovation und Beharrung in der Arbeitspolitik (1993), p. 19 et seq.

Fassmann, Heinz/Münz, Rainer, Einwanderungsland Österreich?, Wien (1995)

Fastenrath, Ulrich (ed.), KSZE: Dokumente der Konferenz über Sicherheit und Zusammenarbeit in Europa, Loseblattausgabe Neuwied

Felderer, Bernhard, Immigration, Geburtenentwicklung und Wirtschaft, Aus Politik und Zeitgeschichte, Beilage zu "Das Parlament", B 18, 39 (1989), p. 16 et seq.

Fenwick, Helen/Hervey, Tamara K., Sex Equality in the Single Market: New Directions for the European Court of Justice, Common Market Law Review 32 (1995), p. 443 et seq.

Florek, Ludwik/Uscinska, Gertruda, Freedom of Movement for Workers and Social Security in View of the Europe Agreement, in Jorens, Yves/Schulte, Bernd (eds.), European Social Security Law and Third-Country Nationals, Brussels (1998), p. 387 et seq.

Fonteneau, Gérard, Proposals for New Improvements, in Council of Europe (ed.), The Social Charter of the 21st Century. Colloquy organised by the Secretariat of the Council of Europe, Human Rights Building 14-16 May 1997, Strasbourg (1997), p. 80 et seq.

Fragomen, Austin T., The Refugee: A Problem of Definition, Case Western Reserve Journal of International Law 3 (1970), p. 45 et seq.

Franssen, Everhardt/Jacobs, Antoine T., The Question of Representativity in the European Social Dialogue, Common Market Law Review 35 (1998), p. 1295 et seq.

Franz, Wolfgang, Zur ökonomischen Bedeutung von Wanderungen und den Möglichkeiten und Grenzen einer Einwanderungspolitik, Konstanz (1993)

Friedrich-Ebert-Stiftung (ed.), Von der Ausländer- zur Einwanderungspolitik, Bonn (1994)

Friedrich-Ebert-Stiftung (ed.), Europäische Einwanderungspolitik, Bonn (1995)

Friedrich-Ebert-Stiftung (ed.), Einwanderungskonzeption für die Bundesrepublik Deutschland, Bonn (1995)

Fritsch-Oppermann, Sybille (ed.), Konkretionen für eine europäische Einwanderungsgesetzgebung, Loccumer Protokolle 69/96 (1997)

Fronhöfer, Dirk, Das Problem der Binnenflüchtlinge im Schnittpunkt der Menschenrechte, des Humanitären Völkerrechts und internationalen Flüchtlingsrechts, Archiv des öffentlichen Rechts (1996), p. 277 et seq.

Frowein, Jochen Abr., The Protection of Property, in Macdonald, Ronald et al. (ed.), The European System for the Protection of Human Rights, Dordrecht (1993), p. 515 et seq.

Frowein, Jochen Abr., European Convention on Human Rights (1950), Encyclopedia of Public International Law II (1995), p. 188 et seq.

Frowein, Jochen Abr./Peukert, Wolfgang (eds.), Europäische Menschenrechtskonvention, EMRK-Kommentar, 2nd ed., Kehl, Straßburg, Arlington (1996)

Frowein, Jochen Abr./Stein, Torsten (eds.), Die Rechtsstellung von Ausländern nach staatlichem Recht und Völkerrecht, Heidelberg (1987)

Fuchsloch, Christine, Das Verbot der mittelbaren Geschlechtsdiskriminierung – Ableitung, Analyse und exemplarische Anwendung auf staatliche Berufsbildungsförderung, Baden-Baden (1995)

Gacon-Estrada, Hélène, The Cooperation Agreements concluded between the European Community and the Maghreb Countries (Algerie, Morocco, Tunisia), in Jorens, Yves/Schulte, Bernd (eds.), European Social Security Law and Third-Country Nationals, Brussels (1998), p. 323 et seq.

Gächter, August, Auswirkungen einer allfälligen Osterweiterung der Europäischen Union auf die Zuwanderung nach Österreich und auf die Akzeptanz von Zuwanderern. Europa 1996. Auswirkungen einer EU-Osterweiterung. Schriftenreihe Europa des Bundeskanzleramts, Wien (1995), p. 47 et seq.

Gargulla, Tanja, Die arbeits- und aufenthaltsrechtlichen Begünstigungen für osteuropäische Arbeitnehmer und Selbständige durch die Europa-Abkommen – Sein oder Schein?, Informationsbrief Ausländerrecht (1995), p. 181 et seq.

Gaudissait, Marc-André/Sinnaeve, Adinda, The Role of the White Paper in the Preparation of the Eastern Enlargement, in Maresceau, Marc (ed.), Enlarging the European Union: Relations between the EU and Central and Eastern Europe, London and New York (1997), p. 41 et seq.

Gelinsky, Katja, Der Schutz des Eigentums gemäß Art. 1 des Ersten Zusatzprotokolls zur Europäischen Menschenrechtskonvention. Eine Analyse der Rechtsprechung der Straßburger Organe, Berlin (1996)

Gerlach, Axel, Asylverträge in der Europäischen Gemeinschaft. Die asylrechtlichen Regelungen des Dubliner und des zweiten Schengener Übereinkommens, AWR-Bulletin (1991), p. 34 et seq.

Gerlach, Axel, Dubliner Asylrechtskonvention und Schengener Abkommen: Lohnt sich die Ratifikation?, Zeitschrift für Rechtspolitik (1993), p. 164 et seq.

Giegerich, Thomas, Luxemburg, Karlsruhe, Straßburg – Dreistufiger Grundrechtsschutz in Europa?, Zeitschrift für ausländisches öffentliches Recht und Völkerrecht 50 (1990), p. 836 et seq.

Gilbert, Geoffrey, Right of Asylum: A Change of Direction, International and Comparative Law Quarterly 32 (1983), p. 633 et seq.
Gilbert, Geoffrey, The Best Early Warning is Prevention: Refugee Flows and European Responses, International Journal of Refugee Law 9 (1997), p. 207 et seq.
Gilsdorf, Peter, Die Kompetenz der Gemeinschaft zur Angleichung asylrechtlicher Bestimmungen in der EG, Europarecht (1990), p. 65 et seq.
Gimbal, Anke I., Die Zuwanderungspolitik der Europäischen Union. Interessen – Hintergründe – Perspektiven, in Das Europäische Einwanderungskonzept – Strategien und Optionen für Europa, edited by Werner Weidenfeld, Gütersloh (1994), p. 49 et seq.
Giraud, Philippe, L'expérience de la France dans la mise en oeuvre de Schengen, in Hailbronner, Kay/Weil, Patrick (eds.), Von Schengen nach Amsterdam – Auf dem Weg zu einem europäischen Einwanderungs- und Asylrecht. Schriftenreihe der Europäischen Rechtsakademie, Vol. 29, Köln (1999)
Göbel-Zimmermann, Ralph, Völker-, verfassungs- und ausländerrechtliche Rahmenbedingungen des Familiennachzugs, Zeitschrift für Ausländerrecht und Ausländerpolitik (1995), p. 178 et seq.
Goerke, Laszlo/Piazolo, Kathrin, Decision-Making under the EU's Social Chapter, International Review of Law and Economics 18 (1998), p. 217 et seq.
Goldman, Alan H., Justice and Reverse Discrimination, Princeton N.J. (1979)
Goldstein, Mara, Die Kompetenzen der Europäischen Gemeinschaften zur Regelung des Asylrechts – Neuere Entwicklungen in den Gemeinschaften sowie eine Untersuchung der EG-Kompetenz, Frankfurt/M. (1994)
Golsong, Heribert, On the Reform of the Supervisory System of the European Convention on Human Rights, Human Rights Law Journal 13 (1992), p. 265 et seq.
Golsong, Heribert, Internationaler Kommentar zur Europäischen Menschenrechtskonvention, Loseblattausgabe, Köln, München
Gomien, Donna/Harris, Davis/Zwack, Leo, Law and practice of the European Convention on Human Rights and the European Social Charter, Strasbourg (1996)
Goodwin-Gill, Guy S., The Refugee in International Law, 2nd ed., Oxford (1998)
Gornig, Gilbert-Hanno, Das Refoulement-Verbot im Völkerrecht, Wien (1987)
Gouloussis, Dimitrious, The Equality of Treatment and the Relationship between Regulations 1612/68 and 1408/71, in Commission of the European Communities (ed.), Social Security in Europe: Equality between Nationals and Non-Nationals, European Conference Oporto November 1994, Lisbon (1995), p. 75 et seq.
Goybet, Catherine, Police, asile, immigration: L'Union est-elle en panne?, Revue du Marché Commun (1995), p. 73 et seq.
Grabitz, Eberhard/Hilf, Meinhard, Kommentar zum EU-/EG-Vertrag, Loseblatt-Ausgabe, München (1999)
Gräfrath, Bernd, Wie gerecht ist die Frauenquote? Eine praktisch-philosophische Untersuchung, Würzburg (1992)
Grahl-Madsen, Atle, The Status of Refugees in International Law, Vol. 1, Leyden (1966)
Greenawalt, Kent, Discrimination and Reverse Discrimination, New York (1983)
Grief, Nicholas, The Accession of the European Community to the European Convention on Human Rights, in Evans, Malcom D., Aspects of Stathood and Institutionalism in Contemporary Europe, Dartmouth (1997), p. 253 et seq.
Griesbeck, Michael, Migration, Asyl und Schleusertum. Zur Bedeutung des Asylrechts und der Asylpraxis bei der Bekämpfung der Schleuserkriminalität, Zeitschrift für Innere Sicherheit in Deutschland und Europa (1998), p. 266 et seq.
Groeben, Hans von der/Thiesing, Jochen/Ehlermann, Claus-Dieter (eds.), Kommentar zum EWG-Vertrag, 4th ed., Baden-Baden (1991)
Groeben, Hans von der/Thiesing, Jochen/Ehlermann, Claus-Dieter (eds.), Kommentar zum EU-/EG-Vertrag, 5th ed., Baden-Baden (1997 et seq.)
Groenendijk, Kees, Verdrag van Amsterdam en de migratie binnen en naar de Europese Unie. Meer flexibiliteit en meer controle, Migrantenrecht (1997), p. 1 et seq.
Guild, Elspeth/Niessen, Jan, The Developing Immigration and Asylum Policies of the European Union, The Hague, London, Boston (1996)
Guild, Elspeth, The Europe Agreements: Natural Persons and Social Security, in Jorens, Yves/Schulte, Bernd (eds.), European Social Security Law and Third-Country Nationals, Brussels (1998), p. 333 et seq.

Guild, Elspeth, The Europe Agreements: The Right of Establishment in the Central and Eastern European Agreements, in Guild, Elspeth (ed.), The Legal Framework and Social Consequences of Free Movement of Persons in the European Union, The Hague, London, Boston (1999), p. 127 et seq.

Guild, Elspeth, Discretion, Competence and Migration in the European Union, European Journal of Migration and Law 1 (1999), p. 61 et seq.

Guild, Elspeth (ed.), The Legal Framework and Social Consequences of Free Movement of Persons in the European Union, The Hague, London, Boston (1999)

Gusy, Christoph, Möglichkeiten und Grenzen eines effektiven und flexiblen europäischen Einwanderungsrechts, in Das Europäische Einwanderungskonzept – Strategien und Optionen für Europa, edited by Werner Weidenfeld, Gütersloh (1994), p. 127 et seq.

Haberland, Jürgen, Die Entschließungen der Justiz- und Innenminister der Europäischen Union im Bereich der Aufnahme (I)/(II), Zeitschrift für Ausländerrecht und Ausländerpolitik (ZAR) 1996, p. 3 et seq./p. 56 et seq.

Hänlein, Andreas, Kommentar: Fehlende unmittelbare Wirkung der Bestimmungen des Assoziationsratsbeschlusses EWG-Türkei über "Invalidität" und Renten bei "Alter und Tod", Europäisches Arbeits- und Sozialrecht (1997), p. 21 et seq.

Hänlein, Andreas, Die Anwendung der Systeme der Sozialen Sicherheit der EG-Mitgliedstaaten auf türkische Arbeitnehmer nach dem Beschluß Nr. 3/80 des Assoziationsrats EWG/Türkei, Zeitschrift für Ausländerrecht und Ausländerpolitik (1998), p. 21 et seq.

Hänlein, Andreas, Problems concerning Decision No. 3180 of the Council of Association: A Point of View from a EU Perspective, in Jorens, Yves/Schulte, Bernd (eds.), European Social Security Law and Third-Country Nationals, Brussels (1998), p. 299 et seq.

Häußer, Otto, Zur europäischen Dimension des deutschen Ausländerrechts, Verwaltungsarchiv 87 (1996), p. 241 et seq.

Häupler, Ulf, Religion und Integration, Zeitschrift für Ausländerrecht und Ausländerpolitik (ZAR) 1999, p. 32 et seq.

Hathaway, James, The Law of Refugee Status, Toronto, Vancouver (1991)

Hailbronner, Kay, Der Nachzug ausländischer Familienangehöriger und die Schutzpflicht für Ehe und Familie, Juristenzeitung (JZ) 1993, p. 574 et seq.

Hailbronner, Kay, Die Freizügigkeit türkischer Staatsangehöriger nach dem Assoziations-Abkommen EWG/Türkei, Europarecht (1984), p. 54 et seq.

Hailbronner, Kay, Möglichkeiten und Grenzen einer Europäischen Koordinierung des Einreise- und Asylrechts – Ihre Auswirkungen auf das Asylrecht in der Bundesrepublik Deutschland, Baden-Baden (1989)

Hailbronner, Kay, Asylrecht und Asylverfahren im Blick auf den europäischen Binnenmarkt, Anwaltsblatt 1989, p. 485 et seq.

Hailbronner, Kay, Ziele und Schranken einer europäischen Asylrechtskoordinierung, Neue Zeitschrift für Verwaltungsrecht (1989), p. 303 et seq.

Hailbronner, Kay, Asyl- und Einwanderungsrecht in der Europäischen Gemeinschaft. Vorträge, Reden und Berichte aus dem Europa-Institut der Universität des Saarlandes, Saarbrücken (1992)

Hailbronner, Kay, Die Rechtsstellung der De-facto-Flüchtlinge in den EG-Staaten – Rechtsvergleichung und Europäische Harmonisierung, Baden-Baden (1993)

Hailbronner, Kay, Migration Law and Policy within the Third Pillar of the Union Treaty, in Bieber/Monar (eds.), Justice and Home Affairs in the European Union: The Development of the Third Pillar, Brussels (1995), p. 95 et seq.

Hailbronner, Kay, Die EU-Sozialpolitik nach Maastricht, in Randelzhofer, Albrecht/Scholz, Rupert/Wilke, Dieter (eds.), Gedächtnisschrift für Eberhard Grabitz, München (1995), p. 125 et seq.

Hailbronner, Kay, Perspektiven einer europäischen Asylrechtsharmonisierung nach der Maastrichter Gipfelkonferenz, Zeitschrift für Ausländerrecht und Ausländerpolitik (ZAR) 1992, p. 51 et seq.

Hailbronner, Kay, Asyl- und Einwanderungsrecht im europäischen Vergleich/Comparative Law of Asylum and Immigration in Europe/Droit comparé de l'asile et de l'immigration en Europe, Schriftenreihe der Europäischen Rechtsakademie Trier 1, Köln (1992)

Hailbronner, Kay, The Concept of "Safe Country" and Expeditious Asylum Procedures: A Western European Perspective, International Journal of Refugee Law 5 (1993), p. 31 et seq.

Hailbronner, Kay, Rechtsfragen der Aufnahme von "Gewaltflüchtlingen" in Westeuropa – am Beispiel Jugoslawien, Schweizerische Zeitschrift für internationales und europäisches Recht 3 (1993), p. 517 et seq.

Hailbronner, Kay, Visa Regulations and Third-Country Nationals in European Community Law, Common Market Law Review 31 (1994), p. 969 et seq.

Hailbronner, Kay, Die europäische Asylrechtsharmonisierung nach dem Vertrag von Maastricht, Zeitschrift für Ausländerrecht und Ausländerpolitik (1995), p. 3 et seq.

Hailbronner, Kay, Perspektiven einer europäischen Asylrechtsharmonisierung nach dem Vertrag von Maastricht, in Piazolo, Michael/Grosch, Klaus (eds.), Festung oder offene Grenzen? Entwicklung des Einwanderungs- und Asylrechts in Deutschland und Europa, München (1995), p. 71 et seq.

Hailbronner, Kay, Privilegierte Drittstaatsangehörige in der Europäischen Union, in Due, Ole (ed.), Festschrift für Ulrich Everling (1995), p. 399 et seq.

Hailbronner, Kay, Neuere Entwicklungen im europäischen Ausländerrecht, Bonn (1997)

Hailbronner, Kay, Visum für Partner einer gleichgeschlechtlichen Lebensgemeinschaft?, Neue Zeitschrift für Verwaltungsrecht (NVwZ) 1997, p. 460 et seq.

Hailbronner, Kay, Die sozialrechtliche Gleichbehandlung von Drittstaatsangehörigen – ein menschenrechtliches Postulat?, Juristenzeitung (JZ) 1997, p. 397 et seq.

Hailbronner, Kay, Die Kontrolle der Entsendung ausländischer Arbeitnehmer und die Dienstleistungsfreiheit, Europäisches Wirtschafts- und Steuerrecht (EWS) 1997, p. 401 et seq.

Hailbronner, Kay, European Immigration and Asylum Law under the Amsterdam Treaty, Common Market Law Review 35 (1998), p. 1047 et seq.

Hailbronner, Kay, Die Neuregelung der Bereiche Freier Personenverkehr, Asylrecht und Einwanderung, in Hummer, Waldemar (ed.), Die Europäische Union nach dem Vertrag von Amsterdam (1998), p. 179 et seq.

Hailbronner, Kay, Asylum: Experiences, Problems and Management Techniques in the European Union, in Monar, Joerg (ed.), The New Transatlantic Agenda and the Future of EU-US Relations, London, The Hague, Boston (1998), p. 127 et seq.

Hailbronner, Kay, The Treaty of Amsterdam and Migration Law, European Journal of Migration and Law 1 (1999), p. 9 et seq.

Hailbronner, Kay, AuslR, Ausländerrecht, Kommentar, 3 Bände, Loseblattsammlung, Stand: 20. Ergänzungslieferung, Heidelberg, August 1999

Hailbronner, Kay/Klein, Eckart/Magiera, Siegfried/Müller-Graff, Peter-Christian, Handkommentar zum Vertrag über die Europäische Union (EUV/EGV), Köln, Berlin, Bonn, München (1998)

Hailbronner, Kay/Ress, Georg/Stein, Thorsten (eds.), Staat und Völkerrechtsordnung, Festschrift für Karl Doehring, Berlin (1989)

Hailbronner, Kay/Klos, Christian/Münz, Rainer/Ulrich, Ralf (eds.), Potentiale für die zukünftige Zuwanderung von Ausländern nach Deutschland, insbesondere im Zusammenhang mit dem Nachzug von Familienangehörigen. Studie im Auftrag der Bundesforschungsanstalt für Landeskunde und Raumordnung, Bonn (1997)

Hailbronner, Kay/Thiery, Claus, Schengen II and Dublin: Responsibility for Asylum Applications in Europe, Common Market Law Review 34 (1997), p. 957 et seq.

Hailbronner, Kay/Thiery, Claus, Schengen II und Dublin – Der zuständige Asylstaat in Europa, Zeitschrift für Ausländerrecht und Ausländerpolitik (ZAR) 1997, p. 55 et seq.

Hailbronner, Kay/Thiery, Claus, Amsterdam – Vergemeinschaftung der Sachbereiche Freier Personenverkehr, Asylrecht und Einwanderung sowie Überführung des Schengen-Besitzstandes auf EU-Ebene, Europarecht 1998, p. 583 et seq.

Hailbronner, Kay/Weil, Patrick (eds.), Von Schengen nach Amsterdam – Auf dem Weg zu einem europäischen Einwanderungs- und Asylrecht. From Schengen to Amsterdam – Towards a European Immigration and Asylum Legislation. De Schengen à Amsterdam – Vers une législation européenne en matière d'immigration et asile. Schriftenreihe der Europäischen Rechtsakademie Trier, Vol. 29, Köln (1999)

Harris, David, The European Social Charter, New York (1984)

Harris, David, A Fresh Impetus for the European Social Charter, International and Comparative Law Quarterly 41 (1992), p. 659 et seq.

Harris, David, The European Social Charter and Social Rights in the European Union, in Betten, Lammigje/MacDevitt, Delma (eds.), The Protection of Fundamental Social Rights in the European Union (1996), p. 107 et seq.

Harris, David, The collective complaints procedure, in Council of Europe (ed.), The Social Charter of the 21st Century. Colloquy organised by the Secretariat of the Council of Europe, Human Rights Building 14-16 May 1997, Strasbourg (1997), p. 100 et seq.

Hartley, Trevor Clayton, The foundations of European Community law: an introduction to the constitutional and administrative law of the European Community, Oxford (1994)

Heckmann, Friedrich/Bosswick, Wolfgang (eds.), Migration Policies: A Comparative Perspective, Bamberg (1994)
Heckmann, Friedrich/Tomei, Veronica (eds.), Freizügigkeit in Europa – Migrations- und europapolitische Aspekte des Schengen-Vertrags, Bamberg (1996)
Heinelt, Hubert (ed.), Zuwanderungspolitik in Europa. Nationale Politiken, Gemeinsamkeiten und Unterschiede, Opladen (1994)
Heinze, Meinhard, Die Rechtsgrundlagen des sozialen Dialogs auf Gemeinschaftsebene, Zeitschrift für Arbeitsrecht (1997), p. 505 et seq.
Hendry, Ian D., The Third Pillar of Maastricht: Cooperation in the Fields of Justice and Home Affairs, German Yearbook of International Law 36 (1993), p. 295 et seq.
Hepple, Bob A., (ed.), Discrimination: The Limits of Law, London (1992)
Hildebrandt, Achim, Das Visumregime im Schengener Vertragswerk, in Heckmann, Friedrich/Tomei, Veronica (eds.), Freizügigkeit in Europa – Migrations- und europapolitische Aspekte des Schengen-Vertrags, Bamberg (1996), p. 43 et seq.
Hillgenberg, Hartmut, Flüchtlinge als Herausforderung für Europa. Ansätze für eine Politik der Schutzgewährung an Kriegs- und Bürgerkriegsflüchtlinge, Europa-Archiv (1994), p. 537 et seq.
Hobe, Stephan, Law of Asylum: A Solution to the Migration Problem? A Study Concerning Aspects of Public International and European Law with Regard to Aliens and Asylum under Special Consideration of the Law of the European States and the United States of America, German Yearbook of International Law (1993), p. 60 et seq.
Höland, Armin, Partnerschaftliche Setzung und Durchführung von Recht in der Europäischen Gemeinschaft – Die Beteiligung der Sozialpartner nach dem Maastrichter Sozialabkommen, Zeitschrift für ausländisches und internationales Arbeits- und Sozialrecht (1995), p. 425 et seq.
Hönekopp, Elmar, Labour Migration to Germany from Central and Eastern Europe – Old and New Trends, in IAB topics No. 23, labour market research, Institute for Employment research, Nürnberg (1997)
Hönekopp, Elmar, The New Labour Migration from Eastern Europe, Nürnberg (1998)
Hof, Bernd, Europa im Zeichen der Migration. Szenarien zur Bevölkerungs- und Arbeitsmarktentwicklung in der Europäischen Gemeinschaft bis 2020, Köln (1993)
Hof, Bernd, Möglichkeiten und Grenzen der Eingliederung von Zuwanderern in den deutschen Arbeitsmarkt, Aus Politik und Zeitgeschichte, Beilage zu "Das Parlament", 44 (1994) B 48, p. 11 et seq.
Hof, Bernd, Zuwanderungsbedarf der Länder der Europäischen Union, in Friedrich-Ebert-Stiftung (ed.), Europäische Einwanderungspolitik, Bonn (1995), p. 7 et seq.
Hoffmann, Holger, Europäische Flüchtlingspolitik – Die Verträge von Dublin, Schengen und Amsterdam – Praxiserfahrungen und Perspektiven, Informationsbrief Ausländerrecht (InfAuslR) 1999, p. 94 et seq.
Hofmann, Rainer, International Humanitarian Law and the Law of Refugees and Internally Displaced Persons, in: European Commission, Law in humanitarian crises (I). How can international humanitarian law be made effective in armed conflict?, Luxembourg (1995), p. 247 et seq.
Holborn, Louise W., Refugees: A Problem of our Time, Vol. 1, Metuchen N.J. (1975)
Holnsteiner, Erich, Die Zusammenarbeit im Bereich der EU-Justiz- und Innenpolitik in der Osterweiterungsperspektive. Europa 1996. Auswirkungen einer EU-Osterweiterung auf die zweite und dritte Säule. Schriften Europa des Bundeskanzleramts, Wien (1995), p. 61 et seq.
Hoogenboom, Thomas, Integration into Society and Free Movement of Non-EC Nationals, European Journal of International Law 3 (1992), p. 36 et seq.
Hornung-Draus, Renate, Erfahrungen und Perspektiven des sozialen Dialogs: Das Beispiel Euro-Betriebsräte, Europäisches Arbeits- und Sozialrecht 1994, p. 14 et seq.
Hornung-Draus, Renate, Die Zukunft des Sozialen Dialogs, Europäisches Arbeits- und Sozialrecht 1996, p. 198 et seq.
Huber, Bertold, Asyl- und Ausländerrecht in der Europäischen Gemeinschaft, Neue Zeitschrift für Verwaltungsrecht (NVwZ) 1992, p. 618 et seq.
Huber, Bertold, Das Schengener Durchführungsübereinkommen und seine Auswirkungen auf das Ausländer- und Asylrecht, Neue Zeitschrift für Verwaltungsrecht (NVwZ) 1996, p. 1069 et seq.
Huber, Bertold, Das Dubliner Übereinkommen, Neue Zeitschrift für Verwaltungsrecht (NVwZ) 1998, p. 150 et seq.
Huber, Bertold, Handbuch des Ausländer- und Asylrechts, 2 Bände, München (1998); Stand: July 1999
Hubert, Patrick, De Schengen à Amsterdam: Questions juridiques et solutions institutionnelles, in Hailbronner, Kay/Weil, Patrick (eds.), Von Schengen nach Amsterdam – Auf dem Weg zu einem

europäischen Einwanderungs- und Asylrecht. Schriftenreihe der Europäischen Rechtsakademie Trier, Vol. 29, Köln (1999), p. 65 et seq.

Hughes, Jane and Liebaut, Fabrice, Legal and Social Conditions for Asylum Seekers and Refugees in Western European Countries, Danish Refugee Council, January 1997

Hughes, Jane and Liebaut, Fabrice, Detention of Asylum Seekers in Europe: Analysis and Perspectives, The Hague, London, Boston (1998)

Hummer, Waldemar, Flüchtlinge im Europäischen Binnenmarkt, Zeitschrift für Rechtsvergleichung, Internationales Privatrecht und Europarecht (1991), p. 129 et seq.

Hummer, Waldemar (ed.), Die Europäische Union nach dem Vertrag von Amsterdam, Wien (1998)

Husmann, Manfred, Europa-Abkommen – dargestellt am Abkommen mit Polen, Zeitschrift für Sozialreform 1998, p. 100 et seq.

Husmann, Manfred, The Right to Freedom of Movement for Workers by Virtue of the Europe Agreements, in Jorens, Yves/Schulte, Bernd (eds.), European Social Security Law and Third-Country Nationals, Brussels (1998), p. 361 et seq.

ICMPD (ed.), Towards a Joint European Visa Regime, Vienna (1998)

Ipsen, Knut, Völkerrecht, 4th ed., München (1999)

Isele, Hellmut Georg, Die Europäische Sozialcharta. Auf dem Weg von den allgemeinen Menschenrechten zu den sozialen Menschenrechten, Wiesbaden (1967)

Jacobi, Otto, Der soziale Dialog in der Europäischen Union, in Mesch, Michael (ed.), Sozialpartnerschaft und Arbeitsbeziehungen in Europa, Wien (1995), p. 257 et seq.

Jacobs, Francis G., European Community Law and the European Convention on Human Rights, in Curtin, Deirdre/Henkels, Ton (eds.), Institutional Dynamics of European Integration, Essays in Honour of Henry G. Schermers, Vol. II, Dordrecht, Boston, London (1994), p. 561 et seq.

Jacobs, Francis G./White, Robin C.A., The European Convention on Human Rights, 2nd ed., Oxford (1996)

Jäger, Markus, The Additional Protocol to the European Social Charter Providing for a System of Collective Complaints, Leiden Journal of International Law 10 (1997), p. 69 et seq.

Jahn, Eberhardt, Migration Movement, Encyclopedia of Public International Law 8 (1985), p. 377 et seq.

Jaspers, Teun, The Perspective of Third-Country Nationals under European Law with Regard to Social Security Issues, in Jorens, Yves/Schulte, Bernd (eds.), European Social Security Law and Third-Country Nationals, Brussels (1998), p. 485 et seq.

Joly, Danièle, The Porous Dam: European Harmonization on Asylum in the Nineties, International Journal of Refugee Law 6 (1994), p. 159 et seq.

Jorens, Yves, Social security, non-discrimination and property, in Van den Bogaert, Stefaan (ed.), Social Security, Non-Discrimination and Property, Antwerpen-Apeldoorn (1997), p. 15 et seq.

Jorens, Yves/Schulte, Bernd (eds.), European Social Security Law and Third-Country Nationals, Brussels (1998)

Joubert, Chantal/Bevers, Hans (eds.), Schengen Investigated: A Comparative Interpretation of the Schengen Provisions on International Police Cooperation in the Light of the European Convention on Human Rights, The Hague, London, Boston (1996)

Kälin, Walter, Das Prinzip des Non-Refoulement, Frankfurt (1982)

Kälin, Walter, Nichteintreten auf Asylgesuche bei fehlenden Ausweispapieren oder illegalem Aufenthalt, Asyl (1988), p. 23 et seq.

Kälin, Walter, Grundriss des Asylverfahrens, Basel (1990)

Kälin, Walter, Refugees and Civil Wars: Only a Matter of Interpretation?, International Journal of Refugee Law 3 (1991), p. 435 et seq.

Kälin, Walter, Towards a Concept of Temporary Protection. A study commissioned by UNHCR (Division of International Protection), Bern, 12 November 1996

Kälin, Walter/Achermann, Alberto, Rückkehr von Gewaltflüchtlingen in Sicherheit und Würde. Ein neues Instrument der Flüchtlingsaußenpolitik?, Bern (1992)

Kahn-Freund, Otto, The European Social Charter, in Jacobs, F.G. (ed.), European Law and the Individual, Amsterdam, New York, Oxford (1976), p. 10 et seq.

Kaligin, Thomas, Tätigkeit von Bauunternehmen aus Polen und der CSFR in Deutschland, Neue Zeitschrift für Arbeitsrecht (1992), p. 1111 et seq.

Karapuu, Heikki/Rosas, Allan, Economic, Social and Cultural Rights in Finland, in Rosas, Allan (ed.), International Human Rights Norms in Domestic Law: Finnish and Polish Perspectives, Helsinki (1990), p. 195 et seq.

Karl, Wolfrum, Vertrag und spätere Praxis im Völkerrecht, Berlin (1983)

Kattau, Thomas, Social Rights in Europe – the Cutting Edge of Human Rights, Romain Journal of International Affairs (1995), p. 72 et seq.

Keller, Berndt, Europäische Arbeits- und Sozialpolitik, München (1997)

Keller, Berndt/Soerries, Bernd, The New Social Dialogue: New Concepts, First Results and Future Perspectives, in Flood, Patrick/Heraty, Noreen/Morley, Michael/McCurtin, Sarah (eds.), The European Union and the Employment Relationship, Dublin (1997), p. 17 et seq.

Keller, Berndt/Soerries, Bernd, The Sectoral Social Dialogue and European Social Policy – More Phantasy Less Facts, European Journal of Industrial Relations 4 (1998), p. 18 et seq.

Kerber, Karoline, Temporary Protection: An Assessment of the Harmonization Policies of European Union Member States, International Journal of Refugee Law 9 (1997), p. 453 et seq.

Kerber, Karoline, Die vorübergehende Schutzgewährung in der Europäischen Union, Leipzig (1998)

Kessler, Francis/Meyer, Francis, La dynamique de l'Article 118a du Traité de Rome, Revue Internationale de Droit Economique 2 (1992), p. 129 et seq.

King, Russel (ed.), Mass Migration in Europe: The Legacy and the Future, Chichester (1995)

Kjonstad, Asbjorn, Social Rights as Property-Cases from Germany, Norway and the European Court of Human Rights, in Van den Bogaert, Stefaan (ed.), Social Security, Non-Discrimination and Property, Antwerpen-Apeldoorn (1997), p. 75 et seq.

Kliemann, Annette, Die europäische Sozialintegration nach Maastricht, Baden-Baden (1997)

Klos, Christian, Rahmenbedingungen und Gestaltungsmöglichkeiten der Europäischen Migrationspolitik, Konstanz (1998)

Klos, Christian, The potential of migrants with family links in Germany, in Hailbronner, Kay/Klos, Christian/Münz, Rainer/Ulrich, Ralf (eds.), Potentiale für die zukünftige Zuwanderung von Ausländern nach Deutschland, insbesondere im Zusammenhang mit dem Nachzug von Familienangehörigen. Studie im Auftrag der Bundesforschungsanstalt für Landeskunde und Raumordnung, Bonn (1997), p. 56 et seq.

Klose, Hans-Ulrich (ed.), Zuwanderung – Möglichkeiten und Grenzen, Bonn (1994)

Koenig, Christian, Europäische Sozialunion als Bewährungsprobe der supranationalen Gerichtsbarkeit, Europarecht (1994), p. 175 et seq.

Koenig, Christian/Pechstein, Matthias, Die Europäische Union. Die Verträge von Maastricht und Amsterdam, 2nd ed., Tübingen (1998)

Koll, Michael/Wirmer, Anton, Arbeitsschutz und europäische Einigung, Zeitschrift für Sozialhilfe und Sozialgesetzbuch (1993), p. 236 et seq.

Kolvenbach, Walter, Vom "Europäischen Betriebsrat" zum "Europäischen Ausschuß", Recht der Arbeit 47 (1994), p. 279 et seq.

Kolvenbach, Walter, Der soziale Dialog in der Gemeinschaft 1995: Eine Bestandsaufnahme, Soziales Europa 2/95, Brüssel (1996)

Kolvenbach, Walter, Mitteilung "Anpassung und Förderung des Sozialen Dialogs auf Gemeinschaftsebene", Brüssel (1998)

Konzen, Horst, Der europäische Einfluß auf das deutsche Arbeitsrecht nach dem Vertrag über die Europäische Union, Europäische Zeitschrift für Wirtschaftsrecht (1995), p. 39 et seq.

Korella, Gina D./Twomey, Patrick M. (eds.), Towards a European Immigration Policy, Brussels (1993)

Koser, Khalid/Lutz, Helma, The New Migration in Europe. Social Constructions and Social Realities, London, Amsterdam (1998)

Koser, Khalid/Walsh, Martha and Black, Richard, Temporary Protection and the Assisted Return of Refugees from the European Union, International Journal of Refugee Law 10 (1998), p. 444 et seq.

Koslowski, Rey, Intra-EU Migration, Citizenship and Political Union, Journal of Common Market Studies (1994), p. 369 et seq.

Kpenou, Cécil, Refugees: A Challenge for Europe, in European Institute of Public Administration (edited by Monica den Boer), The Implementation of Schengen: First the Widening, Now the Deepening, Maastricht (1997), p. 87 et seq.

Kreimer de Fries, Joachim, EU-Teilzeitvereinbarung – kein gutes Omen für die Zukunft der europäischen Verhandlungsebenen, Arbeit und Recht 45 (1997), p. 314 et seq.

Kühne, Hans Heiner, Kriminalitätsbekämpfung durch innereuropäische Grenzkontrollen, Trier (1991)

Kugelmann, Dieter, Spielräume und Chancen einer europäischen Einwanderungspolitik, Zeitschrift für Ausländerrecht und Ausländerpolitik (1998), p. 243 et seq.

Kuhn, Heike, Die soziale Dimension der Europäischen Gemeinschaft, Berlin (1996)

Kuschel, Hans-Dieter, Die Niederlassungsfreiheit für Unternehmen der Europäischen Gemeinschaft in den Europaabkommen der EG mit der CSFR, Polen und Ungarn, Europäische Zeitschrift für Wirtschaftsrecht (1992), p. 511 et seq.

Kyle, David, Transparent Economies and Invisible Workers: Human Smuggling under Global Economic Liberalism. Dilemmas of Immigration Control in a Globalizing World, European University Institute, Florence 11-12 June 1998
Kyriazis, Georgios, Die Sozialpolitik der Europäischen Wirtschaftsgemeinschaft in bezug auf die Gleichberechtigung männlicher und weiblicher Erwerbstätiger, Berlin (1990)
Lambert, Hélène, Seeking Asylum: Comparative Law and Practice in Selected European Countries, Dordrecht (1995)
Lang, Gernot, Das Gemeinschaftsrecht der Drittstaatsangehörigen, Baden-Baden (1998)
Lang, Gernot, Zu den Rechtswirkungen des Vertrags von Amsterdam auf den Rechtsstatus der Drittstaatsangehörigen, Zeitschrift für Ausländerrecht und Ausländerpolitik (ZAR) 1998, p. 59 et seq.
Langenfeld, Christine, Die Gleichbehandlung von Mann und Frau im Europäischen Gemeinschaftsrecht, Baden-Baden (1990)
Langer, Rose, Sozialpolitik, in Bergmann, Jan/Lenz, Christofer (eds.), Der Amsterdamer Vertrag. Eine Kommentierung der Neuerungen des EU- und EG-Vertrages, Köln (1998), p. 93 et seq.
Langer, Rose, Negotiations with Third States, in Jorens, Yves/Schulte, Bernd (eds.), European Social Security Law and Third-Country Nationals, Brussels (1998), p. 441 et seq.
Langhammer, Rolf, Die Assoziierungsabkommen mit der CSFR, Polen und Ungarn: wegweisend oder abweisend?, Kieler Diskussionsbeiträge des Instituts für Weltwirtschaft No. 182 (1992), p. 15 et seq.
Langrish, Sally, The Treaty of Amsterdam: Selected Highlights, European Law Review 23 (1998), p. 3 et seq.
Layton-Henry, Zig (ed.), The Political Rights of Migrant Workers in Western Europe, London (1990)
Lederer, Harald, Illegal Migration: Why does it exist and what do we know about Numbers and Trends?, in Europäisches Forum für Migrationsstudien (ed.), On the Politics and Economics of Illegal Migration, Hamburg (1997), p. 2 et seq.
Legomsky, Stephen H., Immigration and Refugee Law and Policy, Westbury NY (1997)
Lehnguth, Gerold/Maaßen, Hans-Georg/Schieffer, Martin, Rückführung und Rückübernahme – Die Rückübernahmeabkommen der Bundesrepublik Deutschland, Starnberg (1998)
Lemmens, Paul, The decision of 16 September 1996 in the Gaygusuz case situated in the case law of the European Court of Human Rights, in Van den Bogaert, Stefaan (ed.), Social Security, Non-Discrimination and Property, Antwerpen-Apeldoorn (1997), p. 25 et seq.
Lenaerts, Koen, Fundamental Rights to be Included in a Community Catalogue, European Law Review 16 (1991), p. 367 et seq.
Lenaerts, Koen, L'Egalité de Traitement en Droit Communautaire. Un principe unique aux apparences multiples, Cahiers de Droit Européen 27 (1991), p. 3 et seq.
Lepoivre, Marc, Le domaine de la justice et des affaires intérieures dans la perspective de la conférence intergouvernementale de 1996, Cahiers de Droit Européen (1995), p. 323 et seq.
Lidal, Bengt, Proposals for further improvements, in Council of Europe (ed.), The Social Charter of the 21st Century. Colloquy organised by the Secretariat of the Council of Europe, Human Rights Building 14-16 May 1997, Strasbourg (1997), p. 70 et seq.
Lippert, Barbara, Soziale Vergünstigungen und Arbeitnehmerfreizügigkeit in Europa, Aachen (1995)
Lipps, Maren Bettina, Niederlassungsrecht und Unionsbürgerschaft für Drittstaater in der Europäischen Union? Eine vergleichende Studie zur Aufenthaltsverfestigung in Deutschland, Frankreich und Großbritannien, Baden-Baden (1999)
Locheler, Helmut, Die Fortentwicklung des Rechts der EU durch den Amsterdam-Vertrag, Juristische Schulung (JUS) 1998, p. 392 et seq.
Lörcher, Klaus, The social partners' opinion, in Council of Europe (ed.), The Social Charter of the 21st Century. Colloquy organised by the Secretariat of the Council of Europe, Human Rights Building 14-16 May 1997, Strasbourg (1997), p. 130 et seq.
Lyon-Caen, Antoine, Social Security and the Principle of Equal Treatment in the EC Treaty and Regulation 1408/71, in Commission of the European Communities (ed.), Social Security in Europe: Equality between Nationals and Non-Nationals, European Conference Oporto November 1994, Lisbon (1995), p. 45 et seq.
Maaßen, Hans-Georg, Die Rechtsstellung des Asylbewerbers im Völkerrecht – Überlegungen zu den völkerrechtlichen Rahmenbedingungen einer europäischen Asylrechtsharmonisierung, Frankfurt/M. (1997)
Mäder, Werner, Maastricht II – Die soziale Dimension, in Schulte, Bernd/Mäder, Werner (eds.), Die Regierungskonferenz Maastricht II, Perspektiven für die Sozialgemeinschaft, Bonn (1996), p. 66 et seq.

Magiera, Siegfried, Die Beseitigung der Personenkontrollen an den Binnengrenzen der Europäischen Union, in Burmeister, Joachim (ed.), Verfassungsstaatlichkeit, Festschrift für Klaus Stern, München (1997), p. 1317 et seq.
Mahmood, Shiraz, The Schengen Information System: An Inequitable Data Protection Regime, International Journal of Refugee Law 7 (1995), p. 179 et seq.
Maidowski, Ulrich, Umgekehrte Diskriminierung – Quotenregelungen zur Frauenförderung im öffentlichen Dienst und in den politischen Parteien, Berlin (1989)
Majone, Giandomenico, The European Community between Social Policy and Social Regulation, EUI Working Paper SPS No. 92/97, Florence (1993)
Malinverni, Giorgio, La réforme du méchanisme de contrôle institué par la Convention européenne des droits de l'homme, Schweizerisches Zentralblatt für Staats- und Verwaltungsrecht 1997, p. 289 et seq.
Maresceau, Marc, Europe Agreements: A New Form of Cooperation between the European Community and Central and Eastern Europe, in Müller-Graff, Peter-Christian (ed.), East Central European States and the European Communities: Legal Adaptation to the Market Economy, Baden-Baden (1993), p. 209 et seq.
Maresceau, Marc/Montaguti, Elisabetta, The Relations between the European Union and Central and Eastern Europe: A Legal Appraisal, Common Market Law Review 32 (1995), p. 1327 et seq.
Marinho, Clotilde and Heinonen, Matti, Dublin after Schengen: Allocating Responsibility for Examining Asylum Applications in Practice, in European Institute of Public Administration (1998), 3, p. 2 et seq.
Martinez, Miguel Angel, First Session: The Charter of Fundamental Social Rights, in Council of Europe (ed.), The Social Charter of the 21st Century. Colloquy organised by the Secretariat of the Council of Europe, Human Rights Building 14-16 May 1997, Strasbourg (1997), p. 15 et seq.
Marugg, Michael, Völkerrechtliche Definitionen des Ausdrucks "Flüchtling", Basel (1990)
Marx, Reinhard, Temporary Protection: Refugees from former Yugoslavia: International Protection or Solution Oriented Approach?, European Council on Refugees and Exiles (ECRE), London, June 1994
Masing, Johannes, Methodische Grundlagen für die Auslegung der Genfer Flüchtlingskonvention, in Grawert, Rolf/Schlink, Bernhard/Wahl, Rainer/Wieland, Joachim (eds.), Offene Staatlichkeit, Festschrift für Ernst-Wolfgang Böckenförde zum 65. Geburtstag, Berlin (1995), p. 51 et seq.
Matscher, Franz (ed.), The Implementation of Economic and Social Rights: National, International and Comparative Aspects, Kehl am Rhein (1991)
Maydell von, Bernd, Treatment of Third-Country Nationals in the Member States of the European Union and the European Economic Area in Terms of Social Law, in Commission of the European Communities (ed.), Social Security in Europe: Equality between Nationals and Non-Nationals, European Conference Oporto November 1994, Lisbon (1995), p. 137 et seq.
Maydell von, Bernd, Discrimination in domestic social security law of the Member States of the European Union, in Van den Bogaert, Stefaan (ed.), Social Security, Non-Discrimination and Property, Antwerpen-Apeldoorn (1997), p. 89 et seq.
Maydell von, Bernd/Schulte, Bernd (eds.), Treatment of Third-Country Nationals in the EU and EEA Member States in Terms of Social Security Law, Leuven (1995)
Mayer, Udo, Werkvertragsarbeitnehmer aus Osteuropa, Betriebsberater (BB) 1993, p. 1428 et seq.
Mazal, Wolfgang, The Austrian background of the case Gaygusuz and the consequences of the Gaygusuz judgement for Austria, in Van den Bogaert, Stefaan (ed.), Social Security, Non-Discrimination and Property, Antwerpen-Apeldoorn (1997), p. 51 et seq.
McCrudden, Christopher, The Effectiveness of European Equality Law: National Mechanisms for Enforcing Gender Equality Law in the Light of European Requirements, Oxford Journal of Legal Studies 13 (1993), p. 320 et seq.
Meijers, Herman et al., Schengen: Internationalisation of Central Chapters of the Law on Aliens, Refugees, Privacy, Security and the Police, Dordrecht (1991)
Meijers, Herman et al., A new immigration law for Europe? The 1992 London and 1993 Copenhagen Rules on Immigration. Standing Committee of Experts in International Immigration, Refugee and Criminal Law, Utrecht (1993)
Meijers, Herman et al., Democracy, Migrants and Police in the European Union. The 1996 IGC and Beyond, Forum, Utrecht (1997)
Meissner, Doris M. et al., International Migration Challenges in a New Era: Policy Perspectives and Priorities for Europe, Japan, North America and the International Community, New York (1993)

Menke, Matthias, Bedingungen einer Asylgesetzgebung der Europäischen Gemeinschaft, Baden-Baden (1993)
Meyring, Bernd, Die Reform der Bereiche Justiz und Inneres durch den Amsterdamer Vertrag, Europarecht (1999), p. 309 et seq.
Miehsler, Herbert, The European Social Charter and the Civil Servants' Right to Strike: The German Case, in Ius Humanitas, Festschrift für Alfred Verdross, Berlin (1980), p. 547 et seq.
Möschel, Wernhard, Europapolitik zwischen deutscher Romantik und gallischer Klarheit, Aus Politik und Zeitgeschichte, Beilage zu "Das Parlament", 45 (1995), B 3-4, p. 10 et seq.
Monar, Joerg, Justice and Home Affairs in the Treaty of Amsterdam: Reform at the Price of Fragmentation, European Law Review 23 (1998), p. 320 et seq.
Monar, Joerg/Morgan, Roger, The Third Pillar of the European Union: Cooperation in the Fields of Justice and Home Affairs, Brussels (1994)
Moore, Matthew, Freedom of Movement and Migrant Workers' Social Security: An Overview of the Court's Jurisprudence 1992-1997, Common Market Law Review 35 (1998), p. 409 et seq.
Moore, Matthew, Free Movement of Persons: Key Developments in the European Parliament during 1998, European Journal of Migration and Law 1 (1999), p. 103 et seq.
Müller-Graff, Peter-Christian (ed.), East Central European States and the European Communities: Legal Adaptation to the Market Economy, Baden-Baden (1993)
Müller-Graff, Peter-Christian, The Legal Bases of the Third Pillar and its Position in the Framework of the Union Treaty, Common Market Law Review 31 (1994), p. 493 et seq.
Müller-Graff, Peter-Christian, The Dublin Convention: Pioneer and Lesson for Third Pillar Conventions, in Bieber/Monar (eds.), Justice and Home Affairs in the European Union: The Development of the Third Pillar, Brussels (1995), p. 65 et seq.
Müller-Graff, Peter-Christian, Europäische Zusammenarbeit in den Bereichen Justiz und Inneres – Funktion, Ausgestaltung und Entwicklungsoptionen des Dritten Pfeilers der Europäischen Union, in Müller-Graff (ed.), Europäische Zusammenarbeit in den Bereichen Justiz und Inneres – Der Dritte Pfeiler der Europäischen Union, Baden-Baden (1996), p. 11 et seq.
Müller-Graff, Peter-Christian, Justiz und Inneres nach Amsterdam – Die Neuerungen in erster und dritter Säule, integration 20 (1997), p. 271 et seq.
Müller-Graff, Peter-Christian, Legal Framework for Relations between the European Union and Central and Eastern Europe: General Aspects, in Maresceau, Marc (ed.), Enlarging the European Union: Relations between the EU and Central and Eastern Europe, London and New York (1997), p. 27 et seq.
Münz, Rainer, Bevölkerung und Wanderung in Europa, in Bade, Klaus J. (ed.), Das Manifest der 60: Deutschland und die Einwanderung, München (1994), p. 102 et seq.
Münz, Rainer/Ulrich, Ralf, Changing Patterns of Migration: The Case of Germany 1945-1995. Ethnic Origins, Demographic Structure, Future Prospects, Frankfurt (1995)
Münz, Rainer/Weiner, Myron (eds.), Migrants, Refugees and Foreign Policy, Oxford (1997)
Muus, Philip, International Migration within and towards the European Economic Area (EEA) – Past Trends and Expectations for Future International Migration, in Commission of the European Communities (ed.), Social Security in Europe: Equality between Nationals and Non-Nationals, European Conference Oporto November 1994, Lisbon (1995), p. 155 et seq.
Muus, Philip (ed.), Exclusion and Inclusion of Refugees in Contemporary Europe. Comparative Studies in Migration and Ethnic Relations, Utrecht (1997)
Nadifi, Abdeladim, Le statut juridique des travailleurs maghrébins résidant dans la CEE, Revue du Marché Commun (1989), p. 289 et seq.
Nanz, Klaus-Peter, The Harmonization of Asylum and Immigration Legislation within the Third Pillar of the Union Treaty: A Stocktaking, in Monar/Morgan (eds.), The Third Pillar of the European Union, Brussels (1994), p. 123 et seq.
Nanz, Klaus-Peter, Das Schengener Übereinkommen. Personenfreizügigkeit in integrationspolitischer Perspektive, integration 17 (1994), p. 92 et seq.
Nanz, Klaus-Peter, Schengener Übereinkommen und Personenfreizügigkeit, Zeitschrift für Ausländerrecht und Ausländerpolitik (ZAR) 1994, p. 99 et seq.
Nanz, Klaus-Peter, The Schengen Agreement: Preparing the Free Movement of Persons in the European Union, in Bieber/Monar (eds.), Justice and Home Affairs in the European Union: The Development of the Third Pillar, Brussels (1995), p. 29 et seq.
Nanz, Klaus-Peter, Visapolitik und Einwanderungspolitik in der Europäischen Union, in Müller-Graff (ed.), Europäische Zusammenarbeit in den Bereichen Justiz und Inneres – Der Dritte Pfeiler der Europäischen Union, Baden-Baden (1996), p. 63 et seq.

Nanz, Klaus-Peter, Free Movement of Persons according to the Schengen Convention and in the Framework of the European Union, in Institut Européen d'Administration Publique (Sous la direction de Alexis Pauly), De Schengen à Maastricht: Voie royale et course d'obstacles, Maastricht (1996), p. 61 et seq.

Nascimbene, Bruno, Da Schengen a Maastricht, Milan (1995)

Neumann, Gerald L., Buffer Zones Against Refugees: Dublin, Schengen and the German Asylum Amendment, Virginia Journal of International Law 33 (1993), p. 503 et seq.

Nguyen Quoc, Dinh/Daillier, Patrick/Pellet, Alain, Droit International Public, 5th ed., Paris (1994)

Niemeier, Michael, The K.4 Committee and its Position in the Decision Making Process, in Bieber/Monar (eds.), Justice and Home Affairs in the European Union: The Development of the Third Pillar, Brussels (1995), p. 321 et seq.

Novak, Meinhard, Basic Principles in European Social Law Derived from the Case-law of the European Court of Justice, Rivista di Diritto Europeo 2 (1998), p. 255 et seq.

Nowak, Manfred, U.N. Covenant on Civil and Political Rights, CCPR Commentary, Kehl am Rhein, Strasbourg, Arlington (1993)

Nuscheler, Franz, Internationale Migration – Flucht und Asyl, Opladen (1995)

Ohndorf, Wolfgang, Soziale Dimension erheblich gestärkt: Europäische Union, Bundesarbeitsblatt 4 (1998), p. 27 et seq.

O'Keeffe, David, The Schengen Convention: A Suitable Model for European Integration, Yearbook of European Law (1991), p. 185 et seq.

O'Keeffe, David, Comments on the Free Movement of Various Categories of Persons, in Schermers, Henry G. et al., Free Movement of Persons in Europe: Legal Problems and Experiences, Dordrecht, Boston, London (1993), p. 515 et seq.

O'Keeffe, David, European Immigration Law and Policy: The Schengen Conventions and European Community Law, in Institut Européen d'Administration Publique (Edité par Alexis Pauly), Les accords de Schengen: Abolition des frontières intérieures ou menace pour les libertés publiques?, Maastricht (1993), p. 171 et seq.

O'Keeffe, David, The New Draft External Frontiers Convention and the Draft Visa Regulation, in Monar/Morgan (eds.), The Third Pillar of the European Union, Brussels (1994), p. 135 et seq.

O'Keeffe, David, The Emergence of a European Immigration Policy, European Law Review 20 (1995), p. 20 et seq.

O'Keeffe, David, Recasting the Third Pillar, Common Market Law Review 32 (1995), p. 893 et seq.

O'Keeffe, David, The Convention on the Crossing of the External Frontiers of the Member States, in Institut Européen d'Administration Publique (Sous la direction de Alexis Pauly), De Schengen à Maastricht: Voie royale et course d'obstacles, Maastricht (1996), p. 33 et seq.

O'Leary, Siofra, The Relationship between Community Citizenship and the Protection of Fundamental Rights in Community Law, Common Market Law Review 32 (1995), p. 519 et seq.

Partsch, Karl Josef, International Law and Municipal Law, Encyclopedia of Public International Law II (1995), p. 1183 et seq.

Pastore, Ferruccio, L'expérience italienne dans la mise en oeuvre de Schengen, in Hailbronner, Kay/Weil, Patrick (eds.), Von Schengen nach Amsterdam – Auf dem Weg zu einem europäischen Einwanderungs- und Asylrecht. Schriftenreihe der Europäischen Rechtsakademie Trier, Vol. 29, Köln (1999)

Pauly, Alexis, Les accords de Schengen: Abolition des frontières intérieures ou menace pour les libertés publiques?, Institut Européen d'Administration Publique, Maastricht (1993)

Pauly, Alexis, Schengen en panne, Institut Européen d'Administration Publique, Maastricht (1994)

Pauly, Alexis, De Schengen à Maastricht: Voie royale et course d'obstacles, Institut Européen d'Administration Publique, Maastricht (1996)

Peers, Steve, Indirect Rights for Third-Country Service Providers Confirmed, European Law Review 20 (1995), p. 303 et seq.

Peers, Steve, An Even Closer Waiting Room?: The Case for Eastern European Accession to the European Economic Area, Common Market Law Review 32 (1995), p. 187 et seq.

Peers, Steve, The Visa Regulation: Free Movement Blocked Indefinitely, European Law Review 21 (1996), p. 150 et seq.

Peers, Steve, Towards Equality: Actual and Potential Rights of Third-Country Nationals in the European Union, Common Market Law Review 33 (1996), p. 7 et seq.

Peers, Steve, Undercutting Integration: Developments in EU Policy on Third-Country Nationals, European Law Review 22 (1997), p. 76 et seq.

Peers, Steve, European Communities and EEA: Equality, Free Movement and Social Security, European Law Review 22 (1997), p. 342 et seq.
Peers, Steve, Building Fortress Europe: The Development of EU Migration Law, Common Market Law Review 35 (1998), p. 1235 et seq.
Pennings, Frans, Introduction to European Social Security Law: Social Security in the European Community, Deventer (1994)
Pescatore, Pierre, La Cour de Justice des Communautés européennes et la Convention européenne des Droits de l'Homme, in Matscher, Franz/Petzold, Herbert (eds.), Protecting Human Rights: The European Dimension, Studies in honour of Gérard J. Wiarda, Köln (1988), p. 441 et seq.
Petersmann, Ernst U., Struktur und aktuelle Rechtsfragen des Assoziationsrechts, Zeitschrift für ausländisches öffentliches Recht und Völkerrecht 33 (1973), p. 266 et seq.
Piazolo, Kathrin, Der soziale Dialog nach dem Abkommen über die Sozialpolitik und dem Vertrag von Amsterdam, Frankfurt (1990)
Piazolo, Michael/Grosch, Klaus (eds.), Festung oder offene Grenzen? Entwicklung des Einwanderungs- und Asylrechts in Deutschland und Europa, München (1995)
Pieters, Danny (ed.), Introduction into the Social Security Law of the Member States of the European Community, Brussels (1990)
Pieters, Danny (ed.), Social Security in Europe: Miscellanea of the Erasmus-Programme. Social Security in the EC, Brussels (1991)
Pieters, Danny, Europäisches und nationales Recht der sozialen Sicherheit – Zukunftsperspektiven, Zeitschrift für ausländisches und internationales Arbeits- und Sozialrecht (1991), p. 72 et seq.
Pieters, Danny, Enquiry into the Legal Foundations of a possible Extension of Community Provisions on Social Security to Third-Country Nationals legally residing and/or working in the European Union, in Commission of the European Communities (ed.), Social Security in Europe: Equality between Nationals and Non-Nationals, European Conference Oporto November 1994, Lisbon (1995), p. 189 et seq.
Pinder, John, The European Community and Eastern Europe. Chatam House Papers of the Royal Institute of International Affairs, London (1991)
Pitschas, Rainer (ed.), Sozialer Dialog für Europa. Vorträge und Berichte einer internationalen Beschäftigungskonferenz an der Hochschule für Verwaltungswissenschaften Speyer, Berlin (1998)
Pizarro, Sebastiao, The Agreements on Social Security between the Community and Third Countries: Legal Basis and Analysis, in Commission of the European Communities (ed.), Social Security in Europe: Equality between Nationals and Non-Nationals, European Conference Oporto November 1994, Lisbon (1995), p. 103 et seq.
Plender, Richard, Competence, European Community Law and Nationals of Non-Member States, International and Comparative Law Quarterly 39 (1990), p. 599 et seq.
Plender, Richard (ed.), Basic Documents on International Migration Law, The Hague, London, Boston (1997)
Plender, Richard (ed.), Visas and Control of External Borders of the Member States, The Hague, London, Boston (1998)
Plüss-Pozzi, Silvia, Die Entwicklung eines europäischen Asylrechts, AWR-Bulletin (1991), p. 222 et seq.
Polakiewicz, Jörg, Die Verpflichtungen der Staaten aus den Urteilen des Europäischen Gerichtshofs für Menschenrechte, Berlin (1993)
Pollet, Kris, Free Movement of Persons and the Issue of Migration in EU-CEECs Relations: Schengen as an Example?, in Maresceau, Marc (ed.), Enlarging the European Union: Relations between the EU and Central and Eastern Europe, London and New York (1997), p. 209 et seq.
Pooley, Colin G./Whyte, Ian D. (eds.), Migrants, Emigrants and Immigrants: A social history of migration, Routledge (1991)
Prechal, Sacha/Burrows, Noreen, Gender Discrimination Law of the European Community, Dartmouth (1990)
Prieß, Ludger (ed.), Transnationale Migration, Baden-Baden (1998)
Prouvez, Nathalie, Opinion of the non-governmental organisations, in Council of Europe (ed.), The Social Charter of the 21st Century. Colloquy organised by the Secretariat of the Council of Europe, Human Rights Building 14-16 May 1997, Strasbourg (1997), p. 140 et seq.
Pucci di Benisichi, Paolo, Reforms of the Charter since 1989: Reform of the supervisory machinery and reform of the rights guaranteed, in Council of Europe (ed.), The Social Charter of the 21st Century. Colloquy organised by the Secretariat of the Council of Europe, Human Rights Building 14-16 May 1997, Strasbourg (1997), p. 43 et seq.

Rademacher, Ulf, Der Europäische Betriebsrat: Die Richtlinie 94/45/EG des Rates vom 1994-09-22 und ihre Umsetzung in nationales Recht, Baden-Baden (1996)

Rating, Stefan, Mittelbare Diskriminierung der Frau im Erwerbsleben nach europäischem Gemeinschaftsrecht – Richterrecht des EuGH und die Voraussetzungen seiner Rezeption am Beispiel Spaniens und der Bundesrepublik, Baden-Baden (1994)

Reermann, Olaf, Costs of Caring for Foreigners: An EU Comparison. Paper presented at the Conference "Managing Migration in the 21st Century", University of California, Davis, USA, October 10-11, 1997

Reich, Norbert, Bürgerrechte in der Europäischen Union. Subjektive Rechte von Unionsbürgern und Drittstaatsangehörigen unter besonderer Berücksichtigung der Rechtslage nach der Rechtsprechung des EuGH und dem Vertrag von Amsterdam, Baden-Baden (1999)

Remmert, Michael, The Contribution of the Council of Europe to European Coordination Law, in Jorens, Yves/Schulte, Bernd (eds.), European Social Security Law and Third-Country Nationals, Brussels (1998), p. 467 et seq.

Ress, Georg, Die Auswirkungen der Abkommen von Schengen und Dublin auf die Asylpolitik der EG, in Institut Européen d'Administration Publique (Edité par Alexis Pauly), Les accords de Schengen: Abolition des frontières intérieures ou menace pour les libertés publiques?, Maastricht (1993), p. 79 et seq.

Ress, Georg, Menschenrechte, europäisches Gemeinschaftsrecht und nationales Verfassungsrecht, in Haller, Herbert et al. (ed.), Staat und Recht, Festschrift für Günther Winkler, Wien, New York (1997), p. 897 et seq.

Rethmann, Albert-Peter, Asyl und Migration, Münster (1996)

Riegel, Reinhard, Zum Verhältnis von Recht und Wirklichkeit am Beispiel des Datenschutzrechts in der Europäischen Gemeinschaft, Die Öffentliche Verwaltung (DÖV) 1991, p. 311 et seq.

Ringler, Jochen C.K., Die Europäische Sozialunion, Berlin (1997)

Rittstieg, Helmut/Rowe, Gerard C., Einwanderung als gesellschaftliche Herausforderung. Inhalt und rechtliche Grundlagen einer neuen Politik, Baden-Baden (1992)

Rittstieg, Helmut, Einwanderung als gesellschaftliche Herausforderung, Informationsbrief Ausländerrecht (ZAR) 1993, p. 117 et seq.

Roberts, Simon, The Rulings of the European Court of Justice on the Association and Cooperation Agreements in Matters Concerning Social Security, in Jorens, Yves/Schulte, Bernd (eds.), European Social Security Law and Third-Country Nationals, Brussels (1998), p. 209 et seq.

Ronge, Volker, Ost-West-Wanderung nach Deutschland, Aus Politik und Zeitgeschichte, Beilage zu "Das Parlament", 43 (1993), B 7, p. 16 et seq.

Rosas, Allan and Antola, Esko (eds.), A Citizens' Europe: In Search of a New Order, London (1995)

Rossetto, Jean, La Convention de Schengen: Controverses et incertitudes francaises sur le droit d'asile, Revue du Marché Commun et de l'Union Européenne (1994), p. 315 et seq.

Rossetto, Jean, Le contrôle judiciaire dans la Convention de Schengen et le troisième pilier, in European Institute of Public Administration (edited by Monica den Boer), Schengen Implemented: First the Widening, Now the Deepening, Maastricht (1997), p. 27 et seq.

Rudge, Philip, Challenges to Refugee Protection in the 21st Century: Reconciling State Interests with International Responsibilities: Asylum in North America and Western Europe, International Journal of Refugee Law 10 (1998), p. 7 et seq.

Rupprecht, Reinhard, Justiz und Inneres nach dem Amsterdamer Vertrag, integration 20 (1997), p. 264 et seq.

Rupprecht, Reinhard/Osthus-Schroeder, Ulrike, Innere Sicherheit im Europäischen Binnenmarkt, Gütersloh (1992)

Rürup, Bert/Sesselmeier, Werner, Die demographische Entwicklung Deutschlands: Risiken, Chancen, politische Optionen, Aus Politik und Zeitgeschichte, Beilage zu "Das Parlament", 43 (1993), B 44, p. 3 et seq.

Rüthers, Bernd/Dütz, Wilhelm/Hanau, Peter (eds.), Die Euro-Betriebsrats-Richtlinie 94/45/EG: Europäischer Betriebsrat und alternative Verfahren zur Unterrichtung und Anhörung der Arbeitnehmer im transnationalen Unternehmen, Heidelberg (1996)

Saksun, Maija, The Agreements on the European Economic Area, in Jorens, Yves/Schulte, Bernd (eds.), European Social Security Law and Third-Country Nationals, Brussels (1998), p. 399 et seq.

Samuel, Lenia, Fundamental Social Rights: Case Law of the European Social Charter, Strasbourg (1997)

Santel, Bernhard, Migration in und nach Europa. Erfahrungen, Strukturen, Politik, Opladen (1995)

Schattenberg, Bernd, Deutsche Erfahrungen mit Schengen, in Hailbronner, Kay/Weil, Patrick (eds.), Von Schengen nach Amsterdam – Auf dem Weg zu einem europäischen Einwanderungs- und Asylrecht. Schriftenreihe der Europäischen Rechtsakademie Trier, Vol. 29, Köln (1999), p. 23 et seq.

Scheer, Ralph, Der Ehegatten- und Familiennachzug von Ausländern, Heidelberg (1992)

Scheinin, Martin, The meaning of Article 1 of the First Protocol for social security rights in the light of the Gaygusuz judgement, in Van den Bogaert, Stefaan (ed.), Social Security, Non-Discrimination and Property, Antwerpen-Apeldoorn (1997), p. 59 et seq.

Scheller, Susanne M., Das Schengener Informationssystem – Rechtshilfeersuchen "per Computer", Juristenzeitung (JZ) 1992, p. 904 et seq.

Schelter, Kurt, Innenpolitische Zusammenarbeit in Europa zwischen Maastricht und Regierungskonferenz 1996, Aus Politik und Zeitgeschichte, Beilage zu "Das Parlament", 46 (1996), B 1-2, p. 19 et seq.

Schermers, Henry G., The European Communities bound by fundamental Human Rights, Common Market Law Review 27 (1990), p. 249 et seq.

Schermers, Henry G. et al., Free Movement of Persons in Europe: Legal Problems and Experiences, Dordrecht, Boston, London (1993)

Schermers, Henry G., The Legal Character of the Agreement made at Maastricht with Respect to the Social Policy of the European Community, in Ress, Georg/Stein, Torsten (eds.), Europäischer Sozialraum, Baden-Baden (1995), p. 41 et seq.

Schieffer, Martin, Die Zusammenarbeit der EU-Mitgliedstaaten in den Bereichen Asyl und Einwanderung, Baden-Baden (1998)

Schiffer, Eckart, Wie stellt sich Europa zur Einwanderung?, Zeitschrift für Ausländerrecht und Ausländerpolitik (ZAR) 1992, p. 107 et seq.

Schiffer, Eckart, Braucht Deutschland mehr Einwanderung? Verwaltungsrundschau (UR) 1994, p. 178 et seq.

Schlette, Volker, Das neue Rechtsschutzsystem der Europäischen Menschenrechtskonvention, Zeitschrift für ausländisches öffentliches Recht und Völkerrecht (ZaiRV) 1996, p. 905 et seq.

Schmähl, Winfried, Europäische Sozialpolitik und die sozialpolitische Bedeutung der europäischen Integration, Europäische Sozialpolitik (1997), p. 9 et seq.

Schmid, Josef, Die Bevölkerungsentwicklung in der Bundesrepublik Deutschland, in Aus Politik und Zeitgeschichte, Beilage zu "Das Parlament", 39 (1989), B 18, p. 3 et seq.

Schoch, Friedrich, Asyl- und Ausländerrecht in der Europäischen Gemeinschaft, Deutsches Verwaltungsblatt (DVBl) 1992, p. 525 et seq.

Schoenemann, Peter, Das deutsche Asylrecht im Licht der europäischen Asylrechtsharmonisierung und des nationalen Asylrechts in Westeuropa, Neue Zeitschrift für Verwaltungsrecht (NVwZ) 1997, p. 1049 et seq.

Schreiber, Manfred, Europäische Einigung und innere Sicherheit, in Badura, Peter/Scholz, Rupert (eds.), Wege und Verfahren des Verfassungslebens, Festschrift für Peter Lerche zum 65. Geburtstag, München (1993), p. 532 et seq.

Schütz, Raimund, Europaweite Freizügigkeit ohne demokratische Kontrolle? Überwachung der Anwendung der Schengen II – Konvention durch die nationalen Parlamente, Archiv des öffentlichen Rechts (AÜR) 1995, p. 509 et seq.

Schuler, Rolf, Assoziationsratsbeschluß EWG-Türkei Nr. 3/80, Europäisches Arbeits- und Sozialrecht (EuroAS) 1995, p. 167 et seq.

Schulte, Axel, Multikulturelle Einwanderungsgesellschaften in Westeuropa. Soziale Konflikte und Integrationspolitiken, Bonn (1998)

Schulte, Bernd, Sozialhilfe und sozialhilfeähnliche Leistungen und Europäisches Gemeinschaftsrecht, Bundesministerium für Familien und Senioren, Bonn (1994)

Schulte, Bernd, Soziale Sicherheit in der EG. Verordnung (EWG) Nr. 1408/71 und sonstige Bestimmungen, München (1997)

Schulte, Bernd, The Welfare State and European Integration, European Journal of Social Security 1 (1998), p. 7 et seq.

Schulte, Bernd, Treatment of Third-Country Nationals in European Community Law: The Status Quo, in Jorens, Yves/Schulte, Bernd (eds.), European Social Security Law and Third-Country Nationals, Brussels (1998), p. 155 et seq.

Schulte, Bernd, Mäder, Werner (eds.), Die Regierungskonferenz Maastricht II, Perspektiven für die Sozialgemeinschaft, Bonn (1996)

Schulte, Bernd/Barwig, Klaus (eds.), Freizügigkeit und soziale Sicherheit. Die Durchführung der Verordnung (EWG) Nr. 1408/71 über die soziale Sicherheit der Wanderarbeitnehmer in Deutschland, Baden-Baden (1999)

Schulz, Otto, Auf dem Weg der Sozialunion. Die Ergebnisse des Gipfels von Maastricht, Sozialer Fortschritt (1992), p. 79 et seq.

Schulz, Otto, Maastricht und die Grundlagen einer Europäischen Sozialpolitik, Köln, Berlin, Bonn, München (1996)

Schumacher, Christoph, Die soziale Sicherheit von Drittstaatsangehörigen in der Europäischen Union unter besonderer Berücksichtigung der Abkommen des Europarates und der Assoziierungs- /Kooperations- und Europaabkommen, in Barwig, Klaus (ed.), Sozialer Schutz von Ausländern in Deutschland, Baden-Baden (1997), p. 135 et seq.

Schuster, Gunner, Rechtsfragen der Maastrichter Vereinbarung zur Sozialpolitik, Europäische Zeitschrift für Wirtschaftsrecht (EuZW) 1992, p. 178 et seq.

Schutte, Julian J.E., Schengen: Its Meaning for the Free Movement of Persons in Europe, Common Market Law Review 28 (1991), p. 549 et seq.

Schweisfurth, Theodor, Zur Frage der Rechtsnatur, Verbindlichkeit und völkerrechtlichen Relevanz der KSZE-Schlußakte. Ein Diskussionsbeitrag zum Phänomen der außerrechtlichen (non-legal) zwischenstaatlichen Abmachung, Zeitschrift für ausländisches öffentliches Recht und Völkerrecht (ZaöRV) 1976, p. 681 et seq.

Schweitzer, Michael, Europäische Gemeinschaften und Asylrecht, Zeitschrift für Ausländerrecht und Ausländerpolitik (ZAR) 1992, p. 147 et seq.

Sciarra, Silvana, Collective Agreements in the Hierarchy of European Community Sources, in Lyon-Caen, Antoine et al., European Community Labour Law Principles and Perspectives, Liber Amicorum Lord Wedderburn of Charlton (1996), p. 189 et seq.

Sciarra, Silvana, From Strasbourg to Amsterdam: Prospects for the Convergence of European Social Rights and Policy, in Alston, Philipp/Harris, David (eds.), The European Union and Human Rights (1999), p. 473 et seq.

Seidl-Hohenveldern, Ignaz, Völkerrecht, Köln (1994)

Seidl-Hohenveldern, Ignaz/Loibl, Gerhard, Das Recht der internationalen Organisationen einschließlich der supranationalen Gemeinschaften, 6th ed., Köln, München (1996)

Shaw, Josephine, Positive Action for Women in Germany: The Use of Legally Binding Quota Systems, in Hepple, Bob A. (ed.), Discrimination: The Limits of Law, London (1992), p. 386 et seq.

Sidéris, Efstratios, L'égalité de traitement entre nationaux et non-nationaux en droit communautaire de la sécurité sociale, Schweizerische Zeitschrift für Sozialversicherung und berufliche Vorsorge 41 (1997), p. 257 et seq.

Sieveking, Klaus, Migration und Rechtsstatus von Zuwanderern. Bundesrepublikanische und europäische Aspekte, Recht und Politik (1992), p. 135 et seq.

Sieveking, Klaus, Die Anwendung des Assoziationsratsbeschlusses Nr. 3/80 auf türkische Staatsangehörige in Deutschland, Neue Zeitschrift für Sozialrecht (NZS) 1994, p. 213 et seq.

Sieveking, Klaus, Die Rechtsstellung von Drittstaatsangehörigen nach Assoziationsrecht, Zeitschrift für ausländisches und internationales Arbeits- und Sozialrecht 1995, p. 227 et seq.

Sieveking, Klaus, The Rulings of the European Court of Justice on the Legal Position of Non-European Union Nationals under Labour Law and Social Security Law, in Jorens, Yves/Schulte, Bernd (eds.), European Social Security Law and Third-Country Nationals, Brussels (1998), p. 235 et seq.

Simitis, Spiros, Europäisierung oder Renationalisierung des Arbeitsrechts?, in Heinze, Meinhard/Söllner, Alfred (eds.), Arbeitsrecht in der Bewährung, Festschrift für Otto Rudolf Kissel zum 60. Geburtstag, München (1994), p. 1097 et seq.

Simitis, Spiros, Affirming Fundamental Rights in the European Union Time to Act, Brussels (1999)

Simmonds, Kenneth R., The Concertation of Community Migration Policy, Common Market Law Review 25 (1988), p. 177 et seq.

Skran, Claudena M., Refugees in Inter-War Europe, Oxford (1998)

Sörries, Bernd, Fortschritte in der Europäischen Sozialpolitik? Das Sozialabkommen und der Soziale Dialog – eine Zwischenbilanz, Sozialer Fortschritt (1998), p. 303 et seq.

SOPEMI, Trends in International Migration. Annual Report, OECD Paris (1998), p. 53 et seq.

Soysal, Yasemin Nuhoglu, Limits of Citizenship: Migrants and Postnational Membership in Europe, Chicago (1994)

Stanley, Alison/Rowlands, Michael, Die Rechte von Drittausländern in der Neuen Europäischen Ordnung. Ein Bericht über den Begriffswandel der "Grenzen" innerhalb der Europäischen Union, über die Probleme der Illegalität und die Stellung der rechtmäßig ansässigen Drittausländer, Immigration and Nationality Research and Information Charity (1994)

Steenbergen, J.D.M., Schengen and the movement of persons, in Meijers, Herman et al., Schengen: Internationalisation of Central Chapters of the Law on Aliens, Refugees, Privacy, Security and the Police, Dordrecht (1991), p. 57 et seq.

Steenbergen, J.D.M., All the King's Horses...Probabilities and Possibilities for the Implementation of the New Title IV EC Treaty, European Journal of Migration and Law 1 (1999), p. 29 et seq.

Stéfanini, Patrick/Doublet, Frédérique, Le droit d'asile en Europe: La convention relative à la détermination de l'état responsable de l'examen d'une demande d'asile présentée auprès d'un état membre des communautés européennes, Revue du Marché Commun (1991), p. 391 et seq.

Steineck, Alexander, Soll die Europäische Union Einwanderer aus Drittstaaten nach Bildungsmerkmalen auswählen?, Zeitschrift für Ausländerrecht und Ausländerpolitik (ZAR) 1994, p. 177 et seq.

Stenberg, Gunnel, Non-Expulsion and Non-Refoulement, Uppsala (1989)

Stock, Remmert, Aufenthaltsrechtliche Vergünstigungen für polnische Staatsangehörige, Informationsbrief Ausländerrecht (InfAuslR) 1994, p. 392 et seq.

Strasser, Wolfgang, European Social Charter, Encyclopedia of Public International Law 8 (1985), p. 211 et seq.

Streeck, Wolfgang, European Social Policy after Maastricht: The "social dialogue" and "subsidiarity", Economic and Industrial Democracy 15 (1994), p. 115 et seq.

Stüer, Christoph, Personenkontrollen an den europäischen Binnengrenzen und ihr Abbau, Köln (1990)

Sudre, Frédéric, Le Protocole additionnel à la Charte Sociale Européenne prévoyant un système de réclamations collectives, Revue Générale de Droit International Public (1996), p. 715 et seq.

Süß, Gisela, Gemeinschafts- und verfassungsrechtliche Probleme einer europäischen Asylrechtsharmonisierung, Bayerische Verwaltungsblätter (BayVBl) 1990, p. 609 et seq.

Tapiola, Kari, Introduction: The Social Charter of the 21st Century, in Council of Europe (ed.), The Social Charter of the 21st Century. Colloquy organised by the Secretariat of the Council of Europe, Human Rights Building 14-16 May 1997, Strasbourg (1997), p. 23 et seq.

Tardu, Maxime, Migrant Workers, Encyclopedia of Public International Law II (1997), p. 364 et seq.

Taschner, Hans-Claudius, Schengen – Die Übereinkommen zum Abbau der Personenkontrolle an den Binnengrenzen von EU-Staaten, Baden-Baden (1997)

Thiede, Reinhold, Menschliche Ressourcen als Grundlage für ökonomischen Wohlstand und soziale Sicherheit. Bericht über eine internationale Konferenz zum Thema "Human Ressources in Europe", Die Angestelltenversicherung (1992), p. 144 et seq.

Thorburn, Joanne, Transcending boundaries: Temporary Protection and Burden-sharing in Europe, International Journal of Refugee Law 7 (1995), p. 459 et seq.

Thun-Hohenstein, Christoph, Der Vertrag von Amsterdam, Wien, München (1997)

Tomei, Veronica, Europäische Migrationspolitik zwischen Kooperationszwang und Souveränitätsansprüchen, Bonn (1997)

Tomuschat, Christian, A Right to Asylum in Europe, Human Rights Law Journal 13 (1992), p. 257 et seq.

Tomuschat, Christian, The Legal Status of Non-Citizens of the EU: General Introduction Revue Européenne de Droit Public, European Review of Public Law 7 (1995), p. 543 et seq.

Toth, Akos G., The European Union and Human Rights: The Way Forward, Common Market Law Review 34 (1997), p. 491 et seq.

Traxler, Franz, European Trade Union Policy and Collective Bargaining – Mechanisms and Levels of Labour Market Regulation in Comparison, Transfer (European Review of Labour and Research), 2 (1996), p. 287 et seq.

Treber, Jürgen, Sozialer Dialog in der Europäischen Union und Gleichbehandlung bei Teilzeitarbeit: Die Richtlinie des Rates zu der von UNICE, CEEP und EGB geschlossenen Rahmenvereinbarung über Teilzeitarbeit, Zeitschrift für Tarifrecht (1998), p. 250 et seq.

Trechsel, Stefan, The Implementation of the Collective Complaints Procedure, in Council of Europe (ed.), The Social Charter of the 21st Century. Colloquy organised by the Secretariat of the Council of Europe, Human Rights Building 14-16 May 1997, Strasbourg (1997), p. 97 et seq.

Türk, Volker, Das Flüchtlingskommissariat der Vereinten Nationen (UNHCR), Berlin (1992)

Twomey, Patrick, Title VI of the Union Treaty: "Matters of Common Interest" as a Question of Human Rights, in Monar/Morgan (eds.), The Third Pillar of the European Union, Brussels (1994), p. 49 et seq.

Ucarer, Emek M. and Puchala, Donald J. (eds.), Immigration into Western Societies: Problems and Policies, London (1997)

UNHCR, Handbook Voluntary Repatriation: International Protection, Geneva (1996)

UNHCR (ed.), The European Convention on Human Rights and the Protection of Refugees, Asylum Seekers and Displaced Persons, European Series (II), July 1996

Vandamme, Francois, The Revision of the European Social Charter, International Labour Review 133 (1994), p. 635 et seq.

Van de Rijt, Wouter, Schengen depuis le 26 mars 1995, in European Institute of Public Administration (edited by Monica den Boer), Schengen Implemented: First the Widening, Now the Deepening, Maastricht (1997), p. 11 et seq.

Van den Bempt, Paul/Theelen, Greet, From Europe Agreements to Accession: The Integration of the Central and Eastern European Countries into the European Union, Brussels (1996)

Van den Bogaert, Stefaan (ed.), Social Security, Non-Discrimination and Property, Antwerpen-Apeldoorn (1997)

Van den Bogaert, Stefaan, The consequences of the Gaygusuz judgement for Belgian social security, in Van den Bogaert, Stefaan (ed.), Social Security, Non-Discrimination and Property, Antwerpen-Apeldoorn (1997), p. 123 et seq.

Van den Broek, Peter, The Protection of Property Rights under the European Convention on Human Rights, Legal Issues of European Integration 12 (1986), p. 52 et seq.

Van der Steen, Ivo, The meaning of the Gaygusuz judgement for the EC Coordination Regulations and third-country nationals: A reaction from a Member State, in Van den Bogaert, Stefaan (ed.), Social Security, Non-Discrimination and Property, Antwerpen-Apeldoorn (1997), p. 121 et seq.

Van Outrive, Lode, Möglichkeiten zur Realisierung einer Einwanderungspolitik auf europäischer Ebene, in Friedrich-Ebert-Stiftung (ed.), Europäische Einwanderungspolitik, Bonn (1995), p. 29 et seq.

Van Raepenbusch, Sean, La jurisprudence de la cour de justice des Communautés Européennes vis-à-vis des ressortissants de pays tiers, in European Institute of Public Administration (edited by Monica den Boer), Schengen Implemented: First the Widening, Now the Deepening, Maastricht (1997), p. 41 et seq.

Velling, Johannes, Schengen, Dublin und Maastricht – Etappen auf dem Weg zu einer europäischen Immigrationspolitik, ZEW Labour Economics and Human Resources Series Discussion Paper, (1993)

Verdross, Alfred/Simma, Bruno, Universelles Völkerrecht – Theorie und Praxis, 3rd ed., Berlin (1984)

Vermeulen, Hans (ed.), Immigration Policy for Multicultural Society: A Comparative Study of Integration, Language and Religious Policy in five Western European Countries, Brussels (1997)

Verschueren, Herwig, EC Social Security Coordination Excluding Third-Country Nationals: still in line with Fundamental Rights after the Gaygusuz judgement?, in Van den Bogaert, Stefaan (ed.), Social Security, Non-Discrimination and Property, Antwerpen-Apeldoorn (1997), p. 99 et seq.

Verschueren, Herwig, EC Social Security Coordination Excluding Third-Country Nationals: Still in Line with Fundamental Rights after the Gaygusuz Judgment?, Common Market Law Review 34 (1997), p. 991 et seq.

Verschueren, Herwig, The Commission's Proposal to extend Regulation (EEC) No. 1408/71 to Third-Country Nationals, in Jorens, Yves/Schulte, Bernd (eds.), European Social Security Law and Third-Country Nationals, Brussels (1998), p. 187 et seq.

Vevstad, Vigdis, Refugee Protection: A European Challenge, Oslo (1998)

Villiger, Mark, Handbuch der Europäischen Menschenrechtskonvention (EMRK) unter besonderer Berücksichtigung der schweizerischen Rechtslage, Zürich (1993)

Vitzthum Graf, Wolfgang (ed.), Völkerrecht, Berlin, New York (1997)

Vörös, Imre/Droutsas, Dimitri, Die Europa-Abkommen. Rechtliche Fundamente für die Beziehungen der EU mit den mittel- und osteuropäischen Ländern, Zeitschrift für Verwaltungsrecht (ZfV) 1998, p. 1 et seq.

Wagner, Eckart, The Integration of Schengen into the framework of the European Union, Legal Issues of European Integration 25 (1999), p. 1 et seq.

Waldstein, Michael, Das Asylgrundrecht im europäischen Kontext. Wege einer europäischen Harmonisierung des Asyl- und Flüchtlingsrechts, Frankfurt/M. (1993)

Walterskirchen, Ewald, Auswirkungen der Ost-West-Integration auf dem Arbeitsmarkt. Europa 1996. Auswirkungen einer EU-Osterweiterung. Schriftenreihe Europa des Bundeskanzleramts, Wien (1995), p. 287 et seq.

Walwei, Ulrich, Arbeitsmarkt Europa – Probleme und Lösungsansätze, Arbeits- und Sozialpolitik (1996), p. 15 et seq.
Walzer, Michael, Spheres of Justice: A Defense of Pluralism and Equality, New York (1983)
Wank, Rolf, Der Einfluß des europäischen Arbeitsschutzrechts auf die Rechtslage in der Bundesrepublik Deutschland, in von Maydell, Bernd/Schnapp, Friedrich E. (eds.), Die Auswirkungen des EG-Rechts auf das Arbeits- und Sozialrecht der Bundesrepublik, Berlin (1992)
Wank, Rolf/Bögmann, Udo, Deutsches und europäisches Arbeitsschutzrecht, München (1992)
Watson, Philippa, Social Policy after Maastricht, Common Market Law Review 30 (1993), p. 481 et seq.
Weber, Albrecht, Die Harmonisierung der europäischen Einwanderungs- und Asylpolitik, Zeitschrift für Rechtspolitik (ZRP) 1993, p. 170 et seq.
Weber, Albrecht, Einwanderungs- und Asylpolitik nach Maastricht, Zeitschrift für Ausländerrecht und Ausländerpolitik (ZAR) 1993, p. 11 et seq.
Weber, Albrecht, Möglichkeiten und Grenzen europäischer Asylrechtsharmonisierung vor und nach Amsterdam, Zeitschrift für Ausländerrecht und Ausländerpolitik (ZAR) 1998, p. 147 et seq.
Weber, Claus, Reisefreiheit für Drittstaatsangehörige. Welche Kompetenzen besitzen Europäische Gemeinschaft und Europäische Union?, Zeitschrift für Ausländerrecht und Ausländerpolitik (ZAR) 1997, p. 25 et seq.
Weber, Claus, Der assoziationsrechtliche Status Drittstaatsangehöriger in der Europäischen Union, Frankfurt/M. (1997)
Weckel, Philippe, La Convention additionnelle à l'accord de Schengen, Revue Général de Droit International Public 95 (1991), p. 405 et seq.
Wegner, Jörg, Die nichteheliche Lebensgemeinschaft im deutschen Ausländerrecht, Berlin (1998)
Weichert, Thilo, Drittausländer in der Europäischen Gemeinschaft, Informationsbrief Ausländerrecht (InfAuslR) 1990, p. 257 et seq.
Weidenfeld, Werner (ed.), Maastricht in der Analyse – Materialien zur Europäischen Union, Gütersloh (1994)
Weidenfeld, Werner (ed.), Das Europäische Einwanderungskonzept. Strategien und Optionen für Europa, Gütersloh 1994
Weidenfeld, Werner/Hillenbrand, Olaf, Wie kann Europa die Migration bewältigen? Möglichkeiten und Grenzen eines Einwanderungskonzepts, Europa-Archiv (1994), p. 1 et seq.
Weiler, Joseph H.H., Thou Shalt Not Oppress a Stranger: On the Judicial Protection of the Human Rights of Non-EC Nationals – A Critique, European Journal of International Law 3 (1992), p. 65 et seq.
Weiss, Manfred, The Significance of Maastricht for European Community Social Policy, International Journal of Comparative Labour Law and Industrial Relations 1992, p. 3 et seq.
Weiss, Manfred, Die Bedeutung von Maastricht für die EG-Sozialpolitik, in Däubler, Wolfgang/Bobke, Manfred/Kehrmann, Karl (eds.), Arbeit und Recht, Festschrift für Albert Gnade, Köln (1992), p. 583 et seq.
Weiss, Manfred, Der soziale Dialog als Katalysator koordinierter Tarifpolitik in der EG, in Heinze, Meinhard/Söllner, Alfred (eds.), Arbeitsrecht in der Bewährung, Festschrift für Otto Rudolf Kissel zum 60. Geburtstag, München (1994), p. 1253 et seq.
Weiss, Manfred, Zur künftigen Rolle der Europäischen Union im Arbeitsrecht, in Hanau, Peter/Lorenz, Egon/Matthes, Hans-Christoph (eds.), Festschrift für Günther Wiese zum 70. Geburtstag (1998), p. 633 et seq.
Welte, Hans-Peter, Beschlüsse zum Ausländer- und Asylrecht auf der Regierungskonferenz am 16./17. Juni 1997 in Amsterdam (Maastricht II), Zeitschrift für Ausländerrecht und Ausländerpolitik (ZAR) 1998, p. 67 et seq.
Wengler, Wilhelm, Die Unanwendbarkeit der europäischen Sozialcharta im Staat. Ein Beitrag zur Frage des Verhältnisses zwischen Völkerrecht und staatlichem Recht, Bad Homburg, Berlin, Zürich (1969)
Wenig, Marcus, Möglichkeiten und Grenzen der Streitbeilegung ethnischer Konflikte durch die OSZE – dargestellt am Konflikt im ehemaligen Jugoslawien, Berlin (1996)
Werner, Heinz, Wirtschaftliche Integration und Arbeitskräftewanderung: Das Beispiel Europa. Mitteilungen aus der Arbeitsmarkt- und Berufsforschung (1994), p. 232 et seq.
Werner, Heinz, Temporary Migration of Foreign Workers: Illustrated with Special Regard to East-West Migrations, in IAB topics No. 18, labour market research, Institute for Employment research, Nürnberg (1996)

Werner, Heinz/Kehl, Melanie, The Labour Market Situation of EU and of Third Country Nationals in the European Union, in IAB topics No. 32, labour market research, Institute for Employment research, Nürnberg (1998)

Westphal, Volker, Die Voraussetzungen der Einreise und des Aufenthalts von Ausländern nach dem Inkrafttreten des Schengener Durchführungsübereinkommens, Die Polizei 1995, p. 114 et seq.

Westphal, Volker, Die Ausschreibung zur Einreiseverweigerung im Schengener Informationssystem – Voraussetzungen, Wirkungen und Rechtsschutzmöglichkeiten, Informationsbrief Ausländerrecht (InfAuslR) 1999, p. 361 et seq.

Whiteford, Elaine A., Social Policy after Maastricht, European Law Review 18 (1993), p. 202 et seq.

Whittle, Richard, Disability Discrimination and the Amsterdam Treaty, European Law Review 23 (1998), p. 50 et seq.

Wiebringhaus, Hans, Die Sozialcharta des Europarates – Eine Bilanz, in Baer-Kaupert, Friedrich-Wilhelm (ed.), Festschrift für Bernhard C.H. Aubin, Kehl (1979), p. 265 et seq.

Wiebringhaus, Hans, La Charte Sociale Européenne, Annuaire Francais de Droit International 28 (1982), p. 934 et seq.

Wihtol de Wenden, Catherine, Post-Amsterdam Migration Policy and European Citizenship, European Journal of Migration and Law 1 (1999), p. 89 et seq.

Wilke, Axel, Vollendung des EG-Binnenmarktes und Asylrecht, Zeitschrift für Rechtspolitik (ZRP) 1989, p. 225 et seq.

Winkler, Sebastian, Der EGMR zum innerstaatlich und gemeinschaftsrechtlich (RL 65/65/EWG) definierten Arzneimittelbegriff beim Apothekenmonopol, Europäische Grundrechte-Zeitschrift (EuGRZ) 1999, p. 181 et seq.

Winn, David B., Staatsangehörige von Drittländern in der Europäischen Union. Das Recht auf Gleichbehandlung, London (1995)

Winn, David B., Free Movement for Non-EC Workers within the European Community, Utrecht (1997)

Wisskirchen, Alfred, Der Soziale Dialog in der Europäischen Gemeinschaft, in Die Arbeitsgerichtsbarkeit, Festschrift zum 100 jährigen Bestehen des Deutschen Arbeitsgerichtsverbandes, Neuwied (1994), p. 653 et seq.

Wollenschläger, Michael, Grundstrukturen eines europäischen Asylrechts, AWR-Bulletin (1987/88), p. 137 et seq.

Wollenschläger, Michael, Europäische Entwicklungen im Asylrecht und die Einwanderungsproblematik, Nordrhein-Westfälische Verwaltungsblätter (NWVBL) 1992, p. 225 et seq.

Wollenschläger, Michael, Grundlagen und Anforderungen einer europäischen Einwanderungsregelung, in Das Europäische Einwanderungskonzept – Strategien und Optionen für Europa, edited by Werner Weidenfeld, Gütersloh (1994), p. 161 et seq.

Wollenschläger, Michael, Grundzüge eines europäischen Einwanderungskonzeptes, in Friedrich-Ebert-Stiftung (ed.), Europäische Einwanderungspolitik, Bonn (1995), p. 45 et seq.

Wollenschläger, Michael/Becker, Ulrich, Harmonisierung des Asylrechts in der EG und Art. 16 Abs. 2 Satz 2 GG – Rechtsvergleichende Bestandsaufnahme und Reform-Perspektiven in den zwölf EG-Staaten, Europäische Grundrechte-Zeitschrift (EuGRZ) 1990, p. 1 et seq.

Würz, Karl, Das Schengener Durchführungsübereinkommen, Stuttgart (1997)

Zacher, Hans F., Social Security: International Aspects, Encyclopedia of Public International Law 9 (1986), p. 341 et seq.

Zimmer, Willy, Die Reformen des Ausländerrechts, des Asyl- und Staatsangehörigkeitsrechts in Frankreich und Deutschland, Speyer (1996)

Zimmermann, Andreas, Der Vertrag von Amsterdam und das deutsche Asylrecht, Neue Zeitschrift für Verwaltungsrecht (NVwZ) 1998, p. 450 et seq.

Zuleeg, Manfred, Die innerstaatliche Anwendbarkeit völkerrechtlicher Verträge am Beispiel des GATT und der europäischen Sozialcharta, Zeitschrift für ausländisches öffentliches Recht und Völkerrecht (ZaöRV) 35 (1975), p. 341 et seq.

Zuleeg, Manfred, Innerstaatliche Verbindlichkeit völkerrechtlicher Vereinbarungen, in Barwig, Klaus/Lörcher, Klaus/Schumacher, Christoph (eds.), Familiennachzug von Ausländern auf dem Hintergrund völkerrechtlicher Verträge, Baden-Baden (1985), p. 13 et seq.

Zuleeg, Manfred, Europäische Sozialcharta und Familiennachzug, in Barwig, Klaus/Lörcher, Klaus/Schumacher, Christoph (eds.), Familiennachzug von Ausländern auf dem Hintergrund völkerrechtlicher Verträge, Baden-Baden (1985), p. 53 et seq.

Zuleeg, Manfred, Die Rechtsprechung des Europäischen Gerichtshofs zur Stellung der Staatsangehörigen von Drittstaaten in der Europäischen Gemeinschaft, in Barwig, Klaus/Brinkmann,

Gisbert/Huber, Bertold/Lörcher, Klaus/Schumacher, Christoph (eds.), Vom Ausländer zum Bürger, Problemanzeigen im Ausländer-, Asyl- und Staatsangehörigkeitsrecht, Festschrift für Fritz Franz und Gert Müller, Baden-Baden (1994), p. 448 et seq.
Zuleeg, Manfred, International Instruments on Equal Treatment in Social Security Matters, in Commission of the European Communities (ed.), Social Security in Europe: Equality between Nationals and Non-Nationals, European Conference Oporto November 1994, Lisbon (1995), p. 89 et seq.
Zuleeg, Manfred, Das Urteil Taflan-Met des Europäischen Gerichtshofs, Zeitschrift für Ausländerrecht und Ausländerpolitik (ZAR) 1997, p. 170 et seq.

H

Table of Legislation and Preparatory Acts

I. Entry and Admission

COUNCIL DIRECTIVE 72/194/EEC of 18 May 1972 extending to workers exercising the right to remain in the territory of a Member State after having been employed in that state the scope of the Directive of 25 February 1964 on coordination of special measures concerning the movement and residence of foreign nationals which are justified on grounds of public policy, public security or public health, O.J. 1972, L 121/32

COUNCIL DIRECTIVE 75/35/EEC of 17 December 1974 extending the scope of Directive No. 64/221/EEC on the coordination of special measures concerning the movement and residence of foreign nationals which are justified on grounds of public policy, public security or public health to include nationals of a Member State who exercise the right to remain in the territory of another Member State after having pursued therein an activity in a self-employed capacity, O.J. 1975, L 14/14

DECISION of 30 November 1992 of the Ministers of the Member States of the European Communities responsible for immigration setting up a Centre for Information, Discussion and Exchange on the crossing of borders and immigration (CIREFI)

RESOLUTION of 1 June 1993 of the Ministers of the Member States of the European Communities responsible for immigration on the harmonization of national policies on family reunification, SN 2828/1/93 WGI 1497

RESOLUTION of 20 June 1994 adopted by the Council on limitations on admission of third-country nationals to the Member States for employment, O.J. 1996, C 274/3

COUNCIL DECISION of 30 November 1994 on a joint action adopted by the Council on the basis of Article K.3(2)(b) of the Treaty on European Union concerning travel facilities for school pupils from third countries resident in a Member State, O.J. 1994, L 327/1

COUNCIL RESOLUTION of 30 November 1994 on the admission of third-country nationals to the territory of the Member States of the European Union for study purposes, O.J. 1996, C 274/10

COUNCIL RESOLUTION of 30 November 1994 relating to the limitations on the admission of third-country nationals to the territory of the Member States for the purpose of pursuing activities as self-employed persons, O.J. 1996, C 274/7

COUNCIL CONCLUSIONS of 30 November 1994 on the organization and development of the Centre for Information, Discussion and Exchange on the crossing of frontiers and immigration (CIREFI), O.J. 1996, C 274/50

COUNCIL REGULATION (EC) No. 1683/95 of 29 May 1995 laying down a uniform format for visas, O.J. 1995, L 164/1

COUNCIL DECISION of 22 December 1995 on monitoring the implementation of instruments already adopted concerning admission of third-country nationals, O.J. 1996, C 11/1

JOINT ACTION of 4 March 1996 adopted by the Council on the basis of Article K.3 of the Treaty on European Union on airport transit arrangements, O.J. 1996, L 63/8

COUNCIL RECOMMENDATION of 4 March 1996 relating to local consular cooperation regarding visas, O.J. 1996, C 80/1

COUNCIL RESOLUTION of 4 March 1996 on the status of third-country nationals residing on a long-term basis in the territory of the Member States, O.J. 1996, C 80/2

JOINT POSITION of 25 October 1996 defined by the Council on the basis of Article K.3(2)(a) of the Treaty on European Union on pre-frontier assistance and training assignments, O.J. 1996, L 281/1

JOINT ACTION of 28 October 1996 adopted by the Council on the basis of Article K.3 of the Treaty on European Union introducing a programme of training, exchanges and cooperation in the field of identity documents ('Sherlock'), O.J. 1996, L 287/7

JOINT ACTION of 16 December 1996 adopted by the Council on the basis of Article K.3 of the Treaty on European Union concerning a uniform format for residence permits, O.J. 1997, L 7/1

JOINT ACTION of 19 March 1998 adopted by the Council on the basis of Article K.3 of the Treaty on European Union, introducing a programme of training, exchanges and cooperation in the field of asylum, immigration and crossing of external borders (Odysseus-programme), O.J. 1998, L 99/2

COUNCIL DECISION of 3 December 1998 on common standards relating to filling in the uniform format for residence permits, O.J. 1998, L 333/8

COUNCIL REGULATION (EC) No. 574/99 of 12 March 1999 determining the third countries whose nationals must be in possession of visas when crossing the external borders of the Member States, O.J. 1999, L 72/2

COMMISSION COMMUNICATION in pursuance of Council Regulation (EC) No. 574/99 of 12 March 1999 determining the third countries whose nationals must be in possession of visas when crossing the external borders of the Member States, O.J. 1999, C 133/19

COUNCIL DECISION of 20 May 1999 concerning the definition of the Schengen acquis for the purpose of determining, in conformity with the relevant provisions of the Treaty establishing the European Community and the Treaty on European Union, the legal basis for each of the provisions or decisions which constitute the acquis, O.J. 1999 L 176/1.

COUNCIL DECISION of 20 May 1999 determining, in conformity with the relevant provisions of the Treaty establishing the European Community and the Treaty on European Union, the legal basis for each of the provisions or decisions which constitute the Schengen acquis, O.J. 1999 L 176/17.

II. Integration and Social Rights

COUNCIL REGULATION (EEC) No. 1408/71 of 14 June 1971 on the application of social security schemes to employed persons and their families moving within the Community, O.J. 1971, L 149/2

JOINT ACTION of 15 July 1996 adopted by the Council on the basis of Article K.3 of the Treaty on European Union, concerning action to combat racism and xenophobia, O.J. 1996, L 185/5

JOINT ACTION of 24 February 1997 adopted by the Council on the basis of Article K.3 of the Treaty on European Union concerning action to combat trafficking in human beings and sexual exploitation of children, O.J. 1997, L 63/2

COUNCIL REGULATION (EC) No. 1035/97 of 2 June 1997 establishing a European Monitoring Centre on Racism and Xenophobia, O.J. 1997, L 151/1

COUNCIL DECISION of 21 December 1998 relating to the conclusion of an Agreement between the European Community and the Council of Europe for the purpose of establishing, in accordance with Article 7(3) of Council Regulation (EC) No. 1035/97 of 2 June 1997 establishing a European Monitoring Centre on Racism and Xenophobia, close cooperativ between the Centre and the Council of Europe, O.J. 1999, L 44/33

III. Combating Illegal Residence and Repatriation

RECOMMENDATION of 30 November and 1 December 1992 of the Ministers of the Member States of the European Communities responsible for immigration regarding practices followed by Member States on expulsion, SN 4678/92 WGI 11266

RECOMMENDATION of 30 November and 1 December 1992 of the Ministers of the Member States of the European Communities responsible for immigration regarding transit for the purposes of expulsion, 19579/92

RECOMMENDATION of 25 May 1993 of the Ministers of the Member States of the European Communities responsible for immigration concerning checks on and expulsion of third-country nationals residing or working without authorization, SN 3017/93 WGI 1516

COUNCIL RECOMMENDATION of 30 November 1994 concerning a specimen bilateral readmission agreement between a Member State of the European Union and a third country, O.J. 1996, C 274/20

COUNCIL RECOMMENDATION of 30 November 1994 concerning the adoption of a standard travel document for the expulsion of third-country nationals, O.J. 1996, C 274/18

COUNCIL RECOMMENDATION of 24 July 1995 on the guiding principles to be followed in drawing up protocols on the implementation of readmission agreements, O.J. 1996, C 274/25

COUNCIL RECOMMENDATION of 22 December 1995 on harmonizing means of combating illegal immigration and illegal employment and improving the relevant means of control, O.J. 1996, C 5/1

COUNCIL RECOMMENDATION of 22 December 1995 on concerted action and cooperation in carrying out expulsion measures, O.J. 1996, C 5/3

COUNCIL RECOMMENDATION of 27 September 1996 on combating the illegal employment of third-country nationals, O.J. 1996, C 304/1

COUNCIL DECISION of 16 December 1996 on monitoring the implementation of instruments adopted by the Council concerning illegal immigration, readmission, the unlawful employment of third-country nationals and cooperation in the implementation of expulsion, O.J. 1996, L 342/5

COUNCIL DECISION of 26 May 1997 on the exchange of information concerning assistance for the voluntary repatriation of third-country nationals, O.J. 1997, L 147/3

COUNCIL RESOLUTION of 4 December 1997 on measures to be adopted on the combating of marriages of convenience, O.J. 1997, C 382/1

IV. Asylum and Refugee Law

CONVENTION of 15 June 1990 determining the State responsible for examining applications for asylum lodged in one of the Member States of the European Communities – Dublin Convention, O.J. 1997, C 254/1

RESOLUTION of 30 November and 1 December 1992 of the Ministers of the Member States of the European Communities responsible for immigration on manifestly unfounded applications for asylum, SN 4822/92 WGI 1282 AS 146

RESOLUTION of 30 November and 1 December 1992 of the Ministers of the Member States of the European Communities responsible for immigration on a harmonized approach to questions concerning host third countries, SN 4823/92 WGI 1283 AS 147

CONCLUSIONS of 30 November and 1 December 1992 of the Ministers of the Member States of the European Communities responsible for immigration on countries in which there is generally no serious risk of persecution, SN 4821/92 WGI 1281 AS 145

DECISION of 30 November and 1 December 1992 of the Ministers of the Member States of the European Communities responsible for immigration establishing the clearing house (CIREA), SN 2836/93 WGI 1505

COUNCIL CONCLUSIONS of 20 June 1994 on the Commission communication on immigration and asylum policies, O.J. 1996, C 274/49

COUNCIL CONCLUSIONS of 20 June 1994 concerning the possible application of Article K.9 of the Treaty on European Union to asylum policy, O.J. 1996, C 274/34

COUNCIL RESOLUTION of 20 June 1995 on minimum guarantees for asylum procedures, O.J. 1996, C 274/13

COUNCIL RESOLUTION of 25 September 1995 on burden-sharing with regard to the admission and residence of displaced persons on a temporary basis, O.J. 1995, C 262/1

COUNCIL DECISION of 23 November 1995 on publication in the Official Journal of the European Communities of acts and other texts adopted by the Council in the field of asylum and immigration, O.J. 1996, C 274/1

JOINT POSITION of 4 March 1996 defined by the Council on the basis of Article K.3 of the Treaty on European Union on the harmonized application of the definition of the term 'refugee' in Article 1 of the Geneva Convention of 28 July 1951 relating to the status of refugees, O.J. 1996, L 63/2

COUNCIL DECISION of 4 March 1996 on an alert and emergency procedure for burden-sharing with regard to the admission and residence of displaced persons on a temporary basis, O.J. 1996, L 63/10

COUNCIL RESOLUTION of 14 October 1996 laying down the priorities for cooperation in the field of justice and home affairs for the period from 1 July 1996 to 30 June 1998, O.J. 1996, C 319/1

COUNCIL CONCLUSIONS of 27 May 1997 concerning the practical implementation of the Dublin Convention, O.J. 1997, C 191/27

COUNCIL RESOLUTION of 26 June 1997 on unaccompanied minors who are nationals of third countries, O.J. 1997, C 221/23

COUNCIL DECISION of 26 June 1997 on monitoring the implementation of instruments adopted concerning asylum, O.J. 1997, L 178/6

DECISION No. 1/97 of 9 September 1997 of the Committee set up by Article 18 of the Dublin Convention of 15 June 1990, concerning provisions for the implementation of the Convention, O.J. 1997, L 281/1

DECISION No. 2/97 of 9 September 1997 of the Committee set up by Article 18 of the Dublin Convention of 15 June 1990, establishing the Committee's Rules of Procedure, O.J. 1997, L 281/26

COUNCIL RESOLUTION of 18 December 1997 laying down the priorities for cooperation in the field of justice and home affairs for the period from 1 January 1998 to the date of entry into force of the Treaty of Amsterdam, O.J. 1998, C 11/1

JOINT ACTION of 27 April 1998 adopted by the Council on the basis of Article K.3 of the Treaty on European Union, concerning the financing of specific projects in favour of displaced persons who have found temporary protection in the Member States and asylum seekers, O.J. 1998, L 138/6

JOINT ACTION of 27 April 1998 adopted by the Council on the basis of Article K.3 of the Treaty on European Union, concerning the financing of specific projects in favour of asylum-seekers and refugees, O.J. 1998, L 138/8

DECISION No. 1/98 of 30 June 1998 of the Committee set up by Article 18 of the Dublin Convention of 15 June 1990, concerning provisions for the implementation of the Convention, O.J. 1998, L 196/49

JOINT ACTION of 26 April 1999 adopted by the Council on the basis of Article K.3 of the Treaty on European Union, establishing projects and measures to provide practical support in relation to the reception and voluntary repatriation of refugees, displaced persons and asylum seekers, including emergency assistance to persons who have fled as a result of recent events in Kosovo, O.J. 1999, L 114/2

V. ASSOCIATION AGREEMENTS CONCLUDED BY THE EUROPEAN (ECONOMIC) COMMUNITY

EEC-Turkey Association Agreement (64/733/CEE), O.J. 1964, No. 217/3687

COUNCIL REGULATION (EEC) No. 3026/77 of 28 November 1977 on the conclusion of the Supplementary Protocol to the Association Agreement between the European Economic Community and Turkey, consequent on the accession of new Member States to the Community, O.J. 1977, L 361/1

COUNCIL REGULATION (EEC) No. 2210/78 of 26 September 1978 concerning the conclusion of the Cooperation Agreement between the European Economic Community and the People's Democratic Republic of Algeria, O.J. 1978, L 263/1

COUNCIL REGULATION (EEC) No. 2211/78 of 26 September 1978 concerning the conclusion of the Cooperation Agreement between the European Economic Community and the Kingdom of Morocco, O.J. 1978, L 264/1

COUNCIL DECISION of 25 November 1991 denouncing the Cooperation Agreement between the European Economic Community and the Socialist Federal Republic of Yugoslavia, O.J. 1991, L 325/23

DECISION of the Council and the Commission of 13 December 1993 on the conclusion of the Agreement on the European Economic Area between the European Communities, their Member States and the Republic of Austria, the Republic of Finland, the Republic of Iceland, the Principality of Liechtenstein, the Kingdom of Sweden and the Swiss Confederation, O.J. 1994, L 1/1

DECISION of the Council and the Commission of 13 December 1993 on the conclusion of the Europe Agreement between the European Communities and their Member States, of the one part, and the Republic of Hungary, of the other part, O.J. 1993, L 347/1

DECISION of the Council and the Commission of 13 December 1993 on the conclusion of the Europe Agreement between the European Communities and their Member States, of the one part, and the Republic of Poland, of the other part, O.J. 1993, L 348/1

DECISION of the Council and the Commission of 19 December 1994 on the conclusion of the Europe Agreement between the European Communities and their Member States, of the one part, and the Republic of Bulgaria, of the other part, O.J. 1994, L 358/1

DECISION of the Council and the Commission of 19 December 1994 on the conclusion of a Europe Agreement establishing an association between the European Communities and their Member States, of the one part, and the Czech Republic, of the other part, O.J. 1994, L 360/1

DECISION of the Council and the Commission of 19 December 1994 on the conclusion of the Europe Agreement between the European Communities and their Member States, of the one part, and Romania, of the other part, O.J. 1994, L 357/1

DECISION of the Council and the Commission of 19 December 1994 concerning the conclusion of a Europe Agreement establishing an association between the European Communities and their Member States, of the one part, and the Slovak Republic, of the other part, O.J. 1994, L 359/1

Europe Agreement establishing an association between the European Communities and their Member States, of the one part, and the Republic of Estonia, of the other part, O.J. 1998, L 68/3

Europe Agreement establishing an association between the European Communities and their Member States, of the one part, and the Republic of Latvia, of the other part, O.J. 1998, L 26/3

Europe Agreement establishing an association between the European Communities and their Member States, of the one part, and the Republic of Lithuania, O.J. 1998, L 51/3

Europe Agreement establishing an association between the European Communities and their Member States, acting within the framework of the European Union, of the one part, and the Republic of Slovenia, of the other part, O.J. 1999, L 51/3

Agreement with the Republic of Iceland and the Kingdom of Norway concerning the latters' association with the implementation, application and development of the Schengen acquis, O.J. 1999, L 176/35

Agreement in the form of Exchanges of Letters between the Council of the European Union, the Republic of Iceland and the Kingdom of Norway concerning committees which assist the European Commission in the exercise of its executive powers, O.J. 1999, L 176/53

Euro-Mediterranean Interim Association Agreement on trade and cooperation between the European Community, of the one part, and the Palestine Liberation Organization (PLO) for the benefit of the Palestinian Authorithy of the West Bank and the Gaza Strip, of the other part, O.J. 1997, L 187/3

VI. Proposals and Working Documents by the European Commission on Immigration and Asylum

PROPOSAL for a Council Directive on the rights of third-country nationals to travel in the community, COM (1995) 436 final, O.J. 1995, C 306/5

PROPOSAL for a Council Regulation (EC) amending Regulation (EEC) No. 1408/71 as regards its extension to nationals of third countries, COM (1997) 561 final – 1997/0320 (CNS), O.J. 1998, C 6/15

PROPOSAL for a Joint Action concerning solidarity in the admission and residence of beneficiaries of the temporary protection of displaced persons (1998/C 268/14) (Text with EEA relevance) COM (1998) 372 final – 1998/0222 (CNS), O.J. 1998, C 268/22

PROPOSAL for a European Parliament and Council Regulation amending Council Regulation (EEC) No. 1612/68 on freedom of movement for workers within the Community (98/C 344/07) (Text with EEA relevance) COM (1998) 394 final – 1998/0229 (COD), O.J. 1998, C 344/9

PROPOSAL for a European Parliament and Council Directive amending Directive 68/360/EEC on the abolition of restrictions on movement and residence within the Community for workers of Member States and their families (98/C 344/08) (Text with EEA relevance) COM (1998) 394 final – 1998/0230 (COD), O.J. 1998, C 344/12

PROPOSAL for a European Parliament and Council Decision establishing an Advisory Committee on freedom of movement and social security for Community workers and amending Council Regulations (EEC) No. 1612/68 and (EEC) No. 1408/71 (98/C 344/09) (Text with EEA relevance) COM (1998) 394 final – 1998/0231 (COD), O.J. 1998, C 344/16

PROPOSAL for a Council Directive extending the freedom to provide cross-border services to third-country nationals established within the Community (1999/C 67/10) (Text with EEA relevance) COM (1999) 3 final – 1999/0013 (CNS), O.J. 1999, C 67/17

PROPOSAL for a Directive of the European Parliament and of the Council on the posting of workers who are third-country nationals for the provision of cross-border services (1999/C 67/09) (Text with EEA relevance) COM (1999) 3 final – 1999/0012 (COD), O.J. 1999, C 67/12

PROPOSAL of the European Parliament: Second Report of 28 January 1999 on the proposal for a Council Act establishing the Convention on rules for the admission of third-country nationals to the Member States and a draft Convention on rules for the admission of third-country nationals to the Member States of the European Union, COM (1997) 387 final – C4 – 0681/1997 – 1997/0227 (CNS), PE 229.573 fin.

COMMISSION WORKING DOCUMENT: Towards common standards on asylum procedures, SEC (1999) 271 def.

PROPOSAL for a Council Directive on the right to family reunification, COM (1999) 638 final.

I

Table of Cases

I. European Court of Justice

Case Number	*Date*	*Parties to the Case*	*Reference*
C-33/89	2706.1990	Maria Kowalska v Freie und Hansestadt Hamburg	[1990] ECR I-2591
20/59	20.06.1960	Italy v High Authority	[1960] ECR 663
28/68	01.05.1969	Caisse régionale de sécurité sociale du nord de la France v Achille Torrekens	[1969] ECR 125
29/69	12.11.1969	Stauder v Stadt Ulm-Sozialamt	[1969] ECR 419
22/70	31.03.1971	Commission v Council (ERTA)	[1971] ECR 263
51/71 to 54/71	15.12.1971	International Fruit Company NV and others v Produktschap voor groenten en fruit	[1971] ECR 1107
2 and 3/69	13.12.1973	Social Fonds voor de Diamantarbeiders v NV Indiamex et Association de fait De Belder	[1969] ECR 211
152/73	12.02.1974	Giovanni Maria Sotgiu v Deutsche Bundespost	[1974] ECR 153
181/73	30.04.1974	Haageman v Belgian State	[1974] ECR 449
4/73	14.05.1974	J.Nold Kohlen- und Baustoffgroßhandlung v Commission	[1974] ECR 491
9/74	03.07.1974	Casagrande v Landeshauptstadt München	[1974] ECR 773
41/74	04.12.1974	Van Duyn v Home Office	[1974] ECR 1337
78/74	18.02.1975	Deuka v Einfuhrstelle für Getreide und Futtermittel	[1975] ECR 421
67/74	26.02.1975	Bonsignore v Oberstadtdirektor der Stadt Köln	[1975] ECR 297
32/75	30.09.1975	Christini v Société nationale des chemins de fer français	[1975] ECR 1085
24/75	21.10.1975	Teresa et Silvana Petroni v Office national des pensions pour travailleurs salariés (ONPTS), Bruxelles	[1975] ECR 1149
36/75	28.10.1975	Rutili v Ministre de l'intérieur	[1975] ECR 1219
43/75	08.04.1976	Gabrielle Defrenne v Société anonyme belge de navigation aérienne Sabena	[1976] ECR 455
118/75	07.06.1976	Lynne Watson and Alessandro Belmann	[1976] ECR 1185
3, 4, 6/76	14.07.1976	Cornelis Kramer and others	[1976] ECR 1279
41/76	15.12.1976	Suzanne Criel, née Donckerwolcke and Henri Schou v Procureur de la République au tribunal	[1976] ECR 1921
104/76	05.05.1977	Gerda Jansen v Landesversicherungsanstalt Rheinprovinz	[1977] ECR 829
90/76	09.06.1977	S.r.l.Ufficio Henry van Ameyde v S.r.l.Ufficio centrale italiano di assistenza assicurativa automobilisti in circolazione internazionale (UCI)	[1977] ECR 1091

117/76 and 16/77	19.10.1977	Albert Ruckdeschel & Co.et Hansa-Lagerhaus Ströh & Co.v Hauptzollamt Hamburg-St.Annen; Diamalt AG v Hauptzollamt Itzehoe	[1977] ECR 1753
30/77	27.10.1977	Regina v Pierre Bouchereau	[1977] ECR 1999
82/77	24.01.1978	Van Tiggele v Netherlands	[1978] ECR 25
149/77	15.06.1978	Gabrielle Defrenne v Société anonyme belge de navigation aérienne Sabena	[1978] ECR 1365
10/78	12.10.1978	Tayeb Belhouab v Bundesknappschaft	[1978] ECR 1915
103/77 and 145/77	25.10.1978	Royal Schalten-Honig (Holdings) Limited v Intervention Board for Agricultural Produce; Tunnel Refineries Limited v Intervention Board for Agricultural Produce	[1978] ECR 2037
110/78 and 111/78	18.01.1979	Ministère public and another v van Wesemael and others	[1979] ECR 35
115/78	07.02.1979	J.Knoors v Secretary of State for Economic Affairs	[1979] ECR 399
120/78	20.02.1979	Rewe v Bundesmonopolverwaltung für Branntwein (Cassis de Dijon)	[1979] ECR 649
148/78	05.04.1979	Tullio Ratti	[1979] ECR 1629
44/79	13.12.1979	Liselotte Hauer v Land Rheinland-Pfalz	[1979] ECR 3727
792/79	17.01.1980	Camera Care v Commission	[1980] ECR 119
265/78	05.02.1980	Ferwerda c Produktshap voor Vee en Vlees	[1980] ECR 617
53/79	14.02.1980	Office national des pensions des travailleurs salariés (ONPTS) v Fiorante Damiani	[1980] ECR 273
98/79	05.03.1980	Josette Pecastaing v Belgian State	[1980] ECR 691
52/79	18.03.1980	Debauve v Procureur du Roi	[1980] ECR 833
131/79	22.05.1980	Regina v Secretary of State for Home Affairs	[1980] ECR 1585
157/79	03.07.1980	Regina v Stanislaus Pieck	[1980] ECR 2171
32/79	10.07.1980	Commission v UK	[1980] ECR 2403
203/80	11.11.1981	Guerino Casati	[1981] ECR 2595
244/80	16.12.1981	P.Foglia v M.Novello	[1981] ECR 3045
279/80	17.12.1981	A.J.Webb	[1981] ECR 3305
8/81	19.01.1982	U.Becker v Finanzamt Münster-Innenstadt	[1982] ECR 53
62 and 63/81	03.02.1982	Seco v EVI	[1982] ECR 223
53/81	23.03.1982	D.M.Levin v Staatssecretaris van Justitie	[1982] ECR 1035
92/81	10.06.1982	Antonia Caracciolo (née Camera) v Institut nationald'assurance maladie-invalidité and Union nationale des mutualités socialistes	[1982] ECR 2213
35 and 36/82	27.10.1982	Elestina Esselina Christina Morson v State of the Netherlands Head of the meaning of the Vreemdelingenwet; Sweradjie Jhanjan v State of the Netherlands	[1982] ECR 3723
232/82	10.03.1983	Margherita Baccini v Office national de l'emploi (ONEM)	[1983] ECR 583
77/82	23.03.1983	Anastatsia Peskeloglou v Bundesanstalt für Arbeit	[1983] ECR 1085

151/82	13.07.1983	Forscheri v Belgian State de Sciences Humaines Appliquées	[1983] ECR 2323
205-215/82	21.09.1983	Deutsche Milchkontor v Federal Republic of Germany	[1983] ECR 2633
238/83	05.07.1984	Mr.and Mrs.Richard Meade v Caisse d'Allocations Familiales de la Région Parisienne	[1984] ECR 2631
117/83	25.09.1984	Karl Könecke GmbH & Co KG v Bundesanstalt für landwirtschaftliche Marktordnung	[1984] ECR 3291
231/83	29.01.1985	Henri Cullet v Centre Leclerc à Toulouse and Centre Leclerc à Saint-Orens-de-Gameville	[1985] ECR 305
267/83	13.02.1985	Aissatou Diatta v Land Berlin	[1985] ECR 567
94/84	20.06.1985	Joszef Deak v Office national de l'emploi	[1985] ECR 1873
293/83	13.12.1985	Gravier v City of Lüttich	[1985] EJC 593
41/84	15.01.1986	Pietro Pinna v Caisse d'allocations familiales de la Savoie	[1986] ECR 1
59/85	17.04.1986	State of the Netherlands v Ann Florence Reed	[1986] ECR 1283
131/85	07.05.1986	Emir Gül v Regierungspräsident Düsseldorf	[1986] ECR 1573
170/84	13.05.1986	Bilka-Kaufhaus v Weber Von Hartz	[1986] ECR 1607
222/84	15.05.1986	Marguerite Johnston v Chief Constable of the Royal Ulster Constabulary	[1986] ECR 1651
66/85	03.07.1986	Deborah Lawrie-Blum v Land Baden-Württemberg	[1986] ECR 2121
300/84	23.10.1986	A.J.M.van Roosmalen v Bestuur van de Bedrijfsvereniging voor de Gezondheid, Geestelijke en Maatschappelijke Belangen	[1986] ECR 3097
205/84	04.12.1986	Commission v Germany	[1986] ECR 3755
379,380,381/85 and 93/86	24.02.1987	Caisse régionale d'assurance maladie Rhône-Alpes v Anna Giletti, Directeur régional des affaires sanitaires et sociales de Lorraine v Domenico Giardini, Caisse régionale d'assurance maladie du Nord-Est v Feliciano Tampan, Severino Severini v Caisse primaire centrale d'assurance maladie	[1987] ECR 955
316/85	18.06.1987	Centre public d'aide sociale de Courcelles v Marie-Christine Lebon	[1987] ECR 2811
281-287/85	09.07.1987	Federal Republic of Germany and others v Commission	[1987] ECR 3203
12/86	30.09.1987	Meryem Demirel v Stadt Schwäbisch Gmünd	[1987] ECR 3719
314/85	22.10.1987	Foto-Frost v Hauptzollamt Lübeck-Ost	[1987] ECR 4199
20/87	08.12.1987	Ministère public v André Gauchard	[1987] ECR 4879
147/87	17.12.1987	Saada Zaoui v Caisse régionale d'assurance maladie de l'Ile-de-France (CRAMIF)	[1987] ECR 5511
292/86	19.01.1988	Claude Gullung v Conseil de l'ordre des advocats du barreau de Colmar et de Saverne	[1988] ECR 111
197/86	21.06.1988	Steven Malcolm Brown v The Secretary of State for Scotland	[1988] ECR 3205

39/86	21.06.1988	Lair v University of Hannover,	[1988] ECR 3161
143/87	07.07.1988	Christopher Stanton and SA belge d'assurances "L'Étoile 1905" v Inasti (Institut national d'assurances sociales pour travailleurs indépendants)	1988 [ECR] 3877
42/87	27.09.1988	Comission v Belgium	[1988] ECR 5445
186/87	02.02.1989	Ian William Cowan v Trésor public	[1989] ECR 195
389 and 390/87	15.03.1989	G.B.C.Echternach and A.Moritz v Netherlands Minister for Education and Science	[1989] ECR 723
321/87	27.04.1989	Commission v Belgium	[1989] ECR 977
249/86	18.5.1989	Commission v Federal Republic of Germany	[1989] ECR 1263
305/87	30.05.1989	Commission v Hellenic Republic	[1989] ECR 1461
48, 106 and 107/88	27.06.1989	Achterberg-te Riele v Sociale Verzekeringsbank Amsterdam	[1989] ECR 1963
46/87 and 227/88	21.09.1989	Hoechst AG v Commission	[1989] ECR 2859
9/88	27.09.1989	Mário Lopes da Veiga v Staatssecretaris van Justitie	[1989] ECR 2989
374/87	18.10.1989	Orkem v Commission	[1989] ECR 3283
30/88	14.11.1989	Hellenic Republic v Commission	[1989] ECR 3711
C-265/88	12.12.1989	Lothar Messner	[1989] ECR 4209
C-3/87	14.12.1989	The Queen v Ministry of Agriculture, Fisheries and Food, ex parte Agegate Ltd.	[1989] ECR 4459
C-228/88	22.02.1990	Giovanni Bronzino v Kindergeldkase	[1990] ECR I-531
C-12/89	22.02.1990	Antonio Gatto v Bundesanstalt für Arbeit	[1990] ECR I-557
C-113/89	27.03.1990	Rush Portuguesa Lda v Office national d'immigration	[1990] ECR I-1417
C-262/88	17.05.1990	Douglas Harvey Barber v Guardian Royal Exchange Assurance Group	[1990] Ecr I-1889
C-37/89	14.06.1990	Michel Weiser v Caisse nationale des barreaux francais	[1990] ECR I-2395
C-192/89	20.09.1990	S.Z.Sevince v Staatssecretaris van Justitie	[1990] ECR I-3461
C-61/89	03.10.1990	Criminal proceedings against Marc Gaston Bouchoucha	[1990] ECR I-3551
C-297/88 and 197/89	18.10.1990	Massam Dzodzi v Belgian State	[1990] ECR 3763
C-297/88 and C-197/89	18.10.1990	Massam Dzodzi v Belgian State	[1990] ECR I-3763
177/88	08.11.1990	Dekker v Stichting Vorminscentrum Voor Jonge Volwassen	[1990] ECR I-3070
C-18/90	31.01.1991	Office national de l'emploi v Bahia Kziber	[1991] ECR I-199
C-227/89	07.02.1991	Ludwig Rönfeldt v Bundesversicherungsanstalt für Angestellte	[1991] ECR I-323
C-154/89	26.02.1991	Commission v France	[1991] ECR I-659
C-180/89	26.02.1991	Comission v Italian Republic	[1991] ECR I-709
C-198/89	26.02.1991	Comission v Hellenic Republic	[1991] ECR I-727

C-10/90	07.03.1991	Maria Masgio v Bundesknappschaft	[1991] ECR I-1119
C-68/89	30.03.1991	Commission v Netherlands	[1991] ECR I-2637
C-31/90	11.07.1991	Johnson v Chief Adjudication Officer	[1991] ECR I-3723
C-345/89	25.07.1991	Criminal proceedings against Alfred Stoeckel	[1991] ECR I-4047
C-76/90	25.07.1991	Manfred Säger v Denrumeyer & Co.Ltd.	[1991] ECR I-4221
C-349/87	04.10.1991	Elissavet Paraschi v Landesversicherungsanstalt Württemberg	[1991] ECR I-4501
Opinion 1/91	12.12.1991	Draft agreement between the Community, on the one hand, and the countries of the European Free Trade Association, on the other, relating to the creation of the European Economic Area	[1991] ECR I-6079
C-332/90	28.01.1992	Volker Steen v Deutsche Bundespost	[1992] ECR I-341
C-243/90	04.02.1992	The Queen v Secretary of State for Social Security, ex parte Smithson	[1992] ECR I-467
C-370/90	07.07.1992	The Queen v Immigration Appeal Tribunal et Surinder Singh, ex parte Secretary of State for Home Department	[1992] ECR I-4265
C-369/90	07.07.1992	Mario Vicente Micheletti and others v Delegación del Gobierno en Cantabria	[1992] ECR I-4239
C-9/91	07.07.1992	The Queen v Secretary of State for Social Security ex parte Equal Opportunities Commission	[1992] ECR I-4297
C-63 and 64/91	16.07.1992	Jackson v Chief Adjudication Officer	[1992] ECR I-4737
C-78/91	16.07.1992	Rose Hughes v Chief Adjudication Officer, Belfast	[1992] ECR I-4839
C-153/91	22.09.1992	Camille Petit v Office national des pensions	[1992] ECR I-4973
C-240/90	27.10.1992	Federal Republic of Germany v Commission	[1992] ECR I-5383
C-237/91	16.12.1992	Kazim Kus v Landeshauptstadt Wiesbaden	[1992] ECR I-6781
C-206/91	16.12.1992	Koua Poirrez v Caisse d'allocations familiales de la région parisienne, substituée par la Caisse d'allocations familiales de la Seine-Saint-Denis	[1992] ECR I-6685
C-328/91	30.03.1993	Secretary of State for Social Security v Thomas	[1993] ECR I-1247
C-271/91	02.08.1993	M. Helen Marshall v Southampton and South-West Hampshire Area Health Authority	[1993] ECR I-4367
C-66/92	02.08.1993	Genaro Acciardi v Commissie Beroepszaken Administratieve Geschillen in de Provincie Noord-Holland	[1993] ECR I-4567
C-58/93	20.04.1994	Zoubir Yousfi v Belgian State	[1994] ECR I-1353
C-432/92	05.07.1994	The Queen v Minister of Agriculture, Fisheries and Food, ex parte Anastasiru Ltd.and others	[1994] ECR I-3087
C-43/93	09.08.1994	Raymond Vander Elst v Office des Migrations Internationales	[1994] ECR I-3803
C-43/93	09.08.1994	Raymond Vander Elst v Office des Migrations Internationales	[1994] ECR I-3803
C-355/93	05.10.1994	Hayriye Eroglu v Land Baden-Württemberg	[1994] ECR I-5113
C-404/92	05.10.1994	X v Commission	[1994] ECR I-4737

C-165/91	05.10.1994	Simon J.M.van Munster v Rijksdienst voor Pensioenen	[1994] ECR I-4661
Opinion 1/94	15.11.1994	Competence of the Community to conclude international agreements concerning services and the protection of intellectual property-Article 228(6) of the EC Treaty	[1994] ECR I-5267
Opinion 2/92	24.03.1995	Competence of the Community or one of its institutions to participate in the Third revised Decision of the OECD on national treatment	[1995] ECR I-521
C-103/94	05.04.1995	Zoulika Krid v Caisse nationale d'assurance vieilesse des travailleurs salariés (CNAVTS)	[1995] ECR I-719
C-7/94	04.05.1995	Landesamt für Ausbildungsförderung Nordrhein-Weszfalen v Lubor Gaal	[1995] ECR I-1031
C-384/93	10.05.1995	Alpine Investments BV v Minister van Financien	[1995] ECR I-1141
C-116/94	13.07.1995	Meyers v Adjudication Officer	[1995] ECR I-2131
C-450/93	17.10.1995	Eckhard Kalanke v Freie Hansestadt Bremen	[1995]ECR I-3051
C-482/93	26.10.1995	S.E.Klaus v Bestuur van de Nieuwe Algemene Bedrijfsvereniging	[1995] ECR I-3551
C-481/93	26.11.1995	R.Moscato v Bestuur van de Nieuwe Algemene Bedrijfsvereniging	[1995] ECR I-3525
C-272/94	28.03.1996	Michel Guiot and Climatec SA	[1996] ECR I-1905
Opinion 2/94	28.03.1996	Accession by the Community to the European Convention for the Protection of Human rights and Fundamental Freedoms	[1996] ECR I-1759
C-308/93	30.04.1996	Bestuur van de Sociale Verzekeringsbank v J.M.Cabanis-Issarte	[1996] ECR I-2097
C-107/94	27.06.1996	P.H.Asscher v Staatssecretaris van Financien	[1996] ECR I-3089
C-277/94	10.09.1996	Z.Taflan-Met, S.Altun-Baser, E.Andal-Bugdayci v Bestuur van de Sociale Verzekeringsbank and O.Akol v Bestuur van de Nieuwe Algemene Bedrijfsvereniging	[1996] ECR I-4085
C-126/95	03.10.1996	A. Hallouzi-Choho v Bestuur van de Sociale Verzekeringsbank	[1996] ECR I-4087
C-245/94 and C-312/94	10.10.1996	Ingrid Hoever and Iris Zachov v Land Nordrhein Westfalen	[1996] ECR –4895
C- 84/94	12.11.1996	United Kingdom v Council	[1996] ECR I-5755
C-171/95	23.01.1997	Recep Tetik v Land Berlin	[1997] ECR I-329
C-340/94	30.01.1997	E.J.M.de Jaeck v Staatssecretaris van Financien	[1997] ECR I-461
C-344/95	20.02.1997	Commission v Belgium	1997 [ECR] I-1035
C-323/95	20.03.1997	Hayes v Kronenberger	[1997] ECR I-1711
C-351/95	17.04.1997	Selma Kadiman v Freistaat Bayern	[1997] ECR I-2133
C-180/95	22.04.1997	Nils Draehmpaeh v Urania Immobilirnservice OHGl	[1997] ECR I-2195
C-20/91	04.11.1997	Kevin Albert Snares v Adjudication Officer	[1997] ECR I-6057
C-409/95	11.11.1997	Hellmut Marshall v Land Nordrhein-Westfalen	[1997] ECR I-6363

C-309/96	18.12.1997	Daniele Annibaldi v Sindaco del Comune de Guidonia and Presidente Regione Lazio	[1997] ECR I-7493
C-113/97	15.01.1998	Henia Babahenini v Belgian State	[1998] ECR I-183
C-249/96	17.02.1998	Lisa Jacqueline Grant v South-West Trains Ltd.	[1998] ECR I-621
C-85/96	12.05.1998	Sala v Freistaat Bayern	[1998] ECR
C-170/96	12.05.1998	Comission v Council	[1998] ECR I-2763
C-243/95	17.06.1998	Kathleen Hill and Ann Stapleton v The Revenue Commissioners and Department of Finance	[1998] ECR I-3739
C-394/96	30.06.1998	Mary Brown v Rentokil Ltd.	[1998] ECR I-4185
C-154/96	22.10.1998	Louis Wolf v Office national des pension (ONP)	[1998] ECR I-6173
C-411/96	27.10.1998	Margaret Boyle and others v Equal Opportunities Commission	[1998] ECR I-6401
C-66/96	19.11.1998	Handels- og Kontorfunktionærernes Forbund i Danmark, acting on behalf of Berit Høj Pedersen v Fællesforeningen for Danmarks Brugsforeninger and Dansk Tandlægeforening and Kristelig Funktionær-Organisation v Dansk Handel & Service	[1998] ECR I-7327
C-167/97	09.02.1999	Regina v Secretary of State for Employment, ex parte Nicole Seymour-Smith and Laura Perez	[1999] ECR I-623
C-416/96	02.03.1999	Nour Eddline El-Yassini v Secretary of State for Home Department	[1999] ECR I-1209
C-262/96	04.05.1999	Sema Sürül v Bundesanstalt für Arbeit	cf. OJ 1999 C204/12
C-369/96 and C-376/96	23.11.1999	Arblade & Leloup/Sofrage	not yet published in ECR
C-340/97	10.02.2000	Nazli v Stadt Nürnberg	not yet published in ECR
C-329/97	16.03.2000	Ergat v Stadt Ulm	not yet published in ECR

II. Pending Cases of the European Court of Justice

C-158/97		Badeck and others v Hessischer Ministerpräsident and other	pending

III. Judgments of the Court of First Instance

T-135/96	17.06.1998	Union Européene de l'artisanat et des petites moyennes enterprises (UEAPME) v Council	[1998] ECR II-2335

IV. European Court of Human Rights

Case Number	*Date*	*Parties to the Case*	*Reference*
15/1983/71/107-109	28.05.85	Abdulaziz v United Kingdom	Series A 94
117/165-6	27.04.88	Boyle and Rice	Series A 131
3/1987/126/177	21.06.88	Berrehab v Netherlands	Series A 138
1/19989/161/217	07.07.89	Soering v United Kingdom	Series A 161
46/1990/237/307	20.03.91	Cruz Varas v Sveden	Series A 201
45/1990/236/302	20.10.91	Vilvarajah and Others v United Kingdom	Series A 215
53/1995/559/645	19.02.96	Gül v Switzerland	RJD 1996-I 159
39/1995/545/631	16.09.96	Gaygusuz v Austria	RJD 1996-IV 1129
70/195/576/662	15.11.96	Chahal v United Kingdom	RJD 1996-V 1831
45/1995/551/637	15.11.96	Cantoni v France	RJD 1996-V1614
73/1995/579/665	28.11.96	Ahmut v Netherlands	RJD 1996-VI 2017
11/1996/630/813	29.04.97	H.L.R. v France	RJD 1997 III 745
146/1996/767/964	02.05.97	D. v United Kingdom	RJD 1997 III 777

V. European Commission of Human Rights

Case Number	*Date*	*Parties to the Case*	*Reference*
	18.01.78	Ireland v United Kingdom	Series A 25
	16.12.92	Niemitz v Germany	Series A 256
13258/87	09.02.90	M & Co. v Germany	64 DR 138-146 (1990)

J

Table of Abbreviations

AC	Appeal Cases
AEL	Academy of European Law
AFDI	Annuaire Francais de Droit International
AJIL	American Journal of International Law
AJPIL	Austrian Journal of Public and International Law
Ann Eur	Annuaire Européen (European Yearbook)
AöR	Archiv des öffentlichen Rechts
Art.	Article
ASIL	Proceedings of American Society of International Law
ASP	Arbeits- und Sozialpolitik
Asyl	Schweizerische Zeitschrift für Asylrecht und -praxis
AsylVfG	Asylum Procedure Act
AuA	Arbeit und Arbeitsrecht (Zeitschrift)
AuslG	Aliens Act (Ausländugeseh)
AuslR	Ausländerrecht (aliens law)
AVR	Archiv des Völkerrechts
AWR-Bulletin	Association for the Study of the World Refugee Problem
BayVBl	Bayerische Verwaltungsblätter
BB	Betriebsberater
BGBl.	Federal Law Gazette (Bundesgesehblatt)
BGHE	Decisions of the Federal High Court of Justice
BGHR	Reports of the Federal High Court of Justice
BGSG	Federal Border Police Act
BMI	Federal Ministry of the Interior
BPIL	British Practice in International Law
BT-Drs.	Bundestags-Drucksache (official document of Germany's Federal Parliament)
Bull. EC	Bulletin of the European Communities
Bull. EU	Bulletin of the European Union
BVerfGE	Decisions of the Federal Constitutional Court
BVerwGE	Decisions of the Federal Administrative Court
BYIL	British Yearbook of International Law
CA	Court of Appeal
CAHAR	Ad hoc Committee of experts on the legal aspects of territorial asylum, refugees and stateless persons
CDE	Cahiers de Droit Européen
CEPS	Centre for European Policy Studies
cf.	compare
CFI	Court of First Instance of the European Communities
CFSP	Common Foreign and Security Police
CIREA	Centre for Information, Discussion and Exchange on Asylum

CIREFI	Centre for Information, Discussion and Exchange on the Crossing of Borders and Immigration
CJHA	Co-operation in the field of Justice and Home Affairs
CML Rev.	Common Market Law Review
Cmnd.	Command Paper
CMR	Common Market Reporter
CoE	Council of Europe
COM	Commission Document
CONF	Conference of the Representatives of the Governments of the Member States
COREPER	Committee of Permanent Representatives to the European Communities
Cornell ILJ	Cornell International Law Journal
CR	Computer und Recht
CRE	Commission for Racial Equality
CRHC	Comprehensive Response to the Humanitarian Crisis
CSIS	Central Service Computer on behalf of SIS
DC	Dublin Convention
Doc.	Document
DÖV	Die Öffentliche Verwaltung
DVAuslG	Regulation Implementing the Aliens Act
DVBl.	Deutsches Verwaltungsblatt
EA	Europaarchiv
EBC	Convention on External Borders
EC	European Community(-ies)
ECA	European Communities Act
ECHR	European Court of Human Rights
ECHR	European Court of Human Rights Series
ECJ	European Court of Justice
ECR	European Court Reports
ECRE	European Council on Refugees and Exiles
ECSA	European Community Studies Association
ECT	European Community Treaty
ECT	Treaty establishing the European Community
ed./eds.	Editor/editors
EEA	European Economic Area
EEAA	European Economic Area Agreement
EEC	European Economic Community
Efms	Europäisches Forum für Migrationsstudien
EFTA	European Free Trade Association
EHRLR	European Human Rights Law Review
EHRR	European Human Rights Reports
EJIL	European Journal of International Law
EJML	European Journal of Migration and Law
EL Rev.	European Law Review
ELJ	European Law Journal
EP	European Parliament

EPIL	Encyclopedia of Public International Law
EPL	European Public Law
ESC	European Social Charter
et seq.	et sequentes
ETS	European Treaty Series
EU	European Union
EuGRZ	Europäische Grundrechte-Zeitschrift
EuR	Europarecht
EURES	European Employment Service
EuroAS	Europäisches Arbeits- und Sozialrecht
EuZW	Europäische Zeitschrift für Wirtschaftsrecht
EWS	Europäisches Wirtschafts- und Steuerrecht
EZAR	Entscheidungssammlung zum Ausländer- und Asylrecht
FAZ	Frankfurter Allgemeine Zeitung
Fn.	Footnote
FS	Festschrift (Essays in Honour of ...)
GATT	General Agreement on Tariffs and Trade
GG	Basic Law
GYIL	German Yearbook of International Law
Harvard Int'l LJ	Harvard International Law Journal
HR Rev.	Human Rights Review
HRLJ	Human Rights Law Journal
HRQ	Human Rights Quarterly
Ibid./id.	In the same place/the same
ICCPR	International Covenant on Civil and Political Rights
ICLQ	International and Comparative Law Quarterly
ICMPD	International Center for Migration Policy Development
IGC	Intergovernmental Conference
IHRR	International Human Rights Reports
IJRL	International Journal of Refugee Law
ILM	International Legal Materials
Imm AR	Immigration Appeal Reports
InfAuslR	Informationsbrief Ausländerrecht
Int Lawyer	International Lawyer
Integration	Beilage zur "Europäischen Zeitung"
IOM	International Organisation for Migration
IRIRC	International Refugee Integration Resource Center
IRO	International Refugee Organisation
JbchristlSozwiss	Jahrbuch christlicher Sozialwissenschaften
JCMS	Journal of Common Market Studies
JEPP	Journal of European Public Policy
JESP	Journal of European Social Policy
JHA	Justice and Home Affairs
JICL	Journal of International and Comparative Law
JuS	Juristische Schulung
JZ	Juristenzeitung
LIEI	Legal Issues of European Integration

LQR	Law Quarterly Review
MEP	Member of the European Parliament
MittAB	Mitteilungen aus der Arbeits- und Berufsforschung
MJ	Maastricht Journal of European and Comparative Law
MLR	Modern Law Review
Mn.	Marginal Note
MNS	Migration News Sheet
NGO	Non-Governmental Organisation
NJW	Neue Juristische Wochenschrift
No.	Number
NVwZ	Neue Zeitschrift für Verwaltungsrecht
NYIL	Netherlands Yearbook of International Law
NZA	Neue Zeitschrift für Arbeitsrecht
NZS	Neue Zeitschrift für Sozialrecht
NZZ	Neue Züricher Zeitung
O.J.	Official Journal of the European Communities
OECD	Organisation for Economic Cooperation and Development
ÖZöRV	Österreichische Zeitschrift für öffentliches Recht und Völkerrecht
para	paragraph
ParlBeilage	"Aus Politik und Zeitgeschichte", Beilage zu "Das Parlament"
PL	Public Law
RBDI	Revue Belge de Droit International
RdA	Recht der Arbeit
Reg.	Regulation
Res.	Resolution
RIW	Recht der Internationalen Wirtschaft
RJD	Report of Judgments and Decisions
RMC	Revue du Marché Commun
RMCUE	Revue du Marché Commun et de l'Union Européenne
RTDE	Revue Trimestrielle de Droit Européen
SEA	Single European Act
SEC	Document of the Secretariat of the Commission of the European Union
SF	Sozialer Fortschritt
SIC	Schengen Implementation Convention
SIS	Schengen Information System
SOPEMI	Continuous Reporting System on Migration
SZIER	Schweizerische Zeitschrift für internationales und europäisches Recht
TEU	Treaty on European Union
TREVI	Terrorism, Radicalism, Extremism, Violence and Immigration
UDHR	Universal Declaration of Human Rights
UK	United Kingdom
UN	United Nations
UNHCR	United Nations High Commissioner for the Refugees

UNTS	United Nations Treaty Series
VCLT	Vienna Convention on the Law of Treaties
VerwArch	Verwaltungsarchiv
Vol.	Volume
WEU	Western European Union
WGI	(Council) Working Group on Immigration
Yale J Int'l Law	Yale Journal of International Law
YECHR	Yearbook of the European Convention on Human Rights
YEL	Yearbook of European Law
YILC	Yearbook of the International Law Commission
ZaöRV	Zeitschrift für ausländisches öffentliches Recht und Völkerrecht (Heidelberg Journal of Public International Law)
ZAR	Zeitschrift für Ausländerrecht und Ausländerpolitik
ZfA	Zeitschrift für Arbeitsrecht
ZFIS	Zeitschrift für Innere Sicherheit in Deutschland und Europa
ZFSH	Zeitschrift für Sozialrecht in Deutschland und Europa
ZfV	Zeitschrift für Verwaltungsrecht
ZIAS	Zeitschrift für ausländisches und internationales Arbeits- und Sozialrecht
ZRP	Zeitschrift für Rechtspolitik
ZSR	Zeitschrift für Sozialreform
ZTR	Zeitschrift für Tarifrecht
ZVersWiss	Zeitschrift für Versicherungswissenschaft
ZVerwWiss	Zeitschrift für Verwaltungswissenschaften
ZVR	Zeitschrift für Völkerrecht

Index

H